CASES IN COMPARATIVE POLITICS

SECOND EDITION

CASES IN COMPARATIVE POLITICS

SECOND EDITION

PATRICK H. O'NEIL, KARL FIELDS,
AND DON SHARE

W. W. NORTON & COMPANY

New York • *London*

W. W. Norton & Company has been independent since its founding in 1923, when William Warder Norton and Mary D. Herter Norton first published lectures delivered at the People's Institute, the adult education division of New York City's Cooper Union. The Nortons soon expanded their program beyond the Institute, publishing books by celebrated academics from America and abroad. By mid-century, the two major pillars of Norton's publishing program—trade books and college texts—were firmly established. In the 1950s, the Norton family transferred control of the company to its employees, and today—with a staff of four hundred and a comparable number of trade, college, and professional titles published each year—W. W. Norton & Company stands as the largest and oldest publishing house owned wholly by its employees.

Editor: Ann Shin
Copy Editor: Abigail Winograd
Project Editor: Sarah Mann
Editorial Assistant: Robert Haber
Book Design: Chris Welch
Production Manager: Diane O'Connor
Composition by Matrix Publishing Services, Inc.
Manufacturing by Courier Companies

Library of Congress Cataloging-in-Publication Data
    Cases in comparative politics / Patrick H. O'Neil, Karl Fields, and Don Share.—2nd ed.
        p. cm.
    Includes bibliographical references.

    ISBN-13: 978-0-393-92943-0 (pbk.)
    ISBN-10: 0-393-92943-4 (pbk.)
    1. Comparative government—Case studies. I. O'Neil, Patrick H., 1966–
II. Fields, Karl J. III. Share, Donald.

JF51.C32 2006
320.3—dc22   2006045347

W. W. Norton & Company, Inc., 500 Fifth Avenue, New York, N.Y. 10110
www.wwnorton.com

W. W. Norton & Company Ltd., Castle House, 75/76 Wells Street, London W1T 3QT

1 2 3 4 5 6 7 8 9 0

ABOUT THE AUTHORS

Patrick H. O'Neil is Associate Professor of Politics and Government at the University of Puget Sound in Tacoma, Washington. He has a Ph.D. in Political Science from Indiana University. Professor O'Neil's teaching and research interests are in the areas of democratization, conflict and political violence, and the politics of risk and technology. His publications include the books *Revolution from Within: The Hungarian Socialist Workers' Party and the Collapse of Communism* and *Communicating Democracy: The Media and Political Transitions* (editor).

Karl Fields is Professor of Politics and Government and Director of Asian Studies at the University of Puget Sound in Tacoma, Washington. He has a Ph.D. in Political Science from the University of California, Berkeley. Professor Fields's teaching and research interests focus on East Asian political economy, including government-business relations, economic reform, and regional integration. His publications include *Enterprise and the State in Korea and Taiwan.*

Don Share is Professor of Politics and Government at the University of Puget Sound in Tacoma, Washington. He has a Ph.D. in Political Science from Stanford University. He teaches comparative politics and Latin American politics, and has published widely on democratization and Spanish politics. His books include *The Making of Spanish Democracy* and *Dilemmas of Social Democracy.*

BRIEF CONTENTS

CONTENTS

5. JAPAN   147

PREFACE

Cases in Comparative Politics can be traced to an ongoing experiment undertaken by three comparative political scientists at the University of Puget Sound. Over the years the three of us spent much time discussing the challenges of teaching our introductory course in comparative politics. In those discussions we realized that each of us taught the course so differently that our students did not share a common conceptual vocabulary. Over several years we worked to develop a unified curriculum for the introductory comparative politics course, drawing on the strengths of each of our particular approaches.

All three of us now equip our students with a common conceptual vocabulary. All of our students now learn about states, nations, and different models of political economy. All of our students learn the basics about authoritarian and democratic regimes, and they become familiar with characteristics of advanced democracies, communist systems, and developing countries. In developing our curriculum, we became frustrated trying to find cases that were concise, sophisticated, and written to address the major concepts introduced in Patrick O'Neil's brief textbook, *Essentials of Comparative Politics*. Thus, we initially co-authored six cases with the following criteria:

- Each case is concise, making it possible to assign an entire case, or even two cases, for a single class session.
- All cases include discussion of major geographic and demographic features, themes in the state's historical development, political regimes (including the constitution, branches of government, the electoral system, and local government), political conflict and competition (including the party system and civil society), political economy, foreign relations and current issues in each country covered. This conformity allows us to assign specific sections from two or more cases simultaneously.
- The cases correspond to *Essentials of Comparative Politics*, but can also be used in conjunction with other texts.

After the on-line publication of the initial six cases (the United Kingdom, Japan, China, Russia, Mexico, and South Africa), we received positive feedback from teachers of comparative politics. Drawing on their comments and suggestions, we wrote new cases to accommodate individual preferences and give instructors more variety. In our revision of the digital text we added cases on Brazil, France, India, and Iran. With the debut of this printed version (and the corresponding Norton eBook), we have added two additional cases, the United States, and Nigeria.

Selecting only twelve cases is, of course, fraught with drawbacks. Nevertheless, we believe that this collection represents countries that are important in their own right, as well as representative of a broad range of political systems. Each of the twelve cases has special importance in the context of the study of comparative politics. Four of our cases (France, Japan, the United States, and the United Kingdom) are advanced industrial democracies, but they present a wide range of institutions, societies, political economic models, and relationships with the world. Japan is an important instance of a non-Western industrialized democracy, and also an instructive case of democratization imposed by foreign occupiers. While the United Kingdom and the United States have been known for political stability, France has a long history of political turmoil and regime change.

Two of our cases, China and Russia, have in common a past of Marxist-Leninist totalitarianism. Communism thrived in these two large and culturally distinct nations. Both suffered from the dangerous concentration of power in the hands of Communist parties and, at times, despotic leaders. The Soviet Communist regime fell and led to a troubled and incomplete transition to capitalism and democracy. China has retained its Communist authoritarian political system, but has experimented with a remarkable transition to a largely capitalist political economy.

The remaining six cases illustrate the diversity of the developing world. Of the six, India has the longest history of stable democratic rule, but like most countries in the developing world, it has struggled with massive-scale poverty and inequality. The remaining five have experienced various forms of authoritarianism more recently. Brazil and Nigeria endured long periods of military rule. Mexico's history of military rule was ended by an authoritarian political party that held power for much of the twentieth century through a variety of non-military means. South Africa experienced decades of racially discriminatory authoritarianism that excluded the vast majority of its population from the country's government and politics. Iran experienced a modernizing authoritarian monarchy, which was followed by its current authoritarian regime, a theocracy ruled by Islamic clerics.

In writing the cases we have incurred numerous debts. First and foremost, we wish to thank our wonderful colleagues in the Department of Politics and

Government at the University of Puget Sound. By encouraging us to develop a common curriculum for our Introduction to Comparative Politics course, and by allowing us to team-teach the course in different combinations, they allowed us to learn from each other. These cases are much stronger as a result. The University has also been extremely supportive in recognizing that writing for the classroom is as valuable as scholarly publication, and in providing course releases and summer stipends toward that end. Student assistants Brett Venn and Jess Box were extremely helpful in conducting research, and Irene Lim supported us with her amazing technical and organizational skills. Our colleague, Bill Haltom, provided very helpful input throughout the project. Debby Nagusky and Abigail Winograd contributed valuable copy editing assistance, and project editor Sarah Mann helped keep the various materials that went into the book organized. Many thanks to all the folks at Norton— Peter Lesser, Ann Shin, and Roby Harrington—who had faith in this project. Finally, we thank our students at the University of Puget Sound who inspired us to write these cases, and who provided valuable feedback throughout the process.

Don Share
Karl Fields
Patrick H. O'Neil

Tacoma, WA 2006

A note about the data: The data that are presented throughout the text in numerous tables, charts, and other figures are drawn from the CIA World Fact Book, UNDP Human Development Report, Electionworld.org, and Idea.int unless otherwise noted.

1 INTRODUCTION

WHAT IS COMPARATIVE POLITICS?

Comparative politics is the study and comparison of politics across countries. Studying politics comparatively allows us to examine some of the major questions of political science: Why do some countries have democratic regimes while others experience authoritarianism? Why and how do regimes change? Why are some countries affluent and growing while others experience poverty and decline? In this volume, we describe and analyze twelve political systems, focusing on their major geographic and demographic features, the origins and development of each state, their political regimes, their patterns of political conflict and competition, their societies, their political economies, and their relationships with the world. In this introductory chapter, we briefly summarize some key terms and concepts that will help you better understand these cases.

Comparing States

States are organizations that maintain a monopoly of violence over a territory. The term *state* can be confusing because in the United States it also refers to subnational government (i.e., the fifty states), whereas political scientists use *state* to refer to a national organization. In this book, state is used in this broader sense. However, the concept of the state is still narrower than the notion of a *country*, which also includes the territory and people living within a state. As illustrated by our collection of cases, states can differ in many ways, including in their origins, the length of their existence, their strength, and the history of their development.[1] Political scientists also distinguish between the state and the government. The **government** is the leadership or elite that administers the state.

Two of the most obvious differences among states are in their size and their population. The twelve countries included in this book vary considerably in both respects. States also vary in their natural endowments, such as arable land, mineral resources, navigable rivers, and access to the sea. Well-endowed states may have advantages over poorly endowed ones, but resource endowments do not necessarily determine the prosperity of a state. Japan, for example, has become one of the world's dominant economic powers despite having relatively few natural resources. Russia and Iran, on the other hand, are rich in natural resources but have struggled economically.

States also differ widely in their origins and historical development. Some countries (for example, China, France, and the United Kingdom) have long histories of statehood. Many countries in the developing world became states only after they were decolonized. Nigeria, for example, became an independ-

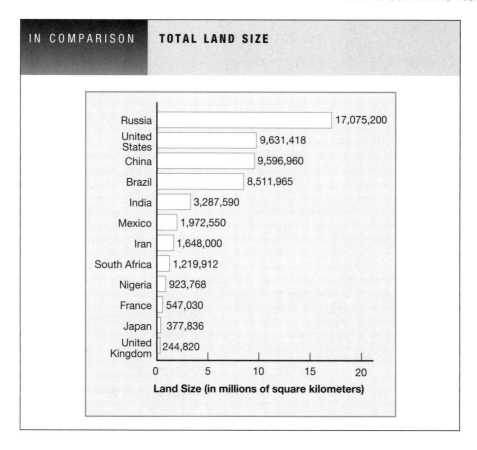

IN COMPARISON   TOTAL LAND SIZE

Russia — 17,075,200
United States — 9,631,418
China — 9,596,960
Brazil — 8,511,965
India — 3,287,590
Mexico — 1,972,550
Iran — 1,648,000
South Africa — 1,219,912
Nigeria — 923,768
France — 547,030
Japan — 377,836
United Kingdom — 244,820

Land Size (in millions of square kilometers)

ent state relatively recently, in 1960. With the end of the cold war in 1989 and the collapse of the Soviet Union two years later, a number of states emerged or reemerged.

States differ, too, in their level of organization, effectiveness, and stability. The power of a state depends in part on its **legitimacy,** or the extent to which its authority is regarded as right and proper. Political scientists have long observed that there are different sources of a state's legitimacy. State authority may draw on *traditional legitimacy,* in which the state is obeyed because it has a long tradition of being obeyed. Alternatively, a state may be considered legitimate because of *charismatic legitimacy,* its identification with the magnetic appeal of a leader or movement. Finally, states may gain legitimacy on the basis of *rational-legal legitimacy,* a system of laws and procedures that become highly institutionalized. Although most modern states derive their legitimacy from rational-legal sources, both traditional and charismatic legitimacy often continue to play a role. In Japan and the United Kingdom, for example, the monarchy is a source of traditional legitimacy that

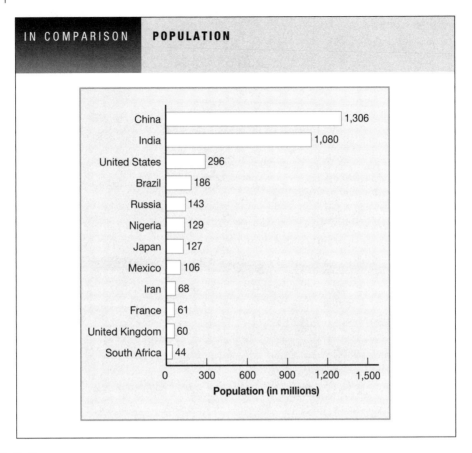

IN COMPARISON   **POPULATION**

Country	Population (in millions)
China	1,306
India	1,080
United States	296
Brazil	186
Russia	143
Nigeria	129
Japan	127
Mexico	106
Iran	68
France	61
United Kingdom	60
South Africa	44

complements the rational-legal legitimacy of the state. Some postcolonial states in the developing world have had considerable trouble establishing legitimacy. Often colonial powers created states that cut across ethnic boundaries or contain hostile ethnic groups, as is the case of Nigeria and Iran.

States differ in their ability to preserve their sovereignty and carry out the basic functions of maintaining law and order. Strong states can perform the basic tasks of defending their borders from outside attacks and defending their authority from internal nonstate rivals. Weak states have trouble carrying out those basic tasks and often suffer from endemic internal violence, a poor infrastructure, and the inability to collect taxes and enforce the rule of law. High levels of corruption are often a symptom of state weakness (see the table on perceived corruption, p. 5). Taken to an extreme, weak states may experience a complete loss of legitimacy and power and may be overwhelmed by anarchy and violence. Political scientists refer to those relatively rare cases as failed states.[2]

Finally, states differ in the degree to which they centralize or disperse political power. *Unitary states* concentrate most of their political power in the

national capital, allocating little decision-making power to regions or localities. Federal states divide power between the central state and regional or local
authorities (such as provinces, counties, and cities). Unitary states like the
United Kingdom and South Africa may be stronger and more decisive, but
the centralization of power may create local resentment and initiate calls for
a **devolution** (the handing down) of power to regions and localities. Federal
states, like Brazil and Russia, often find that their dispersal of power ham-
pers national decision making and accountability.

Comparing Regimes

Political **regimes** are the norms and rules regarding individual freedoms and
collective equality, the locus of power, and the use of that power. It is easiest
to think of political regimes as the rules of the game governing the exercise
of power. In modern political systems, regimes are most often described in
written constitutions. In some countries, however, such as the United Kingdom, the regime consists of a combination of laws and customs that are not

IN COMPARISON	PERCEIVED CORRUPTION, 2005

On a scale of 1 to 10, 1 = most corrupt; 10 = least corrupt.

Country	Score
Nigeria	1.9
Russia	2.4
India	2.9
Iran	2.9
China	3.2
Mexico	3.5
Brazil	3.7
South Africa	4.5
Japan	7.3
France	7.5
United States	7.6
United Kingdom	8.6

Source: Corruption Perceptions Index 2005, Transparency International,
http://www.transparency.org/policy_and_research/surveys_indices/cpi/2005
(accessed 2 March 2005).

incorporated into any one written document. In other countries, such as China and Iran, written constitutions do not accurately describe the extra-constitutional rules that govern the exercise of power.

Democratic regimes have rules that emphasize a large role for the public in governance and protect basic rights and freedoms. **Authoritarian regimes** limit the role of the public in decision making and often deny citizens' basic rights and restrict their freedoms. In the past quarter century, the world has witnessed a dramatic rise in the number of democratic regimes.[3] Over half the world's population, however, is still governed by nondemocratic regimes, which one leading research organization defines as either "partly free," or **illiberal,** (meaning that some personal liberties and democratic rights are limited) or "not free," or authoritarian, (meaning that the public has little individual freedom).[4]

COMPARING DEMOCRATIC POLITICAL INSTITUTIONS

Most political regimes, whether democratic or not, establish a number of political institutions. The **executive** is the branch of government that carries out

IN COMPARISON	FREEDOM HOUSE RANKINGS, 2006

On a scale of 1 to 7, 1 = free; 3 = partly free; 5.5 = not free.

Country	Ranking
China	6.5
Iran	6.0
Russia	5.5
Nigeria	4.0
India	2.5
Mexico	2.0
Brazil	2.0
South Africa	1.5
Japan	1.5
France	1.0
United States	1.0
United Kingdom	1.0

Source: Freedom House, http://www.freedomhouse.org/research/ freeworld/2005/combined2005.pdf (accessed 2 February 2006).

the laws and policies of a given state. We can think of the executive as containing two separate sets of duties. The **head of state** symbolizes and represents the people, both nationally and internationally, embodying and articulating the goals of the regime, and the **head of government** deals with the everyday tasks of running the state, such as formulating and executing policy. The distinction between those roles is most easily seen in systems like those of Japan, the United Kingdom, and France, which have separate heads of state and heads of government. Other systems, like those of Brazil, Mexico, South Africa, and the United States, assign the two roles to a single individual.

The **legislature** is the branch of government formally charged with making laws. The organization and power of legislatures differ considerably. In some political regimes, especially authoritarian ones like China and Iran, the legislature has little power or initiative and serves mainly to rubber-stamp government legislation. In other systems, like that of the United States, the legislature is relatively powerful and autonomous. Unicameral legislatures (often found in smaller countries) consist of a single chamber; bicameral legislatures consist of two legislative chambers. In those cases one chamber often represents the population at large (referred to as the lower house), and the other (referred to as the upper house) reflects the geographical sub-units.

The **judiciary** is the branch of a country's government that is concerned with dispensing justice. The **constitutional court** is the highest judicial body to rule on the constitutionality of laws and other government actions; in most political systems, the constitutional court also formally oversees the entire judicial structure. The power of a regime's judiciary is determined in part by the nature of its power of **judicial review,** the mechanism by which the court reviews laws and policies and overturns those seen as violations of the constitution. Some regimes give the judiciary the power of concrete review, allowing the high court to rule on constitutional issues only when disputes are brought before it. Other regimes give the judiciary the power of abstract review, allowing it to decide questions that do not arise from legal cases, sometimes even allowing it to make judgments on legislation that has not been enacted. In France, the Constitutional Council has only powers of abstract review, while in the United States the Supreme Court has only the power of concrete review. The highest courts in England, by contrast, do not have power to overturn legislation under any circumstances.

The powers of these political institutions and the relationships among them vary considerably across regimes. The most important variation concerns the relationship between the legislature and the executive. There are three major models of legislative-executive relations within democratic regimes. The **parliamentary system** features an executive head of government (often referred to as a prime minister) usually elected from within the legislature. The prime minister is usually the leader of the largest political

PARLIAMENTARY SYSTEMS

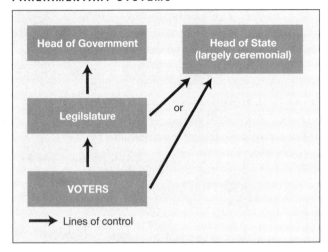

party in the legislature. The prime minister and the cabinet (the body of chief ministers or officials in government in charge of policy areas such as defense, agriculture, and so on) are charged with formulating and executing policy. The head of state in such systems is usually either an indirectly elected or largely ceremonial president or hereditary monarch.

The **presidential system** combines the roles of head of state and head of government in the office of the president. These systems feature a directly elected president who holds most of the government's executive powers. Presidential systems have directly elected legislatures that to varying degrees serve as a check on presidential authority.

There has been much scholarly debate about the advantages and disadvantages of these two legislative-executive models.[5] Parliamentary systems are often praised for reducing conflict between the legislature and the executive (since the executive is approved by the legislature), thus producing more efficient government. In addition, when parliamentary legislatures lack a majority, political parties must compromise to create a government supported by a majority of the legislature. Parliamentary systems are also more flexible because when prime ministers lose the support of the legislature they can be swiftly removed through a legislative "vote of no confidence." The appointment of a new prime minister, or the convocation of new elections, can often resolve political deadlocks. But critics point out that parliamentary systems with a strong majority in the legislature can produce a very strong, virtually unchecked government. Moreover, in fractious legislatures it can be difficult to cobble together a stable majority government.

PRESIDENTIAL SYSTEMS

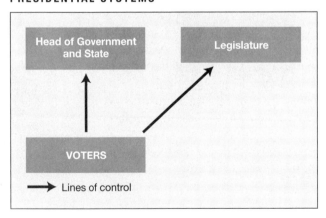

Presidential systems are often portrayed as more stable. There are fixed terms of office for the president and the legislature, which is not the case in most parliamentary systems. Moreover, presidents are directly elected by the public and can be removed only by the legislature and only in cases of criminal misconduct. Nonetheless, presidential systems have been criticized for producing divisive winner-take-all outcomes, lacking the flexibility needed to confront crises, and leading to overly powerful executives in the face of weak and divided legislatures.[6]

In an attempt to avoid the weaknesses of parliamentary and presidential systems, some newer democratic regimes, like those of France and Russia, have adopted a third model of legislative-executive relations, called the **semi-presidential system.** This system includes both a prime minister approved by the legislature and a directly elected president, with the two sharing executive power. In practice, semi-presidential systems tend to produce strong presidents akin to those in pure presidential systems, but the exact balance between the executives varies from case to case.

A final political institution worth mentioning is the **electoral system,** which determines how votes are cast and counted. Most democratic regimes use one of two models. The most commonly employed is **proportional representation (PR).** PR relies upon **multimember districts (MMDs),** in which more than one legislative seat is contested in each electoral district. Voters cast their ballots for a list of party candidates rather than for a single representative, and the percentage of votes a party receives in a district determines how many of that district's seats the party will win. Thus, the percentage of votes each party wins in each district should closely correspond to the percentage of seats allocated to each party. PR systems produce legislatures that often closely reflect the percentage of votes won nationwide by each political party. As a result, they tend to foster multiple political parties, including small ones.

A minority of democracies (mainly the United Kingdom and its former colonies, such as India and Nigeria) rely upon **single-member districts (SMDs).** In these systems, there is only one representative for each constituency,

SEMI-PRESIDENTIAL SYSTEMS

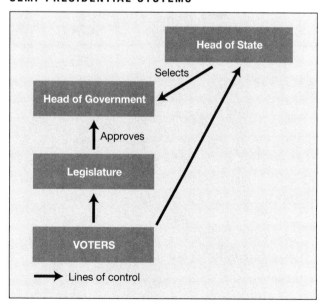

and in each district the candidate with the greatest number of votes—and not necessarily a majority—wins the seat. As opposed to PR systems, SMD votes cast for all but the one winning candidate are "wasted"—that is, they do not count toward any representation in the legislature. SMD systems tend to discriminate against small parties, especially those with a national following rather than a geographically concentrated following.

As with the legislative-executive models, there is a vigorous debate about which electoral system is more desirable.[7] PR systems are considered more democratic, since they "waste" fewer votes and encourage the expression of a greater range of political interests. PR increases the number of parties able to win seats in a legislature and allows parties concerned with narrow or minority interests to gain representation. SMD systems are often endorsed because they allow voters in each district to connect directly with their elected representatives instead of their party, making the representatives more accountable to the electorate. Supporters of SMD argue that it is beneficial to eliminate narrowly based or extremist parties from the legislature. They view SMD systems as more likely to produce stable, centrist legislative majorities.

Some democracies, including a number of newer ones such as Russia and Mexico have combined SMD and PR voting systems in what is known as a

Combinations of Political Institutions				
Country	Type of Regime	Type of State	Legislative-Executive System	Electoral System
Brazil	Democratic	Federal	Presidential	PR
China	Authoritarian	Unitary		
France	Democratic	Unitary	Semi-presidential	SMD
India	Democratic	Federal	Parliamentary	SMD
Iran	Authoritarian	Unitary		SMD
Japan	Democratic	Unitary	Parliamentary	Mixed
Mexico	Democratic	Federal	Presidential	Mixed
Nigeria	Democratic	Federal	Presidential	SMD
Russia	Illiberal	Federal	Semi-presidential	Mixed
South Africa	Democratic	Unitary	Parliamentary	PR
United Kingdom	Democratic	Unitary	Parliamentary	SMD
United States	Democratic	Federal	Presidential	SMD

mixed electoral system. Voters are given two votes: one for a candidate and the other for a party. Candidates in the SMDs are elected on the basis of a plurality while other seats are elected from MMDs and allocated using PR.

COMPARING NON-DEMOCRATIC REGIMES

Many non-democratic regimes have institutions that on paper appear quite similar to those in democratic regimes. In most authoritarian regimes, however, the legislature, the judiciary, and the electoral system do not reveal much about the exercise of political power.

Non-democratic regimes differ from one another in a number of important ways. Common forms of non-democratic regimes include personal dictatorships, monarchies, military regimes, one-party regimes, theocracies, and illiberal regimes. A personal dictatorship, like that of Porfirio Díaz in Mexico (1876–1910), is based on the power of a single strong leader, who usually relies on charismatic or traditional authority to maintain power. In a military regime (such as Brazil from 1964 to 1985 or Nigeria from 1966 to 1979), the institution of the military dominates politics. A one-party regime (like Mexico from 1917 to 2000) is dominated by a strong political party that relies upon a broad membership as a source of political control. In a theocracy, a rare form of government, though the one that characterizes present-day Iran, a leader claims to rule on behalf of God. An illiberal regime (as in present-day Russia) retains the basic structures of a democracy but does not protect civil liberties. In the real world, many non-democratic regimes combine various aspects of these types.

Communist regimes are one-party regimes in which a Communist party controls most aspects of a country's political and economic system. Specific Communist regimes (such as China under Mao Zedong or the Soviet Union under Joseph Stalin) have sometimes been described as **totalitarian.** Totalitarian regimes feature a strong official ideology that seeks to transform fundamental aspects of the state, society, and the economy, using a wide array of organizations and the application of force. (A non-Communist example of totalitarianism is Nazi Germany.)

Non-democratic regimes use different tools to enforce their political domination. The most obvious mechanisms are state violence and surveillance. The enforcement ranges from systematic and widespread repression (as in the mass purges in the Soviet Union or contemporary Iran) to sporadic and selective repression of the regime's opponents (as in Brazil in the 1960s). Another important tool of non-democratic regimes is *co-optation*, whereby members of the public are brought into a beneficial relationship with the state and the government. Co-optation takes many forms, including *corporatism,* in which citizen participation is channeled into state-sanctioned groups; *clientelism,* in which the state provides benefits to groups of its political supporters; and *rent seeking,* in which the government allows its supporters to occupy positions of power in order to monopolize state benefits. The non-democratic regime that dominated Mexico for much of the twentieth century skillfully employed all of those forms of co-optation to garner public support for the governing party, minimizing its need to rely upon coercion. Finally, the mechanism of control that is most often employed in totalitarian regimes is the *personality cult,* or the state-sponsored exaltation of a leader. The personality cult of Stalin in the Soviet Union and that of Mao in China are prime examples, as is the cult of personality that developed around Ayatollah Ruhollah Khomeini, the leader of the Iranian revolution of 1979.

Comparing Political Conflict and Competition

Political scientists can compare and contrast patterns of political conflict and competition in both democratic and authoritarian regimes. In democratic regimes, for example, it is common to compare the nature of elections and other forms of competition among political parties (often referred to as the **party system**).

On the most basic level, political scientists can compare the nature of suffrage, or the right to vote. In democratic regimes and even in many non-democratic ones, such as China and Iran, that right is often guaranteed to most adult citizens.[8] Another important feature of elections is the degree to which citizens actually participate by voting and by engaging in campaign activities (see the table on voter turnout, p. 13). Likewise, party systems can be compared on the basis of the number of parties, the size of their membership, their organizational strength, their ideological orientation, and their electoral strategies.

A comparative analysis of political conflict and competition cannot focus solely on elections. In most political systems, much political conflict and competition takes place in **civil society,** which comprises the organizations outside the state that help people define and advance their own interests. In addition to political parties, the organizations that make up a country's civil society often include a host of groups as diverse as gun clubs and labor unions.

Comparing Societies

The state and the regime exist in the context of their society, and societies differ from one another in ways that can strongly influence politics. For example, ethnic divisions exist within many states. **Ethnicity** refers to the specific attributes that make one group of people culturally different from others; attributes such as customs, language, religion, region, and history. Some states, like China, Japan, and Russia, are relatively homogeneous: one ethnic group makes up a large portion of the society. At the other extreme, countries like Nigeria, Iran,

Average Voter Turnout, 1945–2000	
Country (number of elections)	**Eligible Voters Voting (%)**
South Africa (1)	85.5
United Kingdom (15)	74.9
Japan (21)	69.0
Iran (2)	67.6
France (15)	67.3
India (12)	60.7
Russia (2)	55.0
United States (26)	48.3
Mexico (18)	48.1
Brazil (13)	47.9
Nigeria (3)	47.6
China	NA

Source: "Turnout in the World: Country by Country Performance," International Institute for Democracy and Electoral Assistance

http://www.idea.int/vt/survey/voter_turnout_pop2.cfm (accessed 27 January 2006).

Mexico, and India have a great deal of ethnic diversity. Ethnic diversity can often be a source of political conflict, and even in relatively homogeneous societies the presence of ethnic minorities can pose political challenges (see the table on ethnic diversity, p. 14).[9]

Societies also differ in terms of their political cultures. **Political culture** can be defined as the patterns of basic norms relating to politics. Political scientists have learned a great deal about how political cultures differ in a variety of areas, including citizens' trust in government, respect for political authority, knowledge about politics, and assessment of their political efficacy (the ability to influence political outcomes).[10]

Political scientists also consider **national identity,** or the extent to which citizens of a country are bound together by a common set of political aspirations (most often self-government and sovereignty). Countries with a long history of a consolidated state often have higher levels of national identity than states with a shorter history.

One interesting difference among societies is in the importance they place on religion. In most societies, religiosity has declined with economic prosperity and with the growth of secular values. France, Japan, Russia, and the

Ethnic and Religious Diversity

Country	Largest Ethnic Group (%)	Second Largest Ethnic Group (%)	Largest Religious Group (%)	Second Largest Religious Group (%)
Brazil	55.0	38.0	80.0	20.0
China	92.0	8.0[a]	94–96.0	3–4.0
France[a]	NA	NA	83–88.0	5–10.0
India	72.0	25.5	81.0	12.0
Iran	51.0	24.0	89.0	9.0
Japan	99.0	1.0	84.0	16.0[d]
Mexico	60.0	30.0	89.0	6.0
Nigeria	29.0	21.0	50.0	40.0
Russia	81.5	3.8	54.0	19.0
South Africa	75.0	13.0	78.7	19.8
United Kingdom	81.5	9.6	71.6	2.7
United States	67.0[b]	14.0[c]	52.0	24.0

[a]The French census does not collect data on ethnicity.
[b]Based on the U.S. Census Bureau's 2003 estimate that about 14 percent of citizens are Hispanic.
[c]All other ethnic groups combined.
[d]All other religious groups combined.

United Kingdom are relatively secular societies in which most people do not view religion as very important; the United States continues to be an interesting exception in this regard. In Nigeria and Iran, religion is viewed as important by nearly all citizens.

Individuals and groups within a society can also be distinguished according to their political attitudes and ideologies. **Political attitudes** describe views regarding the status quo in a society, specifically, the desired pace and methods of political change. *Radical* attitudes support rapid, extensive, and often revolutionary change. *Liberal* attitudes promote evolutionary change within the system. *Conservative* attitudes support the status quo and view change as risky. *Reactionary* attitudes promote rapid change to restore political, social, and economic institutions that once existed. Since political attitudes describe views of the status quo, radicals, liberals, conservatives, and reactionaries differ according to their setting. A reactionary in the United

Kingdom, for example, might support the creation of an absolute monarchy, while a reactionary in China might call for a return to Maoist totalitarianism.

POLITICAL ATTITUDES

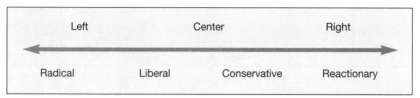

Whereas political attitudes are particular and context specific, **political ideologies** are universal sets of political values regarding the fundamental goals of politics.[11] A political ideology prescribes an ideal balance between freedom and equality. The ideology of **liberalism** (as opposed to a liberal political *attitude*) places a high priority on individual political and economic freedoms, favoring them over any attempts to create economic equality. Private property, capitalism, and protections for the individual against the state are central to liberal ideology. **Communism,** on the other hand, emphasizes economic equality rather than individual political and economic freedoms. Collective property (state ownership) and a dominant state are cornerstones of communism. **Social democracy** (often referred to as democratic socialism) is in some ways a hybrid of liberalism and communism in that it places considerable value on equality but attempts to protect some individual freedoms. Social democrats advocate a mixed welfare state in which an active state exists alongside a largely private economy. **Fascism,** like communism, is hostile to the idea of individual freedom but rejects the notion of equality. **Anarchism,** like communism, is based on the belief that private property and capitalism create inequality, but like liberalism it places a high value on individual political freedom.

The strength of each ideology differs across political systems. For example, opinion research demonstrates that citizens of the United States and, to a lesser extent, citizens of the United Kingdom, have an unusually strong commitment to liberal ideology; large numbers of them support individualism and manifest a notable distrust of state activism. French and Japanese citizens tend to be less individualistic and are more supportive of an active role for the state in the economy. In China, the rise of capitalist economics has eroded popular support for Communist ideology.

Comparing Political Economies

The study of how politics and economics are related is commonly known as **political economy;** this relationship differs considerably in different political systems.[12] All modern states, however, intervene to some extent in the

POLITICAL IDEOLOGIES

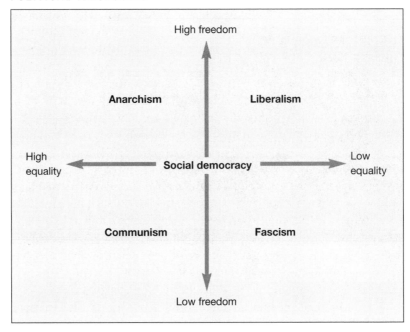

day-to-day affairs of their economies, and in doing so they depend on a variety of economic institutions. Perhaps the most important of these is the *market*, or the interaction between the forces of supply and demand that allocate goods and resources.[13] Markets, in turn, depend on the institution of *property*, the ownership of goods and services. In their attempt to ensure the distribution of goods and resources, states differ in their interaction with the market and their desire and ability to protect private property.

A major political issue in most societies, and a major point of contention among political ideologies, is the appropriate role of the market and the state in the allocation of goods and services. Some goods—for example, air and water quality—are essential to all of society but not easily provided by the market; these are often referred to as **public goods.** Other goods, such as the production of food and automobiles, are more feasibly provided by private producers using the market. In between those extremes is a large gray area. States differ in the degree to which they define a wide array of goods and services as public goods. As a result, government social expenditures (state provision of public benefits, such as education, health care, and transportation) vary widely among countries.

In the political economic systems of countries such as the United States and the United Kingdom, where liberal ideology is dominant, the state plays a significant but relatively small role. In France and Japan, however, the state has played a much larger role in the economy through state ownership (especially in France) and state planning (especially in Japan). Authoritarian regimes have typically had a heavy hand in economic matters, as has certainly been the case in China and Iran. Whereas China's Communist regime has gradually allowed growth in the private sector, the Iranian revolution of 1979 led to an increase in that state's involvement in the economy.

Economies also differ markedly in their size, their affluence, their rates of growth, and their levels of equality. The most commonly used tool for comparing the size of economies is the **gross domestic product (GDP),** the total market value of goods and services produced in a country in one year. GDP is often measured in U.S. dollars at **purchasing-power parity (PPP),** a mechanism that attempts to estimate the real buying power of income in each country using prices in the United States as a benchmark (see the table on GDP at PPP). In terms of the overall size of the twelve economies considered in this volume, the United States, China, Japan, and India dwarf the other cases. It is sometimes more useful, however, to look at *GDP per capita,* which divides

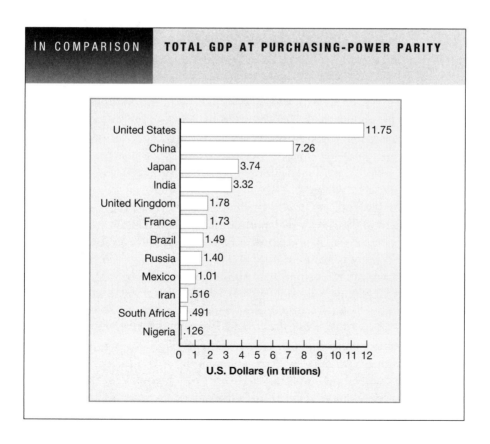

IN COMPARISON   TOTAL GDP AT PURCHASING-POWER PARITY

Country	U.S. Dollars (in trillions)
United States	11.75
China	7.26
Japan	3.74
India	3.32
United Kingdom	1.78
France	1.73
Brazil	1.49
Russia	1.40
Mexico	1.01
Iran	.516
South Africa	.491
Nigeria	.126

U.S. Dollars (in trillions)

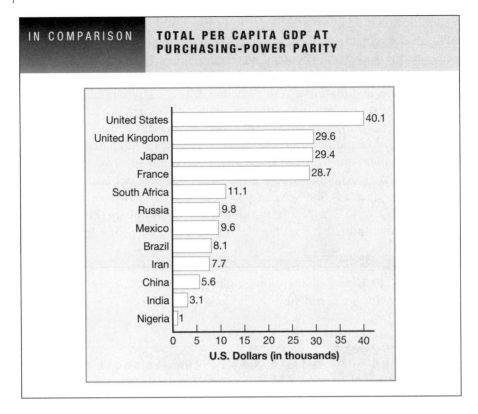

IN COMPARISON   **TOTAL PER CAPITA GDP AT PURCHASING-POWER PARITY**

Country	U.S. Dollars (in thousands)
United States	40.1
United Kingdom	29.6
Japan	29.4
France	28.7
South Africa	11.1
Russia	9.8
Mexico	9.6
Brazil	8.1
Iran	7.7
China	5.6
India	3.1
Nigeria	1

the GDP by total population. GDP is rarely distributed evenly among the population, however, and the **Gini index** is the most commonly used measure of economic inequality, in which perfect equality is scored as 0, and perfect inequality is scored as 100. Endemic inequality has long been a characteristic of developing countries, such as Brazil, South Africa, Mexico, and India (see the table of Gini Index rankings, p. 19). In wealthy countries like the United States, the economic boom of the 1980s and 1990s led to a growing gap between the rich and the poor and a surprisingly large increase in the percentage of the population in poverty.

It is also important to compare the GDP's rate of growth, often expressed as an average of GDP growth over a number of years. Nine of the twelve countries considered in this volume enjoyed economic growth between 1990 and 2002, with China and India growing fastest (see the table on GDP growth, p. 20).

The size and wealth of an economy, and even the distribution of wealth, are not necessarily correlated with the affluence or poverty of its citizens, however. The United Nations produces a Human Development Index (HDI) (see the table on HDI rankings, p. 21) that considers a variety of indicators of affluence, including health and education. When considering GDP per capita and the HDI, one sees that the United States, the United Kingdom, Japan, and France are clearly the most affluent of the countries discussed in this volume.

Governments often struggle with myriad challenges within their economic systems. One concern is the danger of inflation, a situation characterized by sustained rising prices. Extremely high levels of inflation (hyperinflation) can endanger economic growth and impoverish citizens who live on a fixed income. Governments also fear the consequences of high levels of unemployment, which can place a large burden on public expenditures and reduce the tax base.

The Global Context

A country's politics is not determined solely by domestic factors. Increasingly, international forces shape politics in the context of a rapidly expanding and intensifying set of links among states, societies, and economies. This phenomenon, known as globalization, has created new opportunities while pos-

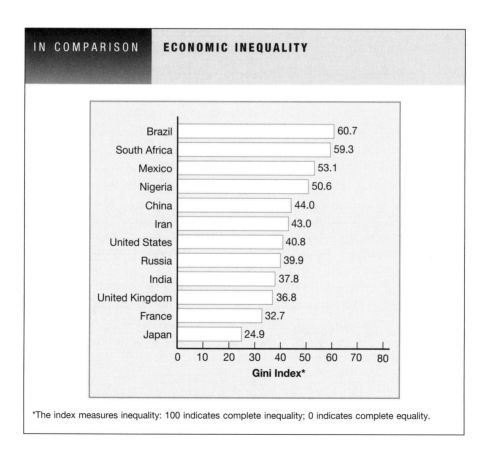

IN COMPARISON   **ECONOMIC INEQUALITY**

Country	Gini Index*
Brazil	60.7
South Africa	59.3
Mexico	53.1
Nigeria	50.6
China	44.0
Iran	43.0
United States	40.8
Russia	39.9
India	37.8
United Kingdom	36.8
France	32.7
Japan	24.9

*The index measures inequality: 100 indicates complete inequality; 0 indicates complete equality.

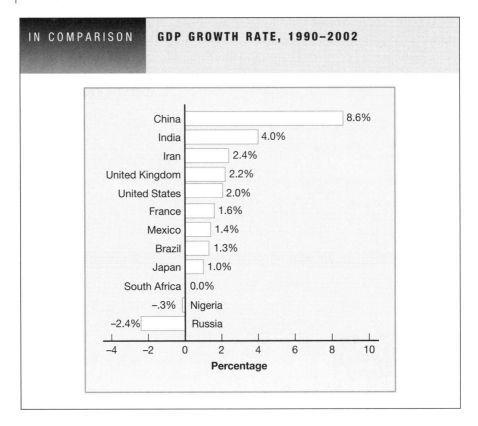

IN COMPARISON   GDP GROWTH RATE, 1990–2002

China — 8.6%
India — 4.0%
Iran — 2.4%
United Kingdom — 2.2%
United States — 2.0%
France — 1.6%
Mexico — 1.4%
Brazil — 1.3%
Japan — 1.0%
South Africa — 0.0%
Nigeria — –.3%
Russia — –2.4%

Percentage

ing important challenges to states. Cross-border interactions have long existed, but the trend toward globalization has created a far more extensive and intensive web of relationships among many people across vast distances. People are increasingly interacting regularly and directly through sophisticated international networks involving travel, communication, business, and education.

It is too early to predict the consequences of globalization for governments and citizens of states. Some observers have argued that globalization may eclipse the state, resulting in global political institutions, whereas others contend that states will continue to play an important, albeit changed, role.[14] Governments are increasingly restricted by the international system, because of both international trade agreements (like those promoted by the World Trade Organization) and the need to remain competitive in the international marketplace.

As a result of globalization, a host of international organizations regularly affects domestic politics, economics, and society. Multinational corporations (MNC), firms that produce, distribute, and market goods or services in more than one country, are increasingly powerful. They are an important source of foreign direct investment, or the purchase of assets in one country by a foreign firm. An array of **nongovernmental organizations** (NGOs)—Amnesty International and the International Red Cross, for example—is increasingly visible. Also active are **intergovernmental organizations** (IGOs), groups created by states to serve particular policy ends. Some important examples are the United Nations, the World Trade Organization, the European Union, the Group of 8 (G8), and the Organization of American States.

A final dimension of globalization, and another example of the growing interconnectedness of states, is the increasing movement of people both within and across borders. Relatively homogeneous societies like France and the United Kingdom have struggled in recent decades to integrate their growing immigrant population. The United States has become dependent on immigrant labor from Mexico and elsewhere. China's opening to the world economy has drawn millions of rural citizens to its booming coastal cities. More than ever, states find that the environment of globalization limits the policy options open to their governments.

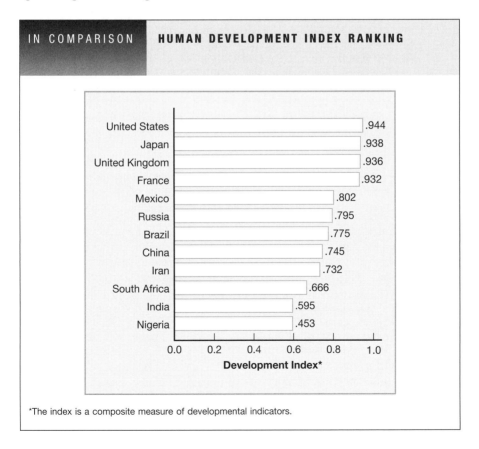

IN COMPARISON   **HUMAN DEVELOPMENT INDEX RANKING**

Country	Development Index*
United States	.944
Japan	.938
United Kingdom	.936
France	.932
Mexico	.802
Russia	.795
Brazil	.775
China	.745
Iran	.732
South Africa	.666
India	.595
Nigeria	.453

*The index is a composite measure of developmental indicators.

CONCLUSION

This introduction has briefly summarized some key concepts and terms used by political scientists to compare political systems. The inquisitive student of comparative politics will find fascinating similarities in the cases that follow. The commonalities across cases give credence to the utility of the comparative enterprise and justify the analytic comparisons offered. But these countries are also diverse and always changing, reminding us of the daunting challenges facing comparative political study.

NOTES

1. For an excellent collection of essays on the state see Peter B. Evans, Dietrich Rueschemeyer, and Theda Skocpol, eds., *Bringing the State Back In* (Cambridge: Cambridge University Press, 1985).
2. Robert I. Rotberg, "Failed States in a World of Terror," *Foreign Affairs* 81:4, (July/August 2002) pp. 127–140.
3. Samuel Huntington, *The Third Wave: Democratization in the Late Twentieth Century* (Norman, OK: University of Oklahoma Press, 1991).
4. Freedom House, http://www.freedomhouse.org/research/freeworld/2005/combined2005.pdf (accessed 2 February 2006).
5. See, for example, Alfred Stepan with Cindy Skach, "Constitutional Frameworks and Democratic Consolidation: Parliamentarism versus Presidentialism," *World Politics* 46:1 (January 1993), pp. 1–22.
6. Juan J. Linz and Arturo Valenzuela, eds., *The Failures of Presidential Democracy: The Case of Latin America* (Baltimore: Johns Hopkins University Press, 1994).
7. One interesting contribution to the debate is Benjamin Reilly, "Electoral Systems for Divided Societies," *Journal of Democracy* 13:2 (April 2002) pp. 156–170.
8. Non-democratic regimes like the Soviet Union or contemporary Iran often feature elections that impose serious limits on the political opposition. In the Soviet Union, only the Communist Party could run candidates. In Iran, the government has often excluded opposition candidates.
9. A good overview is Donald Horowitz, *Ethnic Groups in Conflict* (Berkeley: University of California Press, 2000).
10. Among the many works on public opinion and political participation see Russell Dalton, *Citizen Politics: Public Opinion and Political Parties in Advanced Industrial Democracies* (Washington, DC: CQ Press, 2005).
11. A good overview of political ideologies is Leon Baradat, *Political Ideologies*, 9th ed. (Upper Saddle River, NJ: Prentice Hall, 2005).
12. A classic treatment of political economy is Charles Lindblom, *Politics and Markets: The World's Political Economic Systems* (New York: Basic Books, 1977). The field of international political economics studies the relationships between politics and economics on the international level, and in political science, is a subfield of international relations.
13. Charles Lindblom, *The Market System: What It Is, How It Works, and What to Make of It* (New Haven, CT: Yale University Press, 2001).

14. For an example of the former, see Martin van Creveld, "The Fate of the State," *Parameters* (Spring 1996, pp. 4–18). For an example of the latter, see Saskia Sassen, "The State and Globalization," in Rodney Bruce Hall and Thomas Biersteker, eds., *The Emergence of Private Authority in Global Governance* (Cambridge: Cambridge University Press, 2002), pp. 94–106.

KEY TERMS

anarchism   p. 15

authoritarian regimes   p. 6

civil society   p. 12

communism   p. 15

comparative politics   p. 2

constitutional court   p. 7

democratic regimes   p. 6

devolution   p. 5

electoral system   p. 9

ethnicity   p. 12

executive   p. 6

fascism   p. 15

Gini index   p. 18

government   p. 2

gross domestic product (GDP)   p. 17

head of government   p. 7

head of state   p. 7

illiberal   p. 6

intergovernmental organizations
  (IGOs)   p. 21

judicial review   p. 7

judiciary   p. 7

legislature   p. 7

legitimacy   p. 3

liberalism   p. 15

mixed electoral system   p. 11

multimember districts (MMDs)
  p. 9

national identity   p. 13

nongovernmental organizations
  (NGOs)   p. 21

party system   p. 12

political attitudes   p. 14

political culture   p. 13

political economy   p. 15

political ideologies   p. 15

presidential system   p. 8

parliamentary system   p. 7

proportional representation (PR)
  p. 9

public goods   p. 16

purchasing-power parity (PPP)
  p. 17

regimes   p. 5

semi-presidential system   p. 9

single-member districts (SMDs)
  p. 9

social democracy   p. 15

states   p. 2

totalitarian   p. 11

WEB LINKS

CIA World Factbook   **www.cia.gov/cia/publications/factbook**

Freedom House   **www.freedomhouse.org**

The WWW Virtual Library: International Affairs Resources
   www2.etown.edu/vl

Political Science Resource Pages **www.psr.keele.ac.uk/area.htm**
Inter-Parliamentary Union **www.ipu.org/english/home.htm**
World Bank **www.worldbank.org**
Comparative Politics **web.gc.cuny.edu/jcp**
Journal of Democracy **www.journalofdemocracy.org**

2 UNITED KINGDOM

Head of state: Queen Elizabeth II
(since February 6, 1952)

Head of government:
Prime Minister Anthony (Tony) Blair
(since May 2, 1997)

Capital: London

Total land size: 244,820 sq km

Population: 60 million

GDP at PPP: 1.8 trillion US$

GDP per capita: $29,600

INTRODUCTION

Why Study This Case?

There are many reasons why most introductions to comparative politics begin with a study of the United Kingdom (UK). As the primogenitor of modern democracy, its political system is at once strikingly unique and a model for many other liberal democracies. The UK is the world's oldest democracy. Its transition to democracy was gradual, beginning with thirteenth-century limitations on absolute monarchs and continuing incrementally to the establishment of the rule of law in the seventeenth century and the extension of suffrage to women in the twentieth century. The democratization process persists today, with reforms of the anachronistic upper house of the legislature and ongoing discussions about electoral reform. Unlike many other democracies, the UK cannot attach a specific date or event to the advent of its democracy. At the same time, the United Kingdom is also unusual in that the main political rules of the game have not been seriously interrupted or radically altered since the mid–seventeenth century.

The United Kingdom is one of only a handful of democracies without a written constitution. The longevity and stability of its democracy have thus depended to a large extent on both traditional legitimacy and a unique political culture of accommodation and moderation. Although its constitution is unwritten, many aspects of its democracy have been adopted by a number of the world's other democracies, especially in areas of the globe that were once part of the far-flung British Empire.

Finally, the United Kingdom deserves careful study because it is the birthplace of the Industrial Revolution, which turned it into the world's leading economic and political power for several hundred years. Some have attributed the UK's early industrialization to the emergence of liberal ideology. The UK was also the first major industrialized country to experience an extended economic decline after World War II, the reasons for which have been much debated.

The United Kingdom remains a fascinating case. In 1979, **Margaret Thatcher** of the **Conservative Party** was the first leader of an industrial democracy to experiment with neo-liberal economic policies in an attempt to stem economic decline. The policies were very controversial within the UK but widely emulated in other democracies, including the United States. Even with Thatcher's resignation in 1990, the Conservatives (Tories) remained in power until the 1997 election when they were ousted by the **Labour Party.** Under the leadership of **Tony Blair,** the Labour Party has embraced many of the liberal policies executed by Thatcher and her conservative successors. These policies have become known as the **Third Way.**

Major Geographic and Demographic Features

Since 1801, the **United Kingdom of Great Britain and Northern Ireland** has been the formal name of the United Kingdom. Great Britain itself consists of three nations (England, Scotland, and Wales), and is separated from France by the English Channel. These three nations plus the northeastern part of the island of Ireland constitute the United Kingdom. The remainder of Ireland is called the Republic of Ireland. Confusingly, citizens of the UK are often referred to as British or Britons even if they live in Northern Ireland. Most Welsh, Scots, and Northern Irish consider themselves British, but it would be unwise to call a resident of Edinburgh (in Scotland) or Cardiff (in Wales) English.

The United Kingdom is roughly the size of Oregon and about two thirds the size of Japan. It has approximately 60 million residents, nearly twice the population of California and about half that of Japan. The population is not equally distributed among the four nations (England, Scotland, Wales, and Northern Ireland). Five of six Britons live in England. The UK can be considered a multiethnic state because it contains Scottish, Welsh, and English citizens, who have distinct cultures and languages. Racially, however, the UK is relatively homogeneous; its nonwhite population, composed mainly of immigrants from the UK's former colonies, is only about 3 percent of the total. The majority of those immigrants comes from the Indian Subcontinent, and about one third are from the Caribbean.

The UK's physical separation from the European mainland ended in 1994 with the inauguration of the Channel Tunnel, which links Britain and France. For much of British history, the country's isolation provided some protection from the conflicts and turmoil that afflicted the rest of Europe. A diminished fear of invasion may help explain the historically small size and minimal political importance of the UK's standing army (and the relative importance and strength of its navy). In addition, it may help explain the UK's late adherence to the European Union, its unwillingness to replace the British pound with the euro (the single European currency), and its continued skepticism about European unification.

Historical Development of the State

British citizens owe their allegiance to the Crown, the enduring symbol of the United Kingdom's state, rather than to a written constitution. The Crown symbolizes far more than just the monarchy or even Her Majesty's government. It represents, of course, the ceremonial and symbolic trappings of the British

TIME LINE OF POLITICAL DEVELOPMENT	
Year	**Event**
1215	King John forced to sign Magna Carta, thereby agreeing to a statement of the rights of English Barons
1295	Convening of Model Parliament of Edward I, the first representative parliament
1529	"Reformation Parliament" summoned by Henry VIII beginning process of cutting ties to the Roman Catholic Church
1628	Charles I forced to accept Petition of Right, Parliament's statement of civil rights in return for funds
1642–48	English Civil War fought between Royalists and Parliamentarians
1649	Charles I tried and executed
1689	Bill of Rights issued by Parliament, establishing a constitutional monarchy in Britain
1707	Act of Union put into effect, uniting kingdoms of England and Scotland
1721	Sir Robert Walpole effectively made Britain's first prime minister
1832–67	Reform Acts passed, extending right to vote to virtually all urban males and some in the countryside
1900	Labour Party founded in Britain
1916–22	Anglo-Irish War fought, culminating in establishment of independent republic of Ireland, with Northern Ireland remaining part of the United Kingdom
1973	UK made a member of the European Economic Community (now the European Union)
1979–90	Margaret Thatcher served as prime minister
1982	Falklands War fought with Argentina
1997	Tony Blair becomes prime minister

state. In addition, it represents the rules (or regime) as well as the unhindered capacity (the sovereignty) to enforce and administer these rules and secure the country's borders.

The evolutionary changes of the state over the past eight centuries have been thoroughgoing and not without violence. But in comparison with political change elsewhere in the world, the development of the modern British state has been gradual, piecemeal, and peaceful.

EARLY DEVELOPMENT

Although we commonly think of the United Kingdom as a stable and unified nation-state, the country experienced repeated invasions over a period of about 1,500 years. Celts, Romans, Angles and Saxons, Danes, and finally Normans invaded the British Isles, each leaving important legacies. For example, the Angles and Saxons, Germanic people, left their language, except in areas they could not conquer, like Wales and Scotland, where local languages remained dominant until the eighteenth and nineteenth centuries. Today, we still refer to those areas as the UK's **Celtic fringe.**

In terms of the political development, another important legacy was the emergence of **common law,** a system based on local customs and precedent rather than formal legal codes. That system forms the basis of the contemporary legal systems of the UK (with the exception of Scotland), the United States, and many former British colonies.[1]

The last wave of invasions, by the Normans, occurred in 1066. The Normans were Danish Vikings who occupied northern France. In Britain, they replaced the Germanic ruling class and imposed central rule. Politically, their most important legacy was the institution of feudalism, which they brought from the European continent. Under feudalism lords provided vassals with military protection and economic support in exchange for labor and military service. Though hardly a democratic institution, feudalism did create a system of mutual obligations between lords and peasants on one level, and between monarchs and lords at another level. Indeed, some scholars have seen in these obligations the foundation for the eventual limits on royal power. The most important initial document in this regard is the **Magna Carta,** which British nobles obliged King John to sign in 1215 and which became a royal promise to uphold feudal customs and rights. The Magna Carta set an important precedent by limiting the power of British monarchs and subjecting them to the law. As a result, the United Kingdom never experienced the type of royal absolutism that was common in other countries (for example, in Russia), and this in turn helped pave the way for public control over government and the state.

The UK was fortunate to resolve relatively early certain conflicts that would arise in other states in the modern era. A prime example is the religious divide. During the reign of Henry VIII (1509–47), a major dispute between the British monarch and the Vatican (the center of the Roman Catholic Church) had unintended consequences. When the Catholic Church failed to grant Henry a divorce, he used **Parliament** to pass laws that effectively took England out of the Catholic Church and replaced Catholicism with a Protestant church that could be controlled by the English state instead of by Rome.

The creation of a state-controlled Anglican Church led to a religious institution that was weaker and less autonomous than its counterparts in other European countries. Though supporters of Catholicism fought unsuccessfully to regain power, religion never plagued the UK as a polarizing force the way it did in so many other countries. Northern Ireland, where the split between Protestants and Catholics continues to create political division, is the bloody exception to the rule. A second unintended consequence of the creation of the Anglican Church was that Henry VIII's use of Parliament to sanction the changes strengthened and legitimized Parliament's power. As with the Magna Carta, institutional changes helped pave the way for democratic control—even if that result was not foreseen at the time.

THE EMERGENCE OF THE MODERN BRITISH STATE

As you might have sensed by now, in comparison with its European neighbors the United Kingdom had a more constrained monarchy. This is not to say that British rulers were weak. But in addition to the early checks on monarchic rule, three major developments in the seventeenth and eighteenth centuries decisively undermined the power of British sovereigns and are crucial to understanding why the UK was one of the first nations to democratize.

First, the crowning of James I (a Scot) in 1603 united Scotland and England but created a political crisis. James was an absolutist at heart and resisted limits on his power imposed by Parliament. He sought to raise taxes without first asking Parliament, and his son Charles I, whose reign began in 1625, continued to flaunt royal power, eventually precipitating civil war. The English Civil War pitted the defenders of Charles against the supporters of Parliament, who won the bitter struggle and executed Charles in 1649.

For eleven years (1649–60), England had no monarch and functioned as a republic, known as the **Commonwealth.** Led by Oliver Cromwell, the Commonwealth soon became a military dictatorship. Parliament restored the monarchy in 1660 with the ascension of Charles II, but its power was forever weakened.

Second, when James II, a brother of Charles II, inherited the throne in 1685, the monarchy and Parliament again faced off. James was openly Catholic, and Parliament feared a return to Catholicism and absolute rule. In 1688, Parliament removed James and sent him into exile. In his place, Parliament installed James's Protestant daughter Mary and her Dutch husband, William. A year later, Parliament enacted the Bill of Rights, institutionalizing its political supremacy. Since that time, monarchs have owed their position to Parliament. The Glorious Revolution was a key turning point in the creation of the constitutional monarchy.

Third, in 1714, Parliament installed the current dynastic family by crowning George I (of German royalty). The monarch, who spoke little English, was forced to rely heavily on his **cabinet** (his top advisers, or ministers) and, specifically, on his **prime minister,** who coordinated the work of the other ministers. From 1721 to 1742, Sir Robert Walpole fashioned the position into much of what the office is today. By the late eighteenth century, in large part in reaction to the loss of the colonies in America, prime ministers and their cabinets were no longer selected by monarchs but were instead appointed by Parliament. Monarchs never again had the power to select members of the government.[2]

THE BRITISH EMPIRE

The United Kingdom began its overseas expansion in the sixteenth century, and by the early nineteenth century it had vanquished its main European rivals to become the world's dominant military, commercial, and cultural power. Its navy helped open new overseas markets for its burgeoning domestic industry, and by the empire's zenith in 1870, the UK controlled about one quarter of all world trade and probably had the wealthiest economy. The dimensions of the British Empire were truly exceptional. In the nineteenth century, it governed one quarter of the world's population, directly ruled almost fifty countries, and dominated many more with its commercial muscle.

Paralleling the gradual process of democratization in the UK, the erosion of the British Empire was also slow and incremental. It began with the loss of the American colonies in the late eighteenth century, though subsequently the empire continued to expand in Asia and Africa. By the early nineteenth century, however, it had begun to shrink. Following World War I, the UK granted independence to a few of its former colonies, including Egypt and most of Ireland. With the conclusion of World War II, the tide had turned against the empire. International sentiment favoring self-determination for subject peoples, local resistance in many colonies, the costs of the war, and the burden of maintaining far-flung colonies helped spell the end of the British Empire. Independence was willingly granted to most of the remaining colonial possessions throughout Southeast Asia, Africa, and the Caribbean.

The United Kingdom managed to retain control of a few small colonies, and in 1982 it fought a brief war with Argentina to retain possession of the remote Falkland Islands. One of the UK's last colonial possessions, Hong Kong, was returned to China in 1997. Today, the Commonwealth includes the UK and fifty-four of its former colonies and serves to maintain the economic and cultural ties established during the UK's long imperial rule.

THE INDUSTRIAL REVOLUTION

The United Kingdom lays claim to being the first industrial nation, and industrialization helped support the expansion of its empire. The country's early industrialization was based on its dominance in textiles, machinery, and iron production. It began in the late eighteenth century and developed slowly. By the mid–nineteenth century, most of the UK's workforce had moved away from the countryside urban areas. While industrialization dramatically changed British politics and society, the process did not create the kind of political upheaval and instability that was seen in many late-developing nations, where it occurred more rapidly. Because the British were the first to industrialize, the UK faced little initial competition and therefore amassed tremendous wealth. Its early prosperity may have facilitated its first steps toward democracy.[3]

But the blessing of early industrialization may also have been a factor in the UK's economic decline. As a world leader, the United Kingdom spent lavishly on its empire and led the Allied forces in World Wars I and II. Though the Allies won both wars, the UK was drained economically. The end of World War II also signaled the end of colonial rule, and the UK began to relinquish its empire. As the first industrialized country, the UK would also be one of the first industrialized nations to experience economic decline. When British industries faced new competition and obsolescence after World War II, the country found it increasingly difficult to reform its economy.

GRADUAL DEMOCRATIZATION

We have seen how Parliament weakened the power of the British monarchs, but at the same time we should note that Parliament itself originally represented the interests of the British elite: only the wealthy could vote. The UK had an "upper" **House of Lords,** which represented the aristocracy, and a "lower" **House of Commons,** which represented the interests of the lower aristocracy and the merchant class. In addition, by the time Parliament was established, British monarchs were no longer absolute rulers, although they continued to wield considerable political power. Two factors gradually democratized Parliament and further weakened monarchical power.

The first was the rise of political parties, which emerged in the eighteenth century as cliques of nobles but eventually reached out to a broader sector of society for support. The two largest cliques became the UK's first parties: the Conservatives (Tories) supported the monarch, and the **Liberals** (Whigs) opposed the policies of the monarch. The Whigs were the first to cultivate support among members of the UK's burgeoning commercial class, many of whom were still excluded from the political system.

The second was the expansion of suffrage. In 1832, the Whigs were able to push through a **Reform Act** that doubled the size of the British electorate, though it still excluded over 90 percent of British adults. Over the next century, both parties gradually supported measures to expand the suffrage, hoping in part to gain a political windfall. The process culminated in 1928, when women over the age of twenty-one in the UK were granted the right to vote.

The gradual expansion of the vote to include all adult citizens forced the political parties to respond to demands for additional services. The new voters wanted the expansion of such public goods as health care, education, and housing, and they looked to the state to provide them. It was the Labour Party, as the main representative of the working class, that pushed for policies that would develop basic social services for all citizens, or what we commonly call the welfare state. The British workers who had defended the United Kingdom so heroically during World War II returned from that conflict with a new sense of entitlement, and they elected Labour to power in 1945. Armed with a parliamentary majority, the Labour government quickly moved to implement a welfare state. This was accompanied by the nationalization of a number of sectors of industry, such as coal, utilities, rail, and health care.

POSTWAR POLITICS AND THE EXPANSION OF THE STATE

The Labour Party initiated the welfare state, but British Conservatives generally supported it during much of the postwar period in what has been called the postwar **collectivist consensus.** By the 1970s, however, the British economy was in crisis, and a new breed of Tories (dubbed neo-liberals) began to blame the UK's economic decline on the excesses of the welfare state.

When Margaret Thatcher became prime minister in 1979, she broke with traditional Tory support for the welfare state and pledged to diminish the state's role in the economy. She sought to lower taxes and cut state spending on costly social services, and she replaced some state services (in areas as diverse as housing and mass transit) with private enterprise. Her government thus marked the end of the postwar collectivist consensus. Yet in some ways, a new consensus has formed around Thatcher's reforms. Even the Labour Party, traditionally the staunch defender of an elaborate welfare state, has come to accept the Thatcherite view of more limited social expenditures and privatization.[4]

POLITICAL REGIME

The political regime of the United Kingdom is notable among the world's democracies because of its highly **majoritarian** features. Under the rules of British politics, the majority in Parliament has virtually unchecked power. Unlike political parties in other democracies, even parliamentary democracies, the majority party in the UK can enact policies with few checks from other branches of government. Again unlike other democracies, there are no formal constitutional limits on the central government, no judicial restraints, and no constitutionally sanctioned local authorities to dilute the power of the government in London. Only the historical traditions of democratic political culture keep the British government from abusing its power.

IRON LADY: MARGARET THATCHER AND THATCHERISM

Margaret Thatcher is widely regarded as one of the most important British leaders of the last fifty years, for good or ill. What merits such praise and scorn? Thatcher is noteworthy for the way in which she transformed the Conservative Party and the domestic and international politics of the United Kingdom as a whole.

Defying the Conservative Party's traditional ties to the aristocracy, Thatcher was a grocer's daughter who came to political power through sheer force of will. She rose in the party's ranks in the 1950s, running as the youngest candidate for Parliament in 1951. By the end of the decade, she became a **member of Parliament,** and when the Conservatives gained control of the government in 1970, she was named minister of education. Thatcher quickly became known for her tough demeanor, which many found incompatible with their notion of how a female politician should act. In spite of opposition inside and outside her party, by the mid-1970s Thatcher was able to challenge her Conservative rivals. She gained control of the party and, in 1979, the government.

Thatcher served as prime minister from 1979 to 1990. During that time, the Iron Lady undertook a series of dramatic steps to reverse Britain's economic stagnation and repeal the social democratic policies created under the collectivist consensus. The government privatized many state-owned businesses and allowed numerous ailing firms to go bankrupt. Thatcher also confronted powerful trade unions during controversial and widespread strikes. She took a firm stance in the Falklands War against Argentina and a skeptical approach toward the European Union. The result was a new path of neo-liberalism that would influence economic reforms in the United States, Latin America, and Eastern Europe.

In spite (or perhaps because) of her dramatic reforms, by 1990 Thatcher had alienated many in her own party. The final straw was the ill-advised introduction of a "poll tax," designed to move local governments' tax burden from property owners to all citizens, legislation that generated widespread resentment and even rioting. On November 28, 1990, Thatcher's own party removed her from office and gave her a position in the House of Lords. Though the Conservatives held office until 1997, to this day the party has been unable to find a leader with Thatcher's presence to succeed her.

Political Institutions

THE CONSTITUTION

The United Kingdom has no single document that defines the rules of politics, but the constitution is generally understood to include a number of written documents and unwritten rules that most Britons view as inviolable.[5] In 1215, the Magna Carta set a precedent for limits on monarchical power. Other documents include the 1689 Bill of Rights and the 1701 Act of Union, which united Scotland and En-gland. What makes the UK's constitution particularly unusual is that it also consists of various acts of Parliament, judicial decisions, customs, and traditions. Since Parliament is viewed as sovereign, the democratically elected lower house of the legislature can amend any aspect of the constitution by a simple majority vote. This power extends to the very existence of

---

ESSENTIAL POLITICAL FEATURES

- Legislative-executive system: parliamentary
- Legislature: Parliament
- Lower house: House of Commons
- Upper house: House of Lords
- Unitary or federal division of power: unitary
- Main geographic subunits: England, Scotland, Wales, Northern Ireland
- Electoral system for lower house: plurality
- Chief judicial body: House of Lords

---

the monarchy, the powers of regions or local governments, and the powers of the houses of Parliament. Unlike most other democratic regimes, the UK has no constitutional court.

The absence of written constitutional guarantees has consistently alarmed human rights advocates and has given rise to demands for a more formal constitution or, at the very least, *written* constitutional protections of basic rights. Since 1973, when the UK became a member of the European Union, British citizens have increasingly appealed to European laws to protect their rights. In response to such concerns, in 1998 the government incorporated into law the European Convention on Human Rights, a document that now serves as a basic set of constitutional liberties.

While a source of concern to some, others have lauded the UK's constitution for its unparalleled flexibility and responsiveness to the majority. Changing the constitution in most democracies is a cumbersome and often politically charged process. In the UK, changes can be implemented more quickly and without lengthy political battles. Admirers of the British constitution argue that it has delivered political stability since the late seventeenth century; in their view, a formal document does not necessarily make for a more democratic government.

THE CROWN

We can think of the **Crown,** the legislature, the judiciary, the prime minister, and the cabinet as the main branches of government in the United Kingdom. In most respects, we can think of the British Crown as the head of state. The Crown, embodied by the monarch, is the symbolic representative of the continuity of the British state. The monarch (currently Queen Elizabeth II) thus acts as a purely ceremonial figure, and on matters of importance she must act at the behest of the cabinet even though the cabinet is referred to collectively as Her Majesty's government. The British monarchy is a source of endless popular fascination, in part because the institution and all its pomp and circumstance appear to be a relic in the twenty-first century. The reality, however, is less glamorous. The British monarch today is essentially a paid civil servant: the government allocates a budget to cover the royal family's expenses, and the queen spends much of her time signing papers, dedicating public works, and performing diplomatic functions.

The UK's monarchy has survived for centuries precisely because it has agreed to act constitutionally. Since the nineteenth century, this has meant that it must always follow the orders of elected representatives. For example, although the monarch always selects the head of government, the choice must always be the leader of the majority party in the lower house of Parliament. Only in the unlikely event that no clear majority is present in the legislature could a monarch have any real influence on politics, and even in that case her choice would be severely constrained. Likewise, the monarch is officially the commander of the British armed forces, but it is the prime minister who has the power to declare wars and sign treaties.

The British monarchy is a hereditary institution, following the rule of primogeniture: the oldest son (or oldest daughter if there are no sons) inherits the throne. However, a cardinal principle of the UK's constitution is that Parliament may choose the monarch. In 1701, for example, Parliament imposed a new dynastic family (the Hanovers) to replace the reigning Stuarts. Since that time, only Protestants have been allowed to succeed to the throne. Since 1952, Elizabeth II has been queen, succeeding her father, George VI. Despite the series of high-profile scandals that have rocked the monarchy during her reign, polls consistently show that the institution remains highly popular, as evidenced by the public celebrations of the queen's golden jubilee (fifty years on the throne) in 2002. There have been occasional movements in the UK to eliminate the monarchy, but these have failed to garner much support. In spite of scandals and the costs of royalty, public support for the institution remains strong—a 2006 poll showed nearly three quarters of the public in favor of retaining the institution.[6]

The Branches of Government

THE PRIME MINISTER

Parliament is supreme in the United Kingdom's political system, but real power is concentrated in the prime minister and the cabinet. The prime minister is the head of government and, as in all parliamentary systems, must be an elected member of the legislature. He or she is the head of the largest party in the lower house, the House of Commons. Once named by the monarch (a mere formality), the prime minister selects his or her cabinet.

STRUCTURE OF THE GOVERNMENT

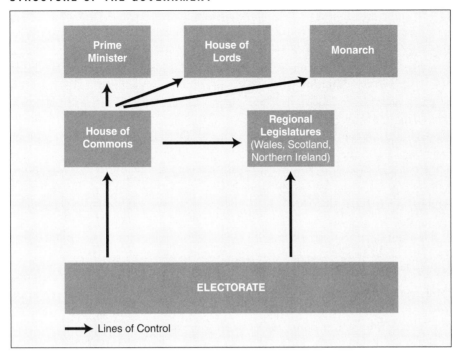

British prime ministers are probably the most powerful heads of government of any contemporary democracy. Because they can expect their parliamentary majority to approve all legislation, because party discipline in the UK is very strong, and because there are few checks on the power of the central government, prime ministers usually get their way. Prime ministers wield less power when their parties hold a slim majority (as was the case with John Major from 1990 to 1997) or when they are forced to depend on a coalition of parties (which is rare). Prime ministers in the UK are, like any member of Parliament (MP), elected to a maximum term of five years, but they alone can decide to call elections at any time before that term has expired. Prime ministers commonly call early elections to take advantage of favorable political conditions. After the UK's victory in the 1982 Falklands War, for example, Margaret Thatcher called an election despite the fact that she had two years remaining on her mandate.

Prime ministers are subject to a legislative **vote of no confidence.** If a government deems a measure to be of high importance and if the measure is rejected by the legislature, either the entire cabinet must resign (and be replaced by a new one) or new elections must be called. But although such a check on the government exists, it is rarely used; over the last seventy years, only one government has been toppled by a legislative vote of no confidence.

In fact, the prime minister can use the threat of a no-confidence vote as a way to rally support. In March 2003, Tony Blair submitted a motion to the House of Commons to support the use of force against Iraq even though a prime minister may take the country to war without parliamentary approval. Yet he chose to submit his decision to the House of Commons, threatening to resign if he failed to win support. The tactic worked: despite widespread opposition to the war among Labour Party backbenchers, a large majority in Parliament supported the war.

Prime ministers play a number of roles. As leaders of their party, they must maintain the support of their fellow MPs, a situation that plagued Thatcher and Major, and more recently, Tony Blair. They must appear in the legislature twice weekly for a televised question time, in which they must defend government policies and answer questions from MPs—and in so doing display strong oratorical skills.[7] As head of government, they must direct the activity of the cabinet and smooth over differences among cabinet members. As politicians, they are expected to guide their parties to victory in general elections. Even though the monarch is head of state and the nation, the prime minister is expected to provide national leadership. British prime ministers are also diplomats and world leaders, roles that Tony Blair has relished, despite the objections of many of his own party members, particularly regarding the war in Iraq.[8]

Prime ministers are always seasoned political veterans with, on average, over two decades of experience in the House of Commons. As a result, British prime ministers are usually outstanding debaters, effective communicators, and skilled negotiators. In the British system, a political outsider has virtually no chance of becoming prime minister—one must move up the ranks of the party before gaining the highest office.

THE CABINET

Cabinets evolved out of the group of experts who originally advised Britain's monarchs. Contemporary British cabinets have about twenty members (called ministers), all of whom must be members of Parliament. They are usually from the lower house but occasionally are members of the upper house, the House of Lords. The prime minister generally appoints leading party officials to the top cabinet positions.

As in most democracies, cabinet ministers in the United Kingdom preside over their individual government departments and are responsible for answering to Parliament (during question time) about actions of the bureaucracies they oversee. The most important ministries are the Foreign Office (which conducts foreign policy), the Home Office (which oversees the judiciary), and the Exchequer (whose minister, called the chancellor, oversees financial policy as head of the central bank).

One unwritten rule of cabinet behavior in the UK is **collective responsibility;** even when individual cabinet ministers oppose a given policy, the entire cabinet must appear unified and take responsibility for the policy. Cabinet ministers who cannot support a decision must resign and return to the legislature (in 2003, three members of Blair's cabinet resigned over the war in Iraq).

THE LEGISLATURE

The British legislature, called Parliament, is perhaps the most powerful legislature on earth, due in large part to the lack of constitutional constraints, which we have discussed above. The concentration of power is even more impressive when it is considered that of the two chambers of the legislature, the House of Commons and the House of Lords, only the former has any real power.

The House of Commons currently consists of 646 members of Parliament representing individual districts in the United Kingdom of Great Britain and Northern Ireland. Members are elected for a maximum term of five years, though new elections may be called before the expiration of the term. Government and opposition parties face each other in a tiny rectangular chamber, with the members of the government and the leaders of the opposition sitting in the front row. The other MPs, called backbenchers, sit behind their leaders. A neutral Speaker of the House presides.

Despite the enormous power of the House of Commons, individual legislators are far less powerful than their counterparts in the United States. They receive relatively paltry salaries and have very small staffs and few resources. In parliamentary systems in general, the largest party elects the prime minister as head of government; as a result, political parties, not individual members, are what matter. Thus, British legislators follow the lead of their party and, for fear of weakening party cohesion, do not undertake the type of individual initiative common to representatives in the United States. Moreover, parties designate certain members to serve as "whips," who are charged with enforcing the party line.

Despite these limitations, MPs do perform important tasks. They actively debate issues, participate in legislative committees (though these are less powerful than their U.S. counterparts), vote on legislation proposed by the government, and have the power to remove the prime minister through a vote of no confidence. Finally, although the government initiates the vast majority of legislation, individual members do propose measures from time to time.

Thus, despite the doctrine of parliamentary supremacy, the legislature in the UK mostly deliberates, ratifies, and scrutinizes policies that are proposed by the executive. The government is usually able to impose its will on its majority in the House of Commons. MPs vote with their parties over 90 percent of the time. Nevertheless, even governments with large majorities lose the occasional vote in the lower house, suggesting that MPs do sometimes act independently.

The House of Lords is another uniquely British institution. Once the more powerful of Parliament's two chambers, it has gradually become virtually powerless, having lost most of its power nearly a century ago. The House of Lords was considered the upper house not only because it represented the top aristocracy but also because it was considered the more powerful of the two houses. As the UK underwent democratization, it made sense for a chamber of appointed members of the aristocracy to lose most of its power. True to the British desire to accommodate tradition, the House of Lords remains as yet another reminder of the UK's pre-democratic past.

The House of Lords is composed of about 700 members, or peers, who have traditionally been appointed in several ways. **Life peers** are distinguished citizens appointed for life by the Crown upon the recommendation of the prime minister. Law lords are top legal experts, appointed for life, who play an important role in legal appeals. About a dozen top officials of the Church of England are also members of the House of Lords. The most controversial aspects of the Lords are the **hereditary peers,** members of the aristocracy (dukes, earls, barons, and so on) who until recently had been able to bequeath their seats to their offspring. In 1999, the Labour government eliminated virtually all of these hereditary peers as part of a reform of the upper chamber.

The House of Lords has no veto power over legislation, but it can delay some legislation up to one year and does occasionally persuade governments to amend legislation. The most important role of the Lords is as the court of last appeal, and the legal expertise of some members of the Lords is often called on to improve legislation. Currently, there is considerable debate in the UK about the future of the upper house; should it be directly elected and/or given greater powers?[9] Reticent to create a second chamber that might limit the power of his own government, Tony Blair has seemed content to eliminate the hereditary peers.

THE JUDICIAL SYSTEM

Compared with the United States and even compared with other parliamentary democracies, the judiciary in the United Kingdom has a relatively minor role. There is no tradition of judicial review (the right of courts to strike down legislation that contradicts the constitution) because the British parliament is always supreme: any law that is passed by the legislature is, by definition, constitutional. Thus the role of the courts in the UK is mainly to ensure that parliamentary statutes have been followed.

Over the last couple of decades, however, a slow move toward greater political involvement of the courts has occurred. In part, this is because British governments have sought legal interpretations that would support their actions. A second factor is the adoption of international laws, such as the European Convention on Human Rights, that codified for the first time a set of basic civil rights. These laws have given the courts new powers to strike down legislation as unconstitutional, though these powers have so far been used sparingly. Still, the days when we could speak of the UK as lacking judicial review may be slowly coming to an end.

Judges are selected from among distinguished jurists by the lord chancellor (the minister who heads the judiciary). They serve until retirement unless they are removed by Parliament (which has never happened). To the extent that the vast majority of judges come from relatively wealthy families and are educated at elite universities, it could be assumed that the judiciary has a conservative bias.

The legal system, based on common law and developed in the twelfth century, stands in stark contrast to the stricter code law practiced in the rest of Europe, which is less focused on precedent and interpretation. Like most democracies, the UK has an elaborate hierarchy of civil and criminal courts, and a complex system of appeals. The House of Lords, many of whose members are distinguished jurists, is the highest judicial authority in the UK, though it does not serve the kind of constitutional-review function that is found in the U.S. Supreme Court.

The Electoral System

Like the United States, the United Kingdom uses the single-member district (SMD) system based on plurality, or what is often known as first past the post (FPTP). Each of the 646 constituencies elects one MP, and that member needs to win only a plurality of votes (that is, more than any other candidate), not a majority. Electoral constituencies are based mostly on population, and they average about 65,000 voters. Constituencies are revised every five to seven years by a government commission.

The implications of FPTP are fairly clear. First, as shown in the table below ("Consequences of the British Electoral System"), the system helps maintain the dominance of the two main political parties, Labour and Conservative. Second, the system consistently penalizes smaller parties. The Liberal Democrats, whose support is spread evenly across the country, regularly get between one fifth and one quarter of votes in many districts but can rarely muster enough votes to edge out the larger parties. In 2005, the Liberal Democrats won 22 percent of the vote but only sixty-two seats (about 10 percent of the total). With well less than three times as many votes as the Liberal Democrats, Labour won about five times as many seats! Small parties that are regionally concentrated, like the Scottish Nationalist Party, do somewhat better, but even they are underrepresented.

Third, the British electoral system has produced clear majorities in the House of Commons even when there was no clear majority in the electorate. Indeed, in the elections of 1951 and 1974, the party with the smaller percentage of the vote won the most seats because of the nature of the electoral system. Even in 1997, Labour won a huge (179-seat) majority in the Commons with only 43 percent of the vote. These distortions occur when more than two parties contest a seat, so that a majority of votes is wasted—that is, the votes are not counted toward the winning party. Since World War II, over 60 percent of all seats have been won with a minority of votes.

In a system that gives virtually unchecked power to the party with the majority of seats, an electoral system that artificially produces majorities could be considered a serious distortion of democratic rule. It is no wonder that the parties most hurt by the electoral system (especially the Liberal Democrats) have called for electoral reform. The Labour government elected in 1997 appointed an independent commission to consider a more proportional electoral system. In 1998, the Jenkins Commission recommended a system that would be a mix of FPTP and proportional representation (PR), as is used in Japan, Russia, Mexico, and a number of other countries. Now that it is the chief beneficiary of the current system, however, Labour has been slow to act on the recommendations.

In contrast, regional legislatures in Scotland and Wales did adopt a mixed electoral system (Northern Ireland uses a rare system known as single-transferable vote). Ironically, the governing Labour Party, which has benefited greatly from FPTP, favored a mixed system for the regional legislatures, fearing that FPTP would produce large majorities for the local nationalist parties.

Local Government

Unlike the United States, the United Kingdom has traditionally been a unitary state: no formal powers are reserved for regional or local government. Indeed, during the Conservative governments of Margaret Thatcher, the autonomy of municipal governments (known as councils) was sharply curtailed. The Labour government elected in 1997 has taken bold steps to restore some political power to the distinct nations that compose the United Kingdom and to local governments.

Although there has never been a constitutional provision for local autonomy, British localities have enjoyed a long tradition of powerful local government. Concerned that local governments, or councils (especially left-leaning ones in large urban areas), were taxing and spending beyond their means, Thatcher's Conservative government passed a law sharply limiting the ability of councils to raise revenue. The struggle between the central government and the councils came to a head in 1986, when Thatcher abolished the Labour-dominated Greater London Council as well as several other urban governments, a move deeply resented by urban Britons. London was now left with councils in each of its thirty-two boroughs, but it had no single city government or mayor. In 1989, Thatcher further threatened local governments by replacing the local property tax with a poll tax, a flat tax levied on every urban citizen. The new policy shifted the tax burden from business and property owners to individuals (rich and poor alike) and was among the most unpopular policies of Thatcher's eleven years in power. In response, rioting broke out in London.

Thatcher's successor, John Major, abandoned the poll tax but continued to limit the financial autonomy of local governments. Since 1997, Tony Blair has restored considerable autonomy to municipal government, enacting reforms that allow Londoners to directly elect a mayor with significant powers and to choose representatives to a Greater London Assembly. Ironically, in the first such election, in 2000, a left-wing Labour opponent of the prime minister was elected. Nevertheless, Blair has maintained the financial limitations on local government that were imposed during Thatcher's tenure.

Representation at the regional level has traditionally been very limited. Of the four nations that constitute the United Kingdom (England, Scotland, Wales, and Northern Ireland), only Northern Ireland had its own legislature—until political violence there caused the central government to disband it in 1972. Each of the four nations had a cabinet minister in the central government, called a secretary of state, who was responsible for setting policies in each region.

As it has with local government, the Labour Party has promoted devolution, or the decentralization of power, to the UK's regions. In 1997, Scotland and Wales voted in referenda to create their own legislatures to address local issues, though their powers are not uniform—Scotland's legislature is more powerful than that of Wales, a reflection of the much stronger nationalist tendencies in Scotland. Meanwhile, the 1998 **Good Friday Agreement** between Catholics and Protestants in Northern Ireland has allowed for the reestablishment of the Northern Ireland Assembly. Some observers view the development of these bodies as the first steps toward a federal UK.[10]

Despite these recent reforms, the UK remains a centralized, unitary state. Regional and local authorities clearly enjoy greater legitimacy and far more powers than in the past, but the central government still controls defense policy, most taxation power, and national economic policy, among other aspects of government. The central government also retains the power to limit (or even eliminate) local government if it so chooses.

POLITICAL CONFLICT AND COMPETITION

The Party System

In the United Kingdom's majoritarian parliamentary system, political parties are extremely important. The majority party controls government and can generally implement its policy goals, which are spelled out in the party manifesto.[11]

From the end of World War II to 1970, the UK had a two-party system. The Conservative Party and the Labour Party together garnered over 90 percent of the popular vote. The two large parties were equally successful during that period, with each winning four elections. After 1974, a multiparty system emerged, which included the birth of a stronger centrist Liberal Party and a surge of support for nationalist parties in Scotland, Wales, and Northern Ireland. But since the Conservatives and Labour continue to prevail, the current system is often dubbed a two-and-a-half-party system, with the Liberal Democratic Party trailing far behind the other two parties.

The UK's party system differs regionally, even for national elections. In England the three major parties (Labour, Conservative, and Liberal Democrat) compete with one another. In Scotland, Wales, and Northern Ireland, important regional parties compete with the three national political parties. In the 2005 elections, the two leading parties together won about 67 percent of the vote, while the remaining votes were divided among a variety of parties. In total, eleven parties won seats in the House of Commons.

The two main parties may be losing votes as a result of the growth of smaller parties. The percentage of the vote cast for parties other than the three major parties has steadily increased over the last three elections, and no party since 1935 has won a majority of the vote. However, the leading parties have not lost control of political power. Since 1945 every government has been run by the Conservatives (Tories) or Labour, and only between 1974 and 1979 did either party fail to have a majority in the House of Commons.

THE LABOUR PARTY

We have discussed the democratization of the United Kingdom as a gradual process that incorporated excluded groups into the political system. The Labour Party is a clear example of this, as it was formed in 1900 as an outgrowth of the trade union movement. Initially, it sought to give the British working class a voice in Parliament. Only after the mobilizing effect of World War I and the expansion of suffrage in 1918 was the Labour Party able to make significant progress at the polls. By 1918, it had garnered almost one quarter of the vote. Labour's turning point and its emergence as one of the

UK's two dominant parties came with its landslide victory in 1945, just after the end of World War II.

Like virtually all working-class parties of the world, the British Labour Party considered socialism its dominant ideological characteristic. British socialists were influenced by Fabianism, however, a moderate ideology that advocated working within the parliamentary order to bring about social democratic change. While Labour championed a strong welfare state and some state ownership of industry, the party's moderate politics never threatened to replace capitalism.

For most of its history the Labour Party depended heavily on working-class votes, winning the support of about two thirds of the UK's manual laborers. Starting in the 1970s, however, the composition of the class structure began to change, with fewer Britons engaging in blue-collar jobs. At that point, the solid identification of workers with Labour began to erode, creating a serious challenge for the party.

By the mid-1970s, the Labour Party was badly divided between radical socialists who wanted the party to move to the left to shore up its working-class credentials and moderates who wanted it to move toward the political center. These divisions involved the party's relationship to the trade unions as well as its stand on economic and foreign policy. This internal division caused the more conservative elements to bolt the party and form the (short-lived) Social Democratic Party in 1981. Most serious, the internal bickering led to the defeat of Labour in every election from 1979 to 1997.

In the 1980s and 1990s, the Labour Party began a process of ideological and organizational moderation. The party's constitution was rewritten in order to weaken severely the ability of trade unions to control party policy. Labour also abandoned its commitment to socialism and advocated a cross-class appeal. Tony Blair, who became party leader in 1994, consolidated these changes and advocated moderate free-market policies along with ambitious constitutional reform, policies that were eventually dubbed the Third Way.[12] Blair's landslide victory in the 1997 elections marked the beginning of a period of party unity and electoral success, what has been termed New Labour, and the election results of 2001 confirmed this success. Blair's victory in the May 2005 elections marked the first time in history that Labour had been elected to office three consecutive times. However, those elections reduced Labour's majority by forty-seven seats, likely as a result of Blair's unpopular policy on Iraq.

THE CONSERVATIVE PARTY

If the Labour Party was never as leftist as some of its Continental counterparts, the Conservatives (Tories) similarly made for a rather moderate right.

The UK's Conservatives emerged in the late eighteenth century and have come to be identified not only with the democratization of the UK but also with the origins of the British welfare state through the collectivist consensus. Because the Tories have usually been pragmatic conservatives and because they have always embraced democratic rule, the party has widespread respect and even electoral support among a wide range of voters. In 1997, about one third of the British working-class vote went to the Conservatives.

Just as the Labour Party developed severe internal ideological divisions beginning in the 1970s, the Tories became divided among advocates of traditional conservative pragmatism, advocates of a limited welfare state, and advocates of radical free-market reforms (known as neo-liberals). The rise to power of Margaret Thatcher in the late 1970s marked the dominance of the neo-liberal faction and the abandonment of support for the collectivist consensus. The party was further split over policy on the European Union, with the so-called Euroskeptics facing off against supporters of continued efforts at European integration.[13]

The Tories struggled in opposition after their defeat in the 1997 elections. William Hague, John Major's successor, was unable to articulate a clear and persuasive alternative to Tony Blair's Third Way policies, and his successor, Iain Duncan Smith, was dumped by his party after the Conservative defeat in the 2001 elections and replaced by Michael Howard in November 2003. Howard, widely viewed as more effective than his two predecessors, was a steady critic of Labour's record on crime, immigration, and European integration. Still, his party performed poorly in the 2004 regional and European Parliament elections. The Tories gained thirty-three seats in the 2005 elections but failed to dislodge Labour. After the electoral results were announced, Howard announced his resignation and was replaced by the young and charismatic David Cameron.

THE LIBERAL DEMOCRATS

The Liberal Democratic Party was formed in 1988 through the merger of the Liberal Party and the Social Democrats. Its ideology is a mixture of classical liberalism's emphasis on both individual freedom and a weak state and social democracy's emphasis on collective equality. The Liberals (Whigs) were displaced by the rise of the Labour Party in the early twentieth century. The current Liberal Democratic Party has been unable to recover the power and influence of the early Whigs. In recent years, the party has won between 17 and 22 percent of the vote but has not been able to break through the barriers imposed by the electoral system. As a result, one of the Liberal Democrats' chief issues is the reform of the electoral law. Without such reform, the future of the Liberal Democrats seems limited.

Consequences of the British Electoral System, 1987–2005

Party	% of Votes	Seats Won	% of Seats
Labour			
1987	31	229	35.0
1992	34	271	42.0
1997	43	419	64.0
2001	41	412	62.5
2005	35	355	54.9
Conservative			
1987	42	375	58.0
1992	42	336	52.0
1997	31	165	25.0
2001	32	166	25.0
2005	32	197	30.0
Liberal Democrat			
1987	23	22	3.0
1992	18	20	3.0
1997	17	46	7.0
2001	18	52	8.0
2005	22	62	10.0
Others			
1987	4	24	4.0
1992	6	24	4.0
1997	9	29	4.0
2001	9	29	4.0
2005	10	32	5.0

Percentages do not always equal 100% due to rounding.

The Liberal Democrats, have been consistent supporters of European integration and fierce opponents of the war in Iraq. Though viewed as a centrist party, the Liberal Democrats have often attacked Tony Blair's policies as too timid and have often called for increased taxation and social spending. Though generally viewed as closer to Labour than to the Conservatives, the party announced in 2004 that it would adopt a policy of strict neutrality vis-à-vis the two major parties and might be willing to form a coalition with either party should the 2005 elections result in a hung Parliament. Liberal Democrats were clearly hoping that the unpopular war in Iraq, backed by a majority of Labour and Tory members of Parliament (MPs), would lead the party to significant electoral gains in the 2005 elections. Indeed, the Liberal Democrats gained 11 seats and won 22 percent of the vote but still earned only about one tenth of the seats in the House of Commons.

OTHER PARTIES

Many small parties vie for seats in British elections, but few of them are successful. All parties must post a small deposit (about US$800), which is returned to parties that win over 5 percent of the vote. The main impediment to the success of small parties remains the structure of the electoral system, since first past the post (FPTP) tends to work against small parties that cannot win a plurality of votes. Only regionally based parties—like the Scottish National Party, the Welsh Plaid Cymru, and several Northern Irish parties (for example, Sinn Féin)—have been able to concentrate enough votes in some districts to win seats in the legislature. Finally, while it has not gained any seats in Parliament, in recent years the extreme right-wing British National Party (BNP) has won a number of council elections in England on an anti-immigration platform.

Elections

British voters select all 646 members of the House of Commons during a general election. Elections must take place every five years but may take place before the end of the five-year term if the prime minister decides to call an early election, as often happens. Usually about 60 to 70 percent of the electorate votes in British general elections, below the European average but far above the U.S. turnout.

British campaigns are short affairs, usually lasting less than a month. The voter has a relatively simple choice: which party should govern? British parties are well disciplined and have clear, published policy manifestos. Compared with voters in the United States, voters in the United Kingdom are far more likely to know what each party stands for and how the parties differ. UK voters tend to focus on differences between parties rather than on differences between candidates. Candidates may not even reside in the district in which they run for office. The notion of one's candidate serving local (rather than party) interests first, concentrating on bringing benefits, or pork, to local constituents in order to secure reelection, is of much less concern than it is in the United States.

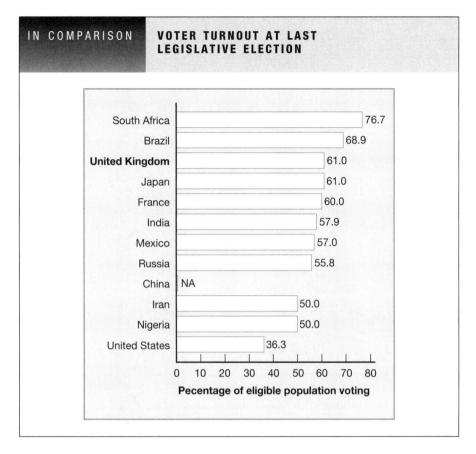

VOTER TURNOUT AT LAST LEGISLATIVE ELECTION

South Africa — 76.7
Brazil — 68.9
United Kingdom — 61.0
Japan — 61.0
France — 60.0
India — 57.9
Mexico — 57.0
Russia — 55.8
China — NA
Iran — 50.0
Nigeria — 50.0
United States — 36.3

0 10 20 30 40 50 60 70 80

Pecentage of eligible population voting

Civil Society

As in virtually all democracies, in the United Kingdom a variety of groups exist to articulate special interests (interests that benefit specific groups instead of the nation as a whole). British interest groups do influence public policy and public opinion, but interest-group lobbying of MPs is far less prevalent than such lobbying is in the United States Congress because British parties are so highly disciplined. Interest groups must focus their attention on the party leadership (since parties, not individual MPs, make key policy decisions) and on the government bureaucracies, which often interpret and apply policies.

Perhaps the greatest influence of British interest groups comes through their participation in **quangos** (quasi-autonomous nongovernmental organizations). Quangos are policy advisory boards appointed by the government that bring government officials and affected interest groups together to help develop policy. First established in the 1960s and 1970s, quangos represented a move toward the neo-corporatist model of public policy making, in which government and interest groups worked together to develop policy. Although attacked in the 1980s by Thatcher (who saw them as empowering special interests and weakening government), there are currently over 5,000 such organizations working in different policy areas.

In sheer numbers, the **Trades Union Congress (TUC),** a confederation of the UK's largest trade unions, is the most important British interest group. For much of the postwar period, the TUC dominated the Labour Party and was thus extremely influential during periods of Labour government. Yet a variety of factors has weakened the TUC over the last two decades. First, as is the case in all industrial democracies, the number of blue-collar workers is shrinking quickly, and the TUC has seen its membership plummet. Only twenty years ago, about one half of British workers belonged to trade unions; today only about one quarter of workers are union members. Second, the Conservative governments of Margaret Thatcher sharply reduced the political power of the TUC by passing laws designed to restrict union activity. Third, reforms within the Labour Party in the 1990s severely eroded the TUC's control of that party. The TUC is still an important source of funding and electoral support, but the TUC-Labour link has been seriously weakened. The TUC can no longer dominate the selection of the Labour Party leader and no longer dominates the formation of Labour policy.

The most important business organization in the United Kingdom, and the main counterweight to the TUC, is the **Confederation of British Industry (CBI).** Unlike the TUC, which has formal links to the Labour Party, the CBI has no direct link to the Tories. The main industrial and financial interests in the UK usually favor Conservative policy, however, and top business leaders have exercised considerable influence in past Conservative governments. Since becoming prime minister in 1997, Tony Blair has been careful to cultivate good relations with the CBI.

SOCIETY

The United Kingdom is in fact divided in many significant ways. The British state is both multinational and multiethnic; British society reveals class, religious, and even linguistic divisions. But while these divisions may appear rather sharp when viewed from the outside, in comparison with most other states they have in fact been relatively benign. Over the centuries, the United Kingdom has demonstrated remarkable national unity and enviable social and political stability.

Class Identity

Class identity remains perhaps the most salient of all social divisions in the United Kingdom and the one perhaps most noticed by outside observers. His-

ETHNIC GROUPS

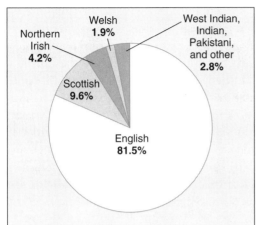

RELIGION

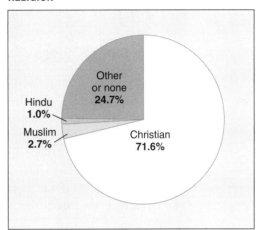

torically, political parties and many key policy debates have reflected class differences, not differences of ethnicity, region, or religion, as is the case in many other states. Certainly the social reforms of the twentieth century largely ameliorated the huge income disparities and rigid occupation-based class lines of nineteenth-century England that preoccupied both Karl Marx and Charles Dickens. But increased social mobility has not yet erased the perception of a two-tier society divided between an upper class and a working class.

Chief among the legacies of the class system has been the education system, which has long channeled a minority of the British elite into "public" schools (which are in fact private schools originally designed to train British boys for public service). Graduates of these elite schools go on to Oxford or Cambridge University before pursuing white-collar careers in government or industry, careers enhanced by elitist old-boy networks. Class differences are also perpetuated by continued self-identification with either the upper class or the working class as manifested in preferred tastes and leisure activities (sherry versus warm beer, cricket versus football, opera versus pub) and variations in speech and accent. Some argue that under the neo-liberal reforms of Margaret Thatcher and Tony Blair, class differences have finally begun to break down. However, with a prosperous and vibrant white-collar southern England and a stagnant and struggling blue-collar north, regional disparities in income remain a source of division.[14]

Ethnic and National Identity

Although we have noted that the United Kingdom is relatively homogeneous, religious, linguistic, and cultural divisions do exist and in some cases are becoming more significant. The UK settled most of its religious differences early on, and its politics are more secular than those in the rest of Europe. Even today, however, Scots are mainly Catholic or Presbyterian, and the English are mostly identified with the Church of England. Religion does remain a source of raw conflict in **Northern Ireland,** however, where the majority is Protestant (of Scottish or English origin) but some 40 percent are Catholic. Northern Ireland comprises the northeastern portion of the island of Ireland (about 17 percent of the island's territory) that remained part of the United Kingdom following the creation of an independent republic of Ireland in 1921. This religious divide was compounded by both national and class differences, with Catholics discriminated against in employment and education. Starting in the 1960s, members of the Irish Republican Army (IRA) turned to violence against British targets in the hopes of unifying the region with the republic of Ireland, and the British army and illegal Protestant paramilitary organizations fought back. Nearly 4,000 individuals on both sides, many of them civilians, died in the conflict. In the 1990s, the British government and the IRA began talks in the hope of establishing peace, resulting in the 1998 Good Friday Agreement, which bound the IRA to renounce its armed struggle in return for political reforms that would give the Catholic population greater say in local government. But the region has not been without setbacks and problems. The 2004 regional elections produced a victory for the Democratic Unionist Party, a Protestant force that opposes the Good Friday Agreement. Several outbreaks of violence in 2004 threatened to destroy the agreement, but to date a tense peace has mostly held. Since 1998, the region has been relatively peaceful for the first time in decades.

Elsewhere, however, new divisions are emerging. Since the 1960s, former colonial subjects (primarily from Africa, the West Indies, India, and Pakistan) have immigrated to the United Kingdom in increasing numbers, giving British society a degree of racial diversity. For the most part, British society has not coped particularly well with this influx. Racial tension between the overwhelming majority of whites and the non-European minority (of less than 3 percent) has sparked conflict and anti-immigrant sentiment, both of which nonetheless remain moderate by American and Continental standards. Lacking proportional representation, the British electoral system has limited the impact of both the nonwhite and the far-right vote in most elections. Parliament has also sought to limit the nonwhite population by imposing quotas that restrict the entrance of nonwhite dependents of persons already residing in the UK. In spite of this, the UK continues to face growing rates of immigration, with some polls predicting another 2 million immigrants will enter the country over the next decade. This will undoubtedly change the social dynamics and may increase xenophobic sentiment, strengthening parties like the British National Party (BNP).

IS PEACE POSSIBLE IN NORTHERN IRELAND?

After years of negotiation, Northern Ireland's status seemed finally determined by the 1998 Good Friday Agreement. Both the British and the Irish governments supported the decision, as did important Northern Irish political groups, including Catholic republicans, who favor Northern Ireland's unification with the republic of Ireland, and Protestant unionists, who favor maintaining Northern Ireland's inclusion in the United Kingdom. Among other provisions, the Good Friday Agreement allows for the institution of a Northern Irish legislature and a voting system that ensures proportional representation (in the past, first past the post had effectively marginalized the Catholic minority).

With this agreement, violence by both republican and unionist paramilitary organizations virtually came to an end. However, one major sticking point remained. As part of the Good Friday Agreement, all paramilitary forces were expected to destroy their weapons. This stipulation was directed primarily toward the republican party (known as Sinn Féin) and its military wing, the Irish Republican Army, which possesses a formidable arsenal. Even as the benefits of the peace became widespread and Sinn Féin assumed a role in local government, the party continued to resist the decommissioning of its military presence. Critics accused Sinn Féin of maintaining a ballots-and-bullets strategy, ready to take up arms if the democratic process did not go its way. Given the long and violent campaign waged by the IRA, immediate disarmament was not an easily achieved goal. Indeed, in the aftermath of the Good Friday Agreement, a car bombing by an IRA splinter group killed twenty-nine civilians in the town of Omagh in 1998.

As a result of the Sinn Féin's failures to decommission its military, the British government suspended Northern Ireland's legislature in October 2002. The IRA has not resumed a violent campaign, but the political future of the region remains uncertain. In October 2003, the IRA announced some limited destruction of weapons and was rewarded with new elections to the regional legislature that November. In July 2005, the IRA finally renounced the use of armed conflict, a move that was widely regarded as crucial to the achievement of a lasting peace Northern Ireland.

In addition to ethnic groups, the UK also comprises of a number of national groups, a fact outsiders tend to overlook. The United Kingdom of Britain and Northern Ireland is made up of four nations—England, Scotland, Wales, and Northern Ireland—with substantial cultural and political differences among them. In fact, most citizens of the UK first identify themselves not as British[15] but as belonging to one of these four nationalities. (The U.S. equivalent to this would be a resident of Los Angeles identifying herself first as a Californian, not as an American.)

Long-standing yearnings for greater national autonomy have gained increasing political significance since the 1960s. Local nationalist parties—including the Scottish Nationalist Party (SNP) and the Welsh Plaid Cymru—with the support of the Labour Party, have advocated devolution—turning over some central-governmental powers to the regions. Tony Blair's Labour government delivered on its campaign promise of devolution in 1999 with the establishment of local legislatures for Northern Ireland, Scotland, and Wales. Some feared that rather than pacify nationalist tendencies, devolution would contribute to the eventual breakup of the country, most notably with an independent Scotland. Yet so far these concerns appear to be unfounded. Nationalist parties, now that they wield power at the local level, have lost much of their appeal. In the 2003 regional elections, both the SNP and Plaid Cymru saw their share of seats in their respective regional legislatures decline.

While persistent regional loyalties and the localization of government have challenged the British national identity, so, too, has the UK's growing dependence on the European Union. As the twenty-first century progresses, British identity (and perhaps even Scottish or Welsh identity) may be eclipsed or at least diluted by an increasing allegiance to Europe. Despite this diffuse loyalty, Britons remain generally very loyal to the Crown and to the notion of a sovereign British people.

Ideology and Political Culture

In terms of the goals of politics, British political values have been strongly influenced by the development of classical liberalism and the conviction that government's influence over individuals ought to be limited. However, the postwar goals of an expanded franchise of full employment and the creation of a welfare state led to a new consensus as many Britons embraced the social democratic values of increased state intervention and less individual freedom in exchange for increased social equality. Economic decline during the 1970s shifted the pendulum back toward personal freedom, which spurned consensus politics, rejected socialist redistributive policies, and advocated privatization.

The electoral success of the Labour Party in 1997 came on the heels of its new policy to reconcile social democratic and liberal ideologies, the so-called Third Way. While this may indicate that British voters did not fully embrace the stark individualism of the Thatcher revolution, much of Labour's success has come from embracing a "kinder, gentler" version of this neo-liberal program. That said, most British—like their Continental neighbors—tend to be more socially and morally liberal than citizens of the United States. The United Kingdom outlawed capital punishment and legalized abortion and homosexuality, all in the mid-1960s. Handguns were banned outright in 1998. Also, there is far less emphasis on religion and "traditional" family values.

Both the consistency and the pendular variation in the UK's political goals and values—as well as the stability of its democratic system—can be attributed in part to its citizens' fundamental attitudes regarding politics, which in turn has been shaped by the country's long history of territorial continuity, political stability, and gradual evolutionary change.

British political culture is typically described as pragmatic and tolerant. In comparison to other societies, British society is thought to be less concerned with adhering to overarching ideological principles and more willing to gradually tinker with a particular political problem. Scholars point to the incremental and ad hoc historical development of British political institutions, noting that there was no defining political moment in British history when founders or revolutionaries sat down and envisioned or established a political system or set of rules based on abstract ideals or theoretical principles. Political radicalism, on either the left or the right, is rare in the UK, with virtually all political actors embracing a willingness to seek evolutionary, not revolutionary, change. This pragmatism is bolstered by a classical liberal tolerance for opposing viewpoints, a strong sense of fair play, and a generally high level of consensus on the political rules of the game.

Although such general characterizations have some utility in accounting for British politics, British political culture in reality comprises multiple subcultures, as is the case in any complex modern or postmodern society. One can certainly still see evidence of an aristocratic culture among the political elite, who share a sense of superiority and noblesse oblige toward those they deem less able to rule, as well as a mass or working-class culture of deference to those in authority. The blurring of class lines has brought with it a greater sense of egalitarianism, however, particularly among the younger generation. These and other long-held values will likely continue to erode in a postindustrial and postmaterial United Kingdom that presumably grows more multiracial and Eurocentric and becomes more concerned with such issues as the environment and other global problems.[16]

POLITICAL ECONOMY

The United Kingdom is noteworthy for its contribution to the liberal economic model. Indeed, most would trace liberalism itself to the UK, where philosophers like John Locke spoke of the inalienable rights of "life, liberty and estate,"[17] setting the stage for such political innovations as the U.S. Declaration of Independence. Yet liberalism in the UK has undergone a number of shifts over the past decades, from a greater emphasis on social democratic values after World War II to the neo-liberalism under Margaret Thatcher, which has been largely continued under the current Labour government.

If there is a common theme that one finds in the UK's economy in the four decades since the end of World War II, it is decline. As we recall, during

LABOR FORCE BY OCCUPATION

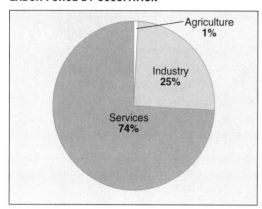

the Industrial Revolution, the UK was "the workshop to the world," the richest country on the planet. Yet over time, this position of dominance deteriorated. As of 2001, the UK's per capita GDP at purchasing-power parity ranked around twentieth in the world, behind once far poorer colonies like Ireland and Australia (though the UK's economy remains one of the ten largest in the world).

Why the decline? There is no single explanation. One basic issue is the downside of the UK's early industrialization. Although early industrialization made the country the world's first industrial power, it was also allowed it to be the first country to face the obsolescence of its technology and the difficulty of shifting to a new economic environment. A second factor is the burden of empire. Although industrialization helped fuel imperialism (and vice versa), the British Empire soon became a financial drain on the country rather than a benefit to it. Related to this is the argument that the UK's orientation toward its empire meant that it was slow to pursue economic opportunities with the rest of Europe when the continent moved toward greater integration after World War II. Finally, many have argued that the collectivist consensus not only blocked meaningful economic reform in the UK for much of the postwar era, but also focused the country on social expenditures while ignoring the simultaneous need to modernize the economy.[18]

Where does this leave the UK's economy in the new century? Like other advanced democracies, the UK is a postindustrial economy. Although industries such as steel, oil, and gas still play an important role, nearly three quarters of the country's wealth is generated by the service sector, in particular, financial services and tourism. Privatization has significantly shrunk the role of the state in the economy, including the sale of a range of assets, among them public utilities and housing, British Airways, Rolls-Royce, and Jaguar. Tony Blair's Labour government has sought to extend privatization to railroads, health care, and even the Underground (London's famous subway system). There have also been substantial changes in the welfare state, moving it from a system that provided direct benefits to the unemployed to one that sponsors "welfare to work" programs emphasizing training in order to find employment. These actions have all required a significant rethinking of Labour Party ideology. The party has ended its traditional call for a greater role for the state in the economy (nationalization of industry was in fact enshrined in the Labour Party constitution until 1995) and has distanced itself from its once close ties with organized labor.

To some observers, the Thatcher revolution and its preservation under Labour have finally helped the United Kingdom turn a corner. The UK's unemployment is half of what it was ten years ago, and the country has enjoyed a decade of economic growth. The UK economy currently looks much better than France, Germany, or Japan. But concerns remain. As in many other countries, neo-liberal economic policies have increased financial inequality in the UK, which has one of the highest levels of inequality in Europe. This inequality also has a regional element, with the country's south growing much faster than the north, the traditional home of heavy industry. Whether this gap is rising or falling is hotly debated. It has also been argued that welfare reform has, in reality, been a costly program that has done little to ease unemployment.[19]

Finally, there is the issue of the UK's economic relationship to the outside world. Historic ties notwithstanding, over the past half century the UK has become closely tied to the rest of Europe, with half of its trade going to other European Union (EU) member states. However, the UK has still not accepted the common currency of the EU, the euro, which was fully introduced in most member states in 2002. British leaders and the public have been cool toward

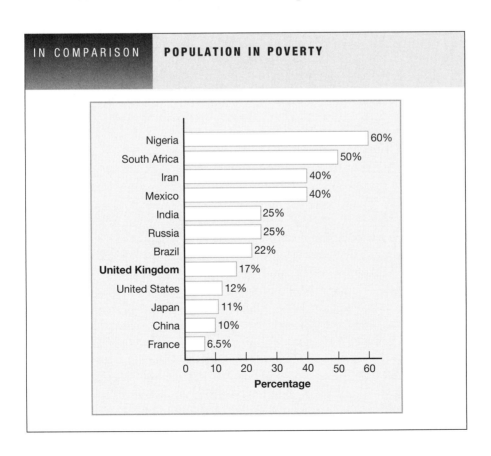

IN COMPARISON   **POPULATION IN POVERTY**

Country	Percentage
Nigeria	60%
South Africa	50%
Iran	40%
Mexico	40%
India	25%
Russia	25%
Brazil	22%
United Kingdom	17%
United States	12%
Japan	11%
China	10%
France	6.5%

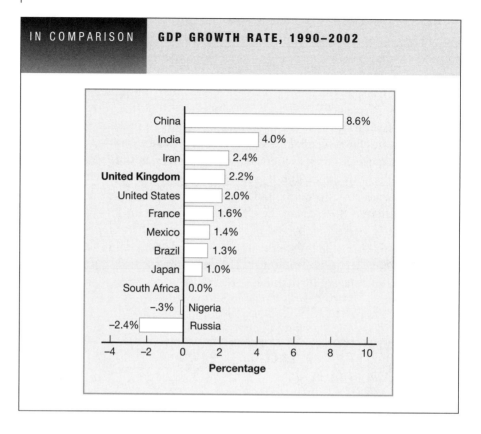

IN COMPARISON   GDP GROWTH RATE, 1990–2002

China   8.6%
India   4.0%
Iran   2.4%
United Kingdom   2.2%
United States   2.0%
France   1.6%
Mexico   1.4%
Brazil   1.3%
Japan   1.0%
South Africa   0.0%
−.3%   Nigeria
−2.4%   Russia

−4   −2   0   2   4   6   8   10

Percentage

the idea of giving up the pound; they fear the change will undermine the country's sovereignty, placing important economic decisions (such as interest rates) in the hands of other member countries and EU bureaucrats. Opponents also argue that the British economy is significantly different from the economies on the Continent and a single currency would reduce the UK's flexibility in responding to the different economic challenges that it faces. Supporters of the euro argue that if the UK were to make the change, the country would avoid the current fluctuations in the exchange rate between the euro and the pound. Adopting the euro would help trade (because there would no longer be the threat of a rising pound, making British goods too expensive for other Europeans) and promote investment (because investors would not worry about how exchange-rate volatility might affect their exports to the rest of Europe). Blair has been a supporter of the euro, and early in his tenure called for an eventual referendum on monetary union. However, he faced resistance not only from the public and the Conservatives but also from his own party, most notably from the chancellor of the exchequer Gordon Brown (who is also Blair's heir apparent). Adoption of the euro does not seem to be an option at this time, though Blair has kept open the idea that a referendum on the issue might be called. In the end, these issues tie into a much broader question: what is the UK's place in the contemporary international system?

FOREIGN RELATIONS AND THE WORLD

The United Kingdom's political future does not rest on domestic politics alone. Although the UK is no longer a superpower, it retains a relatively large army, has its own nuclear weapons, and boasts one of the largest economies in the world. It remains a major player in world affairs but is struggling to define its place and role in a post-cold-war world. The central difficulty lies in the UK's self-identity. As citizens of an island nation and a former imperial power, the British have long seen themselves as separate from continental Europe, which was slower to adopt democracy and remains much more skeptical of the liberal values that first emerged in the UK. Rather than identifying itself with the Continent, the UK built its identity around its empire, orienting itself toward the Atlantic. When the empire eventually declined, the emergence of the United States gave the United Kingdom the sense that its power had in a way been resurrected in a former colony, whose citizens were imbued with liberal values and spoke a common language. During and since the cold war, the United States has counted on the UK as its most dependable ally.

The UK also remains willing to defend its interests militarily. In 1982, the Falkland Islands—a remote British settlement of about 2,000 residents some 300 miles off the coast of Argentina—were seized by Argentina after a long-running dispute over ownership of the islands. The UK dispatched its military to retake the colony and succeeded in driving out the Argentine forces. In the process, over 200 British soldiers and over 600 Argentine soldiers were killed. Many may find the deaths of so many soldiers over two small and sparsely populated islands illogical, but it reflects the UK's postimperial identity and its desire not to surrender its international power. More recently, Tony Blair has strongly supported the U.S.-led war in Iraq, and the UK was the only other country to contribute a significant military force to the conflict. That Blair and President George W. Bush should bond over this issue even though they lead ideologically opposed parties speaks volumes about the historical ties between the United States and the United Kingdom. It also shows the degree to which the UK remains uneasy over its ties to the rest of Europe, most of whose leaders strongly opposed the war.

But despite the government's support of the war, the UK's Atlantic orientation is uncertain. Since 1989, most European countries have engaged in a new effort to expand and strengthen the European Union (EU), which has forged ever-closer political, economic, and social ties among its members. As noted earlier, the UK was a late comer to the EU, initially skeptical of membership and then later kept out by the French (who saw British membership as a Trojan horse through which the United States could influence Europe). The UK has contin-ued to be less than enthusiastic about the EU, especially in respect to its ambi-tions for taking on more power and responsibilities, such as effecting monetary union or a promulgating unified foreign policy. During the 1970s and 1980s, this attitude was less of a problem because the EU had entered a period of relative stagnation. In the last decade, however, many European leaders have moved for-ward to strengthen the EU in order to ensure regional stability and act as a coun-terweight to the "hyperpower" of the United States. New members, a European military force, and even an EU constitution are on the current agenda.

To many Britons, the notion of a stronger EU is unacceptable because they fear the EU will become an unwieldy superstate, undermining national sover-eignty, draining the domestic budget, and imposing Continental values. The fact that half the EU's budget is spent on agricultural subsidies, of which the UK gets relatively little, only underscores this suspicion. According to a 2002 poll con-ducted by the EU, only 31 percent of those surveyed in the UK thought that mem-bership in the EU was a good thing, the lowest ranking of any member state.[20] The UK's reluctance to adopt the euro is further evidence of this skepticism.

Others worry that if the UK remains skeptical of European integration, it will lose even more economic and diplomatic power. Should the UK continue to opt out of monetary union and other EU measures, it may marginalize itself, becoming a peripheral player in the creation of a single European power. Should the UK throw its lot in with the rest of Europe and finally break with the past? This is easier said than done. Having experienced centuries of incre-mental historical development that was relatively free of the revolutions, in-vasions, and wholesale destruction that ravaged the Continent, the British remain resistant to change. In that sense, the country resembles its former colony, the United States.

In short, Britain's position vis-à-vis Europe remains ambiguous. The Con-servatives made opposition to the euro and further European integration a centerpiece of its 2001 electoral campaign, but in 2005 their European policy was moved to the back burner. Once in power, the Labour Party backed away from its initial commitment to the euro, and during the 2005 campaign Blair promised a future referendum on the new EU constitution and, only subse-quently, a referendum on adoption of the euro. Even the Liberal Democrats, the UK's most pro-European party, gave its European policies a low profile during the campaign, appearing to view its position on Europe as an electoral liability. The emergence of a new fringe party, the United Kingdom Indepen-dence Party, which advocates a complete withdrawal from the EU, sought to tap into widespread Euroskepticism in the UK and in May 2005 was able to field candidates in 500 of the UK's 646 electoral districts.[21]

Should the United Kingdom continue to resist European integration its relationship to the United States remains a powerful, if problematic, alterna-tive. As we noted, the UK shares a strong historical affinity with the lone superpower. Even though the disparity in power between the two countries is enormous, British supporters of the Atlantic alliance argue that limited influence over the only superpower is superior to a more equal standing in a body like the EU, whose international authority is rather limited.

But particularly in the aftermath of September 11 and the Iraq war, many Britons have come to the disappointing conclusion that the United States sees the United Kingdom not as a critical ally but rather as a junior partner that is expected to duly follow U.S. foreign policy and provide a veneer of multilateralism no matter what the United States wants to do. This perception has fueled British anti-Americanism much like that seen elsewhere in Europe today. As of 2003, one poll showed that fewer than half of Britons had a favorable view of the United States, down from over 80 percent in 2000 (though this number still remains higher than in most of the rest of Europe). Nearly half of those surveyed also believed that the UK should act more independently of the United States.[22] The UK also finds itself in greater agreement with its European partners on the centrality of resolving the Palestinian-Israeli conflict in order to effect a lasting Middle East peace. This conflict between European and U.S. foreign policies has left the UK in the middle, with diffuse and uneasy ties to both centers of power (see "Current Issues" for further discussion).

The United Kingdom, then, remains unique, as it was centuries ago. Its economic and political systems gave rise to liberalism but remain shaped by centuries-old institutions that have never been fully swept away. Its industrial strength once propelled it to empire status, though now it is overshadowed by its former colony across the Atlantic and an ever-converging Europe. In recent years, the UK has grappled with these issues, hoping to modernize old institutions yet retain its distinct identity and hoping, too, to retain its international stature while reevaluating its relationship to the United States and to the rest of Europe. Will the United Kingdom break from its past, creating a new identity to meet its domestic and international challenges? This will be the critical issue in the UK's immediate future.

CURRENT ISSUES

DEVOLUTION AND CONSTITUTIONAL REFORM

Under the Blair government of Tony Blair, the United Kingdom has seen dramatic institutional changes. Most notable are new legislatures in Wales and Scotland and the restoration of a legislature in Northern Ireland. As part of these reforms, the UK also introduced changes in the electoral system, allowing for the use of proportional systems in local legislatures. Devolution has also included the creation of the office of mayor and a general assembly for London (limiting the power that the central government has traditionally had over the affairs of London). Currently, England is in the process of voting on whether to create its own regional assemblies. At the national level, the government has carried out a dramatic restructuring of the House of Lords, completely eliminating hereditary peers.

Some now argue that the UK should continue the process of political modernization by formalizing the distribution of power within the state and between the state and its citizens. These critics suggest that the UK needs a written constitution that clearly lays out basic rights and responsibilities. Naturally, creating such a document would not be a simple task. Constitutions are not easily revised and are even less easily written, tending to emerge in times of crisis or periods of dramatic regime change. And the fact that the UK's constitution is unwritten does not mean that it does not exist. Numerous informal institutions have long guided British politics and would need to be reconciled with any formal document.

As such, any move toward a formal constitution may come about through traditional incrementalism and European integration. In 1998, the UK incorporated the European Convention on Human Rights into law. While this document did not necessarily extend any new rights to British citizens, it did give judges the power to declare existing and future laws incompatible with the convention, a form of legislative review that they did not previously enjoy. This heightened degree of judicial activism, while still limited, is a direct departure from the British tradition of parliamentary sovereignty. Moreover, further changes may be afoot. The government recently created a Department for Constitutional Affairs, charged with constitutional and judicial reform. Among the proposals being considered by this new committee is the elimination of the 400-year-old office of the lord chancellor, the minister in charge of overseeing the judiciary.

Might the UK finally create a true constitutional court? In the absence of a written constitution, a court with the powers akin to those of the U.S. Supreme Court is unlikely. But over time, the common U.S. notions of federalism and checks and balances may also become a central feature of the British political landscape.

TONY BLAIR AND THE IRAQ WAR

In the immediate aftermath of September 11, the U.S. government viewed the United Kingdom as one of its staunchest allies in the suppression of terrorism. Tony Blair lent his government's unqualified support to the U.S. war against Afghanistan, and British forces played a significant role in the conflict. Blair served as an important conduit between the United States and the rest of Europe, helping to articulate the fight against terrorism and its sponsors. This position was sorely tested with the subsequent war in Iraq. Whereas support for the 2001 war in Afghanistan was relatively easy to garner, the administration of President George W. Bush had a much more difficult time convincing its allies of the necessity and wisdom of deposing Saddam Hussein. Yet Tony Blair once again firmly backed the U.S. foreign policy, helping to convey to the rest of Europe the need and justification for the war. As a result, Blair not only put himself at odds with much of the European and international community, but he also invoked the hostility of much of the British public and members of his own party, including several members of his cabinet who resigned in protest. Though over 100 members of the Labour Party opposed the war, effectively calling for a vote of no confidence against the prime minister, the House of Commons (and most of the opposition Conservatives) eventually voted to support the Blair policy on Iraq. In the aftermath of the invasion of Iraq, Blair has faced harsh criticism. Critics charge him with bringing the UK into an intractable conflict based on questionable intelligence and with putting the country at risk of retaliatory acts of terror. These criticisms were bolstered by the July 2005 terrorist attacks in London.

Why did Blair support Bush's policy in the Iraq war? Common assertions claim that Blair, like many of his predecessors, sees the relationship with the United States as vital, necessitating backing of U.S. policy regardless of the short-term cost. However, other observers have noted that the situation is more complex. Unlike many European politicians, Blair is noted for his moralistic attitude toward international relations, viewing the world in terms of "good" and "evil" in a manner more consistent with that found in U.S. politics.[23] This comes in part from Blair's strong religious faith—again, a departure from the largely unreligious UK. According to this theory, Blair backed the United States in Iraq not only because of the desire to remain close to the United States but also because, correctly or incorrectly, he believed the war was the morally right thing to do.

Whatever the motivation, the war has severely weakened Blair's popularity in both his party and in the UK, and has left many wondering how much longer he will be able to retain his office. The 2005 elections did not provide a clear answer to this question. Labour was "punished" by the electorate: it lost forty-seven seats despite a booming economy. At the same time, Labour retained its parliamentary majority, and the Liberal Democrats, the only major party to oppose the war in Iraq, made some gains but failed to make significant electoral progress.

NOTES

1. R. C. van Caenegem, *The Birth of the English Common Law* (Cambridge: Cambridge University Press, 1989).
2. Jeremy Black, *Walpole in Power* (Stroud, UK: Sutton, 2001).

3. For a discussion of the link between economic and democratic development see Barrington Moore, Jr., *Social Origins of Dictatorship and Democracy* (Boston: Beacon Press, 1966).

4. For a discussion of Thatcherism and its effects see Earl Reitan, *The Thatcher Revolution: Margaret Thatcher, John Major, and Tony Blair, 1979–2001* (Lanham, MD: Rowman & Littlefield, 2003); for her own perspective see Margaret Thatcher, *The Downing Street Years* (New York: HarperCollins, 1993).

5. For a discussion of the constitution in practice see Peter Hennessy, *The Hidden Wiring: Unearthing the British Constitution* (London: Victor Collancz, 1995).

6. Monarchy Poll, MORI, 24 June 2006, http://www.mori.com/polls/2002/granadamedia-topline.shtml (accessed August 3, 2005). For an interesting discussion of the value of the British monarchy to political life see Vernon Bogdanor, *The Monarchy and the Constitution* (Oxford: Clarendon Press, 1996).

7. British question time can be seen regularly on the public-affairs channel C-SPAN, and can be accessed online at http://www.cspan.org.

8. For a good discussion of the role of the prime minister in Britain see Richard Rose, *The Prime Minister in a Shrinking World* (Cambridge: Polity, 2001).

9. For more details see "The House of Lords: Completing the Reform: Department for Constitutional Affairs, 7 November 2001, http://www.dca.gov.uk/constitution/holref/hoelreform.htm (accessed 3 August 2005).

10. "Breaking the Old Place Up," *Economist*, 4 November 1999.

11. To view the manifestos from the recent election, see http://www.psr.keele.ac.uk/area/uk/man/man05.htm (accessed 1 June 2006).

12. Anthony Giddens, *The Third Way: The Renewal of Social Democracy* (Malden, MA: Blackwell, 1998).

13. Mark Garnett and Philip Lynch, *The Conservatives in Crisis* (Manchester, UK: Manchester University Press, 2003).

14. An interesting discussion of the changing nature of class and civil society in Britain can be found in Peter A. Hall, "Great Britain: The Role of Government and the Distribution of Social Capital," in Robert D. Putnam, ed., *Democracies in Flux: The Evolution of Social Change in Contemporary Society* (New York: Oxford University Press, 2002), pp. 21–57.

15. For further discussion, see the MORI/*Economist* poll results at http://www.mori.com/polls/2002/cre.shtml (accessed 5 August 2005).

16. For recent research on British political culture (especially as it relates to freedom equality) see William L. Miller, Annis May Timpson, and Michael H. Lessnoff, *Political Culture in Contemporary Britain* (Oxford, UK: Clarendon Press, 1996).

17. John Locke, *Two Treatises on Government: Of Civil Government Book II*, ch. 7, (1689; Electronic Text Center, University of Virginia, 2002), http://religionanddemocracy.lib.virginia.edu/library/tocs/LocTre2.html (accessed 5 August 2005).

18. A good historical overview can be found in Michael Dintenfass, *The Decline of Industrial Britain, 1870–1980* (London: Routledge, 1993).

19. For further information see *A Modern Regional Policy for the United Kingdom* (London: Department of Trade and Industry, 2003), http://www.dti.gov.uk/europe/consultation.pdf (accessed 5 August 2005).

20. European Commission, *Eurobarometer: Public Opinion in the European Union*, Report 58, March 2003, http://europa.eu.int/comm/public_opinion/archives/eb/eb58/eb58_en.pdf (accessed 3 August 2005).

21. See http://www.independenceuk.org/uk (accessed 3 August 2005).
22. Pew Research Center for the People and the Press, http://people-press.org/reports/display.php3?ReportID=175 (accessed 5 August 2005).
23. Peter Riddell, *Hug Them Close: Blair, Clinton, Bush and the "Special Relationship"* (London: Politico's, 2003).

KEY TERMS ━━━━━━━━━━━━━━━━━━━━━━━

Tony Blair   p. 26
cabinet   p. 31
Celtic fringe   p. 29
collective responsibility   p. 39
collectivist consensus   p. 33
common law   p. 29
Commonwealth   p. 30
Confederation of British Industry (CBI)   p. 50
Conservative Party (Tories)   p. 26
Crown   p. 35
Good Friday Agreement   p. 43
hereditary peers   p. 40
House of Commons   p. 32
House of Lords   p. 32
Labour Party   p. 26
Liberals (Whigs)   p. 32

life peers   p. 40
Magna Carta   p. 29
majoritarian   p. 33
member of Parliament   p. 34
Northern Ireland   p. 52
Parliament   p. 29
prime minister   p. 31
quangos   p. 49
Reform Act   p. 32
Margaret Thatcher   p. 26
Third Way   p. 27
Trades Union Congress (TUC) p. 50
United Kingdom of Great Britain and Northern Ireland   p. 27
vote of no confidence   p. 37

WEB LINKS ━━━━━━━━━━━━━━━━━━━━━━━

British Prime Minister **www.pm.gov.uk**
Parliament **www.parliament.uk**
Foreign and Commonwealth Office **www.fco.gov.uk**
Conflict Archive on the Internet (Conflict and politics in Northern Ireland, 1968 to the present) **cain.ulst.ac.uk**
Scottish Parliament **www.scottish.parliament.uk**
Welsh Assembly **www.wales.gov.uk**
London University page on constitutional reform
   www.ucl.ac.uk/constitution-unit
British Broadcasting Corporation **news.bbc.co.uk**
British Politics Group **www.uc.edu/bpg**
BritainUSA, site of the British Government in the U.S.
   www.britain-info.org

3 UNITED STATES

Head of state and government:
George W. Bush (since January 2000)

Capital: Washington, District of Columbia

Total GDP at PPP:
11.75 trillion US$

Total land size: 9,631,418 sq km

Population: 296 million

GDP per capita: $40,100

UNITED STATES

INTRODUCTION

Why Study This Case?

Some readers may believe that the United States is the standard against which to measure advanced industrial democracies. After all, the United States is governed by the oldest written constitution still in effect. It is the world's greatest military and economic power. Nevertheless, compared with other advanced capitalist democracies, the United States is best viewed as an anomaly full of paradoxes. It is a large and wealthy nation with a relatively weak state. The United States has a highly legitimate political regime and enjoys widespread adherence to the rule of law despite having a political system that was deliberately designed to prevent decisive and coherent policy making. U.S. citizens are deeply proud of their state but distrust it and its bureaucracy in far greater numbers than the citizens of other industrialized democracies distrust theirs. Its political system has long been dominated by two political parties, but those parties are themselves relatively weak, undisciplined, and fragmented. It has a vibrant civil society but very low voter turnout. The United States is a secular democracy in which religion continues to play a comparatively large role in politics and society. It began as a society of immigrants whose national identity is still in flux because of migration and geographic mobility. The United States has more wealth and more social mobility than any other democracy but is plagued by persistent inequality and the presence of an impoverished underclass that is more characteristic of developing countries. The United States leads the world in medical technology but has more citizens without medical insurance than any other advanced democracy. The United States, blessed with peaceful borders and isolation from major world conflicts, initially favored an isolationist foreign policy but has in recent decades intervened militarily in numerous global conflicts.

It is especially important to understand the unusual workings of the U.S. political system given the country's tremendous power in today's world. The importance of U.S. technology, culture, military power, and economic might is undeniable, and the projection of those strengths is often a source of both admiration and resentment by citizens of other countries.

As the United States enters the twenty-first century, it faces new challenges and new questions about its political system. A bitter dispute over a closely contested presidential election in 2000 raised serious doubts about the integrity of the electoral system and the fairness of the political system. A nation that had become assured of its military might and its sovereignty suddenly felt vulnerable after the terrorist attacks of September 11, 2001.

The U.S.-led invasion of Iraq in 2003 has deeply polarized politics in the United States. The painfully slow government response to the hurricane that devastated the U.S. Gulf Coast in the summer of 2005 prompted serious questions about the competence of the U.S. state. Many Americans believe that their country's political and economic systems must undergo major changes in order to respond to the challenges of the future. A question for this case is, can the oldest constitutional democracy in the world deliver such change?

Major Geographic and Demographic Features

By 2005, the population of the United States was nearly 300 million, third in the world after China and India. In terms of area, the United States also ranks third in the world, it is slightly larger than Brazil and China but about half the size of Russia and slightly smaller than Canada. The United States occupies the central portion of the North American continent, between Canada and Mexico, spanning it from the Pacific Ocean to the Atlantic Ocean. It comprises forty-eight contiguous states (and the District of Columbia), Alaska (at the extreme northwest of the continent), and the island state of Hawaii, located about 2,100 miles west of the Califiornia coast. In addition, it possesses numerous overseas territories in the Caribbean and the Pacific. U.S. states are extremely diverse in area, population, geography, climate, and culture.

The United States is blessed with stunning geographic and climatic diversity. Almost half its territory is made up of agriculturally rich lowlands that have become the world's breadbasket. Its climatic diversity allows for the production of food year-round. The United States is divided by several major mountain ranges, but its extensive coastline and navigable river systems facilitate trade and commerce. The United States is richly endowed with natural resources, including minerals, gas, and oil.

For an industrial democracy, its population is unusual in some ways. Replenished by immigration, it has continued to grow more than the population of other industrialized democracies and currently has a birth rate higher than both China's and Brazil's. As a result, unlike Japan and some European countries, the United States does not face a labor shortage in the forseeable future.

The U.S. population is also more geographically mobile than is common in industrialized democracies. Despite a very high level of home ownership, it is estimated that about one in seven Americans moves from one house to another in a given year. In recent decades, this mobility has hurt the old industrial core of the Northeast and the Midwest, whose cities have lost population and wealth, and has favored the Southwest and the West.

Historical Development of the State

AMERICA AND THE ARRIVAL OF THE EUROPEAN COLONIZERS

The origins of the U.S. state can be found in the geographic expansion of European states in the early sixteenth century. A number of European countries began to explore and establish trading missions in the eastern part of the future United States. The French, the Dutch, the Spanish, and the English all attempted to form permanent settlements there.

English citizens migrated to America in search of land, which was becoming scarce in England, and religious freedom. **Puritans,** radical Protestants, constituted a large portion of the early English settlers in North America. English colonists began to establish permanent settlements in the early seventeenth century in present-day Virginia and Massachusetts. The Virginia colony began as a business venture and developed into a slave-based plantation society geared toward the production of tobacco and dominated by white landowners. The Massachusetts colonies were settled largely by Puritans and

	TIME LINE OF POLITICAL DEVELOPMENT
Year	**Event**
1607	First permanent English settlement in America
1754–63	Seven Years' War, ending the French Empire in America
1775–83	American Revolution
1776	Declaration of Independence
1781	Ratification of the Articles of Confederation
1788	Ratification of the U.S. Constitution
1803	Louisiana Purchase, expanding the U.S. frontier westward
1846–48	Mexican War, further expanding U.S. territory
1861–65	Civil War
1865	Ratification of Thirteenth Amendment to the Constitution, abolishing slavery
1903–20	Progressive Era
1933–38	Era of the New Deal
1955–65	Civil rights movement

NATIVE AMERICANS: "ETHNIC CLEANSING" AS THE BASIS FOR WESTERN EXPANSION

Though it is convenient to begin our discussion of the origins of the American political system with the establishment of the English colonies in the seventeenth century, over 100 Indian tribes inhabited what is now the United States, and they had their own political regimes. With the arrival of Europeans, many Native American societies collaborated with or tolerated the colonists, while others violently resisted.

The chief cause of the declining indigenous population after the arrival of Europeans was disease, against which Native Americans lacked resistance. But Native American societies were also subject to military repression, murder, and forced relocation. One infamous example was the 1830 Indian Removal Act, initiated by President Andrew Jackson, which evicted the Cherokees and other tribes from their homelands in the southeastern United States and forced them to relocate on reservations in distant Oklahoma. The forced removal resulted in the death of thousands of Native Americans. The eviction of indigenous peoples by European colonizers in the United States bears numerous similarities to the Afrikaner treatment of blacks in South Africa.

developed into a society of small family farmers. Although Massachusetts was established by settlers who had been persecuted for their religious beliefs, the colonies themselves were characterized by religious intolerance and repression.

By 1640, England had established six of the thirteen colonies that would later form the United States. By the 1680s, the English established six additional colonies, including New York, which was taken from the Dutch, and Pennsylvania. The early colonists faced numerous challenges, including food shortages, disease, isolation from England, and understandable resistance by Native Americans. By the late seventeenth century, the British had begun to assert more control over their remote North American colonies. The British government, with the Navigation Act of 1651, sought to force the colonies to conduct their trade using only English ships, thereby creating colonial dependency. By the early eighteenth century, the British government had allowed elected legislatures to be established in the colonies, transplanting its own embryonic democratic institutions, and had imposed royally appointed colonial governors.

The colonies grew very rapidly, fueled by a high birth rate, the importation of enslaved Africans, mostly to the southern colonies, and continued immigration from England as well as other European countries. For Europeans, the lure of a seemingly endless supply of land was irresistible. Indeed, since colonial days America has been viewed by immigrants worldwide as a land of opportunity and promise.

Between about 1683 and 1763, the English colonists faced numerous foes. They fought indigenous tribes whose land they had taken. They also fought with the growing Spanish and French empires in America, who often allied themselves with Native American tribes and threatened to limit the English settlers' prospects for colonial expansion. In the Seven Years' War (1754–63), the British effectively defeated the French Empire in North America and weakened the Spanish Empire (with Spain giving up claims to Florida in 1763). At the end of the Seven Years' War, Britain inherited a vast empire in America that would prove both costly and difficult to control.

THE REVOLUTION AND THE BIRTH OF A NEW STATE

The United States was the first major colony to rebel successfully against European colonial rule, leading one scholar to call it "the first new nation."[1] At its core, the American Revolution was caused by a conflict between two sovereignties: the sovereignty of the English king and Parliament and the sovereignty of the colonial legislatures that had been established in America. Both believed that they had the exclusive right to raise the taxes paid by the colonists. In the 1760s, the British Parliament had passed a number of taxes on colonists that sparked a spiral of petitions, protests, boycotts, and acts of civil disobedience on the part of the colonists. The British responded by disbanding the colonial legislatures and repressing protest with military force. In the Boston Massacre (1770), British soldiers attacked a mob of colonists, further fueling the colonists' opposition to British intervention in colonial affairs. Colonial militias clashed with British military forces, a precursor to the impending revolution.

In 1774, in response to British repression, anti-British colonial elites convened a Continental Congress in Philadelphia, which was made up of delegates from the colonies. It asserted the exclusive right of the colonial legislatures to raise taxes. The Second Continental Congress, meeting in 1775, created a Continental army, with George Washington at its command. In 1776, the Congress appointed a committee to draft a constitution and approve the **Declaration of Independence.**

The declaration of a new state and a new regime evoked an attack by a large and powerful British army. In the **American Revolution** (1775–83), the colonists were greatly outnumbered but were aided by their knowledge of the terrain and an alliance with France, an enemy of England. With the defeat of the British at Yorktown, Virginia, in 1783, Britain granted independence to the thirteen rebellious American colonies.

THE CONSOLIDATION OF A DEMOCRATIC REPUBLIC AND THE DEBATE OVER THE ROLE OF THE STATE

A unique theme of the American Revolution was its opposition to a British state perceived as overbearing. Distrust of a strong state is still a feature of U.S. politics, but it presented special challenges during the Revolution. Fighting a war against the British required a central authority transcending the thirteen colonial governments, all of which had begun functioning under new constitutions. The **Articles of Confederation,** approved in 1781, created a loose alliance of sovereign states. It featured a unicameral legislature with a single vote for each state. The Confederation Congress assumed important powers regarding conflicts between states and the regulation of settlement to the west, but it required unanimity for the passage of all legislation, lacked a national executive, and did not have the ability to raise taxes or create a national currency. This weak central state made it difficult for the nation to conduct foreign relations, control inflation, and carry out international trade.

In response to those problems, a Constitutional Convention of state delegates was held in 1787 to consider a stronger national state. The resulting constitutional document was a compromise between advocates of a strong federal state and supporters of states' rights. The states ratified the new constitution in 1788, effectively creating a new national state and a new political regime.

The first U.S. Congress met in 1789. It passed legislation that strengthened the state, created a federal judiciary, and imposed a tariff on imports to fund federal expenditures. It also attempted to address the concerns of those who feared the power of a strong central state, by passing twelve amendments to the Constitution, ten of which were ratified by the states and became known collectively as the **Bill of Rights.** The ten constitutional amendments that constitute the Bill of Rights, passed by the first U.S. Congress, in large part aim to protect the rights of individuals against the state.

A major political division in the young American republic was between **Federalists,** led by Alexander Hamilton, President Washington's secretary of the Treasury, and **Democratic-Republicans,** led by the future president Thomas Jefferson. Hamilton, who advocated a strong central state, was responsible for consolidating the Revolutionary War debt incurred by the states, imposing a federal excise tax, and creating a federal bank to print and regulate currency. When Jefferson became president in 1801, he moved to reduce the power of the U.S. state by paying off the national debt, repealing the excise tax, and reducing the size of the federal bureaucracy and the military. At the same time, Jefferson was responsible for a massive increase in the territory of the United States when he acquired much of France's remaining North American territory in the **Louisiana Purchase** (1803). The Louisiana Territory extended America's westward borders to the Rocky Mountains and expedited future westward migration.

THE MOVE WEST AND THE EXPANSION OF THE STATE

With the Louisiana Purchase in 1803, the acquisition of Florida from Spain in 1819, and end of the War of 1812 with Britain in 1815, Americans were free to move westward. This movement came at the expense of Native Americans. As Americans moved westward in search of land to be used for agriculture, the United States used legislation as well as military force to contain, relocate, or exterminate Native Americans. The westward expansion continued with the 1845 annexation of Texas, a Mexican territory prior to a successful separatist movement led by non-Hispanic Americans. The U.S. declared war on Mexico in 1846 (the **Mexican War,** also known as the Mexican-American War) to protect its acquisition of Texas and to lay claim to vast Mexican territories in present-day Arizona, California, Nevada, New Mexico, Utah, Colorado, and Wyoming. In all, the rapidly expanding United States gained one third of Mexico's territory through military conquest, further encouraging the flood of migrants westward.

CIVIL WAR AND THE THREAT TO UNITY

The American Revolution had temporarily united the English colonies, and under Washington's leadership and the work of Federalist leaders the foundations of a strong central state were constructed. But the Federalist project was always controversial, and the creation of a unified United States could not eliminate simmering regional differences that threatened to destroy the Union. These differences culminated in the **Civil War** (1861–65). At its roots were the divergent paths of socioeconomic development in the southern and northern regions of the country. While the North experienced an industrial boom based on its prosperous cities, southern agriculture was still based on slave labor and export-oriented plantations.

In order to gain agreement on a federal constitution, the founders of the republic had largely sidestepped the issue of slavery. Slavery had been abolished in the North after the Revolution, but the Constitution tolerated it. A number of factors brought the issue of slavery to center stage by the mid-nineteenth century: First, the westward expansion of the United States raised the contentious issue of whether new territories would be "slave" states or "free" states. Then, in the first half of the nineteenth century, slavery was banned by England and most of Latin America, and the North increasingly viewed the South as an anachronistic threat to free-market capitalism based on individual liberty and a free labor market. Finally, the early nineteenth century saw the emergence of a rapidly growing abolition movement, largely in the North, which viewed slavery as both undemocratic and anathema to Christian values.

The 1860 election of Abraham Lincoln and the rise to power of the new anti-slavery Republican Party, provoked the secession of eleven southern states and the commencement of the Civil War. The southern states formed a rebel state, called the Confederate States of America, and enacted their own constitution, which guaranteed the institution of slavery.

During the war, the North held important advantages over the South in terms of population (it was over twice as large), wealth, and industry. Nevertheless, the South had the advantage of playing defense on difficult terrain, and it hoped to prolong the war enough to wear down the northern invaders. The long and bloody conflict cost over half a million lives before the South was defeated in 1865 and the Union was preserved. In the same year, the **Thirteenth Amendment** to the Constitution, abolishing slavery, was ratified.

The importance of the Civil War in the development of the U.S. state was immense. The federal government had increased spending and built a huge army in order to subdue the South. The federal government also gained enormous power through its role in reforming the South and reintegrating the southern states into the Union. This use of state power to end race-based slavery and promote democratic values set an important precedent.

THE PROGRESSIVE ERA AND THE GROWTH OF STATE POWER

The U.S. state used its new-found clout to promote democratic reform during the **Progressive Era** (1903–20). Progressives sought to use state (national) power to restrict the power of big business, attack corruption, and address inequality. Under President Theodore Roosevelt (1901–09), the federal government attacked monopolistic businesses and enhanced the ability of the Interstate Commerce Commission to regulate trade between states. In order to protect public land from private development, Roosevelt created a vast system of national parks. Under President Woodrow Wilson (1913–21), laws were passed to curb further the power of large monopolies and to establish a centralized Federal Reserve System as a national lender of last resort. Perhaps the single greatest impetus for the growth of a centralized state was the adoption of the Sixteenth Amendment in 1913, which gave Congress authority to levy a national income tax. In addition, Wilson took the United States into World War I, despite considerable popular opposition, an act that dramatically increased the size and power of the state.

THE GREAT DEPRESSION AND THE NEW DEAL

The stock market crash of 1929 and the Great Depression devastated the U.S. economy. One quarter of the workforce lost their jobs, the GDP dropped by about one third, and there were massive bankruptcies and bank failures. The economic crisis was a pivotal factor in the 1932 election of the Democratic Party candidate Franklin Roosevelt and the implementation of a set of social democratic welfare policies known collectively as the **New Deal.**

The New Deal policies were aimed at ameliorating the economic crisis, but their long-term impact was to increase dramatically the power of the U.S. state. Despite opposition from conservatives and the Supreme Court, Roosevelt, with a Democratic majority in both houses of Congress, passed a series of unprecedented measures. Some of the most controversial pieces of legislation guaranteed workers the right to bargain collectively with employers, created state agencies to generate electric power, provided state payments to farmers who agreed to limit production, and heavily regulated the stock market. In order to carry out these policies, a massive extension of the state bureaucracy and the creation of numerous state agencies, such as the Securities and Exchange Commission and the National Labor Relations Board, were needed. Many of those agencies still exist today. The Social Security Act (1935) established the foundation for the U.S. welfare state (though much later and much less comprehensively than in many northern European countries), creating unemployment insurance, retiree pensions, and other social welfare measures.

The New Deal policies increased the role of the state, and the entry of the United States into World War II enhanced state power even further. The military grew rapidly, the state set wages and prices, and it directly intervened in private enterprise in order to serve the war effort. In wartime, the state trampled on civil liberties, censoring the press and sending thousands of citizens of Japanese ancestry to prison camps. After World War II, in the context of the cold war with the Soviet Union, the state took measures to persecute suspected Communists, firing them from government positions.

THE STRUGGLE FOR DEMOCRATIC RIGHTS: THE CIVIL RIGHTS MOVEMENT AND THE WAR ON POVERTY

Despite constitutional protections and the defeat of the South in the Civil War, U.S. democracy suffered from the legacy of slavery. Widespread discrimination against African Americans continued, most notably in the South but also in the North. After World War II (in which African Americans served and made valuable contributions), a growing **civil rights movement,** often backed by the federal government and the federal judiciary, advocated an end to all forms of racial discrimination.

The struggle for civil rights was only one of the popular reform movements that crystallized in the 1960s. During that decade, many U.S. citizens began to view economic inequality, gender discrimination, and environmental degradation by private business as impediments to democracy. In the mid-1960s, popular movements focused on those concerns combined with growing popular opposition to the **Vietnam War,** contributing to an atmosphere of unrest and rebellion.

Partly in response to popular pressure, the U.S. government attempted to address a number of socioeconomic problems. Under President John Kennedy

(1961–63), the federal government played a crucial role in imposing civil rights legislation on recalcitrant southern states. President Lyndon Johnson (1963–69) announced a War on Poverty, with a dramatic increase in federal spending to combat economic inequality. Johnson launched new programs and founded new state institutions to protect the environment, build low-income housing, fund the arts, and redress racial discrimination. The growing state role in the economy and society even continued under the Republican president Richard Nixon (1969–74), who imposed wage and price controls to stem inflation and signed into law a measure that provided food stamps to the poorest Americans.

In 1980, President Ronald Reagan (1981–89) was elected on a neo-liberal platform of ending the trend toward increased state involvement in the economy. Reagan viewed government as "the problem, not the solution," and rode to power on a wave of conservatism that was critical of the preceding decades of state-led social activism. Reagan cut social spending and reduced taxes while dramatically increasing defense spending. The reform of a welfare state widely viewed as bloated and inefficient continued under the Democratic president Bill Clinton (1993–2001) and the Republican **George W. Bush** (2001 to the present).

In retrospect, it is clear that the United States was fortunate to build and consolidate its state under extremely favorable conditions. It did not have to contend with hostile neighbors and faced no appreciable external threats to its sovereignty. The development of the U.S. state also coincided with the steady success of the economy and the steady expansion of its power abroad.

POLITICAL REGIME

Because of their fresh experience with, and deep distrust of, authoritarian colonial rule, the founding fathers established a democratic regime governed by the rule of law. This means that government can act and citizens can be punished only as authorized by legal statute, all citizens are equal before the law, and no one is above the law, not even political leaders. Those concepts were framed in a written constitution establishing a democratic regime grounded in rational-legal legitimacy.

But the rule of law by itself was judged insufficient. The power

---

ESSENTIAL POLITICAL FEATURES

- Legislative-executive system: presidential
- Legislature: Congress
- Lower house: House of Representatives
- Upper house: Senate
- Unitary or federal division of power: federal
- Main geographic subunits: states
- Electoral system for lower house: plurality
- Chief judicial body: Supreme Court

of legitimate government in the hands of a misguided minority or even a well-intentioned majority could still lead to tyranny. This wariness led the founders to establish a liberal democratic political system with institutions designed to weaken the power and authority of the state. Those institutions included federalism, the separation of powers, and the Bill of Rights. In a sense, the legitimacy of the state was based on its inherent weakness. But that raised a dilemma: How could a state and its elected government manage from a position of weakness the tasks of leading a new and growing nation facing a host of increasingly complex challenges?

The ongoing effort to resolve that dilemma required two regimes in the eighteenth century, a civil war in the nineteenth century, and a dramatic strengthening of central government authority in the twentieth century. In 1777, the Continental Congress established the new nation's first regime under the Articles of Confederation and Perpetual Union. The Articles called for a decentralized confederation of highly autonomous states that vested most authority in the individual states. The ineffectiveness and insufficiency of this confederal regime grew increasingly apparent as the new republic faced potential threats of internal rebellion and costly foreign trade disputes. By 1787, the Articles of Confederation had been jettisoned, replaced by an entirely new constitution, which became the codified embodiment of U.S. rule of law. Inaugurated in 1789, the Constitution established a representative democratic regime governed by a presidential system. The following section examines the institutional components of this regime, including the principles of federalism and separation of powers.

Political Institutions

THE CONSTITUTION

In a nation governed by the rule of law, the 1789 document constituting the regime became all important. The Constitution of the United States of America was passed in large part as a compromise: between less and more populous states, between northern merchants and southern planters, between slaveholders and those not holding slaves, and between "Federalists," who supported a strong central government, and "Anti-Federalists," who advocated states' rights and preferred the decentralized confederal status quo. But the founders and citizens on both sides of the debate shared two characteristics: a fear of too much government in the form of an overbearing central authority, and the recognition that the Articles of Confederation had provided too little government. The constitutional compromise was one of strengthened but nonetheless limited government checked by **federalism,** which divides governing authority between the national and state governments; the **separation**

of powers, which prevents any one branch or office of government from dominating; and the Bill of Rights, which protects the freedoms of individual citizens. In an unprecedented way, this U.S. Constitution created, tempered, and buffered three sovereign spheres within a single political system: national, state, and individual.

The U.S. Constitution also stands out as the oldest written constitution still in force. Although it has been regularly interpreted by judicial action and occasionally amended (in total, twenty-seven times), it has been remarkably durable. Most of it remains fully in effect after more than 200 years, guiding U.S. politics and policy making under circumstances that could hardly have been imagined by its founders. For better or worse, it has served as the model for constituting the regimes of many newly established countries, and its guiding principles of federalism and separation of powers have become standards for numerous democracies.

The Branches of Government

At the national level, the power of government is shared by three institutions: a president, a bicameral legislature, and a judiciary, led by the Supreme Court, which has the power to interpret the Constitution. The framers put in place several institutions designed to "check" and "balance" the powers of each respective branch. For example, the upper chamber of the legislature (the Senate) is given the authority to approve or disapprove executive appointments and ratify or not ratify treaties. Both the **Senate** and the **House of Representatives** (the House) can refuse to pass legislation and can impeach, convict, and remove from office a president or a federal judge (for grievous offenses). The executive (the president) can veto legislation passed by the legislature and appoint judges to the judiciary. The judges, once appointed, have virtually lifetime tenure and serve without political oversight. Most significantly, they have the power of "concrete" judicial review, meaning that they can interpret the Constitution and void any act of the other two branches that they deem unconstitutional if that act is brought before them in a court case. Ultimately, the framers sought to give Congress the upper hand, allowing it to override a presidential veto of legislation (with a two-thirds majority) and overturn a decision of the Supreme Court by amending the Constitution.

The founders also intentionally gave each branch sources of legitimacy. Unlike a parliamentary system, in which executive authority and legislative authority are fused, and only members of parliament are directly accountable to voters, the U.S. system seats its president and members of the legislative chambers in separate elections. Separate branches and separate elections can also allow a third possible check on power: divided government, in which dif-

STRUCTURE OF THE GOVERNMENT

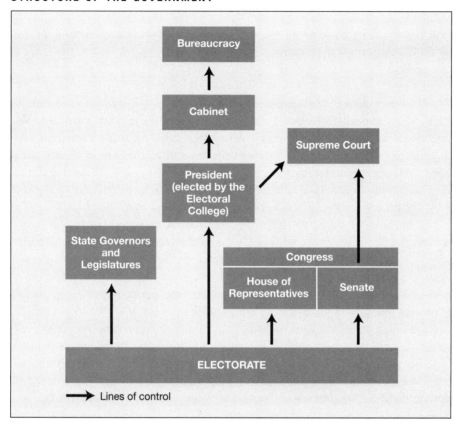

ferent parties control the executive and legislative branches. Although a single party has often dominated both, the United States has experienced divided government over 40 percent of the time since 1830 and, since the end of World War II, nearly 60 percent of the time. Thus what politicians and analysts often criticize as the tendency for American policy-making "gridlock" is an intended consequence of the system of checks and balances. It fosters a state with weak autonomy and a relatively fragmented policy-making process. This formula has led some observers to argue that the United States would be better served by a parliamentary system, which can respond more decisively to threats or needs and can change the executive quickly when it has lost the support of the legislature.

On the other hand, this system reflects the powerful liberal sentiments of both its founders and U.S. political culture today. For many Americans, inefficiency is a price worth paying to keep state power in check. Moreover, in parliamentary systems, coalitions are often needed to form a majority, or a minority government must deal with its own sort of divided government. Coalition and minority governments, it is argued, can be far less stable and far less workable than the U.S. system.

THE EXECUTIVE

The U.S. president is both the head of state and the head of government. As such, the presidency is invested with a great deal of formal authority, and key presidents have expanded the power and influence of the office over time, particularly in the last century. The president is indirectly elected by the Electoral College (based on direct popular vote) to a fixed four-year term and may be elected only twice. All U.S. presidents have been white men and all but one have been Protestant Christians (John Kennedy was Catholic).

As the head of state and the only leader elected to represent the entire citizenry, the president has traditionally taken the lead role in U.S. foreign policy (although treaties are subject to approval of the Senate). The president is also commander in chief of the military. As head of government, the president—like a prime minister—is responsible for managing the day-to-day affairs of the government and makes senior appointments to the executive and judicial branches (again with approval of the Senate). Moreover, the president can initiate proposals for legislative action and veto legislative bills.

The president also manages an enormous bureaucracy, which has mushroomed over the years, with a civilian workforce now approaching 3 million employees. The president does so with the assistance of a **cabinet** composed mostly of the heads of key departments, offices, and agencies. Unlike its parliamentary counterparts, for which the cabinet *is* the government, the U.S. cabinet has no legal authority or standing, and the influence of its officers and the institution has varied from president to president. Some presidents come to rely upon a smaller "inner cabinet" (including, for example, the chief adviser of the National Security Council, a group of officials in the Executive Office of the President) or an informal "kitchen cabinet" of trusted advisers who may not be department heads. The U.S. bureaucracy is technically responsible to the executive branch and is further constrained by the legislature's control of its many budgets. Its civil servants are not fully responsive to either branch, however, and tend to develop close ties to the interest groups they are intended to regulate. In this respect, U.S. bureaucrats lack both the autonomy and the respect historically accorded to their counterparts in countries like France and Japan (*bureaucrat* remains a derogatory term to most Americans).

With few exceptions (such as Andrew Jackson in the 1830s and Abraham Lincoln in the 1860s), presidents prior to the twentieth century were relatively weak leaders who exerted little political influence. As discussed earlier, the

White House and its Oval Office strengthened considerably over the course of the twentieth century. In recent years, the public has expected, and presidents have sought to deliver, a strong executive offering genuine if not dominant leadership. Predictably, both the legislative and the judicial branches have sought to challenge and check this growing influence.

THE LEGISLATURE

The framers of the Constitution intended Congress to be the dominant branch of the U.S. government. And in many ways, despite the growing influence of the presidency and the substantial clout of the Supreme Court, that remains the case. Scholars have argued that the U.S. Congress is in fact "the only national representative assembly that can actually be said to govern."[2] They note that although most countries today have some form of national legislature, the legislatures in authoritarian systems do little more than affirm and legitimate the decisions of the political leadership. And although the parliamentary democracies of western Europe and Japan possess the authority to say no to the executive (at the risk, in many cases, of having the parliament dissolved), those assemblies still lack the power even to modify, let alone initiate, legislation. Only the U.S. Congress has that authority.

The Constitution reserves this supreme power—the power to legislate—for Congress. It also gives Congress the power of the purse—sole authority to appropriate funds—in order to control the way in which its laws are imple-

---

DIFFERENT CHAMBERS, DIFFERENT ROLES

Given the differences in size, tenure, and assigned responsibilities, it is not surprising that the two chambers of Congress play different roles. The Senate is authorized to ratify treaties and approve presidential appointments whereas the House is given exclusive power to originate tax and revenue bills. The Senate tends to be more deliberative, providing a forum for wide-ranging opinions and topics, whereas the House is more centralized and places strict limits on debate. Because they serve a larger and more diverse constituency, senators tend to be less specialized and less partisan and more hesitant to take a position that might offend any major portion of their broad base of voters. Representatives, on the other hand, stand for election every two years and are by necessity more attuned to the needs and interests of their more narrowly defined constituencies. House members tend to be more specialized in their expertise and less reliant on a staff. The House is generally more politicized and partisan. Whereas senators are more likely to cross the aisle to form an alliance or vote with members of the opposing party on an important issue, representatives are generally more likely to vote along partisan lines.

mented. Whereas the U.S. Congress never accepts the president's annual budget without making its own significant adjustments, governments in Britain and Japan can anticipate their parliaments' acceptance of their budgets without any changes.

Another indication of the framers' understanding of congressional power was their decision to divide the legislature against itself by making it bicameral. The House of Representatives consists of 435 members (a number that has remained unchanged since 1910) who are elected to two-year terms in single-member plurality districts. The number of seats and districts allotted to each state is determined by and distributed according to each state's population after each state is allowed one representative. For example, following the 2000 national census, California saw an increase in its allotment of House seats from fifty-two to fifty-three, and New York dropped from thirty-one to twenty-nine seats based on changes in population, and Wyoming retained its single seat. In 1789, there was an average of 1 representative for every 30,000 people; in 1910, the average was over 200,000; since 2000, each member of Congress has represented more than 600,000 citizens on average.

There are 100 members of the Senate, each serving staggered terms of six years with one third of the body elected every two years. Since 1913, senators have also been elected in single-member plurality districts; prior to that, they were elected indirectly by the state legislatures. Each state is allotted two seats regardless of its population, making most senate districts far larger than those in the House. In California, for example, each senator represents approximately 15 million constituents, whereas each of North Dakota's senators represents just over 300,000 constituents.

THE JUDICIAL SYSTEM

This third branch of the U.S. government was the least defined by the Constitution and initially was quite weak. But given the trust and legitimacy vested in the Constitution and the rule of law, it should not surprise us that the U.S. judiciary has come to play a prominent role in the American political system. Over time, the federal court system devised new tools of judicial authority and significantly broadened the scope of its jurisdiction. In 1789, Congress created the federal court system and authorized it to resolve conflicts between state and federal laws and between citizens of different states.

In the landmark decision of *Marbury v. Madison,* the Supreme Court in 1803, established its right of judicial review: the authority to judge unconstitutional or invalid an act of the legislative or executive branch or of a state court or legislature. Although this power of judicial review can be exercised by federal and state courts, the Supreme Court is the court of last resort, the court with the final word on the interpretation of the U.S. Constitution. This kind of judicial review is uncommon but not exclusive to the United States—Australian and Canadian courts also have such authority.

Federal judges are given essentially lifetime appointments, affording them substantial autonomy from both partisan politics and the executive and legislative branches of government. But the Court's power is checked by its reliance upon presidential appointments and Senate approval of nominees to the federal bench, as well as by legislative enforcement of its decisions. Nonetheless, the federal courts have played an increasingly influential role, particularly since the second half of the twentieth century, determining important policy outcomes in such areas as school desegregation and abortion and even determining the winner of the 2000 presidential election. In that case, the Court overturned a decision of a state supreme court (Florida's), and in so doing invalidated a partial recount of ballots in that hotly contested election. It is little wonder that appointments to the Supreme Court have become bitter political struggles as partisan forces seek to project their influence on this now prominent third branch of U.S. government.

The Electoral System

Nearly all elections in the United States are conducted according to a single-member plurality system, in which there is one representative per district, and in which the seat is awarded to the candidate with the most votes (but not necessarily with a majority). This system has favored the emergence of two broadly defined parties and has effectively discouraged the survival of smaller and single-issue parties. Unlike a system of proportional representation, the plurality system in effect "wastes" votes for all but the dominant candidate, forcing coalitions to emerge to compete in the winner-take-all contests.

One way in which parties have sought to enhance their prospects for electoral success has been through the process of drawing up electoral districts, which are used to determine constituencies for Senate, House, and many state and local elections. State legislatures are required to adjust voting districts every ten years to reflect changes in population, and the dominant party in the legislature is able to control the process. Parties seek to influence electoral outcomes by redrawing the districts in ways that will favor their candidates and voting blocs. Political architects often employ gerrymandering, a process named after a Massachusetts governor, Elbridge Gerry, whose fellow party members crafted a district shaped like a salamander. **Gerrymandering** refers to the manipulation of district boundaries by one political party to favor the candidates of that party (nowadays achieved with the aid of sophisticated computer analyses of demographic data).

Although members of both chambers of Congress are elected directly by

National Election Results, 1992–2004					
Legislative Elections					
	House of Representatives* **Total Seats: 435****		**Senate*** **Total Seats: 100****		**Presidential Elections* (party)**
Year of Election	**Democrats**	**Republicans**	**Democrats**	**Republicans**	
1992	258	176	57	43	Clinton (Democrat)
1994	204	230	48	52	—
1996	206	228	45	55	Clinton (Democrat)
1998	211	223	45	55	—
2000	212	221	50	50	Bush (Republican)
2002	204	229	51	48	—
2004	202	232	44	55	Bush (Republican)

*House terms of office are fixed at two years, with all seats elected every two years. Senate terms are fixed at six years, with one third of the seats elected every two years. Presidential terms are fixed at four years, with elections held every four years.

**When Democrats and Republicans together comprise less than the total number of seats, the Independent representatives account for the difference.

a popular vote, the president and the vice president are elected indirectly, by the Electoral College. The founders established the Electoral College as a means of tempering the particular interests (and feared ignorance) of voters. In this system, voters technically do not vote for a presidential candidate but vote instead for a slate of electors from their state, with the electors chosen or appointed by each party from each state. Each state receives a total of electoral votes equal to its combined number of senators and representatives. In addition, the federal District of Columbia has three votes, for a sum of 538 electoral votes (100 plus 435 plus 3). But unlike a plurality system, the Electoral College requires a majority (270) of votes to claim victory. If no candidate obtains a majority, the contest is determined by the House of Representatives (as was the case twice in the early nineteenth century).

Because all but two states use a winner-take-all formula for awarding electoral votes, winning a plurality of the popular vote in a state earns a candidate all of the state's electoral votes. Thus, winning many states by large margins but losing key electoral-rich "battleground" states by narrow margins can lead to a popular victory but a loss in the Electoral College. This has happened three times in U.S. history, most recently in the controversial 2000 election between George W. Bush and Al Gore.

Even before the most recent problem, many observers had called for the elimination of the Electoral College, to parallel the elimination of the indirect election of senators nearly a century ago. Critics charge that this "quasi democratic" vestige of the eighteenth century "undermines both respect for and the legitimacy of electoral results."[3] Nor is this the only electoral reform effort being proposed. Long-standing efforts to reform campaign finance are now being joined by bipartisan calls for changes in the logistics of voter registration, the actual mechanics of voting, and the way in which presidential primaries are conducted, along with a number of smaller issues.

One response to the frustration with the existing electoral and political systems has been the proliferation of state initiatives and referenda. Twenty-seven of the fifty states allow citizen-sponsored statewide ballots called initiatives, and legislature-proposed statewide ballots called referenda (with the ballots themselves often called propositions), in which voters are able to make direct decisions about policy. The Constitution also authorizes a national ballot in the form of a national convention as one means of amending federal law, a method that has never been employed.

Local Government

As noted earlier, the United States has a federal political system dividing authority between self-governing states and a national government, which unites them (hence the "United States of America"). The Constitution authorizes the national, or federal, government to manage both national commerce and foreign policy. Although the granting of those federal powers marked a significant centralization compared with the earlier Articles of Confederation, the states have retained significant powers, including responsibility for many direct social services, such as health, education, and welfare, and authority over internal commerce.

Over time, however, the national government has managed to increase its influence over many of the areas traditionally subject to state sovereignty. The federal government can review the constitutionality of state legislation, impose federal mandates, and make federal grants to states for such things as education and transportation, contingent upon the states' abiding by federal standards. States have given up their sovereignty only reluctantly, however, and in recent years groups advocating states' rights have called for limitations on federal power and returning greater political power to the states, or devolving it on them.

This federal structure of national and state authority has allowed states to experiment with a variety of policies in areas such as welfare restructuring, vehicle emissions standards, domestic partnerships, and educational reforms. But it has also resulted in a lack of standardization in those areas and varying levels of benefits and enforcement across the states. Not surprisingly, the greatest tension comes in areas of conflicting or overlapping authority. A recent tragic example was the government's response to the devastation caused by Hurricane Katrina in the southern Gulf Coast in 2005. Although state and local governments have first responsibility to respond to such a disaster, a state governor can invite the federal government to assist, something that, as one observer noted, the Louisiana governor initially refused to do "out of pride or mistrust or a desire to maintain some degree of control."[4] The lack of a timely response by the federal government further added to the frustration and confusion.

POLITICAL CONFLICT AND COMPETITION

Federalism and the separation of powers have had another important consequence: the multiple levels and branches of elected office in the U.S. political system mean that voters in the United States go to the polls far more often than their counterparts in other democracies. Whereas a typical British or Canadian voter might cast on average four or five votes in as many years, a U.S. voter may go to the polls two or three times as often and cast dozens, if not hundreds, of votes in local, state, and national primary and general elections involving hundreds of candidates for dozens of offices and additional issues presented as initiatives and referenda.

Although this surplus of contests and contestants may be an indication of the health of democracy in the United States, some critics have pointed to it as a cause of "voter fatigue" and one of several reasons for the strikingly lower levels of voter turnout compared with turnout in other democracies. Levels of voter turnout are on average lower in the United States than in all other advanced democracies considered in this volume. And although voter turnout has actually increased in the past two presidential elections—to 52 percent in 2000 and 59 percent in 2004, the highest level since 1968—only about 40 percent of eligible Americans vote regularly.

Suffrage in the United States, as in other democracies, has expanded over time. Limited originally to white male landholders, the franchise was extended first to nonpropertied white males. It was extended to African Americans by the end of the Civil War (though full participation was not possible until Congress passed the Voting Rights Act in 1965), and to adult women in 1920. Most recently, the voting age was lowered from twenty-one to eighteen in 1971.

The Party System

Another factor sometimes blamed for declining rates of voter turnout is the weakness of political parties. Formerly bottom-up organizations linking party members tightly together in purposive grassroots campaigns, political parties in the United States have evolved over time into top-down, candidate-driven national organizations with much looser ties to voters and citizens. American political parties today tend to be weaker and more fragmented than their counterparts in most other countries.

But with much talk recently about the ideological and even geographic polarization of American voters into "red" (Republican) states and "blue" (Democratic) states, it is clear that the U.S. two-party system has certainly endured even as it has evolved. The U.S. plurality system, in one scholar's words, has fostered a "nearly-pure two-party system," in which the Democratic and Republican Parties have won virtually all votes and political offices since their rivalry began nearly 150 years ago.[5]

THE DEMOCRATIC PARTY

The Democratic Party has its roots in the Democratic-Republican Party, which formed in the 1790s with southern agrarian interests as its base. Andrew Jackson led a splinter group to presidential victory in 1828, dubbing it the Democratic Party and portraying it as the party of the "common man." The Democrats dominated the political scene until 1860 and for most of the years between 1932 and 1968.

As a coalition party, like its Republican rival, the Democratic Party is difficult to characterize fully in terms of a set of philosophical principles or even policy preferences. It may be said, however, that the party tends to embrace policies that are more liberal than conservative and draws its support disproportionately from minorities, urban dwellers, organized labor, and working women. Although less so than European socialists or even social democrats, Democrats in the United States generally perceive state intervention designed to temper the market and enhance equality as both legitimate and necessary. As has been the case with liberal parties in Britain and elsewhere, however, neo-liberal trends since the 1980s have weakened the Democratic coalition, causing conflict over traditional New Deal–type social welfare programs providing such entitlements as affirmative action.

THE REPUBLICAN PARTY

The Republican Party, familarly called the Grand Old Party (GOP), is in fact not as old as its rival. It first contested elections in 1856 on an anti-slavery platform that also appealed to northern commercial interests. With Lincoln's presidential victory in 1860, the party dominated national politics until the

1930s, when the Great Depression brought that era of its supremacy to an end. By the late 1960s, the GOP had regained the presidency and by the 1990s had obtained congressional majorities as well.

The Republican Party currently brings together a generally right-of-center coalition that includes both economic and moral conservatives. It draws support disproportionately from rural dwellers, upper-income voters, evangelical Christians, and voters tending to promote freedom over equality, such as owners of small businesses and libertarians. Although there are fewer registered Republican voters than Democratic voters, registered Republicans have tended to vote more regularly than their rivals. Americans identify themselves with both parties in roughly equal numbers, with approximately one third of adults expressing a preference for each of the two parties and most of the remaining one third identifying themselves as independents.

THIRD PARTIES

If fully one third of Americans do not identify themselves with either party, is there political space for a third party? Certainly single-member plurality systems in other countries, such as the United Kingdom, have yielded more than two parties. But in the U.S. setting, establishing the kind of presence essential for national viability has proved difficult, if not prohibitive, for smaller parties. Moreover, the dominant parties have all the advantages of incumbency, including the ability to establish and preserve laws discouraging financing and including on the ballot third-party candidates.

That said, third parties have emerged on the U.S. political scene occasionally as protest voices. And in that sense, third parties and their candidates can claim to have had an impact on the political process even if few of them have had any prospect of national electoral success. Among the third-party movements, the Populists of the late nineteenth century and the Progressives of the early twentieth have been the most successful. More recently, protest voices have emerged from each side of the political spectrum: Ross Perot's populist United We Stand Party earned nearly 20 percent of the popular vote in 1992, and Ralph Nader's pro-environment Green Party garnered nearly 3 percent of the popular vote in 2000. In both cases, one can argue that the third-party candidates took crucial votes from the losing candidate. Nader, for example, garnered nearly 100,000 votes in Florida in the 2000 election. If only 1 percent of his supporters had voted for Gore instead, Gore would have won Florida and the national election.

A factor contributing to the lack of third-party success in the United States is that the dominant parties have routinely embraced key elements of the more successful third-party movements, bringing at least some of the disaffected voters back into the two-party fold, even as they weaken the third parties.

Elections

In the United States, in contrast to countries with parliamentary systems, terms for all elected offices—and therefore the sequencing of elections—are fixed. Each state determines the conduct of the elections, including the rules for any primary elections, preliminary direct elections that are held in many states and are designed to narrow the field of candidates. Since the 1950s, electioneering in the United States has shifted from campaigning done almost exclusively by party leaders and grassroots party workers to highly central-ized and professionalized media campaigns. Election contests today are hugely expensive and marked by media sound bites, talk-show interviews, televised debates, and advertising blitzes, all guided by polls and sophisticated demo-graphic studies.

No campaigns are more illustrative of this American-style electioneering than those for the U.S. presidency. As voters have apparently become less loyal to either party, and in many cases less interested in voting and participating at all, the parties and their candidates have redoubled their efforts (and expen-ditures) to capture this top political prize. In the 2000 presidential election, for example, campaign expenditures totaled some $3 billion, far more than that spent on campaigns in any other country. Campaigns begin early, with an extensive season of primaries, last longer, and involve an all-out effort to both promote the candidate and denigrate the opponents, all in an attempt to mobilize new voters and persuade the "undecided" voters.

Civil Society

Observers since the time of the nineteenth-century French political philosopher Alexis de Tocqueville have marveled at the vibrancy of U.S. civil society and the willingness of its citizens to become civically engaged. Recently, however, ana-lysts have pointed to an apparent weakening of that civic commitment, noting low voter turnout and other signs of growing political apathy among U.S. citi-zens as evidence of a broader, generational decline in social capital.[6] Others argue, however, that the participation of individuals and the organized groups that represent their interests has perhaps not declined as much as it has sim-ply changed: individual citizens associate with one another and seek to influ-ence politics and policy in a variety of new and nontraditional ways.[7]

But precisely because the U.S. policy-making process is so complex and allows so many points of access—including individual officeholders at the national, state, and local level, legislative committees, regulatory agencies, and the initiative process—it has been difficult for individual citizens to influence the political process. And as U.S. political parties have grown weaker and less cohesive, various special-interest groups have emerged and expanded their influence. The remarkable proliferation and enormous influence of these groups in the United States sets this case apart from that of other democracies.

Interest groups are often organized around a single issue or a cluster of issues and therefore typically do not officially affiliate with a particular party or candidate. These organized interests can include a single corporation or business association, public interest groups, and even state or local governments. Perhaps most well known are the political action committees (PACs), political fund-raising organizations authorized by law to raise money for political causes. Although forbidden to support individual candidates, PACs were long permitted to raise unlimited amounts of money in support of political parties. Although a 2002 campaign-finance law banned so-called soft-money, or unregulated donations, even to political parties, organized interests quickly discovered a loophole. Thus was born a new type of tax-exempt organization—known as a 527, for the section of the federal tax code governing its behavior—that can raise unlimited campaign funds as long as the funds are spent on voter mobilization and issue advocacy and do not specifically promote a candidate or a party. Besides seeking to finance campaigns, these interest groups, as well as business corporations and wealthy individuals, exercise their influence through various lobbying techniques, both legal and questionable, to promote the interests of their constituencies.

SOCIETY

Ethnic and National Identity

The first American colonists were largely English-speaking Protestants, but early in the country's history its society was diversified by the importation of enslaved Africans and a steady stream of immigration from Europe. In the mid–nineteenth century, a wave of Asian immigration was spurred by the California gold rush, and another major migration from southern and eastern Europe began in the 1880s. In the 1920s, Congress reacted to the new immigrants by imposing a series of restrictive immigration quotas that favored immigrants from northern Europe. With the amended Immigration and Nationality Act of 1965, Congress abandoned those quotas. As a result, immigration surged again, with the bulk of the new immigrants arriving from Latin America and Asia. The influx of non-European immigrants, especially **Hispanics,** has become an important issue in U.S. politics (see the discussion of Current Issues, p. 101). Currently about 11 percent of U.S. citizens were born abroad.

Contrary to the common perception of the United States as a peaceful "melting pot" of cultures, immigrants have always faced resentment and discrimination. The debate about the impact of immigrants on U.S. society has deep roots in American history.

Ideology and Political Culture

There has been much debate about the distinctiveness of U.S. ideology and political culture. There is broad consensus, however, that the attributes discussed below characterize the dominant U.S. ideology.

INDIVIDUALISM AND FREEDOM

Although citizens of other industrial democracies are more likely to view freedom as resulting from government policy, Americans are more likely to view their individual freedom in terms of what the state can*not* do to them. As a result, whereas many other democracies attempt to specify in their constitutions what the state should provide its citizens, the U.S. Constitution emphasizes citizen's protections from the state.

Like classic liberal thinkers, Americans tend to eschew collective or societal goals in favor of personal or individual goals. Consequently, the role of private property in U.S. society is especially important, and taxes, which are viewed as the state's appropriation of private property, are highly unpopular. Individualism may be one factor that has weakened political parties in the United States and limited their ideological coherence.

PARTICIPATORY CIVIL SOCIETY

An often-observed feature of U.S. political culture is Americans' participation in a plethora of voluntary groups that can be referred to collectively as civil society. Even in the nineteenth century, Tocqueville noted that Americans were "forever forming

ETHNIC GROUPS

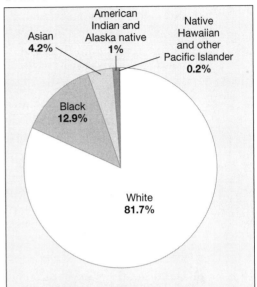

A separate listing for Hispanic is not included because the U.S. Census Bureau considers Hispanic to mean a person of Latin American descent (including persons of Cuban, Mexican, or Puerto Rican origin) living in the United States who may be of any race or belong to any ethnic group (white, black, Asian, and so on). However, the Census Bureau's 2003 estimate of the Hispanic population is about 14 percent.

RELIGION

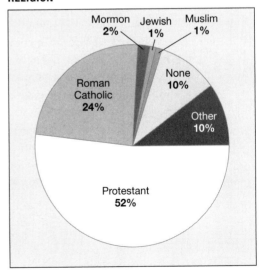

associations."[8] The rich web of civic organizations in the United States exemplifies the notion of self-government and political equality and performs a host of tasks that in other societies might be carried out by the state. In their classic *The Civic Culture*, Gabriel Almond and Sidney Verba found that American citizens, far more than citizens in other democracies, believed that participation in community affairs is part of good citizenship.[9]

As noted previously, some leading scholars have been alarmed by what they see as a rapid decline in the amount of participation in traditional civic groups. Moreover, scholars have noted that the nature of civil society is changing in the United States, with less participation in local grassroots organizations and the emergence of national, professionally managed lobbies (such as the National Rifle Association and the Sierra Club). The terrorist attacks of September 11, 2001, may have revived civic participation, especially among younger Americans, but there is still a debate about whether civil society is in danger.

POPULISM

Populism, the idea that the masses should dominate elites and that the popular will should trump professional expertise, is a key feature of the U.S. creed. As a result, Americans believe in electing public officials at virtually all levels of society, including some law-enforcement officials and judges, and many states have seen an explosion of public initiatives that give the electorate a direct say in a variety of policy issues.

EQUALITY OF OPPORTUNITY, NOT OUTCOME

A deep-seated aspect of U.S. political culture, rooted in the frontier mentality of early America, is the belief that all Americans have, and should have, an equal opportunity to become prosperous and successful. In the nineteenth century, Tocqueville observed that the United States had a far more egalitarian class structure than Europe. While the notions of economic equality and social mobility were certainly exaggerated even in early America—women were second-class citizens, and many others, like African Americans, were excluded altogether—the notions of equality of opportunity and social mobility have endured as part of a fundamental ethos.

Opinion research confirms that Americans today hold true to the notion of equality of opportunity but place less value on equality of actual economic outcomes. Today the reverse of what Tocqueville observed in the nineteenth century is true: disparities of income are greater in the United States than in most of Europe, and they are growing quickly. Indeed, Americans tend to oppose state policies aimed at redistributing income to benefit the poor, and compared with their counterparts in other advanced democracies Americans are more likely to blame the poor for not taking advantage of opportunities open to them. For example, Americans far more than Europeans believe that hard work is likely to lead to success.

IN COMPARISON	FREEDOM VERSUS EQUALITY

Which is more important, freedom or equality? Percent saying freedom:

Country	Percent
United States	71
United Kingdom	65
Nigeria	62
Mexico	61
France	53
South Africa	48
Japan	46
India	45
Russia	45
Brazil	41
China	21
Iran	NA

Source: World Values Survey, 1990. http://www.worldvaluessurvey.org

Despite growing inequality and persistent poverty, Americans evince confidence about their future. Most believe they are better off than their parents, two thirds think that they will achieve the American dream of self-improvement at some point in their lifetime, and 80 percent think that they can start out poor and become rich through their own labors.[10]

Nowhere is the American preference for equality of opportunity over equality of outcome more evident than in the system of public education. A recent comparative survey of education, noting that one quarter of Americans have a college education, concluded that "the quality of intellectual life in America is still the highest in the world."

ANTI-STATISM

The U.S. public has historically viewed its state with relatively high levels of trust and pride. Paradoxically, a deep-seated liberal distrust of "excessive" state power is also a prominent feature of the political culture. The American Revolution began as a rebellion against a powerful British state that was seen as abusing its authority through the unjust taxation of its citizens. The United States is unique in that anti-statism became a founding principle of the new regime. The founders of the U.S. regime consciously sought to embed in the system myriad checks on the power of the central state (a devolution of much power to state and local governments, a powerful and independent judiciary, separations of powers, and so on). As a result, Americans are skeptical of state efforts to promote social welfare, an outlook that largely explains the relatively small size of the U.S. welfare state. Compared with citizens in other advanced democracies, far fewer Americans believe it is the responsibility of the state to provide basic food and housing for every citizen.

THE IMPORTANCE OF RELIGIOUS VALUES

The United States is also unusual among the advanced democracies in the importance it continues to place on religion. A far higher percentage of its citizens belong to a church or other religious organization than do the citizens of other advanced democracies, and Americans are more likely to believe that there are "clear guidelines about what is good or evil."

Some scholars have argued that the high levels of religiosity in the United States stem from the early separation of church and state, which in effect turned religious organizations into voluntary civic groups that competed for

IN COMPARISON	ATTENDANCE OF RELIGIOUS SERVICES

How often do you attend religious services? Percent saying once a month or more:

Country	Percent
Nigeria	95
Brazil	75
Mexico	75
South Africa	68
United States	60
India	51
Iran	47
United Kingdom	19
France	12
Japan	12
Russia	9
China	3

Source: World Values Survey, 2000. http://www.worldvaluessurvey.org

membership.[11] In the United States, new religious groups (most recently, evangelical denominations) constantly emerge to attract congregants who might be disillusioned with more established denominations. Indeed, one could argue that the absence of a state religion led Americans to associate religion with democracy, whereas in other countries state religions have been viewed as inimical to democracy. The importance of religion in the United States has been linked to what has been called utopian moralism, the tendency of Americans to view the world in terms of good versus evil.

POLITICAL ECONOMY

The United States has the world's largest economy in terms of its output, even though Luxembourg has a larger per capita GDP. With less than 5 percent of the world's population, the United States contributes more than 25 percent to its economic output and produces twice as much as Japan (the second largest producer).[12] In the 1990s, while many of the world's economies struggled the United States enjoyed the longest period of sustained economic growth in its history. Since the 1970s, inflation and unemployment have been relatively low.

In general, the U.S. state plays a smaller role in the market than do the governments of most other industrialized democracies. The proportion of GDP controlled by federal, state, and local governments has hovered around 35 percent, less than in most European countries and far less than in Scandinavia (where Sweden, at 67 percent, has the highest proportion); that figure has not varied much over time.[13] Studies of global economic freedom rank the U.S. economy in third place (with only Singapore and Hong Kong deemed to have freer markets).[14] The United States also has some of the lowest tax rates among the industrialized democracies.

Although private enterprise is the main engine of the U.S. economy, the state does play a significant role. Starting with the New Deal reforms of the 1930s, the state's role in the economy increased in order to prevent a market collapse and promote equity. Since the 1980s, governments have attempted to scale back the role of the state in the economy. The Reagan adminis-

LABOR FORCE BY OCCUPATION

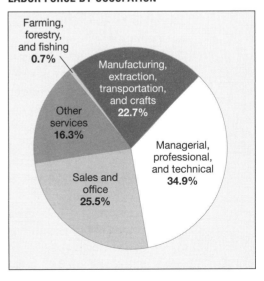

Farming, forestry, and fishing **0.7%**

Manufacturing, extraction, transportation, and crafts **22.7%**

Other services **16.3%**

Managerial, professional, and technical **34.9%**

Sales and office **25.5%**

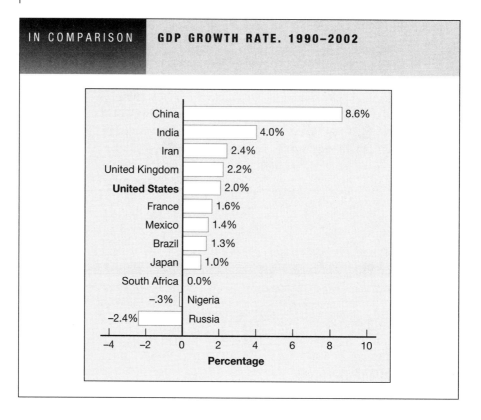

IN COMPARISON   **GDP GROWTH RATE. 1990–2002**

China — 8.6%
India — 4.0%
Iran — 2.4%
United Kingdom — 2.2%
United States — 2.0%
France — 1.6%
Mexico — 1.4%
Brazil — 1.3%
Japan — 1.0%
South Africa — 0.0%
–.3% Nigeria
–2.4% Russia

Percentage

tration, for example, deregulated many sectors of the economy (including telecommunications and the airlines) to make them more competitive. Government regulation of the economy has become a contentious issue as some deregulated sectors (like the savings and loan industry) have experienced massive bankruptcies and economic scandals (such as the late 2001 collapse of the Enron energy conglomerate). Currently, much of the U.S. state's intervention in the economy is aimed at improving the business climate. Over the past forty years, the tax burden has shifted from corporations to individuals while the state has granted huge subsidies to agribusiness and given generous tax breaks to corporations. At the same time, in contrast to many European countries, the state has done little to support trade unions.

Despite its impressive record of economic growth, the United States faces numerous political and economic challenges in the twenty-first century. Foremost is the persistent and growing inequality. More so than in other advanced democracies, poverty remains a stubborn problem in the United States, with about 12 percent of the country's citizens living below the poverty line, including 21 percent of its children (the highest percentage among the advanced democracies) and over 20 percent of African Americans and Hispanics.

Since the Social Security Act of 1935, the U.S. state has provided a safety net of welfare measures, but the provisions have been less extensive than those of other advanced democracies. The United States spends about 12 percent of its GNP on social expenditures, about half the average of the advanced industrial democracies. Legislation in the 1960s expanded welfare measures to include some health-care coverage for the poor and the elderly but stopped short of providing universal health care for all citizens. During the Reagan administration, welfare spending per poor recipient fell by one fifth. Under President Clinton, there was bipartisan support for measures aimed at cutting welfare expenditures. As a result, income inequality in the United States has been a serious and growing problem. Since 1979, the median family income rose by 18 percent while the income of the top 1 percent of the population rose by 200 percent. In 1970s, the poorest one fifth received just over 5 percent of the national income while the richest one fifth received about 40 percent. By 2000, the share of the poorest one fifth had dropped to just over 4 percent while the share of the wealthiest one fifth increased to almost 47 percent.[15] The richest one tenth percent of U.S. citizens now earn two to three times as much as their counterparts in France or the United Kingdom.

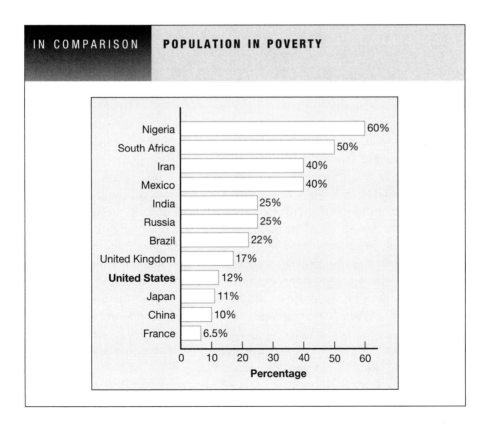

IN COMPARISON   **POPULATION IN POVERTY**

Country	Percentage
Nigeria	60%
South Africa	50%
Iran	40%
Mexico	40%
India	25%
Russia	25%
Brazil	22%
United Kingdom	17%
United States	12%
Japan	11%
China	10%
France	6.5%

Another challenge has been the growing budget deficit over the last two decades. The United States spends far more than it collects in taxes, and the budget deficit has been funded by borrowing. As a result, the United States has a gigantic national debt (over $8 trillion in 2006), with interest payments currently exceeding the entire national budget. The increase in spending since the terrorist attacks of September 11, 2001, and the costly war in Iraq have exacerbated those problems. By 2003, defense spending exceeded the total defense expenditures of the next 13 largest countries combined and was more than double the total defense spending of the remaining 158 countries in the world.[16]

The U.S. economy also faces the challenges of globalization that are common to the other cases in this book. Both Democrats and Republicans have pushed for freer world trade. President Clinton signed the North American Free Trade Agreement (NAFTA), which has further integrated the economies of its largest trading partners, Canada and Mexico. The subsequent administration has pushed for a Free Trade Area of the Americas (FTAA), which would integrate the economies of the Western Hemisphere. Advocates of free trade argue that such agreements create jobs by promoting exports. Opponents have noted the dislocation caused by free trade, as manufacturing jobs are lost to countries with cheaper labor.

FOREIGN RELATIONS AND THE WORLD

The United States is currently the most powerful actor in world politics, due in large part to the size of its military and its economy. The United States plays a major role in a number of multilateral institutions, such as the International Monetary Fund, the World Bank, and the United Nations.

The United States spent its first century after independence relatively removed from world affairs. Governing a country blessed with geographic remoteness from most of the world's major conflicts, U.S. presidents generally sought to avoid what President Thomas Jefferson called "entangling alliances." The rapid growth of the population and the economy drove the projection of U.S. power beyond its borders, however, in what some Americans came to view as the nation's **manifest destiny.** In the early nineteenth century, President James Monroe (1821–25) warned European powers to stay out of the entire Western Hemisphere (this became known as the Monroe doctrine). Later in the century, the United States extended its borders and its power through economic and military means, with victories in the Mexican War (1846–48) and the Spanish-American War (1898) and with the annexation of Hawaii (1898).

By the early twentieth century, the United States was the dominant foreign power in Latin America, and under President Theodore Roosevelt the United States expanded its influence there. Roosevelt, who bragged that he "took" Panama from Colombia in 1903 to build the canal there, preferred economic domination and the threat of U.S. military action (what he called the "Big Stick") as a means of influence, rather than officially acquiring territory. Roosevelt's visit to Panama in 1906, the first-ever foreign trip by a U.S. president, boldly ended the era of isolation.

The long-held preference for avoiding entanglements in Europe was forsaken when the United States belatedly entered World War I. The creation of a national military draft enabled a significant increase in military capability, and the allied victory resulted in a national sense of pride and confidence. At the same time, revulsion at the large number of deaths in a distant war (aproximately 116,700) created a strong popular desire to return to isolationism and avoid future wars. The United States entered World War II only after the Japanese attack on Pearl Harbor, Hawaii, in December 1941. Involvement in World War II was a major turning point in the nation's foreign policy. The United States created a massive army, and its participation was a decisive factor in the Allied victory against the Axis powers. The controversial U.S. decision to deploy its nuclear arsenal against Japan in 1945 heralded its new status as a global superpower.

Almost immediately after World War II, the United States moved to counter the influence of its wartime ally, the Soviet Union, in a growing conflict that came to be known as the cold war. Under the Marshall Plan (1947–1952), the United States invested heavily in the rebuilding of western Europe, in large part to immunize the region against communism. The United States also formed an alliance of industrialized democracies, the North Atlantic Treaty Organization (NATO), in 1949 to ensure the provision of mutual defense in the event of a Soviet attack. In the second half of the twentieth century, the United States acted frequently through direct invasion or covert action to deter Communist threats (real or perceived) in Asia and Latin America.

The U.S. record in its quest to "contain" the global spread of communism was mixed. In the Korean War (1950–1953), it succeeded in protecting South Korea from Communist invasion, and it later helped topple numerous governments it viewed as "dangerous" (such as Guatemala's in 1954 and Chile's in 1973). The United States was unable to prevent a Communist victory in China in 1949, however, though it intervened to preserve the government of Taiwan, and it failed in the Vietnam War (1961–1973), a protracted, costly, and politically unpopular conflict that did not prevent a Communist takeover of Vietnam. Similarly, despite an attempted invasion and decades of covert action and economic pressure, the United States failed to overthrow the Com-

WOULD IT BE BETTER IF ANOTHER COUNTRY RIVALED U.S. MILITARY POWER?

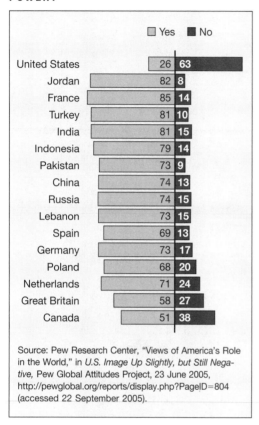

	Yes	No
United States	26	63
Jordan	82	8
France	85	14
Turkey	81	10
India	81	15
Indonesia	79	14
Pakistan	73	9
China	74	13
Russia	74	15
Lebanon	73	15
Spain	69	13
Germany	73	17
Poland	68	20
Netherlands	71	24
Great Britain	58	27
Canada	51	38

Source: Pew Research Center, "Views of America's Role in the World," in *U.S. Image Up Slightly, but Still Negative*, Pew Global Attitudes Project, 23 June 2005, http://pewglobal.org/reports/display.php?PageID=804 (accessed 22 September 2005).

munist regime of Fidel Castro in neighboring Cuba.

The fall of the Berlin Wall in 1989 and the subsequent collapse of the Soviet Union effectively brought the cold war to an end and left the United States as the only world power. This post-Soviet era nonetheless produced serious new challenges. As the undisputed global leader, the United States was called upon to help resolve ethnic violence that erupted in the Balkans and elsewhere. America's cold-war involvement in global conflicts and its enhanced power in the post-cold-war era created considerable global resentment of the United States. One recent global public opinion survey concluded that "anti-Americanism is deeper and broader now than at any time in modern history."[17]

In the 1990s, the United States intervened militarily in the Persian Gulf (to repel the Iraqi invasion of Kuwait) and in the Balkans (to stem ethnic violence), both times taking part in international peacekeeping efforts. After the terrorist attacks on the United States of September 11, 2001, President George W. Bush declared a "war" against global terrorism and announced that the United States would use unilateral pre-emptive force against all possible terrorist threats to the United States. This **Bush doctrine** was viewed by many countries, including some U.S. allies, as a rejection of international law and the United Nations. Some critics viewed it as a dangerous projection of U.S. nationalism and a reassertion of the nineteenth-century view of manifest destiny.[18]

In October 2001, in the first manifestation of the Bush doctrine, the United States led a coalition of forces that invaded Afghanistan and toppled the regime that had harbored Al Qaeda, the organization responsible for the September 11 attacks. The Bush doctrine was further called on in March 2003 with the U.S.-led invasion of Iraq. The Bush administration claimed that Iraq was a threat to the United States and the world because of its possession of weapons of mass destruction and because it, too, harbored terrorists. By 2006, the occupation of Iraq had cost more than 2,300 U.S. lives and hundreds of billions of dollars, and the war had become a divisive domestic political issue.

CURRENT ISSUES

CULTURAL DIVERSITY AND U.S. NATIONAL IDENTITY

The current wave of immigration is a hot political issue. In California, for example, voters in 1994 passed an initiative denying state services to illegal immigrants and their children. One prominent political scientist, Samuel Huntington, contends in a recent book that Mexican immigration is overwhelming, and potentially undermining, U.S. culture.[19] Huntington argues that the United States has enjoyed a unique "creed" that is in part based on the English language and English Protestant culture. He views the most recent wave of Mexican immigration as particularly threatening because it emanates from a neighboring state. Mexican immigrants, he argues, live in cultural enclaves, do not accept the American "creed," and are best understood as an extension of Mexican culture (engaged, he says, in a demographic reconquest of the originally Mexican territories of the U.S. Southwest).

Many scholars disagree with Huntington's assessment. Since the founding of the United States, immigrants have spoken different languages and maintained different cultures, but over time they have assimilated into American culture. Each wave's arrival has been greeted with hostility, fear, and alarm. Even those observers who agree that the current flow of immigration differs in many important respects from those of the past generally disagree with Huntington's assessment that Mexican immigration poses a threat to U.S. society.[20] Much evidence points to the fact that Hispanic immigrants are speaking English and otherwise assimilating into U.S. culture: over 90 percent of second-generation Hispanics are either bilingual or mainly English speakers. One scholar has flatly rejected Huntington's argument, declaring that "Hispanic immigration is part and parcel of broader American patterns of assimilation and integration. Their story, like that of the Irish, Jews, and Italians before them, is an American story."[21]

Nevertheless, public opinion research echoes Huntington's alarm. Most Americans believe that there are too many immigrants, and 85 percent view illegal immigration as a serious problem.[22] Immigrants faced further hostility and suspicion after the terrorist attacks of September 11, 2001. Thus, the United States continues to be a melting pot of cultures fed by a steady stream of immigrants. As in the past, Americans are ambivalent and deeply divided about this aspect of their society.

TERRORISM AND THE WAR IN IRAQ

After the terrorist attacks of September 11, 2001, there was widespread popular approval of President Bush's call for a "war on terrorism." The U.S.-led invasion of Afghanistan to remove the Taliban regime in October 2001 was broadly supported and had United Nations backing as well. In his January

2002 State of the Union address, Bush called Iraq part of an "axis of evil" and vowed that the United States would "not permit the world's most dangerous regimes to threaten us with the world's most destructive weapons." In June of that year, the President stated that the United States would strike first against other states in order to prevent potential threats to U.S. security. In September 2002, Bush called on the United Nations to enforce its own resolutions against Iraq's nuclear weapons program and declared that the United States would act on its own if the UN did not respond.

On October 11, 2002, the U.S. Congress authorized an attack on Iraq. The UN imposed tough new arms inspections in November, but by early 2003 international arms inspectors had made only limited progress. After the United States and the United Kingdom failed to get the UN Security Council to approve a military strike on Iraq, they launched Operation Iraqi Freedom on March 20, 2003. By April 5, 2003, the United States had occupied the Iraqi capital after a relatively easy military victory over the armed forces of the dictator Saddam Hussein. But the occupation of the country would prove far more costly in terms of lives and money. U.S. forces have been subject to a protracted insurgency and have had trouble establishing order. By 2006, over 2,300 U.S. lives and hundreds of billions of dollars had been spent on Iraq. Despite some progress establishing a democratic regime, Iraq remains plagued by violence.

The Bush administration's rationale for invading Iraq has increasingly been called into question. In June 2004, the bipartisan 9/11 Commission concluded that there was no link between the terrorist attacks of September 2001 and the regime of Saddam Hussein. Hussein's alleged support for the Al Qaeda terrorists had been used by the Bush administration as a key justification for the war in Iraq. In June 2004, the U.S. Senate Select Committee on Intelligence released a unanimous bipartisan report on pre-war intelligence on Iraq that harshly criticized U.S. intelligence agencies for the "mischaracterization of intelligence." In September 2004, UN secretary general Kofi Annan called the war in Iraq an illegal violation of the Charter of the United Nations.

Another controversial aspect of the "war on terror" is the USA Patriot Act, passed by Congress in October 2001. The Patriot Act gives the U.S. state new surveillance powers to root out terrorists. It gives government authorities the power to follow citizens' e-mail and Internet use, and it permits the indefinite detention of noncitizens on U.S. soil if there are "reasonable" grounds to suspect that they are involved in terrorist activities. The need to protect U.S. citizens against terrorism was seen by many to justify the diminution of America's much-cherished personal freedom and the privacy of its citizens.

A 2004 survey showed that less than half of Americans approved of President Bush's handling of the war in Iraq.[23] About 60 percent said they thought that Bush was too quick to use military force, and only one third thought that he had tried hard enough to reach diplomatic solutions. By September 2005, the country was evenly divided between those who thought the decision to invade Iraq was a good one and those who opposed it. Americans were similarly divided in their assessments of how the war was going, whether U.S. troops should be withdrawn, and whether the war had facilitated the fight against terrorism. The debate over the war in Iraq appears to have exacerbated an already deeply divided electorate. Most Republicans continue to support both the war and Bush's handling of it while the vast majority of Democrats take the opposite view.

NOTES

1. Seymour Martin Lipset, *The First New Nation: The United States in Historical and Comparative Perspective* (New York: W. W. Norton, 1979), p. 2.
2. This quotation and its subsequent elaboration are drawn from Theodore J. Lowi, et al., *American Government: Power and Purpose*, 7th ed. (New York: W. W. Norton, 2002), p. 162.
3. Lowi et al., *American Government*, p. 454.
4. Nicholas Lehman, "Insurrection," *New Yorker*, 26 September, 2005, pp. 66–67.
5. Ranney, "Politics in the United States," in Gabriel A. Almond, et al., *Comparative Politics Today: A World View*, 8th ed. (New York: Pearson/Longman, 2004), p. 764.
6. Robert Putnam, *Bowling Alone: The Collapse and Revival of American Community* (New York: Simon and Schuster, 2000).
7. See, for example, the recent Pew Internet and American Life Project, http://www.pewinternet.org (accessed 27 January 2006).
8. Quoted in "Degrees of Separation," Survey: America, *Economist*, 14 July 2005.
9. Alan Abramowitz, "The United States: Political Culture under Stress," in Gabriel Almond and Sidney Verba, eds., *The Civic Culture Revisited* (Boston: Little, Brown, 1980), p. 179.
10. "Degrees of Separation."
11. Lipset, *The First New Nation*, pp. 180–81.
12. Andrew L. Shapiro, *We're Number One! Where America Stands—and Falls—in the New World Order* (New York: Vintage, 1992) p. 75; for basic economic data, see "State and Country QuickFacts," U.S. Census Bureau, quickfacts.census.gov (accessed 26 March 2006).
13. Graham K. Wilson, *Only in America? The Politics of the United States in Comparative Perspective* (Chatham, NJ: Chatham House, 1998), p. 61.
14. Erik Gartzke, James D. Gwartney, and Robert A. Lawson, "Economic Freedom of the World: 2003," in *Economic Freedom of the World: 2005 Annual Report*, Fraser Institute, http://www.fraserinstitute.ca/admin/books/chapterfiles/EFW2005ch1.pdf# (accessed 26 March 2006).

15. Data on inequality is from "Middle of the Class," Survey: America, *Economist,* 14 July 2005.

16. Data compiled by the International Institute for Strategic Studies, reported in Charles V. Peña, "A Reality Check on Military Spending," *Issues in Science and Technology Online* (Summer 2005), http://www.issues.org/issues/21.4/pena.html (accessed 6 December 2005).

17. Pew Research Center, "Global Opinion: The Spread of Anti-Americanism," Pew Global Attitudes Project, 24 January 2005, http://pewglobal.org/commentary/display.php?AnalysisID=104 (accessed 22 September 2005).

18. This is the argument of Anatole Lieven, *America, Right or Wrong: An Anatomy of American Nationalism* (New York: Oxford University Press, 2005).

19. Samuel P. Huntington, *Who are We? The Challenges to America's National Identity* (New York: Simon and Schuster, 2004).

20. Tamar Jacoby, ed., *Reinventing the Melting Pot: The New Immigrants and What It Means to Be American.* (New York: Basic Books, 2004).

21. Robert A. Levine, "Assimilation, Past and Present," *Public Interest* (Spring 2005), p. 108.

22. According to a 2003 RoperASW poll, the results of which appear in "Americans Talk about Illegal Immigration," Negative Population Growth, March 2003, http://www.npg.org/immpoll.html (accessed 27 September 2005).

23. Pew Research Center, "Opinion about the Bush Administration's Stewardship," in *Foreign Policy Attitudes Now Driven by 9/11 and Iraq,* Pew Research Center for the People and the Press, 18 August 2004, http://people-press.org/reports/display.php3?PageID=867 (accessed 28 September 2005).

KEY TERMS

American Revolution   p. 71

Articles of Confederation   p. 72

Bill of Rights   p. 72

George W. Bush   p. 76

Bush doctrine   p. 100

cabinet   p. 80

civil rights movement   p. 75

Civil War   p. 73

Declaration of Independence   p. 71

Democratic-Republicans   p. 72

Federalists   p. 72

federalism   p. 77

gerrymandering   p. 83

Hispanics   p. 90

House of Representatives   p. 78

Louisiana Purchase   p. 72

manifest destiny   p. 98

Mexican War   p. 73

Progressive Era   p. 74

Puritans   p. 69

New Deal   p. 74

separation of powers   p. 77

Senate   p. 78

Thirteenth Amendment   p. 74

Vietnam War   p. 75

WEB LINKS

Resource on the U.S. Congress **www.lib.umich.edu/govdocs/fedlegis.html**

U.S. Constitution **supreme.lp.findlaw.com/documents/aofc.html**

U.S. political parties and other resources
  dir.yahoo.com/Government/U_S__Government

Official U.S. government site with links regarding U.S. politics
  usinfo.state.gov/usa/infousa/politics/govlinks.htm

Official source of information on Congress **thomas.loc.gov**

Official site of the Library of Congress, the research arm of Congress
  www.loc.gov/index.html

Site of the National Archives, government repository for documents and
  materials **www.archives.gov**

Nonpartisan site with extensive information on political issues and
  candidates **www.vote-smart.org/index.htm**

4 FRANCE

Head of state: President Jacques Chirac
(since May 17, 1995)

Head of government:
Prime Minister Dominique de Villepin
(since May 2005)

Capital: Paris

Total land size: 547,030 sq km

Population: 61 million

GDP at PPP: 1.73 trillion US$

GDP per capita: $28,700

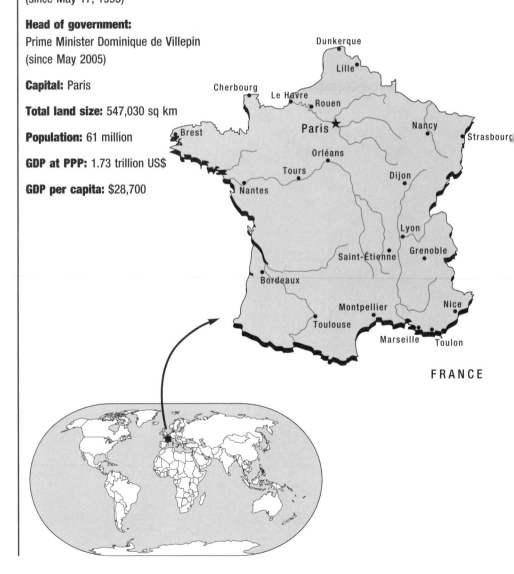

FRANCE

INTRODUCTION

Why Study This Case?

In a fundamental sense, comparative politics is the comparative study of political regimes. The term regime, fittingly, comes from the French word for "rule" or "order" and refers to the norms and rules that govern politics. These norms and rules are institutionalized—often embodied in a constitution—but can and do change as a result of dramatic social events or national crises. Regimes express fundamental ideals about where authority should reside and to what end this authority should be employed.

The French case offers a fascinating study of regimes. In little more than two centuries, France has endured a remarkable range of them, both authoritarian, from absolute monarchy to revolutionary dictatorship, and democratic, including parliamentary and semi-presidential. During this period, France has been governed by no less than three monarchies, two empires, five republics, a Fascist regime, and two provisional governments and has promulgated fifteen separate constitutions! (A popular nineteenth-century joke had a Parisian bookseller refusing to sell a copy of the French constitution to a would-be customer, claiming he did not sell periodicals.)[1] The most dramatic transition was, of course, the **French Revolution** (1789–99) in which French citizens overthrew the *ancien régime* (the European "old order" of absolute monarchy buttressed by religious authority) and replaced it (albeit briefly) with a democratic republic guided by the Declaration of the Rights of Man and of the Citizen.

France can claim title to the birthplace of modern democracy on the European continent, but democracy has not come easily. The French Revolution embraced a set of universal rights for all people and redefined French subjects as citizens. But French revolutionaries concluded that the state had to be strong enough to destroy the old regime, impose the new, and forge a strong national identity. French republicanism established a short-lived revolutionary dictatorship that was followed by Napoléon Bonaparte's coup d'état (a forceful and sudden overthrow of government). Over the next seven decades, French reactionaries battled radicals, and France oscillated between empires, monarchies, and republics (with two more revolutions!).

Not until the present **Fifth Republic** (established in 1958) has France seemed able to break this alternating cycle of stern authoritarian rule and chaotic, or at least dysfunctional, democracy. The Fifth Republic is neither authoritarian nor chaotic and has brought France a thoroughly legitimate democratic regime, a strong economy, relative social stability, and an important role in the European Union (EU), the United Nations, and the world. Indeed, French historian François Furet, a leading authority on the French Revolution, declared in 1978 that "the French Revolution is now ended."[2]

Although revolution is no longer politics-as-usual and today's French citizens are more centrist and less ideologically divided than ever, French political life is far from mundane. French citizens remain skeptical—if not cynical—about politics and politicians and vigorously divided on issues such as immigration, European integration, unemployment, and the proper role of church and state. And whereas most established democracies have vested their constitutions with a certain sanctity and have only cautiously amended them,[3] France's willingness to write and rewrite the rules of the political game offers us a fascinating study in comparative politics and gives us insights into French politics and its political culture, as this case demonstrates.

Major Geographic and Demographic Features

France is a large country—roughly the size of Texas. By European standards, it is substantial, twice the area of Great Britain and in Europe third in size only to Russia and Ukraine. It seems even larger because of its span across much of Western Europe; it shares borders with six countries and is at once an Atlantic, continental, and Mediterranean country.

Although this geography has facilitated foreign commerce, it has also exacerbated French feelings of vulnerability. Protected by mountains on both the southwest (the Pyrenees) and the southeast (the Alps), no such natural barriers exist on its border with Belgium and Germany to the north and northeast. Through the centuries, this corridor has been the locus of repeated invasions and confrontations. Abundant mineral resources (in the Saar region) and productive farmland (in Alsace-Lorraine) have raised the stakes and aggravated the conflicts. This vulnerability has also motivated France's preoccupation with establishing a formidable standing army and a strong centralized state (unlike England, which had a strong navy but a weak army). The French solution to this vulnerability after World War I was the construction of the Maginot Line, a series of concrete fortifications along the Franco-German border designed to prevent the next war. In the event, Nazi forces simply skirted the defenses and invaded France through Belgium. The French solution after World War II—integration with its long-standing German nemesis in the form of the EU—has proved much more effective.

Within France, there are no significant geographic obstacles to transportation or communication. A number of navigable rivers have, over the centuries, been supplemented by canals and railways. France now produces—and uses—the world's fastest trains, making rail travel and shipping within France and across much of Europe fast, convenient, and relatively cheap. This ease of internal travel and communication, combined with France's natural mountain and ocean boundaries, has given the French a strong sense of national identity and facilitated France's economic and political integration.

At the hub of this national integration—both literally and organizationally— lies the capital, Paris. For centuries, Paris has served as the administrative, commercial, and cultural nucleus of France. Generations of Parisian bureaucrats have imposed taxes, corvées (mandatory labor assessments), and even the Parisian dialect of French on all regions of the country. (In fact, France still has an official bureaucratic office charged with the task of determining what new words are to be added to or barred from the national language.) In addition to this linguistic homogeneity, between 83 and 88 percent of all French are at least nominally Catholic. The remainder are Muslim (between 5 and 10 percent), Protestant, or Jewish.

This national unity should not be exaggerated, however. Although metropolitan Paris is home to roughly one sixth (10 million) of France's 60 million citizens, "provincial" life, with its more rustic and relaxed lifestyle, is still preferred by most French people over the hustle and bustle of urban life. Similarly, although French citizens are proud of their national heritage, they are likewise proud of their regional differences. Generally speaking, southern France is more rural, conservative, religious, and agrarian and relatively less prosperous. Northern France is more urban, politically liberal, secular, and industrial.

Historical Development of the State

Whereas French history offers us valuable insights into the study of regimes, this same history is also an essential primer on the rise of the modern nation-state. From Louis XIV's declaration *"L'état, c'est moi"* (I am the state) to Napoléon's establishment of bureaucratic legal codes and the rule of law, the development of the French state offers an archetype for the emergence of the modern state. The French have had an ambiguous love-hate relationship with their state: great patriotism, an embrace of strong leaders, and acceptance of a strong and quite autonomous state coupled with a willingness to revolt against authority and a cynical mistrust of politics. This complexity is in large part the product of France's remarkable political history.

ABSOLUTISM AND THE CONSOLIDATION OF THE MODERN FRENCH STATE

In carving out the Holy Roman Empire in the early ninth century, Charlemagne— leader of a Germanic tribe known as the Franks—established a realm encompassing much of Western Europe. In doing so, he unified the area we know as France earlier than would occur in any of the other European states, including Britain. But with Charlemagne's death, Frankish control was reduced to

TIME LINE OF POLITICAL DEVELOPMENT	
Year	**Event**
800 C.E.	"France" first emerges as an independent power under Charlemagne
1661–1715	Absolute monarchy culminates in rule of Louis XIV
1789	French Revolution launched with storming of the Bastille in Paris
1799	Napoléon Bonaparte seizes power and brings revolution to an end
1848, 1871	Popular uprisings lead to the Second and Third Republics
1940	Third Republic replaced by Vichy (German puppet) regime
1946	The weak Fourth Republic is established
1954	French leave Vietnam in defeat
1958	Threat of civil war over Algeria returns Charles de Gaulle to office, leading to the ratification of his presidency and the Fifth Republic by referendum
1968	The Events of May rioters in Paris demand social and educational reforms
1969	De Gaulle resigns
1981	François Mitterrand and Socialists elected
1986	First period of "cohabitation" between Socialist president Mitterrand and neo-Gaullist prime minister Jacques Chirac
1992	Slim majority of French voters approve Maastricht Treaty establishing the European Monetary Union and the euro
2005	In referendum, French voters reject proposed European Union constitution

an assortment of small feudal kingdoms and principalities well within the confines of what is now France. As with feudal kings elsewhere, the Frankish rulers sought to increase their holdings, stature, and security by squeezing wealth from their subjects. But while this process in England led to a gradual decentralization of power that included first the landed aristocracy and then the middle class, in France it prompted the emergence of absolute monarchs, who centralized authority and developed efficient bureaucracies capable of taxing the subjects and administering the other affairs of state.

Absolute monarchy—that stage in the evolutionary development of Europe between the more decentralized feudal monarchies of the Middle Ages and the constitutional governments of the modern era—made several important contributions to the modern French state.[4] Many of the responsibilities that we associate with a modern state, such as education, welfare, and transportation, were at that time handled by the family, the church, an odd assortment of local authorities, or simply not at all. But three primary duties—making and executing laws, waging war and providing defense, and (largely to pay for the previous task) raising money—became the responsibility of the French kings.

In carrying out those responsibilities, these monarchs did not ignore the social classes outside the court. In fact, the crown initially allied with and—as its autonomy grew—ultimately employed each relevant class, or "estate,"in carrying out its duties. The Catholic clergy, or First Estate, had primary responsibility for administering the legal system; the landed aristocracy, or Second Estate, prosecuted the king's wars; and financiers from the mercantile elite, who came from the Third Estate, made up of commoners (those people not part of either the clergy or the nobility), gathered the taxes that paid for the luxuries of the court, the military, and the rest of the state apparatus. In order to co-opt these groups initially, the crown in the fourteenth century established a rudimentary assembly, or parliament of sorts, known as the Estates General, with representatives from each of the three estates.

By the fifteenth century, Louis XI had sufficiently centralized his authority such that he could wage wars, doubling the size of his kingdom (to roughly the current borders of France), raise taxes to pay for the wars, weaken the influence of the nobility, and largely ignore the Estates General. His successors over the next three centuries reinforced these trends, forging a centralized state with a reputation for administrative efficiency that has largely persisted to this day. The pinnacle of this absolutist authority came during the rule of Louis XIV, who dubbed himself the Sun King and famously declared that *he* was the state. Although that was an overstatement, the absolutist French state of the seventeenth century was remarkable, indeed the envy of all Europe. France had a standing professional army, a mercantilist state-run economy, a ruthlessly efficient tax system, and the extravagant palaces of Versailles. In fact, the Sun King never even convened the Estates General. Why bother?

Neither war nor court life came cheap, and the drains on the royal coffers, combined with the proficient system of taxation, had by the eighteenth century reduced the French commoners to famine and, in turn, had bankrupted the French state. In a desperate attempt to shore up support and seek essential funding, Louis XVI convened the long-dormant Estates General in 1789. Although each estate was to have one vote (allowing the more conservative clergy and nobility to override the commoners), the more numerous representatives of the Third Estate argued that all three houses should meet together as one assembly (allowing the commoners to prevail). The king resisted (understandably), stirring the anger and protests of the commoners. In this revolutionary environment, rising bread prices in Paris prompted Parisians to storm the Bastille, the old Paris jailhouse, on July 14, 1789, launching the French Revolution.

THE FRENCH REVOLUTION, THE DESTRUCTION OF THE ARISTOCRACY, AND THE EXTENSION OF STATE POWER

In the early days of the revolution, the Third Estate established the **Assemblée nationale (National Assembly),** now the lower house of the French parliament), and that body formed a new regime—a democratic republic—and issued the Declaration of the Rights of Man and of the Citizen. Inspired by the French political thinkers Jean-Jacques Rousseau and Baron de Montesquieu and the example of the American Revolution, this document was a powerful and influential statement on liberty that proclaimed the natural rights of the individual in opposition to the tyranny of monarchy. The revolutionaries concluded that the *ancien régime*, with its hereditary and religious privileges, must be destroyed and replaced. No longer should birth or faith determine justice, public office, or taxation.

Rather, in the new French republic, sovereignty was to rest with the people and their elected representatives, church and state were to be separate, and all male citizens could claim the natural and universal rights of both freedom and equality before the law. These revolutionary pronouncements have

---

THE FRENCH REVOLUTION: "NO DINNER PARTY"

When Louis XVI learned of the storming of the Bastille, he commented, "This is [simply] a revolt?" (C'est une révolte?). A member of the court responded, "*Non, Sire, c'est une révolution.*" Another famous revolutionary, China's Mao Zedong, noted that revolution "is not a dinner party . . . it cannot be so refined. [It is] an insurrection, an act of violence by which one class overthrows another." The French Revolution certainly was not a dinner party. It was radical in its fundamental attacks on aristocratic privilege and clerical (church) authority. It was violent, with tens of thousands of French killed in the first five years. Over 20,000 perished under the blade of the guillotine alone, including the king, the queen, and ultimately Robespierre and other leaders of the revolution's Reign of Terror. Most significantly, like other revolutions, it was unpredictable. The decade following the storming of the Bastille unleashed forces and debates that continued to reverberate in France over the next two centuries.

obviously had a profound effect on French politics and the constitutions of nearly all modern nation-states since then. In addition, the revolution fostered popular nationalism as an expression of the natural right of the French nation-state to exist on terms established by its own citizens. But unlike their American counterparts, who feared the tyranny of any centralized authority, French revolutionaries never questioned a powerful, centralized state, just who would control it.

In 1791, French moderates wrote a new constitution limiting the monarchy and setting up a representative assembly that in many ways resembled Britain's constitutional monarchy. But this middle-ground effort was undermined by both monarchists on the right (conservative nobles and clerics) and radical anti-clerical republicans on the left. Led by a militant faction known as the Jacobins, the radicals seized power and launched a class war known as the Reign of Terror, in which all who stood in the way of this radical vision of republicanism risked losing their heads. As in other revolutions—Joseph Stalin's purges in the 1930s Soviet Union and China's chaotic Cultural Revolution come to mind—this terror bred turmoil and paranoia until the very perpetrators became potential suspects and ultimately the victims. The Jacobins' ruthless leader, Robespierre, became the guillotine's final victim as the Reign of Terror came to an end in 1794. Although the violence ended, this ideological and cultural division between two poles—conservative, Catholic, and rural versus progressive, secular, and urban—would resonate in French politics for centuries and in some ways persists today.

In the wake of the Reign of Terror, moderates established a weak and ineffectual government that limped along for five more years (and two more constitutions). In 1799, Napoléon Bonaparte, a brilliant general, seized power in a coup d'état that brought the decade of revolutionary turmoil to an end. Unlike the revolution that had swept away the former social and political institutions, Napoléon's coup retained and indeed codified key elements of the revolution. This Napoleonic Code documented the principles that all men are equal before the law; that the people, not a monarch, are sovereign; and that the church and state are separate domains. Further enhancing France's long bureaucratic tradition, Napoléon established a meritocratic civil service open to all citizens and a system of elite schools to train these functionaries.[5]

THE RETURN TO ABSOLUTISM IN POST-REVOLUTIONARY FRANCE

Napoléon's strong state became even stronger when he was proclaimed emperor for life in a national plebiscite in 1804, and the First Republic was replaced by the First Empire. Clearly, French citizens preferred the peace, stability, and order of Napoléonic France to the chaos that had preceded it. Although the French also valued their civil and property rights, over time—and despite several more plebiscites—Napoléon's rule increasingly resembled the tyranny of the absolute monarchy that had justified the revolution. Napoléon ruled for another ten years, then abdicated the throne for a year in the wake of a series of military defeats at the hands of the hostile conservative monarchies that surrounded France. After a brief comeback, Napoléon was permanently defeated in 1815 by the British at the Battle of Waterloo and was exiled.

With military support from the victorious European powers, absolute monarchy, not democracy, replaced Napoléon's empire, and the bitter ideological divisions of the revolutionary era reemerged. The church and the aristocracy reasserted their privileges until a popular revolt in 1830 forced the crown to establish a constitutional monarchy and promise to pay more respect to the interests of the rising bourgeoisie. A third revolution, in 1848, ended monarchical rule for good, established universal male suffrage, and constituted the short-lived Second Republic. The people elected as their leader Napoléon's nephew Louis-Napoléon, who quickly followed in his uncle's footsteps, using a plebiscite to proclaim himself emperor. In 1852, Louis-Napoléon, or Napoléon III, converted the Second Republic to the Second Empire. Napoléon III ruled for nearly two decades, presiding over a period of peace and rapid industrial growth.

Both peace and prosperity came to an end with France's defeat in the Franco-Prussian War of 1870–1871. Louis-Napoléon's failed efforts to prevent German unification resulted in his capture and the collapse of the Second Empire. Not surprisingly, the absence of central authority once again led to violent struggle—indeed, civil war—between conservative monarchists and radical republicans. Although conservatives came to dominate the National Assembly, radical rioters in Paris, inspired by Marx, established a short-lived rival government in the name of the people, known as the Paris Commune, until French troops crushed the uprising.

DEMOCRATIZATION AND THE WEAK REGIMES OF THE THIRD AND FOURTH REPUBLIC

Out of the ashes and anarchy emerged France's Third Republic, which survived seventy years, until the outbreak of World War II. France's first stable democracy is also, to date, its most enduring. Its endurance should not be mistaken, however, for either strength or legitimacy. The Third Republic was weakened by the persistent and seemingly irreconcilable split between conservatives favoring both monarchy and church and radical socialists, Communists, and anarchists. This division made stable government almost impossible, with successive governments typically lasting less than a year. Despite weak government, the powerful bureaucracy, allied with French business interests, continued to promote economic development and ushered in the *belle époque* ("beautiful epoch," the era of French prominence around 1900).

These political divisions were further polarized by the devastation of World War I (during which over 1.5 million French people died) and the economic depression that followed. These crises provided fertile ground for both fascism and communism, and political extremists of the left and the right proffered Stalinist Russia and Nazi Germany, respectively, as preferable alternatives to France's weak and immobilized Third Republic.

This debate was pre-empted by France's swift defeat at the hands of the overwhelming Nazi military force in the opening weeks of World War II. The Nazi victors collaborated with the French right in setting up the puppet Vichy regime, named after the town in central France where the government was based. Even many French moderates ended up supporting this fascist government, reasoning that the Nazis were better than the Communists.[6] Many other French citizens, however, including members of religious groups and Communists, resisted the Nazi occupation both internally and externally. Although the resistance effort was diverse and at best only loosely linked, the man who came to lead the military resistance and ultimately embody the French anti-Nazi movement was General Charles de Gaulle.

Despite de Gaulle's heroic stature as leader of the resistance effort and the provisional government, after World War II French voters rejected his calls for a strong executive as the foundation of a Fourth Republic. Like the British voters who had voted the equally heroic Winston Churchill from office, the French felt they had seen quite enough of authoritarian leadership at home and abroad. Featuring both a weak executive and a new electoral system of proportional representation, the architects of this Fourth Republic managed to create a regime that was even more paralyzed than the Third Republic had been. No single party or even a stable coalition of parties was able to form a government for long—twenty governments were formed in just twelve years— and thus no political leader was in a position to make difficult or even decisive choices. Economic problems at home and colonial conflicts abroad, particularly in Vietnam and Algeria, were more than the political system could endure. By 1958, French Communists had demanded immediate independence for Algeria, and French generals there had established a provisional government and threatened military action against France if Algeria did not remain French. Under these dire circumstances, the government called on de Gaulle to return to politics and seek a way out of the crisis.

THE RECOVERY OF STATE POWER AND DEMOCRATIC STABILITY UNDER THE FIFTH REPUBLIC

As he had a decade earlier, de Gaulle insisted that he would serve only if the French people would authorize and accept a new constitution that established a strong executive and addressed the other ills of the Third and Fourth Republics. The new constitution was put to a referendum and accepted. De Gaulle,

CHARLES DE GAULLE—A TWENTIETH-CENTURY NAPOLEON?

Although the two were dramatically different in stature (Napoléon was famously short; de Gaulle was over six feet, five inches tall) and dissimilar in many other ways as well, Charles de Gaulle (1890–1970) is often compared with that earlier man on horseback. Like Napoléon, he was a career military man who arrived on the French political scene at a time of crisis and saw himself as a savior of France. Also like Napoléon, de Gaulle graduated from a military academy with a predilection for the use of artillery. In the early weeks of World War II, he led a French tank division against Hitler's attacking armies. When his superiors sued for peace, General de Gaulle opposed the action and escaped first to England and then to Algeria. He became a leader in the resistance movement and in 1944 formed the Free French provisional government that governed liberated France until 1946.

Charged with constituting the Fourth Republic after the war, de Gaulle argued for the establishment of a strong executive that could rebuild war-devastated France and avoid the problems of the weak, polarized Third Republic. French voters rejected his proposal and instead opted for a strong assembly and a largely symbolic presidency. De Gaulle resigned and left politics, warning (accurately) that the Fourth Republic would be no better than its predecessor. Economic problems at home and colonial crises abroad—first in Vietnam and then, most acutely, in Algeria—brought France to the brink of civil war, its government having become immobilized. Amid these crises, de Gaulle returned to the political scene—as Napoléon had in his time—and demanded, and received by referendum, a new constitution that established a strong presidency and formed France's Fifth Republic. Wielding great power, de Gaulle avoided civil war, decolonized Algeria, revived the French economy, and to a great extent restored French prestige. De Gaulle served for eleven years, before resigning after his constitutional reform proposals in response to the 1968 Paris riots were defeated in a plebiscite. He withdrew (again) from politics and died the following year.

who had served briefly as the last **prime minister** of the Fourth Republic, became the first president of the Fifth Republic, in 1958.

We conclude this discussion of the historical development of the French state by noting de Gaulle's significant impact on the republic and his ten-year tenure as its leader. Using sweeping executive authority, de Gaulle granted Algeria independence, established France as an independent nuclear power, withdrew it from the NATO command structure, promoted European integration, nationalized a number of key industries and private firms, and perhaps most surprising, established a substantial welfare state.

Although he averted civil war, revitalized the French economy, and restored French national pride, he was also criticized (particularly by the left) as an authoritarian demagogue. In 1968, Parisians once again took to the streets, in what came to be known as the Events of May. Students erected barricades and demanded educational reforms, and workers seized factories and called for sweeping social reforms. De Gaulle presented a reform program to the French people in a plebiscite, and when the proposals were rejected, he resigned. But rather than prompting a new round of polarized debate, revolution, and yet another constitution, the regime held. Although the French had rejected a leader, they chose not to reject his vision of a republic led by a strong national executive. The extent to which this has been made possible by the hybrid political institutions of the Fifth Republic is the subject of the following section.

POLITICAL REGIME

Political Institutions

THE CONSTITUTION

As noted earlier, France has experienced different types of authoritarian regimes (from absolute monarchy to revolutionary dictatorship) as well as a broad range of democratic regimes (both parliamentary and semi-presidential). The French Third (1875–1940) and Fourth (1946–58) Republics were pure prime-ministerial regimes. Many French viewed those regimes as weak and ineffective because fractious legislatures often resulted in a revolving door of prime ministers (with twenty cabinets in less than twelve years during the Fourth Republic). When fragmented legislatures disagreed with government policies, governments collapsed.

France's current regime, the Fifth Republic (1958–present), is codified in the constitution of 1958. That document was very much the product of Charles de Gaulle's reaction to the perceived instability of the previous two regimes (see "Charles de Gaulle—A Twentieth-Century Napoléon?" on p. 116). The central goal of de Gaulle's 1958 constitution was to eliminate the prime-ministerial system and enhance the power of the executive vis-à-vis France's traditionally powerful and fractious legislature. France thus developed a semi-presidential legislative-executive system that was innovative at the time.[7]

ESSENTIAL POLITICAL FEATURES

- Legislative-executive system: semi-presidential
- Legislature: Parlement
- Lower house: Assemblée nationale (National Assembly)
- Upper house: Sénat (Senate)
- Unitary or federal division of power: unitary
- Main geographic subunits: regions
- Electoral system for lower house: single-member district majority
- Chief judicial body: Cour de cassation (Supreme Court of Appeals)

It created a system whereby political power is shared by the legislature, a directly elected president, and a prime minister who reports to both the president and the legislature.

The French constitution has proved durable and has been amended only three times. It was altered in 1962 to allow direct election of the president and in 1992 to comply with aspects of the European Union's Maastricht Treaty, which created the single European currency. Most recently, in 1993, it was amended to tighten immigration laws.

The Branches of Government

THE PRESIDENCY

Unlike a presidential system, the French **semi-presidential** system includes a dual executive: the president is head of state, and the prime minister is head of the government. However, the constitution of 1958 is ambiguous when it comes to differentiating the powers of the president and the prime minister.[8] Indeed, the French president has relatively few formal powers, but during the course of the Fifth Republic the president has, by precedent, acquired powers somewhat beyond those specified by the constitution.

STRUCTURE OF THE GOVERNMENT

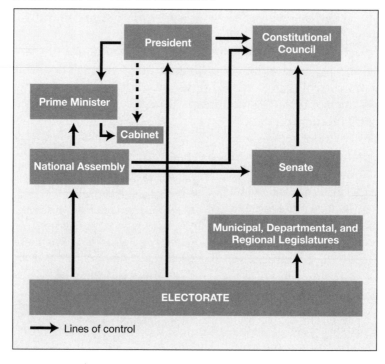

The constitution envisions the French president as a head of state who is to be "above the parties." But unlike the United Kingdom's merely symbolic head of state, French presidents have important political power, though they possess far less formal power than their U.S. counterparts. Much of the authority of the French presidents resulted from the prestige of de Gaulle and from the fact that, since 1962, the president has been the only directly elected political figure with a national mandate.[9] Moreover, French presidents are elected for long terms (five years, reduced from seven years in a 2000 referendum) and can be reelected without limits.

According to the constitution of the Fifth Republic, presidents do not directly govern. Rather, they appoint a prime minister, who must be approved by a majority of the lower house of the legislature and is supposed to select a cabinet (called the **Council of Ministers**) and preside over the day-to-day affairs of the government. In practice, when they enjoy a majority in the legislature, French presidents have selected both the prime minister and the members of the cabinet.

The 1958 constitution would appear to create a potential conflict between a directly elected president and a legislature dominated by the opposition. This is because the constitution requires the legislature to approve the president's choice of prime minister. Many observers predicted that this feature was a recipe for political disaster. The French system has worked rather smoothly, however, due in part to the fact that from 1958 to 1986 the same party dominated the presidency and the legislature, thus reducing the possibility of intra-executive conflict. During these years, the French president developed important *informal* powers, which continue to this day. As noted below, however, even when presidents have lacked a majority in the legislature, they have compromised by appointing prime ministers from the opposition. What might happen should a president refuse to compromise is not entirely clear.

French presidents have assumed some of their powers, but the constitution of the Fifth Republic does give them some formal constitutional tools. Presidents direct the armed forces. They cannot veto legislation, but they can ask the lower house to reconsider it. They can submit referenda directly to the people. They must sign all laws and decrees, but these must also be signed by all members of the Council of Ministers. Presidents also have the power to dissolve the legislature and call new elections, a power that has been employed on five occasions, usually to obtain or reinforce legislative majorities to the president's liking.[10] The president has a powerful staff, housed at the **Élysée Palace** (Palais de l'Élysées), whose members help him develop and initiate policy and work with the prime minister and the cabinet.

Perhaps the most important power of the president is the authority to appoint the prime minister, though the appointment is subject to legislative approval. The president, not the prime minister, selects the members of the cabinet, at least when the president has a majority in the legislature. More-over, presidents have simply asserted the power to remove prime ministers and cabinet members even if those officials have support in the legislature, although the constitution does not specify this authority. In short, and as is the case in Russia, the prime minister has at times become a sort of chief aide whose goal is to carry out the president's political agenda. Consequently, the president chairs the weekly meetings of the Council of Ministers.

In the early years of the Fifth Republic, it was often argued that because of the power and prestige of the president, France was developing a "repub-lican monarchy."[11] Even during de Gaulle's time, however, the presidency was hardly omnipotent. De Gaulle resigned after the electorate rejected his pro-posed reform of the Senate (seen by voters as an attack on the power of local government). François Mitterrand, despite having been president for an unprecedented fourteen years and despite frequent comparisons of his pres-idential style with De Gaulle's, was twice forced to "cohabitate" with an oppo-sition prime minister: in those cases and again from 1997 to 2002, presidential power was severely limited when voters deprived the president of a majority in the legislature. Taken together with judicial limitations on presidential power, French presidents usually have considerably less power than British prime ministers or U.S. presidents.

JACQUES CHIRAC: A PROTOTYPICAL FRENCH PRESIDENT

French president **Jacques Chirac** has been in or around public service for most of his life. His father was an executive in a large, state-owned aviation company. Chirac passed the brutal entrance examination that allowed him to attend **L'École nationale d'administration (ENA),** France's most prestigious administrative train-ing academy, and he graduated near the top of his class. He served in the military during the Algerian War and later served in the colonial bureaucracy in Algeria. He became a loyal follower of Charles de Gaulle and later served on the staff of Prime Minister (and future president) Georges Pompidou. Chirac developed a reputation for toughness; Pompidou called him his bulldozer. He was named prime minister in 1974 by President Valéry Giscard d'Estaing, with whom he had a contentious rela-tionship. Chirac became head of the larger of France's two major conservative par-ties at the time (the other being headed by his rival, Giscard d'Estaing). After resigning as prime minister in 1976, Chirac was elected mayor of Paris. He once again became prime minister in 1986, after Socialist president François Mitterrand appointed him after losing his legislative majority to the conservatives. Chirac ran for president in 1988, losing to Mitterrand. In 1995, Chirac finally won the presidency. Despite alle-gations of corruption in his administration, Chirac, at age seventy, easily won reelec-tion to a five-year term in 2002.

Presidents and Prime Ministers since 1959

President	Dates in Office	Terms	Party	Prime Ministers (Dates)
Charles de Gaulle	1959–69 (resigned in second term)	2		Michel Debré (1959–62)
				Georges Pompidou (1962–68)
				Maurice Couve de Murville (1968–69)
Georges Pompidou	1969–74	1	Gaullist	Jacques Chaban-Delmas (1969–72)
	(died in office)			Pierre Messmer (1972–74)
Valéry Giscard d'Estaing	1974–81	1	Union pour la Démocratie Française (UDF)	Jacques Chirac (1974–76)
				Raymond Barre (1976–81)
François Mitterrand	1981–94	2	Parti Socialiste (PS)	Pierre Mauroy (1981–84)
				Laurent Fabius (1984–86)
				Jacques Chirac (1986–88)
				Michel Rocard (1988–91)
				Edith Cresson (1991–92)
				Pierre Bérégovoy (1992–93)
				Edouard Balladur (1993–95)
Jacques Chirac	1995–present	2	neo-Gaullist	Alaim Juppé (1995–97)
				Lionel Jospin (1997–2002)
				Jean-Pierre Raffarin (2002–2005)
				Dominique de Villepin (May 2005–present)

The fact that the powers of the French president are greater in reality than on paper serves as a reminder that even in established democracies like the UK or France (and not just in authoritarian regimes like China) political regimes are bound by a combination of formal and informal rules.

THE PRIME MINISTER

French prime ministers are appointed by the president but serve with the support of both the president and the legislature. Article 23 of the constitution of the Fifth Republic prevents members of the legislature from serving simultaneously as prime minister, creating an intentional disconnect between the legislature and the government that is more akin to a presidential system than to a prime-ministerial system. The constitution would appear to make the prime minister the most powerful politician in France. In practice, when presidents enjoy a majority in the legislature, French prime ministers are chiefly responsible for cultivating support for presidential policies from within the legislature.[12]

When presidents lack a majority in the legislature, the power of the prime minister is clearly enhanced. Such was the case between 1986 and 1988, 1993 and 1995, and 1997 and 2002. This situation gave rise to an arrangement called **cohabitation,** in which presidents appoint opposition prime ministers who can garner a majority of support in the legislature. Faced with opposition victories in the legislature, Socialist president Mitterrand appointed an opposition neo-Gaullist, Jacques Chirac, as prime minister in 1986 and appointed an opposition head of government again in 1993. Likewise, President Jacques Chirac responded to a Socialist legislative victory in 1997 by naming a Socialist prime minister, Lionel Jospin. In short, such periods of cohabitation serve to limit the power of the French president while enhancing that of the prime minister. Even in those periods, however, French presidents have asserted control over foreign and military policy, a prerogative that was established during de Gaulle's presidency and has never been challenged.

According to the 1958 constitution, it is the Council of Ministers that must collectively "determine and direct the policy of the nation." The Council of Ministers must collectively retain the support of a majority of the lower house. If the prime minister is censured by the legislature, the entire council must resign.

THE LEGISLATURE

France has a bicameral legislature called **Parlement,** composed of the 577-member Assemblée nationale (National Assembly)[13] and a 321-member upper house, the **Sénat (Senate).** Deputies in the National Assembly are elected for five-year renewable terms, and senators are elected for nine-year terms. The constitution of the Fifth Republic clearly weakened the legislature vis-à-vis the executive. As a result, the French legislature is weaker than its counterparts in most advanced democracies, but it still plays an important role in French politics.

The constitution gives the legislature the right to propose legislation, but most bills (about three quarters of the total) originate with the government. The constitution gives the government considerable control over the workings of the legislature, including control of the agenda and the schedule of parliamentary activity. One particularly important limitation is the **blocked vote,** which forces the legislature to accept bills in their entirety and allows votes on only those amendments that have been approved by the government. French legislators have no power to introduce bills or amendments that affect public spending—only the government may introduce such legislation. Moreover, if the Parliament does not approve finance bills and the annual budget within seventy days, they automatically become law.

Another unique constitutional feature allows governments to submit legislation as matters of "confidence." In such cases, the proposed laws are passed unless the legislature passes a motion of censure against the government, an act that would require new elections (and that many legislators are therefore reticent to take). This feature was used frequently during the 1980s and 1990s, often as a way of passing important legislation without legislative debate. It has not been used since 1997, however. The constitution's Article 38 also grants the legislature the right to enable the government to legislate via decrees, known as ordinances. That measure was used twenty-two times between 1958 and 1986 but has been used rarely since then.

The constitution of the Fifth Republic severely reduced the number and powers of the legislative committees, which served as a powerful legislative tool of previous regimes. In recent decades, the legislature has gradually asserted itself more forcefully. Since the 1970s, it has conducted a weekly questioning of government ministers (though not the president) that is somewhat similar to the British routine. The French parliament now regularly amends legislation, and the executive no longer asserts its right to reject all amendments. In 1995, the legislative session was extended from six months to nine months, and extended "special sessions" have become fairly common. Legislative committees have become more important in proposing and amending legislation.

The French upper house, the Senate, is clearly the weaker of the two legislative chambers. It is elected indirectly (by an electoral college of local government officials and members of the lower house), a circumstance that deprives it of legitimacy and power. Like the British House of Lords, it can merely delay legislation passed by the lower house. Important legislation has been passed over the objection of the Senate, most notably during the

Socialist governments of 1981 to 1986, when the more conservative Senate opposed much of the legislation enacted by the leftist government. The Senate's main power resides in its ability to reject constitutional amendments, which require the consent of both houses. The Senate is widely seen as somewhat obsolete and unrepresentative. As with the British House of Lords, there have been regular calls for constitutional reform of the upper house. De Gaulle's failed attempt to reform the Senate via a referendum led to his resignation in 1969.

THE JUDICIAL SYSTEM

As in most democracies, the French judiciary is divided into several branches, including civil, criminal, and administrative. The French judicial system is based on continental European code law, in which laws are derived from detailed legal codes rather than from precedent. During Napoléon's rule, French laws were systematically codified, and much of that original code remains in place today. The role of judges is simply to interpret and apply the codes. Consequently, judges in France have less discretion and autonomy than those in the United States or the UK.

The French court system also operates very differently from that in the United States or the UK. Judges play a much greater role in determining whether charges should be brought and they assume many of the roles of U.S. prosecuting attorneys. In France, judges, not lawyers, question and cross-examine witnesses.

Because the 1958 constitution created a semi-presidential system with built-in potential for deadlock of the legislature and the executive, the Fifth Republic created a **Constitutional Council** to settle constitutional disputes.[14] The council is empowered to rule on any constitutional matter at the request of the government, the head of either house of the legislature, or a group of at least sixty members of either house. The council can rule on the constitutionality of proposed laws only before they are passed, however.

The Constitutional Council is not exactly independent of the executive or the legislature: nine members are appointed to one-year terms, three of whom (including the head member, who has the ability to break tie votes) are appointed by the president; the remaining six members are appointed by the leaders of the two houses of the legislature. In addition, all ex-presidents become lifetime members of the council.

In its early years, the Constitutional Council tended to act rarely and usually backed presidential actions. In recent decades, however, it has shown more independence. In the 1970s, it struck down legislation that would have allowed the government to make certain political organizations illegal. In the 1980s, it invalidated part of Mitterrand's legislation designed to nationalize some private enterprise.

The Electoral System

French presidents are directly elected in two rounds of voting every five years. The first round serves as a national primary, and unless a candidate gets over 50 percent of the vote in the first round (which has never happened in the Fifth Republic), a second round of balloting two weeks later pits the top two candidates against each other.

France also employs a two-round electoral system for its single-member-district elections of members of the National Assembly. In each district, candidates with over 12.5 percent of the vote face off in a second round of balloting (unless a candidate gains over 50 percent of the votes in the first round). During the Socialist administration of François Mitterrand, France experimented with proportional representation for lower-house elections, as it had in the Fourth Republic, but returned to single-member districts two years later. Using two rounds of voting does ensure that winning candidates have a majority of the vote in each district, but it still delivers disproportionate outcomes: in 2002, for example, Chirac's center-right coalition won 64 percent of the lower-house seats with only 47 percent of the nationwide vote.

By using two rounds of voting for presidential and lower-house elections, the French system encourages the existence of numerous parties, especially when compared with single-member-district systems in the UK or the United States. The second round of elections still uses a winner-take-all format, however, and the 12.5 percent threshold for entry into the second round severely limits the number of parties that actually win seats in the legislature.[15]

ELECTORAL SYSTEMS AND THE NATIONAL FRONT

The French case shows us that electoral systems can make an enormous difference. The French **Socialist Party (PS)** had long campaigned for electoral reform, arguing that proportional representation (which was used during the Fourth Republic) is fairer than the single-member-district elections used in the Fifth Republic. When the PS won power in the 1980s, it briefly changed the electoral system for the lower house, adopting proportional representation. The results were shocking to many. The far-right **National Front (FN),** which had previously been shut out of the legislature, took advantage of proportional representation to win thirty-five seats. When the conservatives regained control of the government, they quickly restored single-member districts. As a result the far right was virtually shut out of the legislature (it won only one seat in 1993 and again in 1997 and currently has no seats). The French prefer an electoral system that is less "fair" in its translation of votes into seats, but limits the success of parties deemed to be dangerous to democracy.

France's upper house is elected indirectly, by an electoral college made up of local government officials and the members of the lower house. This explains why France's upper house has often been viewed as the guardian of local interests and as a largely conservative body.

Local Government

France is usually considered a prototypical unitary centralized state with all power concentrated in Paris, the capital and largest city. Compared with most of its neighbors, France has experienced relatively little separatism (with the Corsican independence movement a key exception). While this is a generally accurate picture, France also has a long history of localism and regionalism.

There are twenty-two regions in France (including the island of Corsica), and one hundred departments, much like U.S. counties (four of which are overseas). France's municipalities are known as communes.

Until recently, most political power emanated from the central government to French departments via the powerful **prefect** (a government-appointed local official). In the 1980s, the Socialist government enacted a major decentralization of power. While not eliminating the prefect system, this change gave elected local governments far greater power. French regions, departments, and communes were finally granted the power to levy some local taxes, but local governments still predominantly depend on disbursements from the central government. Local government is now responsible for about one quarter of all public expenditures.[16]

Other Institutions: The French Bureaucracy

The French state developed one the world's earliest and most efficient bureaucracies, and the legacy of this powerful civil service can be seen in contemporary French politics. Compared with that of most other European democracies, the civil service in France retains a high profile and considerable prestige. Graduates of the highly selective École nationale d'administration (ENA) or the École Polytechnic have created a highly skilled cadre of bureaucrats. As in Japan, there is considerable overlap between the administrative elite of the state civil service and the directors of top private corporations. Like Japan's "descent from heaven," the French use the term *pantouflage* (literally, "putting on slippers") to describe the move of administrative elite from the bureaucracy to the top echelons of the private sector. As in Japan, the incestuous links between big business and the bureaucracy has been associated with endemic corruption.

Given the importance of the French bureaucracy, it is little wonder that France's political economy has long been known for a large number of state-owned (or partly owned) enterprises, though the total number of these has been reduced considerably since a wave of privatizations in the 1980s. In addition, the French state has tended to take a high profile in economic planning, similar in many respects to the Japanese case. The French term for administrative guidance is *tutelle*, literally, "tutelage."

It is estimated that about 25 percent of the French workforce is employed in the public sector, and over 2 million French workers are employed by the state. The size of the civil service, large even by European standards, has been a drain on the budget. President Chirac's plans to reduce the size of the civil service and benefits paid to civil servants led to a wave of protests and strikes in early 2005.

POLITICAL CONFLICT AND COMPETITION

The Party System

De Gaulle was deeply suspicious of political parties, blaming them for much of the political turmoil of the Third and Fourth Republics. Indeed, the Union for the New Republic (UNR), which he formed to support the charismatic leader, was never officially a political party. The single-member-district system also narrowed the field of parties and often produced stable majority governments. By the 1960s, the badly fragmented party system of the Fourth Republic had been replaced by a less fragmented multiparty system that featured a bipolar alternation of coalitions of the center right and the center left.[17] By the late 1970s, the political blocs of the right, composed mainly of the **Rally for the French Republic (RPR)** and the **Union for a Popular Movement (UMP)** and the left, composed mainly of the **French Communist Party (PCF)** and the Socialist Party (PS), each earned about half the vote in French elections. The four major parties together won over 90 percent of the vote. Since that time, the dominance of the two blocs has weakened with the emergence of new parties and with the weakening of traditional social cleavages.

The electoral system has been largely responsible for the dominance of the two major blocs during much of the Fifth Republic. The single-member-district system, with its two rounds of voting, requires coalition building in the second round. In the early years of the Fifth Republic, parties of the right usually united behind a single candidate in the first round of elections. The two main parties of the left have competed fiercely in the first round of elections but usually back the surviving leftist candidate in the second round.[18]

Since the early 1980s, the "four party, two bloc" system has weakened somewhat for a variety of reasons, and French elections have become more

Major Political Parties

Party	Description
Union pour un Mouvement Populaire (Union for a Popular Movement; UMP)	Created by a recent merger of the leading parties of the center right (the RPR, the DL, and the remnants of the UDF)
Rassemblement pour la République (Rally for the Republic; RPR)	Founded by Jacques Chirac as the main neo-Gaullist party of the center right; recently merged with the UMP; party of President Chirac and his former prime minister Jean-Pierre Raffarin
Démocratie Libérale (Liberal Democracy; DL)	A small center-right party, recently merged with the UMP
Union pour la Démocratie Française (Union for French Democracy; UDF)	The main non-Gaullist party of the center right, associated with former president Giscard D'Estaing; mostly merged with the UMP
Parti Socialiste (Socialist Party; PS)	The main party of the center left and the only leftist force to win power in the Fifth Republic
Parti Communiste Français (French Communist Party; PCF)	Long the leading party of the left, now in rapid decline
Parti Verts (Green Party; PV)	Environmental party of the left
Front National (National Front; FN)	Party of the far right, anti-immigrant and hostile to the European Union

complex and less predictable. One important change has been the spectacular demise of the PCF. Another factor has been the emergence of the far-right National Front. The French center right held power (both the presidency and control of the legislature) from 1958 to 1981, until the historic victory of the left in the 1981 presidential and 1982 legislative elections. Since then, however, presidents have often lacked majorities in the legislature: French voters supported presidents like Mitterrand and Chirac but then denied them control of the legislature. This suggests that voters are becoming more volatile and less wed to the traditional left-right division.

THE FRENCH LEFT

The PCF and the PS have been the dominant parties of the French left since the end of World War II. The Communist Party played a major role in the French resistance to the Nazi occupation and was rewarded at the polls after the war. The Communists had long been a party staunchly loyal to Moscow, but by the 1960s the PCF had become a leading critic of the Soviet Union, advocating a pro-democratic and reformist line known as Eurocommunism.

Historically, the PCF had a very strong base of support among French workers and in France's trade union movement. For much of the post–World War II period it did well in local elections, usually winning about 20 percent of the vote. It was never able to break through that percentage to win power at the national level, however. By the 1980s, the PCF was already in decline, but the demise of the Soviet bloc spelled its disaster. In addition, Communists had agreed to participate in government coalitions led by the rival Socialist Party, and the PCF briefly held cabinet positions in the early 1980s and from 1991 to 1992. Rather than giving the PCF credibility, government experience only tarnished its image. By 2002, the PCF polled only 5 percent of the votes in the first round of legislative elections. In March 2002, Marie-George Buffet became the party's first female leader.

The PS, formed in 1905, was long divided into social democratic and Marxist camps. In the 1930s, the Socialists were elected to power and led a brief and ill-fated government. After World War II, the PS emerged as the weaker of the two main leftist parties and began a long period of decline. Its fortunes began to change, however, when François Mitterrand became its leader in 1971. Mitterrand forged an electoral alliance with the stronger Communists. Over the years, the PS eclipsed the PCF as the leading party of the left, and its strategy was vindicated by the 1981 election of Mitterrand to the presidency, the first (and only, to date) leftist president of the Fifth Republic. Mitterrand's long presidency (1981–95) was marred by his party's loss of its legislative majority in 1986 and his need to cohabit with a conservative prime minister during most of his two terms in office. His successor, Lionel Jospin, led the PS to a legislative majority in 1997, but the Socialists were dealt a harsh blow when Jospin failed to enter the second round of the 2002 presidential elections, coming in third place behind the far-right National Front.

The French left remains highly fragmented. In addition to the PCF, two old-style Communist parties (the Communist Revolutionary League and the Workers' Struggle Party) attract votes on the left, as does the Green Party (PV). Even the PS is divided between old-style socialists and social democrats.

THE RIGHT

Unity has also proved elusive for the French right, which has yet to develop a dominant conservative party like the UK Conservatives. The most important force on the right consisted of the political heirs of General Charles de Gaulle, often called Gaullists or neo-Gaullists. De Gaulle distrusted political parties, however, and never created a solid party. His heirs thus created competing parties of the right that were more often than not divided more by personality than ideology. The two most important forces were the Rally for the French Republic (RPR), created by Jacques Chirac, and the **Union for French Democracy (UDF),** an alliance of five center-right parties founded in 1978 by Chirac's rival, former president Valéry Giscard d'Estaing. The RPR was seen as more statist, more nationalist (and more skeptical of the European Union), and more socially conservative. The UDF was more supportive of what would be termed today neo-liberalism, including policies that would weaken the role of the state in the market, and more supportive of European integration. Over the years, the differences mostly disappeared, and Gaullists have come to support programs that scale back the French state and have warmly embraced the European Union (EU). In 2002, Chirac encouraged most of the center right to cohere as a single party, now the Union for a Popular Movement (UMP).

Unity among France's two main conservative parties was partly spurred by the emergence and surprising success of the National Front on the far right. The FN's major policy focus has been a reduction in immigration, especially from northern Africa. Led by the fiery **Jean-Marie Le Pen,** the FN made its first real mark in national politics when proportional representation was briefly introduced in the 1980s, enabling it to win its first seats in the lower house. The party was never able to surpass the 15.1 percent it polled in the 1997 legislative elections, however, and since the 1986 election it has never won more than a single seat in the lower house. Nevertheless, in 2002, Le Pen took advantage of the fragmented left to move into a second-round face-off with President Chirac. His dismal performance in that contest (about 18 percent) underscored the fact that the FN is not a viable contender for national power. After that defeat, the party suffered an internal division that is likely to further damage its prospects.

Elections

THE SURPRISING ELECTIONS OF 2002

France's most recent presidential elections did not develop the way most observers had expected. Every presidential campaign in the Fifth Republic has involved a second-round showdown between the candidates of the center right and the center left. Most observers believed that the 2002 elections would involve a second-round runoff between conservative president Jacques Chirac and his former prime minister, PS leader Lionel Jospin. Chirac did lead the first-round field of sixteen candidates, winning about 20 percent of the vote. However, Jospin was narrowly edged out for second place by the candidate of the far-right FN, Jean-Marie Le Pen, viewed by many as a dangerous racist. Jospin failed to win second place because of a combination of factors, including an unusually low turnout and the presence of several competing candidates on the left (including the PV, two Communist parties, and the Workers' Struggle Party). In the second round two weeks later, French voters turned

JEAN-MARIE LE PEN AND THE EMERGENCE OF THE FAR RIGHT

The National Front, created by Jean-Marie Le Pen in 1972, did poorly in its first decade. Only in 1983 did Le Pen make a mark in politics, when he won over 10 percent of the vote in city council elections in a district of Paris. The FN made its first splash nationally in the 1980s when France briefly adopted proportional representation, allowing the party to win a number of seats in France's lower house. Le Pen's appeal had begun to grow, especially in urban suburbs where crime rates were rising, and concentrations of non-European, nonwhite immigrants were growing. Using the slogan "France for the French," Le Pen based his appeal on tough anti-immigrant rhetoric and an emphasis on law and order. He also took a harsh anti-EU stance, opposing the continuing political-economic integration of Europe. The FN again experienced electoral success when it came in second during the first round of France's 2002 presidential elections. Recently it has taken a strong stand against admitting Turkey to the EU. Le Pen dubbed the euro, the EU currency, "the currency of occupation."

The long-term prospects of the FN do not appear promising. Since France abandoned proportional representation and reverted to single-member districts, the party has won only a single seat on two occasions and currently holds no seats in the lower house. Much of the French political spectrum united behind Chirac in the second round of the 2002 elections, signaling a clear repudiation of Le Pen's message. Moreover, the FN, like other parties of the French right, has been badly divided, and an open split of the party in 1999 threatened to destroy it altogether.

Even as a marginal force, however, the FN has had a strong impact on French politics. Its success in legislative elections in the mid-1980s encouraged the legislature to abandon proportional representation. Parties of the center right and center left have attempted to address immigration and law and order, the FN's top issues.

out in large numbers and united behind Chirac in order to hand Le Pen a resounding defeat: Chirac won 82 percent of the vote. The 2002 legislative elections gave Chirac's Union for the Presidential Majority (UMP) and the allied UDF a large majority, which effectively ended the cohabitation that had been in effect since 1997.

REFERENDA

The constitution of the Fifth Republic allows the president to call national referenda. President de Gaulle held five referenda, staking his reputation and political capital on each one. Referenda were used to approve controversial policies, such as independence for Algeria, and to approve the direct election of the president. When de Gaulle lost a 1969 referendum aimed at reforming the upper house of the legislature, he resigned. Since then, referenda have been used less frequently. In 1972, President Pompidou used a referendum to approve the enlargement of the European Common Market, and President Mitterrand asked voters to approve the Maastricht Treaty in 1992. In 2000, President Chirac called a referendum to reduce the presidential term from seven to five years. In 2005, Chirac submitted the proposed European Constitution to a referendum. Voters delivered a resounding rejection of the document despite Chirac's support for it. The defeat prompted the president to fire his prime minister.

Civil Society

As early as the 1830s, the French scholar Alexis de Tocqueville noted the weakness of French civil associations. Most scholars argue that French interest groups and associations remain weaker than those in most advanced democracies. Nevertheless, trade unions and business organizations have been important actors.

LABOR UNIONS

French labor unions have traditionally had a long history of being "divided, weakened, and quarrelsome."[19] Only about 8 percent of the French workforce belongs to a union. Unlike the powerful, unified trade unions of Scandinavia, French labor unions have usually been divided along partisan lines. The most powerful French union confederation is the General Confederation of Labor (CGT), linked to the PCF. The PS has generally backed a smaller French Democratic Labor Confederation (CFDT), while conservatives have most often backed the Force Ouvrière (FO).

The weakness and fragmentation of French unions explain the large number of strikes that occur in France. More powerful unions might engage in productive bargaining with employers or the government. In France, the large number of strikes is a symptom of union weakness, not union strength. Consequently, French unions tend to be more radical than their northern European counterparts.

Despite this numerical weakness, unions continue to play a crucial role in French society. They play a key role, together with employers, in the management of the country's major welfare organizations (health care, retirement, and social security). Their primary strength comes from France's large public-sector workforce, and they are a force to be reckoned with when any French government attempts to reform benefits to those workers.

PRIVATE ENTERPRISE

Compared with French labor, the business sector is well organized by the MEDEF (French Enterprise Movement), and CGPME (General Confederation of Small and Medium-Size Enterprises). It has tended to support lower taxes on business, more flexible laws regarding the hiring and firing of workers, and a reduced role for government in the economy. Business has generally supported the conservatives. Since over half of the CEOs of France's major firms are former civil servants, French business often has privileged access to the state bureaucracy.

THE CHURCH

France is formally a Catholic nation, and despite minorities of Muslims, Protestants, and Jews, over 80 percent of the French are Catholics. Yet despite the predominance of Catholics, France has long been an anti-clerical society, and church and state have been formally separate since 1905. The church continues to play a role in important social rituals (marriage, births, funerals, and so on), but not in the day-to-day lives of most French citizens. The French Catholic Church today lacks an important or central role in French politics. It can, however, rally to the defense of its own institutional issues: in the 1980s, church opposition forced the Socialist government to back away from plans to impose stricter government control over religious schools.

SOCIETY

Ethnic and National Identity

In its ethnic identity, France is a relatively homogeneous society, though historically this was not the case, and it is undergoing change in the present. In centuries past, many parts of France maintained distinct ethnic identities, which included their own languages and cultures—Gascon, Savoyard, Occitan, Basque, and Breton, to name a few. Over time, these unique communities were largely assimilated into a single French identity (though certain ethnic groups, particularly Basques, have retained stronger language and cultural ties).

This assimilation was in part connected to the particular role that the French state played in the development of national identity. One of the important facets of the French Revolution was the idea of a set of universal rights with people identified as citizens rather than subjects of the state. This form of repub-

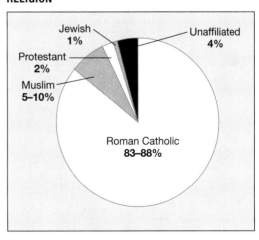

RELIGION

Jewish 1%

Unaffiliated 4%

Protestant 2%

Muslim 5–10%

Roman Catholic 83–88%

licanism was unlike that of the American Revolution, where democracy was predicated on a weak state and a system of federalism. French revolutionaries believed in the necessity of a powerful state to destroy the institutions of the past. A powerful state thus became a key instrument in solidifying and expressing French national identity and patriotism in a way in which it did not in the United States.[20]

Indeed, in contrast to the United States, rivals for public loyalty—most notably, religion—were largely eradicated. Important in this context is the French term **laïcité,** which roughly translates as "secularism." However, *laïcité* implies more than the separation of church and state. Rather, the concept involves the subordination of religious identity to state and national identity—state over church, if you will. This desire to subordinate other identities to French identity is so primary that the national census does not (and is in fact forbidden by law to) record such basic information as ethnicity and religion.

The problem, however, is that this relationship between state and nation is now being challenged. In past centuries, France accepted many immigrants from elsewhere in Europe and was able to assimilate them effectively into the broader national identity. In the past few decades, however, France has seen an influx of people from further afield, often from former French colonies in Africa, the Middle East, and Southeast Asia. The size of this group is uncertain because of the lack of census data but estimates suggest that such immigrants make up over 10 percent of the population and are concentrated in the cities.

Within this debate, the future of the Muslim community takes center stage. Currently, France has the largest Muslim population in Europe outside Turkey, estimated to be at around 5 million to 7 million, or 10 percent of the population. As with many immigrant communities elsewhere, French Muslims often find themselves marginalized in terms of economic and other opportunities due to a lack of education, language barriers, and/or persistent discrimination. Compounding this marginalization is the role of faith. On one level, the growth of a large Muslim population has been disconcerting for a country that historically has been overwhelmingly Roman Catholic, if now only nominally so. This situation is not unlike that of other Western countries. But at another level, the issue is less about Islam itself than the concept of *laïcité*. Muslims are expected to place their faith below that of national and patriotic identity as part of the assimilation process. Yet many do not want to do this, and in the face of persistent marginalization, they turn to their faith as a source of identity and meaning. In fall of 2005 these tensions exploded during a month of rioting in France's heavily immigrant suburbs. The riots revealed the extent to which many immigrants feel marginalized and disrespected by French society.

French elites are loath to embrace multiculturalism, fearing that it will undermine the political fabric that binds the country. At the same time, the government has not been effective at providing opportunities to integrate new minorities into French society (which might require a greater sensitivity toward religion and race, precisely in opposition to traditional state policy). France is not unique in these concerns. However, its particular form of national identity creates a distinct set of problems in relating to an increasingly diverse public.

Ideology and Political Culture

The role of the state in shaping French national identity can be seen in the country's ideological landscape and political culture. Ideological divisions in France are much more fragmented than are those in other European countries, where there tend to be a few coherent and persistent parties that dominate the political scene. Divisive historical events, the weakness of civil society, the importance of the state, Gaullist hostility toward political parties, the two-round electoral system, and the semi-presidential system have all played a part in creating a system in which individual political leaders, rather than ideological groupings, are central.

As a result, while we can speak generally of left and right, social democratic or liberal, in fact the ideological divisions are much more diverse and reflect a range of experiences, such as the battles over the French Revolution and the role of the Catholic Church in French life. In many cases these values cannot be classified as an ideology at all but rather fall under the term *populism*, or within a set of ideas that is suspicious of organized power and places faith in "the common man." From the revolution to Napoléon to de Gaulle, French leaders have often appealed to the masses by seeking to transcend ideology and speak for "the people." This populism has helped keep civil society weak, by fostering an ongoing mistrust of such institutions as political parties.

This residual strength of populist ideas explains not only why ideological divisions in France are as much within groups as between them but also one of the most notable elements of French political culture, the tendency toward mass protests. With civic organizations too weak to articulate public concerns and individuals faithful to the populist notion that the people must struggle against those with power, one of the most common forms of political activity in France is mass protest—marches, demonstrations, and strikes. Between 1998 and 2001, France experienced on average over 1,000 industrial actions per year (compared with around 200 in the United Kingdom), and in 2001 alone there were an additional 800 political protests.[21] This tendency was illustrated in the spring of 2006 when the government of Prime Minister Dominique de Villepin was forced to shelve a controversial labor law reform after millions of students and workers took to the streets to oppose the meas-ure during a month of protest.

POLITICAL ECONOMY

The political economy of France shares with its continental neighbors a strong state role in the economy. Part of this is a function of modern social democratic policies, whereas other elements can be traced over the course of several cen-turies. As far back as the sixteenth century, the absolute monarchy levied heavy taxes on the populace to support a large bureaucracy. At the same time, the French economy was highly mercantilist domestically, divided into a number of smaller markets, each subject to internal tariffs and nontariff barriers like weights and measures. Exports constituted a relatively small portion of the econ-omy.[22] Although the French Revolution and the reign of Napoléon rationalized many of these structures, by the twentieth century France was lagging behind many of its neighbors in terms of economic development. The country retained a large agricultural sector, had few large firms, and had experienced a relatively

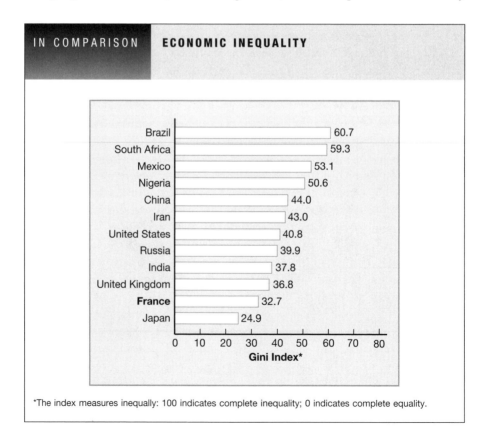

IN COMPARISON   ECONOMIC INEQUALITY

Country	Gini Index*
Brazil	60.7
South Africa	59.3
Mexico	53.1
Nigeria	50.6
China	44.0
Iran	43.0
United States	40.8
Russia	39.9
India	37.8
United Kingdom	36.8
France	32.7
Japan	24.9

*The index measures inequally: 100 indicates complete inequality; 0 indicates complete equality.

low level of urbanization. As one scholar described Paris in 1948, it was "empty of vehicles, needed neither traffic lights nor one-way streets"; electrical services and major consumer goods like refrigerators were little known. He concluded, "France had not really entered the twentieth century."[23]

In the aftermath of World War II, the French government set out to rapidly transform the economy. This took the form of what the French termed *dirigism,* which can be explained as an emphasis on state authority in economic development—a combination of both social democratic and mercantilist ideas. *Dirigism* involved the nationalization of several sectors of the economy (such as utilities), the promotion of a limited number of "national champion" industries to compete internationally, the creation of a national-planning ministry, and the establishment of the ENA to ensure the education of bureaucrats who would be able to direct the economy.[24]

True to its objectives, the *dirigist* system helped bring about a transformation of the French economy. Economic wealth grew rapidly, along with increased urbanization. Through the help of economic subsidies from the European Union, France was also able to change its agricultural sector from one of small farms to one of large-scale production. Whereas in the 1950s France's per capita GDP was approximately half that of the United States, by

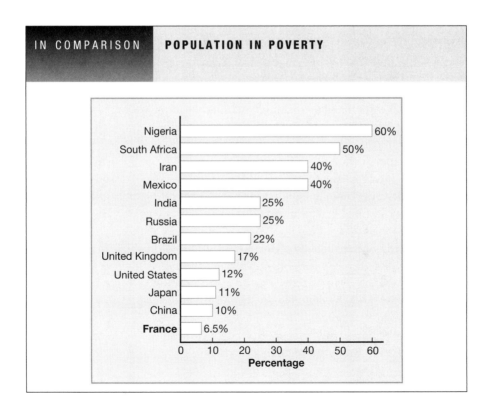

IN COMPARISON   **POPULATION IN POVERTY**

Country	Percentage
Nigeria	60%
South Africa	50%
Iran	40%
Mexico	40%
India	25%
Russia	25%
Brazil	22%
United Kingdom	17%
United States	12%
Japan	11%
China	10%
France	6.5%

LABOR FORCE BY OCCUPATION

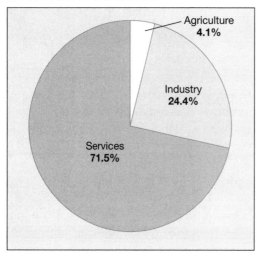

Agriculture
4.1%

Industry
24.4%

Services
71.5%

1973 it was closer to 80 percent that of the United States and surpassed that of its historical rivals, the United Kingdom and Germany.[25]

Under *dirigism*, the French economy was highly dependent on the state's role in subsidizing industry and employment. Total government expenditures as a percentage of GDP were nearly 40 percent in 1973 and over 50 percent in 1998, compared with around 30 percent in the United States. At the same time, while the national-champions policy had helped create a number of high-profile international firms, such as Renault (autos) and Total (oil), the total number of firms per capita remained small relative to other parts of Europe.[26] As a result (or perhaps as a cause) of this, public employment has come to make up around one quarter of the workforce, a number surpassed only by the social democracies of Denmark, Sweden, and Finland. Whether one is working inside or outside the state sector, France provides a generous welfare system, including an extensive range of retirement benefits and a sophisticated health-care system.

As with many other economic systems around the world, in the past twenty years this model has been put to the test. By the mid-1980s unemployment had risen to over 10 percent, a rate that has persisted to the present. Economic growth, which had been double that of the United States from the 1950s to the 1970s, fell below the U.S. and EU averages. Moreover, France faced the European-wide dilemma of an aging population. As the French population has grown older, it has utilized an ever greater share of the welfare system, while fewer young workers are available to fund the expenditures.

The French government has found it difficult to respond to these challenges. Part of the reason is a function of political culture: as the *dirigist* model faces internal stresses, it is also being buffeted by international competition from the EU, the United States, and Asia. Increasing globalization might present new opportunities for France's economy. But from the French perspective, globalization represents a form of economic liberalism extended to the international level—what the French tellingly call the Anglo-Saxon model (by which they mean the United Kingdom and the United States). French politicians and members of the public are suspicious of reforms that will roll back the *dirigist* model and expose the economy more widely to globalization, for they fear that such an approach will essentially destroy existing French institutions and values, replacing them with primarily free-market ones.[27] Such an approach might increase economic growth, but at the cost of surrendering the idea that the French political and economic model is not only worth preserving but is also, like the U.S. system, one with universal application. As a result, reforms are difficult to carry out. In 2005, the government moved to reduce expenditures, seeking, for example, to limit pension benefits and eliminate the thirty-five-hour workweek that was imposed in 2000 in the hope of creating new jobs. This policy prompted widespread public opposition and mass demonstrations. A measure seeking to loosen France's restrictive hiring laws in order to reduce unemployment was withdrawn after massive street protests in 2006.

Perhaps the most interesting facet of the debate over the future of the French economy can be seen in the struggle over agriculture. Though the percentage of the French population engaged in agriculture has shrunk dramatically in the last fifty years, agriculture still plays a central role in French identity. French culture is strongly tied to the concept of rural and agricultural life, and this is also bound up with national identity—locally or nationally produced food is central to the French self-image and to international prestige (think of French wines or cheeses).

But this identity has been sustained in part by large subsidies from the EU, through what is known as the Common Agricultural Policy (CAP). Originally created in part to satisfy French conditions for joining the EU, the CAP became one of the EU's main expenditures, consuming up to 40 percent of its budget. Whereas countries with large agricultural sectors did well under the CAP, member states with smaller or more efficient farms resented the subsidization of agriculture elsewhere, and non-EU countries like the United States opposed the CAP's tariff barriers, which blocked the import of non-EU agricultural products. The growing cost of the CAP (especially with enlargement), combined with pressure from non-EU countries, has intensified this conflict in recent years. But in spite of the pressure, the French government has resisted an elimination or restructuring of the CAP, and French farmers have turned the issue into one of anti-globalization, arguing that reduced support and open trade will lead to the McDonaldization of French food.[28]

In a country where agriculture is central to national identity, such arguments carry weight.

FOREIGN RELATIONS AND THE WORLD

Our discussions have already touched upon the idea that France views itself as a product of revolution with universal application—like the American Revolution before it or the Russian Revolution after. With such a view, France has long seen itself as having a special mission in the international system, to export that revolution's core ideas. This idea could be found as part of the legitimizing force of the French Empire in the eighteenth century, when the concepts of egalitarianism and the importance of the nation-state spread from France across Europe. Modern nationalism as we understand it, in the form of mass volunteer armies and patriotic fervor, was first associated with the French Revolution and Napoléon Bonaparte. Today, the struggles for national identity across Europe are often traced to the Napoleonic Wars.

France's unique view of its place in the world has persisted to the present. France was hardly the only European country to construct an empire, nor was it the first. Yet even after other European states lost or gave up their imperial holdings and retreated from great-power status, France continued to view itself as playing a distinct role in the international system.

This role was brought into sharp focus with the rise of two rivals to universal authority, the United States and the Soviet Union. With the onset of the cold war, France saw itself as caught between two superpowers, both of whom claimed that their ideological mission represented the ultimate political destiny for the rest of the world—including France. As such, over the past fifty years French foreign policy has been consistently driven by the desire to assert and amplify the country's position in the international system.

During the cold war, France played an important role in two Western/European institutions: the European Union (EU) and the North Atlantic Treaty Organization (NATO). In the case of the EU, France was a founding member, along with Germany, Italy, Belgium, the Netherlands and Luxembourg, in 1951. Recall how radical this proposal was at the time, since France and Germany had concluded a bitter war only a few years earlier. But France's motivation was not driven by a sense that its role in the international system had past, requiring it to subsume its powers into a larger, supranational organization. Rather, France saw in the EU the potential to extend its own authority, as a counterweight to the United States and the Soviet Union. With a French-German "motor" at its core, the EU could be a superpower in its own right, changing a bipolar international system into a multipolar one. Thus, the French have always viewed the EU somewhat differently from other member states, particularly Germany and the United Kingdom. For Germany, the EU has been seen as a necessary instrument to prevent another major war by openly refuting the primacy of nationalism and patriotism. For the United Kingdom, the EU is an ongoing threat for precisely the same reason. But for France, the EU has always been an instrument through which French ideals could be pursued. Indeed, under de Gaulle France consistently blocked the UK's membership in the EU, viewing it as a Trojan horse for American interests.

Even NATO, explicitly created to counter Soviet power, was viewed by the French in these terms. For de Gaulle, America's domination of NATO reduced the likelihood that the organization could function as an expression of French policies and values. As a result, the French relationship to NATO was much more distant. Seeking to enhance a European position that would be more independent of the United States, France withdrew from the central military command of NATO in 1966 and developed its own independent nuclear capacity. France failed to achieve its objective of developing Europe as a superpower independent of the United States, but it continued to seek its own path and authority in the international system.

The end of the cold war and the emergence of the United States as the sole superpower has brought a new set of issues and concerns to French foreign policy. Even before 2001, French officials worried about what they termed the United States' "hyperpower." This hyperpower was no longer fettered by the cold war and in the absence of any restrictions would be free to act unilaterally, attempting to remake the world in its own image. Moreover, as we discussed in the section on "Political Economy,"American military hyperpower would be further enhanced by globalization, which at its core is an internationalization of "Anglo-Saxon" values and institutions. As a French foreign minister put it, the United States was like a fish in the sea of globalization, uniquely suited to swim in its waters. For some French observers, then, the end of the cold war and the rise of U.S. hyperpower not only were a challenge to France's international role but also represented an existential crisis, undermining France's place in the world order.[29]

This tension has been evident since September 11. While France expressed strong support for the United States after the terrorist attacks, relations between the two countries grew more tense, especially over the U.S. decision to go to war with Iraq. The debate over the war related to a number of factors important to French foreign policy. First, France saw the war as a clear expression of U.S. hyperpower, a unilateralism that rejects international institutions and thus marginalizes European and other countries. Opposition to the war was therefore driven by a desire to have a say, and by the belief that U.S. force should be part of a multilateral process. Needless to say, the administration of George W. Bush rejected such calls, seeing France's arguments as an attempt simply to stymie U.S. power on behalf of its own interests. A second factor was that France has traditionally cultivated a strong relationship with the Middle East, establishing far friendlier relations with many Arab states than the United States (which has long seen Israel as its main regional ally). France had long had good relations with Iraq and believed that its diplomacy could achieve a more constructive outcome in the region than the use of arms.

Not surprisingly, then, as the United States moved closer to war, France became one of the strongest voices of protest, opposing a United Nations resolution authorizing force. Relations between the two countries soured. Many French observers viewed the U.S. war as a reckless expression of hyperpower that would have disastrous consequences, while many U.S. leaders and pundits responded by accusing France of wanting to bind U.S. power for the sake of its own ends, to keep its cozy relations with the Middle East. Although relations between the two countries have improved somewhat, it would be an overstatement to say that any of the underlying tensions have been resolved.

This conflict feeds into a second major issue for France, which is the future of the EU. The emergence of U.S. power has intensified the French desire for a powerful EU that can stand apart from the United States and play a meaningful role in international relations. This has seemed more likely in recent years, with monetary union and the movement of Germany away from its traditionally strong relationship with the United States (something exacerbated by the war with Iraq). The idea that the EU could truly be a key international player, even a superpower in the classic sense, has never seemed as possible as it does now. And within such a superpower, France believes that it will be the one to give the EU its ideological direction.

But obstacles remain. First, the expansion of the EU to Eastern Europe brought into the organization a number of countries whose view of the international system is quite different from that of France. Their lessons are those of Soviet control during the cold war, and it is the United States, not France or the EU, that is seen as responsible for their liberation. During the run-up to the war in Iraq, a number of Eastern European governments expressed support for U.S. policies, prompting President Jacques Chirac to say that they had "lost an opportunity to keep quiet." France has long been suspicious of enlargement eastward, for fear that more (and more diverse) voices in the EU will dilute the French influence. The French have now emerged as the most strident opponent of Turkish membership. It is likely that similar considerations contribute to this opposition.[30]

Second, the changing nature of the EU also affects France's perception of that body and its place within it. In the past, French leaders have been able to sell deepening membership in the context of expanded influence. But even as the EU moves toward expansion of its power, as in the form of a constitution, many of the French feel that the balance of costs and benefits may be tipping against them. Ongoing pressure to radically reform or eliminate the Common Agricultural Policy pits the EU against French interests, and for some the harmonization of standards at the core of EU regulation seems like little more than globalization at the European level. This has most recently been manifested in the French vote against in a May 2005 referendum seeking approval of the EU constitution. Although observers note that French voters saw this also as a referendum on Chirac's domestic policies, they clearly were also concerned about the potential costs of a united Europe under the current terms. For France, then, the challenge is to maintain its distinct authority in a much changed international environment, even as the traditional tools used to enhance that authority are themselves being transformed. A stronger, more supranational EU that reserves for France a special role in foreign affairs could enhance the country's power. But that is far from certain.

CURRENT ISSUES

THE HEADSCARF CONTROVERSY

Over the past few years, growing tension in politics and society has centered on the place of the headscarf in France. By headscarf, we mean those forms of head covering often worn by Muslim women as an expression of faith and culture. We noted in the discussion of "Society," that in France the principle of *laïcité* means the subordination of faith to the French state and nation. Within *laïcité*, the education system plays an important role as a key institution that socializes the French citizenry and assimilates immigrants, inculcating in them the values of the country.

The growing Muslim community in France, and growing expressions of Muslim identity among some members of this group, have been seen as a challenge to *laïcité*. In 2003, this came to a head in the town of Auberville, where two sisters were threatened with expulsion from school for wearing the headscarf to class. This and other cases of conflict between faith and secularism in the schools led to the French government's establishing a commission to recommend policy on the issue. In 2004, Parlement passed a law based on its recommendation, which forbade the wearing of any "conspicuous religious symbol" in schools, whatever the faith. The law was in fact not entirely new but rather a restatement of existing rules on religious symbols in the classroom.

Domestic and international reactions have varied. For countries with a tradition of greater religious or ethnic diversity, the ban on the headscarf has often been viewed as an overreaction that is likely to intensify conflict within France. This has been a common reaction among many (though not all) in the Muslim world. At the domestic level, however, the ban has been overwhelmingly popular among the non-Muslim French population. Among the French Muslim population, the response has been much more evenly divided, with one survey showing that just over half of Muslim respondents opposed the ban, and over 40 percent favoring it.[31]

The issue is thus less clear than we might think. While there are many Muslim women in France who see the wearing of a headscarf as a case of free expression, the French political system views the act as a conscious challenge to *laïcité* and the French political system. Further confusing the matter is that because of France's large (and often marginalized) Muslim population, domestic Islamic fundamentalism (which rejects the legitimacy of the French state) is viewed as a serious problem and a source of terrorism. There are indications, for example, that some young Muslim women wear the scarf in public schools in France because they have been harassed by fundamentalists for not wearing it. By banning the headscarf, French officials are hoping that the state can continue to play a role in assimilating immigrants into the wider citizenry, bringing other sources of identity under the supremacy of the French national identity. Whether this is still true will become clearer in the coming decades.

NOTES

1. Rolf H. W. Theen and Frank L. Wilson, *Comparative Politics: An Introduction to Seven Countries* (Upper Saddle River, NJ: Prentice-Hall, 2001), p. 101.
2. Quoted in Jeremy D. Popkin, "Not Over After All: The French Revolution's Third Century," *Journal of Modern History* 74 (December 2002), p. 801.
3. Britain has no single document defining its democratic regime but has a constitutional order dating at least to the seventeenth century. The United States has had only one constitution, which it has amended only twenty-six times in more than two centuries. Japan has never changed its postwar constitution.
4. For a useful discussion of these contributions see James B. Collins, *The State in Early Modern France* (Cambridge: Cambridge University Press, 1995).
5. Malcolm Crook and John Dunne, "Napoléon's France: History and Heritage," *Modern and Contemporary France* 8 (2000), pp. 429–31.
6. John Hellman, "Memory, History, and National Identity in Vichy France," *Modern and Contemporary France* 9 (2001), pp. 37–42.
7. Though still relatively rare, semi-presidential systems are used in Russia and Taiwan.
8. Gino Raymond, "The President: Still a 'Republican Monarch'?" in Gino Raymond, ed., *Structures of Power in Modern France* (New York: St. Martin's Press, 2000), pp. 1–18.
9. From 1958 to 1962, presidents were indirectly elected by an electoral college composed of elected officials. De Gaulle sought direct election of the presidency in order to enhance his own power, as well as that of the institution of the presidency.
10. In 1997, President Jacques Chirac's decision to dissolve the legislature and call new elections backfired: the leftist opposition won a majority, and Chirac was forced to appoint the head of the Socialist Party as his prime minister.
11. This was the title of Maurice Duverger's classic work on French politics, *La Monarchie républicaine* (Paris: Robert Laffont, 1974).
12. Robert Elgie, *The Role of the Prime Minister in France, 1981–1991* (New York: St. Martin's Press, 1993).
13. There are 555 deputies representing metropolitan France and 22 representing France's overseas territories.
14. Alec Stone, *The Birth of Judicial Politics in France* (New York: Oxford University Press, 1992).
15. As an example, the Greens won 7.6 percent of the national vote in the first round of the 1993 general elections, but only two Green candidates were able to surpass the 12.5 percent threshold to compete in the second round. Both were defeated. See Alistair Cole, "The Party System: The End of Old Certainties," in Raymond, *Structures of Power in Modern France*, p. 27.

16. Gino Raymond, "Decentralizing or Deconstructing the Republic?" in Raymond, *Structures of Power in Modern France*, p. 165.

17. Alistair Cole, "The Party System," pp. 19–36.

18. Ironically, the Communists had little choice but to accept this arrangement, even though it favored their rivals, the Socialists. Disciplined Communist voters almost always backed Socialists in the second round, but many Socialist voters, distrustful of Communist candidates, often backed candidates of the right in the second round.

19. Susan Milner, "Trade Unions: A New Civil Agenda?" in Raymond, *Structures of Power in Modern France*, pp. 37–69.

20. For a discussion of the differences between the United States and France, see Robert A. Levine, *Assimilating Immigrants: Why America Can and France Cannot*, Rand Occasional Paper (Santa Monica, CA: Rand, 2004).

21. EIROnline, Developments in Industrial Action, 1998–2002, European Foundation for the Improvement of Living and Working Conditions, http://www.eiro.eurofound. eu.int/2003/03/Update/TN0303104U.html (accessed 25 June 2005); "To Have and to Hold," *Economist,* 14 November 2002.

22. Douglass C. North and Robert Paul Thomas, *The Rise of the Western World: A New Economic History* (Cambridge: Cambridge University Press, 1973), ch. 10.

23. David S. Landes, *The Wealth and Poverty of Nations: Why Some Are So Rich and Some So Poor* (New York: W. W. Norton, 1998), p. 468.

24. Peter Hall, *Governing the Economy: The Politics of State Intervention in Great Britain and France* (New York: Oxford University Press, 1986).

25. Angus Maddison, *The World Economy: A Millennial Perspective* (Paris: OECD, 2001), pp. 132, 185.

26. Magnus Henrekson and Dan Johansson, Institutional Effects on the Evolution of the Size Distribution of Firms, Research Institute of Industrial Economics, Stockholm, http://www.iui.se/wp/wp497/IUIWp497.pdf (accessed 25 June 2005).

27. For a discussion of this notion of globalization and Anglo-Saxon economic models see Hubert Vedrine, *France in an Age of Globalization* (Washington, DC: Brookings Institution, 2000).

28. José Bové and François Dufour, *The World Is Not for Sale: Farmers against Junk Food* (London: Verso, 2001).

29. See Hubert Vedrine, *France in an Age of Globalization* (Washington, DC: Brookings Institution, 2000); see also Philip Gordon and Sophie Meunier, *The French Challenge: Adapting to Globalization* (Washington, DC: Brookings Institution, 2001).

30. Maxime Lefebvre, "France and Europe: An Ambivalent Relationship," U.S.-Europe Analysis Series, Brookings Institution, September 2004.

31. Justin Vaïsse, "Veiled Meaning: The French Law Banning Religious Symbols in Public Schools," U.S.-France Analysis Series, Brookings Institution, March 2004, p. 5, n. 16.

KEY TERMS

WEB LINKS

Assemblée nationale   **www.assemblee-nat.fr**
Prime Minister   **premier-ministre.gouv.fr/en**
President   **www.elysee.fr/elysee**
Constitutional Council   **www.conseil-constitutionnel.fr**
Ministry of Foreign Affairs   **www.diplomatie.gouv.fr/en**
Le Monde diplomatique   **mondediplo.com**
Information on national, regional, and local governments
   www.politicalresources.net/france3.htm

5 JAPAN

Head of state: Emperor Akihito
(since January 7, 1989)

Head of government:
Prime Minister Junichiro Koizumi
(since April 26, 2001)

Capital: Tokyo

Total land size: 377,836 sq km

Population: 127 million

GDP at PPP: 3.74 trillion US$

GDP per capita: $29,400

JAPAN

INTRODUCTION

Why Study This Case?

Japan is an essential case for the study of contemporary politics, perhaps foremost to educate a Western audience about what Japan *is not*. Too much of our understanding of Japan is shaped or at least shadowed by dangerously misleading stereotypes. For example, *Japan is not*

- *small:* It has a land mass one third greater than that of Great Britain; a population larger than that of all non-Asian countries other than the United States, Brazil, Russia, and Nigeria; and an economy third only to those of the United States and China.
- *defenseless:* Despite the constitution's famous **Article 9,** which renounces war, Japan possesses a **Self-Defense Force** second only to the U.S. military in terms of technical sophistication and boasts defense expenditures comparable to or greater than those of all member countries of the North Atlantic Treaty Organization except the United States.
- *unique,* or at least no more so than any other country: In terms of political stability, state involvement in the economy, cultural conformity, and even ethnic homogeneity, Japan may be quite different from the United States, but in these and other ways it is more often the United States that is exceptional, not Japan.

If Japan is more "normal" than we might have assumed, it nonetheless remains an intriguing case that defies generalization and begs for further investigation.

Politically, an authoritarian vanguard of low-ranking nobles launched a sweeping revolution from above in the latter half of the nineteenth century, modernizing Japan under the mercantilist slogan **"rich country, strong military."** The nobles and their militarist successors waged wars of imperialist expansion in the name of the Japanese emperor during the first half of the twentieth century, leading ultimately to stunning defeat at the hands of the United States in 1945. U.S. occupiers then launched a second revolution from above, replacing authoritarian rule with a remarkably liberal and democratic constitution written entirely by the Americans (in just six days!) and wholly unaltered by the Japanese in the sixty years since.

But for over fifty of these sixty years, a single political party, the conservative **Liberal Democratic Party (LDP),** has governed Japan. Moreover, elected politicians have historically been subservient to Japan's nonelected career civil servants, who write most of Japan's laws. Has externally imposed democracy taken root in Japan? If not, how do we characterize this type of governance? If so, what lessons might Japan offer for more recently imposed democratic nation-building efforts elsewhere?

Economically, under conditions of state-directed industrialization, imperialism, and war, Japan's authoritarian leaders forged a highly centralized economy in the first half of the twentieth century. But in contrast to the effort placed on political reform, concern with Japan's economic stability in a heightening cold war led the United States to carry out only halfhearted economic restructuring. Japan therefore extended into peacetime its wartime mercantilist economy, which linked career bureaucrats, conservative politicians, and a big-business elite and was spectacularly successful for several decades. By the 1980s, Japan had achieved and in many cases had surpassed the levels of technological prowess, commercial competitiveness, and economic prosperity of the advanced Western industrialized nations.

By the early 1990s, however, this seemingly invincible economy had begun a dramatic and persistent decline that invites comparisons with Great Britain's earlier postwar economic slide. Japan is well into its second decade of stagnant economic growth and lagging industrial production. For much of this period, banks have been in crisis and unemployment has climbed as the stock market has plummeted. How does one account for this dynamic of rapid growth followed by precipitous decline? What have been the causes of Japan's economic success and its more recent failures? And if its mercantilist policies persisted throughout the last century, can they be held responsible for both its rise and its decline? Must Japan change, and if so, how and when?

Finally, Japan may not be exotic, but its balancing of freedom and equality certainly differentiates it to some degree from many other countries. By all measures, Japanese citizens enjoy a very high level of income equality, but this has been managed with low levels of taxation, social services, and other state measures designed to redistribute income (what one political scientist describes as "equality without effort").[1] By the same token, the civil and personal freedoms enshrined in Japan's postwar constitution are unrivaled by all but the most liberal Western regimes, yet Japanese politics remains elitist, its society conformist, and its economy mercantilist.

But even these less stereotypical and more nuanced generalizations now face the prospect of unprecedented if not revolutionary change. In the wake of the economic collapse, long-standing corporate practices such as lifetime employment for white-collar workers are fading. In the face of persistent government scandal and a growing popular sense of political inefficacy, policy-making in a previously harmonious Japan is becoming far more fractious and perhaps even more pluralist. Is Japan facing a third revolution, this time from below? Only by understanding what this country is and where it has come from will we be able to make sense of where it may be going.

Major Geographic and Demographic Features

Even though Japan may not be a particularly small country (it is slightly larger than Germany), its topography and demography certainly make it seem small and have given the Japanese a keen sense of vulnerability and dependency. Although the Japanese archipelago includes nearly 7,000 islands (including several of disputed sovereignty), few are inhabited, and nearly all Japanese reside on one of the four main islands: Hokkaidō, Honshū, Kyūshū, and Shikoku. Even on the main islands, mountainous terrain renders only 12 percent of the land inhabitable, and 80 percent of all Japanese live in an urban setting, with half the population crowded into three megametropolises: Tokyo, Ōsaka, and Nagoya. This means that most of Japan's 127 million inhabitants are crammed into an area about twice the size of New Jersey, making Japan one of the most densely populated countries in the world.

Land (both inhabitable and arable) is not the only scarce natural resource in Japan. Although it has maintained rice self-sufficiency through heroic levels of subsidies for inefficient domestic producers and trade restrictions on foreign rice (Japanese consumers pay about three times the world market price for their rice), Japan remains dependent on imports for nearly three fourths of its food. This critical dependence extends as well to most of the crucial inputs of an advanced industrial economy, including virtually all of its oil and most of its iron ore, other metals and strategic minerals, lumber, coal, and natural gas. This resource dependency has compelled modern Japan to focus on external trade relations and has made it particularly sensitive to the vagaries of this trade.

Such an external focus has been sharpened at crucial junctures in Japan's history by its relative proximity to the Asian mainland. The Korean peninsula in particular served as a ready conduit for importing to ancient and medieval Japan language, technology, religion, and even the popular culture of Korea, China, and places beyond. Over time, Japan adopted (and adapted) from its mainland mentors traditions as varied as Buddhism and bowing, chopsticks and Chinese written characters. At the same time, Japan feared its vulnerability at the hands of its powerful neighbors to the west (particularly China and, later, Russia), and Japanese cartographers and political rulers identified the Korean peninsula as a dagger poised at the heart of Japan.

These fears of vulnerability were not unfounded. In the thirteenth century, a formidable force of Mongols and Koreans mounted two separate attacks on Japan, both of which were repulsed in part by typhoons (dubbed *kamikaze*, or "divine wind" by the Japanese) that blew the attacking ships off course. These incursions and subsequent struggles for power within Japan led rulers first to practice for several hundred years and then to formally impose for two and a half centuries a policy of *sakoku*, or xenophobic isolation. This ended only when Western imperialists forcibly opened Japan in the nineteenth century, reaffirming Japanese fears of weakness.

Japan's insular status has certainly contributed to its racial, ethnic, and linguistic homogeneity. This cultural uniformity should not be overstated, however. Although today virtually all citizens of Japan see themselves as Japanese in language, culture, and race, this image masks the earlier assimilation of the indigenous Ainu (now found almost exclusively on Hokkaidō) and the Okinawans. This homogeneity was also strengthened by the collapse of Japan's multiethnic empire at the end of World War II, when most of the more than 1 million Koreans, Chinese, and Taiwanese living in Japan were sent back to their own countries and more than 7 million Japanese soldiers and civilians were returned home from the colonies. Since the 1980s, Japan has witnessed an influx of Asian migrant workers (predominantly from Southeast Asia, China, and South Asia) who—like the ethnic Koreans and Chinese and even the Ainu and the Okinawans—continue to face varying degrees of political discrimination and social marginalization.

Historical Development of the State

For all the cultural oddities that European traders and missionaries discovered when they first arrived in sixteenth-century Japan, they had actually stumbled upon a nation and society whose historical development bore striking similarities to the development of their own countries. As in Europe, isolated tribal anarchy had gradually given way to growing national identity and the emergence of a primitive state. Aided by clearly defined natural borders and imperial and bureaucratic institutions borrowed from neighboring China, the Japanese state grew in both capacity and legitimacy, particularly after the seventh century C.E. Imperial rule was first usurped and then utilized by a feudal military aristocracy that came to *rule* over an increasingly centralized and sophisticated bureaucratic state for many centuries even as it allowed the emperors to continue to *reign* symbolically.

But whereas weakening feudalism gave way to powerful modernizing monarchs and then to middle-class democracy in Europe, Japan's version of centralized feudalism persisted until Western imperialism provided the catalyst for change in the nineteenth century. A forward-looking authoritarian oligarchy rejected feudalism but consciously retained the emperor as a puppet to legitimate its forced-draft efforts to catch up with the West. These

TIME LINE OF POLITICAL DEVELOPMENT	
Year	**Event**
645 C.E.	Taika Reforms introduced
1192	Minamoto Yoritomo declared first shogun
1603	Tokugawa Shogunate established
1853–54	Forced opening of Japan by Commodore Matthew C. Perry
1867–68	Meiji Restoration
1894–95	First Sino-Japanese War
1904–05	Russo-Japanese War
1918–31	Era of Taisho democracy
1937–45	Second Sino-Japanese War
1941	Pacific War begins
1945	Japan's defeat and surrender in World War II
1945–52	U.S. occupation of Japan
1955	Formation of the Liberal Democratic Party (LDP)
1993	LDP briefly loses majority in the parliament

oligarchs, borrowing this time not from China but from the institutions of modern European states, established a modern Japanese state that grew in autonomy and capacity as it became a formidable military and industrial power. Once again, this new course of imperial expansion and military conquest ended with defeat, this time at the hands of the Americans in 1945, who defanged Japan's militarist state but allowed its mercantilist bureaucracy to remain intact.

Several themes or continuities that emerge from this brief overview and from the narrative that follows are relevant to the development of Japan's modern state and its contemporary politics. First, at critical junctures in its history, outside influence or foreign pressure (what the Japanese call *gaiatsu*) has brought change to Japan.

Second, in the face of this pressure, the Japanese have often chosen not to reject or even resist the external influence but rather have chosen to adopt and then adapt it, deftly assimilating what they perceive as valuable foreign innovations.

was a diverse warrior class, ranging from the wealthy and powerful shogun and daimyo to the lowly retainers barely getting by on a subsistence stipend of rice. Next on the social rung were the peasants, who formed the bulk of the remaining subjects, followed by artisans and craftsmen and finally—at (or near)[2] the bottom of the social hierarchy—the merchants. As in other Confucian societies, commercial activities, including money lending, and those who participated in them were viewed with great disdain. But despite being socially despised, these merchants had established sophisticated and lucrative trading networks throughout Japan by the nineteenth century. Moreover, they had established themselves as the financiers of the lifestyles of the upper ranks of the samurai, who over time grew increasingly indebted to them.

When Commodore Matthew C. Perry steamed into Edo Bay with his fleet of U.S. warships in 1853, he unsuspectingly came upon this system, which was apparently stable but internally ripe for change. The ruling class had status and privilege but was heavily indebted and, in the case of many low-ranking samurai, even impoverished. The merchants were wealthy but socially disdained, lacking both political power and social status. Many Japanese, particularly among the lower ranks of the samurai, had become dissatisfied with what they saw as an increasingly ineffectual if not redundant Tokugawa government and were ready for revolt. Perry didn't cause this revolt, but he certainly facilitated it.

The forceful entry of the Americans and (subsequently) the European powers into Japan and the pressure they placed on the shogunate created a crisis of legitimacy for Tokugawa rule. Virtually free from foreign military threats and isolated from external innovations for centuries, the Tokugawa government lacked the military capacity to resist the unfair trade demands of the Americans and Europeans. The regional daimyo, however, judged these demands as unacceptable and revolted.

A decade of political chaos ensued, prompting a revolution launched not from below, by restive peasants or even aspiring merchants, but from above, by a handful of junior samurai officials. These modernizers were committed to sweeping change cloaked in traditional trappings. They recognized that the maintenance of Japanese independence required the end of the feudal regime and the creation of a modern economic, political, social, and perhaps most important, military system capable of holding its own against the Western powers. But rather than deposing the symbolic leader of the old regime, the modernizers launched their reforms in the name of the sixteen-year-old emperor Meiji, ostensibly "restoring" him to his rightful ruling position.

MEIJI RESTORATION

The vanguard of junior samurai who led the **Meiji Restoration** in 1867 and 1868 came to be known as the **Meiji oligarchs.** What began as a spontaneous xenophobic rejection of the Western threat quickly spawned regime change, a movement for positive reform that involved emulation of and catching up with the West. These oligarchs were well ahead of the rest of Japanese society, establishing the foundations of the modern Japanese state.

Their first priority was to make Japan a strong and wealthy state capable of renegotiating the inequitable treaties the West had imposed on the country. Under the slogan "rich country, strong military," they promoted their mercantilist view that there need be a strong relationship between economic development and industrialization on the one hand and military and political power in the international arena on the other. They dismantled the feudal state, deposing the shogun and converting the decentralized feudal domains to centrally controlled political units. They jettisoned the feudal economy, abolishing hereditary fiefs, returning land to the peasants, and converting samurai stipends to investment bonds. Perhaps most surprisingly, they destroyed their own class, ending samurai privileges.

In 1889, the oligarchs adopted an imperial constitution (patterned after the German constitution), which was presented as a "gift" from the emperor to his subjects. It specified not the rights and liberties of the citizens but the duties and obligations that the subjects owed the emperor and the state. The constitution did create some of the formal institutions of Western democracies, including a bicameral parliament, known as the **Diet,** but its members were chosen by a limited franchise and exercised little ruling authority. The constitution vested all executive power in the emperor, who "appointed" the cabinet ministers (just as reigning emperors had previously appointed the ruling shogun) and retained supreme command over the military. The oligarchs further legitimized this power structure by promoting an emperor-centered form of Shintoism as the mandatory state religion and by inculcating both national patriotism and emperor worship in the education system.

Buttressed by the traditional and charismatic legitimacy of a reigning emperor and the rational-legal legitimacy of an equally symbolic (and largely powerless) parliament, the oligarchs had obtained both the authority and the autonomy to promote painfully rapid development and create a modern military. The highly capable agents for carrying out these goals were threefold:

1. *Bureaucracy:* This revolution from above was envisioned by a handful of elites, but it was carried out by a modern, centralized bureaucracy recruited on the basis of merit. Although the civil service was open to all, it was staffed almost entirely by former samurai who were literate, respected, and had served their feudal lords in similar administrative capacities for generations.

2. *Zaibatsu:* Believing they did not have the luxury to wait for the emergence of an entrepreneurial class, the oligarchs fostered and financed the establishment of huge industrial conglomerates, known as zaibatsu, or "finan-

cial cliques." In so doing, Japan's leaders forged the first of the enduring ties between big business and the state that have persisted to the present.

3. *Military:* Although the military was created initially for defense, the country's resource dependency, the voracious appetite of the zaibatsu, and the example of Western imperialism soon launched Japan on its own successful wave of imperial warfare.

By the end of World War I, the Meiji oligarchs had realized many of their initial goals. In foreign policy, they had successfully renegotiated the inequitable treaties with the West, which now recognized Japan as a rising world power. Japan had not only defeated both imperial China (1894–95) and czarist Russia (1904–05) but had also acquired colonies in Taiwan (1895) and Korea (1910). In the economic realm, by this time Japan had established a fragile but rapidly growing economy.

But these foreign policy and economic successes were not matched in the domestic political realm. By the 1920s, Japan was becoming a nation of diverse economic and political interests that could no longer be easily subsumed under a single banner or slogan, and pressure to change the highly authoritarian system was building. The desire for change became increasingly apparent during the reign of the Taisho emperor (1912–26), particularly in the era of Wilsonian democracy after World War I. By that time, the original Meiji oligarchs had passed from the scene, and efforts by their bureaucratic and military successors to maintain the Meiji political system faced challenges from a middle class demanding democratic rights, laborers organizing for better working conditions, and peasants rioting against onerous taxes.

In an era that came to be known as **Taisho democracy** (1918–31), efforts by these groups and their liberal political proponents to institute democracy were significant but short-lived and ultimately unsuccessful. Different groups increasingly sought to exercise influence in the political realm, with some success, including the election of the first commoner as prime minister in 1918, the granting of universal male suffrage by 1925, and the establishment of political parties.

THE MILITARIST ERA

In fairness, the role of the Diet did expand somewhat, but by the end of the 1920s a number of events had stymied Japan's first attempt at liberal democracy and had once again relegated the parliament to its symbolic reigning role. The Great Depression and the rising global protectionism of the 1930s dealt trade-dependent Japan a harsh blow, leading to increased labor agitation and political unrest as the economy weakened. This domestic instability, combined with anti-Japanese sentiment in China, led to rising nationalist and fascist sentiments at home and reemerging militarism and adventurism abroad. As in Europe and elsewhere, the emergence of these forces led in the early 1930s to a period of political polarization and increased political violence, with democracy the chief victim. One critic labeled this period an era of "government by assassination."

The era of Taisho democracy ended with the Japanese army's seizure of Manchuria in 1931 and the assassination of the last elected head of the government by naval cadets in 1932. Over the next decade, the military steadily expanded its control of the state, ruling in an often uneasy alliance with the bureaucracy and the zaibatsu. Although most historians are not comfortable labeling the Japanese militarist state fascist, the emperor-based system lent itself to the establishment of a near-totalitarian state, one with many similarities to the European Fascist states. The state sought to bring under its auspices or otherwise eliminate virtually all pluralist groups and autonomous organizations, censoring the press, repressing all forms of political dissent, crushing political parties and other forms of free association, and gaining almost complete control over industrial production.

Also, like its Fascist allies in Europe, Japan promoted an ultranationalist emperor-based ideology and expansionist foreign policy, with the intent of

THE JAPANESE EMPIRE, 1942

Source: "The Japanese Empire, 1942." The History Place,
http://www.historyplace.com/united states/pacificwar.gif (accessed 16 July 2005).

extending its empire. It annexed Manchuria in 1932, invaded China proper in 1937, and launched a full-scale conflict in December 1941 with the attack on Pearl Harbor and rapid expansion into Southeast Asia. At the height of its power, Japan's Greater East Asian Co-prosperity Sphere of conquered lands included most of the eastern half of China (including Manchuria), Sakhalin and some of the Aleutian Islands, Korea, Taiwan, the Philippines, Indochina, Thailand, Malaya, Burma, Indonesia, and goodly portions of the South Pacific. As in Europe, Allied forces met, stemmed, and turned back the aggression by 1944. Costly but stunning defeats at sea and on land, followed by the destructive U.S. firebombing of Japanese cities in early 1945 and the atomic bombing of Hiroshima and Nagasaki in August prompted Japan's unconditional surrender on September 2, 1945.

U.S. OCCUPATION

Japan's defeat and destruction were devastatingly complete—militarily, industrially, even psychologically. One historian estimates that the war cost Japan some 2.7 million lives (nearly 4 percent of its population) and that by war's end many more millions were injured, sick, or seriously malnourished.[3] Under these conditions, it was once again foreign—more specifically, American—pressure that provided the impetus for revolutionary change in Japan. Although the seven-year occupation was technically an Allied operation, it remained overwhelmingly a U.S. enterprise managed by a single individual, the **Supreme Commander of Allied Powers** in Japan, General Douglas MacArthur.

Like the arrival of Commodore Perry's ships nearly a century earlier, this American occupation of Japan is significant for both what it changed and what it didn't change. The initial plan called for *demilitarization* to exorcise Japan's militant feudal past and then *democratization* to establish American-style democratic values and institutions. Demilitarization proceeded swiftly and included the purging of all professional military officers, key wartime politicians, and zaibatsu leaders and the disbanding of the ultranationalist associations and political parties. These thoroughgoing purges destroyed the military class and replaced entrenched politicians with technocrats (in most cases, former bureaucrats) and zaibatsu families with professional managers. Most dramatically, the new "Japanese" constitution (quickly drafted by MacArthur's staff and adopted by the Diet in 1947 almost unaltered) included Article 9, the so-called peace clause, by which Japan would "forever renounce war as a sovereign right" and never maintain "land, sea, and air forces, as well as other war potential."

Changing the status of the emperor—in the eyes of the Japanese as well as constitutionally—and eliminating the institution as a political force were key to MacArthur's democratization efforts. The constitution reduced the emperor's stature from godlike and inviolable to simply symbolic, and it transferred sovereignty to the Japanese people. Other measures of this regime change included extending suffrage to women; clarifying relations among the prime minister, the cabinet, and the two houses of the Diet; guaranteeing civil rights and freedoms; breaking up the zaibatsu and imposing anti-trust measures; encouraging labor unions and other interest groups; redistributing land to the peasants; and reforming the education system.

This two-stage approach of demilitarization and democratization remained largely in place for the first two years of the occupation. But the unintended consequences of some reforms as well as external events led to a reverse course, beginning in 1947. That is, continued economic hardship (due in part to war reparations and a policy of little economic aid) combined with the newfound freedom of socialist and Communist activists pushed Japan rapidly toward the left. This, combined with the onset of the cold war (compounded by the Communist victory in China in 1949 and the outbreak of the Korean War in 1950), led to the about-face in occupation policies.

The earlier desire to refashion Japan as a weak and docile "Asian Switzerland" gave way to a plan that would make Japan a full, albeit still unarmed, ally of the West. The deconcentration of industry was scaled back in order to rebuild the economy, and labor strikes were prohibited. Leftist labor activists were purged and in some cases (re)jailed even as numerous conservative politicians were released from prison and rehabilitated. Notably, in all of the twists and turns of occupation policy, the wartime bureaucracy of technocratic planners was left intact, in part because the American occupiers needed it, and in part because they saw the bureaucracy as only the instrument, not the agent, of war.

Today, some occupation reforms are universally considered to have been both successful and beneficial. Others largely failed, whereas some remain highly controversial and even contradictory. For instance, on paper Japan has one of the most liberal political systems in the world. But by default and design, Japan's postwar state featured a core elite of experienced bureaucrats closely allied with conservative politicians (many of whom were former bureaucrats) and big-business executives. This ruling triad, or **iron triangle,** has remained largely intact through good times and bad.

POLITICAL REGIME

Is Japan a democracy? Because of the continuing dominance of the ruling triad of bureaucrats, politicians, and businessmen, much controversy on this issue remains among observers and practitioners of Japanese politics. In important ways, Japan's political structures and procedures are democratic.

The rights and liberties enshrined in Japan's 1947 constitution certainly exceed those of the U.S. Constitution and are perhaps unrivaled. Its citizens are well protected by the rule of law, and its electoral system is probably no more corrupt than that of other advanced liberal democracies. And unlike the United States, Japan has successful Socialist and Communist parties, arguably giving it a greater range of political debate and choice than the United States.

Yet these formal institutions and procedural safeguards of democracy do not tell the whole story. Although democratic practices seldom live up to the ideals of political pluralism in any democratic regime, the initial dominance and persistent power of the postwar bureaucracy and its conservative political and corporate allies have led some to conclude that Japan's democracy is dysfunctional, if not an outright mockery. For most of the postwar era, the conservative Liberal Democratic Party (LDP) has dominated the legislature. And for much of this time, this LDP has been overshadowed in policy making by nonelected career civil servants. Long-standing political practice and informal levers and linkages of power have constrained the full functioning of this imported democracy. This dualism becomes more apparent upon examination of the formal institutions and substantive procedures of Japanese democracy.

IRON TRIANGLE

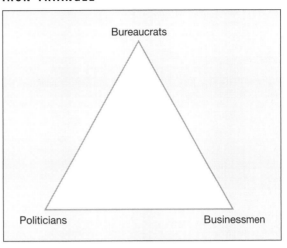

Political Institutions

THE CONSTITUTION

"We, the Japanese people. . . ." The opening phrase of Japan's unamended 1947 constitution reveals what are perhaps its two most significant aspects: its American imprint and the transfer of sovereignty from the emperor to the Japanese people. Although America's allies were calling for the prosecution of Emperor Hirohito

ESSENTIAL POLITICAL FEATURES

- Legislative-executive system: parliamentary
- Legislature: Diet
- Lower house: House of Representatives
- Upper house: House of Councillors
- Unitary or federal division of power: unitary
- Main geographic subunits: prefectures
- Electoral system for lower house: mixed single-member district and proportional representation
- Chief judicial body: Supreme Court

as a war criminal, General Douglas MacArthur insisted that the emperor renounce his divinity but be allowed to retain his throne, to offer continuity and legitimacy to both the occupation government and the new democratic regime. The constitution reduces the emperor's godlike stature to that of a "symbol of the State and of the unity of the people with whom resides sovereign power." In order to empower Japanese citizens, the American framers of the constitution constructed an elaborate system of representative institutions, including universal suffrage, a parliamentary legislature in which the cabinet is responsible to the Diet (rather than the emperor), and an independent judiciary. The constitution also introduced a greater measure of local autonomy, increasing the role of local elected officials.

The Branches of Government

THE HEAD OF STATE

Although invested by the Meiji constitution with total authority, the imperial institution was always controlled by de facto rulers. The 1947 constitution eliminated even this derivative authority, making the role of the emperor wholly symbolic. In fact, unlike the British monarch, the Japanese emperor

STRUCTURE OF THE GOVERNMENT

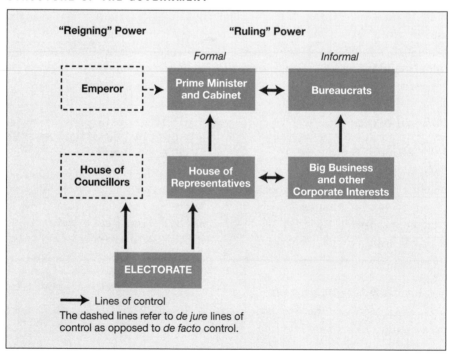

is technically just a symbol of the Japanese state, not the head of state. Like the British queen, however, this standard bearer of the world's oldest imperial dynasty continues to play a significant role in symbolizing the unity and continuity of contemporary Japan. The emperor also performs purely formal tasks, such as appointing the prime minister (who is elected by the Diet) and appointing the chief justice of the Supreme Court (who is designated by the government), and he receives foreign ambassadors and represents the nation on many important ceremonial occasions at home and abroad.

The Japanese throne is both hereditary and patrilineal—therefore, no female heir is permitted to rule in her own right. Emperor Hirohito (who reigned from 1926 to 1989) was succeeded by his eldest son, Akihito, who became Japan's 125th emperor. Akihito's oldest son, Crown Prince Naruhito, and Naruhito's spouse, Princess Masako, have caused some controversy with the birth of their only child, Princess Aiko, in 2001. With speculation that Aiko may remain her father's only heir, many Japanese have called for a change in the laws banning female ascension to the throne.

Although polls show that recent generations of Japanese citizens, like their British counterparts, find themselves increasingly less connected to the throne, significant events, such as the passing of Hirohito and the birth of a prospective female heir, generate enormous public interest and a deeper sense of attachment than the polls seem to indicate. Furthermore, Japan's royal family has faced none of the scandal that has recently challenged the British royals.

THE PRIME MINISTER AND THE CABINET

The prime minister serves as head of government and draws from the Diet cabinet members who serve as ministers, or heads, of Japan's seventeen bureaucratic ministries and other key agencies. The prime minister is always chosen from the lower house and is elected by the members of the Diet. But because the LDP has almost always held a parliamentary majority (or, more recently, has dominated the ruling coalition), its candidate for prime minister— always the party president of the LDP—has typically been elected. This selection process has enhanced the role of LDP internal politics at the expense of parliamentary politics and has diminished to some extent the significance of the office of prime minister.

Successful candidates to the office of prime minister have therefore been required not only to belong to the right party but also to curry sufficient favor and rise high enough in a dominant faction within that party. Thus prominent and prospective LDP party leaders are more concerned with factional ties, personal connections, and back-room bargaining than with promoting a particular policy agenda. Faction leaders have typically brokered this selection process and rotated the office of LDP president (and prime minister) among various factions relatively frequently. Therefore, although Japanese prime ministers are usually experienced and savvy politicians, they tend to be older, have less policy expertise, and serve for far shorter tenures than their counterparts abroad. Cabinet members turn over even more frequently,[4] making them dependent on the expertise, experience, and connections of top bureaucrats within the ministries that they ostensibly head.

Although the cabinet introduces virtually all significant legislation to the Diet, where it is debated, most controversy has already been worked out much earlier in the process. Most legislative drafts originate with the bureaucracy and their expert "advisory councils" and are then passed to LDP policy committees for consideration and emendation. Senior leaders within the LDP (and, more recently, its coalition partners) must then agree on these revised bills and bring them to the cabinet for final approval. Therefore, any bill sponsored by the cabinet has already been formulated, discussed, revised, and approved by the relevant bureaucrats and dominant party before it ever gets assigned to a Diet committee or comes to a vote in the full house. This does not mean that the opposition does not subject legislation and its sponsors to tough questioning, but significantly it is often the bureaucrats, not the ministers who are called on in question time, and the scripted answers of most ministers are written by the bureaucrats, underlining the influence of these career civil servants even in the parliament.

THE LEGISLATURE

The 1947 constitution declares Japan's Diet the "highest organ of state power" and claims exclusive law-making authority for the bicameral parliament. The Japanese Diet has two directly elected chambers, the House of Representatives and the House of Councillors. The **House of Representatives,** the lower house, has 480 members elected for a four-year term. As in other parliamentary systems, the government typically dissolves the lower house prior to the expiration of the term in order to call elections from a position of strength. Alternatively, a vote of no confidence can force dissolution, as it did most recently in 1993 (one of only four successful postwar no-confidence votes). General elections have taken place on average every two to three years since 1947. The upper chamber, the **House of Councillors,** comprises 242 members, elected for fixed six-year terms (staggered so that half the chamber stands for election every three years). Unlike the lower house, the upper house cannot be dissolved.

As in other parliamentary systems, Japan's lower house is far more powerful than the upper, though the House of Councillors is not as inconsequential as the British House of Lords. Although each chamber is technically given comparable powers and responsibilities, in almost all circumstances the lower house can trump the upper. In case of disagreements on virtually any important matter, such as the selection of the prime minister, the wording of legislation, or the passing of budgetary items or treaties, the will of the lower house prevails. In addition, only the lower house can force the resignation of a government. Finally, the prime minister is always selected from the lower house, as are the overwhelming majority of cabinet members.

The Diet convenes for only about eighty days each year, a session roughly half that of the British Parliament. The brevity of the session has enhanced the role and responsibility of the standing committees. Many veteran politicians have established both expertise in particular policy areas and close ties to bureaucrats and interest groups with jurisdiction over or interest in those policy areas. This has given individual legislators a degree of influence over policy formerly reserved for bureaucratic experts and has simultaneously weakened party discipline in voting. The importance of pursuing **pork-barrel** legislation for home-district constituencies has also weakened allegiance to the government. So despite their long-standing dominance of the Diet, LDP governments have been hesitant to provoke the objections of their own members or the extralegal tactics that the opposition often resorted to prior to 1960 (from boycotting to brawling). This has meant that LDP governments have promoted change only gradually, if at all.

THE JUDICIAL SYSTEM

The 1947 constitution established for Japan a court system with a high degree of judicial independence from the other branches of government. In practice, however, the LDP has used its political dominance, appointment powers, and other administrative mechanisms to manipulate the courts and assure judicial decisions in accordance with its political interests. This has been made easier because, unlike the dual system of federal and state courts in the United States, the Japanese system is unitary, with all civil, criminal, and administrative matters under the jurisdiction of a single hierarchy. At the top is the constitutional court, or Supreme Court, whose fifteen members are appointed by the cabinet.

Although politicians in all democracies seek to influence the courts, this combination of a unitary judicial system dominated by a single conservative party has rendered Japan's courts particularly subservient. Perhaps not surprisingly, even though the Supreme Court is invested with the constitutional power of judicial review, it has used this authority sparingly and has been extremely hesitant to declare laws unconstitutional.

The Electoral System

As with other political institutions in Japan, the electoral system is both a cause and a consequence of the LDP's long-standing reign. LDP governments have maintained grossly disproportionate voting districts and established electoral rules that clearly favor the party's interests.[5] Despite reforms enacted by two short-lived opposition coalition governments in the mid-1990s, the LDP has continued to press its advantages.

Representatives in the two chambers of the Diet are elected according to different rules. Although the membership of the weaker House of Councillors has varied slightly during the postwar period, its electoral rules were not affected by the 1990s reforms and have remained unchanged. The 242 councillors serve fixed six-year terms, with half facing election every three years. Elected according to a mixed system, 98 are chosen from party lists using proportional representation (PR) in a nationwide election. The remaining 149 are elected from forty-seven multimember districts (MMD) that coincide with Japan's forty-seven prefectures. Each district returns from two to eight members, but rather than drawing from a party list as in PR, voters have a single, nontransferable vote that they cast for an individual candidate. In other words, rather than first-past-the-post (FPTP) in a single-member district (SMD), as in Great Britain and the United States, the top several-past-the-post (ranging from two to eight members) are elected from each district.

Prior to 1994, the electoral system used to determine membership in the House of Representatives resembled the second part of that used for the upper house.[6] Two significant consequences of the old system should be mentioned. First, because contenders ended up competing for seats not just against opposition candidates but also against members of their own party, the system produced mini-parties, or factions within the LDP and other parties large enough to put forth multiple candidates. Therefore, the most important electoral battles were fought within the LDP, among individuals sharing essentially the same ideology and policy positions, not between parties over policy issues. Second, unable to rely upon simple party or factional affiliations or even policy positions alone in order to succeed, candidates were compelled to form local party machines, known as **koenkai,** to generate essential votes and campaign funds. We return to these and other outcomes when we discuss elections and campaigns (see pp. 178–80).

In the wake of a series of notorious scandals, unpopular tax measures, and precipitous economic decline, thirty-eight years of unchallenged LDP rule gave way in 1993 when a group of LDP legislators defected from the party to support a vote of no confidence. The opposition coalition that replaced the LDP government lost no time in reforming the electoral system, restructuring the rules governing lower-house elections seven months after coming to office. This reform eliminated the old system and established a new mixed system similar to that of Germany and Mexico. Under the new system, the lower chamber still has 480 seats, but 300 are elected from single-member districts (SMDs). The remaining 180 are chosen by PR from eleven regional blocs, in which seats are assigned to the parties according to their share of the total blocwide votes. As in the German system, candidates may run in their own districts and be included in a regional party list, to safeguard their seats in the event of defeat in the home SMD.

This anti-LDP coalition government intended the reforms to shift electoral competition from highly personalized factional politics within the LDP to national party politics between two dominant parties offering genuine policy alternatives. Under the new rules, central party leaders determine who runs in each district and who is included on the lists of PR. Although the PR portion of the ballot provides some seats for smaller parties able to garner the minimal threshold of votes, nearly two thirds of the seats are chosen from single-member districts, favoring well-organized and well-established big parties, as in the United States and Great Britain.

The 1994 reforms also reapportioned districts to reflect demographics more accurately, giving more equitable clout to the much more numerous (and typically less conservative) urban voters. As will be shown in the discussion of interest groups supporting the LDP, these reforms were aimed at rural voters, among the LDP's most loyal supporters. Reflecting the continued elitism of Japanese politics, the reforms were less successful in dealing with (and in fact less concerned about) political corruption, or money politics—precisely the issue that the public and foreign observers most hoped would change. New restrictions on corporate donations to individual politicians were replaced by a system of uniform government subsidies to the parties, not individual candidates. The intent again was to level the playing field among parties and strengthen central party leaders. But as in other capitalist democracies, individual candidates and the corporations and other interest groups that woo them have discovered plenty of loopholes to keep campaign funds flowing.

Because the government registers voters, practically all eligible voters in Japan are registered. Accordingly, voter turnout in national elections has been relatively high, usually between 60 and 80 percent. But significantly, even as the system has become more competitive and politicians have increased their clout vis-à-vis the bureaucracy, voter turnout has declined. Although there are a number of reasons for the decline, popular distrust of politicians and disillusionment with the political process and the Japanese state are paramount.

Local Government

Japan is divided into forty-seven administrative divisions, known as prefectures, each with its own elected governor and legislature. Japan is nonetheless a unitary—not a federal—system, however, in which most political power is invested in the central government. The prefectural governments decide many local issues and are able to raise sufficient taxes to cover about one third of their expenditures (what the Japanese call 30 percent autonomy). These subnational governments depend on the central government for the remainder of their budget, however, and central authorities delegate all local authority (at the prefectural and municipal levels) and can, and sometimes do, retract that authority. The national government can override the decision of any local governor and did so most notably in the case of Okinawa, whose elected local officials have attitudes toward the overwhelming U.S. military presence there that differ significantly from those of the national leaders. Okinawans are not alone, however, in wishing for greater local autonomy.

Other Institutions: Bureaucracy and the Iron Triangle

The Japanese state's most influential, yet entirely extraconstitutional, institution of policy-making authority is the bureaucracy. As in other liberal democracies, the Japanese bureaucracy staffs the dozen or so ministries that make up the Japanese state but is at once both smaller in size and greater in influence than any of its Western counterparts. The prime minister appoints ministers (generally members of the parliament) to head these ministries, who together form the cabinet. The ministers are often not experts in their assignments but rather obtain their appointments based on political criteria and typically have a tenure measured in months, not years. Because of this, these political appointees rely almost entirely upon the career civil servants within their ministries to formulate, facilitate, and ultimately implement and enforce laws and policies. In each ministry, an administrative vice minister with some twenty-five to thirty years of experience in that particular ministry heads these efforts, presiding over a staff of Japan's brightest, who willingly subject themselves to grueling workweeks for relatively meager compensation.

Why, then, is the bureaucracy so powerful and prestigious? There are several answers worth noting. First, the Japanese state has a long-standing tradition whereby those with formal authority do not necessarily exercise power. Rulers and ruled alike are accustomed to legitimate governance by those who may not be vested with formal authority. Nonelected administrators have long had such power in Japan. Second, whereas the U.S. occupation authorities jailed wartime politicians, purged the military, and broke up the zaibatsu, the experienced bureaucrats continued to administrate Japan uninterrupted and unscathed. Third, this political vacuum prompted many veteran bureaucrats to move into leadership positions in Japan's conservative postwar political parties, giving them significant political influence. Chief among these was **Yoshida Shigeru,** a former Foreign Ministry bureaucrat who served as prime minister through most of the occupation and beyond (from 1946 to 1954, with a short hiatus) and profoundly shaped the postwar bureaucracy-dominant political system.

Fourth, the legitimacy and prestige of this dominance have been enhanced by the strictly meritocratic nature of hiring and advancement within the bureaucracy. Aspirants generally finish at the top of their class at Japan's premier national universities and enter their ministries with a cohort of those who have passed the highly competitive entrance exams (approximately 2 percent of those who take the test). The cohort is promoted at the same pace until it advances to the level where there are fewer positions than candidates. In this and subsequent levels of the narrowing bureaucratic hierarchy, only the very best are promoted to senior leadership positions, and those passed over are dismissed from the ministry. At the peak, only one member of the cohort (at most) will be appointed to the position of administrative vice minister, assuring exceptional skill and extensive experience in the upper reaches of each ministry. These senior civil servants exercise extensive policy authority in potent ministries such as the Ministry of Finance and the Ministry of Economy, Trade, and Industry (formerly and famously known as the Ministry of International Trade and Industry, or MITI).

This orderly promotion-and-dismissal policy also helps to explain the willingness of the bureaucrats to work so hard for apparently so little and offers a final reason for the remarkable reach and power of the Japanese bureaucracy. Each year, a contingent of dismissed but highly qualified bureaucrats in their forties and fifties undergo "descent from heaven" (*amakudari*) to try their hand in politics (overwhelmingly as LDP Diet members) or, more commonly, to take senior positions in the very corporations they previously regulated. All but a handful of Japan's postwar prime ministers were former top bureaucrats. Likewise, the corporations that employ retired civil servants gain not just their skills but also their connections. At any given time, Japan's policy elite do not just share a common outlook but often have attended the same prestigious schools and may have worked for decades in the same ministry.

These enduring linkages among senior bureaucrats, conservative politicians, and corporate executives form what has been referred to as an iron triangle, in which the determination and implementation of policies are often facilitated not by negotiations, hearings, and parliamentary votes but by phone calls between former colleagues (dubbed **administrative guidance**) and after-work drinking sessions among friends. In fact, this web of informal connections within the Japanese state consists of hundreds of triangles involving veteran politicians with particular policy expertise, bureaucrats in a particular ministry or division, and the private-sector representatives of interest groups in that policy area. Although "ruling" bureaucrats have traditionally dominated these associations, the "reigning" Diet legitimated the work of the bureaucracy and assured that its policies did not go beyond the range of public tolerance. LDP governments also made sure that the party's most important constituents, including corporations (from which it received massive campaign funds) and rice farmers (on whose overrepresented vote it depended) were well taken care of with producer-oriented industrial and financial policies and protectionist trade policies. Representatives of Japan's large corporations in turn offered firsthand policy advice to the bureaucrats and generally accepted the business-friendly policies and guidance they received in return.

Events over the past decade or so have led some scholars to argue that this "well-oiled, conservative regime" is now undergoing a "regime shift,"[7] in which politicians, interest groups, and even Japanese citizens are gaining political influence at the expense of the bureaucracy and even the elitist triangle. They point to a series of recent bureaucratic scandals and bunglings that have tarnished the reputation and prestige of the bureaucracy, including kickbacks, an AIDS-tainted transfusion cover-up that led to hundreds of deaths, and the poor handling of such national crises as the extended economic downturn, a religious cult's gassing of the Tokyo subway system in 1995 with a deadly poison, and the Kōbe earthquake that same year. They note that politicians were able to take advantage of these and other problems, briefly dislodging the LDP from office and pursuing both electoral reforms and, more recently, administrative changes designed to give the prime minister new leverage over the bureaucracy. Politicians have also gained increasing policy expertise in their own right, making them less dependent on their bureaucratic counterparts in policy making.

Where, then, does power reside in the Japanese state? Even though Japan lacks the United States' formal separation of powers between state and national government and between the executive and legislative branches, it is fair to say that there is no single locus of power in the Japanese state. Even at its strongest, from the 1950s through the 1970s, powerful prime ministers such as Yoshida Shigeru and **Tanaka Kakuei** (see "Tanaka Kakuei and Money Politics," on p. 173) still often held sway over the bureaucracy. Some of Japan's most famous and successful corporations, such as Sony and Honda, achieved their status in part because they defied bureaucratic dictates. And while each bureaucratic ministry may have substantial authority within its own domain, these independent fiefdoms are subject to no overriding direction or guidance.

Scholars critical of this Japanese state have described it as "headless" and susceptible to the kind of uncoordinated drift that led not just to a quixotic war against the United States half a century ago but also to unsustainable trade surpluses with virtually every industrialized country and an inability to reform a twentieth-century mercantilist economy to cope with the challenges it faces in a twenty-first-century globalized economy.[8] Will Japan be able to change, and if so, what will be the impetus? Because those within the iron triangle have demonstrated little willingness or incentive to change, many argue that one must look beyond this ruling triad and perhaps even beyond Japan to locate the forces and pressures capable of bringing about change.

POLITICAL CONFLICT AND COMPETITION

The Party System and Elections

Like Mexico, Sweden, or Italy, postwar Japan offers an example of a predominant party system. In this case, the Liberal Democratic Party (LDP) has dominated all others since it formed as a merger of existing conservative parties in 1955. Its closest rival, the Japan Socialist Party (JSP), is similarly the product of a merger of leftist parties that same year and served for decades as the perennial loyal opposition, until the major reshuffling in 1993. The JSP regularly garnered fewer than half as many votes as the LDP in parliamentary elections and, thanks to LDP gerrymandering, obtained even fewer seats.

During this period, several other parties joined the JSP in opposition by taking advantage of Japan's former multimember-district single-nontransferable-vote (MMD/SNTV) electoral system (in which the fourth or fifth "winner" in a given district need obtain only a small fraction of the districtwide vote) to carve out niches in the Japanese electorate among those who felt excluded by both of the larger parties. These included the Japan Communist Party (JCP), which consistently embraced policies to the left of the JSP, and the more moderate Democratic Socialist Party (DSP) and Clean Government Party (CGP, or New Komeito), which occupied a middle ground between conservative, pro-business LDP politics and the socialist (and pacifist) platform of the JSP. These three and a couple of other short-lived parties typically accounted for roughly 20 percent of the popular vote.

This remarkably stable "one-and-a-half-party system," an important component of the equally stable iron triangle, remained intact for nearly four decades. But in 1993, LDP corruption scandals and inept and unpopular government reaction (or inaction in response) to Japan's drastic economic downturn led to a political revolution of sorts. In order to understand the causes and the nature of this revolt and why it was so long in coming, it is necessary first to examine LDP party politics.

THE LIBERAL DEMOCRATIC PARTY

With the exception of an eleven-month period from 1993 to 1994, the LDP has dominated the Diet from 1955 to the present. The nature of this rule has led some observers to conclude that the LDP is woefully misnamed: It is conservative, not liberal. Its internal politics are highly authoritarian, not democratic. And its factional divisions make it a collection of mini-parties, not a single party.

The LDP can perhaps be best understood as a highly pragmatic electoral machine in which ideological consistency has never taken priority over winning. It has established electoral rules and engaged in campaigns and elections with the express purpose of *staying in power* by maintaining a majority (or at least a healthy plurality) of seats in the parliament. But it has also been more than a political machine for members of the parliament. The LDP's persistent lock on the government has meant that the campaign for the LDP presidency has in almost all cases been the contest for the office of prime minister.

Two organizational features have been key to the LDP's continued dominance, but they have also caused the party significant problems and prevented effective internal reform. The first of these features is the factions, or mini-parties, that have formed within the LDP. Japan's former electoral system compelled contenders for seats in the parliament to compete against candidates not only from other parties but also from their own party. This intra-party competition meant that candidates had to vie for the support of patrons within the party, who provide members with campaign funds, official party endorsements, appointed positions within the party and the government, and other favors. These faction leaders in turn count on the support of their faction members in the party's all-important presidential elections. Five LDP factions emerged in the mid-1950s, have been led by successive generations of LDP kingpins, and have largely survived to the present. Faction members are divided not by ideology, policies, or even the goal of obtaining the party presidency but simply by personal loyalty to the godfather-like leader presiding over each faction.

But even unswerving factional loyalty did not guarantee LDP parliamentary candidates electoral success in their home district under the old system. Because several LDP candidates ran in each district, persuading voters to vote for the LDP was not enough; a sufficient number of voters had to vote preferably for each LDP candidate. In order to help individual candidates obtain enough votes and to ensure that no single candidate received too many votes (therefore "wasting them"), each candidate constructed a local support group, or party "machine," known as a *koenkai*. The *koenkai* are made up of influential district members able to gather votes in their community or, more recently, among members of a particular professional or other special-interest groups within the district.

In the same way that the LDP candidates promised allegiance to their factional patron in exchange for support from above, so they promised policy favors and other pork-barrel enticements in exchange for the votes and campaign donations delivered by their *koenkai*. And just as the factions have outlived individual leaders, so have the *koenkai* been multigenerational. It is not uncommon for an entire *koenkai* to throw its full support behind the son, grandson, or other successor of a retiring member of parliament.

Although these multiple levels of patron-client relations have certainly contributed to the LDP's long-term political dominance, the gifts, favors, and huge sums of money required to lubricate the system and manage the LDP's intense

TANAKA KAKUEI AND MONEY POLITICS

Perhaps the most influential and successful of the postwar Japanese politicians was Tanaka Kakuei, who fostered a powerful LDP faction in the early 1970s and served as prime minister from 1972 to 1974. The consummate Japanese politician, he was nonetheless forced to resign and was ultimately convicted of financial misdeeds involving huge sums of money. By the early 1990s, and several notorious scandals later, the home of a successor to Tanaka as LDP godfather was raided as part of a bribery investigation, and prosecutors found some US$50 million in gold bars and cash hidden in his basement!

intraparty competition (in which purse size, not policy preference, matters) have fostered a system of **money politics,** which has likely made Japanese election campaigns the most expensive in the world. It is estimated that races for the lower house cost incumbents roughly US$1 million and that newcomers may need twice that amount. These sums are even more astounding given Japan's highly restrictive campaign rules, which prevent candidates from advertising on television or radio, severely limit newspapers ads and handbills, prohibit door-to-door canvassing, and confine the official campaign for lower-house elections to just twelve days! These restrictions have meant that personal relationships and the ability to deliver favors are the (very expensive) key to electoral success.

Although many observers speculated that the electoral reforms and the loosening of the LDP's grip on power would eliminate much of the need for local support groups and the value of factions, both have persisted. Put simply, the LDP has been foremost a vote- and money-delivery system, with money being the single most powerful way of obtaining votes. Both money and votes have been secured through expanding circles of corporatist co-optation of businesses and other large interest groups as well as through clientelist currying of favor among local communities and individuals by means of porkbarrel projects, favors, and gifts. As in any democracy, pork-barrel projects in the home district, such as bridges and schools, deliver votes, and the lucrative contracts and licenses awarded to corporations to build these projects bring campaign donations. But LDP politicians and their supporters also attend the funerals, weddings, graduations, and other important events of their loyal constituents (on average over thirty each month), honoring them with their presence and an appropriate (monetary) gift.

Campaign strategies and money politics, both hugely expensive, have plagued the LDP with scandals throughout its history. The most successful politicians are precisely those who are able to generate enough money and connections to rise to the top.

THE 1993 REVOLT

These persistent—indeed, mounting—corruption scandals, combined with general dissatisfaction with LDP governance, prompted widespread calls from outside—and, to some extent, from inside—the party for electoral and campaign reforms. With the LDP old guard continuing to resist, two prominent members of its most powerful faction bolted the party in 1993, taking with them a substantial number of their supporters, and formed the Renaissance Party. Erstwhile LDP Diet members formed two other likewise reformist—but nonetheless conservative—parties around this time, leaving the LDP with (barely) less than a majority of seats in the lower house.

The leader of one of these parties, Hosokawa Morihiro, managed to cobble together a coalition government of all the opposition parties except that of the Communists, which stayed together just long enough (nine months) to enact electoral reforms. A second minority coalition survived for ten weeks, its government cut short when the JSP (now renamed the Social Democratic Party, or SDP), in an act of political expediency, joined its long-time rival, the LDP, in forming a majority coalition in a deal that earned the JSP/SDP the office of prime minister. This coalition lasted from 1994 until 1996, when the LDP, now embracing the newly enacted electoral reforms, was powerful enough in its own right to form a series of coalition governments in which it once again calls (most of) the shots. The opposition, too, has retooled and, under pressure from the new winner-take-all single-member-district (SMD) system to unite, has begun to coalesce around the centrist Democratic Party, which nonetheless remains a distant second behind the LDP in parliamentary seats and popular vote.

Major Political Parties		
Party	Ideology	House of Representatives Election, 2005 (Number of Seats)
Liberal Democratic Party (LDP)	Right	296
Democratic Party (DP)	Center	113
Clean Government Party (CGP)	Center	31
Social Democratic Party (SDP)	Left	7
Japan Communist Party (JCP)	Left	9
Other		33
Total		480

Can this humbled but now apparently revived LDP once again win the loyalty of Japanese voters? The 2001 election of Prime Minister **Junichiro Koizumi** seemed to bode well for the LDP. Koizumi, with his raffish hairdo and populist style, is the antithesis of the traditional LDP politician. He won the LDP presidency without the explicit backing of any major LDP faction and came to office promising to halt Japan's economic malaise and take on the country's conservative bureaucratic and political elite and their deeply entrenched constituencies. But, in the years since his election, Koizumi's popularity has waxed and waned. It appears that his populist style has been no match for the still-powerful remnants of Japan's ruling triad. Just as Mikhail Gorbachev was unable to harness the Soviet Communist Party as a vehicle of reform, Koizumi is finding the LDP and its allies resistant to change. Yet Japanese voters remain hopeful, and Koizumi remains confident that the system can be reformed. Koizumi won reelection bids in both 2003 and 2005. Internal LDP rules require that he step down in 2006.

Civil Society

Because the reforms that brought about Westernization and democracy were imposed from above (and, in many cases, from *outside*), Japan has a centralized bureaucratic society rather than a civil society in which citizens voluntarily organize and participate in political, economic, and social affairs. Like other authoritarian systems, the Meiji and militarist states fostered corporatist and mercantilist institutions to harness Japan's industrial society in the service of modernization and imperialism. Although the U.S. occupiers destroyed many aspects of Japanese authoritarianism and carried out sweeping political, social, and economic reforms, they retained the bureaucracy and, out of fears of communism, squelched many of the nascent civic groups they had initially fostered.

In pursuing economic development and political stability, the postwar Japanese state organized or co-opted interest groups that were important to these goals, such as business and agricultural interest groups, and formed associations for facilitating their political participation. In exchange for their support, these groups have had their interests well represented (and protected) and have prospered. This symbiotic relationship has since been expanded to include many other smaller groups and constituencies in a system of distributional welfare that has prolonged LDP bureaucratic rule, at the increasing expense of both economic health and political flexibility. In addition, labor unions, consumers, and other groups that have often been prominent in the politics of industrialized countries have been notably absent from these arrangements and have in many ways borne the burden of the corporatist system, which is sometimes referred to as Japan, Inc.

The third leg of the iron triangle, Japan's large corporations and the large industrial groupings or conglomerates (often called **keiretsu**) to which they belong, has been both a proponent of and a participant in Japan's postwar development. Big business exercises political influence through Keidanren (Federation of Economic Organizations), which voices the concerns of large corporations and offers policy recommendations to the government. Keidanren has been the conduit through which most campaign contributions have been channeled from large businesses to LDP coffers and therefore has inclined the government to champion business-friendly policies, such as cheap access to capital, investment incentives, and various forms of market protection. Since the economic downturn of the 1990s, businesses have bridled at these campaign contributions and have complained about the use of growing corporate taxes to subsidize inefficient farmers and pork-barrel projects. Analysts point to this divergence of interests as yet another sign of the weakening of the iron triangle.

The other pillar of LDP support has been agriculture, whose highly organized political interests are channeled through local agricultural cooperatives to the national "peak organization" Nokyo (Central Union of Agricultural Cooperatives). Agriculture's key political contribution has been its capacity to provide the LDP with a dependable and geographically concentrated bloc of votes. In exchange, LDP government and bureaucratic policies have favored farmers with protection from agricultural imports, price supports, and relatively low taxes. Although urbanization and electoral redistricting have to some extent weakened the significance of the rural farm vote, Japanese farmers remain an important political force.

Big business and agriculture are not the only interest groups to have offered their campaign contributions and votes to the LDP in exchange for favorable policies and a share of the benefits of Japan's postwar economic boom. Small and medium-size businesses make up most of the Japanese economy, despite their unsung status when compared with high-profile large firms such as Toyota and Sony. These smaller manufacturers and retailers have been very well organized and have parlayed their electoral support into tax breaks, subsidies, and protection from larger firms. For example, the ubiquitous mom-and-pop corner grocery stores effectively kept large retailers out of Japan's neighborhoods for many years. Similarly, Wal-Mart and other large foreign retailers had great difficulty penetrating Japan's market. Another group worth mentioning is the half million construction firms in Japan, most of which are small, unproductive, and well cared for by an inefficient and corrupt government bidding system for public works.

Japan's faltering economy and growing corruption scandals involving the LDP and its supporters have cast new light on the economic and political costs of this corporate welfare system. Critics have argued that the LDP's varied and growing host of constituencies has led to distributional tyranny, furthered Japan's economic crisis, and stifled political change. These corporatist arrangements have also long excluded those deemed potentially harmful to the goals of rapid industrialization, including trade unions, consumers, and women's groups. Because of this, Japan's major labor organizations, including RENGO (Japanese Trade Union Confederation) and the teachers' and public employees' unions, have had adversarial relations with the LDP and have supported the more left-leaning political parties, such as the Socialists and Communists. As Japan's postindustrial and postmaterial society grows more complex and the political marketplace more competitive, many hope that an increasing number of interests will utilize constitutional guarantees to establish a broader range of civic associations.

SOCIETY

Ethnic and National Identity

Few national populations view themselves as racially and ethnically homogeneous as do the Japanese. With immigrants constituting only 1 percent of the population, this perception is grounded in demographic reality. Nonetheless, those of "foreign ancestry" in Japan make up some 5 percent of the population. The notion of a racially pure and monoethnic Japan was largely fostered by the Japanese state from the Meiji period onward as it sought to forge a Japanese nation from the culturally and even linguistically diverse feudal domains of nineteenth-century Japan and to establish Japanese racial

ETHNIC GROUPS

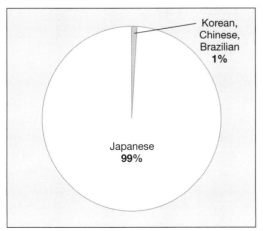

RELIGION

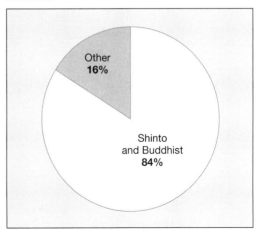

superiority over the peoples of its far-flung empire in the first half of the twentieth century.

This strong ethnic and national identity has come at the expense of several minority groups that have been prevented from both developing a Japanese identity and enjoying the full privileges of citizenship as citizens with a separate ethnic heritage. These minorities include the indigenous Ainu in the north and the Okinawans in the south; descendants of Koreans, Chinese, and Southeast Asians; and the children of mixed ancestry and foreigners. Although not racially separate, the 2 million *burakumin* (social outcasts), whose ancestors worked in the "unclean" occupations, are also seen as a minority group and have faced intense prejudice. Discrimination against these minority groups has been widespread and persistent. Those who have sought to assimilate by taking on Japanese names, mastering the Japanese language, and adopting Japanese cultural mores have generally remained socially marginalized and culturally scorned.

If cultural assimilation is difficult, the naturalization process is nearly as arduous. Being born in Japan does not automatically confer citizenship or voting rights. Non-Japanese can become citizens only after adopting a Japanese name and enduring a series of interviews that include home visits and consultations with neighbors to ensure that the candidate has sufficiently assimilated Japanese culture. This is a process that many find invasive and humiliating. In addition, permanent residents who do not choose citizenship are fingerprinted and required to carry alien-registration identification.

However, economic necessity may bring about the social integration and mobility that cultural obstacles and state policy have prevented. With both a rapidly aging population and dwindling fertility, Japan faces the prospect of having some 30 percent fewer people by the mid-twenty-first century than it has today and a proportionally smaller workforce. Economists and demographers argue that if Japan is not prepared to overcome both its racism and its sexism, which have prevented immigrants and women from fully contributing to the workforce, the country may close the door on its last, best chance to regain its status as an economic powerhouse.

Ideology and Political Culture

Few issues have been as controversial in discussions of Japanese behavior, including political behavior, as cultural values. Max Weber and other early Western social scientists argued that Asia's Confucian culture was inimical to both economic and political modernization. They contended that the Confucian disdain for commerce and emphasis on the group and hierarchy hampered the entrepreneurial initiative and individual freedom that spurred capitalism and democracy in the West. More recently, in the wake of Japan's, and much of the rest of East Asia's, enviable postwar economic growth and relatively peaceful democratic transitions, scholars have pointed to this same Confucian canon, noting these societies' emphasis on diligence, thrift, education, cooperative effort, and deference to authority. Most recently, "Asian values" are once again the villain, accounting for the crony capitalism, nepotism, and inefficient government intervention that are blamed for Japan's—and the rest of Asia's—economic crises of the 1990s.

Equally as controversial has been Japan's own use of cultural values to explain (and at times influence) Japanese behavior. Some of this has been little more than a convenient scapegoat for what would otherwise be seen as illegal trade barriers. For example, Japanese negotiators have argued that American skis were not safe in Japan because Japanese snow forms differently from American snow; that Western foods were not as palatable to the Japanese, who have several more feet of intestines; and that California rice imports would infringe on the Japanese people's sacred relationship with Japanese rice. In other cases, so-called Japanese cultural values have been manipulated or even invented by elites and introduced into the society as a form of "cultural engineering." Political and business elites have extolled Confucian diligence as a Japanese norm to limit leisure time and boost economic production. Militarist leaders used educational indoctrination and state-sponsored religion to invent and inculcate the "time-honored" values of emperor worship and national patriotism.

However, Japan's historical experiences with Confucianism, feudalism, militarism, and bureaucratism have certainly shaped the norms and values that guide Japanese political behavior. So have its experiences with the West, from imposed inequitable treaties and democratic institutions to military defeat and the embrace of Western popular culture. In efforts to attribute political behavior to culture, scholars often point to the group conformity and social hierarchy that pervade most aspects of Japanese life. The basic unit of Japanese society is not the individual but the group, as manifested in such institutions as the family, the company, the political faction, and the nation. Japanese are socialized to defer to the needs of the group and to make decisions through consensus rather than majority vote. Similarly, hierarchy governs most social relationships in Japan, and Japanese are most comfortable in settings in which their social standing in relation to others is clear. Inferiors yield to their superiors' authority, and superiors are obliged to care for their subordinates' needs. In recent decades, advancement in firms, bureaucratic ministries, and LDP factions has been based increasingly on seniority and personalized patron-client relationships and less on merit.

In sum, Japan has undergone political and economic modernization, but on its own (not fully Western) terms. Moreover, individual freedom and social equality remain less important than one's acceptance by the group and one's rightful position in that group's hierarchical division. Japan's remarkably equitable distribution of wealth—on par with that of the European social democracies—is the result of neither cultural norms of egalitarianism nor explicit government policy. In fact, Japan has had a weak labor movement and conservative governments that have promoted low taxation and public spending, conditions that typically foster inequality. This economic and social equality can be attributed in large part to (1) World War II, which reduced all of Japanese society to poverty levels; (2) postwar occupation reforms, including land reform, the breakup of the huge zaibatsu conglomerates, purges of the political, military, economic, and aristocratic elite, and the empowerment of labor unions to bargain collectively for improved working conditions; and (3) Japan's rapid and sustained postwar economic growth, which showered unprecedented prosperity on virtually all social groups in Japan. These factors have consistently weakened the salience of issues of redistribution of wealth as an ideological cleavage in Japan, contributing to the weakness of the Japanese left and shoring up support for the LDP and its pro-growth policies. In a 1994 NHK (Japan Broadcasting Corporation) poll, nearly three fourths of respondents identified themselves as having a political stance ranging from conservative to neutral, whereas less than one fourth saw themselves as progressive or close to progressive.

The current economic malaise (combined with an ongoing generational change in values) may lead to greater diversity of political attitudes and ideologies in Japan. The fading of guaranteed permanent employment—lifetime employment—for Japan's corporate *sarariman* (white-collar "salaryman") and rising unemployment among college graduates (and indeed an increasing number of college and even high-school dropouts) have led to disillusionment with business and politics as usual and mounting calls for change. Such disillusionment is particularly strong among Japanese youth, who have no memory of wartime hardship or postwar poverty and value individual fulfillment through leisure diversions and risky entrepreneurial opportunities rather than through long hours and long years of work for the sake of a company. Younger Japanese have less incentive to remain loyal to a company that can no longer promise them job security. They have little patience for the corruption and authority of long-in-the-tooth LDP bureaucratic rule. In short, change may be initiated by a younger generation that is far more willing and likely to switch both their jobs and their political loyalties.

POLITICAL ECONOMY

Japan's sudden introduction to the global political economy in the nineteenth century fostered the development of a mercantilist political economic system concerned with neither liberal freedom nor Communist equality. Compelled by U.S. gunships to open the country's borders to "free" trade with the West, the Meiji oligarchs recognized that Japan must either modernize quickly or, like China, be overrun by Western imperialism. State-led economic development became not a means of serving the public but rather a means of preserving national sovereignty. The oligarchs' national slogan, "rich country, strong military," acknowledged that Meiji modernizers were fully aware from the outset of the strong relationship between economic development and industrialization on the one hand and military and political power in the international arena on the other.

Even with all the turmoil that Japan experienced in the twentieth century, the basic structure of this "catch-up" mercantilist political economy persists. Forged under conditions of military rigor, refined during the U.S. occupation, and perfected under the aegis of American military and economic protection, this developmental model propelled Japan from the ashes of devastating military defeat to become the second largest economy in the world.

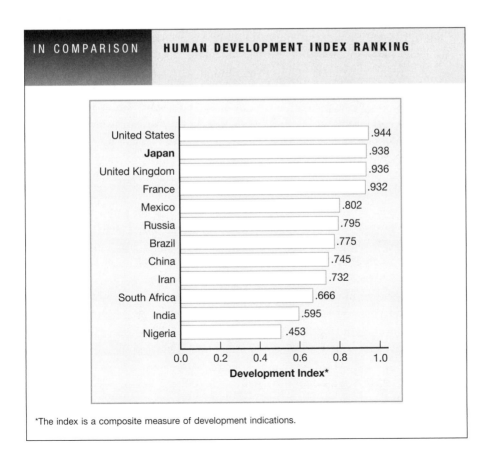

IN COMPARISON   **HUMAN DEVELOPMENT INDEX RANKING**

	Development Index*
United States	.944
Japan	.938
United Kingdom	.936
France	.932
Mexico	.802
Russia	.795
Brazil	.775
China	.745
Iran	.732
South Africa	.666
India	.595
Nigeria	.453

*The index is a composite measure of development indications.

LABOR FORCE BY OCCUPATION

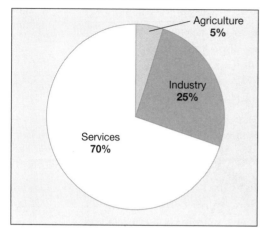

Agriculture
5%

Industry
25%

Services
70%

Not surprisingly, scholars and policy makers alike have sought to understand this developmental "miracle," and the investigation of the model of Japan's **capitalist developmental state** has become an important field of academic study and policy analysis.[9]

Because Japan's capitalist developmental state differs significantly from the liberal capitalist system that Americans often presume to be capitalism's only "true" form, each of the three components of this label is worth examining. The Japanese state may be described as developmental, because its top priority has been economic development, not regulation (as in the United States), welfare (as in Europe's social democracies), or revolution (as in Communist China). But the system is nonetheless capitalist, based on private property and on profit-motivated private firms participating in highly competitive local and global markets. But far more than in the American case, the state has guided the private market.

This guidance has included a host of formal and informal economic measures often grouped under the term **industrial policy.** Industrial policies are formulated and implemented by Japan's elite economic bureaucracy, after consultation and coordination with the private sector. Measures include imposing protective tariffs and nontariff barriers on imports, encouraging cooperation and limiting "excessive" competition in strategic export sectors, and offering low-interest loans and tax breaks to firms willing to invest in targeted industries.

Government guidance hasn't always worked well or as planned. But for many decades, state-led developmental capitalism kept Japan's economy strong, prosperous, and internationally competitive. The prewar family zaibatsu were replaced by professionally managed *keiretsu* conglomerates with ready access to cheap capital. Workers agreed to forgo disruptive labor strikes in exchange for promises of permanent employment, ensuring management a skilled and disciplined workforce. And as early heavy-handed policies of protectionism and explicit control proved unwieldy, bureaucrats came to rely more upon informal directives known as administrative guidance and subtle incentives more suitable for the increasingly internationalized Japanese economy. After growing at an average rate of over 10 percent per year during the 1950s and 1960s, Japan's economy still managed to grow over 5 percent per year during the 1970s and 1980s, substantially faster than the economy of any other advanced industrial democracy. The flagship automotive and consumer-electronics companies within Japan's large conglomerates became multinational giants and household names, and the fruits of Japan's rapid growth lifted the income of and opportunity for nearly all Japanese.

By the 1980s, this very prosperity was masking what now, in hindsight, is much easier to detect as serious structural problems within the model. As the international political economy was becoming ever more integrated and hyper-competitive, the cost of doing business in Japan was mounting. Japan's multi-national automotive and electronics exporters felt this competitive pressure first but kept their heads above water by shifting production overseas and drastically cutting costs at home. Most of Japan's companies were not able to react so nimbly, however, nor was the government prepared to tolerate the kind of unemployment that would have resulted from the wholesale transfer of production abroad. Rather than face global competition, inefficient industries used their influence within the iron triangle to seek protection. They obtained it from a government that had become accustomed to looking after not just economically strategic industries but also politically strategic industries. This government assistance led to waste, overcapacity, and overpricing.

These corporate-welfare measures, combined with a rapid jump in the value of Japan's currency, propelled its stock and real estate markets skyward in the latter half of the 1980s. This led to dangerous overvaluation of both securities and land. At one point in the early 1990s, Japan's stock market was valued at fully half of all the world's stock markets combined. At its peak value, the land under the emperor's palace grounds in central Tokyo was worth as much as the land of the entire state of California! Japan was awash in over-inflated assets and easy money, leading companies, banks, the Japanese Mafia, and even the government to invest in grossly overpriced assets and risky (even foolish) business ventures. When this asset bubble burst in 1992, the value of stock and property plummeted, growth slowed, and already uncompetitive companies were left with huge debts (and dwindling assets and production with which to repay them). The Japanese have labeled these firms **zombies**—essentially dead but propped up by banks and a political system unwilling to force them into bankruptcy. The government slid deeper into debt as it sustained not just these insolvent firms but also the banks that carried their debts (now in the trillions of dollars) even as it attempted to stimulate individual consumption. Although Japan has recently begun moving toward economic recovery—in fits and starts—it is now in its second decade of slow to no growth and slow to no reform of its political economic system.

Although there is no question that government-business cooperation and the state's laserlike focus on economic development fostered Japan's postwar economic boom, that boom was sustained by a political economic structure that is collapsing under its own weight. Producer-oriented industrial and financial policies and protectionist trade measures secured continued Liberal Democratic Party (LDP) rule and guaranteed bureaucrats the autonomy to focus on development. But they also sowed the seeds of destruction in this well-oiled conservative political economy. The corporate welfare that sustained the politicians' positions and the bureaucrats' vision came at the expense of a competitive Japanese economy and led to the collapse of Japan's vaunted lifetime employment. And that same welfare has offered little relief or consolation to Japan's battered consumers. Although the destructive inefficiencies were tolerable during the boom years, they have become a political albatross to the still-powerful LDP and a potential millstone for the Japanese economy.

Just as the loosening of the iron triangle is bringing political competition to Japan, so, it is hoped, will the painful weaning of firms from government protection and the loosening of the bonds of companies to their *keiretsu* alliances and the ties of employees to their firms bring much-needed market competition and efficiency into the Japanese economy. But precisely because changes are painful, Prime Minister Junichiro Koizumi has thus far largely failed to deliver on his bold promises of structural reform in the face of conservative bureaucratic and political resistance.

FOREIGN RELATIONS AND THE WORLD

Despite the vicissitudes of Japan's external relations, its foreign affairs have been marked by several continuities worth noting. First, though insular, the Japanese have been inveterate *borrowers and innovators* of things foreign. From Chinese ideograms to American popular culture, the Japanese have at key periods in their history pragmatically adopted and adapted those foreign elements they deemed beneficial. Second, the Japanese have generally maintained a *hierarchical perception of the world*, in which international entities (countries, empires, races), like internal entities (family members, classes, companies), are seen and ranked in hierarchical terms. Third, Japan's island status and catch-up strategy of mercantilist development have given the Japanese a very strong and sharply delineated sense of *nationalism*, which has made Japanese citizens highly responsive to calls for sacrifice on behalf of the nation when faced with a foreign challenge.

Given these continuities, it should not surprise us that those advocating change in Japan are calling for *gaiatsu* (foreign pressure) or even a "third opening" of Japan (after Perry and MacArthur) as the impetus for change. Although the country's external dealings over the past century and a half have been the source of understandable anxiety and much military disaster, they have also been the impetus for beneficial change. By the same token, Japan's growing international stature has meant that both its economic success and its more recent problems have been spilling over into the rest of the world, with a variety of consequences.

If one were to view Japan's international relations as a series of concentric circles, the most immediate and significant of these would include Japan and its Asian neighbors. These Asian neighbors have felt most acutely both the cost and the benefit of Japan's military, economic, and cultural expansion. Under the promise (or guise) of a Greater East Asian Co-prosperity Sphere, Japan first expanded its empire to Taiwan and Korea, then to the Chinese mainland, Southeast Asia, and the Pacific Islands. Japan brought oppressive colonial rule, imperial exploitation, and military destruction wherever it went but also built the economic infrastructure, transferred technology and training, and exported its version of developmental capitalism to several of its longer-held colonies. Moreover, Japan brought much of Asia into what it dubbed in the 1930s a **flying geese** pattern of economic development, with Japan at the head of a flock of dependent Asian economies. Japan offered leadership by exploiting its comparative advantage in advanced industries and then passing its skills on to the next tier as newer technologies became available. The second tier would do the same for the third, providing a ladder of industrial progress for (and Japanese dominance of) all of Asia.

Since Japan's defeat and its embrace of American-directed pacifist prosperity, the rest of Asia has viewed Japan with understandable ambivalence. On the one hand, though its constitution renounces war, Japan has never been required to atone for or even acknowledge its colonial and wartime legacies in the way that Germany has faced and frequently reexamined its Nazi past. The Japanese imperial army forced thousands of Korean and other Asian "comfort women" to serve as sexual slaves for its troops in the field, and—like most conquering armies—committed a host of war-related atrocities. Koreans, Chinese, and other Asians are troubled that Japanese textbooks have largely glossed over these events and that many of Japan's conservative politicians and prime ministers (including Koizumi) have made annual pilgrimages to Yasukuni, a controversial shrine honoring Japan's war dead. Chinese and Korean patriots regularly take to the streets demanding Japanese apologies and threatening boycotts of Japanese products.

On the other hand, the past benefits and future fruits of investment in and trade with the world's second-largest economy make it difficult for the rest of Asia to turn its back on Japan. Despite memories of war, many Asians are more interested in educational opportunities in Japan or employment in a Japanese factory than they are in an apology for past offenses. Despite historical tensions, its own economic woes, and the growth of other economies in the region, Japan remains by far the head goose as the region's leading provider of trade, technology, and investment capital.

But Japan's very real economic clout in Asia must be placed in the broader context of its continued economic—and, particularly, military—dependence on the United States. Within the context of Japan's overwhelming defeat in World War II and America's decades-long struggle with the Soviet Union, this patron-client relationship made good sense and good foreign policy for both the United States and Japan. For the United States, Japan offered a shining (if still superficial) example to the world of American-sponsored liberal capitalist democracy and was certainly worth the cost of military protection and the toleration of mercantilist trade policies. For their part, most Japanese (with notable exceptions on the left and the right) were content to develop the economy under this military and economic protection.

During the 1950s and 1960s, the United States and Japan were happy with their roles in the relationship. The United States sponsored Japan's return as a member in good standing of the U.S.-sponsored world trading system and cold-war alliance while Japan turned its full attention to rebuilding its economy. But by the 1970s, its very success as dutiful client led to a divergence in Japan's economic and security relations with its American patron. Whereas both the United States and Japan have been willing to retain a relationship of military protection and dependence, Japan's rapid economic growth has made it a full-fledged economic competitor. Over the past three decades, the United States and Europe have engaged in trade wars with Japan and have increased their demands that Japan end its economic protectionism and shoulder the burdens of an economic colleague, demands to which Japan has acceded, albeit at times reluctantly.

Japan, the rest of Asia, and the rest of the world have changed too much to allow the persistence of Japan's status quo. Critics inside and outside Japan express frustration over the country's split personality as "economic giant" and "political pygmy" and call for Japan to become a "normal" or "ordinary" country. These terms mean different things to different advocates but typically entail the *liberalization* of Japan's economy and society, opening the country's borders to trade, investment, immigrants, and students, as well as the *militarization* of Japan, developing the ability to both defend itself and contribute to regional and global security. We have already discussed the obstacles to and prospects for economic and social change in Japan. Here, we turn finally to Japan's security and its political role in the world.

Despite a constitution that prohibits the use or threat of war in resolving conflicts (Article 9) and the presence of 47,000 U.S. troops on its soil, Japan is not without its own means of defense. It currently has a Self-Defense Force (SDF) of some 240,000 personnel and an annual military budget of nearly US$50 billion, ranking it fourth in the world in terms of military expenditures. Although sentiment in Japan since World War II has been decidedly pacifist, rising tensions on the Korean peninsula and the growing capacity of China's military (which ranks third in the world in expenditures) have shifted public opinion quite dramatically. Although only 16 percent of Japanese respondents in a 2003 opinion poll favored changing Article 9 of the constitution for reasons related to defense; this is nearly twice the percentage who advocated such a change in 1995 and a third more than in 2001.

At the same time, the United States and other countries are pressuring Japan not only to bear more of the burdens of its own defense but also to participate more fully in regional and global peacekeeping operations. They criticize Japan's "checkbook diplomacy," by which, for example, Japan offered US$13 billion to compensate for its inability to participate militarily in the Gulf War of 1991. Conservative Japanese politicians (including Prime Minister Koizumi) are responding, using this convergence of *gaiatsu* with their own political and ideological interests to bolster Japan's technological sophistication and the capacity to project force beyond its borders. Despite a great deal of controversy at home, Koizumi deployed naval forces to the Indian Ocean in support of U.S. operations in Afghanistan and sent more than 500 troops to help rebuild Iraq.

But while a growing minority of Japanese is willing to accept a greater role for Japan's armed forces, most Japanese—and certainly most Asians—remain highly wary of Japanese militarism. Advocates of a nonmilitarized Japan argue that the country can and indeed has projected its power and influence abroad in a host of beneficial ways and that striving for twentieth-century militarized "normalcy" is contrary both to the intent of Japan's pacifist constitution and to the interests of Japan and the world. They argue that Japan need not be a military power to be a global power and point to a host of areas in which Japan has already shown global leadership. They note that Japan has (until very recently) been the world's top donor of international aid, giving over US$10 billion in foreign-development assistance annually. They contend that Japan ought to focus its efforts on areas of global benefit, such as the environment, technology transfers to developing countries, and even weather prediction and climate control, rather than engage in a dangerous and costly arms race with China or other countries.

Can Japan use its unique constitutional restrictions to create a new kind of nonmilitary hegemony? More fundamentally, can it implement the economic and political reforms necessary to right its economic ship in time to maintain its international influence? Will these reforms come from above, from below, from the outside, or perhaps not at all (or not in time)? In this, as in other areas, Japan's capacity and willingness to change as it faces the twenty-first century will prove crucial to its future security, as well as to its economic prosperity and political stability.

CURRENT ISSUES

ARTHRITIC JAPAN

Japan faces an additional economic challenge, which is not yet as acute as the structural problems prolonging its current recession, but could be even thornier. It is at the forefront of a problem that many advanced industrial societies now confront: the convergence of an aging population and dwindling fertility rates. Like Italy, Germany, and other European societies, Japan has a population aged sixty-five and older that is rapidly increasing relative to the rest of its society. As noted in the table below ("Population over Age Sixty-five"), the ratio of Japanese senior citizens to the total population was only 12 percent in 1990 and is currently less than 20 percent but is expected to climb to more than 35 percent by 2050. By midcentury, demographers predict, Japan will have 1 million centenarians and 30 percent fewer people overall, and nearly 1 million more people will die each year than are born.

This "graying" of society brings a host of economic challenges, which the United States and other countries are certainly concerned with as well, including health and financial care for the growing aged population. But the most acute problem that Japan faces, far more so than other advanced countries, is that of a declining workforce. The size of Japan's workforce peaked in 1998 and is expected to decline rapidly as fewer and fewer Japanese reach maturity each year to replace retiring and dying workers. Japan is certainly not alone in this problem, but whereas most advanced societies have expanded

Percentage of the Population over Age 65

Year	Japan	United States	Germany	France	Italy	United Kingdom
1990	12.05	12.39	14.96	13.99	15.32	15.72
1995	14.54	12.47	15.47	15.09	16.62	15.74
2000	17.37	12.30	16.40	15.97	18.07	15.75
2010	22.54	12.89	20.19	16.62	20.63	16.95
2020	27.85	16.29	22.51	20.45	23.85	20.21
2030	29.57	20.17	27.70	23.85	28.58	24.34
2040	33.23	21.00	30.92	26.16	34.53	27.24
2050	35.65	21.09	30.97	26.73	35.87	27.31

Source: "International Comparison: Ratio of 65 Years Old and Over among Total Population," Statistics, Web Japan: Gateway for All Japanese Information, http://web-japan.org/stat/stats/01CEN2C.html (accessed 16 July 2005)

their labor pools by more fully integrating women and immigrants into the workplace, Japan has not been willing to embrace either group.

In fact, experts have argued for years that one of the quickest boosts to Japan's economic slowdown would be the expansion of work opportunities for women, particularly in management and other professional roles. Only 40 percent of Japanese women currently work (compared with nearly 47 percent in the United States and 48 percent in Sweden), and these women hold only 9 percent of the managerial positions (compared with 46 percent in the United States and 32 percent in Sweden). Women's advocates in Japan contend that the relative lack of women's economic participation may be reducing Japan's economic growth by over half a percentage point annually. In those few Japanese companies in which women constitute at least half of all workers, profits are double those in which female employees account for 10 percent or less. But resistance to expanding women's role in the workforce remains high in this traditionally patriarchal society. In 2003, Japan ranked sixty-ninth among the seventy-five members of the World Economic Forum in terms of empowering women. In the meantime, advocates argue, Japan is forced to compete economically with one hand tied behind its back.

Even if women were fully empowered, economists and demographers agree that the only long-term hope for stabilizing Japan's population and workforce is to increase and sustain immigration over many years. Absent this source of workers, consumers, and taxpayers, experts predict that Japan's economy will not just decline but may very well collapse! As its traditional views toward the role of women have kept women at home, Japan's conservative attitudes toward ethnic purity and the insular nature of Japanese society have severely restricted immigration. Whereas the United States accepted an average of 1 million immigrants a year during the 1990s, it took Japan a quarter century to absorb 1 million immigrants into its society. Moreover, most of these immigrants are brought in from other Asian countries to fill low-paying "dirty, dangerous, and difficult" jobs. Japan has done little to attract immigrants with specialized knowledge and skills, once again handicapping its economy.

These issues pose the question of whether Japan is willing or indeed even able to make the changes necessary to compete in a twenty-first-century world that has changed so considerably while aspects of Japan have not.

NOTES

1. Margaret A. McKean, "Equality," in Takeshi Ishida and Ellis S. Krauss, eds., *Democracy in Japan* (Pittsburgh: University of Pittsburgh Press, 1989), p. 203.

2. There was also an underclass or outcast segment of society known as the *eta* or *burakumin*, discriminated against for their work in the ritually impure trades, such as tanning and butchering.

3. John Dower, *Embracing Defeat: Japan in the Wake of World War II* (New York: W. W. Norton, 1999), p. 45.

4. Prime ministers have served, on average, just over two years, and cabinet members' tenure has averaged less than one year (finance ministers have averaged approximately sixteen months).

5. Although the population of voting districts was relatively balanced when districts were originally set up after the war, the LDP never reapportioned them even as the countryside became depopulated. In exchange for their voting loyalty, farmers were assured high prices for their rice and were given voting clout as much as three times greater than that of urban voters, who were less likely to vote for the LDP. In the 1990 lower-house elections, for example, opposition parties won nearly 54 percent of the popular vote but garnered only 44 percent of the seats.

6. Under the old system, all representatives were elected from multimember districts (MMDs) in which voters had a single nontransferable vote (SNTV) that they cast for a specific candidate instead of a party list. This unusual MMD/SNTV system created a variety of incentives and consequences, both for the LDP, which benefited immensely from the rules, and for opposition parties struggling to compete.

7. T. J. Pempel, *Regime Shift: Comparative Dynamics of the Japanese Political Economy* (Ithaca, NY: Cornell University Press, 1998).

8. See, for example, Karel van Wolferen, *The Enigma of Japanese Power* (New York: Alfred Knopf, 1989).

9. The seminal study in this field is Chalmers Johnson, *MITI and the Japanese Miracle: The Growth of Industrial Policy, 1925–1975* (Stanford, CA: Stanford University Press, 1982).

KEY TERMS

administrative guidance   p. 169
amakudari   p. 169
Article 9   p. 148
capitalist developmental state   p. 182
Diet   p. 156
flying geese   p. 185
House of Councillors   p. 164
House of Representatives   p. 164
industrial policy   p. 182
iron triangle   p. 160
Tanaka Kakuei   p. 170
keiretsu   p. 176
koenkai   p. 166
Junichiro Koizumi   p. 175
Liberal Democratic Party (LDP)
   p. 148

Meiji oligarchs   p. 155
Meiji Restoration   p. 155
money politics   p. 173
pork-barrel   p. 165
"rich country, strong military"
   p. 148
samurai   p. 153
Self-Defense Force   p. 148
Yoshida Shigeru   p. 168
shogun   p. 154
Supreme Commander of Allied
   Powers   p. 159
Taisho democracy   p. 157
Tokugawa   p. 154
zombies   p. 183

WEB LINKS

Japanese Constitution **www2.gol.com/users/michaelo/Jcon.index.html**
Japanese Prime Minister and Cabinet
  www.kantei.go.jp/foreign/index-e.html
Japanese Statistical Data **web-japan.org/stat/index.html**
  This site, affiliated with Japan's Ministry of Foreign Affairs, provides regularly updated statistical information in 23 different categories including
  aging, crime, elections, media, and women, and others.
National Diet of Japan **www.lib.duke.edu/ias/eac/Kokkai.htm**
  Includes useful links to House of Councillors and House of Representatives, with extensive information on membership, relative strength of
  parties, and electoral and legislative procedures.

6 RUSSIA

Head of state:
President Vladimir Vladimirovich Putin
(since December 31, 1999)

Head of government:
Prime Minister Mikhail Yefimovich Fradkov
(since March 5, 2004)

Capital: Moscow

Total land size: 17,075,200 sq km

Population: 143 million

GDP at PPP: 1.40 trillion US$

GDP per capita: $9,800

INTRODUCTION

Why Study This Case?

For decades, Russia stood out from all other countries in the world. Established in 1917, the Soviet Union (which included present-day Russia and many of its neighbors) was the world's first Communist state. The Soviet Union served as a beacon for Communists everywhere, a symbol of how freedom and equality could be transformed if the working class could truly gain power. It provoked equally strong responses among its opponents, who saw it as a violent, dangerous, and power-hungry dictatorship. The rapid growth of Soviet power from the 1930s onward only deepened this tension, which eventually culminated in a cold war between the United States and the Soviet Union following World War II. Armed with thousands of nuclear weapons and ideologically hostile, these two states struggled to maintain a balance of power and avoid a nuclear holocaust. Until the 1980s, many observers believed that humanity would eventually face a final, violent conflict between these two systems.

Yet when the Soviet Union's end did come, it was not with a bang but a whimper. In the 1980s, the Soviet Union saw the rise of a new generation of leaders, who realized that their system was no longer primed to overtake the West, economically or otherwise. The general secretary of the Soviet Union's Communist Party, Mikhail Gorbachev, attempted to inject limited political and economic reforms into the system in order to overcome these problems, but the reforms seemed only to exacerbate domestic problems and polarize the leadership and the public. Gorbachev's actions culminated in the actual dissolution of the Soviet Union and the formation of fifteen independent countries, one of which is Russia.

How would Russia be reconstructed from these ruins? Like many of the other post-Communist countries, Russia has had to confront the twin tasks of forging democracy and establishing capitalism in a country that had little historical experience of either. How does a nation go about creating a market economy after Communism? How does it go about building democracy? Russia has proved an amazing experiment in building new institutions that reconcile freedom and equality in a manner far different from that of the previous regime. We can learn a lot from Russia's attempt at meeting this awesome challenge.

Some fifteen years on, Russia's success is open to debate. Many have argued that its transition to democracy and capitalism has been uneven at best. Democratic institutions remain weak, public cynicism regarding politics is high, and many of the basic civil freedoms expected in a democracy, such as a free press, have declined in recent years. In economic terms, too, the outcome is unclear; much of the society has grown much more unequal in terms of wealth, and many Russians have grown poorer over the past fifteen years, while much economic power has been concentrated in the hands of an elite. Optimists reject many of these concerns. They note that for a country with no real history of democracy or capitalism, Russia has done amazingly well in a few years and far better than many doomsayers predicted in the 1990s. Its problems may be numerous, but they are not much different from those of many other middle-income countries. Russia has built a democratic system that has managed to conduct elections and respond to basic political necessities, albeit in fits and starts. These optimists point to the growing number of private businesses and a growing middle class.

It is hard to reconcile these two views of the same country, and travelers to Russia might get either impression (or both), depending on where they go, what they see, and with whom they speak. Russia's reconstruction is by no means complete; it remains in transition, and the path it takes will shape its role in the global community as a whole.

Major Geographic and Demographic Features

As we study Russia's geography, the first thing we notice is the country's vast size. Even when viewed separately from the various republics that made up the Soviet Union, Russia is nearly four times the size of the United States and covers eleven time zones. Yet for all its size, much of it is relatively unpopulated. With some 146 million people, Russia's population is far smaller than that of the United States or the European Union (with 296 million and 450 million, respectively). Much of the Russian population is concentrated in the western, geographically European part of the country. Russia's east, Siberia, is a flat region largely uninhabited because of its bitterly cold weather. Siberia represents an interesting comparison to the American frontier experience. While Americans moved westward toward the Pacific Ocean in the nineteenth century to find new lands to settle, Russians moved eastward toward the same ocean. Alaska was part of the Russian Empire until it was sold to the United States in 1867. But Russian and American experiences of the frontier were quite different. In America, the amenability of the climate and soil helped spread the population across the country and reinforce a sense of "pioneer individualism." In contrast, the harsh conditions of Siberia meant that only the state could function effectively in much of the region, where it developed infrastructure and created populated communities. Many of those who were to "settle" Siberia, before and after 1917, were political prisoners sent into exile.

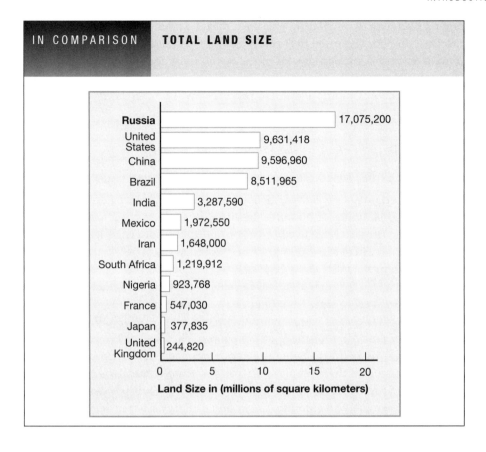

IN COMPARISON   **TOTAL LAND SIZE**

Russia — 17,075,200
United States — 9,631,418
China — 9,596,960
Brazil — 8,511,965
India — 3,287,590
Mexico — 1,972,550
Iran — 1,648,000
South Africa — 1,219,912
Nigeria — 923,768
France — 547,030
Japan — 377,835
United Kingdom — 244,820

Land Size in (millions of square kilometers)

Russia's vastness has other implications as well. By virtue of its size and location, Russia has many neighbors. Unlike the relative isolation of North America, Russia shares borders with no fewer than fourteen countries. Many of these countries were part of the Soviet Union and are considered by Russians to remain in their sphere of influence (not unlike the way in which many Americans view Latin America). But Russia also shares a long border with China, a neighbor with whom it has often had poor relations. Russia also controls a series of islands in the Pacific that belonged to Japan until 1945, a situation that remains a source of friction between the two countries. Russia has long felt uneasy about its neighborhood. Over the centuries, unable to rely on oceans or mountains as natural defenses, it has been subject to countless invasions from Europe and Asia. Physical isolation has never been an option.

While Russia may suffer from some intemperate climates and uneasy borders, it benefits in other areas. The country is rich in natural resources, among them wood, oil, natural gas, gold, nickel, and diamonds. Many of these resources are concentrated in Siberia and are thus not easy to extract, yet they remain an important component of the economy. Though there are concerns as to what the economic and environmental repercussions will be, there is no doubt that the exploitation of these resources will be central in the ongoing development of the Russian economy.

Historical Development of the State

FOREIGN INVASION, RELIGION, AND THE EMERGENCE OF A RUSSIAN STATE

Any understanding of present-day Russia and its political struggles must begin with an understanding of how the state has developed over time. While ethnically Slavic peoples have lived in European Russia for centuries, these peoples are not credited with founding the first Russian state. Rather, credit is usually given to Scandinavians (Vikings) who expanded into the region in the ninth century C.E., forming a capital in the city of Kiev. Nonetheless, the true origins of the Russian state remain open to debate. This issue is highly politicized, as many Russians reject the notion that foreigners were first responsible for the organization of the Russian people. The dispute even involves the very name of the country. Scholars who believe in the Viking origin of the Russian state argue that the name Russia (or **Rus**) comes from the Finnish word for the Swedes, *Ruotsi,* which derives from a Swedish word meaning "rowers." Those who dispute this claim argue that the name is of a tribal or geographic origin that can be traced to the native Slav inhabitants.[1]

Whatever its origins, by the late tenth century the Kievan state had emerged as a major force, stretching from Scandinavia to Central Europe. It had also adopted **Orthodox Christianity,** centered in Constantinople (modern-day Istanbul). Orthodoxy developed distinctly from Roman Catholicism in a number of practical and theological ways, among which was the perception of the relationship between church and state. Roman Catholics came to see the pope as the central leader of the faith, separate from the political power of Europe's kings. Orthodoxy, however, did not draw such a line between political and religious authority, a situation that, some argue, stunted the idea of a society functioning independently of the state.

Another important development was the Mongol invasion of Russia in the thirteenth century. The Mongols, a nomadic Asian people, first united under Genghis Khan and controlled Russia (along with much of China and the Middle East) for over two centuries. During this time, Russians suffered from widespread economic destruction, massacres, enslavement, urban depopulation, and the extraction of resources. Some scholars view this occupation as the central event that set Russia on a historical path separate from that of the West, one leading to greater despotism and isolation. Cut off from European

TIME LINE OF POLITICAL DEVELOPMENT

Year	Event
1237–40	Mongols invade
1552–56	Ivan the Terrible conquers the Tatar khanates of Kazan and Astrakhan; establishes Russian rule over the lower and middle Volga River
1689–1725	Peter the Great introduces reforms, including the subordination of the church, the creation of a regular conscript army and navy, and new government structures
1798–1814	Russia intervenes in the French Revolution and the Napoleonic Wars
1861	Edict of Emancipation ends serfdom
1917	Monarchy is overthrown and a provisional government established; Bolsheviks in turn overthrow the provisional government
1918–20	Civil war takes place between the Red Army and the White Russians, or anti-Communists
1938	Joseph Stalin consolidates power; purges begin
1953	Stalin dies
1956	General Secretary Nikita Khrushchev denounces Stalin
1985	Mikhail Gorbachev becomes general secretary and initiates economic and political reforms
1991	Failed coup against Gorbachev leads to the collapse of the Soviet Union; Boris Yeltsin becomes president of independent Russia
1993	Yeltsin suspends the parliament and calls for new elections; legislators barricade themselves inside the parliament building, and Yeltsin orders the army to attack parliament; Russians approve a new constitution, which gives the president numerous powers
1994–96	In war between Russia and the breakaway republic of Chechnya, Chechnya is invaded, and a cease-fire is declared
1996	Yeltsin reelected
1999	Yeltsin appoints Vladimir Putin prime minister and resigns from office; Putin becomes acting president
1999	Russia reinvades Chechnya following a series of bomb explosions blamed on Chechen extremists
2000	Putin elected president
2004	Putin reelected

intellectual and economic influences, Russia would not participate in the Renaissance, feel the impact of the Protestant Reformation, or develop a strong middle class.

Not all scholars agree with this assessment, however. For some, the move toward despotism had its impetus not in religion or foreign invasion but in domestic leadership. Specifically, they point to the rule of Ivan the Terrible (1533–84), who came to power in the decades following Russia's final independence from Mongol control. Consolidating power in Moscow rather than Kiev, Ivan began to assert Russia's authority over that of foreign rulers and began to destroy any government institutions that obstructed his consolidation of personal power. In a precursor to the Soviet experience, Ivan created a personal police force that terrorized his political opponents. Though Ivan is viewed in much of Russian history as the unifier of the country, many historians see in him the seeds of repressive and capricious rule.[2] Whatever his legacy, it was with Ivan's rule that we can see the emergence of a single Russian emperor, or **czar** (from the Latin word Caesar), who exercised sovereignty over the nation's lands and aristocrats.

In sum, we might argue that no one factor led to Russia's unique growth of state power and its dearth of democratic institutions. Religion may have shaped political culture in a way that influenced the way Russians viewed the relationship between the individual and the state. Historic catastrophes like Mongol rule may have stunted economic growth and cut the country off from the developments that occurred elsewhere in Europe. Political leadership might also have solidified certain authoritarian institutions. None of these conditions may have been enough individually, but taken together they served to pull Russia away from the rest of the West.

Ivan's death left Russia with an identity crisis. Did it belong to Europe, one of numerous rival states with a common history and culture? Or did differences in history, religion, and location mean that Russia was separate from the West? Even today Russia continues to confront this question. Some rulers, most notably Peter the Great (r. 1689–1725), saw Westernization as a major goal. This was typified in the relocation of the country's capital from Moscow to St. Petersburg, to place it closer to Europe. Peter consulted with numerous foreign advisers in his quest to modernize the country (particularly the military) and carry out administrative and educational reforms. In contrast, reactionaries like Nicholas I (r. 1825–55) were hostile to reforms. In Nicholas's case, the hostility was so great that in the last years of his reign even foreign travel was forbidden. Reforms proceeded over time, such as the emancipation of the serfs in 1861, but these lagged behind the pace of changes in Europe. As Russia vacillated between reform and reaction, there was continuity in the growth of a centralized state and a weak middle class. Industrialization came late, emerging in the 1880s and relying heavily on state intervention. This inconsistent modernization caused Russia to fall behind its international rivals.

THE SEEDS OF REVOLUTION

The growing disjunction between a largely agrarian and aristocratic society and a highly autonomous state and traditional monarchy would soon foster revolution. As Russia engaged in the great power struggles of the nineteenth and twentieth centuries, it was battered by the cost of war, and national discontent grew. In 1904, Russia and Japan came into conflict as each sought to gain control over portions of China. To Russia's surprise, Japan asserted its military strength and quickly proved itself the more modern power, defeating Russia. In 1905, Russia experienced a series of domestic shocks in the form of protests by members of the growing working class, who had migrated to the cities during the rapid industrialization of the previous two decades. The Revolution of 1905 forced Nicholas II to institute a series of limited reforms, including the creation of a legislature (the **Duma**). Although these reforms did quell the revolt, they were not revolutionary (the changes themselves were limited), nor did they bring stability to Russia. Shortly thereafter, the czar began to weaken the very rights and institutions he had agreed to. Meanwhile, many radical political leaders refused to participate in these new institutions and sought the removal of the czar himself.

World War I was the final straw. The overwhelming financial and human costs of the war exacerbated domestic tensions, weakening rather than strengthening national unity. As the war ground on, Russia faced food shortages, public disturbances, and eventually a widespread military revolt. The czar was forced to step down in March of 1917, and a non-Communist, republican leadership took control, unwisely choosing to remain in the war. This provisional government had little success asserting its authority. As disorder and public confusion grew, Communist revolutionaries, led by Vladimir Ilich Lenin (1870–1924), staged a coup d'état. This was no mass rebellion but rather an overthrow of those in power by a small disciplined force. After a subsequent civil war against anti-Communist forces, Lenin would begin the transformation of Russia, renamed the Soviet Union—the first Communist state in world history.[3]

THE RUSSIAN REVOLUTION UNDER LENIN

In many aspects Lenin's takeover was a radical, revolutionary event, whereas in other ways the new Communist government fell back on the conservative institutions of traditional Russian rule. Under Lenin, local revolutionary authority (in the form of **soviets,** or workers' councils) was pushed aside, though it was given superficial recognition in the new name of the country— the Union of Soviet Socialist Republics. Similarly, while the Communist Party embraced Russia's multinational character by creating a federal system around its major ethnic groups, the new republics had little power. Authority was vested solely in the Communist Party, which controlled all government and state activity. Alternative political parties and private media were banned. A secret-police force, the **Cheka,** was formed to root out opposition; it would later become the **KGB,** the body that would control domestic dissent and supervise overseas surveillance. The "commanding heights" of industry were nationalized, seized by the state in the name of the people. Managing all of this newfound power was a growing bureaucratic system, composed of the ***nomenklatura***—a term that refers to the politically influential jobs in the state, society, or economy and the Communist Party appointees who staffed them. The Communist state took on an enormous task of managing the basic economic and social life of the country. This helped justify the state's high degree of capacity and autonomy.

Yet even under Lenin's harsh leadership, the Soviet state did not reach its zenith. For the Soviet leadership, 1917 was intended to be simply a first step in a worldwide process. The historian Mary McAuley writes evocatively of Soviet telephone operators ready to receive the call that revolution had broken out elsewhere in the world in response to their triumph.[4]

As the years passed without other successful revolutions, the Soviet Union had to confront the possibility that it alone might have to serve as the vanguard of world revolution. Its focus had to shift so that domestic politics, not spreading revolution, would be paramount. Yet many old revolutionaries (those who had taken part in the 1917 events) had little interest in the day-to-day affairs of the party and state. One exception was Joseph Stalin (1879–1953), whose power over the party grew after Lenin died. By appointing loyal followers to positions of power and slowly consolidating his control over party and state institutions through increasingly brutal means, Stalin was able to force out other revolutionary leaders. One by one, those who had fought alongside Lenin in the revolution were removed from power, demoted, exiled, imprisoned, and/or executed.

STALINISM, TERROR, AND THE TOTALITARIAN STATE

By the late 1930s, Stalin had consolidated control over the Soviet party-state and was thus free to construct a totalitarian regime that reached across politics, economics, and society. As a central-planning bureaucracy was created to allocate resources and distribute goods, the last vestiges of private property were wiped away. The impact of this was particularly dramatic in agriculture, which was forcibly collectivized. Farmers often destroyed their livestock and crops rather than surrender them to the state, and many wealthy peasants were executed. Agricultural production collapsed, and as many as 7 million lives were lost in the resulting famine. In industry, the government embarked on a policy of crash industrialization in an attempt to catch up with and overtake the capitalist countries.

Power was thus centralized to a degree unknown before Soviet rule.[5] This growing power of the bureaucratic elite was enforced by the secret police, who turned their attention to anyone suspected of opposing Stalin's rule, whether outside the party or within. Millions of people were imprisoned or executed. Terror became a central feature of control, and the innocence or guilt of those arrested was often largely irrelevant. Finally, Stalin's power was solidified through a cult of personality that portrayed him as godlike, incapable of error and infinitely wise.

STABILITY AND STAGNATION AFTER STALIN

With Stalin's death, the Soviet leadership moved away from its uses of unbridled terror and centralized power, and Stalin's excesses were publicly criticized to a certain extent. The basic feature of the Soviet system remained in place, however. Power was vested in the Politburo, the ruling cabinet of the Communist Party. At its head was the general secretary, the de facto leader of the country. Government positions such as national legislators, the head of the government, and the head of state were controlled and staffed by the Communist Party and simply implemented the decisions of the Politburo. The economy also remained under the control of a central-planning bureaucracy, and although Russians were no longer terrorized, security forces continued to suppress public dissent through arrest and harassment. All basic aspects of Soviet life were decided by the *nomenklatura*. The party elite became, in essence, a new ruling class.

For a time, this system worked. The state was able to industrialize rapidly by controlling and directing all resources and labor. Moreover, in its infancy, Soviet rule enjoyed a high degree of legitimacy among the public. Even in the darkest years of Stalin's terror, citizens saw the creation of roads, railways, massive factories, homes and schools, and the installation of electricity, where none had existed before. If freedom was nonexistent, a rough level of equality was created, and many people were given education, jobs, health care, and retirement benefits, often for the first time. The Soviet people saw their standard of living increase dramatically.

But by the 1960s, some party leaders had begun to realize that a system so controlled by a central bureaucracy would become too institutionalized and conservative to allow necessary change or innovation. General Secretary Nikita Khrushchev, who took office in 1953, after Stalin's death, made an initial attempt at reform. But Khrushchev was thwarted by the party-state bureaucracy and was forced from his position by the Politburo in 1964. He was replaced by Leonid Brezhnev, who rejected further reform and placated the *nomenklatura* by assuring them that their power and privileges were protected. Under these conditions, economic growth slowed, and those in power became increasingly corrupt and detached, using their positions to gain access to scarce resources. Public cynicism grew as economic development declined. In the 1960s, it was still possible to believe that Soviet development might match or even surpass that of the West. But by the 1980s, it was clear that in many areas the Soviet Union was in fact stagnating or falling behind.

THE FAILURE OF REFORM AND THE COLLAPSE OF THE SOVIET STATE

Upon Brezhnev's death, in 1982, a new generation emerged from the wings, seeking to transform the Soviet state. Among its members was Mikhail Gorbachev, who became general secretary in 1985. Unconnected to the Stalinist period, Gorbachev believed that the Soviet state could be revitalized through the dual policies of **glasnost** (political openness) and **perestroika** (economic restructuring). Gorbachev believed that a limited rollback of the state from public life would encourage citizen participation and weaken the *nomenklatura's* powerful grip. Similarly, economic reforms would increase incentives and reduce the role of central planning, thus improving the quality and quantity of goods. Overall, the Soviet people would be better off, and the legitimacy of the Communist Party would be restored.

In hindsight, we can see that this attack on state power would turn out to be disastrous for the Soviet system. Gorbachev unleashed forces he could not control, leading to divisive struggles inside and outside the party. Nationalism grew among the many ethnic groups in the various republics, with some going so far as to demand independence. Critics attacked the corruption and incompetence of the party, calling for greater democracy, and others demanded a greater role for market forces and private property. Still others were disoriented by the changes, upset by the implication that the Soviet past had in fact been a historical dead end.[6]

At the same time, party leaders became polarized over the pace and scope of reform. Among them was **Boris Yeltsin,** an early protégé of Gorbachev's who was sidelined as his calls for change grew more radical. Ejected from the Politburo, Yeltsin was elected president of the Russian Soviet Socialist Republic (the largest republic in the ostensibly federal Soviet system). The moderate Gorbachev was now under attack from two sides: Yeltsin and other reformers, who faulted his unwillingness to embrace radical change, and conservatives and reactionaries, who condemned his betrayal of Communism. The very institutions of the party-state, unresponsive and unchanged for decades, began to unravel. In some ways, the Soviet Union began to resemble the chaotic Russia of pre-1917, and the tensions eventually came to a head. In August 1991, a group of anti-reform conservatives sought to stop the disintegration of Soviet institutions by mounting a coup d'état against Gorbachev, hoping that the party-state and the military would join their ranks. With

Gorbachev under arrest by the conspirators, Yeltsin led the resistance, famously denouncing the takeover while standing atop a tank. The army refused to back the coup, and it unraveled within two days.

As the coup collapsed, so did Gorbachev's political authority. The public blamed him for the chaos that had led up to the takeover (in fact, the conspirators were members of his cabinet, appointed to solidify his power). Moreover, Gorbachev was eclipsed by Yeltsin, whose authority was bolstered by his heroic stance against the coup. Yeltsin seized the opportunity to ban the Communist Party, effectively destroying what remained of Gorbachev's political base. In December 1991, Yeltsin and the leaders of the various Soviet republics dissolved the Soviet Union, and Yeltsin became president of a new, independent Russia. He would hold this position until 1999, when he named his prime minister, **Vladimir Putin,** acting president. Putin went on to win the presidential elections in 2000 and again in 2004.

POLITICAL REGIME

Is Russia a democracy? Certainly it enjoys a much higher degree of freedom than its Soviet predecessor. But while a number of democratic structures have been built since 1991, they remain weakly institutionalized. Democracy is being challenged from above, by those in power, and is being weakened from below by political cynicism and a weak civil society. Russia is perhaps best described as an illiberal democracy, in which many of the routines and procedures of democracy exist but are insecure and subject to sudden change or restriction. Clearly, the political regime is still in motion, but toward what end? Of late, the direction seems to be away from democracy, with changes that consolidate power in the hands of the state in general and the presidency in particular.

Political Institutions

THE CONSTITUTION

The Russian constitution is a document borne of violent conflict. As discussed above, Russia emerged in the aftermath of a failed coup d'état by opponents of radical

---

ESSENTIAL POLITICAL FEATURES

- Legislative-executive system: semi-presidential
- Legislature: Federal Assembly
- Lower house: State Duma
- Upper house: Federation Council
- Unitary or federal division of power: federal
- Main geographic subunits: republics, provinces, territories, autonomous districts, federal cities (Moscow and St. Petersburg)
- Electoral system for lower house: mixed plurality–proportional representation
- Electoral system for upper house: indirect election by local executive and legislature
- Chief judicial body: Constitutional Court

reform. This history is different from the recent history of most other Eastern European Communist countries, where Communist leaders were removed from power through public protest and elections. Although the Soviet state was dissolved, many elements of the old regime, including its political leaders, remained intact and in power. Boris Yeltsin thus faced a set of political institutions that were largely unchanged from those of the previous era. This carryover led to conflict. Most problematic was the battle between President Yeltsin and the existing parliament. At first, the parliament was a bicameral body consisting of the Congress of People's Deputies and the Supreme Soviet, both of which remained packed with former party members. The parliament initially supported Yeltsin but soon clashed with him over the speed and scope of his economic reforms.

As Yeltsin sought increased reform, the parliament grew so hostile that it sought to block his policies (including constitutional reform) and impeach him. In September 1993, Yeltsin responded by dissolving the parliament. Yeltsin's parliamentary opponents barricaded themselves in their offices, attempted to seize control of the national television station, and called for the army to depose the president. The army sided with Yeltsin, however, containing his opposition and suppressing the uprising with force. This support paved the way for Yeltsin to write a new constitution, which was enacted in 1993. Though the new constitution formally swept away the old legislative order, it could hardly be described as an auspicious beginning for democracy and facilitated the development of a system that emphasized presidential power.

The Branches of Government

THE KREMLIN: THE PRESIDENCY AND THE PRIME MINISTER

For centuries, Russians have referred to executive power—whether in the form of the czar or in the form of the general secretary—as the **Kremlin.** Dating back to the eleventh century, the Kremlin is a fortress in the heart of Moscow that has historically been the seat of state power. Today, much of the Kremlin's power is vested in the hands of the presidency, as elaborated in the 1993 constitution. That constitution created a powerful office through which the president could press economic and political changes despite parliamentary opposition. The result is a semi-presidential system in which the president serves as head of state while a prime minister serves as head of government. Power is divided between the two offices, but the president holds an overwhelming amount of executive power. The president is directly elected to serve a four-year term, may serve no more than two terms, and may be removed only through impeachment. Vladimir Putin, the current president, was elected in 2000, after serving as Boris Yeltsin's last prime minister, and was reelected in 2004, having faced little serious competition for the office.

The president's powers are numerous. It is the president, not parliament, who chooses and dismisses the prime minister and other members of the cabinet. Although the lower house of parliament, the State Duma, may reject the president's nominee, if it does so three times, the president must dissolve the Duma and call for new elections. The president cannot dissolve the Duma in the year following parliamentary elections, however, or in the last six months of his term. The president also appoints leaders to seven federal districts that constitute all of Russia, allowing him to oversee the work of local authorities.

The president may propose and veto bills and can issue decrees, laws that do not require legislative approval, are often not made public, and may not be challenged by citizens in the courts. President Yeltsin frequently relied on decrees to bypass his obstreperous legislature, and even with a more compliant body, Putin has often used the power of the decree to enact law.[7]

Another source of power lies in the president's control of important segments of the state. The president has direct control over the Foreign Ministry, the Defense Ministry, and the Interior Ministry (which handles the police and domestic security) as well as the armed forces. The president also controls the successor to the KGB, the **Federal Security Service (FSB),** which manages domestic and foreign intelligence. Presidential control over these

STRUCTURE OF THE GOVERNMENT

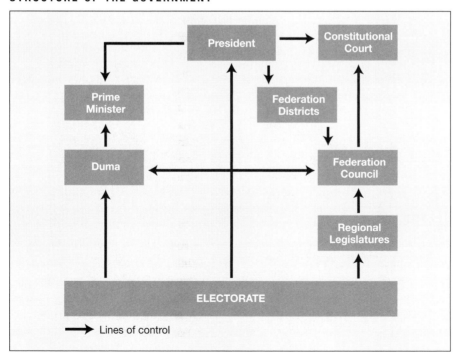

WHO IS VLADIMIR PUTIN?

Vladimir Putin's rapid rise to power caught virtually every observer by surprise. Few were aware of his existence just a few years before his election to the presidency. Putin was born in 1952 in Leningrad (now St. Petersburg) and studied law at the state university there. From his early years, he showed an interest in the security services, and in 1975, upon graduation, he joined the KGB, the Soviet intelligence agency. What exactly Putin did during his time in the KGB is unclear. It is known that from 1984 to 1990 he was stationed in East Germany, where he learned German and was charged with recruiting KGB agents and keeping tabs on opposition movements in that country.

In 1991, Putin left the KGB to work for the new mayor of Leningrad, Anatoly Sobchak. Sobchak had been one of Putin's college professors and supported Yeltsin during the 1991 coup. In 1994, Putin became deputy mayor of the city (by then renamed St. Petersburg) and was soon after made deputy chief administrator for the Kremlin, charged in part with helping to implement presidential decrees. In 1998, Yeltsin made Putin head of the Federal Security Service and in 1999 appointed him prime minister.

In December 1999, Yeltsin resigned from office, naming Putin acting president in advance of the 2000 presidential elections. During that time, Putin was viewed as a decisive actor, in contrast to the increasingly unstable (and often drunk) Yeltsin. Of particular importance for Putin's career was the second Chechen war, which he initiated in 1999 after a series of terrorist apartment-house bombings in Russia killed more than 300 people. Since becoming president, Putin has filled many of the top posts in his administration with the so-called *siloviki,* "men of power" whose careers began in the military or the KGB. To some observers, Putin's reliance on military and security officials is moving the country in a dangerous direction, emphasizing order and control over (sometimes chaotic) democracy.

so-called "power ministries" allows the office a great deal of influence in foreign affairs and domestic security.

As in the United States and other presidential or semi-presidential systems, it is difficult to remove the Russian president, with impeachment possible only on a charge of high treason or another "grave" crime. The impeachment process must first be approved by the high courts, after which two thirds of both houses of parliament must vote in support of the president's removal. In 1999, the parliament attempted to impeach President Yeltsin on various charges, including his 1993 conflict with the legislature, economic reform, and the war in **Chechnya.** None of the charges passed.

In contrast to that of the president, the prime minister's role is to supervise those ministries not under presidential control and propose legislation to parliament that upholds the president's policy goals. The Russian prime minister and other members of the cabinet, unlike their counterparts in many other parliamentary systems, are not appointed from and do not reflect the relative powers of the various parties in parliament. Because of the president's ability to choose the prime minister and other members of the cabinet, there is less of a need to form a government that represents the largest parties in parliament. Instead, Russian prime ministers to date have largely been career bureaucrats chosen for their technical expertise or loyalty to the president rather than party leaders who have climbed the ranks in parliament. This description includes the current prime minister, Mikhail Fradkov, originally a Soviet bureaucrat who worked on economic affairs. This dependent relationship weakens the prime minister's power, as the office does not wield a parliamentary base of support that could be mobilized independent of the president.

THE LEGISLATURE

Given the power of the Russian presidency, does the national legislature have any real role? The absence of clout would certainly be consistent with the Soviet past. Under Communist rule, the legislature served as little more than a rubber stamp, meeting for a few days each year simply to pass legislation drafted by party leaders. Today, Russia's parliament has little direct influence over the course of government, but it would be an exaggeration to say that nothing has changed since Soviet times.[8]

Russia's bicameral parliament is known officially as the Federal Assembly. It comprises a lower house, the 450-seat State Duma, and an upper house, the 178-seat **Federation Council.** Members of both houses serve four-year terms, with power residing in the lower house. The Duma has the right to initiate and accept or reject legislation and may override the president's veto with a two-thirds vote. The Duma also approves the appointment of the prime minister, though repeated rejections can lead to its dissolution. As in other legislatures, the Duma can call a vote of no confidence in opposition to the prime minister and his government. Should a no-confidence vote pass, the president may simply ignore the decision. If a second such vote passes within three months, however, the president is obliged to dismiss the prime minister and cabinet and call for new Duma elections.

In the instances of prime-ministerial approval and votes of no confidence, then, the Duma wields unpredictable weapons. The Duma's opposition to the prime minister (and, by extension, the president) could lead to its own dissolution. Under the right circumstances, however, the Duma's opposition could lead to elections that strengthen the position of opposition parties. Of course, the exact opposite could also occur. Thus far, the Duma has not put this power to use, though in 1998 the Yeltsin administration was forced to withdraw a candidate for prime minister after he was rejected twice. In that case, the president feared new elections would only bring more anti-Yeltsin representatives into the Duma.

Another area in which the Duma wields some power is in the drafting of legislation. During the Yeltsin administration, the majority of legislation originated in the Duma, much of it dealing with substantial public issues. This has changed under the Putin administration, however, and most legislation now originates with the president or prime minister. This is in keeping with most European parliamentary systems and is perhaps a sign that there is now greater legislative-executive cooperation than existed under Yeltsin. Others might contend that it reflects the increased power of the executive in recent years.

As the upper house, the Federation Council's powers are less extensive than those of the Duma. The Federation Council primarily serves to represent local interests and act as a guarantor of the constitution. The body represents each of the eighty-nine federal administrative units, with two representatives from each. Since 2002, one representative has been selected by the governor of each region and another by the regional legislature. Although the Federation Council does not produce legislation, it must approve bills that deal with certain issues, including taxation and the budget. Other Duma legislation may also be considered by the Federation Council if it acts within two weeks of the proposal's passage by the lower house. If the Federation Council rejects legislation, the two houses compromise in order to approve it, or the Duma may override the upper house with a two-thirds vote. The Federation Council also has the ability to approve or reject presidential appointments to the Constitutional Court, declarations of war and martial law, and international treaties.

THE JUDICIAL SYSTEM

One of many tasks that Russia faces in the coming decades is the establishment of the rule of law. By this we mean a system in which the law is applied equally and predictably, with no individual being exempt from its strictures. Prior to Communist rule, Russia had not developed any real traditions of a law-bound state: the czar acted above the law, viewing the state, society, and economy as his subjects and property. This continued into the Soviet era. Under Stalin, any legitimate legal structures were undermined by the arbitrary use of terror and the vast secret-police force that maintained its own courts and jails. While these excesses were curbed after Stalin's death, the legal system remained an important means by which opposition to the Communist regime could be checked. Moreover, no constitutional court existed. By definition, the party represented the true expression of the people's will and therefore by definition could not act in an unconstitutional manner. In reality, the party was not representative of the people's interests. The lack of legal safeguards served only to undermine public confidence in the political order.

Given the history of weak legal institutions, it has been difficult to generate the rule of law in the post-Communist era. Since 1991, Russia has faced an explosion in corruption, as privatization and marketization have generated new fortunes and allowed those with political power to gain access to new sources of wealth. Organized crime has also become a serious problem, with criminals actively trafficking in drugs, prostitution, money laundering, and private-business "protection." Meanwhile, the public has little faith in the state to protect it or mete out justice.

At the top of the Russian legal structure lies the **Constitutional Court.** First developed under Mikhail Gorbachev's reforms in the late Soviet era, the Constitutional Court has nineteen members, nominated by the president and confirmed by the Federation Council to serve fifteen-year terms. As in other countries, the court is empowered to rule on such matters as international treaties, relations between branches of government, violations of civil rights, and the impeachment of the president. It has the power of both abstract review (the ability to rule on constitutional issues even when a case has not been brought before it) and concrete review (the ability to rule on specific cases). One role the Constitutional Court does *not* play is that of a court of last appeal for criminal cases; this is the responsibility of the Supreme Court.

In the 2000 presidential campaign, Putin promised to implement a "dictatorship of law," leading observers to debate whether the president hopes to strengthen the legal system (and thus democratic institutions) or build police powers that would check crime, but at the risk of authoritarian rule. Thus far the results are open to interpretation. The international corruption-watchdog group Transparency International ranks countries on a 10-point scale, with 1 being the most corrupt; in 2004, Russia was given a rating of 2.8, similar to that of India and below China. This is up from 1999, when Putin entered office; then Russia had a rating of 2.4, but the improvement has been modest.

Other areas of Russia's legal system have seen less progress. One notable problem is that regional authorities (such as governors, regional legislatures, and local courts) often disregard Constitutional Court rulings and operate according to laws that have been declared unconstitutional. However, President Putin's recent efforts to centralize power may mean that this independence will become a thing of the past. At the same time, the wide and growing scope of presidential powers has escaped challenge by the court. Part of this may be a function of the court's support for Putin, but another important factor is that as an institution the Constitutional Court remains very weak. Should it challenge a powerful president and be ignored, it would undermine its own credibility.[9]

The Electoral System

Like its other institutions, Russia's electoral structure has changed dramatically over the past fifteen years. In the late Soviet period, the president of Russia was indirectly elected by the republic's Congress of People's Deputies. Just prior to the 1991 coup, the presidency was made a directly elected office; Yeltsin won the election and retained the office when Russia became an independent country. Since that time, Russians have elected their president directly. Elections were held in 1996, when Yeltsin was reelected; in 2000, when Putin came to office; and in 2004, when Putin was reelected. Presidential elections are relatively straightforward: if no candidate wins a majority in the first round, the top two candidates compete against each other in a second round. In 2000 and 2004, Putin won a majority (over 70 percent in 2004), eliminating the need for a runoff. As mentioned earlier, no president can serve more than two terms, with each term lasting four years. In all three presidential elections, voter turnout was over 60 percent.

The Duma has also held regular elections. Between 1990 and 1993, these elections were conducted using a plurality system of single-member districts (SMDs), as in the United Kingdom and the United States. With the 1993 constitution, however, Russia adopted a mixed system similar to that found in Japan and Germany. That is, half the seats in the Duma are elected through a plurality system, and the other half are selected in multimember districts (MMDs) using proportional representation (PR), in which the share of the vote given to a party roughly matches the percentage of seats it is allotted. In addition, Russia relies on a 5 percent threshold for the PR section of the ballot, to keep smaller parties out of the parliament. Parties that do not win at least 5 percent of the PR vote are not awarded any seats, though they may still win individual seats in the SMDs.

A mixed electoral system such as Russia's typically generates two large parties, with several smaller parties usually necessary to form a ruling coalition. However, these provisions have not yet led to the consolidation of political parties that one might expect. Political parties (and the Duma) have remained highly fragmented and subject to dramatic turnover from election to election. In the 1993, 1995, and 1999 elections, six or more parties held at least 5 percent of the seats in the Duma, and only once did a party win even one third of the total seats. Overall, parties remain weakly institutionalized and unstable. Perhaps as a result, voter turnout for the Duma elections has been lower than that for the president: 65 percent in 1995, 60 percent in 1999, and 56 percent in 2003.

This current electoral system is facing dramatic change. Putin has submitted legislation to eliminate all SMDs, to be replaced in the 2007 elections with a pure PR system and a 7 percent threshold. The president has explained this reform as a way to make the system more efficient by consolidating political parties. Critics see instead another means by which the president can keep independent candidates from winning seats, as is more likely in the SMDs, where unaffiliated independents can run for office.

Local Government

One of the greatest battles within the institutional framework of Russia over the past fifteen years has been between the central government and local authorities. Just as tensions between Soviet central power and the republics contributed to the dissolution of the Soviet Union, so, too, has Russia confronted centrifugal tendencies since 1991. Like the Soviet Union that preceded it, Russia is a federal system, with a bewildering array of eighty-nine different regional bodies: twenty-one republics, 50 *oblasts* (provinces), six *krays* (territories), ten autonomous *okrugs* (districts), and two federal cities (Moscow and St. Petersburg).

Each of these bodies has different rights, not just for each category, but within the bodies in each category as well. The twenty-one republics, for example, represent particular non-Russian ethnic groups and enjoy greater rights, such as the ability to have their own constitution and a state language alongside Russian. In the early 1990s, several republics went so far as to make claims of sovereignty that amounted to near or complete independence; in Chechnya, the result was outright war against the central authorities, which continues today (see "Current Issues"). Other federal bodies are much weaker. Thus there is **asymmetric federalism,** a system in which power is devolved unequally across the country and its constituent regions, often as the result of specific laws negotiated between a region and the central government. Each of the eighty-nine territories, regardless of its size or power, has its own governor and local Duma; as described above, the governor appoints one representative to the Federation Council, and the Duma appoints the other.

The Putin administration has taken several steps to reduce regional power and make the territories comply with national laws and legislation. As mentioned earlier, one major step in 2000 was the creation of seven new federal districts that encompass all of Russia and its constituent territories. Each region is headed by a presidential appointee, who serves to bring the local authorities more directly under presidential control. Shortly after the creation of these districts, Putin also managed to change the Federation Council. Previously, membership comprised the governors and Duma heads of each region. Since 2002, however, these individuals may only appoint representatives to the Federation Council, not serve in it themselves. Again, this can be seen as an attempt by Putin to weaken local authorities' power by removing them from the national legislature.

In 2004, Putin enacted a new round of changes to further curb local power. Following this decree, all local governors were appointed by the president rather than elected directly, with their appointments subject to confirmation by the local legislatures. Putin clearly sought to rationalize legal and administrative structures in the country as a way to increase overall state capacity and efficiency. At the same time, it is apparent that Putin believes that greater state capacity can come only through greater state autonomy, subordinating local authorities to a chain of command that leads directly to the president. This again raises the danger of an overly powerful president whose authority reaches all the way to the local level.

POLITICAL CONFLICT AND COMPETITION

The Party System and Elections

The Russian transition from a one-party system to a multiparty democracy has not been easy. Russia has yet to see the institutionalization of political parties with clear ideologies and political platforms. In most democracies, parties serve to articulate and aggregate preferences and hold elected officials accountable. It is hard to say that such a system currently exists in Russia. Instead, multiple parties rise and fall between elections, for a number of reasons. The relative weakness of ideology among the public (see "Society") contributes to some extent. A second factor is the power of the presidency. Largely divorced from the legislature and its party politics and standing alongside a weak prime-ministerial office, the presidency has contributed to the creation of parties that largely serve one individual's presidential ambitions. Making clear distinctions between the parties—or even keeping track of them—is thus difficult.[10] However, we can create a few categories.

COMMUNIST AND LEFTIST PARTIES

Since 1991, the strongest and most institutionalized party has been the **Communist Party of the Russian Federation (CPRF),** successor of the Soviet-era organization. Though banned by Yeltsin in 1991, the party was allowed to reorganize and draws support from a substantial portion of the population that is ambivalent about or hostile to the political and economic changes that have taken place since the 1980s. The CPRF has done consistently well since the 1993 elections, when it captured 10 percent of the Duma's seats; in the 1995 elections it increased this share to one third, becoming the largest sin-

Average Voter Turnout, 1945–2000	
Country (number of elections)	**Eligible Voters Voting (%)**
South Africa (1)	85.5
United Kingdom (15)	74.9
Japan (21)	69.0
Iran (2)	67.6
France (15)	67.3
India (12)	60.7
Russia (2)	**55.0**
United States (26)	48.3
Mexico (18)	48.1
Brazil (13)	47.9
Nigeria (3)	47.6
China	NA

Source: "Turnout in the World: Country by Country Performance," International Institute for Democracy and Electoral Assistance

http://www.idea.int/vt/survey/voter_turnout_pop2.cfm (accessed 27 January 2006).

gle party in the Duma. Although its vote share declined in the 1999 elections, it remained the single largest party in the Duma. CPRF's head, Gennady Zyuganov, also did well in the 1996 and 2000 presidential elections, coming in second on both occasions. The party also boasts a membership of approximately a half million members, far larger than any of the other Russian parties.

The CPRF differs from most other post-Communist parties in Eastern Europe; many of these parties broke decisively from their Communist past in the 1990s and successfully recast themselves as social democratic organizations. In contrast, the CPRF remains close to its Communist ideology, though it has recently attempted to move in a more social democratic direction. Although the party has cooperated to some extent with the Putin administration, it remains largely an oppositional force. The CPRF has benefited from its organizational strength and membership base, though this legacy from the Soviet era is also a liability. As the Russian population ages, the CPRF will be forced to recast its ideological message to appeal to a younger base or risk (literally) dying out.

In the 2003 elections, the CPRF was also challenged by the new Motherland Party, an umbrella of left-wing and nationalist organizations led by a former CPRF member of the Duma. Motherland's combination of nationalist and leftist rhetoric cut deeply into the CPRF's base of support, and there were widespread accusations that the party had in fact been created by the Putin government to weaken the CPRF.

LIBERAL PARTIES

In spite of Russia's move to capitalism, liberalism has made relatively few inroads into political life. Liberalism has had a standard bearer in **Yabloko,** however, formed in 1993 and led by Grigory Yavlinsky, a former economic adviser to Mikhail Gorbachev. As a party, Yabloko is pro-Western and pro-market economy, favoring stronger ties to the North Atlantic Treaty Organization and the European Union and criticizing the war in Chechnya. Yabloko draws support from white-collar workers and urban residents in the major cities, and its orientation can be described as somewhere between liberalism and social democracy.

Since 1999, Yabloko has faced competition from a new liberal party, the **Union of Right Forces (URF).** A coalition of smaller parties and groups, the URF is headed by Boris Nemtsov and Anatoly Chubais, who were members of Boris Yeltsin's cabinet. In the 1999 elections, the URF gained 7 percent of the seats in the Duma, and some expected that the URF and Yabloko might merge in order to boost their electoral chances. This did not occur, and in the 2003 elections neither party made it over the 5 percent proportional-representation (PR) threshold required for a seat in the Duma (though each won a handful of seats in single member districts).

Why has liberalism found such rocky soil in Russia? Several factors are at work. First, given the historically statist and collectivist nature of Russian politics, a liberal political ideology is not likely to find a wide range of popular support. Second, Russia's middle class, a likely base of liberal support, remains relatively small. Third, the division of votes between two liberal parties has not helped matters. Finally, both Yabloko and URF have been tainted by accusations that they were instruments of the **oligarchs,** individuals who became rich in the aftermath of Communism, often through connections to the government. One such oligarch who supported Yabloko and URF was Mikhail Khodorkovsky, former head of the Yukos oil company, who was arrested in October 2003 on questionable charges (see "Current Issues"). This is ironic, given that every major party, including the Communists, actively courted top Russian businessmen as parliamentary candidates for the 2003 elections. Prompted by their poor showing in the 2003 elections, Yabloko and URF continue to discuss a merger in advance of the 2007 elections.

NATIONALIST PARTIES

During the 1990s, one of the most infamous aspects of the Russian party spectrum was the strength of nationalism, as manifested by the ill-named **Liberal**

Democratic Party of Russia (LDPR), headed by Vladimir Zhirinovsky. Neither liberal nor democratic, the LDPR espoused a wild rhetoric of xenophobia and anti-Semitism, the reconstitution of the Soviet Union (by force if necessary), and a general hostility toward liberal capitalism and democracy.[11] In the 1993 elections, many observers were shocked by the LDPR's electoral strength, when it gained 14 percent of the seats in the Duma. Since that time, the LDPR's fortunes have waned to the point where it barely met the 5 percent PR threshold in the 1999 elections. In the 2003 elections, however, the LDPR staged something of a comeback. This resurgence can be attributed in part to the party's consistent support in the Duma for Putin and his government.

PARTIES OF POWER

Although the **parties of power** represent the largest segment of parties in the Duma, they cannot be described in ideological terms. Russia's parties of power can be defined as those parties created by political elites to support their political aspirations. Typically, these parties are highly personalized, lack specific ideologies or clear organizational qualities, and have been created by prime ministers during or following their time in office. For example, the Our Home Is Russia Party was created in advance of the 1995 Duma elections as a way to bolster support for Prime Minister Victor Chernomyrdin and President Yeltsin. Lacking any specific ideology, the party nevertheless took the second largest share of seats (after the CPRF). Once Chernomyrdin left office, in 1998, the party's share of support rapidly declined. Subsequently, in the 1999 elections, two contending parties of power emerged. Fatherland–All Russia was formed to advance the presidential aspirations of former prime minister

DUMA ELECTION, 1995–2003 (% OF SEATS WON)			
Party	**1995**	**1999**	**2003**
Communist Party of the Russian Federation	33	20	11
Yabloko	10	5	<1
Union of Right Forces	*	7	<1
Liberal Democratic Party of Russia	11	4	8
Fatherland–All Russia	*	10	*
Our Home Is Russia	14	*	*
Unity and United Russia	*	18	49
Motherland Party	*	*	8
*Party either disbanded or did not exist at this election.			

Yevgeny Primakov and Moscow mayor Yuri Luzhkov. Meanwhile, Unity was created to bolster Putin's campaign. After Unity beat Fatherland–All Russia handily in the Duma elections, Primakov and Luzhkov withdrew from the presidential campaign, and in 2001 the two parties merged to form United Russia, essentially climbing on to the bandwagon of power. Former Interior Minister Boris Gryzlov currently leads United Russia. Drawing on Putin's popularity and the government's increased control over the electoral process, United Russia swept the 2003 elections.

Overall, the 2003 Duma elections showed a disturbing move away from democracy. Ideologically oriented parties declined in favor of the current party of power and its nationalist allies, all of which appeared interconnected by business and government ties. The media, now largely in the hands of the state, clearly served those parties favored by Putin and his allies. While international observers could not point to any examples of voter fraud, the use of state resources to favor some parties clearly distorted the outcome to such an extent that it is difficult to call this a free and fair election.

Civil Society

As with political parties, civil society in Russia has developed in fits and starts, starting largely from scratch. Prior to the 1917 Russian Revolution, civil society was weak, constrained by low economic development, authoritarianism, and feudalism. With the revolution, what little civil society did exist quickly came under control of the Soviet authorities, who argued that only the party could and should represent the "correct" interests of the population. A wide range of corporatist institutions were thus created to link the people to the party, through the workplace, the media, culture, and even leisure activities. Those few remnants of independent organized life, such as religion, were brought under tight control. With the advent of glasnost in the 1980s, however, civil society slowly began to reemerge. The first independent group that resulted from liberalization may have been the fan club of a Moscow soccer team, established in 1987. By late 1989, tens of thousands of groups had appeared and were playing an important role in eroding Soviet rule.

Since that time, civil society has continued to grow in Russia, and over 300,000 organizations—focused on such issues as health care, the environment, human rights, gender, and ethnicity—are currently registered with the Russian authorities. But this growth has come with difficulties, and it faces new challenges. One problem is financial: many groups find it difficult to raise money and often turn to international organizations for support. Although this is not necessarily a bad thing, it weakens the link between local organizations and their constituents and raises the danger that such groups will be viewed as instruments of foreign concerns.

A second problem is that the growth of civic groups has heightened tensions in some areas. This is particularly the case in the area of religion. Historically, Russians have been overwhelmingly, if nominally, Orthodox Christians, with smaller numbers belonging to other faiths, such as Islam. Although Soviet-imposed atheism seriously weakened the role of religion, in recent years Orthodox Christianity has to a degree reclaimed its role in public life. At the same time, however, new religious movements have emerged, ranging from evangelical Christians to various New Age groups. The Orthodox Church has strongly criticized them, and in 1997 the Russian government placed restrictions on the ability of new religious groups to pros- elytize or build seminaries and educational programs. Many have criticized this restriction on the democratic right to express one's faith, but others have defended it as a necessary step to defend the public against "danger- ous cults."

This leads us to a third concern: that through such regulations the gov- ernment is seeking to co-opt civil society, pulling it into a tighter orbit around the state by legislating what kinds of organizations can and cannot exist and what they can and cannot say. The government has been particularly aggres- sive in opposing civic groups that are openly critical of current policy in such areas as the environment and the war in Chechnya. Tools to control civil soci- ety include the tax code, used to investigate sources of income; the process of registering with the authorities, which can be made difficult; and police harassment. The government has also brought espionage charges against envi- ronmental activists who have called attention to such issues as the dumping of radioactive waste by the Russian military. Compounding matters, Russian civil society has seen much of its financial and human capital dry up as inter- national donors have been discouraged from supporting Russian nongovern- mental organizations.

Whatever the fate of civil society in Russia, it will have little success if it is unable to express views and promote agendas openly. This requires not only basic civil rights but also independent institutions that can amplify these con- cerns, such as the press. Here, too, Russia faces problems. The collapse of Communism saw the emergence of a lively Russian media that for the first time was able to speak critically on an array of issues. Many of the most pow- erful segments of the media, however, such as radio and television, remained in the hands of the state or came under the control of oligarchs with ties to Yeltsin. Indeed, Yeltsin's victory in the 1996 elections was attributed in part to the strong support he received in the media, whose owners feared the reper- cussions should the Communist candidate come to power. Similarly, the media were seen as strong supporters of Putin in recent parliamentary and presidential elections. In spite of this support, Putin has put strong economic pressure on many independent stations since 2000, employing economic and legal tactics to acquire them and curb their editorial independence. In the past few years, all of the largest private television stations have come under direct or indirect state ownership. To be fair, these were hardly objective stations in their previous lives—most of them served as the mouthpiece of their oligarch owners. But with their nationalization, the Russian media have become much less diverse and clearly oriented toward supporting those in power. Although a few open media outlets remain, particularly newspapers, their audience pales in comparison with radio and TV audiences, and they are often under pressure from the Kremlin to provide a more pro-government slant. Given the overwhelming support that the electronic media gave to Putin's allies in the 2003 Duma elections, the muzzling of the press is an important development.

SOCIETY

Ethnic and National Identity

The Soviet Union, like the Russian Empire before it, was an ethnically diverse country made up of a number of republics, each representing a particular ethnic group. The dissolution of the Soviet Union eliminated much of this ethnic diversity, however. Today Russia is overwhelmingly composed of ethnic Russians, part of a larger family of Slavic peoples in Eastern Europe who are linked by similarities in language (and, to a lesser extent, culture and religion). Inside and outside the borders of the former Soviet Union there are Slavic peoples, such as Ukrainians, Poles, Belarusians, Serbs, Czechs, and Slovaks. In some areas, there is a strong affinity among the Slavs; in others, animosity is more the norm.

Over 80 percent of the Russian population is ethnically Russian, and although there are scores of minority groups, none represents more than 4 percent of the population. These minorities include other Slavic peoples, indigenous Siberians who are related to the Inuits of North America, and a host of others whose communities were absorbed into Russia as part of its imperial expansion over time. Russia is also dominated by a single religious faith, Orthodox Christianity, a branch of Christianity that is separate from the Roman Catholicism and Protestantism that dominate Europe.

NATIONAL IDENTITY AND CITIZENSHIP

The fact that ethnic Russians make up an overwhelming percentage of the Russian population has not helped the country avoid ethnic conflict. As in many other countries, Russia faces the problem that some of its ethnic groups have developed nationalist aspirations and seek greater autonomy from the central authorities, even to the point of outright independence. Serious eth-

ETHNIC GROUPS

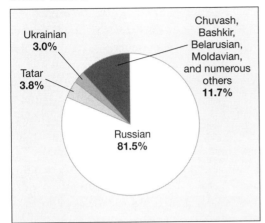

RELIGION

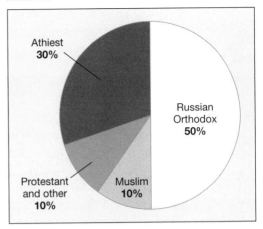

nic conflicts have been most prominent among non-Russian populations in the mountainous region known as the **Caucasus,** in southwestern Russia, near the Black Sea and Turkey. This area is home to a diverse mixture of non-Slavic peoples with distinct languages, customs, and religious faiths. Whereas only about 10 percent of the Russian population is Muslim, Islam is the dominant faith in many parts of the Caucasus.

Most notable is the case of Chechnya (see "Current Issues"). With the collapse of the Soviet Union in 1991, the various republics broke off to form independent states. Chechnya, however, was not a republic in its own right but rather part of now-independent Russia. Many Chechens believed that they, too, should have the right of independence and so began to agitate for an independent state. The conflict eventually led to outright warfare between Russian military forces and Chechen rebels, in which much of the Chechen capital was demolished and tens of thousands of civilians were killed or left homeless. During the mid-1990s, an uneasy peace allowed Chechnya to function as a de facto independent country, but in 1999 Russian forces reinvaded Chechnya in the aftermath of a series of apartment-house bombings in Russia that may or may not have been the work of Chechen rebels. Indeed, it was the second invasion of Chechnya during Putin's tenure as acting president that helped pave the way for his 2000 presidential victory. Although Russian forces have regained nominal control over the region, the conflict continues.

Ideology and Political Culture

Consistent with our discussion of political parties, political ideologies in Russia are also very much in flux. Since 1917, essentially one ideological viewpoint was legally tolerated—that of communism. Alternative views on the relationship between freedom and equality were long suppressed by the Soviet system. People could read Marx but not Jefferson or any other political thinker with a different view. Since 1991, Russia has experienced a much greater diversity of ideas, but in many ways those ideas have not made a deep impact on political life. This is particularly true in the case of democratic values. Although public opinion surveys indicate that people do believe that individual freedom has increased, it is not clear that such freedoms are fully valued. For example, a 2004 survey indicates that the protection of democratic rights is of far less importance to Russians than economic and social concerns.

Perhaps not surprisingly, then, the one clear ideology that remains powerful in Russia is Communism, though it, too, attracts only a minority of public support. Alternative concepts such as liberalism and social democracy have fared even worse. And as we have seen, parties attempting to campaign on the basis of these ideas have been unable to communicate with the public effectively or succeed at the ballot box. Instead, parties that are built more on current issues and personalities than objective or lasting values predominate. Overall, Russians tend not to identify themselves with any package of values that we might recognize as an ideology.

Again, part of this situation may simply be a question of time. After more than seventy years of one dominant ideology and a painful economic and political transition, Russians have yet to fully adapt debates over freedom and equality to their own circumstances. But might there be broader factors at work? Some observers argue that the development of economic order and a stable democracy are not simply functions of time or generational change. Rather, the Russian ideology may largely be shaped by the country's political culture, which is not so easily overcome or transformed. According to this view (and one that we alluded to in the introduction), the Russian political culture has come to emphasize a number of values that conflict with Western democratic institutions. These "Russian values" include deference to hierarchy, trust in a single powerful leader,

THE CHECHNYA CONFLICT

Source: University of Texas at Austin, http://www.us-history.org/images/chechMaps.jpg (accessed 27 July 2005)

hostility toward individual ambition and risk taking, and general suspicion of institutions. All these factors, it is argued, lead to weak support for the rule of law and democracy as a whole. Does Russia remain outside the West? Is it unlikely to join the advanced democracies in embracing similar political, economic, and social institutions? We will turn to this question again as we speak of Russia's place in the world.

POLITICAL ECONOMY

How does one build capitalism—with its private property and open markets—in a country that historically has had little of either? This is the challenge now facing Russia as it moves away from communism, and as with other aspects of the new nation, the results have been mixed: the new economic system is neither

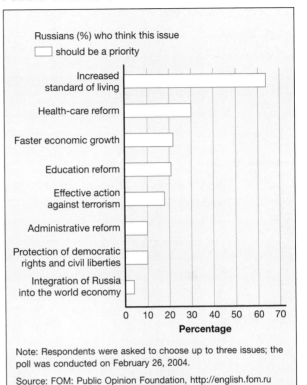

PUBLIC OPINION ON KEY ISSUES

Russians (%) who think this issue should be a priority

- Increased standard of living
- Health-care reform
- Faster economic growth
- Education reform
- Effective action against terrorism
- Administrative reform
- Protection of democratic rights and civil liberties
- Integration of Russia into the world economy

Percentage

Note: Respondents were asked to choose up to three issues; the poll was conducted on February 26, 2004.

Source: FOM: Public Opinion Foundation, http://english.fom.ru

Communist nor fully capitalist. Russia's political economy remains in a state of transition—or, more skeptically, in a state of paralysis or stagnation.

Like other former Communist countries, Russia undertook a series of dramatic reforms in the 1990s in order to privatize state assets and free up market forces. Looking to the lessons of Poland and acting on the advice of Western economic advisers, Russia opted for a course of **"shock therapy,"** rapidly dismantling central planning and freeing up prices with the hope that these actions would stimulate competition and the creation of new businesses. The immediate result was a wave of hyperinflation—in 1992 alone, the inflation rate was over 2,000 percent. Savings were wiped out, the economy sank into recession, and tensions between President Boris Yeltsin and the parliament deepened, helping to foster the violent clash between the two branches of government in 1993. The GDP contracted dramatically; only in the late 1990s did it begin to grow again.

At the same time, Russia began the process of privatization, which was equally problematic. Privatization started with the distribution of vouchers to the public so that Russians could purchase shares that would give them ownership in formerly state-owned businesses. In many cases, however, businesses were not sold off to a large number of shareholders but became subject to **insider privatization,** with the former directors of these firms acquiring the largest shares. Therefore, wealth was not dispersed but concentrated in the hands of those who had strong economic and political connections. Despite the power of this old *nomenklatura* elite, however, a small number of new businessmen quickly emerged from various ranks of society, taking advantage of the environment to start new businesses and buy old ones, amassing an enormous amount of wealth in the process. It is this group that came to be known as the oligarchs. The oligarchs were noted for their control of large amounts of the Russian economy (including the media), their close ties to the government, and the accusations of corruption surrounding their rise to power.

The problem of the oligarchs was compounded in 1996, when the government instituted the loans-for-shares program. Strapped for cash (and fearful of a Communist Party victory in the 1996 presidential elections), the Yeltsin administration chose to borrow funds from the oligarchs in return for shares in those businesses that had not yet been sold off by the state—in particular, the lucrative natural-resources industry and the energy sector. Overall, foreign investment played a very small role in the Russian privatization process.

Debate continues over whether the particular policies of marketization and privatization were a mistake. Critics argue that market reforms failed to take into account the institutional constraints of Russia, among them the absence of private enterprise, a weak civil society and a risk-averse culture, the absence of the rule of law, and the centralization and large scale of industry. Moreover, the privatization process was not geared toward encouraging foreign investment and a greater distribution of assets but toward empowering a narrow elite that could support those in power. Others retort that given the weakness of the economic and political institutions in Russia, no reform was likely to be easy and that, if anything, Russia suffered from reforms that were too conservative rather than too radical. Despite these differences of opinion, Russia's ongoing economic problems are not simply the result of economic reform. Many of them were a function of the Soviet order that had reached a crisis stage, an event that any policy would have been forced to confront.

LABOR FORCE BY OCCUPATION

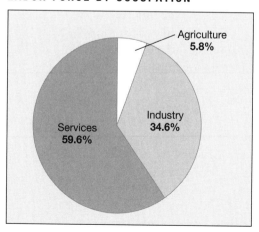

Agriculture 5.8%

Industry 34.6%

Services 59.6%

Where do the economic reforms of the 1990s leave Russia today? Certainly, we can point to a number of gloomy statistics and observations. Poverty rates in Russia are high, ranging from 20 to 50 percent of the population, depending on how the numbers are calculated. Inequality is another problem, with rates more comparable to those in less developed countries than to those in Western Europe or North America. Economic growth, while on the rise after a number of years of contraction, has been predicated largely on the export of natural resources such as oil and gas rather than the development of finished products or services. Businesses by and large continue to be hindered by state regulations, high taxes, corruption, organized crime, and insider connections. Observers have noted that one result of these hindrances is that Russia has become a country of many very small businesses and a few very large ones. Small enterprises are able to fly under the radar, escaping the detection of state officials and organized crime, while very large firms wield enough clout to manage problems with the state or the crime world on their own (and are themselves often connected to government, criminal activity, or both). But medium-size firms lack the ability to either escape notice or fend off adversaries. This is bad for Russia; according to one government estimate, poor regulations alone cost the country nearly US$6 billion a year. These problems limit foreign investment, serving as a form of protectionism or quasi mercantilism. As a result, foreign direct investment in Russia is half that of far smaller ex-Communist countries in Eastern Europe, like Hungary and the Czech Republic.

Still, there is room for optimism. In spite of the chaotic nature of privatization and marketization, approximately 80 percent of Russia's GDP is now in private hands, and the country does have a growing middle class. Still, many worry that Russia's recent growth, driven as it is by high oil prices, will prove an unsustainable source of economic development in the long run.

As part of its reform plans, the administration of President Vladimir Putin has sought to boost economic activity through a variety of new policies. Some tax and property-rights reforms have been implemented, and further changes in this direction could help establish a predictable climate for business and foreign investment. At the international level, Russia is negotiating entry into the World Trade Organization as a way to promote exports and investment and may join by 2007. Finally, Putin has gone after a number of the oligarchs (see "Current Issues") in order to restrict their power, though this action seems directed less at fostering economic development than at bringing under heel those who might use leverage to influence the government. It also raises the question of whether even large firms can fend off the interference of the Russian state.

The Russian economy faces a number of thorny issues, such as the decline of its older infrastructure, education, and social services. Liberalizing markets

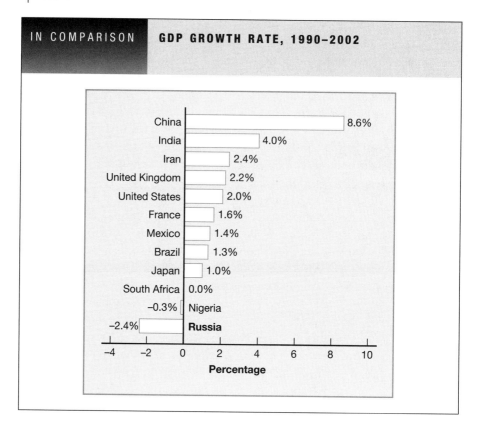

IN COMPARISON

IN COMPARISON   GDP GROWTH RATE, 1990–2002

China — 8.6%
India — 4.0%
Iran — 2.4%
United Kingdom — 2.2%
United States — 2.0%
France — 1.6%
Mexico — 1.4%
Brazil — 1.3%
Japan — 1.0%
South Africa — 0.0%
Nigeria — –0.3%
Russia — –2.4%

Percentage

and property rights alone will not be enough to make Russia prosperous—doing so will also require investments in society. For a state with relatively limited budgetary resources, this is a major challenge.

FOREIGN RELATIONS AND THE WORLD

Like the United Kingdom, Russia must deal with its status as a former super-power. Yet unlike the United Kingdom, Russia has been forced to confront this change suddenly and dramatically. Not long ago, the Soviet Union was one of the world's most powerful countries, boasting an impressive military, a nuclear arsenal, and a network of allies around the world. One of Mikhail Gorbachev's reforms was to reduce hostility between the Soviet Union and the West in order to foster greater cooperation between the superpowers. Lit-tle did he (or others) expect that this reconciliation would create such tur-moil. The collapse of the Soviet Union has left Russia in an odd situation as it considers its role in the international community.[12] Russian pride was dealt a blow when the Soviet Union splintered and the United States emerged as an unequaled international military power. Thus, while Russia can benefit from a strong relationship with the United States, there is a sense that it is no longer an international actor that must be taken seriously.

This can be seen in part in the slow eastward expansion of the North Atlantic Treaty Organization (NATO) and the European Union (EU). NATO was founded in 1949 as an international alliance that stood in opposition to the Soviet Union, but since 1989 many post-Communist countries have sought membership in it in order to cement their relationship with Western Europe and the United States. Russia has cooperated with NATO but has also criticized it, still viewing it as an organization opposed to Russian interests. One specific source of tension was the 1990s wars in the former Yugoslavia, in which Russia expressed greater sympathy with the Serbs, a Slavic people who share the culture and Orthodox Christianity of many Russians. In contrast, NATO eventually intervened on behalf of the Muslims in Bosnia and Kosovo. Russia also strongly opposed NATO's eastward expansion, in which it incorporated a number of former Communist countries, arguing that this action would increase tension and instability in the region. Yet NATO continued to expand in spite of Russian pressure, with the Czech Republic, Hungary, and Poland (all former Soviet satellites) joining in 1999. In 2004, Lithuania, Estonia, and Latvia (all once part of the Soviet Union) gained full NATO membership, alongside the former Soviet allies Bulgaria, Romania, Slovakia, and Slovenia.

Today NATO is less oriented toward defending its members against a Russian attack than it is focused on generating stability among the member states and fostering cooperation to defend against threats to regional stability (such as terrorism). Yet Russia remains outside NATO, and the two entities remain wary of each other's intentions. As part of its enlargement, NATO created a council designed to give Russia a voice in its policy. This did not extend any real power over NATO actions, however; that would require Russia's membership in the body, which is unlikely. Some NATO members (particularly those formerly under Soviet control) continue to harbor fears that Russia could again turn hostile toward its European neighbors. Russia, too, has reservations: NATO membership would symbolize (and in some ways finalize) its loss of power and final submission to U.S. supremacy. Clearly, Russia's international role is complicated by internal and external uncertainties about its relationship to the world. Yet in spite of sporadic tensions, Russia, NATO, and the United States have continued to build a cooperative relationship. This is an impressive feat considering that not long ago these entities were poised to wipe one another off the face of the earth.

Just as Russia confronts an ever-larger NATO alliance on its western border, it must also contend with the enlargement of the European Union. In May 2004, the EU accepted ten new countries into its ranks, including three (Estonia, Latvia, and Lithuania) that had once been part of the Soviet Union, bringing the EU up to the borders of Russia. However, there are no expectations or beliefs that Russia can (or will) join the EU. As with NATO, Russian membership would require the country to surrender its self-perception as an independent world actor and transfer sovereignty to international institutions. It would also necessitate substantial reform of all levels of domestic institutions and demand a political solution to the ongoing crisis in Chechnya. But expanding EU integration threatens to further marginalize Russia from Europe. Already, formerly Communist EU candidate countries have reoriented their economies, turning them away from the Russian market; the political, cultural, intellectual, and even linguistic ties that once linked Russia to Eastern Europe are quickly disappearing. Both the EU and NATO continue to move inexorably eastward, incorporating countries once allied with or part of the Soviet Union and further isolating Russia in the process.

If Russia's international future is not (yet) wedded to the West, what role might it play? Russia has thus far been content to function on the periphery of the international community, seeking to restore and maintain relations with its Soviet-era allies. Russia also retains connections with the world's few remaining Communist states, such as North Korea, and with Iran. It has also improved its ties with China, though it fears China's growing power.

In seeking to reassert its power over the former Soviet republics, Russia has joined the **Commonwealth of Independent States (CIS),** a loose integrationist body that incorporated many former Soviet republics after 1991. The CIS has little power, however, and is hardly an EU in the making. Russia has also been involved militarily in civil conflicts in the former Soviet Union, stationing troops in Central Asia and the Caucasus, thereby exerting influence over these regions and their important commodities, such as oil. Yet even in these areas, Russia's authority has been threatened. In 2001, the U.S. military stationed troops in Uzbekistan in advance of its invasion of Afghanistan, and in 2005 a series of mass demonstrations in the Ukraine dislodged the pro-Russian presidential candidate after charges of voter fraud and Russian meddling. Increasingly, leaders across the CIS who once supported Russia are looking more toward the EU as well as toward the United States. For Russia, this is humiliating.

Russia still holds a vast arsenal of nuclear weapons, a fact that might alone qualify it as a superpower—except that its military has shrunk so dramatically that it can no longer assume any significant international role. Russia's soldiers are underpaid and untrained, and their equipment is outdated. This decline raises fears that Russia's weapons of mass destruction—chemical, biological, and nuclear—could be (or already have been) stolen or sold to other states or to terrorists. Western observers are particularly concerned about Russia's bioweapons capacity, which was actively developed under the Soviet regime despite the international treaties in which it promised to abandon such research.

KALININGRAD: A RUSSIAN ISLAND IN A EUROPEAN SEA

The complicated relationship between Russia and the European Union is symbolically represented in the case of Kaliningrad, a Russian port city seized from Germany during World War II. After the region's Germans were forcibly expelled, it was made an important Soviet naval base. With the dissolution of the Soviet Union, however, the city was cut off from continental Russia and has since lagged behind its neighbors in economic and social development. The average wages in Kaliningrad are one third those in Poland, and its rate of AIDS infection is among the highest in Europe. To make matters worse, when the bordering states of Lithuania and Poland joined the EU in 2005, Kaliningrad was surrounded by an international organization to which it does not belong. The main benefits of the EU, such as free trade and the free movement of peoples, do not apply to the residents of Kaliningrad, leaving them isolated from both Europe and Russia. Some in Kaliningrad now speak of seeking a more autonomous status within Russia, so that they might increase their integration into the EU. In a way, Kaliningrad symbolizes Russia as a whole. While Russia is not removed from Europe, its connections are tentative and ambivalent, and these ties could either deepen or decline as the EU grows in size and expands its powers.

Some observers fear that a Russian strain of weaponized anthrax or smallpox could fall into the wrong hands or that Russian technicians might be tempted to sell this scientific expertise.[13] Russia and the international system as a whole continue to deal with the legacies of Russia's superpower status, legacies that represent not only changes in policy and organization but also a shift in Russia's understanding of its place in the international system.

Russia has historically vacillated between the poles of international engagement and isolationism. During its isolationist phases, Russians have argued that their country is somehow separate from Europe and the West, different in culture, religion, and historical traditions—and to a certain extent, this is true. Public opinion surveys have indicated that nearly half of all Russians do not consider themselves European and think that Russia confronts a worldwide conspiracy against them.[14] Still, at many points in its history Russian leaders sought to learn from and engage in the outside world, modernizing their institutions with the goal of becoming an important international actor. Under Soviet rule, these divergent tendencies were fused to create a great revolutionary power with global aspirations. This outward-looking ideology eventually dissipated, however. Now that the union has been dissolved and Russia's Communist ideology abandoned, it cannot pursue isolationism while aspiring to the status of an international power. The country may break with its superpower past and seek to become a "normal" state, with the diplomatic and military capabilities commensurate with a country at its level of development. If it does not, Russia may remain trapped as a shadow of its former self, caught between the nostalgia of its former stature and the painful realities of the present.

CURRENT ISSUES

THE WAR AGAINST THE OLIGARCHS

One of ongoing issues in Russia over the past fifteen years has been the rise of the so-called oligarchs. This term is often used to describe anyone with a large amount of wealth in Russia, but more specifically it refers to those individuals who (through a combination of smart business moves and political connections) amassed large fortunes in the early 1990s. Most of this wealth is directly connected to the loans-for-shares deal of 1996, in which many of the crown jewels of the economy (such as oil and minerals) were sold off to a new business elite. By the mid-1990s, the oligarchs were playing a powerful role in Russia through their share of the economy, their ownership of media, and their close ties to the administration of Boris Yeltsin.

Under President Vladimir Putin, the situation has changed, though not necessarily for the better. When he assumed the presidency, Putin made clear his view of the oligarchs: they stood as obstacles to his plans for reform and consolidation of power. Putin moved quickly to curb their power. Charges of tax evasion and various other crimes were brought against a number of the most powerful business owners, forcing several to flee the country to avoid arrest. The Kremlin also forced many oligarchs to sell off their assets, including the television stations they owned. To be sure, many Russian and international observers approved of these measures, viewing the oligarchs as robber barons who had enriched themselves at the expense of the country.

But this battle is not simply a case of a new government cleaning up a corrupt economic system. What appears to be important for Putin is not that the economy functions with a level playing field but rather that those with economic power be subordinate to the Kremlin. A good example of this can be found in the October 2003 arrest of Mikhail Khodorkovsky, who was head of the Yukos oil firm, on charges of fraud and tax evasion. Khodorkovsky, like most oligarchs, had amassed his wealth in the 1990s through rather questionable means. But over the past several years, his firm was frequently noted for its high standard of corporate governance. So why was he arrested? The answer, it would seem, is that Khodorkovsky (like several fallen oligarchs before him) had begun to use his wealth to support political organizations like Yabloko and the Union of Right Forces and the few media outlets still critical of the Kremlin. In contrast, oligarchs who have aligned themselves with Putin's United Russia or affiliated parties have not undergone investigation, and many have become part of Putin's administration. This campaign against the oligarchs, then, raises the issue of the rule of law in Russia: if the law is to be respected, it must be applied equally to all citizens, including political rivals. In the aftermath of Khodorkovsky's arrest, many investors worried that any private business could be subject to attack if it threatened the Kremlin in any way. Others have worried that Putin is effectively renationalizing parts of Russia's economy by using fabricated legal charges to seize control of private firms. Putin's war against the oligarchs may be part of his quest for a "dictatorship of law," but the result may be more dictatorship than law. Recently, Putin has stated that he will no longer review the privatizations of the 1990s with an eye toward prosecution. This may help build domestic and international confidence in the economy, if his promises are kept.

CHECHNYA, ISLAMIC FUNDAMENTALISM, AND TERRORISM

The Chechen war is important to understand not only because of its impact on Russian politics but also for the way in which it has become part of the larger battle over terrorism and Islamic fundamentalism. The origins of this war are similar to other nationalist struggles in the Soviet Union: by 1990, nationalist Chechens, who had long resented their subordination to Soviet rule, began to agitate for greater autonomy (some for outright independence from Russia). In 1991, nationalist Chechens declared independence, and rising tensions between Russia and Chechnya led to all-out war from 1994 to 1996.

Until that time, this struggle was clearly nationalist in nature, with Chechens viewing themselves as a distinct ethnic and cultural group with their own nationalist aspirations. The first Chechen war quickly took on religious overtones, however. Islamic militants, many of whom had fought the Soviets in Afghanistan, came to Chechnya "to defend Islam" against Russian forces. With their arrival came a fundamentalist view of Islam much more militant and literal than that of the Sufi branch of the faith that had been practiced in the region for centuries. The brutal nature of the conflict, in which thousands of innocent Chechens were killed and much of the region was destroyed, radicalized many who remained.

By 1999, when Russia invaded again, the Chechen war had taken on a fundamentalist quality, and with it the use of terrorism became a more common practice. In 2002, Chechen rebels seized control of a theater in Moscow, threatening to kill their hostages if the war was not ended immediately. Russian forces eventually stormed the building, first administering a powerful narcotic gas, which killed over 100 hostages. In 2004, two passenger planes were downed by suicide bombers, killing 89, and the Moscow-installed president of the Chechen Republic was assassinated. In 2005, Chechen terrorists seized a school in the town of Beslan, taking over 1,000 hostages. When a terrorist bomb apparently went off prematurely, the chaos inside and outside the school led to an open firefight between terrorists, military forces, and armed civilians who had gathered at the scene. In the end, 300 died, mostly children. There are few prospects for the resolution of this conflict anytime soon. If anything, Russia's recent assassination of one of the Chechens' more moderate rebel leaders means that leadership may pass into the hands of more radical figures, who take Al Qaeda and its notion of international jihad (rather than national independence for Chechens) as their inspiration.

NOTES

1. Hakon Stang, *The Naming of Russia*, Meddelelser Occasional Paper, no. 77 (Oslo: University of Oslo, 1996), www.hf.uio.no/east/Medd/PDF/Medd77.pdf (accessed 26 July 2005); see also Nicolas Riasanovksy, *A History of Russia* (New York: Oxford University Press, 1963).

2. A fascinating Soviet-era interpretation of Ivan's leadership can be seen in the Sergei Eisenstein film *Ivan the Terrible* (1945).

3. For a discussion of this period, see Richard Pipes, *Three "Whys" of the Russian Revolution* (New York: Vintage, 1995).

4. Mary McAuley, *Soviet Politics: 1917–1991* (New York: Oxford University Press, 1992), pp. 26–27.

5. See Robert Conquest, *The Great Terror: A Reassessment* (New York: Oxford University Press, 1991), and Anne Applebaum, *Gulag: A History* (New York: Doubleday, 2003).

6. For a discussion of the last days of Soviet rule, see David Remnick, *Lenin's Tomb: The Last Days of the Soviet Empire* (New York: Random House, 1993).

7. Oleh Protsk, "Ruling with Decrees: Presidential Decree Making in Russia and Ukraine," *Europe-Asia Studies* 56 (July 2004): 637–60.

8. For more on the Russian legislature see Thomas F. Remington, *Politics in Russia*, 2nd ed. (New York: Pearson-Longman, 2002).

9. See Alexei Trochev, "Implementing Russian Constitutional Court Decisions," *East European Constitutional Review* (Winter/Spring 2002), pp. 95–102, and "Less Democracy, More Courts: A Puzzle of Judicial Review in Russia," *Law and Society Review* (September 2004), pp. 513–48.

10. For more on political parties in Russia see Michael McFaul, "Party Formation and Non-Formation in Russia," *Working Papers* 12 (May 2000), Carnegie Endowment for International Peace, http://www.ceip.org/files (accessed 27 July 2005).

11. See Vladimir Petrovich Kartsev and Todd Bludeau, *Zhironovsky* (New York: Columbia University Press, 1995).

12. For a discussion see Gabriel Gorodetsky, ed., *Russia between East and West: Russian Foreign Policy on the Threshold of the Twenty-first Century* (Portland, OR: Frank Cass, 2003).

13. Geoff Brumfiell, "Russia's Bioweapons Labs: Still Out in the Cold," *Nature*, 12 June 2003, pp. 678–80.

14. Russia Votes, Centre for the Study of Public Policy, University of Strathclyde, Glasgow, and Levada Center, Moscow, http://www.russiavotes.org/ (accessed 27 July 2005).

KEY TERMS ════════════════════════════════

asymmetric federalism   p. 211

Caucasus   p. 219

Chechnya   p. 206

Cheka   p. 200

Commonwealth of Independent
   States (CIS)   p. 226

Communist Party of the Russian
   Federation   p. 212

Constitutional Court   p. 209

czar   p. 198

Duma   p. 199

Federation Council   p. 207

Federal Security Service (FSB)
   p. 205

glasnost   p. 202

insider privatization   p. 222

KGB   p. 200

Kremlin   p. 204

Liberal Democratic Party of Russia
   p. 215

nomenklatura   p. 200

oligarchs   p. 214

Orthodox Christianity   p. 196

parties of power   p. 215

perestroika   p. 202

Vladimir Putin   p. 203

Rus   p. 196

siloviki   p. 206

soviets   p. 199

shock therapy   p. 221

Union of Right Forces   p. 214

Yabloko   p. 214

Boris Yeltsin   p. 202

WEB LINKS ════════════════════════════════

Russian and East European Network and Information Center
   inic.utexas.edu/reenic/countries/russia.html

Carnegie Endowment for International Peace, Russian and EurAsian
   Program   **www.carnegieendowment.org/programs/russia**

Russia Daily Journal **www.russiajournal.com**

Russian Center for Public Opinion and Market Research
   www.wciom.ru/default_e.htm

Transitions Online, News source covering the former Soviet Union and
   Eastern Europe   **www.tol.cz**

Mikhail Gorbachev's Web site   **www.mikhailgorbachev.org**

PBS Special on post-Communist Russia
   www.pbs.org/newshour/bbeurope/russia/1991/index.html

Kremlin Government Site, English-language version   **www.kremlin.ru/eng**

The Federation Council   **www.council.gov.ru/index_e.htm**

Yabloko, English-language version   **www.eng.yabloko.ru**

Open Society Institute   **www.soros.org**

7 CHINA

Head of state: President Hu Jintao
(since March 15, 2003)

Head of government: Premier Wen Jiabao
(since March 16, 2003)

Capital: Beijing

Total land size: 9,596,960 sq km

Population: 1.306 billion

GDP at PPP: 7.26 trillion US$

GDP per capita: $5,600

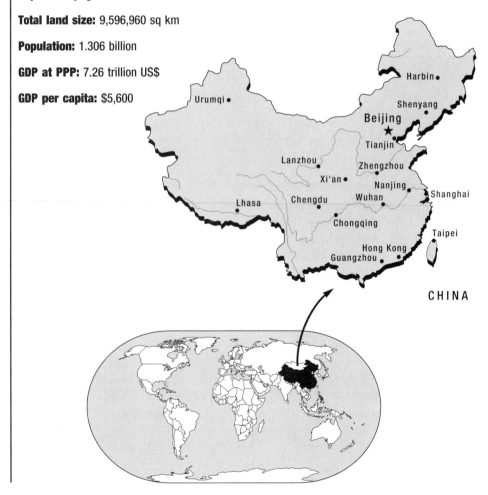

CHINA

INTRODUCTION

Why Study This Case?

Napoléon Bonaparte is said to have described China as a "sleeping giant." Centuries later that description continues to resonate, though with every passing year it seems less and less appropriate. Today, most observers agree, China is finally stirring after centuries of slumber, with repercussions that are transforming the world. But it is not simply these changes that draw our attention; after all, China is not the first, nor the only, country to undergo dramatic change. Rather, it is that these changes are taking place in a country that we tend to speak of in superlatives, qualities no other country can easily match.

The first of China's superlatives is its history, which extends back at least 4,000 years. Several millennia before most modern nations and states existed in even rudimentary form, China had taken shape, creating a relatively unified country and people. To be certain, China was torn apart innumerable times during this process by civil strife and external invasion. Yet in spite of these difficulties, a continuous Chinese civilization has existed for thousands of years and directly shapes and informs modern Chinese society and politics.

Second is China's sheer size. It is the most populous country in the world, with over 1.3 billion people. This is four times the population of the United States, which totals approximately 287 million. With the exception of India (whose population is also more than 1 billion), no other country's population even comes close to China's. Overpopulation has been both a source of concern for the Chinese government and a lure for foreign businesses that have dreamed for centuries of the profits that could be gained if they could somehow tap this vast market.

This leads to a third superlative quality, China's recent and rapid development. In centuries past, China was one of the most powerful empires in the world, easily dominating its much smaller neighbors. China saw itself as the center of the world. Over time, this superiority would lead to isolation and from isolation to stagnation. Foreign imperialism in the nineteenth century would force China open but would also lead to war and revolution. By the time of the Communist takeover in 1949, foreign powers had finally been expelled, and China was once again enjoying a period of isolation. But starting in the late 1970s, the ruling Chinese Communist Party introduced more liberal economic policies while maintaining its tight control over political power. Known as **reform and opening,** these changes would lead the country to a period of growth unmatched in the world. Between 1975 and 2000, China's GNP grew at an average rate of 8 to 9 percent a year—*double* the current rate of the other fast-growing Asian tigers such as South Korea and Singapore and *quadruple* the average growth rates of the United States, Japan, and Great Britain.

This amazingly rapid economic development is underlined by the fact that six of the ten tallest buildings in the world can now be found in China. Visitors to the city of Shanghai stand awestruck before the massive skyscrapers that now line the banks of the Huangpu River. At the same time, political reform has been much more limited, and public protests for change, such as the Tiananmen Square protests in 1989, have garnered violent reactions from the Communist regime. In this sense, China stands in stark contrast to Russia, whose transition from Communism made way for greater democracy but came at the expense of economic decline and marginalization from the rest of the world.

As a result of reform and opening, millions of Chinese have risen out of poverty over the last several decades. At the same time, these economic reforms have led to the closure of many inefficient state-owned businesses and have jeopardized the livelihoods of millions of workers. China is thus engaged in a precarious race to reform itself before the shock of these changes overwhelms the country. This economic modernization is not only transforming the physical and social landscape of the country but also reshaping international finance and trade. While it often goes unrecognized, China is becoming a central factor in globalization. Indeed, the recent flood of cheap Chinese exports into the world market has displaced numerous workers beyond China's borders and has substantially lowered global inflation. At the same time, its voracious consumption of oil and other raw materials has raised concerns of global shortages. Now that the giant is awake, its development will have profound effects on the world.

Major Geographic and Demographic Features

We have already noted that China boasts the largest population in the world. Not surprisingly, it is also one of the largest countries in terms of landmass, exceeded only by Russia, Canada, and the United States. Its physical size allows for a range of climates and geographic features. The southwestern portion of the country, including Tibet, is known for its mountain ranges (the Himalayas and the Altai), and most of the northwestern Xinjiang region is desert. The northeastern portion, bordering Mongolia and Russian Siberia, is marked by bitterly cold winter temperatures. Not surprisingly, most of the Chinese population is concentrated in the southern and seaboard portions of

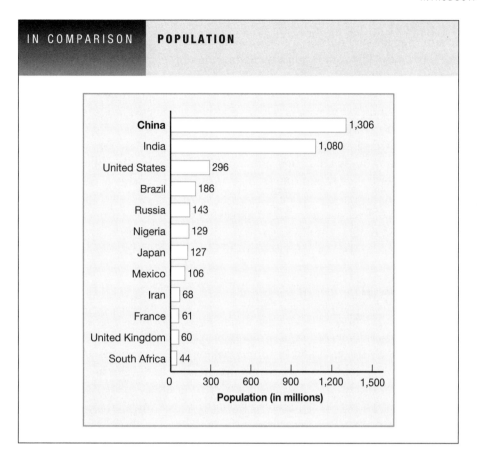

IN COMPARISON   **POPULATION**

China — 1,306
India — 1,080
United States — 296
Brazil — 186
Russia — 143
Nigeria — 129
Japan — 127
Mexico — 106
Iran — 68
France — 61
United Kingdom — 60
South Africa — 44

0   300   600   900   1,200   1,500

Population (in millions)

the country, where the climate is more temperate and there is greater rainfall, yielding the majority of China's arable land. Intersecting this region are the two lifelines of China, the Yellow (Huang He) and Yangtze (Chang Jiang) Rivers, which flow east toward the Pacific Ocean. The Yangtze is currently the focus of much domestic and international attention due to the ongoing Three Gorges Dam project. The largest ever constructed, by 2009 this dam will generate millions of kilowatts of electricity (something desperately needed in China) and will help prevent the flooding that has been a recurrent problem. Critics have argued that the dam will destroy countless historic sites, displace millions of people, and cause major environmental damage. Moreover, failure of a dam this size would have catastrophic results.

Given the country's large population and landmass, the Chinese are a puzzlingly homogeneous population, with over 90 percent of the population considered part of the main ethnic group, known as Han. This stands in contrast to the persistence of ethnic diversity in Europe, Africa, and South Asia, even within individual countries. What explains the difference? The answer lies in the geography. The southern portion of the country is not only more amenable to human habitation but also lacks the extreme geographic barriers, such as high mountains and deserts, that impede travel and migration. Historically, the Yellow and Yangtze Rivers connected much of the country, allowing knowledge, foods, animals, and culture to spread more easily than in other parts of the world. Such connections helped foster the emergence of a single Han identity, though not always intentionally. The lack of land barriers made it much easier for early empires to develop and bring a large area under their control. China was first unified as early as 221 B.C.E., and with political centralization the diverse cultures and languages of southern China were slowly absorbed into the larger Han identity. It is at this point in history that we can begin to speak of the emergence of a singular Chinese state.

Historical Development of the State

The paradox of China's political development is how a country with such an ancient civilization and such early political centralization could become such a weak state by the twentieth century, lacking both capacity and autonomy. But a closer examination reveals that China's early development and later weakness are closely related. The country's first political leaders can be traced to the Shang dynasty, which reigned from the eighteenth to the eleventh century B.C.E., two thousand years before European states would appear in their earliest forms. It was during this time that written Chinese (characters) first appeared. Power in the country was decentralized, however, and wars between various rivals were commonplace. It was only much later, during the Qin dynasty (221–206 B.C.E.), that a single Chinese empire (and the name China) would emerge. During this period, China first experienced political centralization, with the appointment of nonhereditary officials to govern provinces, the minting of currency, the development of standard weights and measures, and the creation of public works such as roads, canals, and its famous Great Wall.

CENTRALIZATION AND DYNASTIC RULE

This centralization and expansion of sovereign power was carried on by the subsequent Han dynasty (206 B.C.E.–220 C.E.), a reign marked by great cultural development, the rise of domestic and international trade, foreign exploration, and conquest. At this time, China was far ahead of Europe in its understanding of timekeeping, astronomy, and mathematics. The philosophy of **Confucianism** influenced the imperial leaders, with its emphasis on a fixed

TIME LINE OF POLITICAL DEVELOPMENT

Year	Event
1700 B.C.E.	Beginning of Chinese civilization under Shang dynasty
221 B.C.E.	Unification of China under Qin dynasty
1839–42	First Opium War
1911	Overthrow of Qing dynasty
1919	May Fourth movement
1921	Founding of Chinese Communist Party (CCP)
1934–35	Long March
1937–45	Second Sino-Japanese War
1949	Founding of the People's Republic of China (PRC)
1958–60	Great Leap Forward
1966–76	Cultural Revolution
1978	Deng Xiaoping launches reform and opening
1989	Tiananmen Square massacre
2001	China's accession to the World Trade Organization (WTO)

set of hierarchical roles, meritocracy, and obedience to authority. Confucianism in turn helped foster the development of the Chinese civil service, a corps of educated men chosen on the basis of exams testing their familiarity with Confucian thought. The notion of a professional civil service based on competitive exams would not emerge elsewhere in the world for centuries.

With the collapse of the Han dynasty, China would be divided for nearly four centuries, until the Sui and Tang dynasties (591–907 C.E.). With these dynasties, the unity of the empire was restored, the bureaucratic institutions of the Han period resurrected, and the economic and cultural life allowed to flourish once again. The institutionalization of the bureaucracy also helped foster the development of a gentry class, made up of landowners and their children, who were groomed from birth to join the bureaucracy. This bureaucratic class would become the glue that held China together. Subsequent dynasties would continue to rely upon the bureaucracy to maintain Chinese unity, even when new dynasties were established by foreign conquerors, as under the Yuan (Mongols) and the Qing (Manchus). Such continuity helped foster economic development and innovation, which continued to advance faster than in Europe and other parts of the world.

AFFLUENCE WITHOUT INDUSTRIALIZATION—AND THE FOREIGN CHALLENGE

At the advent of the Ming dynasty (1368–1644), China still led the world in many areas of science, economics, communication, technological innovation, and public works. Such knowledge laid the foundation for modernization and industrialization, yet these processes did not take place. During these three centuries, Europe experienced the Renaissance, international exploration, and the Industrial Revolution, while Chinese innovation and economic development began to stagnate around 1400. By the mid-1400s, the Chinese empire had banned long-distance sea travel and showed little interest in developing many of the technological innovations it had created. Why did this occur?

There are several possible reasons. One argument is cultural. Confucian thought helped establish political continuity and a meritocratic system in China, but over the centuries these ideas became inflexible and outdated. During the early twentieth century, bureaucratic examinations were still based on 2,000-year-old Confucian texts. Rigid Confucian ideology placed China at the center of the world (and universe), viewing any new or outside knowledge as unimportant and rejecting changes that might disrupt the imperial system.

A second argument is economic. During the early centuries of the Chinese Empire, entrepreneurialism was the main path to wealth. But with the rise of the bureaucratic elite, this role became a more powerful means of personal enrichment, particularly through rent seeking and corruption. The financial rewards of public employment led many in the upper classes to divert their most talented children to the civil service. It also concentrated economic power in the hands of the state, while business activity was stunted by a Confucian distain for commerce and steep, arbitrary taxation (naturally, the bureaucracy opposed any reforms that might threaten its privileges).

A third argument is geographic and furthers the points above. The geographic factors that facilitated early unification and continuity also limited competition, since there was less danger that a lack of innovation might lead to destruction by outside forces. In Europe, by contrast, innumerable states continuously vied for power, making isolation impossible and conservatism a recipe for economic and military defeat. No one power in Europe could ban seafaring or abolish the clock; states that resisted progress and innovation soon disappeared off the map. China, however, could reject technology and embrace isolationism since there were no rival powers to challenge such policies. In short, a combination of cultural, economic, and geographic forces allowed China's lengthy isolation.

Europe's economic and technological development continued, and its age of exploration and conquest began just as China was closing itself to the outside world. The Portuguese first reached China by 1514, and during the sixteenth and seventeenth centuries other European traders tried to expand these initial contacts. These remained tightly controlled by the Chinese, however, and attempts to expand connections were futile. In perhaps the most famous example, a British trade mission led by Lord Macartney was rebuffed by the Chinese emperor, whose reply to King George III read: "I set no value on objects strange or ingenious, and we have no use for your country's manufactures."[1]

But the Chinese Empire was losing its ability to ignore the outside world, and external forces were beginning to test China's power. The First Opium War (1839–42), with Great Britain, resulted in a resounding Chinese defeat, forcing China to cede Hong Kong to the British and pay restitution. Various western powers quickly demanded similar access, and subsequent wars with the French and the Japanese only further extended the control of imperial powers over the country. Foreign pressures in turn contributed to growing domestic instability.

THE EROSION OF CENTRAL AUTHORITY: CIVIL WAR AND FOREIGN INVASION

By the beginning of the twentieth century, the centralized authority of the Chinese state, developed over two thousand years, effectively crumbled. In 1911, a public revolt finally swept away the remnants of the Qing dynasty, and China was declared a republic, but it soon fell under the control of regional warlords. In the midst of this chaos, two main political organizations formed to compete for power. The Nationalist Party, also known as the **Kuomintang (KMT),** slowly grew in strength under the leadership of **Sun Yat-sen.** The party was aided by student protests in 1919, known as the **May Fourth movement.** These nationalist revolts rejected foreign interference in China and called for modernization, radical reform, and a break with traditional values and institutions, including Confucianism.

The second organization was the **Chinese Communist Party (CCP),** formed in 1921 by one of the leaders of the May Fourth movement. Though the KMT's Sun had been educated in the United States, both parties received support from the recently established Soviet Union. In fact, the Soviets saw the KMT as a more likely contender for power than the CCP and hoped to move the KMT into the Soviet orbit. Following Sun's death in 1925, relations between the KMT and the CCP unraveled. Chiang Kai-shek, head of the KMT's armed forces, took control of the party and expelled pro-Soviet and pro-CCP elements. Chiang also ensured that both warlords and the CCP were brutally suppressed in areas under KMT control. By 1928, the KMT had emerged as the effective leader of much of the country, while the CCP was pushed out of the cities and into the countryside. The KMT quickly shed any pretense of democracy, growing even more dictatorial and corrupt.

During the repression of the CCP, power within the party began to pass into the hands of **Mao Zedong** (1893–1976). Deviating from the Marxist convention that revolutions be led by the urban proletariat, Mao believed that a Communist revolution could be won by building an army out of the peasant class. Mao and the CCP established their own independent Communist republic within China, but KMT attacks forced the CCP to flee westward in what was later called the **Long March** (1934–35). This circuitous retreat would take the CCP and its loyal followers over 6,000 miles and cost many lives (indeed, of the 100,000 who set out on the Long March, only 10 percent would arrive at their final destination, in Yan'an). The Long March represented a setback for the CCP but strengthened the idea that the party should reorient itself toward the peasant majority. The CCP fostered positive relations with the peasantry during the Long March, which contrasted strongly with the more brutal policies of the KMT. The revolutionary ideology of the CCP and its call for equality drew all classes of Chinese to its ranks.

In 1937, both the KMT and the CCP faced a new threat as Japan launched a full-scale invasion of the country after several years of incursions. The two parties formed a united front, though they continued to battle each other even as they resisted the Japanese advance. While the war weakened KMT power, which was based in the cities, it helped bolster the CCP's nationalist credentials and reinforced its ideology of a peasant-oriented Communism of the masses. The war also forged a strong Communist military, the People's Liberation Army (PLA), geared to fight the enemy and win public support. This Chinese birth of Communism is quite different from the Soviet experience, in which a small group of urban intellectuals seized control of the state through a coup d'état. In fact, the CCP and PLA were a new state and regime in the making.

THE ESTABLISHMENT AND CONSOLIDATION OF A COMMUNIST REGIME

The end of World War II found the CCP much strengthened and the KMT in disarray. The Communists now commanded the support of much of the countryside, while the KMT's traditional urban base of support was shattered by war and tired of corruption. Communist attacks quickly routed the KMT, and in 1949 the Communist forces entered Beijing unopposed and established the People's Republic of China (PRC). Chiang and the remnants of the KMT fled to the island of Taiwan, declaring themselves the true government of China— which the United States recognized (rather than the PRC) until 1979. Taiwan continues to function independently of China, though the PRC has never recognized it and asserts that eventually the "rebel province" will return to mainland control.

The new Communist regime faced the challenge of modernizing a country that was far behind the West and ravaged by years of war. The CCP's assets, forged during the war, were its organizational strength and a newly established reservoir of public legitimacy. Forming a close alliance with the Soviet Union, China began a process of modernization modeled after the Soviet experience under Joseph Stalin: nationalization of industry, collectivization of agriculture, and central planning. At the same time, the CCP began to ruthlessly repress anyone viewed as hostile to the revolution, including landowners, KMT members and sympathizers, and others suspected of opposing the new order. Several million were killed.

EXPERIMENTATION AND CHAOS UNDER MAO

Within a few short years, however, China would diverge from the typical Soviet-style path of Communist development. This resulted partly from growing tensions between the Soviet Union and China and partly from the particular ideological facets of Chinese Communism that had developed in the wake of the Long March. Stalin died in 1953, bringing to an end his ruthless terrorizing of the Russian people. His successor, Nikita Khrushchev, openly denounced Stalin in 1956, taking tentative steps toward allowing greater personal liberty and bringing an end to the unbridled use of violence against the public.

In China, too, some liberalization took place. Mao's **Hundred Flowers campaign** of 1956 encouraged public criticism and dissent, though it was soon ended and the most prominent critics removed from their positions of authority. Mao and other Chinese leaders began to see Soviet de-Stalinization as a retreat from Communist ideals and revolutionary change, and they upheld China as the true vanguard of world revolution. China's own experience in constructing peasant-based Communism in a largely agrarian country provided China's leaders with justification for assuming this leadership role. After all, its experiences were not dissimilar to the many anti-imperial struggles taking place across the less developed world at the time.

China's first major break from the Soviet model was the **Great Leap Forward** (1958–60). Departing from the model of highly centralized planning, Mao reorganized the Chinese people into a series of communes that were to serve all basic social and economic functions, from industrial production to health care. Each commune was to set its own policies for economic development within the guidelines of general government policy. In Mao's view, revolutionary change could be achieved by putting responsibility directly into the hands of the public, which would move the country rapidly into Communism. State capacity was thus devolved, albeit within an authoritarian system.

In the absence of clear directives and organization, the Great Leap Forward quickly faltered. For example, a campaign to increase steel production led not to the creation of large foundries staffed by skilled employees, as had happened in the Soviet Union, but produced a million backyard furnaces built by unskilled communes, which consequently produced worthless metal. Overall economic and agricultural production declined, leading to disorder and famine. In the face of this debacle, Mao stepped down as head of state in 1959 (though he remained head of the CCP), and China recentralized production and state control. Poor relations with the Soviet Union compounded these setbacks, which culminated in 1960 with the Soviet withdrawal of technical and financial support.

From this, Mao drew the conclusion that the problem was not that the CCP had been too radical but that it had not been radical enough. Soviet history proved, Mao reasoned, that without an unwavering commitment to radical change, revolution would quickly deteriorate into conservatism (as Mao saw occurring in China). He thus sought to place himself back at the center of power and re-ignite revolutionary fervor through the construction of a cult of personality. This was first captured in the publication of *Quotations from Chairman Mao*, the "Little Red Book" of Mao's sayings that became standard reading for the public.[2]

In 1966, the cult took shape as Mao and his backers accused the CCP itself of having "taken the capitalist road" and encouraged the public (particularly students) to challenge the party-state bureaucracy at all levels. Schools were closed, and student radicals, dubbed the **Red Guard,** took to the streets to act as the vanguard of Mao's **Cultural Revolution.** Authority figures (including top party and state leaders, intellectuals, teachers, and even parents) were attacked, imprisoned, tortured, exiled to the countryside, or killed. Historic buildings, writings, and works of art condemned as "bourgeois" and "reactionary" were destroyed.

By weakening all social, economic, and political institutions in China, Mao made himself the center of all authority and wisdom. The result of this new vision was years of chaos and violence as the country slid into near civil war among various factions of the state, society, and the CCP. State capacity and autonomy largely disappeared. The only remaining institution of any authority, the PLA, was finally used to restore order. The excesses of the Cultural Revolution were largely curbed by 1968, though factional struggles within the party continued until Mao's death, in 1976.

REFORM AND OPENING AFTER MAO

With Mao's death, the incessant campaigns to whip up revolutionary fervor ended, and the party came under control of leaders who had themselves been victims of the Cultural Revolution. Most important was **Deng Xiaoping** (1904–97), a top party leader from the earliest years of the CCP who had been stripped of his posts during the Cultural Revolution. In the race to take control of post-Mao China, Deng outmaneuvered Mao's widow, Jiang Qing, and her allies (known as the Gang of Four) and consolidated power. By 1979, Deng had set the nation on a very different course.

In contrast to Mao's emphasis on revolutionary action for its own sake, Deng pursued modernization at the expense of Communist ideology, in what became known as reform and opening. The government encouraged private business and agriculture and cultivated foreign relations with capitalist countries, continuing a process that began under Mao with U.S. president Richard Nixon's visit to China in 1972. It also expanded foreign investment and trade while de-emphasizing ideology. To quote Deng, "Whether a cat is black or white makes no difference. As long as it catches mice, it is a good cat." Ironically, the destruction of much of the party-state under the Cultural Revolution made these reforms easier. China began to embrace the market economy, with all of its benefits and difficulties.

One reform that did not take place, however, was political. In spite of the downgrading of Communist ideology, the CCP still maintained complete control over political life, and attempts at public debate in the 1970s were quickly silenced. Although reform and opening lifted millions out of poverty, by the 1980s serious problems had emerged, among them inflation, unemployment, and widespread corruption (particularly within the CCP). As with the May Fourth movement and the Red Guards of the Cultural Revolution, students would once again play a major role in expressing discontent over this situation. In April 1989, students gathered at Tiananmen Square, in front of the Forbidden City (the former imperial palace), to mourn the death of Hu Yaobang, a former general secretary of the CCP who had been dismissed after student protests in 1987. The eulogy quickly grew into a general protest against corruption and a call for political reform. These were calls not for an end to Communist rule but for greater public participation in decision making, not unlike what was occurring in the Soviet Union under Mikhail Gorbachev at the same time.

The demonstrators' ranks swelled rapidly. On the historically significant May 4, an estimated 100,000 students and other citizens marched in the streets of Beijing, and by May 17 an estimated 1 million people had occupied Tiananmen Square. Martial law was declared, but many protesters remained, and on June 4, the party leadership brought in the military. Several hundred protesters were killed and thousands were arrested in various clashes around the city, though those gathered at the square itself were allowed to leave. This same formula of economic reform and opening combined with persistent political authoritarianism, continued throughout the 1990s under Deng's successor, **Jiang Zemin,** and under Jiang's successor, current leader **Hu Jintao.**

POLITICAL REGIME

Despite China's past quarter century of economic reform and global trends of democratization, the country remains stubbornly authoritarian. In fact, approximately half of the world's population that does not democratically

ESSENTIAL POLITICAL FEATURES

- Legislative-executive system: Communist Party authoritarian regime
- Legislature: Unicameral National People's Congress (nominal authority only)
- Unitary or federal division of power: unitary
- Main geographic subunits: provinces
- Electoral system for lower house: NA
- Chief judicial body: Supreme People's Court

elect its leaders resides in China.[3] Certainly China's historical legacy of over 2,000 years of centralized authoritarian rule (legitimized by Confucian precepts) has buttressed the current regime. But in order to understand the nature and resilience of China's Communist authoritarianism, we must examine the ways in which political control is organized and exercised in a Communist party-state.

In spite of China's economic liberalization, its Communist party-state retains the essential organizational structure that the Chinese Communist Party (CCP) adopted from the Soviet Union. Though China's reformist leaders have almost fully rejected Marx in their embrace of market freedoms, their decision to retain a closed political system is very much in accord with Lenin's vision of the Communist party-state. Lenin contended that for the Communist revolution to succeed in Russia, a self-appointed Communist Party elite, enlightened with wisdom and imbued with revolutionary fervor, would need to serve as a vanguard on behalf of the masses. This group alone would have the organizational capacity and resolve to lead the revolutionary transition from feudalism and capitalism to state socialism and ultimately utopian Communism. The need to allow the process to unfold, Lenin argued, justified the party in maintaining a political monopoly and serving as a "dictatorship of the proletariat."

This ideological and organizational logic has had several consequences for the exercise of political control in China (as was true in the Soviet Union and other Communist party-states). Most important, it means that political authority flows *from* the party elite to those within the party, the state, and society, who are expected to submit to this authority. We examine each of these in turn.

Political Institutions

THE PARTY

The CCP is governed according to Lenin's principle of **democratic centralism,** in which "the individual Party member is subordinate to a Party organization, the minority is subordinate to the majority, the lower level organization is subordinate to the higher level, each organization and all members of the whole Party are subordinate to the Party's National Congress and the Central Committee."[4] And while party leaders have a moral obligation to provide opportunities for party members to discuss, consult, and even criticize, in fact, leaders impose all important decisions on those below them, who are expected to fully abide by decisions made at the center. In short, centralism always prevails over democracy.

THE STATE

The party elite exercise control over state (and party) officials through the *nomenklatura* system, by which party committees are responsible for the appointment, promotion, transfer, and firing of high-level state, party, and even public-industry personnel (in China's case, this comprises some 10 million positions). The party also maintains direct control over the government and bureaucracy through a political structure of "organizational parallelism," in which all government executive, legislative, and administrative agencies are matched or duplicated at every level of organization by a corresponding party organ (see the table on p. 247). These CCP bureaus supervise the work of the state agencies and assure that the interests of the party prevail. This means that although the Chinese political system has a premier, a parliament, and bureaucratic ministries, *party* officials and organizations orchestrate the policy process and direct the votes of all party members who hold elected and appointed government offices (typically more than four-fifths of all officeholders).

SOCIETY

Scholars describe ruling Communist parties as "greedy institutions" that are not satisfied with simply controlling the political process but seek to control all aspects of public and even private life. This was particularly true during the Maoist era of mass campaigns and totalitarian penetration of society. Control was maintained through the **danwei** ("unit") system, which gave all Chinese citizens a lifetime affiliation with a specific industrial, agricultural, or bureaucratic work unit that dictated all aspects of their lives, including housing, health care, and other social benefits. This organizational plan was reinforced by the *hukou* ("household registration") system, which tied all Chinese to a particular geographic location. Economic liberalization and the freedoms of private employment are gradually breaking down these traditional methods of social control, however, and China now has a **floating population** of between 100 million and 150 million itinerate workers who have abandoned their *hukou* and have no *danwei* affiliation. But the party-state is attempting to keep pace. In 2003, officials announced a plan to distribute microchip-embedded national identification cards to all 960 million eligible Chinese citizens that will store vital information and allow for the tracking of China's increasingly mobile citizenry.

We need to be very careful, however, not to overestimate the authoritarian grasp of China's political leaders. Despite these herculean efforts at control, the opening of the economy and the growing complexity of Chinese society have inevitably weakened China's authoritarian regime. Economic and financial decentralization has given local authorities and private firms the autonomy to resist central policies and develop greater independence. These changes, combined with the long-standing inefficiency of China's enormous bureaucracy and growing problems of corruption and nepotism at all levels of government (as well as the sheer size, diversity, and backwardness of much of China), also call state capacity into question. These centrifugal pressures for decentralization and general weakening of the party's power have led scholars to label China's current political regime one of "fragmented authoritarianism." Before exploring the potential consequences of this fragmentation, we first examine the political institutions of China's authoritarian rule.

THE CONSTITUTION

China is ostensibly governed by a constitution that is designated "the fundamental law of the state" and vests formal authority in both party and state executive and legislative offices. However, under the conditions of elite authoritarian rule in China, political power has not been highly institutionalized. Just as the party always prevails over the state, so Mao Zedong and his successors have been little deterred by any checks or balances inherent in the formal institutions of either the party or the state. China's supreme leaders have relied as much or more on their informal bases of power (including personal connections, age, experience, and patronage) than on their formal positions or titles. Although there has been collective agreement among current leaders to avoid a return to the tyranny of the Maoist era, political rule in post-Mao China has remained largely vested in a single "paramount" leader surrounded by a key group of twenty-five to thirty-five highly influential political elites. Though these leaders hold key positions in the party and the state, their stations simply affirm (but do not decide) their status and authority.

More fundamentally, this has meant that the Western notion of the rule of law (in which all citizens are equal under the law and are protected from arbitrary state power) has generally not prevailed in China. Most significantly during the Maoist period but even to the present, the country's legal issues have been highly politicized. Most legal institutions have been subject to the ideological priorities of the party-state and the personal motivations its leaders. Reform and opening, however, have had growing influence on legal reform as foreign investors, local entrepreneurs, and now the World Trade Organization (WTO) have begun pressing the Chinese authorities to abide by contracts and respect property rights. This newfound legal adherence is spilling over into other aspects of policy making and portends an even greater role for some of China's other formal political institutions, discussed below.

Parallel Organization of the Chinese Communist Party and the Chinese Government, 2003			
Party Office or Organ	Officeholder or Number of Members or Departments	Corresponding Government Office or Organ	Officeholder or Number of Members or Departments
Chairman	Office abolished in 1982	President (head of state)	Hu Jintao
General secretary	Hu Jintao	Premier (head of government)	Wen Jiabao
Politburo Standing Committee (PSC)	9 members	State Council Standing Committee	10 members
Politburo	24 members	State Council	43 members
Central Committee (CC)	198 members	National People's Congress Standing Committee	159 members
National Party Congress	2,979 members	National People's Congress (NPC)	2,120 members
Central Military Commission (CMC)	8 members	Central Military Commission	7 members
CMC chairman	Hu Jintao	CMC chairman	Hu Jintao
Secretariat	Large staff of the party cadre	State Council General Office	Large staff of civil servants
Party departments	Approximately 46 departments	Bureaucratic ministries	Approximately 46 ministries, bureaus, and commissions
Central Discipline Inspection Commission	121 members	Supreme People's Court	1 president and 8 vice presidents

Source: Adapted from Melanie Mannion, "Politics in China" in Gabriel Almond et al., *Comparative Politics Today: A World View* (New York: Pearson/Longman, 2004), p. 428.

STRUCTURE OF THE GOVERNMENT

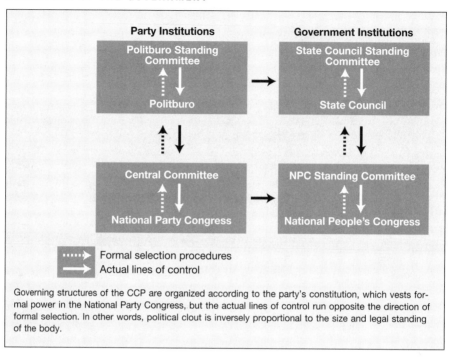

Governing structures of the CCP are organized according to the party's constitution, which vests formal power in the National Party Congress, but the actual lines of control run opposite the direction of formal selection. In other words, political clout is inversely proportional to the size and legal standing of the body.

Communist Party Institutions and Organs

Although the National Party Congress "elects" its Central Committee (CC), which in turn "selects" the Politburo, in fact the nine or so members of the Politburo Standing Committee (PSC) make up the top political leadership of China. The PSC convenes in weekly meetings headed by the general secretary of the party, currently Hu Jintao. PSC members are "elected" by the twenty-five or so Politburo members, but it is the PSC (or its dominant senior members) that typically makes national decisions. The Politburo effectively serves as China's governing cabinet, with each member of the Politburo responsible for a particular set of policy areas or issues that roughly corresponds to the ministerial portfolios of the State Council.

Technically, the Politburo, the PSC, and the general secretary are all "elected" by the CC of the National Party Congress, but in reality party leaders determine the makeup of both the Politburo and the PSC prior to the actual casting of ballots. When the 200 or so CC members vote, they do so on a ballot on which all candidates run unopposed. The CC typically meets annually and carries out the ongoing approval and endorsement of the National Party Congress between its sessions. Despite the largely ceremonial role of the CC, its members constitute the pool of China's party officials who are groomed for top leadership. However, in this system of largely informal and not-yet-institutionalized power, membership in the CC affirms, but does not bestow, this elite status.

The CC in turn is elected by the **National Party Congress,** which is the party's cumbersome legislative body, parallel to the government's National People's Congress. With nearly 3,000 members, it is far too unwieldy and meets too infrequently to conduct any real policy making. Instead, its "plenary," or full, sessions have been used as the venue for announcing changes in policies and leadership and formally endorsing the ideological "line" of the party. In recent decades, the National Party Congress has regularly convened at five-year intervals. There have been a total of sixteen party congresses from the founding of the party in 1921 through the Sixteenth National Party Congress, held in 2002, at which Hu Jintao replaced Jiang Zemin as general secretary, and the pace and focus of economic reform were reconfirmed.

Delegates to the National Party Congress ostensibly represent the more than 66 million members of the CCP organized at the provincial and local levels. In both the National Party Congress and its CC, delegates are left with few if any choices of candidates for the higher-level bodies, and their senior leaders heavily influence the choices they can make. Since 1982, however, members of the CC have been elected by secret ballot, and since the late 1980s there have actually been more candidates than seats available for the CC.

There are several other party organs worth noting. Like the government, the CCP also staffs its own bureaucracy, known as the Secretariat. The Secretariat oversees the implementation of Politburo decisions and, just as important, the distribution of propaganda in support of these decisions through its Propaganda Department. Given the important political role of China's military, party leaders have used the Central Military Commission (CMC) to retain tight control over the armed forces. The CMC reports directly to the Politburo and has always been chaired by China's paramount leader or his designee. Significantly, Jiang Zemin first relinquished his positions as general secretary of the CCP in 2002 and president of the People's Republic of China (PRC) in 2003, but retained his office of chairman of the CMC for another year. A final party organ, the Central Discipline Inspection Commission, is charged with maintaining party loyalty and discipline and rooting out corruption.

Each of the institutions discussed above is part of the central party structure located in Beijing. Each province also has a party committee with a secretary and a standing committee with departments and commissions in the pattern of the central party apparatus. Below this the party is represented by comparable organizations at the county, city, district, township, and village levels. The lower-level party leaders have often exercised a degree of autonomy, with potentially significant consequences for the devolution of authority and the political liberalization of China.

The Branches of Government

Although the national constitution designates China's legislature—the **National People's Congress (NPC)**—the highest organ of the state, government and state institutions remain subservient to party oversight. Nonetheless, day-to-day responsibilities for managing the affairs of the country are largely in the hands of the executive State Council's ministries and commissions and the NPC.

THE HEAD OF STATE

The president of the PRC is China's head of state, an entirely titular office. During the reform era, the supreme leader or his designee has always held this office. Jiang Zemin held the office from 1993 to 2003 concurrently with his positions as General Secretary of the CCP and head of the CMC. As noted above, Jiang has resigned from all three of these positions, handing them one by one to his designated successor, Hu Jintao.

THE STATE COUNCIL

The State Council, China's executive branch, is the primary organ of daily government activity and is led by the premier (who serves as head of government). The premier is recommended by the party's Central Committee and then formally elected by the NPC, which has never yet failed to choose the recommended candidate. The premier, currently **Wen Jiabao,** is typically the second- or third-ranking member of the PSC. With the assistance of several vice premiers, the premier and his cabinet of ministers and commissioners (collectively, the State Council) govern China. The council oversees the work of China's fifty or so bureaucratic ministries and commissions, which manage the country's economy, foreign relations, education, science, technology, and other affairs of the state. The ministers who lead each ministry or commission may also serve as vice premiers or hold party offices as members of the Politburo or even the PSC. Like the CCP's Politburo, the State Council also has its own standing committee, which meets twice weekly.

Historically, the State Council's primary responsibility was the management of China's socialist economy, devising the annual and five-year economic plans and managing the state-owned enterprise system. But learning perhaps from the Soviet Union's failed efforts at *perestroika*, China's State Council has shown administrative flexibility in adapting to the needs of a more open economy. Under the guidance of its party counterparts, the council's ministries and commissions formulate and implement most of China's laws and regulations.

THE NATIONAL PEOPLE'S CONGRESS

The State Council is formally appointed by China's parliament, the National People's Congress (NPC), which serves as China's legislative branch. NPC elections are held every five years, a schedule observed faithfully only since Mao's death. The NPC's nearly 3,000 delegates represent both geographic and functional constituencies (e.g., industry and the military). As with many other government and party organs, delegates are typically selected by party officials and run unopposed, rather than being democratically elected from below. The NPC typically meets annually for about two weeks and "elects" a standing committee of approximately 150 members, usually headed by a member of the PSC. This NPC Standing Committee then meets regularly as a legislative assembly roughly every two months throughout the year.

Despite having the constitutional authority to pass laws and even amend the constitution, the NPC has never had an independent or influential role in policy making. Rather, it has most often served to ratify policies already determined by central leaders. In more recent years, however, as China's economy and society have become more complex, the NPC and its standing committee have gradually become venues for delegates to offer opinions, express dissatisfaction with government policy, and even occasionally cast dissenting votes. Rival party leaders have also used the body in recent years either to promote or to slow the reform process. As its constituent committees and specialized policy groups have become more knowledgeable and sophisticated, the NPC has started to shape these policies of reform. The full NPC is, of course, still far from a democratic parliament. Like its party counterpart, the institution is too large and meets too seldom and too briefly to exert substantial influence. And while its standing committee is gaining substance, it, too, remains far weaker than both the executive State Council and (of course) the CCP.

THE JUDICIAL SYSTEM

Under China's system of authoritarian rule, the law is subject to the leaders, not the other way around. In fact, for the most part the PRC's legal system did not function under Mao, and no criminal code existed prior to 1978. Legal reforms since that time have established of a judicial system, but it remains subservient to the party hierarchy, which routinely protects officials from the law. At the same time, party leaders have often applied corruption or abuse-of-office statutes selectively and have fabricated or exaggerated crimes in order to snare political opponents or hold up one deviant as an example to others.

China has come under severe criticism from human rights groups both for its eagerness to employ capital punishment for a variety of crimes (including corruption, smuggling, theft, bribery, and rape) and for its extensive incarceration of political prisoners. Observers estimated in 2005 that some 300,000 prisoners were being held in labor reeducation camps with no access to the legal system. Amnesty International noted that during one of China's periodic "strike hard" campaigns in 2001, Chinese authorities executed more criminals (1,781) in three months than did the rest of the world in the previous three years.[5] Amnesty International also contends that an estimated 50,000 practitioners of the outlawed **Falun Gong** meditation sect have been detained as political prisoners, with many of them and numerous other prisoners of conscience subjected to torture and other inhumane conditions.

Local Government

Unlike both Japan and Europe, which experienced decentralized feudalism in the not-so-distant past, China has been unified and ruled centrally for over 2,000 years. This has led successive authoritarian regimes, including the current one, to resist notions of federalism, believing that unity and stability are possible only under strong central leadership. Central control over such a huge and diverse nation has been far from complete but has been managed through the central structure of parallel party and government rule replicated throughout the descending levels of government. This includes 27 provinces, almost 3,000 counties, 45,000 townships, and nearly 1 million villages![6] Each level is modeled on the central government, with party and government councils, administrative departments, and congresses at the provincial, county, and township levels.

But if China's authoritarian rule has always been somewhat fragmented, the increased social and political demands brought on by reform and opening are making their mark on local politics. In an effort to both shore up the legitimacy of Communist rule and address growing discontent within local communities, central political leaders have been experimenting over the past two decades with gradually increasing measures of local democratization. Initial ventures, during the 1980s, granted rural villages the right to secret ballot elections for county-level government congresses; later they were allowed to popularly elect relatively powerless "village committees" and "village heads." But by the late 1990s, increasingly brazen farmers, workers, and entrepreneurs had begun demanding the right to elect their local party secretaries who are the real locus of power at the village level.[7] Although this political liberalization has not yet "trickled up" in any formal way, its impact on the nearly 1 billion Chinese still living in local villages ought not be underestimated.

Other Institutions: The People's Liberation Army

Chairman Mao famously stated, "Political power grows out of the barrel of a gun." Later he claimed that he had not meant that military might is the means of obtaining political power but rather that "the Party commands the gun, and the gun must never be allowed to command the Party."[8] Although the CCP has sought to abide by Mao's admonition, the **People's Liberation Army (PLA),** which comprises China's army, navy, and air force, has played a significant role not just in China's revolutionary history but also in contemporary Chinese politics. Mao used the prestige and heroic stature the PLA garnered in battle prior to 1949 to add legitimacy to the Communist party-state once the PRC was established. The PLA played a key role in economic reconstruction in the 1950s, brought the Red Guard to heel during the chaotic Cultural Revolution, and smashed the protests at **Tiananmen Square** in 1989. The crackdown on the Tianamen Square demonstration left hundreds (some say thousands) of protestors dead, capturing the world's attention. In the reform period, party leaders have sought to narrow both the economic and the political roles of the military. Party leaders have forced the military to sell off its extensive industrial and commercial interests, reduce its manpower, and upgrade the PLA's professionalism and technological prowess. Even with its new "leaner" status, the PLA remains the world's largest military force, with some 2.5 million troops and a military budget of nearly US$50 billion. As discussed earlier, the party established the Central Military Commission (CMC) first within the party and later as a government agency in order to guarantee party-state control over the gun. This control seems more certain now than perhaps at any other time in PRC history.

POLITICAL CONFLICT AND COMPETITION

The Party System: The Chinese Communist Party

Although reform and opening have created new avenues of economic and social mobility in China, membership in the Chinese Communist Party (CCP) remains essential for acquiring political influence and status. Because it offers the primary path to political advancement and is also an obligatory creden-tial for many careers and appointments, membership in the CCP is both sought after and selective. In 2002, there were over 66 million registered members in the party, which is roughly 7 percent of China's adult population. Between 2 million and 3 million new members are accepted into the CCP every year. Sig-nificantly, nearly a quarter of its current members are under age thirty-five and nearly one fifth have college degrees.

While party membership has always been the chief pathway to elite recruit-ment, over time different sectors of society have gradually been targeted for inclusion in the party as the needs and priorities of the party-state have evolved. Mao Zedong's most significant contribution to Communist doctrine was his inclusion of peasants as an integral component of Communist revolution. Whereas Lenin described the Russian peasants as backward "vermin," Mao glo-rified the peasants' role in the Chinese revolution and recruited peasants to take political office in the new People's Republic of China (PRC). During the 1950s, the CCP sought to first create and then recruit a sector of industrial workers in order to establish a more orthodox (Marxist) Communist party. During the Cultural Revolution, the keys to political advancement were ideological purity and a background untainted by either feudal or bourgeois heritage.

Since Mao's death, China's reformist leaders have successively broadened the definition of political correctness in an effort to co-opt those deemed important to the reform program into the ranks of the party. Deng Xiaoping emphasized that an "ability to catch mice" (expertise), and not the "color of the cat" (political correctness), was the true measure of contribution to China's progress. He welcomed professionals, scholars, and intellectuals into the party. And in a move sure to have Marx rolling in his grave, Premier Jiang Zemin broadened the definition of the CCP in a policy known as the "Three Represents" to include not just workers and peasants, but even private entrepreneurs! Such moves have led critics to wonder how long a ruling party founded on the principle of destroying the very social class it has now chosen to embrace can endure.

But even as increasing numbers of scholars and other interested observers inside and outside China predict the collapse of CCP rule, it has managed thus far to resist both external challenges and internal decay.[9] Although the CCP's original heroic stature and revolutionary legitimacy may have little hold on China's younger generations, recent party leaders have effectively employed a mixture of authoritarian controls, patriotic nationalist appeals, and economic benefits to maintain the party's monopoly of political power.

THE SUCCESSION AND CIRCULATION OF ELITES

One of the greatest challenges to perpetuating this political dominance has been the issue of political succession. As in most authoritarian systems, China faces the problem of having no institutionalized "vice office" to ease the transition to a successor when the top leader dies. The passing of longtime leader Mao Zedong in 1976 led to a leadership crisis and caused a rancorous struggle among several elite factions. In an effort to avoid repeating this problem, Deng Xiaoping did not assume formal leadership positions in either the party or the government when he came to power two years later and launched his reforms. Although he retained his position on the Politburo Standing Committee until 1987 and chaired the Central Military Commission until 1989, Deng's only official title, until his death in 1997, was honorary president of the China Bridge Society.[10] From behind the scenes, he served as the paramount leader of China. "Third-generation" leader Jiang Zemin followed a variant of this model. After some ten years, in 2002, 2003, and 2004, respectively, Jiang stepped down from his positions as party general secretary, national president, and chairman of the CMC. Each of these positions was surrendered to his "fourth-generation" successor, Hu Jintao, who in 1992 had already been chosen by Deng Xiaoping as Jiang's successor.

In explaining the apparent success of this smooth transition from the third to the fourth generation of party leaders and the continued resilience of

China's authoritarian rule, scholars point to a number of factors. These include the willingness and ability of the party elite to follow established norms of succession, promote elites within the party based more on merit than on personal or factional connections, and carefully balance the co-opting of elites and masses by repressing organized opposition to the party.[11] The party-state's careful management of this increasingly complex society is the focus of the next section.

Civil Society

Because the CCP claims to represent all legitimate social interests, officially there is no civil society in China. By definition, any organized interests outside the party are illegitimate and potentially harmful. Accordingly, the party-state has organized a number of mass organizations to control society and mobilize social groups to fulfill national goals. Legitimate "mass organizations" formed by the CCP include, among others, the Women's Federation and the All-China Federation of Trade Unions. Such groups are led by party officials and assist the party-state in disseminating information and implementing policies. In addition, the government has organized numerous nongovernment associations during the reform period to facilitate state control of emerging economic and social interests, including small and large businesses, laborers, and other sectors. Although these are still firmly under state control, scholars point to these interest groups as potential elements of an independent Chinese civil society.

By far, the CCP's greatest gamble to date has been its 2001 decision to welcome capitalists as members of the party. In a move of political expediency that would have been incomprehensible to both Marx and Mao, Jiang Zemin argued that under the current conditions of "socialism with Chinese characteristics," the CCP ought to represent not just the interests of workers and peasants but also those of the private agents of China's "advanced productive forces." This open (if awkward) embrace of what was long considered socialism's class enemy acknowledges the growing economic influence (and political potential) of China's capitalist class. Nearly one fourth of China's GNP is produced by private companies, and when public-private joint ventures are included, these firms account for over half of China's production. China's leaders recognize that, one way or another, capitalist interests will be heard. However, their determination that such interests be heard from within the party rather than from without may indeed have "revolutionary" consequences.

It should also be noted, however, that the illegality of independent civil associations has not prevented their emergence. This was perhaps most apparent in the 1989 demonstrations of students and their supporters at Tiananmen Square. But there have been many other efforts both prior to and since that event to organize social interests outside the official confines of the party-state (in fact, the events at Tiananmen Square in 1989 were the site's third such protest during the reform era).

To date, all significant attempts to form unauthorized political or social interest groups have been swiftly repressed. After the crushing of the student movement at Tiananmen Square, perhaps the most notable instance of repression has been the party-state's campaign against practitioners of the meditative martial arts movement Falun Gong. Founded in 1992, this traditional Chinese martial arts sect was initially tolerated by the party-state as it rapidly gained adherents in small gatherings for exercise in parks and other public spaces. But in 1999, the regime labeled the sect an "evil cult" and banned the organization as it began to mount larger demonstrations and rallies, including a day-long silent protest outside the Beijing residential compound of China's top leaders. Falun Gong now reports some 60 million Chinese followers, but the regime asserts that the number of participants is less than 2 million. The party-state's determination to squelch a social movement that claims no political agenda demonstrates both the extent of state paranoia and the remarkable organizational capacity and compelling attraction of this social movement under daunting circumstances.

The increasing complexity and openness of China's twenty-first-century society—coupled with the inevitable growing pains of its ongoing economic revolution—almost guarantee that this cycle of subversive rebellion, state repression, and renewed social resistance will continue to grow. A case in point is internet usage in China, where more than 110 million Chinese netizens regularly surf and blog. The government, recently with the cooperation of the corporate giants Yahoo and Google, has assiduously sought to censor access to politically dangerous resources on the web and prevent its use for unapproved political activity. Moreover, many of these potential movements will not be easily repressed. Peasant protests against onerous taxes, local corruption, and environmental hazards, and urban workers' strikes against layoffs and horrific working conditions are both increasingly common and well organized. The Chinese government officially acknowledged some 74,000 such protests in 2004 alone. Potentially even more destabilizing is China's floating population of migrant workers, estimated at between 100 million and 150 million, numbers that may now exceed the population of Japan. These nomadic laborers have little job security, no legal residency beyond their abandoned villages, and no authorized access to housing, health care, or education.

Although none of these groups is yet an organized movement like Falun Gong or the separatist movement in Tibet, some observers predict that such grassroots movements could combine with ongoing intellectual dissidence to rekindle demands for democratization and the end of CCP rule. Can this juxtaposition of an increasingly open economic system and a persistently closed political system endure? Although there is much debate over whether China's authoritarian political system is moving toward greater liberalization or inevitable collapse, most conclude that this volatile combination is far too contradictory to prevail for long.

SOCIETY

Ethnic and National Identity

Though the Chinese commonly view themselves as a homogeneous society, China is not without ethnic diversity. China is populated mostly by Han Chinese (who make up about 92 percent of the total population) but recognizes at least fifty-five minority nationalities. Although minorities make up only a small percentage of the population, many reside in strategic "autonomous areas" (such as Tibet and Xinjiang) that make up more than 60 percent of China's territory and have a long and often violent history of resistance to the Chinese state. Even among Han Chinese there is tremendous linguistic diversity, as the map on p. 259 illustrates. For thousands of years, Han Chinese have shared a written language, but Han speakers are divided into eight main language groups and hundreds of dialects. The majority of Chinese (about 800 million) speak Mandarin, but many also speak some form of Wu (90 million) or Yue (also known as Cantonese; 70 million).

Since the twentieth century, Beijing has sought to make Mandarin (and the Beijing dialect of Mandarin) the official language of government and education. Despite these attempts, Mandarin is not spoken universally in rural China, and its use has actually declined in prosperous urban areas along China's southern coast. Indeed, the inability of China's Communist regime to

ETHNIC GROUPS

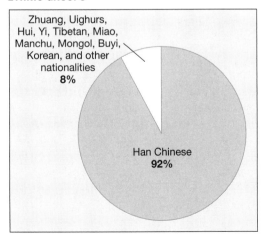

Zhuang, Uighurs, Hui, Yi, Tibetan, Miao, Manchu, Mongol, Buyi, Korean, and other nationalities
8%

Han Chinese
92%

RELIGION

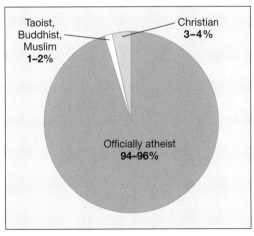

Taoist, Buddhist, Muslim
1–2%

Christian
3–4%

Officially atheist
94–96%

impose a uniform national language calls into question its capacity and suggests that local resistance to central control is stronger than often assumed.

Ideology and Political Culture

Chinese political culture is in a state of flux, and much will remain unknown until more extensive public-opinion data (banned until very recently) are available. During the rule of Mao Zedong, the Chinese Communist Party (CCP) attempted to reshape China's traditional political culture through massive propaganda, mobilization, and repression. The importance of Communist ideas has waned since the time of Mao's death, especially as a capitalist economy has come to coexist with state socialism. Communist ideology still has strong rural influence, but China's cities reflect a growing diversity of information and ideas.

TRADITIONAL CENTRALIZED AUTHORITARIANISM

Mao viewed China's "poor and blank" population as ripe for the party-led makeover of political culture, but traditional Chinese political culture was far more resilient than Mao had imagined. Before the Communists took power in 1949, China had a long history of centrally imposed authoritarian politics. Mao's Communists moved the capital from Nanjing back to Beijing (which had been the imperial capital for centuries) and in doing so directly connected their rule to traditional Chinese authoritarianism. In many ways, the Communist regime replicated elements of the rigid and hierarchical imperial system. For example, China still administers extremely competitive national examinations that determine university admission, and under Communist rule the tradition of respect for one's elders was reflected in the elevated average age of party leaders. Despite significant efforts by some to improve the status of Chinese women, the male domination of China's Communist leadership continues to expose the traditional paternalism of Chinese politics.

CONFUCIANISM

One significant influence over the political culture and ideology of Chinese has been the thought of the scholar Confucius (551–479 B.C.E.). Under the tenets of Confucianism, the role of government is to impose a strict moral code and to foster "correct" thought. Key to the Confucian view of the world are the ideas of hierarchy and subservience to one's superiors, with respect radiating out from one's family (the elders) to the national leader (the emperor).

MAOISM

While Mao's ideas were firmly rooted in Marxism-Leninism, Mao gave those ideas a decidedly Confucian spin. He believed that the key to revolutionary

CHINESE LANGUAGE DIALECTS

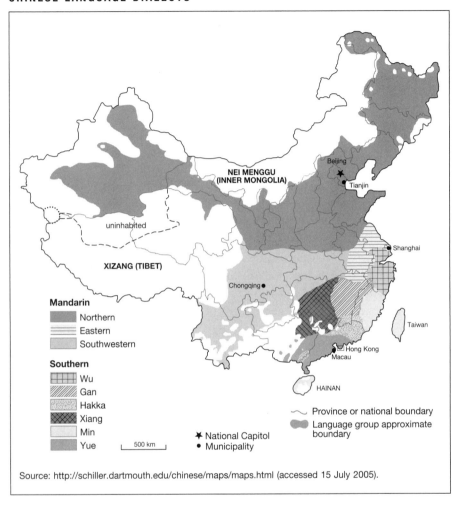

NEI MENGGU
(INNER MONGOLIA)

Beijing

Tianjin

uninhabited

Shanghai

XIZANG (TIBET)

Chongqing

Taiwan

Mandarin

Northern

Eastern

Southwestern

Southern

Wu

Gan

Hakka

Xiang

Min

Yue

500 km

Hong Kong
Macau

HAINAN

✶ National Capitol
● Municipality

⌒ Province or national boundary
Language group approximate
boundary

Source: http://schiller.dartmouth.edu/chinese/maps/maps.html (accessed 15 July 2005).

prosperity lay in the ability of the Communist Party to create a "new socialist man" and alter the way people think. While building on traditional Chinese political culture, Mao introduced some radical concepts. For example,
instead of rallying to the traditional Confucian notion of harmony, Mao promoted constant class struggle. Maoism emphasized the collective over the individual, again drawing on traditional Confucian notions. However, where
traditional Chinese values favored loyalty to the extended family, Mao sought
to transfer that loyalty to the larger community, as embodied by the party,
the state, and, locally, the work unit (*danwei*). The Communists also claimed
to promote egalitarianism, thus improving the lot of the nation's poor, peasants, and women.

XINJIANG: A FUTURE POWDER KEG?

Chinese support for the U.S. war on terrorism after the events of September 11 can partly be explained by China's concern about its northwestern province of Xinjiang. Xinjiang is home to numerous Muslim groups, the foremost of whom are the Uighurs, who form a slim majority of the province's population. The Uighurs have long resented Chinese control and the steady growth of Han Chinese, who now account for 38 percent of the province's population. Xinjiang lags behind the rest of China in economic and social development, a fact that has only encouraged resentment of Chinese rule. A small and loosely organized separatist movement has undertaken several minor acts of terror against the Chinese. The Chinese government has reacted with harsh repression[12] and the U.S. State Department for the first time in 2005 recognized one of these groups as a foreign terrorist organization.

In Mao's view, revolutionary thought (as decreed by the party leadership) could replace Chinese values, and the party could promote these ideas through constant propaganda and slogans, mass campaigns, and the education system. Likewise, economic development could be "willed" through massive acts of voluntarism. Mao regularly favored political correctness over technical expertise, often at great cost to China's economy, most infamously during the Cultural Revolution.

Given the dearth of modern opinion research in Communist China, it is impossible to know whether Maoism has changed Chinese political culture or merely reinforced traditional Chinese characteristics. The ease with which the Chinese have embraced capitalist reforms, increased individualism, and allowed the growth of inequality suggests that Mao's ideas were accepted more out of deference to central authority than out of any deep convictions.

Since Mao's death, the importance of Maoism has waned. China's current leaders neither demand nor desire the type of mass mobilization that was a hallmark of Mao's China. The current leadership instead prefers a largely depoliticized public that is more common in third world authoritarian regimes, as it was in pre-Communist China.

NATIONALISM

Nationalism was a dominant feature of twentieth-century China and remains so today. The country's long and powerful imperial past (and its humiliation at the hands of foreigners in the nineteenth and twentieth centuries) has bred a strong sense of national pride. Mao's Communists capitalized on this sense of nationalism by melding the struggle for communism with the bitter struggle to expel the Japanese occupiers during World War II. Fierce nationalism— often manifested as xenophobia—is a cornerstone of Chinese political culture and is frequently used by Communist leaders to maintain support for the political system. The unexpectedly confrontational official reaction to the mistaken U.S. bombing of China's embassy in Yugoslavia in 1999 and the anti-Japanese street protests in 2005 are two recent manifestation of Chinese nationalism.

CHALLENGES TO CHINA'S COMMUNIST POLITICAL CULTURE

There is growing evidence that the strict party control of Chinese political culture is steadily eroding. The widespread support for the pro-democracy student movement in Tiananmen Square in 1989 was the first major sign that the Communist Party no longer had a monopoly on political ideas (even as the party's crushing of the protests demonstrated that the state retained a monopoly of force). Subsequent years have seen steady growth in dissent and protest by China's rural poor, disgruntled industrial workers, and disaffected ethnic minorities. The health and spirtuality movement Falun Gong has frightened the Chinese government with its ability to attract and mobilize followers independent of state control. Internet usage vital to China's economic growth, has exploded in China and created a venue for Chinese political opposition. For better or worse, booming trade and tourism have released a flood of Western ideas and values. In sum, it is unclear how long China's leaders can depend on a largely passive and compliant public, especially as rapid economic growth and globalization create new tensions and opportunities.

POLITICAL ECONOMY

From 1949 to 1978, China adopted a Soviet-style Communist political economic model. In choosing this model, Mao Zedong and the Chinese Communist Party (CCP) leadership consciously opted for equality over freedom, promising all Chinese an **"iron rice bowl"** (cradle-to-grave health care, work, and retirement security), as well as retaining state ownership of all property and full control of the economy through central planning. State bureaucrats assigned targets and quotas to producers at all levels of the economy and allocated basic goods to consumers.

As was the case in the Soviet Union, this centrally planned political economic model favored the development of heavy industry at the expense of consumer goods. It also led to the creation of a massive state

LABOR FORCE BY OCCUPATION

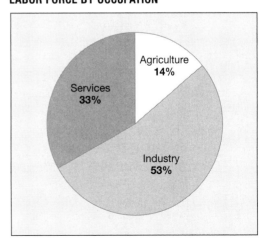

Agriculture 14%

Services 33%

Industry 53%

economic policy-making bureaucracy not present in capitalist political economies. Between 1949 and 1952, the state gradually nationalized most private industries and mobilized the economy to recover from the eight years of war with Japan and four years of civil war. By 1952, the Communist state had redistributed land to over 300 million landless peasants. In the mid-1950s, peasants were strongly encouraged to form larger agricultural cooperatives, pooling land, equipment, and labor and sharing profits; such cooperatives gave the state greater political control over the countryside.

Despite the agrarian roots of the Chinese revolution, Mao and the CCP sought to emulate Stalin's successful crash industrialization policy by launching the Great Leap Forward (1958–60). Mao believed that Communist-led mass campaigns could be marshaled for rapid industrial growth, and to pursue that goal he favored a policy of **Reds versus experts,** or politically indoctrinated party cadres (Reds) over those with economic training (experts). Vowing to progress "twenty years in a day" and to catch up with the industrialized West in fifteen years, Mao promoted the creation of small-scale, labor-intensive industry (so-called backyard industries) in both cities and the countryside. The Great Leap Forward further collectivized agriculture by creating gigantic communes that became party-controlled providers of education, health care, public works, and industrial production. The Great Leap Forward was a gigantic failure. The diversion of energy to industry and from agriculture and a drop in food production caused by the forced collectivization of agriculture were largely responsible for a three-year famine that killed as many as 30 million people.

By the early 1960s, Mao had been marginalized from the realm of economic policy making, and most of his Great Leap policies had been abandoned. Large-scale agricultural communes were disbanded, and peasant households were allowed to operate as independent producers, supplying their goods directly to the state and selling their surplus on the free market. Industries began to emphasize expertise over political correctness and material over moral incentives.

Responding to his own marginalization, Mao attacked these new policies as "capitalist" and in 1966 launched the Great Proletarian Cultural Revolution. The persecution unleashed during the next decade targeted those with the most expertise; the impact on the economy was devastating. Once again, Mao's disastrous policies were shelved.

In the mid-1970s, China's was still a poor and isolated economy, and the CCP leadership focused on creating rapid economic growth rather than traditional Communist goals of equity. After the death of Mao in 1976, and under the leadership of Deng Xiaoping, economic reform began gradually.[13] Agricultural communes were disbanded and replaced with the **household responsibility system,** a euphemism for largely private farming. Individual farmers still had to sell a set amount of their produce to the state but were free to sell any surplus on the open market. Food production improved dramatically, and famine became a thing of the past. Industries were decentralized; in their place, "collective" and "town and village" enterprises were allowed greater economic freedom and encouraged to generate profits. The importance of China's state sector gradually diminished, dropping from about 80 percent in 1980 to under 20 percent by 1996. By the mid-1980s, private industry was permitted (though initially heavily regulated), and the state gradually eliminated price controls. Hoping to end China's economic isolation, the government created **special economic zones** in 1979, offering tax breaks and other incentives to lure foreign investment to a handful of coastal enclaves.

By the 1990s, China's socialist command economy had been transformed into a "socialist market economy." The reforms sparked two decades of astounding economic growth. From 1980 to 2000, China's economy grew nearly 10 percent annually, and its GNP quadrupled. Millions have been lifted out of poverty, but China remains a poor country. Its per capita GDP at purchasing power parity in 2000 was only $3,976, compared with $34,142 in the United States, $9,037 in Mexico, and $8,377 in Russia.

The reforms have created both rapid growth and huge problems. As China's enterprises have become more profit oriented, they are free to lay off unproductive labor. As a result, Mao's "iron rice bowl" (the promise of lifetime employment and state-provided social services) has given way to massive unemployment. The Chinese leadership is betting that China's growing private sector will be able to absorb the unemployed. After decades of Communist emphasis on equality, the reforms of the last two decades have made China much less equal, magnifying inequality between individuals, between urban and rural Chinese, and between regions.[14] China's Gini index (a measure of inequality where a score of 0 equals perfect equality and 1 equals total inequality) rose from .386 to .462 between 1988 and 1995.[15] Most direct foreign investment has been concentrated along China's eastern coast, especially in Guangdong Province, Shanghai, Beijing, and Tianjin, while China's poorer interior has received very little of this investment. The growing inequality is partly responsible for the estimated 100 million to 150 million Chinese who comprise China's floating population (rural migrants seeking greater prosperity in urban areas) and has also been blamed for rising crime rates.[16] The Chinese no longer enjoy guaranteed access to health care, and even the traditional benefit of free universal education has been eroded.

In the increasingly competitive economic environment, state-owned enterprises (SOEs) have struggled. The state attempted to restructure the SOEs through mergers and consolidation, and the number of such firms has been reduced from 100,000 in the mid-1990s to about 60,000 today. Today, 74 percent of industrial output is produced by the private sector. The state sector is still enormous, however, and continues to suffer from inefficiency, corruption, and surplus labor—while consuming a disproportionate amount of credit granted by state-owned banks. The Chinese state subsidizes unprofitable state industries, in large part through the state-owned banking system, because it wants to avoid politically dangerous levels of unemployment.

RURAL UNEMPLOYMENT AND TRANSITION

Seventy percent of China's population lives in the countryside. Economic reforms have benefited the countryside, but not as much as urban areas, and rural China is still desperately poor. As a way of favoring industrialization, China has kept prices for farm products artificially low, and as the country modernizes its agriculture, hundreds of millions of Chinese have migrated to the cities to escape rural poverty. Such immigration is technically illegal, and rural Chinese who migrate to cities face harsh conditions and discrimination, but the state has been unable to stem the tide, despite recent efforts to redress the imbalance between urban and rural benefits from reform and opening.

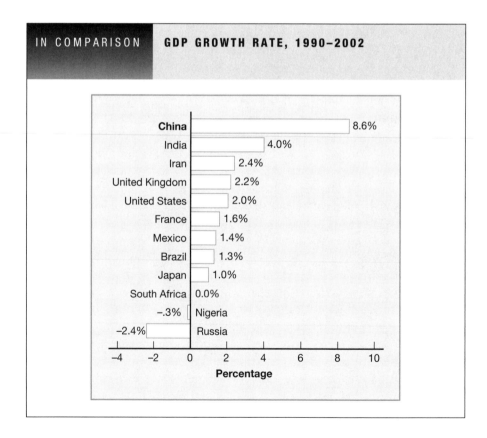

IN COMPARISON　　**GDP GROWTH RATE, 1990–2002**

China: 8.6%
India: 4.0%
Iran: 2.4%
United Kingdom: 2.2%
United States: 2.0%
France: 1.6%
Mexico: 1.4%
Brazil: 1.3%
Japan: 1.0%
South Africa: 0.0%
Nigeria: –.3%
Russia: –2.4%

Percentage

China's entry into the World Trade Organization (WTO) in 2001 promised greater challenges to its economy. WTO membership requires China to further liberalize its economy, and domestic firms, especially SOEs, face growing competition from foreign enterprises. Most recently, even China's debt-ridden state-banking sector has begun to feel the harsh winds of foreign competition. Despite the tremendous liberalization of the Chinese economy, the country's economic system remains substantially closed. China's economy is freer than Russia's but is still more restricted than the economies of Mexico, Japan, the United Kingdom, and the United States.

FOREIGN RELATIONS AND THE WORLD

During much of their long history, the Chinese viewed themselves as economically and culturally superior to the rest of the world. When nineteenth-century incursions by more economically advanced Western powers shattered that perception, Chinese society entered an extended period of crisis and self-doubt. The defeat of the Japanese in 1945 ended the humiliation of Japan's brutal occupation of China, and in 1949 the victorious government sought to restore China's past grandeur. China's return to isolation reached its zenith during the Cultural Revolution, when Mao Zedong attacked all foreign cultural and economic influences. China was not only isolated from Western capitalist nations and most of its neighbors but had also been estranged from its erstwhile mentor, the Soviet Union, beginning in the late 1950s, as Soviet and Chinese policies diverged after Stalin's death.

Since Mao's death in 1976, China has steadily emerged from decades of isolation. U.S. president Richard Nixon's historic visit to China in 1972 marked the beginning of China's opening to the West and the rest of the world. By the end of the 1970s, the United States and most other countries had normalized relations with Communist China and had, in effect, ceased to recognize the anti-Communist regime in Taiwan. Today, China's military might, the size of its economy, and its status as a permanent member of the United Nations Security Council make it an important international power. However, the country's long legacy of isolation continues to color its foreign relations and inform its official rhetoric.

Throughout the 1990s, China continued to improve its relations with much of the world, signing major accords with the European Union, Russia, Japan, and the Association of Southeast Asian Nations (ASEAN). These treaties are part of what the Chinese leadership has referred to as "strategic partnerships."[17]

Despite persistent bitter memories of the brutal Japanese occupation during World War II, China has to a large extent made peace with Japan. The two nations now share substantial and mutually important economic relations, although Japan's unwillingness to apologize for its past to China's satisfaction continues to fuel strong anti-Japanese sentiment in China. China's bitter rivalry with India, with whom it fought a border war in the early 1960s, has been replaced by a growing trade relationship and a 2005 agreement to resolve outstanding border disputes. These two regional nuclear powers are poor countries with populations exceeding 1 billion, and the potential for a dangerous confrontation between them has diminished in recent decades. India has recognized Chinese sovereignty over Tibet but has also provided refuge for the Dalai Lama and the exiled Tibetan government. China once supported Pakistan in its conflict with India but is now officially neutral. In 2001, China and Russia signed their first friendship treaty in fifty years, ending their bitter cold-war rivalry for world Communist leadership.

China has played an important role in the growing global concern about the nuclear capabilities of North Korea, its neighbor and traditional ally. North Korea shows only vague interest in the Chinese model of gradual economic liberalization and maintains a closed state and a Communist political economy similar to those of Maoist China. Nevertheless, since the end of the cold war, China has been North Korea's only reliable ally and its chief source of economic aid. This special relationship has given China a key role in diplomatic efforts to address North Korean threats. China must balance this relationship with its now-booming trade and investment ties with capitalist South Korea.

Ever since President Richard Nixon's historic 1972 visit, China's volatile rela-

THE EP-3 INCIDENT

Relations between China and the U.S. have vastly improved since the end of the cold war, but the Maoist legacy of distrust and hostility toward the United States unexpectedly surfaced in April 2001. The Chinese air force attacked a U.S. Navy EP-3 surveillance aircraft flying in international airspace off China's coast. The damaged aircraft was forced to make an emergency landing on Hainan Island in China. U.S. officials were surprised by the hostile Chinese response and aggressive rhetoric. Initially, China refused to free the EP-3 and its crew and demanded a U.S. apology for the incident. Only protracted diplomacy and a vaguely worded "apology" avoided serious damage to Sino-U.S. relations. This occurence demonstrates that China remains deeply sensitive about perceived foreign threats to its sovereignty. Reservoirs of historic anti-Americanism run deep for some members of the Communist Party. Moreover, the incident must be understood in the context of President George W. Bush's statements, soon after taking office, that the United States would not hesitate to use military force to protect Taiwan from a Chinese attack. The Chinese view such statements as foreign interference in domestic politics.

tionship with the United States has been characterized by periodic tension and mistrust. When U.S. pilots mistakenly bombed the Chinese embassy in Belgrade in 1999, China's leadership responded with bellicose rhetoric that alarmed U.S. leaders. In 2001, China and the United States faced off over China's capture of a U.S. surveillance plane that was forced to make an emergency landing on Chinese soil (see "The EP-3 Incident," on p. 266). China's leaders made statements that incited nationalist sentiment and smacked of the Maoist era. Since the events of September 11, however, relations between China and the United States have steadily improved.[18] Although some Chinese intellectuals viewed the attacks on the United States as understandable retaliation for its imperialist behavior, China supported the U.S. invasion of Afghanistan and the broader war on terrorism (though not its invasion of Iraq in 2003).[19]

At the heart of Sino-U.S. relations is the estimated US$220 billion in two-way trade and direct investment that bind the two countries. China is currently America's third largest trading partner, and the United States is second on China's trade list. But one central question threatens this relationship: Does China pose a threat to world peace? Although China's leaders speak often of China's "peaceful rise," some scholars have pointed to Chinese leaders' frequent outbursts of nationalist, anti-U.S., and anti-Japanese rhetoric. They doubt that economic liberalization and increased trade will moderate Chinese behavior toward its neighbors and make it a more peaceful member of the international community. Instead, the confidence created by China's spectacular economic growth, combined with some of the negative domestic consequences of that growth (such as unemployment), could provoke China to deal more aggressively with Taiwan, Tibet, and its other Asian neighbors.[20]

CURRENT ISSUES

THE TAIWAN QUESTION

At the center of China's relationship with its neighbors are a number of territorial disputes. By far the most serious regards the future of Taiwan, which is located only 100 miles off the Chinese mainland. After the victory of the Communists in 1949, Nationalist troops under Chiang Kai-shek retreated to Taiwan. Taiwan prospered as a capitalist authoritarian state and, during the cold war, gained the military protection of the United States. But at the urging of the People's Republic of China (PRC), Taiwan lost its United Nations seat in 1971. The United States (along with most other nations) effectively ceased to recognize Taiwan after formal diplomatic relations were established with China in 1979. By the 1980s Taiwan appeared increasingly vulnerable to Chinese attack.

The Chinese leadership has always regarded Taiwan as a renegade province of the mainland, and it has always sought the full re-integration of

Taiwan into the PRC.[21] China has continually threatened Taiwan, first with bombardment and subsequently with harsh rhetoric and military displays. The Chinese have repeatedly claimed that they would view any declaration of independence by Taiwan as an act of war. Tensions over Taiwan have continued to grow since it democratized in the late 1980s. In late 1995, the PRC sought to intimidate voters in Taiwan's presidential election with aggressive military action and veiled threats. The United States' unique relationship with Taiwan has often proved to be a thorn in the side of Sino-U.S. relations. Despite the continued tension between Taiwan and China, however, Taiwanese investment in and trade with China, estimated at US$150 billion in 2002, is quickly drawing the economies closer together.

The case of Hong Kong may provide a model for peaceful resolution of the Taiwan issue. Hong Kong is a tiny territory that was ceded by the Chinese to the United Kingdom in the mid-1800s, largely as a result of China's losses in wars intended to open China to foreign trade. The United Kingdom ruled Hong Kong as a colony for over a century, and it became a successful capitalist economic powerhouse on the doorstep of Communist China. In the 1980s, China and the United Kingdom agreed on a plan that would relinquish Hong Kong to Chinese sovereignty in 1997 under the principle of **"one country, two systems."** The Chinese guaranteed Hong Kong virtually total autonomy for a transitional period of fifty years, a pledge that it has thus far respected in most regards. China has argued that a Hong Kong-style re-integration of Taiwan into the PRC would involve little or no disruption for the Taiwanese.

HUMAN RIGHTS AND FOREIGN RELATIONS

China's repeated violations of human rights (and especially the Tiananmen Square events of 1989) have been a source of tension between China and the rest of the world. The Chinese view any criticism of their domestic politics as foreign meddling, and they tend to react defensively. The U.S. attempt to link China's human rights behavior to trade benefits was deeply resented by the Chinese and was abandoned in the mid-1990s. China's main trading partners have been reluctant to focus too much attention on human rights issues as their economic stakes in China increase. Free-trade advocates contend that increased trade and contact with the West—constructive engagement—not economic sanctions, will most effectively improve human rights in China. Others contend that globalization will increase economic disparities and tensions within China and that the leadership may respond with even greater political repression. Whether or not China's entry into the World Trade Organization in 2001 and Beijing's hosting of the 2008 Olympics will lead to greater international scrutiny of human rights issues remains a topic for debate. To date, China has been remarkably successful in balancing its reform and opening with harsh political repression.

NOTES

1. Quian Long, letter to George III (1793; Internet Modern History Sourcebook, Fordham University, 1998), www.fordham.edu/halsall/mod/1793quianlong.html (accessed 16 June 2005).

2. For a list of quotations, see Mao Tse-tung, *Quotations from Chairman Mao Tse-tung*, http://www.marxists.org/reference/archive/mao/works/red-book (Mao Tse-tung Internet Archive, 2000) (accessed 18 June 2005).

3. Bruce Gilley, "The Limits of Authoritarian Resilience," *Journal of Democracy* 14 (2003), p. 18.

4. China Internet Information Center, "China's Political System: The Party in Power," http://www.china.org.cn/english/Political/25060.htm (accessed 19 August 2003).

5. See Amnesty International, "China: 'Strike Hard' Anti-Crime Campaign Intensifies," press release, 23 July 2002, http://web.amnesty.org/library/Index/engASA17029 2002?Open (accessed 17 November 2003).

6. The first figure includes twenty-three actual provinces and the four "municipalities," or megacities of Beijing, Shanghai, Tianjin, and Chongqing.

7. Charles Hutzler, "Elections: Winding Road to Reform," *Far Eastern Economic Review* (5 September 2002), p. 27.

8. Mao Tse-tung, "Problems of War and Strategy" in *Selected Works* vol. 2 (Beijing: Foreign Language Press, 1965), p. 225.

9. See, for example, Gordon G. G. Chang, *The Coming Collapse of China* (New York: Random House, 2001), and Minxin Pei, "Contradictory Trends and Confusing Signals," *Journal of Democracy* 14 (2003), pp. 73–81.

10. Like many Chinese, Deng Xiaoping was an avid bridge player.

11. Andrew J. Nathan, "Authoritarian Resilience," *Journal of Democracy* 14 (2003), pp. 6–17.

12. Dru Gladney, "Xinjiang: China's Future West Bank," *Current History* (September 2002), pp. 267–70.

13. Gordon White, *Riding the Tiger: The Politics of Economic Reform in Post-Mao China* (Stanford, CA: Stanford University Press, 1993).

14. Tony Saich, "China's New Leadership: The Challenges to the Politics of Muddling Through," *Current History* (September 2002), pp. 250–55.

15. Carl Riskin, Zhao Renwei, and Li Shi,eds., *China's Retreat from Equality* (New York: M. E. Sharpe, 2000), p. 75.

16. Michael Dorgan, "Growing Rich-Poor Gap, Economic Growth, Spur Crime in China," Knight Ridder/Tribune Business News, 27 March, 2002.

17. Zhang Y. S. Wankun, "Patterns and Dynamics of China's International Strategic Behaviour," *Journal of Contemporary China* 11, no. 31 (May 2002), p. 235.

18. David Shambaugh, "Sino-American Relations since September 11: Can the New Stability Last?" *Current History* (September 2002), pp. 243–49.

19. Ying Ma, "China's America Problem," *Policy Review* (February–March 2002), pp. 43–56.

20. Emma Broomfield, "Perceptions of Danger: The China Threat Theory," *Journal of Contemporary China*, 12, no. 35 (May 2003), p. 265.

21. Kurt M. Campbell and Derek J. Mitchell, "Crisis in the Taiwan Strait?" *Foreign Affairs* 80 (July/August 2001), p. 14.

KEY TERMS

Chinese Communist Party (CCP)
  p. 239
Confucianism   p. 236
Cultural Revolution   p. 242
danwei   p. 245
democratic centralism   p. 244
floating population   p. 245
Great Leap Forward   p. 241
Falun Gong   p. 252
household responsibility system
  p. 262
Hundred Flowers campaign   p. 241
"iron rice bowl"   p. 261
Wen Jiabao   p. 250
Hu Jintao   p. 243
Kuomintang (KMT)   p. 239
Long March   p. 240

May Fourth movement   p. 239
National Party Congress   p. 249
National People's Congress (NPC)
  p. 250
"one country, two systems"   p. 268
People's Liberation Army (PLA)
  p. 252
Red Guard   p. 242
Reds versus experts   p. 262
reform and opening   p. 233
special economic zones   p. 263
Tiananmen Square   p. 253
Deng Xiaoping   p. 242
Sun Yat-sen   p. 239
Mao Zedong   p. 239
Jiang Zemin   p. 243

WEB LINKS

China's Political System   **www.china.org.cn/english/Political/25060.htm**
  Official government site describing the political structure, fundamental
  laws, rules, regulations, and practices of China since its founding.
A Country Study: China   **lcweb2.loc.gov/frd/cs/cntoc.html**
  Library of Congress's *Country Studies Series* presents a description and
  analysis of the historical setting and the social, economic, political, and
  national security systems of China
China General Information Base   **www.chinatoday.com/general/a.htm**
  Unofficial site offering useful general information

8 INDIA

Head of state:
President A. P. J. Abdul Kalam
(since July 26, 2002)

Head of government:
Prime Minister Manmohan Singh
(since May 2004)

Capital: New Delhi

Total land size: 3,287,590 sq km

Population: 1.080 billion

GDP at PPP: 3.32 trillion US$

GDP per capita: $3,100

INTRODUCTION

Why Study This Case?

India presents a remarkable and instructive case for the study of comparative politics. This South Asian nation will, within several decades, eclipse China as the world's most populous country. Already it is the world's largest democracy, with more voters in a typical election (some 400 million) than the entire population of any other country in the world except China.

Besides being the largest, India is also one of the most improbable of democracies, and herein lies one of the key puzzles of the case. Scholars most often associate democracy with critical levels of prosperity, mass literacy, urbanization, and national unity. India seemingly disproves every one of these factors. One fourth of all Indians live on less than US$1 a day, and less than half of all Indian women are literate. Paradoxically, poor and illiterate Indians—most often living in rural areas, not cities—are three times as likely to vote as the national average. And despite the backwardness of rural India, satellite dishes have brought television to more than 80 percent of the country's half million villages.

Most puzzling, perhaps, is how democracy can survive and thrive in a country so dangerously divided by history, language, religion, and **caste.** India has thousands of years of history as an authoritarian, hierarchical culture that has stratified, segmented, and compartmentalized its society. Today, over 1 billion Indians speak some 33 major languages with over 1,500 dialects. They worship over 5,000 gods, and six religions have at least 50 million adherents each. Caste divisions still segregate India socially, economically, and culturally. At times, these ethnic and social divisions have erupted into violent conflict and dramatic threats of secession. Given these circumstances, some observers marvel that the country can even stay together, let alone accommodate the cacophony of demands that are presented.

Others argue that democracy may not be so much the puzzle as the solution. A ponderous but flexible democracy may be the only way of holding this patchworked nation together. Prior to gaining its independence, in 1947, India had already been introduced to—if not allowed to participate in—the liberal practices of its British imperial master. As a sovereign nation, India fully adopted the political institutions of British democracy—the Westminster parliamentary model. This system has taken root but remains distinctly Indian. India thus offers comparative political scientists a useful Petri dish for studying the transplantability of democratic institutions to a postcolonial setting and the challenges facing such a transplant.

In recent years, the greatest challenge to Indian democracy and political stability has come from persistent religious conflict and increasing fundamentalism. As this case will demonstrate, Sikh and Muslim separatism and Hindu chauvinism have threatened the very democratic system that has sought—so far successfully—to accommodate them. India prevailed in its struggle for colonial independence in large part because of one devout Indian's ability to combine the Hindu concept of nonviolence with the liberal notions of tolerance and the separation of religion and state. The charismatic leadership of Mahatma (Mohandas K.) Gandhi and the secularism of his followers successfully united an ethnically diverse colony in the common cause of democratic nation building.

But as has been the case in nearly all other postimperial countries, modernization has come neither quickly nor easily to India. This huge and still impoverished nation must juggle the maintenance of its notable democracy with the challenges of development and increasing globalization. Although India's urban centers can boast a prosperous and technically savvy elite minority standing very much in the twenty-first century, its rapid economic development over the past two decades has left much of the rest of the nation behind. So to the many other divisions threatening India's democracy and political integrity, we must add the inequalities of income and opportunity.

To some extent, India shares with most other less developed and newly industrializing countries these multiple and simultaneous threats of ethnic conflict, political instability, and economic inequality. India is important not just because of its relative ability to manage these challenges democratically but also because its sheer size and growing international prominence guarantee it will have increasing influence in the rest of the world.

Major Geographic and Demographic Features

India looms large in both size and population, surpassed only by China as Asia's largest and most populous country. The country divides relatively neatly into two triangles stacked on top of each other, with the sharp angles pointed to the north and the south. The northern triangle is home to territorial disputes that have led to three wars with Pakistan to the west and ongoing tension with China to the east. The northernmost state of Jammu and Kashmir at the apex of the northern triangle, is claimed by both Pakistan and India and remains a volatile tinderbox of ethnic and nationalist dispute. The southern triangle is a huge peninsula that juts into the Indian Ocean, historically buffering the area from India's neighbors but opening the region to Western trade and, ultimately, imperial conquest.

Both India's climate and its politics have been profoundly shaped by geography. The Himalayas serve as towering sentinels on the northern border,

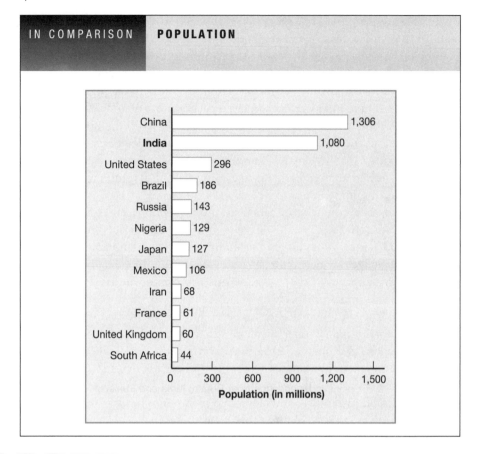

IN COMPARISON   POPULATION

China — 1,306
India — 1,080
United States — 296
Brazil — 186
Russia — 143
Nigeria — 129
Japan — 127
Mexico — 106
Iran — 68
France — 61
United Kingdom — 60
South Africa — 44

Population (in millions)

shielding the subcontinent (comprising India, Pakistan, and Bangladesh) over the millennia from Siberian winds and Central Asian invaders. The Himalayas (Sanskrit for "abode of snow") are also the source of India's two most important river systems: the Indus, long the cradle of Indian civilization, and the Ganges, a river Hindus value as sacred and worship as a goddess. These rivers and the sheltered climate of India's northern plains have made the north remarkably fertile, sustaining dense levels of civilization.

Crop production in the more arid regions of southern India is no less important but riskier because of its dependence on the monsoons—the four summer months of heavy rains. A successful monsoon season—neither too little nor too much rain—can make the difference between drought or flood and famine or feast for many Indians. The **green revolution** of the 1960s and 1970s, with its technologically enhanced crops and cropping methods, improved production dramatically. Nonetheless, India's rapidly growing population remains highly dependent on an agricultural economy, often called a gamble in rains.[1]

And although India possesses a wide range of natural resources, its per capita endowment of oil, timber, minerals, and petroleum reserves is relatively low. More than half of all Indians remain dependent on an agrarian livelihood—only China has more peasants. And only China has more people. The United Nations predicts that India will surpass China as the world's most populous country by 2035 and will continue to grow until 2050, when, it is estimated, its population will peak at roughly 1.5 billion, or one fourth the world's total.

The product of numerous waves of empire building, India's population is racially, ethnically, and linguistically diverse. The simplest division of Indian society is between the Aryans to the North and the Dravidians to the South, though this division is amplified by linguistic differences. In the North, most Indians speak some variety of Indo-Aryan, which is part of the Indo-European family of languages. Most common among these is **Hindi,** now one

	TIME LINE OF POLITICAL DEVELOPMENT
Year	**Event**
1857–58	Sepoy Mutiny put down, and formal British colonial rule established
1885	Indian National Congress created
1947	India gains independence from Britain; India and Pakistan partitioned
1948	Mahatma Gandhi assassinated
1947–64	Jawaharlal Nehru serves as prime minister until his death
1971	India-Pakistan War leads to creation of Bangladesh
1975–77	Indira Gandhi institutes emergency rule
1984	Indira Gandhi launches military operations at Amritsar and is assassinated by Sikh bodyguards
1984–86	Rajiv Gandhi serves as prime minister
1991	Rajiv Gandhi assassinated
1992	Ayodhya mosque destroyed
1996	Electoral victory of the Bharatiya Jamata Party (BJP) leads to the rise of coalition governments
1998	Nuclear weapons tested
2002	Muslim-Hindu violence breaks out in Gujarat
2004	Congress-led coalition defeats BJP coalition; Manmohan Singh becomes prime minister

of two national languages, the other is English. Most people in the South speak one of four dialects of the Dravidian language, almost completely distinct from Hindi. English has become the only universal language, but one that is spoken in large part by the elite. Even so, there are more English speakers in India (33 million) than in Canada, a fact that U.S. companies drawn to the **outsourcing** of their technology support are well aware of.

Historical Development of the State

Civilization on the Indian subcontinent predates a unified Indian state by several thousand years. Three religious traditions and nearly 1,000 years of foreign domination mark the contours of this gradual formation of a sovereign Indian state.

HINDUISM, BUDDHISM, AND ISLAM

Over 3,000 years ago, nomadic Indo-Aryans began migrating eastward from Persia into the northern and central plains of present-day India, subduing the darker-skinned Dravidians, many of whom moved southward. From the fusion of the two cultures emerged the customs, philosophical ideas, and religious beliefs associated with **Hinduism.** Like other traditional religions, Hinduism governs not just worship practices but also virtually all aspects of life, including the rituals and norms of birth, death, marriage, eating, and livelihood. For roughly the next 2,000 years, India enjoyed relative freedom from outside influence as Hindu traditions such as polytheism, reincarnation, and the social and political hierarchy of caste infused Indian society (see "Indian Caste System," on p. 277).

It was under the auspices of Buddhism—a second religious tradition, originating in India in the sixth century B.C.E.—that rulers commenced India's first efforts at nation building. Spreading Buddhism's message of peace and benevolence to subjects of all ethnic groups and social ranks, dynastic rulers unified much of what is now India by the fourth century B.C.E. and remained in power for several hundred years. The development of the silk route by the first century C.E. spread Buddhism to China and beyond. At home, however, Hinduism gradually reemerged as the religion of state and has remained India's dominant faith, with over 80 percent of Indians identifying themselves as Hindu. Today, Hinduism is the world's third largest religious tradition, after Christianity and Islam.

These 2,000 years of relative isolation gave way to a millennium of foreign domination beginning with marauding Muslim invaders in the eighth century. (Foreign invasion and occupation did not end until India gained its independence from British imperialism and colonialism in 1947.) The arrival of this third religious tradition at the hands of martial Muslim rulers never fostered the kind of tolerance shared by Hindus and Buddhists. But the intro-

INDIAN CASTE SYSTEM

Like many other pre-modern societies, India's was compartmentalized and divided for thousands of years according to occupation and social obligations. India's system was at once more complex and more flexible than it is often portrayed as being, with some 3,000 separate but not wholly rigid divisions. Each category possessed its own rules for the social behavior and interactions involved in activities such as eating, communicating, and marrying. More generally, Indian society was divided into four main castes, or *varnas*, including Brahmans (priests), Kshatriyas (warriors and rulers), Vaishyas (traders and merchants), and Sudras (peasants and laborers). At the bottom of—technically outside—the hierarchy were the so-called **untouchables.** These included two groups: those who performed duties deemed unclean, which involved handling the dead and disposing of human waste, and those aborigines who lived outside village life, in the mountains or forests. The touch or even shadow of the "outcastes" was considered polluting by high-caste Hindus.

Sanctioned and legitimized by the Hindu religion, these social divisions grew increasingly rigid over time, with strictly defined behaviors and little prospect of mobility. Independent India has made efforts to ease the discrimination associated with caste and, in particular, its deleterious effects on the "untouchables." Mahatma Gandhi worked tirelessly on their behalf, referring to them as harijans, the children of God. India's 1950 constitution not only banned the "untouchable" status but also legislated special "reservations," or affirmative actions, designed to improve the status of these "scheduled castes." Calling themselves **Dalits** (Suppressed Groups), they now number some 140 million people, or 16 percent of the population.

duction of Islam to India gave birth to a new religious tradition, **Sikhism,** which combines Hindu and Muslim beliefs. It also sowed the persisting seeds of mutual animosity among India's Hindus, Muslims, and Sikhs. A final wave of Muslim invaders, descendants of Genghis Khan known as **Mughals** (Persian for "Mongol"), ruled a relatively unified India for several hundred years beginning in the sixteenth century. But by the eighteenth century, Mughal rule had weakened at the hands of growing internal Hindu and Sikh dissatisfaction and expanding Western imperialism.

BRITISH COLONIALISM

The lucrative spice trade beckoned European powers to the Indian Ocean, beginning with the Portuguese and the Spanish in the sixteenth century and then the Dutch and the British by the seventeenth century. Lacking a strong, centralized state, India was vulnerable to foreign encroachment, and the British in particular made significant commercial inroads. In 1600, the British crown granted a monopoly charter to the private East India Company, which over the years perfected an imperial strategy of commercial exploitation. This private merchant company cultivated trade first and then cheap labor and ultimately succeeded in controlling whole principalities. It did so through a strategy of setting up puppet Mughal governorships, known as nabobs, with British merchant advisers at their side. This **nabob game** greatly facilitated the plundering of Indian wealth and resources.

The British introduced the concept of private property and the English language, and with it science, literature, and—perhaps most revolutionary— liberal political philosophy. Also, as the East India Company lost its monopoly on Indian trade, a growing number of British merchants sought Indian markets for British manufactures, particularly cotton cloth. With British cotton selling at less than half the price of local handmade cloth, this "free" trade put millions of Indian cloth makers out of work. Communication and transportation technology—the telegraph, print media, the postal system, and the railroad (the British laid some 50,000 miles of track)—did much to unify India and give its colonial subjects a shared recognition of their frustrations and aspirations. This was particularly true of those native Indians employed in the colonial military and civil service who were beginning to develop and articulate a sense of Indian nationalism.

Growing economic frustration, political awareness, and national identity led to the **Sepoy Mutiny** of 1857–58, a revolt sponsored by the Indian aristocracy and carried out by Indian *sepoys*, soldiers employed by the British. The mutiny failed in large part because the Indians were too divided, both by British design and by the long tradition of religious animosity that split Hindu and Muslim conscripts. The failure convinced the growing number of Indian nationalists that independence from British colonialism would first require national unity. To British authorities the mutiny signaled the weakness of nabob rule and the threat of Indian anti-colonialism. In 1858, the British Parliament's Government of India Act placed India under direct colonial rule. Under this British raj, or rule, modern British civil servants replaced private merchants and puppet nabobs, and the colony became the "brightest jewel in the crown of the British empire."[2]

THE INDEPENDENCE MOVEMENT

By the end of the nineteenth century, calls for self-rule had become louder and more articulate, though they were still not unified. Two local organizations came to embody the anti-colonial movement: the **Indian National Congress** (INC, also referred to simply as Congress or Congress Party) founded in 1885, and the **Muslim League,** founded in 1906. But hopes for a gradual transfer of power after World War I were instead met with increased colonial repression culminating in a 1919 massacre in which British troops opened fire on unarmed and innocent Indians, murdering hundreds and wounding over 1,000.

This massacre galvanized Indian resistance and brought **Mohandas K. Gandhi,** a British-trained lawyer, to the leadership of Congress and the independence movement (see " Gandhi," on p. 279). Gandhi led successful protests and nationwide boycotts of British imports and such British institutions as the courts, schools, and civil service employment. Perhaps most successful of these protests was his 1930 boycott of British salt, which was heavily taxed by the colonial raj. In declaring the boycott, Gandhi led a group of followers on a 200-mile march to the sea to gather salt, a violation of the British monopoly. Upon their arrival, Gandhi and many others were jailed, and the independence movement garnered national and international attention.

Gandhi's integrity and example, the charismatic draw of his remarkable strategy of nonviolence, and the growing repressive and arbitrary nature of colonial rule swelled the ranks of the independence movement. Among those who joined was a younger generation of well-educated leaders schooled in the modern ideas of socialism and democracy. Chief among them was **Jawaharlal Nehru,** who would succeed Gandhi as the leader of the INC and become independent India's first prime minister.

Weakened by both economic depression and war, Britain was in no shape to resist Indian independence and entered into serious negotiations toward this end following World War II. The biggest obstacle to independence now became not British foot-dragging but disagreements and divisions among India's many interests, particularly Hindus and Muslims. Fearful that Muslims, who constituted 25 percent of the population, would be unfairly dominated by the Hindu majority, Muslim leaders demanded a separate Muslim

---

GANDHI

Mohandas K. Gandhi, affectionately known by Indians as Mahatma or "Great Soul," was born in 1869 and studied law in Britain. He first experienced racism while practicing law in South Africa and was thrown out of the first-class compartment of a train because of his skin color. That event prompted his tactics of revolutionary nonviolent resistance, first practiced against South African discrimination and then perfected in India after his return there in 1914. Upon his return, he adopted the simple dress, ascetic habits, and devout worship of a Hindu holy man and developed his philosophies of *satyagraha* (holding firmly to truth) and *ahimsa* (nonviolence, or love). He argued that truth and love combined in nonviolent resistance to injustice could "move the world." He also taught that Western industrial civilization must be rejected in favor of a simpler life. He led a charismatic nationalist movement that was embodied in his example of personal simplicity and campaigns for national self-sufficiency. The movement was punctuated by dramatic instances of nonviolent resistance, hunger strikes, and periods of imprisonment. Successful in his campaign to end colonialism, even the Great Soul could not prevent either Hindu-Muslim violence, or ultimately, the partition of Pakistan and India, despite his best efforts. Five months after India achieved independence, a Hindu militant assassinated Gandhi to protest his efforts to keep India unified.

state. Negotiations collapsed as civil war broke out between militant adherents of the two faiths.

Against this background of growing violence, the British chose **partition,** creating in 1947 the new state of Pakistan from the Muslim-dominated northeast (what would become independent Bangladesh in 1971) and from the northwest and forming independent India from the remaining 80 percent of the colony. This declaration led to the transmigration of up to 10 million refugees—Muslims to Pakistan, Hindus and Sikhs to India—across the hurriedly drawn boundaries. It is estimated that as many as 1 million Indians and Pakistanis were killed in the resulting chaos and violence. Among the victims of this sectarian violence was Gandhi himself, assassinated in 1948 by a militant Hindu who saw the leader and his message of religious tolerance as threats to Hindu nationalism.

INDEPENDENCE

Like many of the other newly minted countries that would became part of the postwar decolonization movement, independent India faced a host of truly daunting challenges. In India, these included settling some 5 million refugees from East and West Pakistan, resolving outstanding territorial disputes, jump-starting an economy torn asunder by partition in an effort to feed the country's impoverished millions, and creating democratic political institutions from whole cloth. This last task, promised by Nehru and his INC, had to be carried out in the absence of the prosperity, literacy, and liberal traditions that allowed democracy to take hold in the advanced democracies and seemed to many an unlikely prospect. Given India's particular circumstances and its kaleidoscopic social, political, and economic interests—what one author called "a million mutinies now"[3]—such an endeavor seemed particularly foolish.

But unlike many other postcolonial countries, India brought to the endeavor of democratization several distinct advantages. First, its lengthy, gradual, and inclusive independence movement generated a powerful and widespread sense of national identity. Although India had not experienced a thoroughgoing social revolution in the style of Mexico or China, most Indians had come to identify themselves not just by their region, caste, or even religion, but also as citizens of the new republic. The legacy of Gandhi's charismatic outreach to all Indians, including outcastes, Muslims, and Sikhs, brought much-needed (if perhaps ultimately short-lived) unity to its disparate population.

Second, although Indians did not control their own destiny under the British raj, the Indian intellectual class was well schooled in both the Western philosophies and the day-to-day practices of liberal democracy. Generations of the Indian elite had not just been taught in the British liberal tradition; many of them had also served faithfully in the colonial bureaucracy. By the time of

independence, Indians for most practical purposes were in fact governing themselves on a day-to-day basis, albeit following the dictates of a colonial power.
Indeed, their appreciation of and aptitude for the virtues of democracy made
its denial under British imperial rule seem all the more unjust.

Finally, the long-standing role of the INC as the legitimate embodiment
of the independence movement and Nehru as its charismatic and rightful
representative gave the new government a powerful mandate. Like Nelson
Mandela's African National Congress, which took its name from its Indian
predecessor and swept to power in South Africa's first free election in 1994,
Nehru led the INC to a handy victory in India's first general election, in
1951. This afforded the INC government the opportunity to implement
Nehru's vision of social democracy at home and mercantilist trade policies
abroad. The INC would govern India for forty-five of its first fifty years of
independence, led for nearly all those years by either Nehru, his daughter,
or his grandson.

A NEHRU DYNASTY

"Uncle Nehru," as Jawaharlal Nehru was affectionately called, led the INC to
two subsequent victories in 1957 and 1962. But by his third term, Nehru had
realized the intractability of many of India's economic and foreign policy challenges and his own inability to transform the nation as quickly as he had
hoped. As one scholar has observed, "In India, nothing changed fast enough
to keep up with the new mouths to be fed."[4] Nehru died in office in 1964, and
with his death the INC began to lose some of its earlier luster and its ability
to reach across regional, caste, and religious divisions to garner support.

Within two years, Nehru's daughter, **Indira Gandhi** (no relation to
Mahatma), assumed leadership of a more narrowly defined INC and became
India's first woman prime minister. Far more authoritarian than her father,
Gandhi's first decade of rule divided the party between her supporters and
her detractors. With her popularity within the party weakening in the 1970s,
Gandhi sought support from India's impoverished masses with a populist campaign to abolish poverty. Although the program was highly popular and initially successful, the global oil crisis reversed many of the early economic
gains. Riots and strikes spread throughout India, with citizens of all classes
complaining of the dangerous dictatorship of the "Indira raj."

Facing declining support, charges of corruption, and calls to step down,
Gandhi instead chose in 1975 to suspend the constitution by declaring martial law, or **emergency rule.** The Indian constitution does authorize such a
measure, and during the two years of emergency rule, riots and unrest ceased,
and economic efficiency improved. Nonetheless, Gandhi's swift suspension of
civil liberties, censorship of the press, banning of opposition parties, and jail-
ing of over 100,000 political opponents (including many of India's senior

statesmen), chilled Indian democracy and prompted widespread (albeit largely silent) opposition to her rule.

When Gandhi surprisingly lifted emergency rule in 1977 and called for new elections, virtually all politicians and the overwhelming majority of voters rallied to the cause of the new Janata (people's) Party in what was seen as an effort to save Indian democracy. But the members of the Janata coalition shared little beyond their opposition to Gandhi's emergency rule. After two years of indecisive and inept governance, the INC was returned to office—with Gandhi as its leader. Indian voters had spoken, indicating their preference for the order and efficiency of Gandhi's strong hand over the Janata Party's ineptitude.

During Indira Gandhi's second tenure, persistent economic problems were compounded by increasing state and regional resistance to central control and growing ethnic conflict. Demands for the devolution of central authority were sharpest in the Sikh-majority Punjab, whose leaders had become increasingly violent in their political and religious demands. Violence escalated, and demands for an independent Sikh state of Khalistan heightened. In 1984, Gandhi declared martial law, or **presidential rule** (the state-level equivalent of emergency rule, which is also constitutionally authorized), in the state of Punjab. She then launched a military operation on the Golden Temple in **Amritsar,** Sikhism's holiest shrine. Sikh separatists' firebrand leader and some 1,000 of his militant followers ensconced in the temple were killed in the operation, and loyal followers swore vengeance. The vengeance came months later, when Gandhi's Sikh bodyguards assassinated her. In what was to become a motif of communal violence, the assassination sparked violent retribution as angry Hindus murdered thousands of innocent Sikhs throughout India.

Nehru had led the INC and governed India for some seventeen years. His daughter, Indira, presided over Indian politics for almost as long. But whereas Nehru's legacy was one of national inclusion and consensus building among a wide range of regional interests, Gandhi's rule was far more divisive, intolerant, and heavy-handed. The Indian state she bequeathed to her son Rajiv, who replaced her as leader of the INC, was more centralized and its party politics far more divided. This was not necessarily a bad thing for Indian democracy, however. For the first time, a viable political opposition was emerging, one capable of standing up to the powerful INC.

Widespread sympathy in the wake of Gandhi's assassination made it natural for the INC to select her younger son, Rajiv (her older son and heir apparent, Sanjay, having been killed in a plane accident) and assured the Congress Party its largest (and last) majority in the 1984 election. Rajiv Gandhi governed for five years, beginning the shift of India's economic focus away from the social democratic and mercantilist policies of his mother and grandfather. He promoted more liberal market measures, which have been expanded in the subsequent two decades. Ethnic violence and political divisiveness persisted, with trouble simmering between Hindus and Muslims in the Punjab and in new hot spots in the border region between India and Bangladesh to the east and between Hindus and ethnic Tamil separatists to the south. During a 1991 campaign, two years after Rajiv Gandhi had been turned out of office by a weak opposition coalition, he was assassinated by a Tamil suicide bomber. The Nehru dynasty had ended (at least for the time being), and coalition governments had become the norm.

COALITION GOVERNMENTS

The decline of the INC's dominance has led to a series of coalition governments typically led by a national party such as Congress but shored up by regional partners. Coalitions of all political stripes have maintained the reforms begun under Rajiv Gandhi and the INC, including economic liberalization and increased political devolution to state governments. The INC's strongest competition has come from the **Bharatiya Janata Party (BJP),** a party with the potential for nationwide scope and appeal. The BJP has been able to articulate a Hindu nationalist vision, an alternative (some would say a dangerous one) to the vision of a secular India established by the INC at the time of India's founding. Drawing its strength initially from upper-caste Hindu groups, by the late 1990s the BJP was attracting Hindus of all castes under the banner of Hindu nationalism.

The event that began to galvanize this support was yet another incident of sectarian violence at yet another temple site. Babri Mosque, located in the northern Indian city of **Ayodhya,** had been built by Mughals on a site alleged to be the birthplace of a major Hindu god. The site was deemed sacred by Muslims and Hindus and for decades has been a point of controversy for local adherents of both faiths. By the 1990s, various Hindu nationalist groups had seized on Ayodhya as both a rallying political issue and a gathering place. In 1992, BJP supporters and other Hindu extremists destroyed the mosque, vowing to rebuild it as a Hindu shrine. This act ignited days of Hindu-Muslim rioting and violence and the killing of many Indians across the country. Repercussions have persisted. In the state of **Gujarat** in 2002, on the tenth anniversary of the event, Muslims set fire to railcars carrying Hindu activists back from a ceremony at Ayodhya, killing fifty-eight people. Hindu retaliatory violence incited by religious militants killed thousands. The issues continue to simmer.

This communal violence has served to harden positions on both sides and polarize political support. A BJP coalition that had come to power in 1998 remained in office until 2004, when it was turned out by a surprisingly resurgent INC and assorted coalition partners. Organizations loosely affiliated with the BJP have continued to promote divisive Hindu nationalist rhetoric in order to garner support and have sponsored violence and discrimination against a variety of minority religious and ethnic groups. During its six years in office, however, the BJP coalition governed relatively moderately. It did so both to retain its coalition partners and to promote India's national goals of economic growth and stable relations with neighboring countries. These current domestic and international priorities will be taken up in subsequent sections.

Significantly, the leader of the INC at the time of its surprise return to office in the 2004 election was **Sonia Gandhi,** the Italian-born widow of Rajiv Gandhi. Although she would have been the logical choice to assume the office of prime minister (and extend the Nehru dynasty), the BJP made her foreign birth a divisive campaign issue. Thus, she stepped aside and allowed **Manmohan Singh** to become the country's first Sikh prime minister. It should be noted, however, that Sonia Gandhi continues to lead the INC and has two grown children, both of whom have expressed interest in a political career.

POLITICAL REGIME

With an electorate approaching 700 million voters, India can easily claim title to the world's largest democracy. But is this democracy genuine, and does it work? Certainly in form it is democratic. Its constitution and other political institutions were modeled explicitly on Britain's Westminster parliamentary system, and few changes to the original blueprint have been enacted. And with the exception of Indira Gandhi's authoritarian interlude of the 1970s, the institutions seem in practice to function more effectively and legitimately in India than in many other former British colonies that share a similar institutional inheritance. Indian democracy nonetheless differs in important ways from that of its colonial mentor and other advanced Western industrialized democracies, as our discussion will make apparent.

Why has democracy fared better in India than, for example, in neighboring Pakistan, a country that shares many of the same cultural and historical legacies? Although a full answer to this question is beyond the scope of this survey, the well-established stability and near-universal legitimacy of the institutions surveyed here provide an important part of that answer. Now three generations of Indian politicians and citizens from across the ideological spectrum have been schooled in the lessons of parliamentary democracy. They function and participate in a system that maintains civil parliamentary debate, a politically neutral bureaucracy, an independent judiciary, and firm civilian control over the military.

ESSENTIAL POLITICAL FEATURES

- Legislative-executive system: prime ministerial
- Legislature: Sansad
- Lower house: Lok Sabha (People's Assembly)
- Upper House: Rajya Sabha (Council of States)
- Unitary or federal division of power: federal
- Main geographic subunits: states
- Electoral system for lower house: single-member district plurality
- Chief judicial body: Supreme Court

Political Institutions

THE CONSTITUTION

Perhaps befitting India's size and population, its constitution is one of the world's longest, enshrining in writing the fundamental principles of Britain's unwritten constitutional order of parliamentary democracy. It establishes India as a federal republic, reserving significant but subordinate authority for the state governments. During the nearly fifty years of hegemonic rule by the Indian National Congress (INC), however, state governments had little independence. The weakening of the INC and the onset of coalition governments have begun a process of devolution, allowing regional political parties and the states they represent to wrest significant authority from the Center (a term referring to India's national government and its capital in New Delhi).

Two controversial tenets of the Indian constitution have certainly enhanced the power of the Center. The first of these authorizes the central government to suspend or limit freedoms during a "grave emergency," when India faces threats of "external aggression or internal disturbance." This emergency rule (nationwide martial law) was invoked twice during international conflicts, with China in 1962 and with Pakistan in 1971. More controversially, Indira Gandhi invoked this clause to institute emergency rule from 1975 to 1977, using it as a blunt (but nonetheless effective) tool against her political opponents. After her defeat in the subsequent election, the constitution was amended to limit such a decree to conditions of external aggression or domestic armed rebellion.

Indira Gandhi was not the only prime minister to invoke the second measure, that of presidential rule, which allows the central government to oust a state government and assert direct rule. National governments have employed this measure on a number of occasions when ethnic unrest, local resistance, or simply a political stalemate has rendered a state, in the judgment of the Center, ungovernable. Although these measures may seem unusual and have at times been imposed for purposes of political expediency, the violence, disorder, and corruption often associated with regional Indian politics have made presidential rule an important and generally legitimate tool of the central government.

The Branches of Government

THE PRESIDENT

As a republic, India has as head of state a president, not a monarch, and as in most other parliamentary systems, the president's role is largely symbolic. The president is authorized to "appoint" the prime minister, but as with the monarchs of Britain and Japan, this is simply an affirmation of the leader of the dominant party or coalition in the parliament. Similarly, while it is the president's role to "declare" national or state emergency rule, this declaration can be made only on the "advice" of the prime minister.

The substantive exception to these symbolic tasks has been the president's role following elections that have produced no majority party (nowadays increasingly the rule). Under these circumstances, the president seeks to identify and facilitate the formation of a workable governing coalition. If that is not possible, the president dissolves the parliament and calls new elections. An electoral college, made up of the national and state legislators, elects presidents to five-year renewable terms, though many presidents have in effect been appointed by powerful prime ministers. All presidents to date have been men; several have been Muslims, and one recent president, Kocheril Raman Narayanan, is a member of the "untouchable" Dalit caste.

THE PRIME MINISTER AND THE CABINET

As in the British system, the Indian prime minister and cabinet constitute the executive branch. The prime minister, as head of the government, is respon-

STRUCTURE OF THE GOVERNMENT

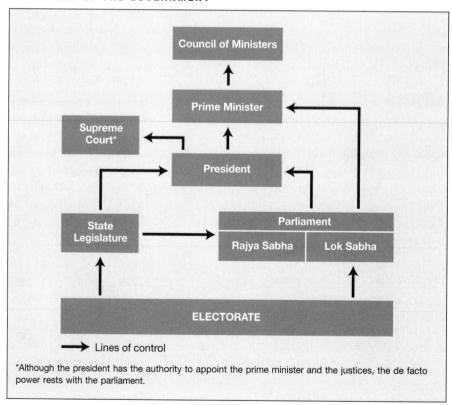

*Although the president has the authority to appoint the prime minister and the justices, the de facto power rests with the parliament.

sible for managing the day-to-day affairs of government and is the state's most important political figure. The prime minister has typically been the leader of the party with a majority in the lower house of the legislature or, more recently, a leader from within a coalition of parties that can garner sufficient support to constitute a majority, or even a minority, government. To remain in office, the prime minister must retain the confidence of the lower house and may choose to dissolve it at any point and call elections in order to solidify support for the government.

The prime minister chooses members of the parliament to serve in a Council of Ministers that presides over all government ministries and departments. From this larger council, a smaller and more manageable group of the fifteen to twenty most important ministers meets weekly to formulate and coordinate government policy. The current prime minister, Manmohan Singh, is the country's first Sikh to serve in that office and began his tenure in 2004 as the leader of a Congress coalition.

During the years of Congress dominance, the three generations of Nehru prime ministers wielded overwhelming executive power. Although this was most apparent during Indira Gandhi's authoritarian tenure, her father and even her son were also dominant prime ministers who left their personal imprints on the office and on Indian politics. Even during the more recent era of coalition governments in which the prime minister's influence has weakened, the office has remained the primary source of policy making and political power.

THE LEGISLATURE

As is the case in many parliamentary systems, the lower house, or **Lok Sabha (House of the People),** dominates India's bicameral legislature. This lower chamber seats 545 members, all but two of whom are elected by voters for terms not to exceed five years (the final two seats are reserved for Anglo-Indians appointed by the president). Although its size may seem to weaken its effectiveness, India's huge population remains relatively underrepresented. Each representative serves nearly 2 million people, four times that of a member of the U.S. House of Representatives and twenty times that of a member of Britain's House of Commons!

Like the British lower house, the Lok Sabha serves primarily as a chamber of debate between the government and the opposition. It has adopted many of the rituals and institutions of its colonial model, including a neutral Speaker of the House who presides over question time. Seen during the era of the INC's dominance as little more than window dressing for the party in power and its prime minister, the Lok Sabha has had an increasingly important political role since the emergence of multiparty coalition governments and the strengthening of regional parties.

As its name denotes, the upper house, or **Lok Rajya (House of States),** represents India's twenty-eight states and seven territories. All but twelve of its 250 members are elected (the remaining twelve being appointed by the president) to fixed six-year terms. Although the upper chamber technically possesses most of the same powers as its lower counterpart—including the right to introduce legislation—in practice it has been much weaker. Only the Lok Sabha can introduce bills to raise revenue and any financial measure the Lok Rajya votes down can be enacted with just the support of the lower house. Any other deadlocked legislation is put to a majority vote of a joint session, assuring the more numerous lower chamber the upper hand. Most significantly, the prime minister and cabinet are responsible only to the lower house, which can force the prime minister from office by a vote of no confidence.

THE JUDICIAL SYSTEM

Unlike Britain and more like the United States, India has a Supreme Court with a bench of twenty-six justices, who are appointed by the president and may serve until age sixty-five. Typically, the most senior judge serves as chief justice.

India's Supreme Court is a constitutional court with the authority of judicial review (the right to rule on the constitutionality of acts of the parliament). This power to interpret the constitution is limited, however, by the comprehensive nature of the Indian constitution. Its power has also been limited by the parliament's ability to reverse court decisions by amending the constitution, as it has done on a number of occasions (ninety-two times in fifty-four years). With the exception of the two-year period of Indira Gandhi's emergency rule in the 1970s, when the judiciary was seen as having yielded to the prime minister's political influence both in the appointment of justices and in the suspension of constitutionally guaranteed civil rights, the Supreme Court has enjoyed (and earned) a reputation for fairness and independence.

The Electoral System

As with many of the other political institutions we have covered, India's electoral system closely resembles the British model. At the national level, voters use a plurality system to elect representatives to the Lok Sabha, as in Britain and the United States. The country is divided into 543 single-member districts (SMDs), in which the candidate who earns a plurality of votes on the first ballot is elected. The districts are based primarily on population, but some districts are reserved for the so-called scheduled castes, which include the "untouchables" and tribal minorities. Members of the upper house are elected for staggered six-year fixed terms by the state legislatures, with seats apportioned according to each state's population.

Whereas this plurality system in the United States and Britain has favored the emergence of two nationally based large parties and has penalized smaller parties, this is increasingly not the case in India. The INC certainly used the electoral system to its advantage during its period of dominance, winning clear majorities in the Lok Sabha in most elections even though it never won a majority of the popular vote (nor has any other party in India's history) and often received little more than a plurality. The largest of the other parties, including the Janata Party and the Baratiya Janata Party (BJP) have also benefited, winning a higher percentage of seats than votes. The weakening of the INC's hegemony since the 1990s has splintered the national vote, however, and has given new significance to regional parties based on ethnic, linguistic, or religious identity. The 2004 Lok Sabha elections seated representatives of nearly forty different political parties, none with over one third of the seats and ten parties with over ten seats each.

Local Government

Because of the extensive regional diversity (and undoubtedly influenced by the religious conflicts troubling India at the time of its founding), the framers of India's constitution established a federal republic but preserved a decidedly powerful center. In fact, the Center's constitutional power to declare a national emergency or impose presidential rule on an obstreperous state in many ways makes India's system more unitary than federal. Less dramatically, the federal government is also authorized to challenge any state legislation that contradicts an act of the parliament and can even change the boundaries of states as it sees fit.

India is now divided into twenty-eight states and seven territories, whereas the original division had fourteen states and six territories. This expansion is in large part a nod to powerful state interests and speaks to another way in which India's federalism differs from the American model. State borders in India reflect in most cases linguistic divisions that have at times taken on ethno-religious significance, pitting non-Hindu regional interests against the Center. This conflict has been most pronounced in states such as Punjab, dominated by the Punjabi-speaking Sikhs, and **Kashmir,** where Urdu-speaking Muslims constitute a majority. But other ethnic groups have also wielded the mechanisms of state authority to assert state interests against the federal government.

Perhaps the best comparison with Indian federalism is not the United States but rather the historically diverse and linguistically distinct European Union (EU).[5] Like the English and the Greeks, the Hindi speakers of Bihar in the north and the Tamil speakers of Tamil Nadu in the south converse in mutually unintelligible tongues and share little common history and equally little interaction. Like the citizens of Sweden and Portugal, their customs, cultures, and traditions vary widely, as do their social and economic profiles. Bihar is impoverished and largely illiterate whereas Tamil Nadu is prosperous and technologically advanced. There is no similar contrast in the U.S. setting.

This comparison with the EU also points to one of the crowning accomplishments of India's democratic resilience. For all of the local conflict and secessionist violence that India has experienced, the Center has held, and the strife has remained localized. With larger populations and religious, linguistic, and territorial disputes sufficient to rival any of those that led to the numerous wars of Europe (and ultimately prompted the formation of the EU), India has for the most part managed these disputes peacefully and democratically. This is no small feat. And as state-based regional political parties and movements in India continue to strengthen and call for increased devolution, it gives hope not just to the emerging democratic federal system in Europe, but to that in Iraq, Russia, and other areas threatened by centrifugal dissolution.

POLITICAL CONFLICT AND COMPETITION

Despite occasional heavy-handed government restrictions on civil rights and periodic demonstrations of communitarian intolerance and even violence, Indian politics remains vibrant, open, and generally inclusive. Voter turnout typically averages around 60 percent for parliamentary elections. The nonpartisan Freedom House in 2003 deemed India "free," with ratings of 2 in its political rights and 3 in civil rights (on a scale of 1 to 7, with 1 the most free).

In fact, given India's size and diversity, some might argue that political competition has been too inclusive. As one Indian journalist complained, "Everyone in India gets a veto."[6] The competition and conflict—typically but not always healthy—reflect the dualism and diversity of India: a prosperous, cosmopolitan, and highly literate minority voting side by side with roughly two thirds of the electorate who cannot read, have their roots in rural villages or urban slums, and may survive on less than a US$1 a day. Both are important components of Indian democracy.

The Party System

During the first few decades of independence, India's party system was stable and predictable. Like Japan's Liberal Democratic Party or Mexico's Partido Revolucionario Institucional, Congress presided over a one-party-dominant system that effectively appealed to a broad range of ideological and social groups and co-opted numerous disaffected constituencies, including the poor and minorities. More recently, this system has become far more fragmented, complex, and unpredictable as national opposition parties and regional and even local interests have gained ground in both state and national elections.

THE CONGRESS PARTY

More than just a political party, the Indian National Congress (INC), from its founding in 1885, became the flagship of national independence, commanding widespread appeal and support across the political and even the ethnic spectrum. After independence, Jawaharlal Nehru and the INC pursued a slightly left-of-center ideology of social democracy. This included social policies of "secularism"(more a program of religious equal opportunity than a separation of religion and state) and social reform, continuing the efforts of Mahatma (Mohandas K.) Gandhi to eliminate caste discrimination through a program of affirmative action for the lower castes.

The party's economic program was marked by democratic socialism, including national five-year plans and state ownership of key economic sectors. These policies earned the support of workers, peasants, and particularly members of the lower castes. At the same time, the INC retained the support of business by respecting private property and supporting domestic industry with mercantilist policies of import substitution. It remained for decades the only party with national appeal.

The INC's dominance began to weaken after Nehru's death, as disagreements grew between Indira Gandhi and party elders in the late 1960s. These disagreements led to divisions within the party and to Gandhi's capture of the dominant faction, known as Congress (I) for Indira, during the 1970s. Gandhi made populist promises to India's poor, vowing to abolish poverty through government programs, but she never fulfilled those promises. By the 1980s, the INC had begun to move away from its traditional priorities of democratic socialism and religious neutrality. Indira Gandhi began promoting Hindu nationalism, and her son Rajiv launched neo-liberal economic reforms. Their legacies have outlived the architects and have been embraced even more enthusiastically by other political parties.

By the late 1980s, the INC had surrendered its position of primacy, and the single-party-dominant system gave way to a regionalized multiparty system and coalition governments. During this time, the INC alternated rule with various permutations of Hindu nationalist coalitions, controlling the government in the first half of the 1990s and then returning to power in 2004. Although the INC continues to embrace in principle the neo-liberal reform program first launched by Rajiv Gandhi, its most recent return to government was in large part a result of its progressive appeal to India's peasantry, a nod to both Nehru's democratic socialism and Indira Gandhi's populism.

THE BHARATIYA JANATA PARTY

As opposition to the INC grew during Indira Gandhi's 1970s autocratic interlude, a number of contending parties began to emerge or take on new importance. A coalition of some of these opposition parties, under the name Janata (People's) Party, ultimately wrested the government from the INC in the late 1970s. One of the smallest of these coalition partners was Jana Sangh, a Hindu nationalist party that left the Janata coalition in 1980 and changed its name to the Bharatiya Janata Party (BJP), or Indian People's Party.

Since that time, the BJP's popularity has climbed rapidly as support for secularism has given way to increasing sentiment for ethnic and religious parties. The BJP won only two seats in the Lok Sabha elections of 1984, but increasing Hindu nationalist sentiment (manifested most violently in clashes with Sikhs at Amritsar in 1984 and with Muslims in Ayodhya in 1992 and in Gujarat in 2002) allowed it to expand its representation to 161 seats by 1996 and form a coalition government, led by Atal Behari Vajpayee. Although this first BJP coalition lasted only twelve days, by 1998 the BJP had become the largest party in the parliament, and Vajpayee and his BJP-led coalition governed from 1998 until turned out of office in the 2004 elections. Despite this recent decline in support (the BJP held on to only 138 seats in 2004), it remains, with the INC, one of India's two largest parties.

From its founding, the BJP has been an outspoken advocate of Hindu national identity. It is a member of a larger constellation of more than thirty loosely tied Hindu nationalist organizations known as the RSS (the acronym for National Association of Volunteers in Hindi). These religious, social, and political associations vary widely in their acceptance of violence and militancy in promoting Hindu nationalism, but all embrace **Hindutva,** or Hinduness, as India's primary national identity and ideal. Whereas some of the more moderate RSS member organizations promote benign patriotism, other reactionary or fundamentalist association members teach a Hindu chauvinist version of Indian history and condone and even train their members in violent tactics of religious and racial discrimination.

Similarly, the BJP itself has both moderate and militant elements. Its elected national leaders tend to downplay the BJP's religious ties, promote the BJP as a more honest alternative to the INC, and emphasize its neo-liberal economic policies of privatization, deregulation, and foreign investment. This reputation of honesty and neo-liberalism has appealed in particular to India's growing middle class, which is more interested in economic freedom and prosperity than in secular equality. This predominantly Hindu middle class has become frustrated with what it perceives as the reverse discrimination of the INC's secular policies of tolerance of minority religion and caste-based affirmative action.

The more extremist and fundamentalist elements in the BJP are more overtly anti-Muslim, contending that India's Muslims were forced to convert by foreign invaders and would naturally revert to their native Hinduism in an India that was allowed to promote its true heritage. They are more prone to violence, praising the assassin of Mahatma Gandhi and the combatants of Ayodhya and Gujarat as heroes and protectors of Indian heritage. Their leaders have been more successful politically at the local and state levels (particularly in the region of India's so-called cow belt in the Hindu-majority north) but have become important allies in the BJP's efforts to form national ruling coalitions. Secularists fear that this influence will weaken the moderate wing of the party.

PARTIES OF THE LEFT

India's so-called Left Front consists of a collection of Communist and other left-leaning parties whose popularity seems unfazed by the declining success of Communist parties and countries elsewhere in the world. These parties together have managed to garner on average between 7 and 10 percent of the national vote and typically over fifty seats in the Lok Sabha. This bloc of seats has given the Communist parties a decisive role in the making and breaking of recent coalitions and therefore a certain leverage in government policy, despite their minority status. In the 2004 elections, the INC was not able to form a government without their support.

The leftist parties have in large part remained successful because of their willingness to evolve and seek alliances with other parties. Although both of the major leftist parties, the Communist Party of India and the Communist Party of India (Marxist), initially supported violent revolution, over the years both have ultimately embraced peaceful means to achieve communism. More recently, both have come to look and act much more like social democratic parties, embracing a mixture of state and private ownership and even promoting foreign investment. Their strength has in large part been localized as they have succeeded as the dominant regional party in several key states.

REGIONAL PARTIES

The declining dominance of the INC and the rise of coalition governments have given new prominence to regional and local political parties, which have come to dominate in many states and tip the balance in national elections. Moreover, as INC-supported secularism has waned, ethnic, linguistic, and religious identities have become increasingly important rallying points for political interests that are often concentrated by region. For example, states with predominant ethnic or religious identities, such as the Dravidian Tamils in the southern state of Tamil Nadu and the Punjabi Sikhs, have often been led by these regional and state parties. Another party has drawn its support from lower-caste Indians in several of India's poorer states. In only one of India's six most populated states does either the INC or the BJP hold a majority in the state parliament.

GENERAL ELECTIONS, 1989–2004

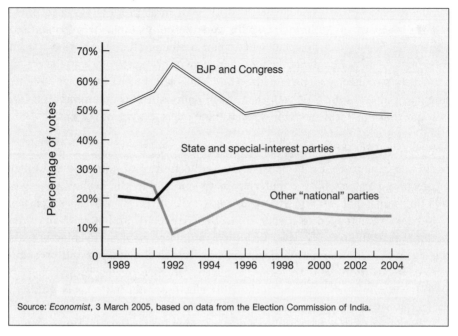

Source: *Economist*, 3 March 2005, based on data from the Election Commission of India.

The localized parties often have sufficient voting strength to control small but influential blocs of seats in the national parliament as well. In the 2004 election, the INC and the BJP won less than half the total vote, and state and special-interest parties won nearly 40 percent, as noted in the above figure ("General Elections"). This reflects in one sense a devolution of central power that could be healthy for Indian democracy. But given the diversity of India's interests, it also speaks to the secessionist aspirations and highly localized interests of Indians and may be a sign of a dangerous centrifugal force.

Elections

Campaigns and elections are essential democratic procedures and often-times dramatic theatrical events. Certainly this is true of India, where all aspects of an election must be measured in superlatives. For instance, in the spring of 2004 nearly 400 million of the eligible 690 million voters flocked to the 700,000 polling stations to cast votes (using over 1 million new electronic voting machines). They selected their favored parliamentary candidates from the thousands of choices, representatives of one of six "national" parties or the dozens of regional ones. The task was so huge that polling was spread out over four weeks as election officials and their machines migrated across the country, harvesting votes. Indeed, this four-week election period was longer than the government-limited three-week campaign that preceded it.

Perhaps most amazing was the outcome itself, again testament to the authenticity of Indian democracy. Prior to the 2004 election, it was a foregone and universally held conclusion that the BJP-led coalition would retain its majority and extend its six-year tenure. With strong national economic growth and thawing relations with Pakistan over the troubled issue of Kashmir, the governing coalition called early national elections to capitalize on these successes, campaigning under the motto "India Is Shining." In the weeks prior to the election, BJP leaders were already busy divvying up potential cabinet posts, and INC leaders were offering justifications for their party's anticipated weak showing.

But Indian voters had different plans, allowing the INC to edge ahead of the BJP with just over one fourth of the total seats. With its coalition partners, the INC gained control of 40 percent of the seats, compared to 34 percent for the BJP alliance. And after several days of negotiations, the INC expanded the coalition to include a number of regional, state, and left-of-center parties and secured the outside support of the Communist Party of India (see "Lok Sabha Election Results," below). Thus, the INC formed a government, naming Manmohan Singh as prime minister.

Civil Society

As the dominance of the INC has faded and political authority has become decentralized, more—and more diverse—interests and elements of Indian society have demanded influence. Although India does have conventional civil

Lok Sabha Election Results, 2004

Party or Coalition	Vote (%)	Seats
India National Congress (INC)	26.8	145
Bharatiya Janata Party (BJP)	22.2	138
INC and allies (United Progressive Alliance; UPA)	34.6	217
BJP and allies (National Democratic Alliance; NDA)	35.3	185
Left Front (LF)	7.6	59

organizations representing business, labor, and even peasants, these groups tend not to be particularly effective in influencing policy. Labor unions are organized by political party and are therefore highly fragmented and politically ineffective. Business certainly does influence both politics and politicians—corruption is a serious problem among members of India's parliament—but the reputation for corruption seems to confirm both the traditional Hindu and the more modern socialist biases against the influence of private business. Peasants are plentiful and at times vocal, but their political demands are episodic and particular.

Communal groups representing ethnic, religious, and caste groups have been far more influential in Indian politics. Hindus, Muslims, and Sikhs all have well-organized groups representing their political interests, and each supports its own political party or parties. This is also true also of the Dalits, or "untouchables," who have their own political party and constitute one of India's largest mass movements. Although there is good reason to be concerned about the destabilizing and divisive potential of these religious- and caste-based groups, there is also evidence that their multiple demands have more often been addressed substantially (if not met) through the political process, thereby defusing civil discord and strengthening the legitimacy of the system.

Less traditional divisions and demands are also taking shape in contemporary Indian civil society, including significant environmental and women's movements. Environmental protests include resistance to development projects such as the Narmada dam and deforestation and advocacy of redress for industrial accidents such as the Union Carbide disaster in Bhopal in 1984. Women's movements that have bridged class and ethnic divisions have organized to protest so-called dowry-deaths, which claim the lives of as many as 25,000 Indian women annually.

Another important voice of Indian civil society is the media establishment, arguably one of the largest and most active in the world. It includes 40,000 newspapers and other periodicals, including some 4,000 dailies, all of which enjoy a significant degree of editorial and political freedom. These figures are all the more impressive when one remembers that nearly one third of Indian men and over half of Indian women are illiterate. Given these figures, India's extensive radio and television networks are even more important conduits of information and have been subject to more careful government scrutiny and control. This oversight has become increasingly difficult, however, as satellite television—now available in 80 percent of India's half million villages—has introduced new competition into the market. India's substantial investment in networking the entire country with broadband cable will also certainly expand avenues for civic communication.

SOCIETY

Ethnic and National Identity

Contemporary India is a "complicated jigsaw"[7] of astounding ethnic and social diversity cobbled together by centuries of imperial conquest. Independent India has sought to create from this patchworked imperial raj a unified and secular nation-state. This has required of India and its citizens a measure of social tolerance that has not always been available, seemingly leaving the country on the edge of disintegration. Yet for all the communitarian conflict and threats of secession, national unity has prevailed. Before noting the political culture that has at least to some degree preserved this unity, we turn first to the ethnic and social divisions that threaten it.

When the lighter-skinned Indo-Aryans migrated into what is now northern and central India thousands of years ago, they pushed the native, darker-skinned Dravidians southward. Each culture retained separate linguistic and cultural identities that persist to some extent today. Roughly two thirds of Indians (virtually all in the north) speak some variation of the Sanskrit-based language brought by the Indo-Aryans, which now forms some ten distinct languages. The most common of these is Hindi, one of two official national languages, which is spoken by over one third of all Indians. Approximately one fourth of all Indians speak one of the four main Dravidian languages. In all, the constitution recognizes fourteen languages, but at least another thirty languages claim over 1 million speakers each. The only other national language is English. Although only some 3 percent of the population speaks it fluently, as in other polyglot postcolonies it has become an essential medium for national politics and commerce.

ETHNIC GROUPS

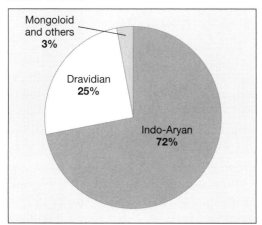

RELIGION

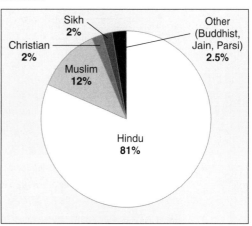

INDIAN LANGUAGES

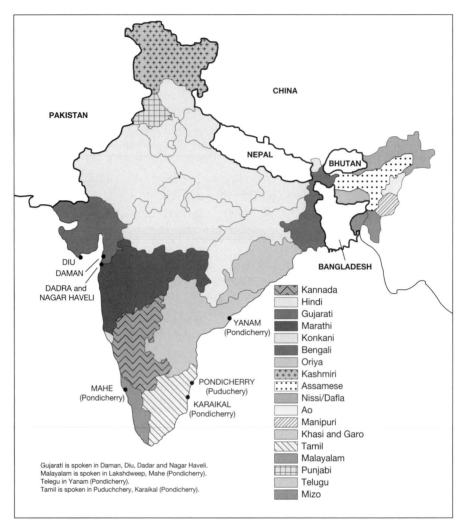

PAKISTAN

CHINA

NEPAL

BHUTAN

DIU
DAMAN

DADRA and
NAGAR HAVELI

YANAM
(Pondicherry)

BANGLADESH

MAHE
(Pondicherry)

PONDICHERRY
(Puduchery)

KARAIKAL
(Pondicherry)

Kannada
Hindi
Gujarati
Marathi
Konkani
Bengali
Oriya
Kashmiri
Assamese
Nissi/Dafla
Ao
Manipuri
Khasi and Garo
Tamil
Malayalam
Punjabi
Telugu
Mizo

Gujarati is spoken in Daman, Diu, Dadar and Nagar Haveli.
Malayalam is spoken in Lakshdweep, Mahe (Pondicherry).
Telegu in Yanam (Pondicherry).
Tamil is spoken in Puduchchery, Karaikal (Pondicherry).

Source: http://www.mapsofindia.com/maps/india/indianlanguages.htm (accessed 30 June 2005).

Note: Map is not to scale.

These divisions are at once exacerbated and moderated by religious differences. Although over 80 percent of Indians share a common faith, regional
and linguistic groups practice their Hinduism differently. The promotion of
Hindu nationalism has brought a degree of unity to these groups, but at the
expense of some 12 percent of Indians who are Muslim and 2 to 3 percent

who are adherents of Sikhism (an amalgam of Hindu and Muslim theologies) and the comparable percentage who are Christian. These religious differences have often acquired political significance, leading at times to assassinations, violent pogroms and bitter reprisals, and secessions and threats of secession. The most dramatic flare-ups of sectarian violence have been between Hindus and Muslims, including the initial partitioning of Muslim Pakistan and Hindu India and ongoing territorial disputes in Kashmir as well as the events at Ayodhya in 1992 and Gujarat in 2002, described earlier. Less dramatically but perhaps even more significantly, India's democracy has fostered the emergence and growth of religious-based political parties that have rallied around these nationalist and separatist sentiments.

As if the linguistic and religious differences were not sufficiently divisive, the hierarchical separation of Indian society into castes remains the most significant of India's social divisions. Although industrialization and urbanization have made the caste system today more permeable and flexible than it once was, it remains socially, politically, and economically important. Although neither class identity nor income inequality are as severe in India as in many other developing countries, those in the lower ranks of India's caste system are typically also the poorest, with the scheduled castes the poorest of the poor. In an effort to redress this discrimination against the outcastes, or Dalits, the government established affirmative action programs reserving jobs, scholarships, and even seats in the parliament for members of this group.

Although not fully effective in leveling the playing field, these measures have helped the Dalits achieve a degree of social mobility and even political organization (including the formation of a regional political party). Moreover, the policies have become contentious, angering many higher-caste Hindus, who see the measures—along with special protections afforded to minority religious groups—as reverse discrimination. The Hindu nationalist Bharatiya Janata Party (BJP) has seized on this issue in expanding its constituency among the growing Hindu middle class and stirring the embers of Hindu fundamentalism.

Ideology and Political Culture

As with many other elements of Indian politics, India's political culture defies generalization. Nonetheless, two somewhat contradictory values are worth mentioning. On the one hand, Indians identify themselves and their politics *locally*. Indians are tied most importantly to family, occupational group, and their immediate regional linguistic and religious associates. These immediate ties tend to segment and even fragment politics in India, which promotes political awareness and cooperation locally but also causes political friction and even violence between groups. And while this localization may limit the scope of conflict, it also constrains the kind of mobilization that could address pressing national needs.

On the other hand, despite its cultural diversity and contentious politics, Indians continue to identify themselves as Indians and generally support and see themselves as an important part of Indian *national* democracy. So while the bonds of national unity are less powerful than local ties, India's "bewilderingly plural population" nonetheless sees itself as "capable of purposeful collective action."[8] Mahatma (Mohandas K.) Gandhi and Jawaharlal Nehru remain national heroes for most Indians who take their role as citizens seriously and see Indian democracy as legitimate.

Some see in this combined sense of local power and political efficacy a dangerous tendency toward identity politics in Indian democracy. Nehru's secular nationalism has ceded ground to political movements that mobilize supporters in the name of religion or region. Majority Hindus perceive themselves as threatened by minority religions, the prosperous middle class depicts itself as victim of India's poorest outcastes, and Punjabi Sikhs and Kashmiri Muslims clamor for independence. Yet democracy and unity prevail, speaking to India's remarkable capacity to adopt and adapt foreign institutions for its own use. An Indian adage claims that "democracy is like cricket—a quintessentially Indian game that just happened to have been invented elsewhere." There is no question that India has made democracy its own.

POLITICAL ECONOMY

By the time India finally obtained its independence from British imperialism, it had had quite enough of the West's version of free trade. For nearly four decades, successive (mostly INC) governments adopted a foreign policy of mercantilist economic nationalism, promoting **import-substitution industrialization** and restricting foreign investment and trade. Governments also promoted social democratic policies domestically in order to limit the private sector, redistribute wealth, and give the state the leading role in guiding the economy. These policies were in some ways successful. By 1979, through the technological gains of the green revolution, India had become one of the largest agricultural producers in the world and for most years since then has been a net exporter of food. India established a relatively large—if not broad—middle class, and some niches in the economy and some regions of the country truly prospered.

However, by the mid-1980s, frustration with poverty, corruption, and continued slow growth at home coupled with the popularity of export-led growth and structural-adjustment programs abroad, led successive governments to

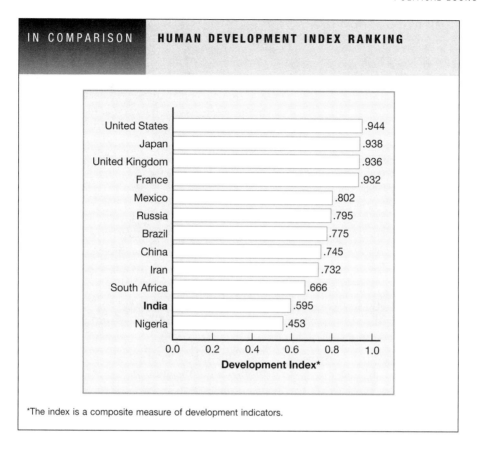

IN COMPARISON   **HUMAN DEVELOPMENT INDEX RANKING**

	Development Index*
United States	.944
Japan	.938
United Kingdom	.936
France	.932
Mexico	.802
Russia	.795
Brazil	.775
China	.745
Iran	.732
South Africa	.666
India	.595
Nigeria	.453

*The index is a composite measure of development indicators.

adopt neo-liberal policies of economic reform. Although the process has been more gradual than the "shock therapy" adopted in Poland or Russia and the results have been less thorough than the reform and opening of China, measures to liberalize foreign trade and investment and privatize the economy have been significant. Governments weakened India's notorious **permit raj,** the mercantilist holdover requiring licensing and approval processes for operating a business and importing and exporting products. Restrictions on foreign investment have been eased, and many state-owned companies have been sold to the private sector.

The results of this liberalization effort have been impressive. In the two decades since the reforms were launched, economic growth in India has averaged nearly 6 percent per year (compared with an average of less than 2 percent per year for the previous twenty years). Even as the population continued to grow rapidly, the total number of poor Indians declined by 69 million from 1979 to 2000. Trade and investment are up, and Western outsourcing (moving the production of goods and services to another country to take advantage of cheap

LABOR FORCE BY OCCUPATION

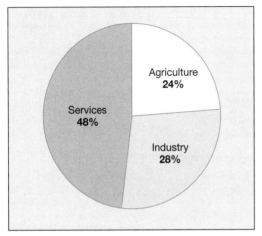

Agriculture
24%

Services
48%

Industry
28%

labor or other savings) has brought jobs and growth to some segments of the Indian economy.

Yet huge economic problems persist. Fully one quarter of India's population remains mired in poverty, living on less than US$1 per day. Half of India's children under the age of five are underweight, and the total number of malnourished Indians has hardly dropped in the last ten years. Fully one fourth of the world's undernourished reside in India. Corruption and protectionism persist; it still takes on average eighty-nine days to secure the permits necessary to start a business in India.

A comparison with China in this regard is instructive.[9] Although China was poorer than India when both countries were established in the late 1940s and remained so through the 1970s, China has dramatically outperformed India since then. Its growth rates have hovered near 10 percent for the past twenty years, population growth has slowed, and trade and investment have skyrocketed. In recent years, China's annual increases in trade have exceeded India's total annual trade.

Part of the explanation for this difference rests in two challenges that continue to perplex India: too many people and too little education. Whereas the growth rate of China's population has slowed to less than 1 percent per year, India's remains closer to 2 percent. This has meant fewer mouths to feed in China and more wealth to spread around. The World Bank has concluded that extreme poverty has been nearly eradicated there.

In addition, China has done a far better job of providing basic education for its citizens. Over 90 percent of Chinese adults are literate, compared with less than 60 percent of Indians. More troubling, less than half of Indian women are literate, compared with over 85 percent of Chinese women. Economists and demographers argue, however, that there may be a silver lining: if India can educate its population, particularly its women, population pressures will ease. More important, this demographic liability could become an asset as mouths to feed develop into skilled, competitive workers in the twenty-first century global economy.

Like China and many other developing countries that have been drawn into this global economy, India faces an additional problem. Although the economy is growing, it is doing so unevenly. Much has been made of India's recent information technology (IT) boom, and for good reason. Several large Indian computer firms are now globally competitive, and Western companies have flocked to cities such as Bangalore in the south and Hyderabad in the north to take advantage of India's wealth of service workers and English-speaking engineers.

But the IT industry remains largely irrelevant to most Indians. As a whole, it employs only about 1 million out of a labor force of some 500 million and makes up only 4 percent of India's GDP. Six of India's twenty-eight states receive virtually all of India's foreign investment. Thus it has created for India a dual economy that exacerbates both regional and class tensions. An elite, urban, prosperous, and Westernized middle-class minority sits precariously on top of a huge lower class that is largely rural, illiterate, and in many cases unemployed or underemployed.

If India is to eliminate or at least address this persistent poverty and inequality, stay ahead of its rapid population growth, and perhaps catch up to China and other competitors, scholars and policy makers agree that it must do several things. Among them are improving conditions for its rural population; improving roads, telecommunication, and other aspects of the

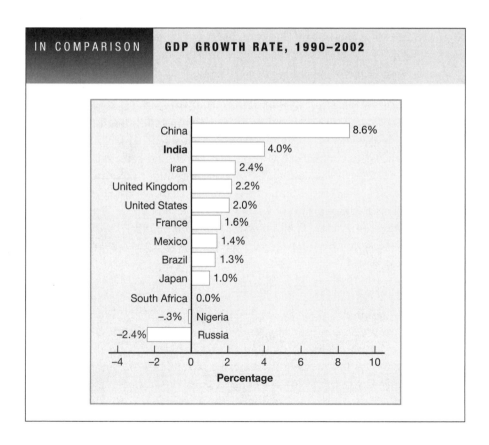

IN COMPARISON   GDP GROWTH RATE, 1990–2002

infrastructure, increasing foreign investment; and above all providing elementary education and basic health care, particularly to its girls and women.

There is evidence that this can be done. The state of Kerala, in southwestern India, boasts female literacy rates of nearly 90 percent and fertility rates and population growth far lower than the national average. These are the result, however, not of neo-liberal market reforms but of several decades of socialist state policies in education, health care, and land reform that emphasize equality over freedom. Although India is not likely to return fully to the social democratic policies of the 1950s, its voters in 2004 chose the INC and its leftist coalition partners with a mandate not to forget them—the majority of Indian voters whom recent economic growth has in many ways left behind.

FOREIGN RELATIONS AND THE WORLD

Once India had gained its independence, Jawaharlal Nehru charted for the country a foreign policy of "peaceful coexistence" with its neighbors and "nonalignment" in the superpower cold war that was just then taking shape in the postwar world. In fact, Nehru became a leader of the nonaligned movement of postcolonial developing countries seeking to create a neutral "third world" separate from the American-led Western nations (the first world) and the Soviet-led Eastern bloc (the second world). Unfortunately, the ethnic politics of partition and the geopolitics of big-power relations derailed this course. In the decades that followed, India fought three wars with Pakistan and maintained frosty relations with both Communist China and the capitalist United States. With the end of the cold war, however, and under conditions of much higher (nuclear) stakes (first China, then India and finally Pakistan joined the United States as nuclear powers), India's relations have recently thawed with all three of these countries. With growing economic and political clout, India is beginning to command the respect of an emerging great power in both the region and the world.

PAKISTAN

No issue has haunted India's foreign relations as much as the legacy of partition. This bitter division into Muslim Pakistan and Hindu India in 1947 not only soured relations between these erstwhile partners in the independence struggle, but it also left jagged and festering wounds in the very boundaries between them. At the center of the conflict is the contested region of Kashmir, situated on the northern portion of the border between the two countries. At the time of partition, Kashmir was the largest of three principalities that had not committed themselves to joining one country or the other. The

INDIA'S BORDER CONFLICTS

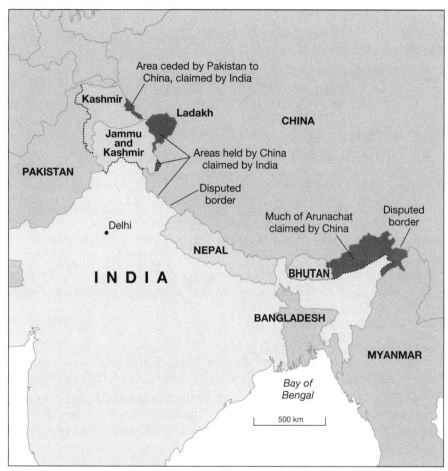

Source: *Economist*, 3 March 2005.

majority of its subjects were Urdu-speaking Muslims whose ethnic sentiments leaned toward Pakistan, but its prince was a Hindu who hoped Kashmir could remain independent. This ambivalence gave way to armed conflict—the first of three undeclared wars between India and Pakistan—within months of partition.

A year of armed conflict ground to a halt in 1949, and the line of conflict has remained the de facto border between the two countries (see map). Pakistan launched a second war in 1965, hoping to sever Kashmir from the rest of India, but the Pakistani advantage of surprise was no match for India's superior forces, and the hostilities ended in three weeks. The third war was waged not over Kashmir but over the struggle for independence in Bangladesh, what was then East Pakistan. Although the original partition created one Pakistan, its eastern and western halves were linked only by a shared religion and were divided by language, culture, and—most troubling—nearly 1,000 miles of Indian territory. Backed by newly acquired Soviet armaments, India came to the aid of the secessionist movement in 1971, forcing Pakistan to accept liberation and Bangladeshi independence.

The Kashmir region remains the world's most militarized border dispute. The level of tension has waxed and waned, but as one author notes, the cease-fire line has continued "to serve as a target range"[10] claiming on average 3,000 lives per year. With nuclear weapons now potential ammunition for both sides, many hope that caution will prevail over the "pathological politics" of ethnic hatred.[11] There is reason for hope. Peace talks were restarted in 2004, and the two countries have also restarted cross-border bus travel and are considering a gas pipeline from Iran to India that will pass through Pakistan. To much fanfare, India's and Pakistan's political leaders met in India in 2005 to view a cross-national cricket match (India won), proving again that in this region of the world cricket is serious politics. A devastating earthquake that struck the Kashmiri region later that year killed some 74,000 Pakistanis and Indians and led to a humanitarian crisis, spurring negotiators on both sides to agree to soften restrictions on the border and seek a more permanent solution to the territorial dispute.

SEPTEMBER 11 AND GREAT-POWER RELATIONS

India's early hopes for peaceful relations with China, its neighbor to the north, were dashed by Chinese expansion into areas of India's northeastern Himalayan region. Tensions led to the Chinese invasion of India in 1962 to resolve what China viewed as "border disputes" but what India deemed outright aggression. India claims several territories now held by China—mostly Kashmiri land ceded to China by Pakistan—that are larger in area than Switzerland. China, in turn, claims three times as much real estate to the east that is now in the hands of India. Efforts since 1998 to resolve these disputes finally yielded positive results in 2005, when both sides agreed to allow a cross-national committee to resolve this conflict. Despite this recent thawing of relations and China's support of India's bid for a permanent seat on the United Nations Security Council, the relationship is complicated by China's long-standing ties with Pakistan, including its helping Pakistan keep pace with India's nuclear capabilities.

The September 11 terrorist attacks in the United States and subsequent "war on terror" launched by George W. Bush's administration have brought a new dynamic to India's dealings with China, the United States, and even Pakistan. Historically, India's relationship with the world's second largest democracy has been cool at best. But like China, India saw the benefits of recasting its own struggle with Muslim insurgents as part of a larger global war on terror. The United States has responded warmly, lifting sanctions in place since India's nuclear tests in the 1990s, expanding trade, and—to Pakistan's chagrin—increasing military sales. Most significantly, in 2006 President Bush signed a nuclear cooperation deal with Prime Minister Singh that allowed India to purchase nuclear technology for the first time in three decades, despite India's refusal to sign the Nuclear Non-Proliferation Treaty. These actions have put Pakistan in an awkward position: after all, India's Kashmiri terrorists have been viewed by Pakistan as freedom fighters. But Pakistan has had little choice but to go along with this "war on terror," and India has been impressed with Pakistan's recent efforts to rein in Kashmiri insurgents and facilitate peace efforts between the rivals.

Today, India's diplomatic relations with its neighbors and other powers in the region are more cordial than they have been at any time since independence. Trade and investment with both China and the United States are booming, and talks between India and Pakistan on opening and expanding transportation and trade links across the bloodstained region of Kashmir are under way. India is one of only a handful of nuclear powers and enjoys a growing economy and increasing influence in global forums. India—with good reason—sees itself, and is increasingly seen by others, as an emerging great power.

CURRENT ISSUES

PIPELINE POLITICS AND ENERGY ALLIANCES

Although improving education and addressing poverty may be primary public policy concerns for India's economic development, an issue of almost equal concern is India's growing energy needs. Already facing desperate shortages of electricity and fossil fuels to feed its industrial and consumer demands, analysts project that India will need to double its capacity to generate, transmit, and distribute energy in the next ten years. Just as India's green revolution in the 1960s and 1970s doubled its food production, many are pointing to the need for a comparable energy revolution today.

Although India has substantial coal and natural gas reserves and the potential for a great deal of domestic hydropower, it is also aggressively pursuing energy resources from abroad and has brokered a deal with the United States to acquire nuclear technology. India envisions an Asian pipeline grid that would bring natural gas west from Myanmar through Bangladesh to India and from Central Asia and Iran east to India. In addition to substantially boosting its own resources, India hopes to push this pipeline on to China, brokering natural gas to energy-hungry China. Many in the region laud this initiative in effect to reopen the ancient Silk Route and update it with a vital twenty-first-century commodity. Proponents note not only its economic value, but also the potential it has for easing political tensions between India and its regional neighbors, Pakistan and China. The European Union, after all, began as a coal and steel arrangement among European rivals.

The United States has been less enthusiastic about India providing Iran with a lucrative outlet for its natural gas and has sought to increase its own favor and influence in India, agreeing in 2006 to life curbs on the sale of nuclear technology and nuclear reactors to India. Those critical of this agreement argue that India has never signed the Nuclear Non-Proliferation Treaty and tested its own nuclear weapons in 1998 outside of the treaty. India has sought to assure the United States that its nuclear ambitions are entirely peaceful, but at the same time has resisted American pressure to break off pipeline negotiations with Iran.

CAN SECULAR DEMOCRACY PREVAIL?

In early 2005, a bus station in Indian-controlled Kashmir went up in flames on the eve of the Indian and Pakistani governments' launching of bus links across the contested border. Later that year, three simultaneous bomb blasts rocked New Delhi; once again hours before the two governments announced a landmark agreement easing border resitrictions designed to facilitate relief efforts in the region following a devastating earthquake. Kasmiri-based Muslim insurgent groups claimed responsibility for both actions, seeking to stymie peace efforts in this war-torn region and fearing that these confidence-building measures would undermine their efforts to end Indian rule and unite the area with Pakistan or declare Kashmiri independence.

These flames are both symbol and substance of the most pressing issue facing India today: Can pluralist politics prevail? Can Mahatma (Mohandas K.) Gandhi and Jawaharlal Nehru's vision of a secular nation embracing all Indians and a democratic policy giving voice to all identities survive? Or will the rise of Hindu chauvinism, the press of communitarian violence, and the stress of separatist demands fray India at its borders and tear it apart from the center?

Certainly there are reasons for grave concern. The embers from one sectarian clash hardly cool before the next spark is ignited. The fires that destroyed the mosque in Ayodhya and the bloody siege at the Sikh Golden Temple in Amritsar compete with images of the charred corpses of Hindu pilgrims in railcars at the station in Gujarat. Each of these becomes the justification for yet another round of bloody reprisals and increasingly inflammatory political demands.

Yet the very survival of Indian democracy is its greatest hope. Despite the violence, Indian pluralist politics has given voice and legitimacy to a welter of demands and preserved relative peace in this multiethnic nation. Even the Kashmiri bus-station fire offers good evidence. Despite the arson and the murder of one local official, the Indian government resolved that the bus service would go on as planned, and it has. Local citizens are overwhelmingly in favor of this effort to reunite families that have been separated in some cases for over fifty years. The government has painted streets in the villages along the bus route in the Islamic holy color of green. And the sides of the buses are adorned with an ancient Kashmiri saying that holds promise for all Indians: "I broke the sword and made sickles out of it."

NOTES

1. Stanley Wolpert, *India* (Berkeley: University of California Press, 1991), p. 14.
2. Wolpert, *India*, p. 55.
3. V. S. Naipaul, *India: A Million Mutinies Now* (New York: Penguin, 1990).
4. Wolpert, *India*, p. 212.
5. The following comparisons are taken from Susanne Hoeber Rudolph and Lloyd I. Rudolph, "New Dimensions of Indian Democracy,"*Journal of Democracy* 13 (2002), pp. 52–66.
6. Arun Shourie, "Two Concepts of Liberty," Economist, 3 March 2005, http://www.economist.com/displaystory.cfm?story_id=3689308 (accessed 1 July 2005).
7. Kesavan Mukul, "India's Embattled Secularism," *Wilson Quarterly* 27 (Winter 2003), p. 61.
8. Kesavan, "India's Embattled Secularism."
9. A number of the comparative figures for China and India in this and subsequent paragraphs are drawn from "The Tiger in Front," Survey: India and China, *Economist*, 3 March 2005.
10. Wolpert, *India*, p. 235.
11. Ishtiaq Ahmed, "The 1947 Partition of India: A Paradigm for Pathological Politics in India and Pakistan,"*Asian Ethnicity* 3 (March 2002), pp. 9–28.

KEY TERMS

WEB LINKS

GOI Directory of Indian government Web sites   **goidirectory.nic.in**
Parliament   **parliamentofindia.nic.in**
The Times of India   **timesofindia.indiatimes.com**
Government and Politics of South Asia: South and Southeast Asian Studies,
   Columbia University Libraries
   www.columbia.edu/cu/lweb/indiv/southasia/cuvl/govt.html
India Democracy   **www.indiademocracy.com** A non-profit, pro-democracy
   site facilitating communication between citizens and elected representatives
Outlook, a popular weekly news magazine   **outlookindia.com**

9 IRAN

Head of State: Ayatollah Ali Khamenei
(since June 4, 1989)

Head of Government:
Mahmoud Ahmadinejad
(since August 6, 2005)

Capital: Tehran

Total land size: 1,648,000 sq km

Population: 68 million

GDP at PPP: .516 trillion US$

GDP per Capita: $7,700

IRAN

INTRODUCTION

Why Study This Case?

Like many of our cases, Iran nicely illustrates some of the most important dynamics of comparative politics. Most important, Iran is associated with what we think of as **Islamism, or Islamic fundamentalism.** When we speak of Islamic fundamentalism, we mean an approach to the faith marked by a belief that literal interpretation of the faith should be the basis of the political regime. In other words, Islamic fundamentalism transforms faith into ideology.

In 1979, the authoritarian, secular Iranian monarchy fell to revolution, inspired in part by the charismatic leadership of the religious leader **Ruhollah Khomeini.** This Islamic revolution dramatically transformed all aspects of Iranian life, as Khomeini and his followers sought to create a theocracy, in which the regime is dominated by a religious elite. In this "Islamic Republic," law and politics are expected to flow from the **Koran,** the main spiritual text of Islam. The Iranian revolution became a source of inspiration for Islamist movements around the world. As numerous countries struggle with Islamic fundamentalism, the Iranian revolution remains an important example of the power of Islam as a political vision.

When one looks more deeply, however, one finds that Iran is atypical and unrepresentative of the politics of Islam or even the politics of the Middle East. Contrary to what we might think, Iran is not an Arab country—the major ethnicity of Iran's population is Persian. Nor do Iranians speak Arabic, the common language of the Middle East. Indeed, Iranians see themselves as a distinct nation and look upon Arab countries as foreign. Iranians do not see themselves as part of some broader group of Arab peoples.

This difference in ethnicity and national identity is further compounded by religion. Again, at first glance Iran's revolution might be seen as the first spark in the current wave of Islamic fundamentalism, and there can be no doubt that the revolution did inspire a new wave of radicalism across the region. But the impact of the revolution was also tempered by the fact that Iran practices **Shiism,** a minority form of Islam that differs in its belief in the rightful religious heir of **Muhammad.** As a result, many followers of Islam around the world (especially fundamentalists) reject the Iranian theocracy for avowing a heretical form of the faith. In spite of this division, Iran has certainly influenced modern debates about the relationship between politics and Islam, especially among Shiite groups elsewhere in the region (as in Iraq and Lebanon). For some, Iran remains the model for political change; for others,

Iran is an example of how religion and politics should not mix. Such views can be found not only among average Shiites but also among the top clergy.

These complexities help shape Iran's role in the international system. In recent years, Iran has moved toward developing its own nuclear-weapons capacity, thus putting itself on a collision course with the United States and the European Union. Fears are that Iran might use nuclear weapons against Israel (which has its own nuclear arsenal) or that the regime might transfer weapons or weapons technology to terrorists. Such tensions occur against the backdrop of growing domestic turmoil. A quarter century after the Islamic revolution, reform-minded leaders have sought greater liberty and democracy, supported by former president **Mohammad Khatami** (1997 to 2005). Hopes were high that Khatami's election would pave the way for dramatic political change. Religious conservatives managed to beat back the reformers and limit Khatami's powers, however. The June 2005 election of the conservative Mahmoud Ahmadinejad as president dealt a serious blow to the reformers and the conservatives appear to have the upper hand for now. But is their hostility to change a recipe for future domestic conflict? And if so, how might it help improve, or even destabilize, international relations? In spite of its unique institutions, Iran may give us a glimpse into the potential power of Islamic fundamentalism, as well as the sources of resistance to it.

Major Geographic and Demographic Features

Iran occupies an important position in Middle East politics, yet in many ways it is an outlier. As we have already noted, Iran is a Persian rather than an Arab country, with its population speaking **Farsi** instead of Arabic. Iran itself is on the eastern periphery of the Middle East, sharing borders with Afghanistan and several states that were once part of the Soviet Union. But its geographic position does not mean that Iran is insignificant. It is about the size of Alaska or somewhat smaller than Mexico and has a population of about 70 million—larger than that of the United Kingdom. For both its size and its population, Iran ranks in the world's top twenty nations. Not only is it large, but it is also young. The median age is less than twenty-five, and nearly one third of the population is under fifteen. Compare this to Japan, for example, where the median age is over forty and less than 15 percent of the population is under fifteen. The youthful nature of Iran matters. A large percentage of the population has no memory of the country before the Islamic Republic and has largely experienced only economic decline under the current regime. Related to this is the fact that the state must deal with a large influx of young people into the education and economic sectors. This segment of the population currently represents the greatest challenge to the regime, and the government responded harshly to a wave of student protests for reform that first broke out in 1999.

POPULATION BY AGE, 2000

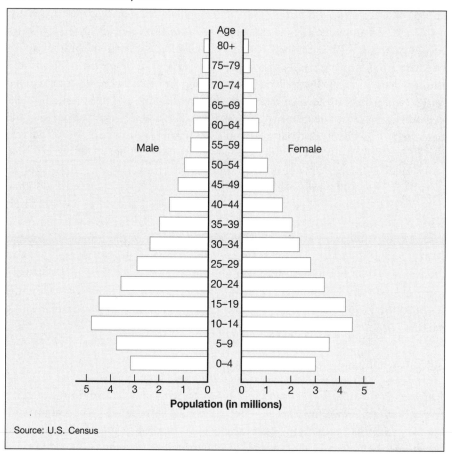

Source: U.S. Census

In addition to being young, Iran's population is diverse. Only about half the population is ethnically Persian. One quarter is Azeri, members of a Turkic-speaking people, who are concentrated in the northwest of the country, near the borders of Armenia and Azerbaijan. The remaining quarter of the population is made up of several smaller ethnic groups, including Kurds, Arabs, Turkmen, and Gilaki. There were various conflicts between these groups and the new government in the aftermath of the 1979 revolution. Although the conflicts have largely dissipated, there remain internal and external tensions over the place of the ethnic groups in Iranian society and politics.

As important as what lies above the ground in Iran is what lies beneath it. Iran is the fourth largest producer of oil in the world, after Saudi Arabia, the United States, and Russia, and it is the fourth largest exporter of oil as well. As in many other countries, oil has been a boon and a curse. It was oil that drew imperial attention at the start of the twentieth century and helped bring about modernization—as well as corruption and revolution. Oil has also helped keep the current regime in power, even as other parts of the economy have stagnated. Yet oil has its limits. Some observers project that at its current rate, Iran will go from exporting oil to importing it within a decade. Nonetheless, Iran possesses a large reserve of natural gas, perhaps the largest in the world after Russia. As more countries seek cleaner alternatives to oil, natural gas is likely to become central to Iran's development.

Historical Development of the State

THE PERSIAN LEGACY AND THE ISLAMIC EMPIRE

Modern Iran can be traced back thousands of years, to the second millennium b.c.e. Around that time, a number of people migrated into the region from Central Asia, among them the ethnic group we know as the Persians. Persian continues to be the name used for the majority population of Iran, and up until 1935 the country itself was known as **Persia.** Over the centuries, the Persians were able to extend their influence in the region, subduing other groups and creating an empire in the process. By the fifth century b.c.e. the Persian Empire under the Achaemenid dynasty was vast, stretching from modern-day Afghanistan to Greece and Egypt. This empire was noted for its wealth and technical sophistication and would become an important symbol of Iranian might that resonates with Iranians even today. Although the empire would collapse after two centuries, the country continued to develop under a series of ruling dynasties. Their kings, or *shahs*, would rule through the sixth century c.e. During this time, Persia would be shaped not only by its own innovations but also by its connections to neighboring cultures.[1]

The most dramatic transformation of Persia by outside forces occurred in the seventh century, with the arrival of Islam. Shortly after the death of the prophet Muhammad, in 632 C.E., his successors began to spread the faith through the region by military conquest. By 650, Persia was essentially under Islamic control. The new Islamic empire, under the Umayyad Dynasty (661–750 C.E.), brought Persia into the Arabian fold while adopting some Persian practices and institutions. Arabic became the language of the state, while Farsi remained the tongue of the people, and the population slowly converted to the new faith. In the seventh century, a major schism occurred within Islam, led by the followers of Muhammad's son-in-law, Ali, who developed their own allegiances to Ali's line of descendants. This "party of Ali," or shiat Ali, had its stronghold in neighboring southern Iraq and would become the state religion of Persia several centuries later.[2]

Up through the eleventh century, Persia would be part of this powerful Islamic empire, which was headed by a caliph, or supreme political and religious figure.

TIME LINE OF POLITICAL DEVELOPMENT

Year	Event
1905–6	Constitutional revolution seeks to limit power of the monarchy
1921	Reza Khan seizes power
1925	Reza Khan proclaimed shah and changes his name to Reza Shah Pahlavi
1941	British and Soviet forces occupy Iran; the shah is forced to abdicate in favor of his son, Mohammad Reza Pahlavi
1951	Parliament votes to nationalize the oil industry
1953	Struggle between the shah and Prime Minister Mohammad Mosaddeq culminates in Operation Ajax, in which Mosaddeq is overthrown with U.S. help
1963	White Revolution begins
1979	Iranian revolution: the shah is desposed; Ayatollah Ruhollah Khomeini returns from exile; U.S. Embassy seized, and hostages held for 444 days
1980	Iraq invades Iran
1988	Iran-Iraq War ends
1989	Ayatollah Khomeini dies
1997	Reformer Mohammad Khatami elected president
1999	Pro-reform student protests lead to rioting and mass arrests
2001	President Khatami reelected for a second term
2002	Russia begins work on Iran's first nuclear reactor, at Būshehr
2004	Conservatives regain control of parliament, routing reformers

From the thirteenth to the fifteenth century, Persia, like much of the Middle East, was devastated by the Mongols, who similarly subjected much of Russia to their rule. Persia was economically devastated and depopulated. Only with the death of the last major Mongol leader did a new Persian dynasty emerge.

DYNASTIC RULE AND THE ADOPTION OF SHIISM

The period from the sixteenth to the early twentieth century saw the rise of two long-standing Persian dynasties: the Safavids (1502–1736) and the Qajars

(1794–1925). Under the Safavids, the country adopted Shiism as the state religion and tightly connected religion and state. Shiism deviated from dominant Sunni Islam not only in its views on the proper descendants of the Prophet, but also in its development of a messianic view that the true descendant of Ali, known as the Hidden Imam, would reappear at the appointed time. In this regard, Shiism resembles Christianity. Also akin to Christianity is Shiism's emphasis on martyrdom, in particular its reverence of those seen as the true successors of Muhammad who died at the hands of their rivals. Finally, the Safavids cultivated a powerful clergy, sometimes compared with that found in Roman Catholicism. This, too, deviates from Sunni Islam, and it is this clergy that would come to play a critical role in modern Iranian politics.

Although Persia was able to maintain its power in the face of regional rivals, such as the Turkish Ottoman Empire, it inevitably came under pressure from the expanding Western powers. In the early nineteenth century, Russia squeezed Persia from the north, seizing territories, while the United

UNDERSTANDING ISLAM

Along with Judaism and Christianity, Islam is one of the three monotheistic faiths that trace their belief in one god to the biblical figure Abraham. Islam's central figure is Muhammad (c. 570–632 C.E.), known as the Prophet, who in 610 began to receive a series of revelations from God (Allah), which were delivered through the archangel Gabriel. These revelations were set down in the Koran, the central holy book of Islam. In these revelations, Muhammad came to understand that Judaism and Christianity, while originally prescribing proper relationships with God, had strayed from the true path. Facing persecution, Muhammad fled Mecca (in present-day Saudi Arabia) but eventually returned and took control of the city with the help of his followers. Mecca subsequently became the spiritual center of the faith.

Islam is built on five fundamental tenets, known as the pillars of Islam: the declaration of faith in Allah as the one God and Muhammad as his prophet, ritual daily prayers, almsgiving, fasting during the religious holy month of Ramadan, and the hajj, the pilgrimage to Mecca. Islam also comprises a system of religious laws, known as **sharia,** which regulates the conduct of believers.

In the centuries after Muhammad, Islam spread rapidly through the Middle East, Africa, Asia, and Europe. At the present time, nearly 1 billion people are Muslims. As with other faiths, Islam is divided into several sects. Ninety percent of Muslims belong to the Sunni branch, which identifies with the Islamic leadership that succeeded Muhammad. Shiism breaks with Sunni Islam on this issue of leadership and relies to a greater extent on a clerical hierarchy of religious leaders (the imams and **ayatollahs**). Sufism, another branch of the faith, emphasizes mysticism and ritual as a means of making a connection with Allah. Many Sunnis do not recognize Shiites or Sufis as Muslims, branding them heretical and idolatrous.

Kingdom conquered neighboring India and attempted to gain control over Afghanistan. Thus, by the mid–nineteenth century, Persia faced a crisis that extended across the region. How to confront the Western powers, given their superiority in military and economic might? How could Persia modernize and still preserve its sovereignty?

FAILED REFORMS AND THE EROSION OF SOVEREIGNTY

In the last decades of the Qajar dynasty, the monarchy enacted various reforms, learned from the West, meant to modernize the state. It experimented with Western-style economic and political institutions even as it surrendered ever more sovereignty to the British and the Russians. Public animosity grew in the face of government weakness and the perception that the monarchy was selling off the country to Westerners. In 1906, religious and business leaders led protests calling for limitations on the monarchy, which resulted in an elected assembly that drew up the country's first constitution and legislative body (known as the **Majlis**).

This "constitutional revolution" did not live up to expectations. The monarchy quickly sought to reassert its power and disband the Majlis, and in the subsequent chaos the United Kingdom and Russia divided the country into spheres of influence, all but eliminating Persian sovereignty. With the outbreak of World War I, Persia became entangled in the conflict as Russian, Turkish, and British troops fought or supported various Persian factions that were vying for power. After the Russian Revolution and the collapse of the Ottoman Empire, the United Kingdom became the dominant foreign power in Persia. The Majlis sought to oppose British imperialism, however, rejecting a 1919 agreement that would have granted the United Kingdom significant control over the state and the economy, including Persia's oil industry.

The Majlis's anti-British stance did not pave the way for the establishment of democracy. In 1921, an obscure military officer, Reza Khan, marched into Tehran. Although the coup d'état does not appear to have been planned by the United Kingdom, it did receive support from British officials in Persia, and is widely considered by Iranians to be the direct result of an imperialist plot.

THE CONSOLIDATION OF POWER UNDER REZA SHAH

Reza Shah Pahlavi, as Reza Khan would come to call himself, proved to be more than a mere puppet of the British. Once head of the armed forces, he quickly moved to consolidate his power, removing his fellow conspirators from office and neutralizing threats within and without Iran. Centralizing the military, he was able to quell several regional rebellions and limit British and Soviet interference in the country's affairs. In 1923, the last shah of the Qajar dynasty appointed Reza Khan prime minister and promptly went into exile in Europe; in 1925, the Majlis formally deposed the Qajar dynasty and appointed Reza Khan the new shah.

As a monarch with limited constraints on his power, the shah pursued a course of dramatic Westernization, going far beyond the country's previous flirtation with Western innovations. This course included bureaucratic reform, the institution of primary and secondary education as well as a university system, the development of road and rail systems, and the establishment of a number of state-owned businesses to develop monopolies in important domestic and export-oriented markets. Persia also exerted greater control over its burgeoning oil industry, which had been dominated by Britain since its inception. In addition, Reza Shah instituted national conscription as part of his effort to centralize military might and extend state control over what had been a fractious and tribal country. The shah complemented this political centralization with efforts to build a modern national identity. Persia's extensive history was used to promote the idea of a single people whose glory extended back thousands of years.

Finally, as part of his modernization, the shah greatly extended the rights of women, giving them the right to education, including at the university level. He also sought to root out traditional customs seen as holding back the emancipation of women. One important symbol was the headscarf, or chador. In 1934, inspired by similar reforms in Turkey, Persia forbade the wearing of the chador in schools, a proscription that was later extended to other public facilities. The shah's efforts in regard to women were part of a broader attack on religious institutions, whose power was limited in such areas as education and law. Like the Safavids, the shah sought to bring Shiism under political authority, in order to bolster the legitimacy of the state and the regime.

Modernization came at the expense of democratization. The shah's objective was to rapidly develop the country along Western lines. Democratic institutions, such as the press and the Majlis, were curtailed, and religious and political opponents were jailed, exiled, or killed. By the eve of World War II, Iran, as the country was by then known, had made significant progress in establishing modern political institutions and independence from foreign interference. Yet it had come at the cost of increased repression of civic life and traditional institutions and identities.

World War II again drew the country unwillingly into conflict, as the United Kingdom and Russia invaded in 1941 to open a land corridor between Allied territories and gain access to Iranian oil. Reza Shah was forced to abdicate in favor of his son, Mohammad Reza Pahlavi. While Iran did not become a literal battleground, as World War II gave way to the cold war, the United States, the United Kingdom, and the Soviet Union sought to consolidate their power over the weakened country and its oil supplies. Political activity also resurfaced in the face of the weakened state.[3]

THE NATIONALIST CHALLENGE UNDER MOSADDEQ, AND THE U.S. RESPONSE

In response, the Majlis (which had regained some of its power in the face of the war and the change in the monarchy) increasingly supported nationalization of the oil industry. Nationalization was advocated in particular by the new prime minister, **Muhammad Mosaddeq,** who represented the National Front, a party that favored reducing the shah's role in the government. The shah reluctantly conceded to nationalization, provoking British anger and leading to the withdrawal of Britain's technical support, essentially halting oil production. As the crisis deepened, Mosaddeq moved leftward, allying himself with the Marxist Tudeh Party. He also grew more authoritarian in his politics, dissolving the Majlis in 1953 on the basis of a questionable referendum. The United States, which initially had been sympathetic to Iran's dispute with the United Kingdom, now began to see Iran through the lens of the cold war, fearing Communist rule. With the support of the shah, the United States and the United Kingdom moved to overthrow Mosaddeq, through a covert program known as **Operation Ajax.** Several days of conflict between supporters of the prime minister and supporters of the shah, including rival elements of the military finally culminated in a victory for the shah and his backers. In the aftermath of Operation Ajax, hundreds of National Front and Tudeh leaders and supporters were arrested, and several key leaders were executed.[4]

The shah then reconcentrated power in the hands of the monarchy. At the same time, the United States replaced the United Kingdom as Iran's most powerful strategic ally. The shah repressed Tudeh, the National Front, and other opposition parties and strengthened the secret police (known by its acronym, **SAVAK**). The position of the prime minister and the powers of the Majlis were also weakened.

AUTHORITARIANISM AND MODERNIZATION DURING THE WHITE REVOLUTION

Having brought the political system under his control, the shah turned to the policy of top-down modernization that had earlier been promoted by his father. In 1963, the government began a series of reforms in what came to be called the **White Revolution.**[5] The policy included land reform, privatization of state-run industries, a literacy campaign, and the enfranchisement of women. Some reforms, in particular land reform and the enfranchisement of women, faced strong opposition from religious leaders and in June of that year led to rioting, which the government suppressed. A subsequent and much weaker protest in 1964 over Iran's growing alliance with the United States was also quickly quelled. Connected to both protests was Ruhollah Khomeini, a charismatic ayatollah, or senior Shiite cleric. Khomeini was sent into exile, settling eventually in neighboring Iraq, where he continued to criticize the Iranian regime and articulate an alternative vision: an Iran governed by Islam.

For the next fifteen years, the shah would rule without serious challenge. All remaining pretenses of democracy were swept away, leaving a one-party state with all power concentrated in the hands of the monarchy. Rapid if uneven modernization continued, fostered by state policy as well as rising oil revenues (by the mid-1970s, upwards of US$20 billion a year). Iran built a large military in response to the shah's desire to project the country as a major regional force and a "great civilization" to be reckoned with on the world stage.

All of the rapid change did little to legitimize or support the shah's rule. Although billions of dollars in oil revenue flowed into Iran, much of it disappeared into the pockets of those in power or went to support the lavish lifestyle of the shah and his family. Economic improvements were not experienced widely across the population, and the influx of oil money led to inflation and the erosion of the middle class. That so much disruption and misery was tied to oil, and that so much of the oil industry was directed and run by foreigners, helped foster the sentiment that the United States and other Western powers were plundering the nation and leading to its ruin.

OPPOSITION TO THE SHAH AND THE IRANIAN REVOLUTION

The erosion of the economy during the mid-1970s eventually translated into public opposition. In 1977, the new U.S. president, Jimmy Carter, with his greater emphasis on human rights, began to criticize the shah for his repressive practices. Hoping to pacify his ally, the shah carried out a limited set of reforms, freeing some political prisoners and allowing banned organizations, like the National Front, to reorganize. The Carter administration did not press the shah further, however, and in the eyes of many hopeful Iranians seemed to retreat from its earlier criticisms in favor of political stability.

As U.S. pressure on the shah flagged, Iranians found another source of external opposition to his repressive rule in the form of the Ayatollah Khomeini. Still in Iraq, in the Shiite holy city of Najaf, Khomeini had over the course of his exile elaborated a vision of an Islamic political system for Iran. In particular, he argued that Islamic government should be constructed around the concept of **velayat-e faqih,** or rule by Islamic jurists. Whereas a monarchy was a usurpation of Allah's rule on earth, a system of government by a clergy trained in Islamic jurisprudence would be a continuation of the political system first established by the Prophet. Since such a form of government was the only regime consistent with the will of God, secular forms, such as that of the shah, should be overthrown. Khomeini's writings and sermons began to attract a large following in Iran, where, despite his absence, his reputation continued to grow.[6]

The shah, Khomeini, and the United States were now on a collision course. In 1978, the Iranian government attempted a smear campaign against

Khomeini, which only increased the ayatollah's support and touched off a series of protests over the course of several months that resulted in many deaths. Yet there was little expectation that these events would seriously threaten the shah's rule. As in the case of Eastern Europe and the Soviet Union, observers saw the Iranian opposition as too weak to match the power of the state.

Yet they were wrong. Three events turned public protest into revolution. First, in August 1978 a fire at the Rex Cinema in Abadan killed some 400 people. Many latched on to the rumor that SAVAK had torched the theater in order to blame the religious opposition. Others suggested that protesters had been chased into the theater by the police and then set ablaze. The funerals for the victims became another flash point for massive public protest.

In response to the public protests, the shah declared martial law. Yet the protests continued. In September, a massive protest in Tehran in defiance of martial law called for the end of the monarchy and the return of Ayatollah Khomeini. The army fired on the protesters, and some fired back. Hundreds were killed, and the violence took on increasingly religious symbolism, with allusions to martyrdom and the coming of a messiah.

The shah, realizing that even in exile Khomeini was a dangerous force, persuaded the Iraqi government to remove him to France. Rather than isolating him, however, the move to Europe only improved Khomeini's connections to Iran and the outside world. By November, Tehran was racked by widespread public violence, and the shah, while increasing his reliance on force, appeared to fear for his political survival. A series of crackdowns and attempts at co-optation of the opposition had no effect. The United States, too, vacillated in its support for the shah, criticizing the use of violence while continuing to give him its support.

In December 1978, millions of protesters took to the streets of Tehran in defiance of a government ban on such public gatherings. Then military units began to defect. The shah fled to Egypt and was replaced by a provisional government with a tenuous hold on the country. On February 1, 1979, millions gathered to welcome the Ayatollah Khomeini as he returned to Iran.[7]

THE CONSOLIDATION OF AN ISLAMIC REPUBLIC

Khomeini quickly moved to undermine the secular provisional government in his quest to create an Islamic state. Outflanking the various political and religious factions that had sprung up during the revolution, Khomeini used his charismatic power to gain control of the government and implement a regime that would enshrine his notion of the *velayat-e faqih*. The constitution of December 1979 allowed for not only a president and a prime minister, but also a *faqih*, a religious leader who is an expert in Islamic law, who would have supreme political authority. This position would be filled by Khomeini until his death.

THE U.S. EMBASSY HOSTAGE CRISIS

On February 14, 1979, a group of Iranian students associated with a Marxist political group temporarily seized control of the U.S. Embassy in Tehran. From the perspective of many Iranians, the embassy represented the power behind the throne that had propped up the shah's rule and acquiesced in his despotic ways. Khomeini denounced the takeover and forced the students' retreat. On November 4, the embassy was stormed a second time, and sixty-six Americans were taken hostage. On this occasion, however, the students were followers of Khomeini and were inspired by the belief that the United States was preparing a counterrevolution that would restore the monarchy, akin to operation Ajax in 1953. Most observers believed that the seizure would not be a prolonged affair. Within a matter of days, however, Khomeini formally endorsed the takeover, helping to project the new regime's staunch anti-Americanism and sideline more moderate forces who sought better relations with the United States. The crisis would last for 444 days, generating frustration and a deep animosity in the United States toward Iran while serving as a source of revolutionary pride for many Iranians. In April 1980, President Carter approved a military operation to rescue the hostages, only to have the mission scuttled after sandstorms, equipment failure, and a helicopter crash that killed eight servicemen. Only after Carter had been defeated by Ronald Reagan in the 1980 presidential election did Khomeini agree to allow the hostages to leave. To this day, the United States does not have formal diplomatic relations with Iran.

The creation of the new **Islamic Republic of Iran** would not be peaceful. The new government suppressed all opposition, including monarchists, members of Marxist and other secular political groups, ethnic minorities, and members of other faiths. From 1979 to 1980, hundreds if not thousands were executed in the name of "revolutionary justice." Student supporters of Khomeini seized control of the U.S. Embassy, holding much of its staff for over a year (and leading to an ill-fated rescue attempt by the Carter administration).

Yet the violence would pale in comparison with the Iran-Iraq War. As the revolution unfolded in Iran, in Iraq Saddam Hussein looked on these developments as a threat to his own rule over a country in which over half the population was Shiite. Khomeini himself hoped to spread his Islamic revolution beyond Iran's borders, and Iraq was the logical next choice. At the same time, Iraq saw in Iran's chaos an opportunity to extend its power in the region and seize territory. In September 1980, Iraq launched a full-scale invasion of Iran, initiating the Iran-Iraq war, which lasted until 1988.

The war caused widespread destruction on both sides. Iraq had superior firepower and the support of such countries as the United States, which feared the spread of the Iranian revolution. Iran, in contrast, had the greater population and its revolutionary fervor—leading it to send unarmed children to fight the Iraqis, promising them rewards in the afterlife for their certain martyrdom. In 1982, realizing that he had miscalculated his chance of success, Hussein sought to end the war, but Khomeini refused, hoping to carry his revolution to Iraq. In 1988, when the war finally ended, neither side emerged victorious, and nearly 1 million Iranians and Iraqis had died. Shortly thereafter, Khomeini himself died, leaving the Islamic Republic to govern without him.

POLITICAL REGIME

Since 1979, the Islamic Republic of Iran has sought to follow the ideas of Ruhollah Khomeini in creating a political system built around his idea of the *velayat-e faqih*, which would replace the sovereignty of men and women with the sovereignty of God as transmitted by the clergy. Yet Khomeini had come to power in the wake of a popular revolution that was driven by the public's demand for a political system that responded to their needs and desires. The new regime would thus have to reconcile the will of the people with what was seen as the will of God. Finally, as with the Russian Revolution of 1917, the new Iranian system was seen as a temporary set of institutions to serve until the return of the Hidden Imam, or true descendant of the Prophet (some Iranians in fact initially saw Khomeini as this figure). Since the death of Khomeini, however, the regime has faced the challenge of what Max Weber termed "the routinization of charisma." That is, how does a nation maintain the ideals of the leader once the leader is gone? The result is a political system quite unlike any other, a mixture of institutions that seek to balance the word of man with the word of God.

Political Institutions

THE CONSTITUTION

As we know, the Iranian constitution is a product of the 1979 revolution. Since that time, the only major changes to the document occurred ten years later, when Khomeini sought to ensure that the principles of the Islamic Republic would be maintained after his death. In its preamble, the constitution lays out the origins of the current regime, which is viewed as a revolt against the "American conspiracy" of the White Revolution. According to the constitution, the Islamic Republic exists not to serve the individual or mediate between diverse interests but to guide the people toward Allah. The Koran (the holy book of Islam) therefore serves not only as a spiritual text but also as the foundation for a unified national ideology that is to be embodied in the political system. Allah is sovereign over the Iranian people and state, and all political acts are expected to flow from the word of Allah. As the constitution itself states, "All civil, penal, financial, economic, administrative, cultural, military, political, and other laws and regulations must be based on Islamic criteria." This concept is consistent with religious fundamentalism in general, including Islamic, Christian, and Jewish forms. In each one, sovereignty in the form

> ### ESSENTIAL POLITICAL FEATURES
>
> - Legislative-executive system: semi-presidential theocracy
> - Legislature: Majlis
> - Lower house: Majlis
> - Upper house: (none)
> - Unitary or federal division of power: unitary
> - Main geographic subunits: ostanha (provinces)
> - Electoral system for lower house: single-member district majority
> - Chief judicial body: Supreme Court

of statehood and democracy is seen as blasphemous, with humans arrogating to themselves powers and rights that should reside only with God. The rule of law is heresy, as it is God's law, or *sharia,* that should reign supreme. As such, the Iranian constitution and political institutions are (at least in theory) an attempt to express God's will rather than instruments of human will.

The Branches of Government

THE SUPREME LEADER AND THE PRESIDENCY

The particular nature of the Iranian constitution has resulted in a set of political institutions that to outsiders are fascinating and bewildering. This can be seen in what is typically one of the less complex institutions, the executive branch of the government. As in many other countries, Iran has a dual executive, with power divided across two offices. In most other cases, such divisions break between head of state and head of government, with the former a monarch or president and the latter prime minister. The former reigns while the latter rules.

Iran's executive does not follow this pattern. The dominant executive is the **supreme leader,** a position created for Khomeini following the revolution as an expression of his charismatic power. As befits the title, the supreme leader is the most powerful office in Iran, created to ensure that a senior cleric is at the helm of Iranian politics, directing both political and spiritual life. The supreme leader serves for life, though the **Assembly of Experts** can theoretically remove him for incompetence or failure to uphold his religious duty.

The powers of the supreme leader are numerous. First, he may decide who may run for the office of president, eliminating rivals in the process. He is also commander in chief of the armed forces and appoints the heads of the various branches of the military. The supreme leader also appoints the chief

STRUCTURE OF THE GOVERNMENT

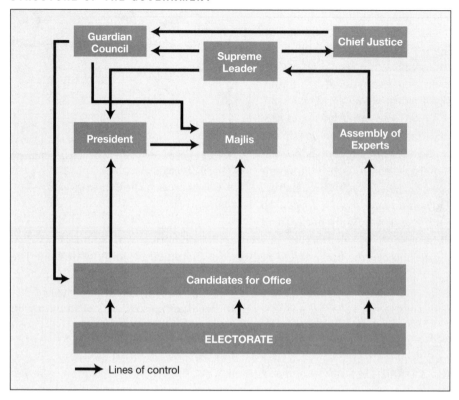

justice, and the directors of radio and television broadcasting. The supreme leader, while not directly involved in legislation, is given the power to supervise policy and, if necessary, call referenda. In some ways, the supreme leader may be seen as the head of state, embodying the people (through the word of Allah) and representing the nation in such areas as national defense. The supreme leader's role in policy is also much more that of reigning than ruling. Yet given the powers that do reside with the office, it is hardly ceremonial. If anything, the supreme leader looks much more like a traditional monarch than any corresponding modern political executive.

Following Khomeini's death, the office of supreme leader was to be held by a high-ranking Iranian ayatollah, just as Khomeini had been. Even at the time of the revolution, however, few of the most powerful ayatollahs accepted Khomeini's notion of the *velayat-e faqih,* and Khomeini's heir apparent, Ayatollah Hussein Ali Montazeri, was sidelined for his criticism of the regime's dictatorial nature. Since 1989, the supreme leader has been **Ali Khamenei,** a midlevel cleric who rose to the rank of ayatollah just before taking office.

Khamenei lacks the charismatic appeal of Khomeini and the religious training and reputation of Iran's most senior clerics.

How is the supreme leader chosen? The role falls to the Assembly of
Experts, a body of eighty-six members who are themselves popularly elected
for eight-year terms. Candidates for the assembly are vetted in advance of
elections, limiting the people's choice and ensuring that its membership is
dominated by clerics who accept the political status quo. In a way, this is not
unlike the power that Communist parties have held over elected positions,
vetting candidates on the basis of their loyalty to communism.

If the supreme leader functions as a powerful head of state, the presidency
is (confusingly) more akin to a head of government. The president is directly
elected, serving four-year terms with a two-term maximum. Within his scope
of responsibilities lie managing the budget, initiating legislation, and selecting a cabinet of ministers charged with directing various facets of policy. The
president is also in charge of foreign policy, appointing ambassadors, signing
treaties, and helping to foster diplomatic relations. Given the president's lack
of control over the military, however, his powers in this area remain circumscribed, and the supreme leader does not refrain from making his own foreign policy statements. In general, the president is charged with the task of
executing the laws, making certain that specific policies are carried out. After
1979, there was an expectation that the president would be a nonreligious figure, more in keeping with an office concerned with "worldly" affairs. Since
1981, however, the position has been held primarily by clerics.

THE LEGISLATURE

The Islamic Republic retains one political institution from Iran's past: the legislature, or Majlis, remains a unicameral body whose members are directly
elected on the basis of universal suffrage of men and women over the age of
fifteen. Its 290 members serve four-year terms. As one might suspect, this
Majlis, like its predecessors, has a limited amount of power. Its powers include
initiating and passing legislation, overseeing the budget, and approving the
members of the president's cabinet. Cabinet members may also be removed
by a vote of no confidence, though the Majlis's power in this area does not
extend to the president himself.

The inherent supremacy of God's law in the Iranian constitution raises
questions about the very functioning of the legislature. Since man-made laws
are essentially a deviation from *sharia,* the role of the Majlis is technically to
create statues that are an expression of that divine law. This condition raises
the question of who is to ascertain whether legislation is consistent with religious law and to what extent it limits real legislative authority.

These limitations can be seen in the presence of two additional bodies, the **Council of Guardians** and the **Expediency Council.** The Council of Guardians is made up of twelve individuals who serve six-year terms: six lawyers, who are nominated by the chief justice and approved by the Majlis, and six clerics specializing in religious law, who are appointed by the supreme leader. The powers of the Council of Guardians are significant; among them is the power to review all legislation that derives from the Majlis, to "ensure its compatibility with the criteria of Islam and the Constitution."[8] It may send legislation back to the Majlis for revision if it finds it incompatible; if the Majlis is unable to revise the legislation to the Council of Guardians's satisfaction, a third body, the Expediency Council, mediates. The Expediency Council is made up of members appointed by the supreme leader and currently is headed by Ali Akbar Hashemi Rafsanj, who was president from 1989 to 1997. The final decision of the Expediency Council cannot be overturned. The Council of Guardians (and, to a lesser extent, the Expediency Council) serves as a kind of unelected upper house, one with substantial powers to restrict the work of the Majlis.

THE JUDICIAL SYSTEM

The way in which political authority stems from religious tenets naturally has a profound effect on the nature of the law itself. The legal system in Iran, derived from *sharia*, serves to defend itself against deviation—not to interpret the law or expand its boundaries, as is often the case in secular democracies. Of course, even *sharia* is not always clear, and new circumstances require reconciling current policy and practices with the religious text.

At the apex of this branch of government is a chief justice, a single figure whose qualifications require an understanding of *sharia* (making the appointment of a cleric necessary). The chief justice is appointed by the supreme leader for a five-year term. His role is to manage the judicial institutions and oversee the appointment and removal of judges. Beneath the chief justice is the Supreme Court, which serves as the highest court of appeal. Like the position of chief justice, this office is entirely staffed by high-ranking clerics chosen for their familiarity with religious law.

The Electoral System

In spite of the theocratic limitations, Iran would seem to enjoy some superficial elements of democracy. In particular, there are direct elections for the Majlis, the Assembly of Experts (which selects the supreme leader), and the presidency. The constitution gives the Council of Guardians the power to oversee all elections, however, which in practice means that this unelected body may reject any candidate for each elected office. In the 2004 Majlis elections, for example, the Council of Guardians barred some 2,000 candidates from standing for office, including 80 who were already members of the legislature. This action helped stifle the growing reform movement that had emerged in the mid-1990s. Similarly, only half the candidates for the 1998 Assembly of Experts election were allowed to stand, and in the 2001 election of the president only 10 candidates were allowed to run from a list of over 800 who applied.

Elections for all three institutions are based on a single-member district majority system. Candidates compete in districts for a majority of the vote (for the presidency, the country serves as a single district); if no single candidate wins a majority, a runoff is held between the two top vote getters. Interestingly, given the strong support for reform among the youth, the voting age has become a political tool. During the 1990s, the reformist-dominated Majlis lowered the legal voting age from sixteen to fifteen (the lowest in the world), seeking to enfranchise millions of voters they hoped would help consolidate their position. Conservatives, meanwhile, sought (and failed) to raise the voting age to undercut the reformers.

Local Government

Iran's history, like that of many countries, has been one of a struggle by the state to centralize power. Though the country is currently divided into thirty ostanha, or provinces, these bodies, like the local institutions below them, have little independent power, a condition that existed long before the current regime. Although the constitutional revolution of 1905–1906 was driven in part by local associations with the goal of creating representative local government, this goal was never realized. The 1979 revolution similarly made claims about the need for local government, though again no changes were instituted. After taking initial steps toward creating a local government, the theocracy moved away from devolving power. The demands of institutionalizing the theocratic regime, going to war with Iraq, nationalizing industry, and quelling ethnic unrest drove the regime to centralize power even more. It rejected any notions of regional autonomy or federalism and suspended elections to the local and regional councils that were first started in 1980.

This situation, like much about politics in Iran, is currently in flux. In 1997, the government passed a law on decentralization that moved power away from the Ministry of the Interior. Prior to that time, the ministry had been responsible for local affairs, appointing regional governors and mayors. As a result of the new law, local councils were created at the village, city, and province level, to manage local politics and the election of mayors. In a further departure from the past, these councils—with some 200,000 offices in all—were to be directly elected.

The first elections to the newly created council positions took place in 1999, with over 500,000 candidates competing at the local level for the first time in Iranian history. Iranian reformers saw the elections as an important step toward democratization, since they expected that the new councils would help wrest power from conservatives at the center of the state. The fact that candidates for council seats do not have to be vetted by the Council of Guardians, as they are for the Majlis, further increased expectations that reformist candidates would win many of the new seats. And as expected, in many areas (especially the large cities, including Tehran), reformists swept the elections. Hopes that these victories would help foster democratization, however, turned out to be overly optimistic. The inability of reformers to push through changes at the national level, combined with new limits on the council's authority, has limited local power and contributed to public skepticism about the possibility of change. Council elections in 2003 saw low voter turnout, and in Tehran conservatives routed reformist city council members. So long as liberalization at the national level is blocked, local democracy will remain restricted.[9]

Other Institutions: The Revolutionary Guard and the Basij

Alongside the wide reach of state power and the role of the theocratic revolution in Iran, there are a number of institutions with significant political power that operate largely outside normal state authority. Of these, two merit particular mention: the **Revolutionary Guard** and the **Basij,** or People's Militia.

The Revolutionary Guard is a paramilitary force that emerged from the 1979 revolution. It originally comprised several thousand men from various militias and groups that had sprung up in response to particular events, and it was independent of the armed forces, which Khomeini mistrusted because of their role during the Pahlavi dynasty; it answered only to the supreme leader. As a "corps of the faithful," the Revolutionary Guard was assigned the immediate task of defending the new regime, destroying rival groups and movements, such as Marxists and supporters of greater ethnic autonomy. Later, during the Iran-Iraq War, the Revolutionary Guard expanded in size in order to fight on the front lines as a military force. It did this by forming a large people's volunteer militia, the Basij, in which young boys played a prominent role. With its members poorly trained and ill equipped but imbued with religious fervor, the Basij was known for its "human wave" attacks against the Iraqi front lines, sometimes even clearing minefields with its soldiers' own bodies.

The end of the war and the consolidation of the revolution undercut the justification for the Revolutionary Guard and the Basij, but both organizations have continued to play an influential role in Iranian politics, as political actors outside the state, controlled only by the supreme leader and his allies. The Revolutionary Guard remains a potent force, with its own ministry, army, navy, and air-force units, and appears to have a hand in the development of Iran's nuclear program, calling into question to the extent to which the president has any real authority in this area. The Guard is becoming an increasingly independent and direct player in Iranian domestic and international affairs as well, with its top leaders taking on important additional roles in the state and government. Given the Guard's hostility to reform, its military power, and its control over potential weapons of mass destruction, this is worrisome development.

In contrast, the Basij is no longer a significant military force, though it has maintained its importance by shifting its focus to domestic repression. Basij members, still 1 million strong, serve in public works, doing disaster relief and other civil projects. More disturbing is their role as a public-morals police force, taking responsibility for such things as preventing public displays of affection and seizing illegal satellite dishes, which can receive foreign broadcasts. In recent years, the Basij have also violently dispersed student protests. In July 2005, Supreme Leader Khamenei appointed the commander of the Basij to the position of chief of Iran's national police force, leading some observers to predict a wave of repression against political and social freedoms.

POLITICAL CONFLICT AND COMPETITION

For many reasons, political competition in Iran is a confusing matter to outside observers. The nature of the revolution and the role of religion in the course of that radical change constitute one factor, as they helped create political differences that do not easily fit on our usual matrix of ideologies. In addition, Iran largely lacks formal political parties, a result of the regime's desire to stifle dissent and safeguard the revolution against "un-Islamic" policies and ideas.

It was not always this way. In the immediate aftermath of the 1979 revolution, there was an outburst of activity, with political organizations and parties representing a diverse array of views. Organizations that had been suppressed by the shah also resurfaced, such as the Marxist Tudeh Party and the Mojahedin, an armed anti-shah movement that combined radical Marxism with Shiism. Among these groups emerged two dominant parties. The first, the Islamic Republican Party (IRP), was closely allied with Ayatollah Ruhollah Khomeini and his desire to establish a theocracy. The second, the Liberation Movement, was more pro-Western and favored a more limited role for religion in politics. Numerous parties stood for the first postrevolutionary elections in 1980, but the electoral system eliminated virtually all groups but the IRP, which gained a majority of seats. Some independent parliamentarians and members of the Liberation Movement sought to resist this consoli-

Average Voter Turnout, 1945–2000	
Country (number of elections)	**Eligible Voters Voting (%)**
South Africa (1)	85.5
United Kingdom (15)	74.9
Japan (21)	69.0
Iran (2)	**67.6**
France (15)	67.3
India (12)	60.7
Russia (2)	55.0
United States (26)	48.3
Mexico (18)	48.1
Brazil (13)	47.9
Nigeria (3)	47.6
China	NA

Source: "Turnout in the World: Country by Country Performance," International Institute for Democracy and Electoral Assistance

http://www.idea.int/vt/survey/voter_turnout_pop2.cfm (accessed 27 January 2006).

dation of power while groups like the Mojahedin turned their weapons on the IRP, destroying their headquarters and much of their leadership in 1981. The government responded with increased repression of opposition groups, imprisoning and executing thousands of political activists while marginalizing the increasingly critical Liberation Movement.

With the 1984 and 1987 elections, the theocratic hold on the Majlis was made complete. In advance of the 1984 elections, all parties other than the IRP were banned. In 1987, even the IRP was eliminated, having become factionalized in the debate over the role of the state in the economy and now a possible threat to Khomeini's rule.

The Rise and Fall of Political Reform

After 1987, political debate within the Majlis was limited primarily to economic concerns, with competition between those who favored a more free-market economic approach and those who supported more statist policies. (See the section on "Society" for a discussion of these different political tendencies).

Debates on the nature of the political system itself were not allowed. Change was afoot, however, made possible in part by the death of Khomeimi in 1989 and the government's realization that some reform was necessary in the face of a stagnating economy. In 1992, Majlis elections saw a victory for the free-market faction over the statists, who in turn supported the 1997 presidential candidacy of the pro-reform Mohammad Khatami, whose victory, with over 70 percent of the vote, surprised Iranians and outside observers alike. Finally, in 1998 the government rescinded its ban on political parties, allowing the registration of the Servants of Construction, a pro-Khatami group.

By the late 1990s, political debate and competition had become more diverse. Prior to this time, conflicts within the Majlis had skirted the issue of political change. Supporters of both free markets and state intervention in the economy were united in their opposition to greater democratic participation and a limit to religious rule. In some ways, this situation is similar to many early forms of political transition. In the Soviet Union in the 1980s, General Secretary Mikhail Gorbachev hoped to use limited reforms to revitalize communism, not to scrap it. China has embraced much more radical economic reforms even as it has tightened political control. Often, however, limited pragmatic reforms take on a life of their own.

President Khatami's call for greater democracy in Iran, as well as improved relations with the outside world, particularly the United States, catalyzed public support. In addition to the movement for free-market reform, there quickly developed a movement for democratic change and a reduction of religious authority, led in part by intellectuals and young people. Demands for change grew more strident and in 1999 led to violent protests by tens of thousands of university students, during which hundreds were arrested and several killed.

The Servants of Construction Party and other reform groups coalesced to form the **Second Khordad Front** to contest the 2000 Majlis elections. The Council of Guardians, perhaps wary of provoking more protests, used its power sparingly in disqualifying Khordad candidates (though several prominent leaders were prevented from standing for office). The Khordad Front went on to win 189 of the 290 parliamentary seats, dealing a stunning blow to religious conservatives. In 2001, President Khatami was again overwhelmingly reelected with over 70 percent of the vote. Many expected that these twin victories would solidify reformist power and pave the way for a political transition.

That belief would be short-lived. While reformers controlled the Majlis and the presidency, these remained relatively weak political institutions. Religious conservatives still controlled or had the support of the Council of Guardians and the Expediency Council, the Revolutionary Guard and Basij, and the supreme leader. Soon after the elections, a wave of repression was directed against reformists. Numerous journalists and pro-democracy activists were arrested, and a number of pro-reform newspapers were shut down. In the Majlis, while reformers passed a wide array of legislation to limit state power and increase democratic rights, the bills were mostly vetoed by the Council of Guardians. Meanwhile, President Khatami lacked the power and the political skills to outflank the conservatives and was increasingly seen as an impotent and indecisive leader.

Using their legal and coercive powers, conservatives have effectively brought the reforms in Iran to an end. The final blow was dealt in advance of the 2004 Majlis elections, when the Council of Guardians banned some 2,000 reformist candidates, including 80 reformist members of parliament. Reformers subsequently called for a boycott of the elections, and voter turnout, which during the 1990s had been in the 70 percent range, dropped to around 50 percent. With fewer reformists competing or turning out to vote, religious conservatives, campaigning under a variety of names, swept to power, gaining over 150 seats. Reformists saw their number of seats drop to fewer than 50.

The last piece in the puzzle is the presidency. In the June 2005 presidential elections, former president Ali Akbar Hashemi Rafsanj was expected to return to power. In spite of Rafsanj's conservatism, there were expectations from his campaign that he would focus on limited economic reforms and improved relations with the West—a model some have called "China lite."[10] To the surprise of many Iranians and outside observers, however, the presidency was won by the conservative mayor of Tehran, Mahmoud Ahmadinejad. Rafsanj claimed that the Council of Guardians and the Republican Guard (the latter of which Ahmadinejad was once a member) interfered illegally with the elections. Yet even if the claim is true, it is clear that many voters turned to Ahmadinejad because of his modest background and concern for social issues like poverty and corruption, as a contrast to those like Rafsanj who had come to power after 1979 and had become rich through their positions in government. Ahmadinejad's victory is another sign of the population's frustration with the Islamic Republic, but his hard-line positions on relations with the West and the primacy of religion will only complicate external relations and further limit domestic liberalization.

Civil Society

As might be expected, civil society in Iran has mirrored the changes and challenges of political competition discussed above. Over the past century, Iran has seen the rise of organized civil activity during periods in which the state was weak, as during the constitutional revolution in 1905–06, immediately after World War II, and during the 1979 revolution. After the creation of the Islamic Republic of Iran this nascent civil society was again stifled, viewed as anathema to the supremacy of religious rule and the need for national unity during the war with Iraq. Most civic organizations were either absorbed into the state or outlawed. This was consistent with the theocracy's emphasis on the notion of the **ummah,** or community, whose members were expected to act as a unified group that embodied and served the revolution. Plurality and autonomy were anathema to religious rule and revolutionary ideals.

After Khomeini's death and the end of the war, however, civil society began to reemerge, though it remained marginal and beleaguered. A handful of intellectuals, clerics and others questioned the current regime and advocated reform, but this activity was frequently met with arrest, torture, and even death. One notable example is Ayatollah Hussein Ali Montazeri, whom Khomeini had handpicked to serve as supreme leader upon his death. Montazeri eventually fell out of favor, however, having criticized the government for human rights abuses. In 1997, he was placed under house arrest, in part for suggesting that the supreme leader should be a popularly elected position and many of its powers transferred to the presidency.

Khatami had made the reinvigoration of Iran's civil society a major plank of his campaign, and when he was elected president in 1997, civil society began to flourish. In the aftermath of his victory and the 2000 Majlis election, there was a torrent of public discussion about the scope and pace of reform as old taboos were challenged.

This debate was most notable in the case of the media. New publications rapidly proliferated at all levels of society, from academic journals to daily newspapers. In the early 1990s, for example, Tehran had five newspapers; by 2001, there were over twenty. Across the country, the total number of printed media numbered over 1,000. In addition, numerous scholarly works were published that sought to articulate the role of civil society in Iran and its importance in helping to establish democracy and the rule of law. Alongside the growth of free expression, numerous civic organizations began to spring up, dealing with such issues as local government, human rights, the environment, women's rights, and poverty.

Yet all of these forms of civil society were under sustained attack from their inception. In 1998, several newspapers were raided by the police, following their criticism of the arrest of Tehran's mayor, an ally of President Khatami. Shortly thereafter, Supreme Leader Khamenei attacked the press as "the base of the enemy," and numerous publications were closed or attacked by government-sponsored militants. A 2000 law, passed prior to the Majlis elections, restricted the ability of the press to operate and new publications to form. By 2003, over 100 publications had been closed, and over forty journalists had been arrested. At least five journalists were killed in 1998 and 1999, events the government blamed on "rogue" intelligence agents, and in 2003 the Canadian Iranian journalist Zahra Kazemi died in prison after being beaten. Numerous others were detained, harassed, and tortured.

Internet Usage in Three Middle Eastern Countries, 2000–2004				
Country	Population	Usage, 2000	Usage, 2004	Usage Growth, 2000–2004 (percentage)	Penetration (percentage population)
Iran	67,477,500	250,000	4,800,000	1,820	7.1
Saudi Arabia	22,287,100	200,000	1,500,000	650	6.7
Turkey	75,058,900	2,000,000	5,500,000	175	7.3

Source: http://www.itu.int and http://www.internetworldstats.com

Similar pressure was made against nongovernmental organizations, with many being attacked, their offices destroyed, and an unknown number of their members detained, often without charges. After the student protests of 1999, a number of prominent student leaders were arrested. These detainees are often held at a detention center known as Prison 59, which is under the control of the Revolutionary Guard.

This suppression has helped move civil action to a new arena—the Internet. In the past few years, Internet access and use have exploded, growing faster than in any other country in the Middle East. Of particular interest has been the expansion of blogs frequently written by Iranian women, to whom few other outlets of expression are open. While most blogs focus on the personal lives of their authors, as in the West, many tackle social and political subjects that are not covered in the largely weakened media. This may explain their widespread popularity; it is estimated that as of 2004 there were as many as 100,000 Iranian blogs. The development of a virtual public discourse has not escaped the notice of the authorities: they have begun banning access to Web sites seen as hostile to the government and have recently begun to arrest popular bloggers whose postings are critical of the regime, charging them with "moral crimes."

SOCIETY

Ethnic and National Identity

We noted earlier that Iran is distinct from other Islamic states in the Middle East, not only it its embrace of the minority Shia branch of Islam but also in that the majority population is ethnically Iranian (or Persian) rather than Arab. With their distinct language, history, and culture, ethnic Iranians view themselves as quite separate from the Arab states of the Middle

East, contributing to a sense of nationalism that is in many ways much stronger than anything found elsewhere in the region. It was this nationalism that in part helped sustain Iran in its long war against Iraq, which was often portrayed by both sides as part of a long struggle between Persians and Arabs.

At the same time, Iran is not the homogeneous state that its nationalism or distinctive identity might lead us to believe it is. While Persians make up a majority of the population, it is a bare majority. The rest of the population is composed of various other ethnic groups. Some are close to the Persian majority in language and religion. Others are much more distinct and have at times complicated the creation of a centralized Iranian state. Among these groups, the two largest, the Azeris and the Kurds, are particularly important. This is not only because of their size but also because of their connection to ethnic kin outside Iran. In both cases, turmoil and political change in surrounding countries have affected these ethnic minorities and, as a result, the way in which Iran deals with its neighbors.

The largest and most important minority ethnic group in Iran is the Azeris, who make up around one quarter of the population (perhaps more) and are concentrated in the north of the country. Like the majority Persians, the Azeris follow Shiism, but they speak a Turkic language related to the languages of Turkey and Central Asia. Historically, the Azeris resided entirely within the Persian Empire, but with the expansion of Russia in the nineteenth century their region was divided between the two countries. With the collapse of the Soviet Union in 1991, an independent Azerbaijan emerged, propelled by a nationalist movement that included calls for unification with the Azeri regions of Iran, a call that had some resonance with the Iranian Azeris. Iran, not surprisingly, saw this as a clear threat to its territorial integrity. Around this time,

ETHNIC GROUPS

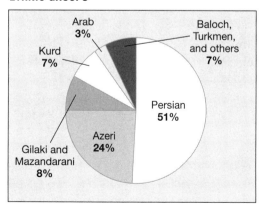

RELIGION

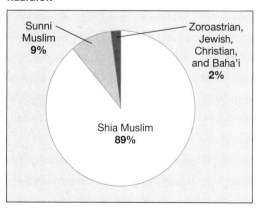

Azerbaijan fought a war against another ex-Soviet republic, Armenia, over an ethnic Armenian enclave in Azerbaijan; in this conflict, Iran sided with Christian Armenia over its Azeri co-religionists. Even in Iran, power politics and nationalism can trump religious solidarity.[11]

Relations with the Kurdish population have at times been similarly tense. Less than 10 percent of the population, Kurds carried out an armed revolt against the new Islamic Republic of Iran in 1979, demanding greater autonomy, though their opposition has been far less violent than that of the Kurds in neighboring Turkey and Iraq. All three countries have long feared the desire among some Kurds to carve an independent Kurdistan out of their territory. The U.S. invasion of Iraq has added a new level of complexity and uncertainty to this issue, with Kurds in Iraq exercising de facto autonomy and many seeking to secede from the country.

Ideology and Political Culture

In the absence of political parties and free expression, it is hard to speak of any coherent spectrum of ideologies in Iran. A confusing array of terms is used—hard-liners, radicals, conservatives, traditionalists, reformers, pragmatists, technocrats. In spite of this confusion, we can speak of several loose political attitudes or tendencies, some of which are more ideologically coherent than others. As in other countries, these divisions tend to fall along the axis of freedom and equality, though they combine in ways that are quite different from the combination commonly found in the West.

One major division has been between so-called religious conservatives and religious radicals, though even within these camps there are subdivisions. Conservatives (sometimes called traditionalists) have tended to support free markets and private property and improved relations with the West, while favoring a strict approach to moral issues. Many of them are uncomfortable with the very notion of the *velayat-e faqih,* which they see as a dangerous fusion of temporal and spiritual power, favoring a more **quietist** approach to Islam. This quietist Shiism holds that the role of the faith is to act as an intermediary between the state and society until the return of the Hidden Imam, influencing spiritual and social values but not getting directly involved in politics. Politics is viewed as a corrupting influence on faith, something to be kept at a distance.[12] In contrast, radicals (sometimes called hard-liners) have tended to favor a greater role for the state in the economy, in order to redistribute wealth. They have also opposed reconciliation with the West, and have been less interested in strict moral regulation. Radicals have held important positions in the state since 1979. An additional division that took shape in the 1990s was associated with pro-reform ideas, with a general consensus on the need to develop democracy and limit the role of religion in public life. Each

IN COMPARISON   SUPPORT FOR AUTHORITARIAN RULE

Respondents saying that it is a very or fairly good idea to have a strong leader who does not have to bother with parliament and elections

China	United Kingdom	Japan	United States	South Africa	France	Iran	Russia	Mexico	India
19%	25%	28%	30%	34%	35%	39%	49%	56%	59%

Source: World Values Survey, 2000.

of these tendencies draws on historical precedents and Iranian and foreign ideas to support their objectives.[13]

At a second level, we can observe more fixed elements of political culture. Many have argued that the 1979 revolution radically transformed Iranian political culture, and certainly the dramatic reordering of the state and society, along with the devastating effects of the war with Iraq, changed the way in which ordinary Iranians viewed the role of politics, authority, and religion. But these changes may not have developed in the way we expected. One area in which this is the case is nationalism. Public opinion surveys show that Iranians have a stronger sense of national identity than do citizens of Arab countries and are more likely to identify themselves as Iranians first and Muslims second. Unlike their neighbors, Iranians view themselves as a distinct culture with its own important pre-Islamic past, and the revolution did little to undermine this attitude. Indeed, if anything, the Iran-Iraq War only strengthened national identity. In addition, fewer than 40 percent of those surveyed

IN COMPARISON   PRIDE IN NATIONALITY

Respondents saying that they are very proud of their nationality

Japan	China	Russia	France	United Kingdom	India	United States	South Africa	Mexico	Iran
23%	26%	31%	40%	51%	71%	72%	75%	80%	92%

Source: World Values Survey, 2000.

expressed support for authoritarian rule. This compares favorably with Mexico and Russia and advanced democracies like France and the United States.[14] The existence of a strong national identity, support for democracy, and a weaker presence of religion in people's lives may be the groundwork necessary for a democratic transition in the future.

POLITICAL ECONOMY

Iran's economic system reflects the dilemmas of late modernization, authoritarianism, and war. It is also a good example of what is sometimes called the "resource trap," the situation that occurs when a resource makes a country poorer rather than richer.

As discussed in the section on "Historical Development of the State," Iran's modern economic development lagged well behind that of the West, beginning

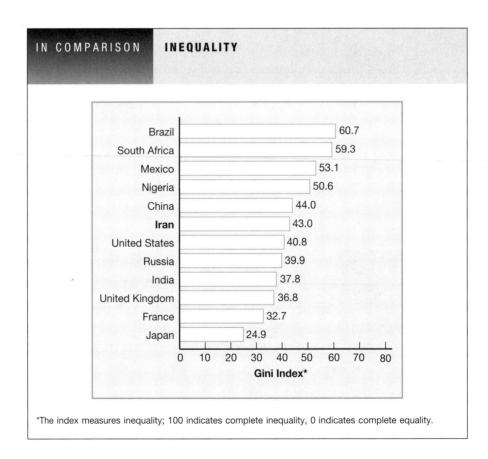

IN COMPARISON   INEQUALITY

Country	Gini Index*
Brazil	60.7
South Africa	59.3
Mexico	53.1
Nigeria	50.6
China	44.0
Iran	43.0
United States	40.8
Russia	39.9
India	37.8
United Kingdom	36.8
France	32.7
Japan	24.9

*The index measures inequality; 100 indicates complete inequality, 0 indicates complete equality.

only in the 1920s under the Pahlavi dynasty. **LABOR FORCE BY OCCUPATION**
It was not a late embrace of liberalism, how-
ever, but rather an attempt at top-down
industrialization, following the mercantilist
pattern adopted by many countries in the
less developed world. Nor should such a
path have been surprising; given the imperialist designs of many Western powers on
the Middle East, an attempt by the state to
generate domestic wealth was a logical
response—and was not unlike the Western
powers' own past. Iran's mercantilism did
help modernize the country, such that by the

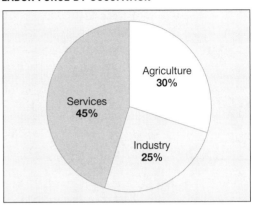

1970s half the population was living in urban areas. At the same time, it led
to social dislocation as the country made a rapid jump from an agrarian, isolated, and semi-nomadic system in just a few decades.

Top-down mercantilist development led to similar problems in other less
developed countries, though in Iran the problems were compounded by the
discovery of oil. At first glance, one would expect that oil reserves to be the
salvation of any country, providing it with the resources to develop its infrastructure and generate new industries. In reality, the opposite tends to be the
case. Oil is often more a curse than a blessing, especially when controlled by
the state. Rather than direct resources toward the goal of development, leaders give in to a seemingly irresistible temptation, which leads to corruption as
they siphon off the wealth to line their pockets or serve their own policy
predilections. Moreover, since the public is eliminated as the major source of
state revenue, those in power can effectively ignore the public and repress or
co-opt any opposition. The issue of "taxation without representation" becomes
meaningless—the state can do without either, and is able to avoid having to
make the trade-off. This became evident during the time of the White Revolution, when economic development coincided with growing inflation and
inequality. This uneven development, built on oil exports and Western imports,
also fueled hostility toward Western materialism, or what was termed "West-
oxication" or "Weststruckness" by one critical Iranian scholar of the era.[15]

Reflecting the economic factors that helped bring about the 1979 revolution, the new constitution explicitly stated that "the economy is a means, not
an end." This stood in contrast to liberal capitalist systems, in which the quest
for wealth and profit becomes "a subversive and corrupting factor in the course
of man's development." The oil and other state-owned industries were to
remain in the state's hands, with the profits redirected toward presumably
more equitable goals. In addition, numerous private industries were nationalized after their owners fled the revolution. In many cases, their assets were

turned over to several **bonyads,** or parastatal foundations. The objectives of the *bonyads* are ostensibly to help the disadvantaged, such as war veterans and the poor. Over time, however, the *bonyads* have become major economic players in their own right, controlling substantial assets and industries while operating independently of any government oversight (other than that of the supreme leader).[16] Thus, the Iranian economy is heavily controlled by the state, directly or indirectly. By one estimate, some 60 percent of the economy is directly controlled by the state while another 10 to 20 percent is owned by the *bonyads*.

Another important distinction in Iran's economic system is its autarky, or economic independence. Opponents of the shah accused him of selling the country to foreigners, exporting their oil wealth for the benefit of a few. Just as the 1979 constitution describes profit and wealth as corrupting influences, the postrevolutionary government has seen foreign trade as a means of enslavement by Western imperialism. Oil could be exported to develop the economy, but the government, at least initially, sought a policy of self-suffi-ciency in economic production to secure the country from the effects of "West-oxication." In reality, trade with the West continued, as autarky proved an unsustainable policy for economic development.

The results of the post-1979 economic model have been poor. To be fair, Iran's economy was devastated by the long war with Iraq, which destroyed infrastructure, drained the national treasury, and killed many of the country's young men. By 1988, when the war ended, Iran's per capita GDP had fallen to just over half its 1979 level. Since that time, the economy has steadily rebounded, although as of 2003 it remained below its level of some twenty years before. In addition, the reliance on oil means that the economy is dependent on the international market; at times when oil prices have been in a slump, the state has lacked the revenues necessary to keep the economy moving. Oil production itself has been in decline, with the country producing probably around half what it did in the 1970s. Some 40 percent of the popu-lation lives below the poverty line and unemployment is estimated to be 15 to 20 percent. Iran's economic equality, a cornerstone of the revolution, is no better than that of the United States. Finally, compounding matters is the fact that the Iranian economy faces the challenge of providing employment for millions of young Iranians who enter the workforce each year; for members of the labor force under age twenty-four, the unemployment rate is over 30 percent. This economic marginalization of the young in turn increases their hostility to the regime, as occurred under the shah.

Solutions to these economic problems are not easy. Iran can expect that revenues from its existing oil reserves and the development of natural gas will help sustain the state budget. This is not likely to diversify the economy or provide new sources of employment, however. Under the presidency of Mohammad Khatami, there were efforts at privatization of state-owned indus-

VARIATIONS IN IRAN'S GDP*, 1974–2001

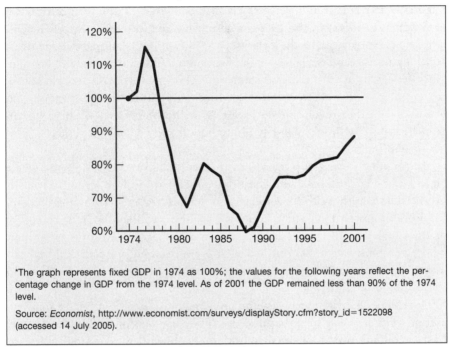

*The graph represents fixed GDP in 1974 as 100%; the values for the following years reflect the percentage change in GDP from the 1974 level. As of 2001 the GDP remained less than 90% of the 1974 level.

Source: *Economist*, http://www.economist.com/surveys/displayStory.cfm?story_id=1522098 (accessed 14 July 2005).

tries, as well as encouragement of direct foreign investment. But both policies are controversial. The bonyads are loathe to give up their firms, even if they are unprofitable, since they are a source of power. Greater government oversight is similarly unwelcome. And the idea of foreigners investing in the development of natural resources is unacceptable to much of the clerical ruling elite, as it smacks of the pre-revolutionary period of imperial domination. Until these obstacles to reform are overcome, Iran is unlikely to make any significant improvement in its economy.[17]

FOREIGN RELATIONS AND THE WORLD

Iran's foreign relations are a function of its revolutionary aspirations, the limits of that revolution, and the nature of power at the international level. After 1979, Iran's leaders believed that theirs was the first in a series of revolutions that would sweep the Islamic world. Like the Russian and Chinese revolutions before it, the Iranian revolution was thought to be the vanguard of a political movement that would extend beyond Iran's borders. In the early postrevolutionary years, Iran served as a beacon for Muslims everywhere, helping to give voice to their grievances against the West and against their own despotic rulers. Iran became associated with radical movements and terrorism,

including the use of suicide attacks and the idea of martyrdom as their justification. Iran's role in this regard was first and most clearly seen during the
civil war in Lebanon in the 1980s, where it backed the Shiite group Hezbollah in its efforts against the occupying Israeli forces. During that conflict,
Hezbollah was responsible for a suicide bombing of U.S. Marines in Lebanon,
killing over 200 servicemen, and some observers have asserted that the bombing took place on the direct orders of Iran. Iran's long struggle against Iraq
was also shaped by revolutionary fervor. As we noted earlier, Ayatollah Ruhollah Khomeini saw Iraq's majority Shiite population as the logical next step in
his revolution.

Iran's hope to spread its vision of political Islam to the rest of the world
faced several major obstacles. The first was Shiism itself, a minority variant
of the Islamic faith. With its emphasis on the descendants of Ali, messianism,
a culture of martyrdom, and a hierarchy of clerics, Shiism limited the ability
of the revolution to spread among the majority Sunni Muslim population
worldwide. Only in a few countries, such as Iraq and Lebanon, do Shiites exist
in any significant numbers, and for many Sunnis, Shiites are heretics who do
not truly follow Islam.

A second major obstacle was ethnicity. The obvious goal of the Iranian revolutionary policy was to spread the revolutionaries' vision within the Middle
East, helping to overthrow secular leaders, establish Islamic states, and drive
out Western influence in the process. But Iranians are not Arabs; their culture
is not Arabic, nor is their language. Just as the revolution had difficulties speaking in terms of one Islam, it could not speak in terms of one Middle Eastern
people. Here, too, Iran was the outlier. This was only reinforced by the **Iran-
Iraq War,** in which Iran relied in part of nationalistic fervor to maintain public support and Iraq's Arab but Shiite majority largely fought against Iran.

Yet while Iran failed to serve as the lodestar for revolution, many of the
ideas and symbols of the revolution would influence a second wave of political conflict, beginning with the war in Afghanistan in 1980 and continuing
through the emergence of Al Qaeda. The current wave of terrorism owes much
of its ideology and mythology to Iran, though ironically a movement like Al
Qaeda views Shiism as a form of idolatry even more pernicious than Christianity or Judaism.[18]

With these limits to its revolutionary goals, Iran's foreign policy reverted
to a more defensive position. As with most revolutionary states, Iran spoke of
the need for vigilance to defend the revolution against those reactionaries who
would destroy it if given a chance. Such a view can generate a foreign policy
focused on insecurity and isolation and a domestic policy that justifies oppression and deprivation by blaming them on the enemy. For Iran, from 1979 to
the present that enemy has been the "Great Satan," or the United States. Since
the seizure of the U.S. embassy in Tehran, the United States has not had for-

mal diplomatic relations with Iran and has forbidden virtually all economic, cultural, and other ties to the country. The Iranian leadership has shared this antipathy.

During the last few years, several major developments have changed and complicated Iran's relationship to the outside world, especially the United States. The first was President Mohammad Khatami's election in 1997. Khatami took a foreign policy line quite different from that of either his predecessor or the supreme leader, Ali Khamenei. Khatami, picking up on American political scientist Samuel Huntington's belief in an emerging "clash of civilizations,"countered with the idea of a "dialogue among civilizations." Such a dialogue, Khatami argued, could help strengthen relations between countries and avert conflict. Prior to Khatami's election, Iran had already taken steps toward normalizing its relations with the outside world, but these actions were more pragmatic and based largely on economic need. In contrast, Khatami's ideas went much further in intent, seeking positive relations rather than simply the absence of overt hostility. Such an idea ran counter to the notion of the revolution itself, which saw conflict as an inevitable part of the restoration of Islam. Khatami looked to be positioning himself as Iran's Mikhail Gorbachev, bringing an end to the U.S.-Iranian "cold war."

The second major development was September 11, 2001. With the terrorist attacks on the United States, the administration of President George W. Bush hardened what were already uncharitable views of countries considered "rogue states" that is, countries viewed as outside the predictable norms of international behavior. The Bush administration coined its now (in)famous phrase "the axis of evil," which included Iraq, Iran, and North Korea. In each case, the Bush administration saw an authoritarian regime with an implacable hostility toward the United States, the pursuit of weapons of mass destruction, and a record of supporting terrorist or military attacks on its neighbors. Iran was not considered a major supporter of Al Qaeda (in part for reasons mentioned above), but the Bush administration feared that the sectarian division that inhibited their cooperation could always be overcome, just as Nazi Germany and the Soviet Union (briefly) overcame their mutual hatred to join as allies in the early stages of World War II. Although Khatami's international initiative was already foundering before September 11, checked by conservatives in the government and the state, the U.S. position further weakened his position and strengthened leaders who opposed any improved ties with the United States.

The final developments were the U.S. wars in Afghanistan and Iraq, countries that share borders with Iran. In the case of Afghanistan, the Iranian government had long opposed the Taliban, puritanical Sunnis who opposed Shiism and the Shiite communities in their country. However, the war also meant that U.S. forces now sat next door. The war in Iraq was even more complicated.

After the Iran-Iraq War, Saddam Hussein suppressed the Shiite population, fearing that they might pose a threat to his Sunni-dominated government (in spite of their general support for the war against Iran). During the 1991 Gulf War, some Shiites did rise up, though they were quickly crushed after receiving no help from the coalition forces, who they believed would come to their aid. When Iraq was invaded in 2003, the Shiite majority quickly reasserted itself, with power coalescing around its religious leaders, many of whom were originally from Iran or had trained there. This gave Iran a new source of leverage in Iraq, but at the same time the Iranian leadership worried that the wars in Afghanistan and Iraq were a prelude to a U.S.-led "regime change" in Iran.

Iran thus finds itself with a set of opportunities and dangers. In both Afghanistan and Iraq, Iran is able to influence domestic affairs through local political and/or religious leaders who are tied to Iran by ethnicity or religion. This is especially the case in Iraq, given that the Shiites represent some 60 percent of the population. Whatever the outcome of the current conflict, it is expected that Iraqi Shiites will come to dominate politics. What is not certain is the model they will follow. Some Iraqi Shiites look to Iran for inspiration in creating their own theocracy, while others favor a quietist model that limits the role of religion in political life. Still others are strictly secular. Finally, Arab-Persian differences divide the Shiite communities of Iraq and Iran. There is no doubt that Iran exercises significant influence over the Iraqi Shiite community, however, and if Iran actively sought to undermine U.S. efforts to stabilize the country, it easily could. But for Iran, the choice is not so clear. A destabilized Iraq could marginalize the Shiite population once again and/or spread violence into Iran. At the same time, a democratic Iraq, especially one dominated by Shiites, could be an inspiration for the Iranian people that their leaders would rather they not have. And across all of this lies the U.S. military presence, whose forces now sit just across much of Iran's border. All of these concerns play into and are shaped by Iran's nuclear question, which is discussed in detail below. Forces and developments inside and outside the country could lead Iran to play a major, and positive, regional and international role in the coming years. Intensified conflict, however, in Iran, in neighboring countries, or across the region, could prove disastrous for the local and the global communities.

CURRENT ISSUES

THE NUCLEAR PROGRAM

One of the most critical issues that confronts the international community at the present is Iran's apparent nuclear weapons program. How this issue is resolved—whether diplomatically or through force—could have profound repercussions for Iran, the region, and the rest of the world.

Even before the 1979 revolution, as part of an extensive plan to develop nuclear energy for peaceful purposes, Iran showed interest in developing a nuclear weapon. These ideas were largely underdeveloped, however, and were completely halted with the overthrow of the shah. Yet by the mid-1980s, the Iranian leadership had begun to revive its research into nuclear power. Part of the reason may have been Iraq's own nuclear weapons program, which might have been directed against Iran. Even though Iran is a signatory to the Nuclear Nonproliferation Treaty (NPT), there is widespread evidence that it has been pursuing several steps to produce enriched plutonium and uranium, necessary ingredients for making a nuclear weapon. Furthermore, these actions have been untaken without notifying the International Atomic Energy Agency (IAEA), which oversees the NPT and obliges nonnuclear signatories to report any such activities and allow inspection.

The growing international concern over Iran's nuclear program has been deepened by what appears to be an expansion of Iran's program. In 1995, Russia agreed to finish a nuclear-reactor project at Bushehr and provide the reactor fuel. While ostensibly commercial in nature (Iran claims the plant is intended solely to produce electricity), the particular design of the reactor makes it much easier for Iran to refine plutonium and in large amounts. Russia has asserted that it will reprocess the spent fuel, thus preventing the extraction of bomb-making material, but even if this promise is upheld, there is the possibility that Iran will be able to make its own fuel in future.

The IAEA, the United States, and Europe have all expressed concern about this project but are divided on how to respond. The United States has favored a much harder line toward Iran, warning it to abandon its nuclear program or face serious consequences. The Europeans have favored a more diplomatic approach, hoping to provide incentives (such as energy alternatives and improved economic relations). So far, neither the carrot nor the stick approach has proved effective, and there are concerns that Iran will "go nuclear" even as international efforts are under way. For Iran, a nuclear weapon may represent the ultimate safeguard against U.S. intervention or invasion; for many U.S. officials, such a weapon in the hands of Iran is only a short step from the hands of terrorists. Both beliefs may be a dangerous misconception.

How to resolve this situation? A verifiable agreement might help end Iran's international isolation and promote better relations with Europe and the United States. Or Iran may succeed in creating a nuclear weapon in secret, unbeknownst to the international community. A third possibility is that the United States or Israel might carry out pre-emptive strikes against suspected nuclear facilities in Iran, such as the one in Bushehr, before it comes online.

Israel did just that in 1981 in Iraq, destroying a nuclear reactor that was under construction. It is unlikely that all nuclear sites could be located or destroyed, however. Moreover, Iran could retaliate by inciting violence in the Shiite community in neighboring Iraq or sponsoring terrorist attacks further afield. The stakes are high for all involved.[19]

NOTES

1. Elton L. Daniel, *The History of Iran* (Westport, CT: Greenwood Press, 2001).
2. For a discussion of Shiism in Iran and elsewhere, see Heinz Halm, *Shi'ism* (New York: Columbia University Press, 2004).
3. For a discussion of this period and the increasing U.S. influence in Iranian politics, see Kenneth M. Pollack, *The Persian Puzzle: The Conflict between Iran and America* (New York: Random House, 2004).
4. Stephen Kinzer, *All the Shah's Men: An American Coup and the Roots of Middle East Terror* (New York: John Wiley & Sons, 2003).
5. Ali M. Ansari, "The Myth of the White Revolution: Mohammad Reza Shah, 'Modernization,' and the Consolidation of Power," *Middle Eastern Studies* 37:3 (July 2001), pp. 1–24.
6. Ruhollah Khomeini, *Islamic Government* (Tehran: Institute for Compilation and Publication of Imam Khomeini's Works, n.d.); see also Karen Armstrong, *The Battle for God* (New York: Alfred A. Knopf, 2000).
7. For an analysis of these events, see Charles Kurzman, *The Unthinkable Revolution in Iran* (Cambridge, MA: Harvard University Press, 2004).
8. From International Constitutional Law, http://www.oefre.unibe.ch/law/icl (accessed 14 July 2005).
9. Kian Tajbakhsh, "Political Decentralization and the Creation of Local Government in Iran: Consolidation or Transformation of the Theocratic State?" *Social Research* 67, no. 2 (Summer 2000), pp. 377–404.
10. Afshin Molavi, "Buying Time in Tehran," *Foreign Affairs* (November/December 2004), pp. 9–17.
11. Nazrin Mehdiyeva, "Azerbaijan and Its Foreign Policy Dilemma,"*Asian Affairs* 34:3 (November 2003), pp. 271–85.
12. Graham E. Fuller, *Islamist Politics in Iraq after Saddam Hussein*, Special Report 108, United States Institute of Peace, August 2003, http://www.usip.org/pubs/special reports/sr108.html (accessed 11 July 2005)
13. Ali Banuazizi, "Iran's Revolutionary Impasse: Political Factionalism and Societal Resistance," *Middle East Report* 191 (November–December, 1994), pp. 2–8.
14. Ronald Inglehart et. al., *Human Beliefs and Values: A Cross-Cultural Sourcebook Based on the 1999–2002 Value Surveys* (Mexico City: Siglo XXI, 2004), and Monsoor Moaddel, "Public Opinion in Three Islamic Countries," *Footnotes: Newsletter of the American Sociological Association* 31, no. 3 (January 2003), http://www.asanet.org/footnotes.
15. Jalal Al-e Ahmad, *Weststruckness*, trans. John Green and Ahmad Alizadah (Costa Mesa, CA: Mazda, 1997).
16. Suzanne Maloney, "Islamism and Iran's Postrevolutionary Economy: The Case of the Bonyads,"in Mary Ann Tétreault and Robert A. Denemark, eds, *Gods, Guns,*

and Globalization: Religious Radicalism and International Political Economy. (Boulder, CO: Lynne Reinner Publishers, 2004), pp. 292–334.

17. Jahangir Amuzegar, "Iran's Unemployment Crisis,"*Middle East Economic Survey* 41 (11 October 2004), http://www.mees.com (accessed 11 July 2005).

18. Michael Scott Doran, "The Saudi Paradox,"*Foreign Affairs* (January–February 2004), pp. 35–51.

19. For more on this issue, see Henry Sokolski and Patrick Clawson, eds. *Checking Iran's Nuclear Ambitions* (Carlisle, PA: Strategic Studies Institute, 2004).

KEY TERMS

Assembly of Experts   p. 325

ayatollah   p. 317

Basij   p. 330

bonyads   p. 342

Council of Guardians   p. 328

Expediency Council   p. 328

Farsi   p. 313

Iran-Iraq War   p. 344

Islamic Republic of Iran   p. 323

Islamism, or Islamic fundamentalism   p. 312

Ali Khamenei   p. 326

Mohammad Khatami   p. 313

Ruhollah Khomeini   p. 312

Koran   p. 312

Majlis   p. 318

Muhammad   p. 312

Muhammad Mosaddeq   p. 320

Operation Ajax   p. 320

Reza Shah Pahlavi   p. 318

Persia   p. 315

quietist   p. 338

Revolutionary Guard   p. 330

SAVAK   p. 320

Second Khordad Front   p. 333

sharia   p. 317

Shiism   p. 312

supreme leader   p. 325

ummah   p. 335

velayat-e faqih   p. 321

White Revolution   p. 320

WEB LINKS

Web site of the Supreme Leader Ayatollah Khamenei   **www.leader.ir**

Ministry of Foreign Affairs, Islamic Republic of Iran   **www.mfa.gov.ir**

Middle East Economic Survey   **www.mees.com**

Islamic Republic News Agency   **www.irna.com/en**

Iran Daily   **www.iran-daily.com**

Middle East Network Information Center, University of Texas, Austin
   menic.utexas.edu/menic/Countries_and_Regions/Iran

10 MEXICO

Head of state and government:
President Felipe Calderón
(since December 1, 2006)

Capital: Mexico City

Total land size: 1,972,550

Population: 106 million

GDP at PPP: 1.01 trillion US$

GDP per capita: $9,600

MEXICO

INTRODUCTION

Why Study This Case?

For over eight decades, stability was the feature that differentiated Mexico's political system from that of most of its Latin American neighbors and from its own turbulent pre-1917 history. Unlike the political atmosphere of most other third world countries, Mexico's post-1917 political atmosphere was relatively peaceful: power was transferred between leaders after regular, peaceful elections, and the military was thoroughly subordinate to civilians. This stability resulted from a highly effective and remarkably flexible semi-authoritarian regime dominated by a single party, the **Partido Revolucionario Institucional (PRI).** That model delivered impressive rates of economic growth but also produced an economy plagued by severe economic inequality and massive poverty.

In July 2000, the PRI's long tenure came to a sudden end, marking the start of a new era in Mexican politics. The decline of the PRI's political hegemony had begun in the early 1980s, when the Mexican economy narrowly averted bankruptcy. In response to a severe economic crisis, the PRI leadership had begun to dismantle the prevailing protectionist and statist economic model. Mexico opened up its economy to the world and began a transition to a neo-liberal economic political economy. It quickly became one of Latin America's most open economies. The hallmark of this new era was Mexico's 1994 entry into the **North American Free Trade Agreement (NAFTA)** with the United States and Canada.

The economic crisis of the 1980s (and the PRI's response to it) created new sources of political opposition, and the party's power was seriously threatened for the first time in seventy years. In 1988, the PRI resorted to massive fraud to avoid losing the presidency, and it increased the use of fraud to prevent the opposition from taking control of state legislatures. In January 1994 armed Mayan peasants shocked Mexico when they seized control of a southern Mexican town. In March of that year, the PRI's presidential candidate was assassinated while campaigning for office, the first such political murder since 1928. There were allegations that the murder had been ordered by members of the governing party, and the inability of the government to solve the crime added to a sense of crisis. The emergence of a strong political challenge to the PRI, the presence of an armed guerrilla movement, and a high-profile political murder destroyed the image of Mexico's system as stable and peaceful.

The political turmoil was alarming to Mexicans and Americans alike. Participation in NAFTA only ratified a growing (but highly asymmetrical) interdependence between the U.S. and Mexican economies. Mexico and the United States share a 2,000-mile border, and Mexican immigration to the United States has long provided a steady stream of labor that is vital to the U.S. economy. In addition, the United States is the chief consumer of Mexico's oil exports, and Mexico is now the United States' second biggest trading partner, after Canada.

After two decades of political and economic crisis, the July 2000 victory of **Vicente Fox Quesada,** the first non-PRI president since 1917, provided new hope for Mexico's future, even as it raised new questions. Fox took power vowing to shake up the Mexican system but soon discovered that the PRI's loss of the presidency did not give him a blank check. The PRI maintained strongholds of political power in a variety of federal and state political institutions. The hotly contested elections of July 2006 revealed that six years after its democratic transition, Mexico was deeply polarized between left and right. The conservative **Felipe Calderón** won a razon-thin victory over a leftist candidate who was critical of free trade, and whose main priority was to address Mexico's endemic poverty. The election was so close that Calderón's opponent, Andrés Manuel Lopéz Obrador, demanded a recount, and launched a legal challenge to the results. Our study of Mexico will raise several important questions: Has Mexico had a democratic transition, or is it still best viewed as a semi-authoritarian regime? Has Mexico's embrace of a neo-liberal economic model been a success, or has it merely exacerbated inequality and worsened poverty? Is Mexico likely to remain a close and trusted ally of the United States?

Major Geographic and Demographic Features

Mexico's stunningly diverse geography includes tropical rain forests, snow-capped volcanoes, and rich agricultural regions. Historically, the two major mountain ranges that divide Mexico, the eastern and western Sierra Madres, have made transportation and communication difficult. Only 12 percent of Mexico's land is arable, and the most productive agricultural areas are in northern Mexico, close to the U.S. border. There, large and highly mechanized export farms provide much of America's winter produce. The proximity of Mexico's agricultural export to the U.S. market has been a major boost to Mexico's economic growth. Agriculture in southern Mexico is characterized by smaller farms and less efficient production. Mexico is well endowed with minerals and has major oil reserves.

With 106 million people, Mexico has the second largest population in Latin America (after Brazil). Its population is racially quite diverse: about 60 percent are **mestizos,** people of mixed Spanish and indigenous blood, and another 30 percent, living primarily in the central and southern parts of the country, are considered indigenous because they speak an indigenous language. The largest indigenous groups are the Maya, located in Mexico's far south (along the Guatemalan border), and the Nahuatl, concentrated in central Mexico. On Mexico's Caribbean coast is a large population of African decent.

Nearly three quarters of Mexico's population lives in an urban setting, a relatively recent change. Mexico City has dwarfed all other Mexican cities—it now has about 18 million residents. Population growth has slowed with economic development, but Mexico's large population still strains the country's resources. As a result, Mexicans still migrate in very large numbers. Many have left the impoverished countryside for the cities, often leaving the poor south for the wealthier north, especially the factory towns along the U.S. border. At the same time, a steady stream of Mexicans has migrated across the border to the United States.

Historical Development of the State

The history of the modern Mexican state can be viewed as a struggle between political order, which has almost always been achieved by authoritarian rulers, and periodic political anarchy.[1]

When the Spanish conquistador **Hernán Cortés** arrived in Mexico in 1519, he encountered well-established and highly sophisticated indigenous civilizations. The country had long been home to such peoples as the Maya, Aztecs, and Toltecs, who had relatively prosperous economies, impressive architecture, sophisticated agricultural methods, and powerful militaries. Within three years of their arrival, the Spanish conquerors had defeated the last Aztec leader **Cuauhtémoc,** destroyed the impressive Aztec capital Tenochtitlán, and decimated the indigenous population. By the early seventeenth century, the indigenous population had been reduced from about 25 million to under 1 million.

Historical Period and Political Conditions		
Dates	**Period**	**Political Condition**
1519–1810	Colonial	Order
1810–76	Independence	Anarchy
1876–1910	Porfiriato	Order
1910–20	Mexican Revolution	Anarchy
1917–2000	The PRI Regime	Order

TIME LINE OF POLITICAL DEVELOPMENT

Year	Event
1810–21	War of Independence fought against Spain
1846–48	One third of Mexico's territory lost in war with the United States
1910–17	Mexican Revolution
1917	Revolutionary constitution adopted
1929	Official revolutionary party created, later becoming the Partido Revolucionario Institucional (PRI)
1934–40	Presidency of Lázaro Cárdenas, during which land reform is promoted, the oil industry is nationalized, and the state is given a larger role in the economy
1939	Partido Acción Nacional (PAN) formed as a conservative opposition to the revolution
1968	Student protest movement against the Mexican government violently repressed
1981–82	Economic collapse caused by sudden drop in oil prices and Mexico's inability to pay its foreign debt
1988	Assumption of power by President Carlos Salinas de Gortari after elections widely viewed as fraudulent
1994	North American Free Trade Agreement (NAFTA) put into effect
	Rebellion of Zapatistas, indigenous peasants in the southern state of Chiapas
	PRI presidential candidate Luis Donaldo Colosio assassinated while campaigning, replaced by Ernesto Zedillo
1994–2000	Presidency of Ernesto Zedillo
2000	Election of PAN candidate Vicente Fox Quesada, marking the first defeat of the PRI in seventy-one years

The surviving indigenous peoples of Mexico, concentrated in the central and southern parts of the country, became a permanent underclass of slaves and landless peasants.

The Aztec Empire was replaced by the equally hierarchical, authoritarian, and militaristic Spanish Empire, which created a legacy very different from that imparted to the United States by British colonialism. Mexico was the richest of Spain's colonial possessions, and Spain ruled the distant colony with an iron first, sending a new viceroy to the colony every four years. Colonial

viceroys were absolute dictators: armed with the terror of the Spanish Inqui-
sition, they were able to stamp out most political dissent. Lacking any civilian oversight, rampant corruption thrived in the colonial administration.

INDEPENDENCE AND INSTABILITY: THE SEARCH FOR ORDER

The struggle for independence can be viewed as a conflict over control of the
state between the aristocracy loyal to Spain and the increasingly powerful and
wealthy criollos (Mexican-born descendants of the Spanish colonists). Though
inspired by the French and American Revolutions, the Mexican independence
movement was mostly a response to the sudden blow that Napoléon's invading armies delivered to Spain. When Spain adopted a progressive liberal constitution in 1820, conservative Mexican elites accepted independence as the
only means by which to preserve order and the status quo. The leading rebels
and political conservatives agreed that an independent Mexico, declared in
1821, would preserve the role of the Catholic Church and implement a constitutional monarchy with a European at the head. Mexico's **War of Independence** lasted eleven years and cost 600,000 lives.

Mexico's independence was dominated by political conservatives. As a
result, independence did nothing to alleviate the poverty of Mexico's indigenous people and its large mestizo population. Indeed, the violence of the War
of Independence and the elimination of the minimal protections of the Spanish crown worsened their plight. The power of the large landholders, or *lati-
fundistas,* grew with independence, and the newly independent Mexico grew
more economically disparate and politically unstable. Much of the turmoil
and political chaos that plagued Mexico over the next half century was caused
by a dispute between conservative monarchists and more liberal republicans.
With the end of Spanish rule and the strong centralized government of the
viceroy, Mexico was dominated by local military strongmen, known as
caciques. Mexico's weak central state could not impose its authority.

Independent Mexico's first leader, Colonel Agustín de Iturbide, had himself crowned emperor in 1822 but was overthrown by General Antonio López
de Santa Ana, Mexico's first in a series of **caudillos** (national military strongmen), and executed two years later. Santa Ana dominated the politics of Mexico for the next thirty years, but despite his considerable power he was unable
to impose his authority over the local caciques or prevent the secession of
Texas in 1836. The impotence of a fragmented Mexico became even more
apparent in the 1840s, when a rising imperial power, the United States,
defeated the country in the **Mexican-American War** (1846–48), which resulted
in Mexico's loss of half its territory (present-day Arizona , California, Colorado, Nevada, New Mexico, Texas, and Utah) to the United States. In the
aftermath of the defeat, Mexico's weakened government faced a massive uprising, known as the War of the Castes, by the indigenous Mayan population in
the south. It took several years of fighting to subdue the rebellion.

Over the next several decades, Mexican liberals, led by a Zapotec Indian, Benito Juárez, attempted to centralize, modernize, and secularize Mexico. Juárez, who occupied the presidency on three separate occasions, imposed a fairly progressive constitution in 1857 and is today considered one of Mexico's first proponents of democracy. Juárez was unable to bring stability to Mexico, however. In 1864, Mexican conservatives, backed by French troops, imposed an ill-fated and short-lived monarchy ruled by an Austrian emperor, Maximilian, who was captured and executed in 1867. Juárez regained power, but his reforms alienated Mexican conservatives, and Mexico soon succumbed to a long dictatorship.

THE PORFIRIATO: ECONOMIC LIBERALISM AND POLITICAL AUTHORITARIANISM

From 1876 to 1910, Mexican politics was dominated by **Porfirio Díaz,** a general who had backed the liberal reforms of Juárez and fought to expel the French-imposed monarchy. Díaz assumed power in 1876 and had himself reelected repeatedly until 1910. Díaz ruled Mexico with an iron fist, imposing a brutal authoritarian regime (known as the porfiriato), which gave Mexico its first taste of stability since independence. Díaz was also responsible for Mexico's first real economic development and was the first Mexican ruler to impose the power of the state on remote areas.

THE REVOLUTION

The **Mexican Revolution** (1910–20) can be viewed as a struggle between two groups attempting to seize control of the state. The first included middle-class Mexicans resisting the dictatorship of Díaz. The second included radical social reformers who sought agrarian reform, among other things.

In the first phase of the revolution, middle-class political reformers, led by the landowner Francisco Madero, defeated the Díaz dictatorship. Madero's victory promised democratic reforms and minimal economic change. The second phase of the revolution involved a struggle between these political reformers and advocates of radical socioeconomic change. The most famous revolutionary advocate of the poor was **Emiliano Zapata,** a young mestizo peasant leader. Zapata organized a peasant army in Morelos, south of Mexico City, to push for agrarian reform. In the north of Mexico, **Francisco (Pancho) Villa** had organized an army of peasants and small farmers.

The often contradictory aspects of the Mexican Revolution help explain why it was so protracted and so bloody: Mexico soon descended into political chaos, in which armed bands led by regional caciques fought one another over a period of ten years. About 1.5 million Mexicans (about 7 percent of the total population) died in the conflict, and thousands more fled north to the United States. Order was restored only in 1917, under the leadership of a northern governor, Venustiano Carranza. Carranza defeated not only his supporters who wanted a return to a dictatorship but also Zapata and Villa, the more radical voices of the revolution.

The constitution of 1917 reflected some of the contradictions of the revolution. The document was written not by peasants and workers but by middle-class mestizo professionals who had suffered under the Díaz dictatorship. That some of their values were largely "liberal" explains provisions that call for regular elections as well as harsh measures to weaken the Catholic Church. The constitution sought to prevent the reemergence of a dictatorship by devolving political power to Mexico's states, adopting federalism, and barring presidents and other elected leaders from reelection. Reflecting the power of the emerging mestizo class and the role played by indigenous Mexicans in unseating the dictatorship, the 1917 constitution provided elaborate protection of indigenous communal lands and called for land reform. It was also a nationalist document, prohibiting foreign ownership of Mexican land and mineral rights.

Although Carranza successfully seized power and fostered the new constitution, he was unable to implement many of the reforms or stem Mexico's endemic political violence. His government was responsible for the murder of Zapata in 1919, and Carranza himself was assassinated by political opponents in 1920.

Mexico's next two elected presidents, Álvaro Obregón (1920–24) and Plutarco Elías Calles (1924–28), finally put an end to the political bloodshed and developed a political system capable of maintaining order. Obregón promoted trade unions but brought them under the control of the state. He also promoted land reform while tolerating the presence of haciendas. He managed to gain the support and recognition of the United States, which had feared the revolution as a socialist experiment. Most significant, he purged the army and weakened the revolutionary generals who had continued to meddle in politics. Calles consolidated state power by imposing the first income tax and investing in education and infrastructure. He vigorously enforced the constitution's limit on the power of the Catholic Church. The church was a major landowner, and its support for the dictatorship of Díaz and the enemies of the revolution made it a prime target for reform. Religious processions were banned, clergy could not appear in public in religious garb, the church could not own any property, and control over education was given to the state.

When Calles left power, he also left Mexico his most enduring legacy: the Revolucionario Partido Nacional, later renamed the Revolucionario Partido Institucional (PRI). From the outset, the PRI was conceived as a party of power and a party of the state. Its colors (red, white, and green) are the colors of the Mexican flag. Its goal was to encompass all of those who supported the revolution, and its members thus ranged from socialists to liberals. Moreover, it was designed to incorporate and co-opt the most important organizations in Mexican society, starting with the army. The PRI's main purpose was to end political violence by controlling the political system and the process of presidential succession. After decades of instability and violence, the revolution's leaders brought Mexico an unprecedented period of political peace.

STABILITY ACHIEVED: THE PRI IN POWER, 1917–2000

For decades, the PRI provided Mexico with the much-desired political stability that its founders had sought. Under the PRI, Mexico held national elections every six years, and new presidents took power without violence or military intervention. The PRI regime featured a strong president, directly elected for a single six-year term. Though not stipulated in the 1917 constitution, PRI presidents claimed the power to name their successors by officially designating the PRI candidate for the presidency, and for over eighty years no official PRI candidate ever lost a presidential election. During most of the PRI's tenure in office, the Mexican president enjoyed the reverence and aloofness of monarchical heads of state while possessing far more power than the typical democratic president. Most important, until 2000 Mexican presidents controlled the vast machinery of the PRI and used the state to dispense patronage. Unlike U.S. presidents, they faced no effective check on their power from the legislature, judiciary, or state governments, all of which were controlled by the PRI.

Under the PRI, regular elections were held for national, state, and local offices, and opposition parties actively contested these elections. During most of this period, there was no formal censorship of the press, and Mexicans were free to voice their opinions and criticize the government. Mexicans were free to live where they wanted, and according to their constitution, they were living as in a democratic state.

But under its surface, the Mexican regime had clear authoritarian tendencies. The PRI held an inordinate amount of power. It won every presidential election between 1917 and 2000 and during that time won the vast majority of seats in the legislature and at the state and local level. The PRI dominated major trade unions and peasant organizations. Through its control of the state, the PRI dominated major pieces of the economy, including Mexico's vast oil wealth. The PRI became expert at co-opting possible sources of opposition, including the press and the weak opposition parties. Unlike many authoritarian regimes, the PRI did not often need to revert to harsh measures of repression, but when necessary the regime used a variety of tactics to stifle the opposition. Most notorious was the selective use of electoral fraud in order to preserve its political dominance, a tactic that was employed increasingly in the 1970s and 1980s as its grip on power began to erode.

Since the Mexican Revolution, scholars have struggled to characterize the Mexican regime. It is perhaps most accurate to view Mexico under the PRI as an authoritarian regime dominated by a single political party, but one that afforded far more civil liberties than its authoritarian counterparts elsewhere. Mexico held regular (though not always free and fair) elections, tolerated and even encouraged political parties (although those parties began to win office only in the 1980s), and formally protected basic civil liberties. Compared with almost any other authoritarian regime, the PRI kept human rights abuses to a minimum. The PRI maintained its power almost exclusively through co-optation, inclusion, and corruption. Its unparalleled success meant that it did-n't often need to resort to brute repression. The Peruvian novelist Mario Vargas Llosa thus viewed the PRI regime as the "perfect dictatorship."[2]

THE SLOW EROSION OF PRI POWER, 1980–2000

By the early 1980s, the vaunted stability of the Mexican regime was called into question by a series of interrelated economic and political challenges to PRI rule. The economic crisis of the 1980s unleashed numerous challenges to

CARLOS SALINAS AND THE POWER OF THE PRI

The history of Carlos Salinas de Gotari illustrates well the workings of the PRI. Salinas, a Harvard-educated technocrat, rose steadily through the ranks and was appointed by his political patron, President Miguel de la Madrid Hurtado, to a top cabinet post. De la Madrid then handpicked Salinas for the PRI presidential nomi-nation. In 1988, Salinas won the presidency in elections widely thought to have been stolen from the opposition. Despite a questionable popular mandate, Salinas con-tinued de la Madrid's neo-liberal economic reforms and signed the landmark 1994 NAFTA with the United States and Canada.

Mexican presidents traditionally completed their terms and once out of power scrupulously avoided the political limelight and were treated with considerable respect. The tradition was broken with Salinas, however, who found himself vilified after leaving office in 1994. His economic policies were blamed for the economic depression of 1994–95, and his administration was accused of massive corruption. In March 1995, Salinas's brother Raúl was arrested and later sentenced to prison for the 1994 murder of a PRI deputy leader. Subsequent investigations revealed that the former president's brother had stashed millions of dollars in hidden bank accounts and had not paid taxes on most of that wealth. As a sign of the growing disarray within the PRI, Carlos Salinas then committed a political taboo by publicly attacking the policies of his handpicked successor, President Ernesto Zedillo. At the request of Zedillo, Salinas went into voluntary exile in Ireland. For many Mexicans, the Salinas episode was symbolic of everything that was wrong with PRI rule.

the party's political hegemony. The conservative opposition in northern Mexico, long an advocate of free-market economic policies, began to seriously contest local and state elections. The PRI was then forced to revert to ever-increasing and ever-more-overt electoral fraud to deny power to the opposition. The watershed election of July 2000 ended the PRI's seventy-one-year control of the presidency. Vicente Fox, candidate of the conservative **Partido Acción Nacional (PAN),** handily defeated Francisco Labastida of the PRI, despite an expensive and elaborate PRI campaign.

POLITICAL REGIME

Political Institutions

THE CONSTITUTION

On paper, the Mexican regime does not differ markedly from that of the United States, although much more power is granted to Mexico's president. The constitution of 1917 calls for a presidential legislative-executive system, a separation of judicial, legislative, and executive power, and a system of federalism that gives Mexico's states considerable power. The seventy-one-year domination of the political system by the Partido Revolucionario Institucional (PRI) rendered this formidable Constitution largely meaningless, however. Mexican presidents enjoyed near-dictatorial powers with few checks on their authority. Through their domination of the PRI, they not only controlled the judiciary but also handpicked state governors. The Mexican legislature might have served as a check on the PRI, but until July 1997 it was controlled by it.

Elections at all levels were largely a charade, serving mainly to validate PRI appointments to elective offices. Even the president was not truly elected, since incumbent presidents ritually designated their successor. Campaigns were more celebrations of PRI's power than genuine political contests.

How, then, did the opposition manage to win local and state elections in the 1980s, and how did the opposition unseat the PRI in the 2000 presidential election? Part of the answer to these

---

ESSENTIAL POLITICAL FEATURES

- Legislative-executive system: federal republic
- Legislature: Congreso de la Union (National Congress)
- Lower house: Camara Federal de Diputados (Federal Chamber of Deputies)
- Upper house: Camara de Senadores (Senate)
- Unitary or federal division of power: federal
- Main geographic subunits: estados (states)
- Electoral system for lower house: mixed single-member district and proportional representation
- Chief judicial body: Suprema Corte de Justicia de la Nación (National Supreme Court of Justice)

questions lies in the growing illegitimacy of the regime during the 1970s, when Mexico's economy began to deteriorate. But the erosion of PRI legitimacy was also the result of widespread outrage in reaction to the PRI's blatant and unabashed disregard for the rule of law in the 1980s and 1990s. As opposition to the PRI grew and as the PRI resorted more openly and more regularly to widespread electoral fraud, sectors of the party pushed for democratization. Seeking to polish its image, the PRI passed a number of reforms that favored the opposition.

One important set of reforms passed in 1993 changed the electoral law (implementing some element of proportional representation, or PR) in order to guarantee the presence of the opposition in the legislature. Other reforms passed under the last PRI president, Ernesto Zedillo, gave the legislature control over judicial appointments and imposed electoral safeguards that greatly reduced the ability of a government to steal an election.

The Branches of Government

THE PRESIDENCY

Because of their immense power and unchallenged authority, Mexican presidents have often been viewed as elected monarchs. The 1917 constitution created a far more powerful president than that conceived in the U.S. model. The Mexican president can issue executive decrees that have the force of law. He can directly introduce legislation in **Congress** and can veto legislation initiated by Congress. Until 1994, Mexican presidents had extensive power to appoint and remove judges. As late as 1982, President José López Portillo essentially decreed the nationalization of Mexico's banking system.

Mexican presidents serve a single six-year term. They must be at least thirty-five years old and native born and cannot be a member of the clergy or an active member of the military. During the seventy-one-year reign of the PRI, the power of the president was greatly enhanced by the tradition of handpicking his successor, who was generally chosen from among the cabinet members. Mexican presidents also enjoyed enormous power because the state played a leading role in the economy. Control over key natural resources and infrastructure (for example, oil, electricity, and communications) historically put the key economic lever in the hands of the executive.

Mexican presidents appoint and preside over a large cabinet of ministers, who oversee the various government departments. In recent decades, the Secretariat of Government, which controls internal political affairs, and the Secretariat of the Treasury, which oversees the economy, have been the highest-profile cabinet posts and have often been stepping-stones to the presidency. The reorganized cabinet of Vicente Fox Quesada included nineteen cabinet secretaries, in addition to seven policy coordinators whose job is to

STRUCTURE OF THE GOVERNMENT

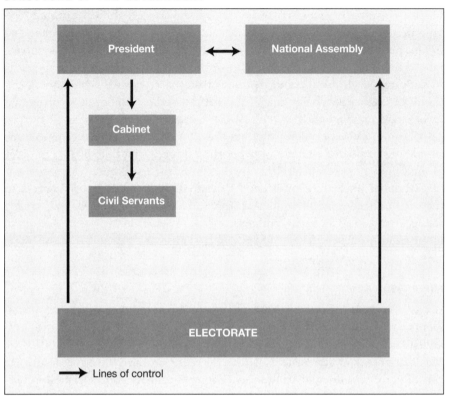

ease communication among ministries.[3] In the first two years of Fox's administration, his inexperienced cabinet was characterized by chaos and confusion, a radical departure from the PRI era. Since Fox's historic victory in 2000, Mexico's president has been faced with an unprecedented lack of a majority in Congress. As a result, some of the constitutional checks on presidential power that were long absent in the Mexican system have become more effective. One sign of the waning of presidential power was Fox's inability to obtain his party's nomination for his favored candidate, Interior Minister Santiago Creel, in the 2006 elections.

THE LEGISLATURE

Mexico has a bicameral legislature, called Congress, which is composed of a lower house (the **Chamber of Deputies**) and an upper house (the **Senate**).[4] The 500-member Chamber of Deputies has the power to pass laws (with a two-thirds majority), levy taxes, and verify the outcome of elections. Mexico's upper house is composed of 128 members, with three senators from each state and the Federal District of Mexico City, and an additional 32 senators selected from a national list on the basis of proportional representation. The upper house has fewer powers than the lower house, but it does have the power to confirm the president's appointments to the **Supreme Court,** approve treaties, and approve federal intervention in state matters.

Both houses have a committee system that on paper looks much like the U.S. system. In practice, however, Mexican legislators and the legislative committees lack the teeth of their northern counterparts because of one key difference: according to Article 59 of the constitution, Mexican legislators cannot be reelected to consecutive terms. As a result, from 1970 to 1997 only about 17 percent of Mexican deputies entered the lower house with any legislative experience, effectively depriving Mexico of the kind of senior lawmakers who dominate the U.S. system.[5] Most legislators were members of the PRI and could not afford to cross the leadership because they depended on the party for future political appointments. Even after the PRI's loss of the presidency in 2000, single-term legislators were reluctant to disobey their party leadership if they hoped to be nominated for another post in local or state government. Ironically, the PRI (whose founding principle was no reelection) is now the strongest advocate of ending term limits.

The Mexican legislature is currently in transition. Until 1988, the PRI regularly won over 90 percent of lower-house seats and never lost a Senate seat. Between 1970 and 2003, it averaged 66.9 percent of the seats in the lower house, dwarfing the presence of its nearest rival, the Partido Acción Nacional (PAN, Vicente Fox's National Action Party), which averaged about 17 percent during that period).[6] In 1997, the two main opposition parties were able to form a coalition and take control of the lower house. After the 2000 elections, the PRI remained the strongest party in the lower house but fell well short of a majority of seats. In the Senate, the opposition controlled 53 percent of the seats.

Before 1997, the lower house approved about 97 percent of the legislation submitted by the executive. That percentage dropped precipitously after 1990 and has continued to fall. Moreover, the number of laws originating in the legislature (instead of in the president's office) has increased dramatically. With its internal divisions and a president who does not enjoy complete control over deputies from his own party, the lower house has resisted many of Fox's policies. Despite his inaugural pledge to respect Congress, Fox began his term acting very much like the PRI presidents in his relationship with Congress: he designed legislative proposals without any congressional input.[7] Fox's imperious behavior only emboldened the legislature. Congress blocked some legislation and radically altered other measures. For example, the lower house modified Fox's indigenous-rights bill, which emerged from the legislature so weakened that the Zapatista guerrillas rejected it. Fox's proposed reform of Mexico's tax structure was torpedoed by PRI and PRD (Partido de la Revolución Democrática) opposition, and Congress blocked his effort to negotiate a reduction of tariffs on imported sugar. Mexico's upper house even used its constitutional power to bar Fox from traveling to the United States in April 2002, complaining that the president was not paying enough attention to domestic politics.

Since Mexican legislators can't be reelected and the majority of them are unlikely to receive presidential patronage, there is little to incline them to end the executive-legislative gridlock. The stubborn opposition to Fox by PRI and PRD legislators could have been predicted. The lukewarm support for Fox's legislative proposals by members of his own party has been more surprising. In short, Fox has attempted to govern like the PRI presidents, but without the benefit of the PRI's system of political control.

THE JUDICIAL SYSTEM

Mexico's judiciary is structured according to the U.S. model. Like the United States, Mexico has a Supreme Court as well as courts at the local and state levels. The eleven Supreme Court justices are appointed by the president and are confirmed by a two-thirds vote of the Senate. They serve terms of up to fifteen years. The Mexican judiciary has important formal powers, but under the PRI the Supreme Court never overturned any law, and it tended to view its jurisdiction in very limited terms. During the last PRI presidency, dramatic changes were introduced to give the Supreme Court far greater jurisdiction and power.[8] The Supreme Court can now determine the constitutionality of legislation upon the request of one third of the lower house, but it can strike down a law only if a supermajority of eight out of eleven justices agrees. The reforms have increased the independence of the judiciary by creating a seven-member Federal Judicial Council to oversee the administration of justice.

During the last years of PRI rule and in the early years of the Fox administration, the Supreme Court assumed a much more activist role. For example, it ordered President Zedillo's administration to release records relating to the banking industry, and it struck down Fox's attempt to privatize electricity generation. Despite this progress, Mexico's judicial system is severely hampered by a widespread perception that judges, especially at the local level, are corrupt. Both Zedillo and Fox made it a priority to enhance the prestige and power of the beleaguered court system.

The Electoral System

During the last two decades of PRI, rule elections were widely viewed as corrupt. The 1988 presidential election was probably the zenith of PRI electoral fraud: over 30,000 ballot boxes disappeared, and in an effort to cover up the thievery the federal government declared the final ballots a state secret. Only in 1996 did the PRI succumb to pressure and create a truly independent **Federal Electoral Institute,** taking power away from the government-controlled Secretariat of the Interior. It also created the Federal Electoral Tribunal to adjudicate all electoral disputes. Mexico now has a sophisticated and transparent electoral system featuring a national electoral register and voter identification cards, public funding for electoral campaigns, and strict limits on private contributions.

Voting is compulsory in Mexico, although enforcement of the law is sporadic. In part because of this law and in part because the PRI traditionally used its power to encourage electoral turnout, Mexican elections have generally had very high turnout, usually between 60 and 80 percent.

Mexico's current electoral system for the legislature dates from reforms implemented by PRI president Miguel de la Madrid Hurtado in 1986. Mexico now has a mixed electoral system for the lower house, with 300 single-member districts (SMDs) and 200 proportional representation (PR) seats. Deputies in the lower house serve three-year terms. Mexico's electoral system for the upper house is unique. Senators serve six-year terms, and three are elected from each state and the federal district. The party with the most votes wins two senate seats, and the party finishing second is automatically awarded the third seat. An additional thirty-two seats are allocated according to PR. Mexican presidents are directly elected every six years in a single round of voting. Elections to the Senate take place at the same time as the presidential elections. Parties must get at least 2 percent of the national vote in order to win seats from the PR lists.

Local Government

Despite being formally federal, Mexico operated very much like a unitary political system under the PRI. Excessive localism and a history of instability and political violence caused by the absence of a weak central authority favored the PRI's centralizing tendencies, despite the federalist constitutional rhetoric. Federal authorities controlled local elections, local budgets, local police forces, and so forth. Until 1997, the mayor of Mexico City was a cabinet member appointed directly by the president.

Mexico currently has thirty-two states and a Federal District of Mexico City, each with its own constitution and unicameral legislature.[9] States are subdivided into county governments (called **municipios**). State governors, county councils, and county presidents are elected directly, although until recently PRI leaders handpicked them. Until 1988, all governors were from the PRI, although in the 1980s only widespread electoral fraud prevented

LOCAL RESISTANCE TO GLOBALIZATION

Mexico's federal government has enthusiastically embraced foreign investment as a way to provide jobs for Mexico's poor. No region needs jobs more than the poverty-stricken state of Oaxaca, home to many of Mexico's indigenous poor. But in December 2002, the city council of Oaxaca voted to prohibit the construction of a McDonald's restaurant in the city's historic and picturesque zócalo (town square). Oaxaca has long prided itself on its reputation as Mexico's culinary capital, and the zocalo has been an important venue for protests against federal policy. The city council responded to a grassroots protest movement that collected almost 10,000 signatures, another sign of the reemergence of an autonomous civil society after decades of PRI rule.

opposition victories. Indeed, some of the first serious opposition to PRI hegemony came at the local level, especially in Mexico's prosperous north, when unpopular PRI local leaders and state governors were successfully defeated by opposition candidates. The PRI's use of widespread electoral fraud at the local level helped ignite regional opposition to the party's heavy-handed centralist policies. The first opposition governor took power in 1989 in the state of Baja California Norte. In the 1990s, the PRI began to accept opposition victories in numerous local elections, and by the end of that decade opposition parties controlled seven governorships.

Mexican states do have important powers, but their sovereignty is far more circumscribed by federal authorities, especially the federal bureaucracy, than in other federal systems, like the United States, Canada, and Germany. The PRI regime limited local autonomy by retaining tight control over public funds, controlling about 85 percent of all revenues collected. Under Fox, this figure has been substantially reduced, suggesting that local government will play an enhanced role in Mexico's future.

Although in the 1980s and 1990s state and local politics provided the first opportunities for Mexico's anti-PRI opposition, some local and state offices (especially in rural areas) remained PRI strongholds long after the party lost the presidency in 2000. A good example is the rural west-coast state of Guerrero, where the PRI retained a lock on state government until being ousted by the leftist PRD in the gubernatorial elections of 2005.

As in most Latin American political systems, the military has been a key political actor. Before the Mexican Revolution, military strongmen repeatedly intervened in politics. But one of the revolution's greatest achievements was to tame Mexico's military. Since 1946, all presidents have been civilians, and the military no longer plays a direct role in politics.

POLITICAL CONFLICT AND COMPETITION

The Party System

Under the Partido Revolucionario Institucional (PRI), opposition parties were mostly tolerated; some were even encouraged to exist in order to give legitimacy to the PRI-dominated system. The Party skillfully cultivated and selectively co-opted all the opposition parties, which were, in general, weak and divided until the 1980s. The PRI periodically altered the election laws to increase the presence of the opposition in the legislature while using electoral fraud to retain control of the presidency and key governorships.

THE PARTIDO REVOLUCIONARIO INSTITUCIONAL

The PRI was founded in 1929 as a way of ending Mexico's often violent struggle for political power. From the start, the PRI was viewed as a party representing the interests of the Mexican state. During its long rule, the PRI became increasingly indistinguishable from the state, and the immense power of Mexico's presidents resulted from their effective control over both the Party and the state.

Average Voter Turnout, 1945–2000	
Country (number of elections)	**Eligible Voters Voting (%)**
South Africa (1)	85.5
United Kingdom (15)	74.9
Japan (21)	69.0
Iran (2)	67.6
France (15)	67.3
India (12)	60.7
Russia (2)	55.0
United States (26)	48.3
Mexico (18)	**48.1**
Brazil (13)	47.9
Nigeria (3)	47.6
China	NA

Source: "Turnout in the World: Country by Country Performance," International Institute for Democracy and Electoral Assistance

http://www.idea.int/vt/survey/voter_turnout_pop2.cfm (accessed 27 January 2006).

> ### PRI: CLIENTELISM FROM TOP TO BOTTOM
>
> During the PRI's long rule, millions of Mexicans lived in extreme poverty. During the 1990s, over 17,000 people survived as *pepenedores*, garbage pickers who live and work in Mexico City's rat-infested garbage landfills. The journalist Alma Guillermoprieto described how the PRI web of patron-client relationships extended all the way down to the lowly *pepenedores*.[10] She argued that garbage-dump caciques were able to use patron-client relationships to provide services for the garbage pickers and, most important, to protect their jobs from government officials seeking to move them out of the dumps. One community of *pepenedores* was awarded a neighborhood of homes across the street from a dump, complete with a school and running water. With this extension of aid, the PRI secured the support of some of Mexico's most destitute voters.

A key element of the PRI's exercise of power was the use of **patron-client relationships,** in which powerful government officials delivered state services and access to power in exchange for the delivery of political support. The patron-client relationships operated from the top of the hierarchy, dominated by the PRI-controlled presidency, down to the very poorest segments of society (see the box above). At the elite level, vast informal networks of personal loyalty, known as **camarillas** (political cliques), were far more important than ideology.

The PRI also maintained control over the state through its ability to mobilize and control mass organizations. During the presidency of Lázaro Cárdenas, worker and peasant organizations were created and then integrated into the PRI structure. By using the state to channel patronage to PRI mass organizations, independent mass organizations were rendered marginal and impotent. Mexico's business elite duly lavished the PRI with campaign donations. One notorious example was a 1993 dinner, hosted by President Carlos Salinas, at which two dozen of Mexico's top business leaders were asked to give US$25 million each to the PRI.

The PRI has no clear or consistent ideology other than political opportunism. Over the last century, it sought mainly to control political power, and PRI governments varied greatly with each presidency. For example, redistributive and nationalist economic policies implemented during the Cárdenas presidency (1939–40) were directly contradicted by subsequent PRI presidents. All PRI leaders claimed to represent the legacy of the Mexican Revolution, but as we have seen, that legacy is ambiguous.

Given that PRI presidents supported very different types of political economic policies, why wasn't there more open dissent within the PRI? In part, there wasn't more dissent because the PRI wrote electoral rules that made it virtually impossible for dissident PRI factions to form new parties and win elections.

Beginning in 1982, the PRI slowly but steadily lost support in presidential, congressional, and local elections. Some of the decline was a direct result of Mexico's rapid urbanization: while rural Mexicans were particularly susceptible to local PRI bosses, urbanites were better educated, wealthier, and more politically independent. The PRI also suffered from a reduction in the state's ability to dispense patronage during tough economic times. The economic-austerity policies of the 1990s, a cornerstone of the government's neo-liberal policies, undoubtedly cost it a number of votes.

Ironically, the erosion of the PRI's political power in the 1990s was also a partial consequence of its attempt at democratic reform. Seeking to enhance its democratic legitimacy, the government in the 1990s spent over US$1 billion to implement a high-tech electoral system that greatly reduced electoral fraud.

Even with its historic defeat in the July 2000 presidential elections, the PRI remains Mexico's strongest political party. It holds a majority of seats in the Senate and the largest plurality of seats in the Chamber of Deputies and controls more than half of Mexico's governorships. It is the only party with a truly national reach and the only one capable of running candidates for every nationwide political office. The PRI gained sixteen seats in the July 2003 midterm lower-house elections, but its share of the vote (at 35.6 percent, still the largest of any party) continued the steady decline that had begun in the mid-1990s.

Since losing the presidency in 2000, the PRI has been rudderless. As a party designed to serve sitting presidents, it no longer has a clear leader. The official party leadership, the PRI legislative delegation, and PRI governors have all wielded considerable power and have produced what one observer has called "a hydra-headed behemoth."[11] Recent changes in the PRI structure have led to the direct election of a party president, however.[12] Whether the PRI can transform itself from the perennial party of the state to an effective force of political opposition remains to be seen. Its 2006 presidential candidate, Roberto Madrazo, ran a lackluster campaign and was widely perceived as an old-style PRI machine politician.

THE LEFT

After the revolution, the PRI attempted to occupy the political space traditionally occupied by leftist parties, even though it usually pursued economic policies traditionally identified with the right. Because the PRI regime had its leftist phases, especially during the presidency of Lázaro Cárdenas, and because Mexico's foreign policy often supported leftist governments and leftist movements elsewhere in Latin America, there was little real political space to be occupied by leftist parties.

Nevertheless, parties of the left existed in Mexico, though most of them supported the PRI. Although the Communist Party was banned until 1979, the Popular Socialist Party (a moderate socialist party) and a few other leftist parties regularly won a few seats in the legislature. A serious leftist political force emerged only in the 1980s, when a leftist faction within the PRI, led by Michoacán governor Cuauhtémoc Cárdenas, bolted from the party.[13] Cárdenas, the son of the former president, then led the newly formed PRD (Partido de la Revolución Democrática) in a coalition of four opposition parties in the 1988 elections.

Bolstered by the high-profile leadership of Cárdenas and boosted by the PRI's loss of popularity, the PRD performed extremely well in the 1988 elections. Many observers believe that had there not been significant electoral fraud, the PRD would have won those elections. Despite this auspicious start, the PRD struggled as a leftist opposition party. It has been plagued by internal infighting and has been unable to capture enough voters outside its strongholds in Mexico City and the south.

The PRD clearly stands to the left of the PRI. During the 1980s and 1990s, it attacked the PRI's neo-liberal reforms and neglect of poor Mexicans. It advocated more nationalist and protectionist policies than had traditionally been pursued by the PRI. PRD candidates at the state and local level have had considerable success, and the PRD has controlled Mexico City's government since 1997, but the party's performance in the 2000 presidential elections was certainly a disappointment. Cárdenas won just over 16 percent of the presidential vote, and the PRD did only slightly better in elections to Congress. The 2000 elections left the PRD as a minor political force whose seats in Congress are not sufficient to build a majority, even if combined with the Partido Acción Nacional (PAN).

The PRD's prospects improved considerably after the 2003 legislative elections. With its allies on the left, it saw its support increase moderately, to about one quarter of the electorate, and it gained thirty-six seats, the biggest gain of any party. The PRD defeated the PRI in key gubernatorial elections in Guerrero and Baja California del Sur in February 2005, although the PRD still controlled only five of Mexico's thirty-two states. The PRD mayor of Mexico City, Andrés Manuel López Obrador, a charismatic populist, emerged as the front-runner in the 2006 presidential election but saw his lead slip away as the conservative opposition portrayed him as a dangerous radical who would threaten Mexico's prosperity and harm relations with the United States.

THE RIGHT

Mexico's main conservative party, the Partido Acción Nacional (PAN), was founded in 1939 by defectors from the PRI. It became the only opposition party to develop a strong organizational presence, especially in its strongholds in northern Mexico and the state of Yucatán. The party emerged as a con-

THE CLOSEST MEXICAN ELECTION

During the long rule of the PRI, elections were usually lopsided affairs, and when necessary, elections were rigged to preserve the PRI's power. Given this history of electoral fraud, the victory of conservative Felipe Calderón over the leftist Andrés Manuel López Obrador in the July 2006 elections raised serious doubts about the fairness of the electoral process. After all, in 1988 the PRI resorted to massive electoral fraud to prevent a victory of the leftist PRD presidential candidate. In the lead-up to the 2006 presidential election the PAN government (with help from the PRI) unsuccessfully tried to block López Obrador's candidacy on questionable legal grounds. Although most observers pointed to the huge improvements in the safeguards protecting Mexico's electoral system from fraud, the razor-thin victory of Calderón over López Obrador (about 220,000 votes, under 0.5 percent) raised serious suspicions, and López Obrador vowed to contest the results.

servative response to the leftist policies of the PRI during the late 1930s and early 1940s. It advocated Christian democratic ideas, opposing the PRI's anticlericalism and supporting pro-business policies. Since its base of power was state politics, the PAN became an early advocate of state's rights and opposed the centralization of power that was a feature of Mexican politics under the PRI.

Like many conservative parties, the PAN has been divided historically between Catholic conservatives and more progressive technocrats. The more progressive wing has dominated the party since the late 1980s, but the PRI's adoption of neo-liberal economic strategies during that decade threatened to steal the PAN's thunder. The PAN continues to be plagued by internal division, and PAN legislators have been much less willing to follow their own leadership than have PRI legislators.

In the 1990s, the PAN won the governorship of seven states. As the PRI fought harder to deny the PAN electoral victories, it unwittingly gave the PAN an issue that garnered support among Mexicans of all classes: the need to end corruption and guarantee free elections. Its leaders now preside over one third of all Mexicans. Nonetheless, the PAN suffers from its geographic concentration of the vote (mostly in northern Mexico) and its relative weakness among rural voters, who continue to overwhelmingly support the PRI.

Vicente Fox was not a prototypical PAN leader and did not share much of the social conservatism that is typical of many PAN leaders. His roots were in local government, having served as governor of his home state after a stint in Congress. His charisma and his personal-support network allowed him to overcome much opposition within his own party and helped expand the PAN's appeal to new voters. In the 2000 presidential campaign, Fox created his own campaign organization. That organization did not depend on the official PAN hierarchy, which was dominated by Fox's political rivals.[14] Once in office, Fox formed a cabinet that included no members of the PAN's traditionalist wing, and his closest advisers are non-PAN members. He has had stormy relations with the more conservative "traditionalist" wing of the PAN, which dominates the legislature and the party hierarchy.

Fox's record in office has been viewed as a mixed bag, but on the whole his administration has had trouble meeting the very high expectations that accompanied his historic victory in 2000. His administration delivered on some concrete reform promises.[15] Fox passed a transparency law to facilitate public oversight of government, and he restructured and purged Mexico's powerful and corruption-riddled Federal Judicial Police. He passed legislation to allow some 10 million Mexicans living abroad (many in the United States) to vote in elections. Some progress has been made on health care and pension reform, and the Fox administration has been praised for containing inflation. These successes, however, were outweighed by numerous policy failures, due in large part to Fox's inability to work with the opposition-dominated legislature, as well as with the opposition within his own party. Fox failed to solve the Zapatista rebellion in Chiapas, was unable to pass a badly needed tax increase to raise revenue for social spending and other public investment, and has a disappointing record on rooting out government corruption. After the PAN's drubbing in the 2003 legislative elections, when the governing party lost one quarter of its seats in the lower house, Fox's status as a lame-duck president was exacerbated, and his government was accused of losing focus. For the 2006 elections the PAN nominated former Energy Minister Felipe Calderón to be its presidential candidate, rejecting Fox's preferred candidate.

Since the earthquake of the 2000 election, the Mexican party system has been in flux. Recent data suggest that only about one quarter of Mexican voters have a strong identification with any party. Beginning in the 1990s, there was a significant partisan "dealignment," in which many voters abandoned the PRI. Not all of those voters have realigned themselves with other parties, however, and a large segment of the Mexican electorate remains "fluid."[16]

This fluidity can be witnessed in the legislative elections since 2000. The 2000 presidential elections were a clear victory for Vicente Fox, but the PRI emerged from the legislative elections as the dominant political force, though it suffered setbacks in its percentage of votes and in the number of seats it won in the lower house. The big loser in those elections was the leftist PRD, which was relegated to third place. The 2003 election dealt a severe blow to the governing PAN and signaled a comeback for the left: the PRD and its allies picked up thirty-six seats in the lower house. The PRI continued to suffer a loss of votes but was able to exploit the electoral system to win sixteen additional seats. The 2006 elections confirmed the steady rise of the PAN and PRD at the expense of

SEATS IN THE CHAMBER OF DEPUTIES, 2003 AND 2006

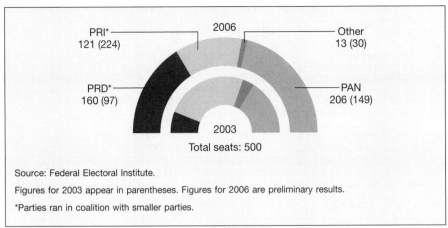

PRI*
121 (224)

2006

Other
13 (30)

PRD*
160 (97)

PAN
206 (149)

2003

Total seats: 500

Source: Federal Electoral Institute.

Figures for 2003 appear in parentheses. Figures for 2006 are preliminary results.

*Parties ran in coalition with smaller parties.

the waning PRI. Like his predecessor, President-elect Calderón will have to govern without a majority in the lower house.

Mexico has had a highly competitive electoral system since 2000. The current system has three major parties but operates as a two-party system in most of the country.[17] In Mexico's north and west, the PAN and PRI fight for votes, while in southern Mexico the PRD and PRI are chief rivals. Only in Mexico City and the surrounding areas do all three parties really compete on an equal footing. The PRI remains the only party with support in all regions, while the PRD and the PAN have more regionally concentrated bases of support.

A variety of smaller parties compete for, and regularly win seats in, the Mexican legislature. The most important of these is the Mexican Green Party (PVEM), an environment-oriented party that has little in common with its European counterparts. The PVEM was allied with the leftist PRD in the 1997 elections, then backed the conservative PAN in 2000. In 2003 and 2006, it ran in an alliance with the PRI.

Elections

During most of the PRI's long reign, elections were more national celebrations of PRI power than competitive electoral campaigns. Every six years, the country was decked out in the PRI's colors, patronage was dispensed on a massive scale, and the PRI nominees (in effect the presumed winners) toured their constituencies and made speeches.

The 2000 presidential campaign broke with the tradition. The opposition candidates (Cuauhtémoc Cárdenas of the PRD and Vicente Fox of the PAN) had announced their intention to run for the presidency several years before the election, and both candidates were widely assumed to have a lock on their parties' nominations. The PRI candidate, traditionally named quite late in the six-year presidential term, was determined for the first time by a PRI primary vote. As a result, several PRI candidates began campaigning for the nomination early in Zedillo's presidential term, with Francisco Labastida winning the party primary in a hotly contested race.

The 2000 campaign was also the first to be governed by new electoral-finance rules, which not only sharply limited private contributions but also provided candidates with public financing. Access to the media by all political parties was far more equitable than ever before. While PRI candidates still enjoyed an advantage, the playing field was more level than it had been in past elections. The first truly fair and competitive election was also the first national campaign in which U.S.-style mudslinging was widespread. The PRI portrayed Fox as a U.S. lackey, while Fox questioned Labastida's "macho" credentials. Some of the most negative campaigning took place between the two PRI contestants for the nomination. The 2000 campaign was also the first truly modern campaign in Mexican history. Television took on a pivotal role, culminating in two televised presidential debates, which the charismatic and engaging Fox won handily over the more wooden Labastida and Cárdenas.

In the 2000 campaign, Mexico's three major political parties presented voters with a fairly wide range of choices. The PRI, under the campaign slogan "Power will serve the people," represented the legacy of the Mexican Revolution and nationalism. The PAN shared the PRI's enthusiasm for neo-liberal reforms but offered itself as the party of democratization, as captured by its campaign slogan "Ya!" ("enough already"). Only the leftist PRD criticized neo-liberal economic policies and the North Atlantic Free Trade Agreement (NAFTA).

The midterm elections of 2003 were viewed by the government and the opposition as a referendum on the record of the PAN. Fox and his supporters hoped that the PAN would get a majority in the legislature so that it could implement its reform agenda without having to deal with a "do-nothing" lower house. The opposition sought a popular mandate for its strategy of opposing reforms that were seen as damaging to Mexico's economy and society. The results were not encouraging for the PAN, but gains made by the PRI and, especially, the PRD seemed to portend an especially competitive presidential election in 2006.

The 2006 presidential campaign was Mexico's first "normal" presidential contest. In 2000 the main issue had been democratization and the defeat of the PRI's semi-authoritarian regime. In 2006, Mexicans faced their first real choice between parties of the right and left. The early frontrunner, Andrés Manual López Obrador (of the leftist PRD) ran a campaign aimed at improving the plight of Mexico's poor. His main opponent, the PAN's Felipe Calderón, advocated a pro-business set of policies aimed at increasing employment. Calderón chipped away at López Obrador's initial lead by questioning his commitment to democracy and by portraying him as a dangerous leftist who would threaten Mexico's economic stability. The campaign was characterized by an unprecedented level of mudslinging and U.S.-style attack advertisements, ending the relatively benign political discourse that characterized the political campaigns of the PRI era. The outcome of the 2006 election revealed a polarized and divided electorate; Calderón and López Obrador each won just over 35 percent of the vote, and Calderón won by just over 200,000 votes.

Civil Society

Under the PRI, Mexican groups and associations were often incorporated into the state in a system known as corporatism. The paternalistic PRI would then mediate among different groups while making sure that no one group challenged government power. The PRI was formally divided into three sectors (labor, peasants, and the "popular" middle class), each dominated by PRI-controlled mass organizations. It would be a mistake to assume that the Mexican state could control all autonomous groups in society, however. To cite one example, the private-sector Confederation of Employers of the Mexican Republic (COPARMEX) became an important voice of opposition to the PRI, instead of supporting the governing party.

BUSINESS

Although the PRI successfully co-opted Mexico's private sector for decades, it can be argued that business groups later emerged as the most powerful source of opposition to PRI rule. Under the PRI, most private-sector interests were channeled into a variety of semi-official organizations, including the National Chamber of Industries and the National Chamber of Commerce. Until 1996, private-sector membership in these organizations was mandatory. Even though the PRI never gave business organizations formal representation within the governing party, business interests wielded power through more informal organizations and channels. The secretive Business Coordinating Council (CCE), which represents some of Mexico's wealthiest capitalists, had close ties to the Fox government.

The relationship between the business sector and the PRI was complex and often contradictory. In general, the policies of the PRI favored the private sector, especially big business. At the same time, business leaders bitterly opposed attempts by some PRI presidents to enact the social agenda of the Mexican Revolution. In the 1970s, Presidents Luis Echeverría Alvarez and José

López Portillo sought to expand the role of the state in the economy, and their policies damaged business-government relations. Although those policies were short-lived, they served to garner opposition to the PRI among northern business interests. The election of a business-sector president in 2000 will likely enhance the political power of the private sector. The prospect of a PRD victory in 2006 clearly alarmed much of the business sector.

LABOR

The PRI actively supported the unionization of Mexican workers, but the unions were thoroughly integrated into the corporatist system. They received massive subsidies from the state, which made them politically pliant. They enjoyed privileged treatment under the PRI, in part because they were never able to incorporate much of the workforce (about 16 percent, at their peak) and because one third of their members were government employees. The labor movement in Mexico was highly centralized. The dominant labor organization, the **Confederation of Mexican Workers (CTM),** was created by the PRI and became one of the main pillars of the governing party. The CTM was dominated for over fifty years, until his death in 1997, by Fidel Velázquez Sanchez, a PRI die-hard.

Unions independent of the PRI are a relatively new phenomenon. In 1997, Mexico's independent unions formed the National Union of Workers (UNT) to compete with the CTM. Since the mid-1990s, a series of laws and court decisions have weakened the grip of the formerly official unions. The neo-liberal economic policies pursued by the PRI over the last two decades and the PRI's recent loss of national power have created new dilemmas for the CTM. Its membership has clearly suffered from the economic reforms, and its leadership no longer benefits from government patronage. On the one hand, democratic reforms promoted by the PAN are likely to give labor unions more autonomy and a greater ability to contest government policy. On the other hand, the PAN is even more committed to neo-liberal economic reform than is the PRI.

THE MEDIA

The PRI maintained a political lock on the media by co-optation more than by coercion. Rather than imposing censorship, the government courted the favor of Mexico's media by purchasing advertisements in pro-PRI media outlets, giving supportive media voices cheap access to infrastructure and bribing reporters outright. Mexico's largest media conglomerate, Televisa, was extremely close to the PRI. By the early 1990s, the PRI had loosened its control of the media somewhat. The government stopped bribing reporters, and the wave of privatizations created a more competitive media environment, allowing for criticism of the PRI.

SOCIETY

Ethnic and National Identity

Alan Riding has described Mexico as a nation proud of its Indian past but ashamed of its Indian present.[18] Under the Partido Revolucionario Institucional (PRI), Mexico glorified and embraced its indigenous ancestry and inculcated pride in the *mestizaje,* or blending of cultures produced by the conquest. Indigenous peoples who have not assimilated into mestizo Mexico have been politically marginalized and have been victims of Mexico's worst poverty, whereas Mexico's wealthy elite have tended to be lighter skinned and of European origin.

The PRI's success in perpetuating the myth of *mestizaje* may help explain how it avoided the kind of ethnically based violence that has plagued Guatemala, its neighbor to the south, as well as other Latin American nations. But that myth was violently shattered on January 1, 1994, when a rebel army made up mostly of Mayan Indians, the **Zapatista Army of National Liberation (EZLN),** occupied several towns in Mexico's southernmost state of Chiapas.[19]

Many viewed the EZLN as solely an indigenous group seeking greater autonomy for Mexico's long-neglected Indian population. It soon became clear, however, that the EZLN included among its demands the democratization of the Mexican political system and an end to the neo-liberal reforms that had ravaged the indigenous poor. Chief among the EZLN's concerns was the abrogation of Article 27 of the constitution of 1917, which had mandated land reform. On a more general level, the EZLN was reacting to the devastation caused by neo-liberal trade policies that had exposed the inefficient peasant farmers to competition from cheaper foreign imports. The call for

ETHNIC GROUPS

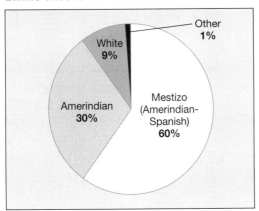

RELIGION

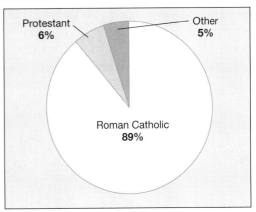

COMANDANTE MARCOS

When the Zapatistas burst into the public view in 1994, their spokesperson was a masked rebel known only as Comandante Marcos. He was later identified as a former university professor, a mestizo. The enigmatic rebel leader captured the imagination and support of Mexicans with his unconventional style and his regular dispatches from the jungle, which were often marked by wit and humor. In many ways, Marcos can be viewed as the first post-cold-war guerrilla. Under his leadership, the EZLN relied heavily upon electronic media and the Internet to disseminate its political message. (The EZLN continues to maintain a Web site; see Web Links on p. 391.)

democratization was partly a response to the political lock that the PRI maintained on some of Mexico's poorest and most heavily indigenous regions.

The Zapatista uprising was surprisingly popular within Mexico and, together with the economic crisis, helped erode PRI political dominance and accelerate electoral reforms. In 1996, the Zedillo government signed the San Andres Peace Accords with the EZLN, promising protection of indigenous languages and granting indigenous communities political autonomy. These provisions were never implemented, however, and Vicente Fox Quesada, who claimed he could resolve the Chiapas conflict "in fifteen minutes," was unable to make peace with the Zapatistas. Fox's proposed constitutional amendment aimed at addressing some Zapatista demands was watered down by Congress, and the Zapatistas rejected the outcome. As of this writing, the standoff between the government and the Zapatistas continues.

Ideology and Political Culture

Perhaps the most important aspect of Mexican political culture is a profound distrust of the state and the government. Opinion research demonstrates that Mexicans have a far more negative view of their political system and state than their U.S. counterparts do. In 2000, Congress was viewed favorably by only 20 percent of Mexicans, compared with about 80 percent in the United States.[20] Mexicans' high level of disenchantment with their state and political system has been exacerbated by the government's poor response to many national crises over the last two decades. A high-profile split within the PRI, the massive electoral fraud of 1989, corruption charges against former president Carlos Salinas de Gortari, the Chiapas uprising, and the murder of the PRI's designated presidential candidate were all factors that helped to erode popular confidence in the Mexican system.

These scandals and decades of authoritarian rule may explain why a majority of Mexicans express little or no interest in politics, notwithstanding a temporary surge of interest around the historic 2000 presidential elections. Mexican men express far more interest in politics than women do, and interest in politics increases with levels of education and income. Mexicans on the left of the political system (supporters of the Partido de la Revolución Democrática, or PRD) generally express much higher levels of interest in politics than do Mexicans in the center and on the right.

A serious problem confronting Mexico's attempt to construct a stable democracy is the very low level of political efficacy (the belief that one can make a difference), as expressed in opinion polls. Whereas about one third of U.S. respondents claim to have no ability to influence political outcomes, over half of Mexicans express this view. One positive sign is that the 2000 PRI electoral defeat appears to have restored Mexicans' faith in the fairness of elections, and recent data show that levels of electoral efficacy have risen dramatically.

Unlike Communist regimes, which actively promoted political mobilization, Mexico under the PRI was an authoritarian regime that sought to contain and limit popular participation in politics. Mexico's political culture continues to show the effects of decades of authoritarian rule: the country has very low levels of participation in politics, party membership, and political activism. Although there is some evidence of a steady increase in popular political activity since the 1980s, declining voter turnout has continued to be a concern. Turnout for the 2003 elections was only 41.7 percent down from 63.7 percent in 2000. The declines may be explained by the weakening of the PRI electoral machine, the return to "normal" politics after the excitement surrounding the 2003 elections, and the fact that midterm elections usually draw fewer voters.

During the authoritarian regime of the PRI, the majority of Mexicans professed sympathy for no political party. The erosion of PRI hegemony and the increasing competitiveness of elections have led far more Mexicans to identify with a political party. By 2000, the PRI and the Partido Acción Nacional (PAN) each enjoyed the support of about one third of the electorate, and the PRD was supported by about 10 percent. Opinion data show quite clearly that the Mexican electorate is anchored on the center right. The leftist PRD suffers from the fact that only about 20 percent of Mexicans identify themselves as being on the left. Although more Mexicans define themselves as being on the left or right than do U.S. respondents, Mexicans have been steadily gravitating toward the center.

The erosion of PRI political hegemony has also been accompanied by a dramatic shift in the social-class basis of Mexico's parties. Wealthy and middle-class Mexicans abandoned the PRI in droves between 1989 and 2000. By 2000, the PRI depended mostly on the support of lower-class Mexicans, though the PAN had nearly the same amount of support among poor voters. Indeed, one of the remarkable changes between 1989 and 2000 was the PAN's ability to garner support from all classes.

Opinion research reveals that most Mexicans favor democracy over authoritarianism. When compared with U.S. respondents, however, Mexicans are far more likely to define democracy in terms of equality than in terms of freedom. The inability of democracy to remedy Mexico's staggering inequality could potentially undermine Mexican support for democracy.

POLITICAL ECONOMY

As noted earlier, the leaders of the Mexican Revolution had a complex and often contradictory set of goals. Some of the revolutionaries were middle-class landowners who sought greater political democracy, others sought major socioeconomic (especially land) reform, and others were mostly interested in restoring political order while eliminating the dictatorship of Porfirio Díaz.

Between 1917 and 1980, leaders of the Partido Revolucionario Institucional (PRI) did agree on some main features of the Mexican economy. First, Mexico's industrialization would be encouraged through import-substitution policies, which employed high tariffs to protect Mexican industries and agriculture. Government policies provided Mexican entrepreneurs with subsidized credit and energy and very low taxes. The PRI's ability to control labor and therefore labor costs also benefited Mexico's entrepreneurs. Second, Mexico was to have a capitalist economy, but the Mexican state played an important role in key sectors of the economy, though far less than in socialist economies.

Despite this general consensus, economic policies of the PRI presidents between 1917 and 2000 fluctuated a great deal. The nationalists, usually associated with the left wing of the PRI, placed more emphasis on redistribution of income, plenty of state social spending, and a strong state presence in the economy. Their economic policies tended to be strongly nationalistic, and they sought greater economic independence from the United States.

President Lázaro Cárdenas (1934–40) was the most important nationalist. Cárdenas was a mestizo revolutionary general who became governor of the state of Michoacán. He used the PRI to organize and mobilize Mexico's workers and peasants, and he was the first president to implement

LABOR FORCE BY OCCUPATION

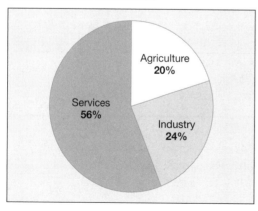

- Agriculture 20%
- Services 56%
- Industry 24%

the land reform called for in the constitution of 1917. Cárdenas gave 180,000 peasant communities grants of land, called *ejidos*, providing land to some 750,000 landless Mexicans. He integrated peasants and workers into state-controlled unions, and he strengthened the Mexican state by nationalizing the foreign-dominated oil industry and creating a state oil monopoly **(Pemex).** More than any other Mexican president, Cárdenas embodied the socialist aspects of the Mexican Revolution. At the same time, his policies won the PRI the enduring political loyalty of Mexico's workers and peasants. Future Mexican presidents never addressed the socioeconomic aspirations of the Mexican constitution as much as Cárdenas did, but the presidencies of Adolfo López Mateos (1958–64), Luis Echeverría Álvarez (1970–76), and José López Portillo (1976–82) followed policies that mirrored the views of the PRI nationalist left.

The liberals—including Miguel Alemán Valdés (1946–52), Gustavo Díaz Ordaz (1964–70), Miguel de la Madrid Hurtado (1982–88), and Carlos Salinas de Gortari (1988–94) favored economic growth over redistribution. They tended to favor freer trade, increased foreign investment in the Mexican economy, and better relations with the United States. President Díaz Ordaz strongly favored economic growth over distribution, and his policies favored big business and agricultural exporters. De la Madrid and Salinas undertook a major change in Mexico's political economic policies by liberalizing its statist economy, abandoning long-entrenched social commitments (like land reform), and entering the General Agreement on Tariffs and Trade (GATT) in 1986 and the North American Free Trade Agreement (NAFTA) with the United States and Canada in 1994. Fox has generally continued these liberal economic policies.

THE DIMENSIONS OF THE ECONOMY

In terms of its aggregate wealth, Mexico is a relatively prosperous developing country and, compared with other developing countries, fairly industrialized. It is currently the world's eighth largest exporter. Industry accounts for about one quarter of its GDP, and agriculture now accounts for only 8 percent. The country is also rich in natural resources, especially oil, which is its chief economic asset. Since the presidency of Lázaro Cárdenas (discussed above), Mexican oil has been controlled by the state monopoly, Pemex.

From the 1940s to about 1980 the Mexican economy grew spectacularly, in what has often been called the Mexican miracle. Bolstered by the peace and stability of the PRI regime, and benefiting from a steady increase in U.S. investment, Mexico became more industrialized, urban, and educated. Its economy also became more heavily dependent on the United States. By 1962, the United States accounted for 85 percent of all foreign investment in Mexico. Mexico sent two thirds of its exports to the United States, and the same percentage of its imports came from the United States. The U.S.-Mexican economic relationship was (and remains) *asymmetrical*, however: the U.S. economy is far more vital to Mexico than Mexico's is to the United States.

ECONOMIC CRISES OF THE 1970S AND '80S

In the 1970s, Mexican presidents used the country's vast oil wealth to support massive government spending in an attempt to alleviate chronic inequality and poverty. The spending fueled inflation and began to erode the value of the peso, Mexico's currency. Mexico incurred vast debts from foreign lenders, who viewed the oil-rich country as a trustworthy borrower. By the 1980s, oil accounted for over two thirds of the value of Mexico's exports. A major drop in world oil prices in 1981 exposed the shaky foundation of Mexico's economy, and Mexico came close to defaulting on its international debt in August 1982.

The response by Presidents de la Madrid and Salinas was to abandon the decades-old mercantilist model of protectionism and state interventionism and embrace neo-liberal economics, thus beginning a reversal of the country's political economy. By terminating the constitution's promise of land

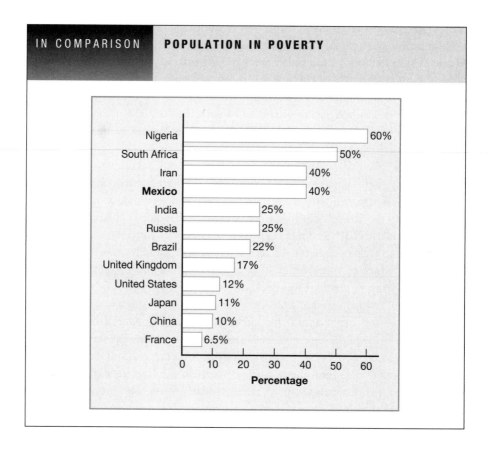

IN COMPARISON   **POPULATION IN POVERTY**

Country	Percentage
Nigeria	60%
South Africa	50%
Iran	40%
Mexico	40%
India	25%
Russia	25%
Brazil	22%
United Kingdom	17%
United States	12%
Japan	11%
China	10%
France	6.5%

reform and opening up Mexico to a flood of cheap agricultural imports, the government in effect devastated many of Mexico's poorest peasants. The country's steady economic recovery in the late 1980s and early 1990s was upset in 1994 and 1995 by its most severe economic depression since the 1930s. In December 1994, the value of the Mexican peso collapsed, and the Mexican economy was saved only by the International Monetary Fund's largest bailout ever. Between 1994 and 1996, real wages dropped 27 percent, and an estimated 75 percent of Mexicans fell below the official poverty line.[21] Mexico had embraced free trade and globalization as a response to the economic crisis of the early 1980s, but its response had made it even more vulnerable to economic instability.

NAFTA AND GLOBALIZATION

The North American Free Trade Agreement has drastically reduced (and will soon eliminate) most tariffs on agricultural goods traded among Mexico, Canada, and the United States. As a result, Mexico has been flooded by U.S. products (such as corn and pork) that cost one fifth as much to produce as similar Mexican products. NAFTA has doubled the amount of food that Mexico imports from the United States, thereby lowering Mexican food prices but creating a massive crisis for millions of Mexico's farmers. About one fifth of Mexicans work in agriculture, and the vast majority are poor subsistence farmers who will be hurt the most by NAFTA competition. As a result, Mexico will lose millions of jobs in agriculture. NAFTA has also exacerbated the gap between the wealthy north and the impoverished south.[22]

In many ways, NAFTA benefits Mexico. Manufacturing exports to the United States have skyrocketed, growing at an average rate of 75 percent annually since NAFTA went into effect.[23] Greater access to U.S. markets has been a boon to Mexico's fruit and vegetable producers, who now supply much of the U.S. winter market, although exports of agricultural goods have grown very modestly compared with those of manufactured goods. Cheaper imports have benefited a wide variety of Mexican producers and consumers.

Mexico's embrace of NAFTA has clearly created a more diversified economy. In the 1980s, oil made up about two thirds of the country's exports. Mexico now exports a wider variety of goods, but it is extremely dependent on the U.S. market, to which it sends 90 percent of all its exports.

Mexico's entry into NAFTA has attracted more direct U.S. investment in Mexico. Much of the investment has gravitated toward **maquiladoras,** factories that import materials or parts to make goods that are then exported. These factories, concentrated along the Mexican-U.S. border, account for about half of all of Mexico's exports, and they now generate more foreign exchange for Mexico than any other sector, including oil.[24] The maquiladoras have added half a million jobs to Mexico's north, but some critics argue that the operations add relatively little to the Mexican economy, since most materials and technology are imported. Average maquiladora wages are above Mexico's minimum wage but far below the average wage in the manufacturing sector. The concentration of maquiladoras in Mexico's wealthier north has exacerbated the country's severe north-south income gap.

Whether NAFTA has created more winners than losers is a hot topic of debate within Mexico.[25] The government of Vicente Fox Quesada has been reluctant to increase social spending, a move that might mitigate the effects of NAFTA. One result of the new pressures created by NAFTA has been the previously discussed increased flow of Mexicans to the United States in search of employment. What is clear, however, is that NAFTA has dislocated millions of Mexicans and will create new political and economic challenges for future Mexican administrations.

ECONOMIC POLICIES AND ISSUES

Despite the Mexican Revolution's commitment to greater equality and the efforts of some reformist presidents to help the poor, Mexico was and is a country of massive inequality. The Mexican novelist Carlos Fuentes has called Mexico a country "where 25 people earn the same as 25 million."[26] The pre-1980s mercantilist policies were unable to address the persistence of massive poverty in Mexico, and the more recent shift to neo-liberal policies has only increased the gap between rich and poor. In 2000, the poorest 40 percent of the population earned about 12 percent of Mexico's income while the wealthiest 10 percent earned about 40 percent, and the gap has widened since 1984.[27] *Forbes* magazine listed twenty-four Mexicans in its 1994 annual report on the "swelling roster of global billionaires." Only the United States, Germany, and Japan had more billionaires at the time. A year earlier, there had been thirteen, and in 1987, when the magazine first began compiling its list, there had been only one.[28] These huge inequalities in income are mirrored by a variety of social indicators. For example, in 1998 infant mortality was four times higher among the poorest 20 percent of Mexicans than among the richest 20 percent, and the poorest 10 percent of Mexicans averaged only 2.1 years of education, whereas the richest 10 percent average over 12 years of education.[29]

The Mexican government has estimated that about one fourth of Mexicans lack enough money for food and clothing. One third of all workers earn less than the minimum wage (about US$4 per day). Poverty in Mexico is most pronounced in rural areas, still home to some 23 million people. Despite the legacy of land reform, most rural Mexicans cannot support themselves on their tiny plots of land, and many are forced to seek work as migrant laborers. Millions have migrated to already overcrowded urban areas, seeking employment and a better life, and millions more have immigrated to the United States for the same reasons.

Mexico's wealth is also geographically unequal. Northern Mexico is far wealthier than the central and southern regions. While the north is characterized by large-scale export agriculture (benefiting from proximity to the U.S. market), land use is much more fragmented in the south. Southern Mexico has a far poorer infrastructure, lower levels of education, and more poverty.

Another indicator of the degree of inequality in Mexico is the tremendous size and importance of the informal sector. A conservative estimate is that over 9 million Mexicans (perhaps as much as one third of the total workforce) are employed in the underground economy as informal vendors of goods and services. Mexican cities are full of *ambulantes* (street vendors), which local governments have fought unsuccessfully to regulate. These workers pay no taxes on their earnings but enjoy few protections and benefits.

Efforts to redress these inequalities through increased social spending have been hampered by Mexico's inability to collect taxes, especially when compared with wealthier industrialized countries. Attempts to raise taxes meet with widespread skepticism in part because Mexico's traditionally corrupt state is simply not trusted.

FOREIGN RELATIONS AND THE WORLD

Mexico's foreign relations have always been heavily molded by its complex relationship with the United States. In the political turmoil of the nineteenth century, Mexico lost half its territory to an expanding United States. Indeed, Mexico's humiliation at the hands of the United States has been a major theme in the Mexican psyche. Even Porfirio Díaz, whose dictatorship promoted closer ties to the U.S., is reported to have lamented, "Poor Mexico! So far from God and so close to the United States." One goal of the Mexican Revolution (and the aim of much of its official rhetoric) was to restore the sovereignty and power of Mexico on the global stage. The Partido Revolucionario Institucional (PRI) leadership clearly sought a system that would restore stability to the Mexican system and prevent future attacks on Mexican sovereignty. In the early years of the revolution, foreign economic interests were sharply curtailed, and foreign oil companies were nationalized. Mexico under the PRI began to assert itself as an independent and autonomous state, gradually gaining the status of a regional power within Latin America.

During and after World War II, Mexico became a closer ally of the United States while still asserting an independent voice in its foreign policy. From the 1960s through the 1980s, Mexico opposed U.S. foreign policy in Latin America, fostered a close relationship with Fidel Castro's Cuba (a U.S. archenemy), and supported revolutionary movements in the region that often opposed the United States.

Many Mexicans were proud that their country could act so independently of the United States in the arena of foreign policy. The economic catastrophe of the 1980s and Mexico's decision to abandon revolutionary economic policies and liberalize its economy made clear the limits to Mexican independence in its foreign affairs. In exchange for massive economic aid in the 1980s, Mexico was pressured to curtail its opposition to U.S. foreign policy in Latin America.

Since the election of Vicente Fox Quesada in 2000, Mexico has moved closer to the United States on most foreign policy issues.[30] Fox has sought to work closely with President George W. Bush in the hope of gaining new agreements on immigration and trade. Since the 1994 North American Free Trade Agreement (NAFTA), Mexico's increased economic dependence on the United States has clearly limited its international assertiveness. That did not stop the Fox administration from opposing Bush's invasion of Iraq in 2003, a stance that led to a cooling of U.S.-Mexican relations.

Mexico today is clearly at a crossroads. With its first democratically elected president in decades and a booming economy based on exports to the United States, Mexicans can feel proud of their accomplishments. At the same time, now that Mexico has vanquished authoritarian rule, it must deal with a number of historical problems. It must find a way to reestablish the legitimacy of the state (by reducing corruption), restore public order (by reducing crime and improving the judiciary), and perhaps most important, address the growing inequality between the winners and the losers in its political economic transition.

CURRENT ISSUES

CRIME AND CORRUPTION: THE COLOMBIANIZATION OF MEXICO?

The Mexican Revolution successfully strengthened state power and autonomy and ended endemic violence in Mexico. Yet the long domination of the Partido Revolucionario Institucional (PRI), its dependence on patron-client relations, its co-optation, and its electoral fraud all fostered a culture of corruption and lawlessness that now increasingly threatens the state and its capacity, autonomy, and legitimacy. The ability of the state to impose its authority has eroded because of the explosion of crime since the 1980s. In Mexico City, reported crimes doubled from 1993 to 1997, and an estimated 90 percent of all crime in the city goes unreported. Over 1 million muggings were reported there in 1997, and 3,000 Mexicans were kidnapped and held for ransom in 1998.[31] Statistics like these have led some to wonder whether Mexico is heading the way of its unruly southern neighbor—whether it is in effect undergoing a "Colombianization."[32]

The spectacular increase in crime has a variety of causes. To some extent it coincides with the economic crisis that began in the 1980s and was exacerbated by the 1994–1995 economic depression. The governments of the 1980s and 1990s pursued painful neo-liberal economic reforms while weakening the welfare state established by the PRI. The rise in crime rates may also be related to the steady decline in the PRI's hegemony and the decentralization and democratization of the political system. In the case of most postauthoritarian democracies, crime tends to flourish when the power of an authoritarian state is weakened and a painful economic transition is under way. The increase of drug trafficking has also been accompanied by a dramatic increase in violent crime.

What is perhaps most alarming from the perspective of the legitimacy of the state is that Mexico's various police forces (local, state, and federal) contribute directly to the problem. Mexican police are generally poorly trained and poorly paid, making them susceptible to corruption. Even worse, the police have been known to be involved in a wave of kidnapping and extortion crimes that have shocked the country. In 2002, Mexico City officials invited former New York City mayor Rudolph Giuliani to advise them on how to stem the twin problems of crime and corruption. A survey in the 1990s showed that between 1981 and 1990, the proportion of Mexicans who thought it acceptable to accept a bribe or buy stolen goods rose from 32 percent to 55 percent.[33]

DEMOCRATIZATION, IMPUNITY, AND THE EMERGENCE OF CIVIL SOCIETY IN GUERRERO

From 1929 to 2005, the PRI held power in the state of Guerrero, where international human rights organizations had long complained that the PRI government, the police, and the judiciary, in collusion with powerful landowners (caciques), were conspiring to repress all types of civic groups. A good example was the repression of a variety of environmental groups that sought to stop powerful logging companies from clear-cutting the forests of the Sierra Madre. Felipe Arreaga, an environmental activist who had been particularly successful in his opposition to powerful logging interests, had led a group of farmers who successfully blockaded logging trucks. Local landowners threatened Arreaga and his followers and accused them of being leftist guerrillas. Arreaga was jailed in November 2004 on what human rights groups claim were trumped-up charges of murdering the son of a wealthy landowner who opposed the activists. Arreaga's defenders claim he was jailed as a vendetta for having stopped lucrative logging projects favored by powerful landowners. The defeat of the PRI state government by the leftist Partido de la Revolución Democrática (PRD) in early 2005 gave rise to hopes that Arreaga would be released. The PRD has long claimed that hundreds of Guerrero activists were harassed and killed during the decades of PRI rule. Human rights activists are hopeful that the new PRD state government will signal a democratization of Guerrero politics and break the nexus linking powerful landowners, the judiciary, the police, and the state government.

Crime and corruption not only weaken the capacity of the state but also weaken its autonomy. A good example is President Fox's aggressive prosecution of corrupt union workers at the state oil monopoly, Pemex. Many of the accused leaders are also members of the PRI's legislative delegation in Congress. The PRI retaliated by threatening to block Fox's proposed partial privatization of Mexico's inefficient energy sector.

Over the last two decades, Mexico has seen an alarming rise in drug trafficking, driven by the growing market for illegal drugs north of the border and facilitated by a Mexican legal system that is both weak and corrupt.[34] Mexico has experienced a dramatic growth of drug-related gang violence and a steady stream of corruption scandals involving drug money. The United States has been alarmed by the growing drug traffic across the U.S.-Mexican border: it is estimated that about 70 percent of all marijuana and cocaine entering the United States arrives through Mexico. American attempts to undertake anti-narcotics operations in Mexico have been attacked as abridging Mexico's sovereignty, and U.S. criticism of Mexico's anti-narcotics efforts has often raised tensions between the two neighbors.

MIGRATION

There is a long history of Mexicans' emigrating across the 2,000-mile U.S.-Mexico border.[35] Mexicans have long argued that the United States depends on their immigrants and that their right to work in the United States should be guaranteed through bilateral agreements. But many Americans have focused on the negative effects of Mexican immigration to the United States. Why has there been such a steady flow of Mexicans into the United States? Most immigrants come because of the higher standard of living in the United States, although the first wave of immigrants also fled the violence of the Mexican Revolution. During the severe labor shortages of World War II, the United States established the Bracero Program, which allowed over 4 million Mexicans to work temporarily in the United States between 1942 and 1964. Today, there are almost 11 million Mexicans living in the United States (about 10 percent of Mexico's total population and 4 percent of the U.S. population). According to some estimates, the amount of foreign exchange sent to Mexico by Mexicans living outside the country has grown to almost US$20 billion annually, making it the largest single source of foreign exchange (even larger than revenue earned from oil exports).[36]

From 1965 to 1986, an estimated 5.7 million Mexicans immigrated to the United States, of whom 81 percent were undocumented.[37] The United States operated a "de facto guest-worker program," whereby border enforcement was tough enough to prevent a flood of immigration but not so strict as to prevent a steady flow of cheap and undocumented labor.[38] The costs of illegal immigration were raised just enough that only about one in three undocumented Mexicans could be caught and returned. Most immigrants who tried to enter the United States succeeded, although not on the first try. The U.S. attempt to enforce border control was largely symbolic, but it never threatened the availability of cheap labor. The dramatic growth of undocumented Mexican immigrants, especially after the economic crisis in Mexico during the early 1980s, became a political crisis in the United States during the 1980s and 1990s. The result was the 1986 U.S. Immigration Reform and Control Act (IRCA), which imposed sanctions on employers of illegal aliens and toughened the enforcement of immigration laws. At the same time, it provided an amnesty for longtime undocumented workers and legalized about 2.3 million Mexican immigrants.[39] In the late 1990s, however, illegal immigration continued to skyrocket. In 2006, the U.S. administration of George W. Bush proposed tougher border controls as well as measures aimed at giving legal status to more Mexicans living in the United States.

NOTES

1. A good overview of the development of the Mexican state is Alan Knight, "The Weight of the State in Modern Mexico," in James Dunkerley, ed., *Studies in the Formation of the Nation State in Latin America* (London: Institute of Latin American Studies, 2002), pp. 212–52.

2. Quoted in http://www.libertyhaven.com/countriesandregions/latinamerica/mexicomyths. shtml (accessed 25 July 2005).

3. Pamela Starr, "Fox's Mexico: Same As It Ever Was?" Current History, (February 2002), pp. 58–65.

4. The best English-language overview is Luis Carlos Ugalde, *The Mexican Congress: Old Player, New Power* (Washington, D.C.: Center for Stategic and International Studies, 2000).

5. Ugalde, *The Mexican Congress*, p. 102.

6. Ugalde, *The Mexican Congress*, p. 146.

7. Ginger Thompson, "Congress Shifts Mexico's Balance of Power," *New York Times*, 21 January 2002, p. A6.

8. Jodi Finkel, "Judicial Reform as Insurance Policy: Mexico in the 1990s," *Latin American Politics and Society* 47, no. 1 (Spring 2005), pp. 87–111.

9. Wayne Cornelius, Todd Eisenstadt, and Jane Hindley, eds., *Subnational Politics and Democratization in Mexico* (San Diego, CA: Center for U.S.-Mexican Studies, 1999), and R. Andrew Nickson, *Local Government in Latin America* (Boulder, CO: Lynne Reinner, 1995), pp. 199–209.

10. Alma Guillermoprieto, *The Heart That Bleeds* (New York: Alfred A. Knopf, 1994), pp. 47–67.

11. Pamela Starr, "Fox's Mexico: Same As It Ever Was?" *Current History* (February 2002), p. 62.

12. Joy Langston, "Why Rules Matter: Changes in Candidate Selection in Mexico's PRI, 1988–2000," *Journal of Latin American Studies* 33 (2001), pp. 485–511.

13. Kathleen Bruhn, *Taking on Goliath: Mexico's Party of the Democratic Revolution* (University Park, PA: Penn State Press, 1997).

14. Starr, "Fox's Mexico," p. 60.

15. A good overview is Chappell Lawson, "Fox's Mexico at Midterm," *Journal of Democracy* 15 (2004), pp. 339–50.

16. Lawson, "Fox's Mexico at Midterm," p. 144.

17. Joseph Klenser, "Electoral Competition and the New Party System in Mexico," paper presented at the annual meeting of the Latin American Studies Association, Washington, D.C., 6–8 September 2001.

18. Alan Riding, *Distant Neighbors* (New York: Vintage, 1989), p. 199.

19. Three excellent overviews are Tom Hayden, ed., *The Zapatista Reader* (New York: Thunder's Mouth Press, 2002); Lynn Stephen, *Zapata Lives: Histories and Cultural Politics in Southern Mexico* (Berkeley: University of California Press, 2002); and Chris Gilbreth and Gerardo Otero, "Democratization in Mexico: The Zapatista Uprising and Civil Society," *Latin American Perspectives* 28, no. 4 (July 2001), pp. 7–29.

20. Data in this section are drawn from Roderic Ali Camp, *Politics in Mexico*, 4th ed. (New York, Oxford University Press, 2003), ch. 3.

21. Paul Cooney, "The Mexican Crisis and the Maquiladora Boom: A Paradox of Development or the Logic of Neoliberalism?" *Latin American Perspectives* 28, no. 3 (May 2001), pp. 55–83.

22. Rafael Tamayo-Flores, "Mexico in the Context of the North American Integration: Major Regional Trends and Performance of Backward Regions," *Journal of Latin American Studies* 33 (2001), p. 406.

23. Tamayo-Flores, "Mexico in the Context of the North American Integration," pp. 377–407.

24. Cooney, "The Mexican Crisis and the Maquiladora Boom."

25. Thomas J. Kelly, "Neoliberal Reforms and Rural Poverty," *Latin American Perspectives* 28, no. 3 (May 2001), pp. 84–103.

26. Quoted in Nicolas Wilson, "What's Wrong with This Picture?" *Business Mexico* 4 (April 1997), p. 22.

27. Roderic Ali Camp, *Politics in Mexico*, 4th ed. (New York: Oxford University Press, 2003), p. 251.

28. John Summa, "Mexcio's New Sugar-Billionaires," Multinational Monitor, November 1994, http://multinationalmonitor.org/hyper/issues/1994/11/mm1194_09.html (accessed 23 July 2005).

29. "Rich Is Rich and Poor Is Poor," Survey: Mexico, *Economist*, 26 October 2002.

30. Stephen Morris and John Passé-Smith, "What a Difference a Crisis Makes: NAFTA, Mexico, and the United States," *Latin American Perspectives* 28, no. 3 (May 2001), pp. 124–49.

31. Michael J. Mazarr, *Mexico 2005: The Challenges of the New Millennium* (Washington, D.C.: Center for Strategic and International Studies, 1999), p. 102.

32. Mazarr, *Mexico 2005*, uses that term on p. 105.

33. Mazarr, *Mexico 2005*, p. 103.

34. Victoria Malkin, "Narcotrafficking, Migration, and Modernity in Rural Mexico," *Latin American Perspectives* 28, no. 4 (July 2001), pp. 101–28.

35. Douglas Massey, Jorge Durand, and Nolan Malone, *Beyond Smoke and Mirrors: Mexican Immigration in an Era of Economic Integration* (New York: Russell Sage Foundation, 2002).
36. "Rise Report in Remittances to Mexico," *Seattle Times*, 15 April 2005, p. A14.
37. Massey, Durand, and Malone, *Beyond Smoke and Mirrors*, p. 45.
38. Massey, Durand, and Malone, *Beyond Smoke and Mirrors*, p. 45.
39. Massey, Durand, and Malone, *Beyond Smoke and Mirrors*, p. 49.

KEY TERMS

caciques   p. 355

Felipe Calderón   p. 352

camarillas   p. 368

caudillos   p. 355

Chamber of Deputies   p. 362

Confederation of Mexican Workers (CTM)   p. 376

Congress   p. 361

Hernán Cortés   p. 353

Cuauhtémoc   p. 353

Porfirio Díaz   p. 356

Federal Electoral Institute   p. 365

Vicente Fox Quesada   p. 352

maquiladoras   p. 383

mestizos   p. 352

Mexican-American War   p. 355

Mexican Revolution   p. 356

municipios   p. 365

North American Free Trade Agreement (NAFTA)   p. 351

Partido Acción Nacional (PAN)   p. 360

Partido Revolucionario Institucional (PRI)   p. 351

patron-client relationships   p. 368

Pemex   p. 381

Senate   p. 362

Supreme Court   p. 363

Francisco (Pancho) Villa   p. 356

War of Independence   p. 355

Emiliano Zapata   p. 356

Zapatista Army of National Liberation (EZLN)   p. 377

WEB LINKS

Mexican government offices and agencies
   www.mexonline.com/mexagncy.htm
Latin American Network Information Center: Mexico
   www.lanic.utexas.edu/la/mexico An encyclopedic collection of links maintained by the University of Texas, Austin
Zapatista Army of National Liberation **www.ezln.org.mx**
La Jornada **www.jornada.unam.mx** A Mexican daily newspaper
El Universal   **english.eluniversal.com** A Mexican daily newspaper
Reforma **www.reforma.com** A Mexican daily newspaper

11 BRAZIL

Head of state and government:
President Inácio Lula da Silva
 (since January 1, 2003)

Capital: Brasília

Total land size: 8,511,965 sq km

Population: 186 million

GDP at PPP: 1.49 trillion US$

GDP per capita: $8,100

INTRODUCTION

Why Study This Case?

When Brazil successfully launched a rocket into space in October 2004, it became the first Latin American country to do so. Brazil has ambitious plans to sell rockets to the European Space Agency, adding to its already impressive list of high-tech exports. Brazil's successful entry into space exemplifies its many paradoxes. It is the ninth largest economy in the world, with a dynamic industrial sector. It has strikingly modern cities, like São Paolo and Rio de Janeiro. But it is also plagued by some of the worst poverty, inequality, and indebtedness on the planet, and its cities are burdened by sprawling slums and violence. One Brazilian economist dubbed Brazil **"Belindia"** to denote this odd combination of Belgium's modernity and India's underdevelopment.[1]

Brazil is a highly urbanized society, with over 80 percent of its population living in its cities (six of which have over 2 million residents), but about half of its land consists of the sparsely populated **Amazon basin.** The Amazon rain forest is often considered to be the lungs of the world and its rapid destruction has become a major focus for environmentalists. Within Brazil, the Amazon has until recently been viewed most often as a rich resource that needs to be more efficiently exploited in order to reduce inequality and poverty and enhance Brazil's *grandeza* (national greatness).

Given Brazil's history of extreme inequality and its large mass of poverty-stricken citizens, one might expect it to have experienced a mass revolution along the lines of Russia, Mexico, and China. At the very least, one might have assumed a history of political violence similar to that of South Africa during apartheid. But Brazilian history is mostly devoid of such organized violence. For the most part, the country's political elite have retained power skillfully, and Brazil's poor have remained politically disorganized. Since its independence, Brazil has alternated between weak democratic regimes dominated by economic elites and authoritarian rule, usually presided over by the military. From 1964 to 1985, a military dictatorship quashed a growing mass movement and suspended most political freedoms. Nevertheless, Brazil experienced a gradual and remarkably peaceful transition to democracy in the mid-1980s, and today it is the world's fourth largest democracy. Brazilian democracy is characterized by regular elections and broad civil liberties and has enabled a peaceful succession of power. In 2003 Brazilians elected a leftist president, **Luiz Inácio Lula da Silva,** known popularly as Lula, and despite fears surrounding his election, democracy has proved remarkably durable. Lula is Brazil's first working-class president (see "Lula," on p. 406).

Despite this admirable political record, serious questions remain about the long-term viability of Brazilian democracy. Can a democratic regime persist when there are extraordinarily high levels of economic inequality? Will the growing wave of crime and lawlessness erode confidence in democracy and the rule of law? Will Brazil's legacy of statism, clientelism, corruption, and political deadlock prevent democratic reforms?

Brazil is a fascinating case in part because of its relatively successful multiracial society. It has the largest African-origin population outside Africa. Despite a brutal history of slavery that lasted until quite late (ending in 1888) and persistent racism, Brazilian blacks are more comfortably integrated into society than their U.S. counterparts are. Brazilian society has also integrated Europeans (initially Portuguese and later Italians, Germans, and Spaniards), Africans, indigenous Americans, and other immigrants with relatively little ethnic tension. Endowed with a gigantic and geographically insulated country and blessed with formidable natural resources, Brazilians have a strong sense of national identity that makes Brazil unlike many of its Latin American neighbors.

Major Geographic and Demographic Features

Brazil's immense size gives it special importance: slightly larger than the continental United States, it is the world's fifth largest country and occupies almost half of the South American continent. With almost 170 million citizens it is home to one third of Latin America's population.

Brazil shares borders with ten other South American countries, but because most of its population has always been concentrated on its east coast, it historically has had surprisingly little interaction with its neighbors. Brazilians have often looked to Europe instead of their Latin American neighbors. (Brazil's main population centers are geographically closer to Europe than to some parts of South America.)

The concentration of population on the coast has been a major theme in Brazilian politics. In the 1950s, Brazilian leaders sought to shift Brazil's energy westward and open its vast Amazon frontier. In 1960, the capital was moved from the cosmopolitan, coastal Rio de Janeiro to the barren and isolated interior location of **Brasília,** where a futuristic planned city was created. Today Brasília has a population of over 2 million.

Brazil's Amazon has only 13 percent of its population but makes up over 60 percent of its landmass. In the 1960s, Brazil's military government began building roads west into the Amazon jungle, seeking to promote a demographic shift westward to alleviate the landless problem, exploit the natural resources of the region, and extend the power of the state into the hinterlands. Waves of impoverished northeasterners migrated to the Amazon to claim land

and eke out a living, with mixed success. This colonization of the Amazon region came at a tremendous cost to the natural environment and to its indigenous inhabitants.[2]

Brazil is now an overwhelmingly urban country, but this is a fairly recent development. The economic miracle of the late 1960s and early 1970s drew much of Brazil's rural population into its already overcrowded cities. Immigrants from the countryside helped fuel Brazil's industrial growth but were forced to live in the sprawling *favelas* (urban shantytowns) that ring Brazil's cities. Nowhere is the phenomenon of rapid urbanization more apparent than in São Paolo, Brazil's industrial capital and largest metropolitan area, with over 17 million residents.

Industrialization has also exacerbated a geographic schism in terms of socioeconomic development. Brazil's southeast, originally the center of the coffee boom, has become wealthy, industrialized, and populous; the three southeastern states of Rio de Janeiro, São Paolo, and Minas Gerais now contain nearly half of Brazil's population, generate well over half of its wealth, and contain its most important cities. Meanwhile the northeast, the old center of sugar production, has become less populated and poorer. What once was the population center of Brazil now contains only 28 percent of its inhabitants and has the lowest per capita income. The region is now plagued with depleted soil, fierce international competition in the sugar market, and periodic droughts.

Historical Development of the State

THE RELUCTANT COLONY

Pedro Álvares Cabral first arrived in Brazil in 1500 when he was blown off course on his way to India. He claimed the territory for the Portuguese crown, but Portugal initially paid little attention to it. Unlike the Spaniards, who encountered sophisticated empires and vast mineral wealth in their Latin American colonies, the Portuguese found the land sparsely populated (by between 1 million and 6 million indigenous Americans), and it offered no apparent mineral resources. While the Spaniards focused much of their energy on populating and exploiting their newfound territories, the Portuguese crown continued to focus on the lucrative spice trade with the East, and they built few permanent colonies.

Despite this neglect the Portuguese did establish trading posts along their new territory's coast. The early explorers discovered a hardwood that produced a valuable red dye; its Latin name was *Brasile*, for which the new territory was named. In response to incursions by the French in the 1530s, the Portuguese crown attempted to take more permanent control of Brazil. The

TIME LINE OF POLITICAL DEVELOPMENT	
Year	**Event**
1500	Portuguese arrive in Brazil
1690s	Gold is discovered
1763	Capital transferred from Salvador to Rio de Janeiro
1822	Pedro I declares Brazilian independence from Portugal
1822–89	Empire, a semi-authoritarian monarchical regime
1899–1930	First Republic, a quasi-democratic regime
1930	Military overthrows the republic and establishes authoritarian rule
1937–45	Rule of Getulio Vargas's Estado Nôvo (New State), an authoritarian regime
1945–64	Second Republic, a democratic regime
1960	The capital is transferred from Rio de Janeiro to Brasília
1964–85	Authoritarian military regime
1985–present	New Republic, a democratic regime
2003	Luiz Inácio Lula da Silva assumes presidency

government doled out massive territories (often larger than Portugal itself) to *donatarios* (nobles) who were willing to settle the remote land and defend it from foreigners. Brazil's first capital was established in 1549 in the northeast coastal town of Salvador, also called Bahia.

The Portuguese crown's decision to cultivate sugar in Brazil first transformed the colony from a backwater into a more vital part of the Portuguese Empire. Brazil had unlimited rich land on which to cultivate sugar, but it lacked the necessary labor pool. Initial attempts to enslave the indigenous population backfired: the relatively small population was quickly decimated by European-borne disease, war, and harsh treatment, and the survivors fled deep into Brazil's interior.

By the late sixteenth century, the Portuguese had come to depend on African slaves to maintain the sugar economy. Between 1550 and 1850, between 3 and 4 million African slaves were shipped to Brazil, and at that time Brazil's African population was far larger than its tiny white minority. Almost half of all Brazilians today have African ancestry.

Unlike the United States, Brazil soon developed a large **mulatto** popula-tion (Brazilians of a mixed white and black ancestry). Portuguese settlers also mixed with indigenous people in the interior, resulting in a smaller but still significant *caboclo* population.

The institution of slavery turned Brazil into the world's first great planta-tion export economy. The slave-based sugar economy generated massive wealth for the white minority and established a pattern that persists today: a tiny (mostly white) elite controls the vast majority of wealth while much of the population lives in poverty.

By the mid-seventeenth century, Brazil's sugar economy had begun a steady decline, caused in part by fierce competition from Spanish, French, and Dutch colonies in the Caribbean. The presence of the Portuguese crown was relatively small and was largely concentrated in the sugar-producing areas of the northeast coast.

THE GOLD AND DIAMOND BOOM AND THE RISE OF BRAZIL

The discovery of gold in the 1690s and diamonds in the 1720s forever changed the fate of Brazil. Mineral wealth was concentrated in the southeast and led to a demographic shift southward that has continued to this day; the central interior region, called Minas Gerais, (General Mines) became the country's most populous area. The Portuguese began to establish settlements in the inte-rior, and in 1763 the capital was moved south from Salvador to Rio de Janeiro. The seventeenth-century gold boom generated massive wealth, but much of Brazil's gold ended up in Europe.

By the end of the seventeenth century, the Portuguese Empire had weak-ened in the face of growing British, French, and Dutch power. The Portuguese crown reacted by attempting to tighten its control of its Brazilian colony, imposing unpopular taxes on the colonists. These measures provoked a rebel-lion in the gold-mining capital of Vila Rica in 1789, but unlike the outcome of the rebellion in the United States, the Portuguese crown quickly crushed the uprising. Moreover, the colonial elites, frightened by Haiti's slave rebel-lion in 1791, were too fearful of the Afro-Brazilian majority to push for out-right independence.

THE PEACEFUL CREATION OF AN INDEPENDENT BRAZILIAN STATE

Although Brazilian colonial elites did not advocate independence, the eco-nomic development spurred by mineral wealth created demands for increased autonomy and helped establish a distinct Brazilian identity. Furthermore, the colonial elites in the huge territory developed strong regional identities. Iron-ically, events in Europe more than colonial dissatisfaction paved the way for independence.

Napoléon Bonaparte's invasion of the Iberian Peninsula in 1807 was the catalyst for independence movements in Spanish America. Portugal's monarchy fled the invading French and moved the royal court to Brazil, a de facto recognition that Brazil had become the center of the Portuguese Empire. The arrival of the Portuguese monarch entailed transplanting the Portuguese state bureaucracy to Brazil, and Rio de Janeiro soon became a modern, cosmopolitan capital. Recognizing the importance of its colony, King João VI designated Brazil a kingdom, co-equal with Portugal. The king returned to Portugal in 1821 after the end of the Napoleonic Wars, but he left his son Pedro on the Brazilian throne with instructions to support independence.

In this unusual manner, Pedro I became the leader of Brazil's transition to independence and spared the country the kind of bloody wars experienced by much of Spanish America. Pedro declared independence on September 7, 1822, and Portugal offered little resistance. Without its own armed forces and facing the prospect of rebellion by powerful regional elites, Brazil depended heavily on the British, who quickly became its major trading partner.

It was important that Emperor Pedro I promulgated a constitution in 1824 and did not behave as an absolutist monarch. Nevertheless, the constitution of the Empire was essentially authoritarian with a very strong executive. In 1826 Pedro I inherited the Portuguese throne from his father, but shortly thereafter he returned to Portugal and left his own son, Pedro II, on the Brazilian throne. Pedro I's official abdication in 1830 greatly weakened the power of the central state and further enhanced the power of regional elites. Pedro II formally assumed the throne in 1840 from a caretaker regency when he was only fourteen years old, and he ruled Brazil until 1889.

Brazil's peaceful independence movement as well as the presence of reasonably enlightened monarchs during the nineteenth century were crucial to solidifying the Brazilian national identity and, most important, were essential for stemming the countless regional rebellions that plagued the country during its first half century of statehood. Under the Empire (1822–89), the foundations were laid for a strong central state dominated by the monarch. Brazil was also fortunate to find a new export product to replace sugar and minerals: coffee cultivation began in the 1820s in central and southern Brazil, further drawing economic development southward toward the coffee capital of São Paolo. Bolstered by the continued importation of slaves (which continued until the British banned the slave trade in 1850), Brazil quickly became the world's leading coffee producer.

Although the emperor opposed slavery, the Brazilian state did little to end it, in large part because the economy depended so heavily on slave labor. When the monarchy finally decreed the abolition of slavery in 1888, the conservative Brazilian rural elite begrudgingly accepted the new reality rather than risk a U.S.-style civil war. Slave labor was partly replaced by a massive influx of immigration from Europe.

Politically, Brazil was remarkably stable during the nineteenth century (especially when compared with much of South and North America), in part due to the presence of a reasonably progressive monarchy that played a moderating role in Brazilian society. The monarchy promoted competition and alternation between Brazil's main conservative and liberal political parties. Pedro II purposely kept Brazil's military weak, fearing its involvement in politics, and he actively worked to limit the power of Brazil's Roman Catholic Church.

By the 1880s, the monarchy had a variety of opponents. Urban intellectuals, influenced by European positivism and republicanism, saw the monarchy as antiquated. Abolitionists, frustrated by the monarchy's prolonged acceptance of slavery, viewed it as a reactionary force. Powerful interests, including the military, the Catholic Church, and some regional elites, came to resent it. Faced with a military coup d'état in 1889, Pedro II chose exile instead of war, once again sparing Brazil from the violence that plagued the rest of Latin America.

REPUBLICANISM AND THE CONTINUATION OF OLIGARCHIC DEMOCRACY

Brazil's military overthrew the monarchy and established the Old Republic (1889–1930), whose motto, "Order and Progress" still adorns the Brazilian flag. It turned the republic over to civilian political elites (oligarchs) but replaced the monarchy as arbiter of Brazilian politics. A new constitution, modeled almost entirely on the U.S. Constitution, established a federal system composed of powerful states, a directly elected president, and separation of power between the branches of government. Voting was restricted to literate male adults, and only 3 to 6 percent of the population voted in elections.

Although the monarchy was abolished, political power continued to be held tightly by a somewhat expanded political elite. At the state level, the governorships were controlled by economic oligarchs and their network of local bosses (known as *coroneis*, or colonels). The most powerful states, São Paolo, dominated by the coffee oligarchs, and Minas Gerais, dominated by dairy farmers, competed and cooperated to control the presidency and the national legislature in an arrangement that has been called "the politics of the governors" and "the alliance of coffee and cream." Presidents selected their successors and then used a vast web of patronage and clientelism to deliver the vote.

During the First Republic the state governments, particularly the most important states of São Paolo, Minas Gerais, Rio de Janeiro, and Rio Grande do Sul, became more powerful at the expense of the federal government. The weak federal government and the decentralization of power suited Brazil's powerful economic interests. The republic effectively mediated and contained political conflict between and within powerful economic interests while excluding all others. But by the early twentieth century, the elitist regime had alienated the growing urban middle class, who sought increased participation; the nascent industrial working class in São Paolo, who sought the creation of a welfare state; and immigrants inspired by radical European ideologies. Demands for political and economic reform were met with harsh repression. New forces of opposition weakened the Old Republic, but the increased infighting between regional leaders was the root cause for the regime's failure.

GETÚLIO VARGAS AND THE NEW STATE

In October 1930, the military once again intervened in politics, this time to end the First Republic. Military leaders installed **Getúlio Vargas,** an elite politician from Rio Grande do Sul who had been a losing candidate for the presidency. Vargas acted quickly to enhance the power of the federal government, replacing elected governors with his appointees. In 1933, a new constitution reduced the autonomy of individual states (revoking their power to tax, for example), while maintaining the elected president and congress. Vargas broke his pledge to hold democratic elections and in 1937 created a new dictatorial regime he called the **Estado Nôvo** (New State).

The Estado Nôvo was clearly inspired by fascist Italy and Germany, whose regimes featured a strong, authoritarian central state, as well as by Franklin Roosevelt's New Deal policies. But Vargas is best viewed more as a typical Latin American **populist** (similar in many respects to Argentina's Juan Perón, or Mexico's Lázaro Cárdenas) than as a fascist or social democrat. Unlike both the monarchy and the First Republic, which largely catered to the agricultural elite, Vargas's bases of support included the urban industrialists, middle class professionals, workers, and sectors of the military. Politically, Vargas favored a model of **state corporatism,** whereby all sectors of society were strongly encouraged to organize within state-controlled associations. Vargas viewed this system as a way to cultivate his base of support among different sectors of society while limiting the ability of civil society to challenge the state. Unofficial unions, groups, and parties were marginalized and harassed. Vargas viewed the state as a paternalistic arbiter of societal conflict.

The authoritarian Estado Nôvo was responsible for some of the first protections and welfare benefits for Brazil's urban workers, and Vargas's regime mobilized labor and raised wages. Vargas established state firms to promote industrialization in key sectors such as steel and imposed protectionist policies to shield Brazilian industry from foreign competition (import-substitution industrialization). As a result, Brazil experienced an industrial boom after 1930. Vargas modernized and professionalized the Brazilian military, creating the

ARE POPULISTS ON THE LEFT OR THE RIGHT?

L atin American populism is hard to label on a left-right spectrum, and populism is a complex, contradictory, and controversial movement. Latin American populists usually challenged established agrarian elites, who had previously dominated politics. They mobilized and sought to improve the lives of urban workers as a way of promoting industrial growth. At the same time, populists were hostile to socialists and Communists, the traditional parties of the left. Unlike those groups, populist leaders advocated capitalist development with a large role for the state. Moreover, the authoritarian methods of populist leaders alienated many leftist intellectuals. Vargas' Estado Nôvo nicely illustrates the many contradictions of populism. His pro-worker rhetoric alarmed entrepreneurs, and his pro-industrial policies alienated traditional rural oligarchs. At the same time, Vargas never implemented badly needed agrarian reform, and his regime effectively weakened the Communist and socialist left. Indeed, at the time some called Vargas the "father of the poor and the mother of the rich."[3] Key elements of Latin American populism were statism and nationalism, as well as the charismatic nature of the populist leaders. Vargas believed that state sponsorship of industrialization was a way to modernize and enhance the power and prestige of Brazil. The question of how to view populism is not just a historical debate: It has informed the current controversy created over the presidency of Venzuela's Hugo Chávez.

Escola Superior de Guerra (Superior War College), an institution that further bolstered the confidence and autonomy of the military.

After 1945, pressure mounted for Vargas to convene free elections. In the aftermath of World War II, during which Brazil had sent troops to help defeat fascism in Europe, dictatorships fell out of favor. In October 1945, Brazil's military, emboldened by its enhanced role in the dictatorship and its successful contribution to the Allied war effort, deposed Vargas and convened elections.

THE DEMOCRATIC EXPERIMENT: MASS POLITICS IN THE SECOND REPUBLIC

During the Second Republic (1945–64) Brazilians had their first real taste of democracy, and for the first time there was real competition for control of the state. The Brazilian masses, mobilized by Vargas during the Estado Nôvo, were now a force to be reckoned with. Suffrage was expanded dramatically (though only about one fifth of the electorate participated during elections), and new national parties, including the Communist Party of Brazil, attempted to appeal to voters.

In 1950, Vargas, the former dictator, was elected to the presidency in a deeply polarized election. He attempted to continue the populist policies of the Estado Nôvo but now faced a vigorous opposition that controlled the legislature and the press and stymied his policy proposals. In 1954, Vargas broke the deadlock by resigning and shortly after stunned the nation by committing suicide.

In the aftermath of Vargas's death, Juscelino Kubitschek, a follower of Vargas's, was elected president. Often considered Brazil's greatest president, Kubitschek was responsible for a number of grandiose public works, including the moving of Brazil's capital from Rio de Janeiro, on the coast, to Brasília, deep in the interior.

THE BREAKDOWN OF DEMOCRACY AND THE MILITARIZATION OF THE STATE

Following Vargas's dictatorship, democracy was established but never consolidated. Brazil's democracy was deeply polarized between supporters and opponents of Vargas's populist policies. Opponents of Vargas and his successors increasingly called on the military to end democracy in order to prevent a return to populism. They sought to reduce the role of the state in the economy. Supporters of Vargas and his successors increasingly viewed Brazil's democracy as weak, ineffective, and beholden to the country's wealthy elite. They increasingly advocated leftist policies that called for a growth in the role of the state in the economy through a wave of nationalizations.

This political polarization crystallized during the presidency of **João Goulart** (1961–64), a minister of labor under Vargas. In the context of the cold war, the military and much of the right viewed Goulart as a dangerous leftist and a potential dictator who reminded them too much of Vargas. His term began inauspiciously, as the military insisted that the Brazilian legislature curtail the president's power before allowing him to take office. Goulart spent much of his first years in power, and a great deal of political capital, passing a national plebiscite that restored his full powers, further alarming his opponents. The political crisis also developed in the context of a severe economic crisis caused by rampant inflation and growing debt. In 1964, after Goulart attempted to rally workers and peasants to his defense and after he clumsily alienated the military by backing some mutinous officers, the Brazilian military, with U.S. support, once again seized power.

The military had intervened in Brazilian politics six times since 1889, but in each instance soldiers had quickly retreated to their barracks, leaving politics to civilian leaders. By 1964, the Brazilian military believed it was time to take control of the state and hold on to it. Encouraged by the United States and politicians on the right, Brazilian military leaders thought they possessed the leadership skills to preserve political order, the power to prevent a feared Communist revolution, and the technical skills to run the economy.

Brazilian military leaders presided over a regime that has often been described as **bureaucratic authoritarian.**[4] Military leaders suspended the constitution and then decreed a new authoritarian one, banned existing parties and replaced them with two official ones to contest local and congressional elections (eliminating direct elections for governors and the president), took control of trade unions, and severely restricted civil liberties. They sought to erase for good the populist legacy of Vargas. The presidency, held by a series of military leaders, issued numerous decrees that gradually stripped the political system of its democratic features. Torture, disappearances, and exile became commonplace, though they never reached the horrific dimensions experienced during bureaucratic authoritarian regimes in Argentina or Chile.[5]

Although it initially attempted to reduce the role of the state in the economy, the Brazilian military eventually adopted policies of state-led industrialization that were in many ways a continuation of Vargas's statism. The state spent lavishly on major infrastructural projects, including hydroelectric dams, a paved highway to penetrate the Amazon rain forest, and even a nuclear power program. Military rule coincided with the decade of sustained spectacular economic growth that averaged over 10 percent annually—dubbed the economic miracle.

GRADUAL DEMOCRATIZATION AND THE MILITARY'S RETURN TO THE BARRACKS

Beginning in the mid-1970s, faced with an economic crisis and growing domestic opposition, the military began to slowly loosen its political grip on the country while maintaining ultimate control. This process, known as *abertura* (gradual opening), coincided with the global energy crisis that hit Brazil particularly hard, raising its already high level of international debt. Inflation skyrocketed to levels that exceeded those under Goulart. The "official" opposition party tolerated by the regime became more vigorous in its call for regime change and more successful in legislative elections.

Under the presidency of General João Figueiredo (1979–85), political prisoners were released, censorship was reduced, and political parties were allowed

History of Regimes			
Regime	**Years**	**Type**	**Outcome**
Empire	1822–89	Quasi-democratic constitutional monarchy	Military coup
Old Republic	1889–1930	Quasi-democratic republic	Military coup
Provisional government	1930–37	Semi-authoritarian republic	Gétulio Vargas seized power with military backing
Estado Nôvo	1937–45	Semi-authoritarian republic	Military coup
Second Republic	1945–64	Democratic republic	Military coup
Military regime	1964–85	Military dictatorship	Controlled, negotiated transition
New Republic	1985–present	Democratic republic	

to reemerge. These measures and the growing economic crisis led to a surge of opposition demands for direct presidential elections and democratic reform. The military's carefully laid plans for controlling the transition unraveled in 1984, when members of the pro-military party in the legislature backed a civilian democratic reform candidate, Tancredo Neves. Neves died shortly after his election and was replaced by the more conservative José Sarney, but the momentum of political reform could not be stopped. In 1987, a constituent assembly was elected to write a new democratic constitution, formally adopted in 1988.

Thus, democratization came gradually to Brazil and began when the military sought to begin a controlled process of reform. It was encouraged by a severe economic crisis, facilitated by political miscalculation, and supported by a widespread popular fatigue with military rule.

POLITICAL REGIME

Political Institutions

THE CONSTITUTION

Brazil has been a democracy since the adoption of its current constitution in 1988. The constitution was written in the waning days of the country's authoritarian regime and made important compromises in a number of areas. In many ways, the constitution is similar to that of the Second Republic. However, reacting to the long period of authoritarian rule, the framers of the current constitution established a set of rights that could not be amended or curtailed—for example, the principles of federalism, the separation of powers, and certain individual rights. Compared with previous documents, the current constitution imposes very strict limits and controls on the ability of the government to declare a state of siege or take wartime measures. Constitutional amendments are possible and can be initiated by the legislature (if one third of the members of either house agree), the state legislatures (if a majority of them agree), or the president. Such amendments can pass only with the support of separate two-thirds majority votes in both houses of the legislature.

A major debate raged during the writing of the constitution in 1987. Most members of the

---

ESSENTIAL POLITICAL FEATURES

- Legislative-executive system: presidential
- Lower house: Chamber of Deputies
- Upper house: Federal Senate
- Unitary or federal division of power: federal
- Main geographic subunits: states
- Electoral system for lower house: proportional representation
- Chief judicial body: Supreme Federal Tribunal and Higher Tribunal of Justice

constituent assembly favored abandoning Brazil's traditional presidential system for a parliamentary model. The conservative president at the time did not
want to see his own powers diminished and he resisted vigorously but did
agree to hold a plebiscite on the issue. In 1993, voters rejected the proposed
parliamentary system. Brazilians were wary of losing their ability to elect their
head of government directly, and distrusted their political parties, the linch-
pin of the parliamentary model.[6]

The Branches of Government

THE PRESIDENCY

The Brazilian president is both head of government and head of state and on
paper is among the most powerful leaders in Latin America. The president
and a vice president are elected for four-year terms and may serve a second
term.[7] The Brazilian president has the line-item veto, allowing for the rejection of select aspects of legislation. The president has the power to initiate

STRUCTURE OF THE GOVERNMENT

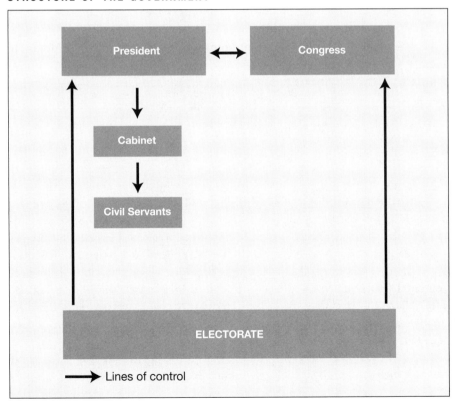

Lines of control

LULA

Brazil's new president breaks with a long line of leaders who come from the powerful, wealthy elite. Luiz Ignácio Lula da Silva, known as Lula, was born in the poverty-stricken rural northeast. The sixth of seven children, Lula was raised in a shack by a single mother. The family moved to a *favela* of São Paulo in search of employment when Lula was seven, and he immediately began to participate in Brazil's vast informal sector, shining shoes and selling candy to help support his family. By the age of twelve, Lula was working full-time in a screw factory, where he eventually began his involvement in the trade union movement. Lula's life bears many of the marks of Brazil's endemic poverty. Formally, he has only a fifth-grade education (though he earned his high-school equivalency and a technical degree). His first wife died in childbirth because she could not afford medical care.

In the 1970s, just as Brazil's union movement began a wave of strikes aimed at pressuring the military government to democratize, Lula became a local union leader, a position that earned him a prison term. In 1980, he was elected the first leader of the new **Worker's Party (PT),** a democratic socialist party. By the mid-1980s, Lula had become a member of congress and the best-known politician in Brazil. He was especially admired by Brazil's large underclass. Lula ran unsuccessfully for president three times and was defeated mainly because Brazil's upper-class politicians closed ranks to defeat what they viewed as a socialist threat. In the 2002 elections, Lula moderated his image, donned a business suit, and made an effort to reassure business leaders, the church, and the military, the sectors most frightened by his candidacy. To explain these changes he quipped, "I changed, Brazil changed."

With his resounding victory in the 2002 elections, Lula becomes the first Brazilian president directly touched by the poverty afflicting so many of his fellow citizens. One of his inauguration goals was to assure every Brazilian one plate of food a day. His election was in many ways as momentous as the election of Nelson Mandela in South Africa or Vicente Fox in Mexico.

---

and push legislation through the legislature (about 80 percent of all legislation is initiated by the president) and is the only individual capable of initiating budgetary legislation. However, the formal power of Brazilian presidents has to date been weakened by the fragmentation of the legislature. Brazilian heads of government need to cobble together legislative majorities from fractious and poorly disciplined political parties. Faced with the lack of legislative majorities, Brazilian presidents have often resorted to legislating by emergency decree, thereby circumventing the legislature altogether.[8] President Fernando Collor de Mello won the presidency in 1999 as an "outsider," and his political party held only 3 percent of the seats in congress. In his first year in office, he used 150 such emergency decrees to pass a variety of important economic reforms, whose dubious legality were justified by the president

Presidents since 1985

President	Dates in Office	Party	Description
José Sarney	1985–89	Social Democratic Party (PSD)*	A conservative who took office after the sudden death of a popular civilian democrat, who had been elected according to the cumbersome rules of the military regime
Fernando Collor de Mello	1989–92	National Order Reconstruction Party (PRONA)	Resigned after being impeached by Congress on charges of corruption
Itamar Franco	1992–95	National Order Reconstruction Party (PRONA)	Collor's vice president, who took office after Collor resigned
Fernando Henrique Cardoso	1995–2002	Brazilian Social Democracy Party (PSDB)	First two-term president, responsible for major market and social reforms
Luiz Inácio Lula da Silva	2002–present	Workers' Party (PT)	First working-class president

*The PSD was a party that broke from the military party at the end of the dictatorship and is now defunct.

as a necessary response to an economic crisis and whose legality went unchallenged by Brazil's highest court.[9]

Perhaps the greatest power of Brazilian presidents comes from their ability to make appointments to the cabinet and top levels of Brazil's vast bureaucracy. The ability to appoint key ministers, especially the powerful minister of the economy (who controls economic policy and the budget), gives presidents enormous patronage power.

THE LEGISLATURE

Brazil's legislature, the **National Congress (Congresso Nacional)** is composed of two co-equal houses. The 513-member **Chamber of Deputies (Câmara dos Deputados)** is the lower house (whose members are elected to four-year terms), and the 81-member **Federal Senate (Senado Federal)** is the upper house (whose members are elected for eight-year terms). There are no term limits for members of either house.

Both houses must approve all legislation before it is sent to the president, and when the houses disagree on legislation, they convene joint committees to iron out differences. The legislature can override presidential vetoes with a majority vote of both houses and can, with a two-thirds vote in both houses, amend the constitution with the agreement of the president. As in the United States, the Senate has the power to try a president or cabinet members for impeachable offenses and must approve top presidential appointments.

The actual power of the Brazilian legislature is a complex matter. On the one hand, legislators do not play a key role in most policy making, for many reasons, including the dominance of the president, the weakness of the political parties, the individualism of legislators, and the relatively weak committee system. A persistent problem limiting the effectiveness of the legislature has been an inability to reach a quorum on key matters. Legislators often view their jobs as stepping-stones to more prestigious and lucrative occupations, such as state governor or top bureaucratic posts.

On the other hand, the constitution does allocate significant power to Congress, and Brazil's legislature has played an important, if not the leading, role from time to time.[10] Several high-profile congressional hearings (called parliamentary commissions of investigation) have exposed fraud and corruption, even at the highest level of government. In 1992, Congress successfully impeached President Fernando Collor de Mello on corruption charges. On the whole, Congress has not achieved the popular legitimacy that might be expected given its formal power.[11]

THE JUDICIAL SYSTEM

Along with the legislature and executive branches, the judiciary is the third branch of government in Brazil. At the highest level is the **Federal Supreme Court (Supremo Tribunal Federal),** whose eleven justices are appointed by the president and approved by a majority vote in the Senate for a term not to exceed thirty years. The thirty judges of the Superior Court of Justice are similarly appointed and approved and also serve no more than thirty years. Brazil's federal judicial structure is replicated at the state and local level. The court system also features a Supreme Electoral Court (Tribunal Superior Eleitoral), an increasingly common institution in developing countries that is designed to prevent fraud. Most observers agree that elections in Brazil have been remarkably transparent and fair in large part because of the Electoral Court.

As is the norm in Latin America, Brazil employs code law, a rigid system in which judges apply the penal code rather than broadly interpret laws based on historical precedent. As a result, the Brazilian judiciary has less power than its U.S. counterpart, and the Supreme Federal Court has been reticent to challenge the ongoing use of presidential emergency decrees.

At the lower levels, the Brazilian legal system is regularly criticized as beholden to economic elites and riddled with corruption. Many poor Brazilians feel that they cannot be fairly represented within the system. A survey taken in 1996 reported that 96 percent of respondents believed that a poor person would be dealt with more harshly in the legal system than a wealthy one.[12] In rural areas, for example, powerful landowners are often successful at influencing legal decisions to the detriment of the peasants. An old Brazilian expression summarizes this unequal access to the judicial system: "For my enemies, the law; for my friends, anything." There have been particularly harsh criticisms, backed by reports by international human rights organizations, of the judiciary's inability to hold Brazil's numerous security forces responsible for a host of human rights abuses.

The Electoral System

Brazil is an excellent example of how an electoral system can fundamentally influence the way in which legislatures and executives interact. A distinct feature of Brazil's democracy is the multiplicity of relatively weak parties. This has made it almost impossible for Brazilian presidents to gain the support of a stable legislative majority and has created a built-in conflict between the executive and the legislature. The electoral system is largely to blame.

All Brazilians over the age of sixteen can vote, and since 1988 illiterate citizens have been allowed to vote. Voting is mandatory for all literate citizens between the ages of eighteen and seventy. Partly as a result, Brazil has regularly enjoyed a turnout of around 70 percent in legislative and presidential elections. Presidents, state governors, and mayors of large cities must receive a majority of the vote in a first round of voting or face their strongest opponent in a second round. For Senate races, the three candidates with the most votes win seats.

It is the electoral system used for Brazil's lower house (and for all state legislatures) that has been most controversial. In this highly unusual system, called **open-list proportional representation (PR),** voters may choose *either* a party list (as in normal proportional representation) or write in names of candidates. Votes for each party (and for candidates associated with each party) are then tallied, and seats are allocated to each party proportionally. However, the determination of how seats are allocated to individual party members is based on the number of votes they receive. Candidates must therefore campaign under their own names (not just their party labels) and have an incentive to promote their own candidacies at the expense of their party colleagues. The system serves to weaken the power of political parties and the ability of those parties to enforce internal discipline. The fragmentation of parties is exacerbated by the fact that state-level parties, not the federal party hierarchy, determine the composition of party lists. The tendency has been for individual candidates to seek the backing of powerful state-level politicians, further enhancing Brazil's tradition of clientelism and pork barrel

politics. Moreover, unlike many systems that employ proportional representation, Brazil has no threshold for gaining seats, meaning that even the smallest political parties can easily gain representation in the legislature.[13]

Districts for both houses of the legislature are the twenty-six states plus
the federal district. For the lower house, the number of legislators per district
is determined roughly according to population and ranges from a low of eight
to a maximum of seventy. This minimum allocation has overrepresented the
least populated (and most conservative) sectors of Brazil and has underrepresented urban Brazil, but attempts to change the allocation have been blocked
by representatives of all parties from the overrepresented regions.[14] The fact
that each state also sends three senators to Congress has, as in the United
States, added to the overrepresentation of sparsely populated, rural, and generally more conservative states.

Local Government

Brazil is a large and diverse country, and since colonial times there has been
a tension between control by the federal government and the desire for regional
autonomy. For much of Brazil's history, local authorities have enjoyed considerable autonomy, but during the Estado Nôvo and the military regime, the
pendulum swung decisively toward the federal government. During the transition to democracy, Brazil's first directly elected heads of government were
the state governors chosen in 1982. Brazil's new democracy has firmly reestab-
lished the principle of **robust federalism,** and Brazilian federalism devolves
more power to the states than in most other federal systems.[15]

Each of Brazil's twenty-six states (plus the federal district) has an elected
governor and a unicameral legislature. Since 1997, governors have been allowed
to be reelected to a second term. Brazilian states are further divided into over
5,000 *municípios* (municipalities), similar to U.S. counties, that are governed
by elected mayors and elected councils. Brazilian states have historically owned
their own banks and have even run some industries. The constitution allocates
to state and local governments a huge chunk of all federal tax revenue. State
governors have largely been free to spend as they please, and many states have
run up huge debts with the federal government. In 1998, the governor of the
powerful state of Minas Gerais (former president Itamar Franco) stopped repay-
ment of his state's massive debt (over US$15 billion) to the federal government,
provoking a severe budgetary crisis. Brazil differs from most other federal systems in that the constitution of 1988 does not spell out specific spending responsibilities in areas such as health and education. Nor did it regulate the spending
of state banks, which continued to fund excessive spending at the state level.

Governors and mayors of big cities thus have a lot of money to use to help
federal legislators gain election. Those legislators, in turn, work at the federal

level to promote pork barrel federal spending on infrastructure projects for their states. Some of those expenditures have ended up in the pockets of corrupt local officials.

Beginning in the Collor de Mello administration, the federal government began to reassert itself vis-à-vis the states, intervening in (and in some cases privatizing) the state banking systems. The federal government forced some states to sell state-owned utilities and rein in state spending. During the two terms of President Cardoso, states and municipalities were forced to assume a greater portion of welfare spending. The 2000 Fiscal Responsibility Law further limited state and local spending by specifically preventing the federal government from refinancing state-government debt.[16]

Nevertheless, much of Brazilian politics can still be seen as the politics of the governors, and Brazilian presidents must negotiate with powerful state governors much as they must horse-trade with the Brazil's fractious legislature.

Other Institutions: The Military and the Police

We have seen that Brazil's military played an important role in its domestic politics. From the late nineteenth century until 1964, the military acted mainly as an arbiter, intervening in politics to depose leaders it found unacceptable and then returning to the barracks and returning power to the hands of the civilians. By the mid-1960s, however, the military no longer saw itself as a simple arbiter of domestic conflict. Its officer corps, trained at the influential U.S-supported Escola Superior da Guerra (Superior War College, or ESG) during the cold war, began to view its role as a domestic guardian of order against the "foreign" ideological threats of socialism and communism. Many of these ideas were fused into a national security doctrine, which focused the military's attention domestically and deflected it from threats on Brazil's borders. Not only were the military elite trained in war strategy, but increasingly they also gained expertise in public administration and economics. By 1964, military leaders believed that Brazil's democratic regime, with its weak and polarized parties, had become chaotic and would be susceptible to Communist subversion. Between 1964 and 1985, Brazil's military held power directly, in an alliance with conservative business elites and technocrats and, at least initially, with the tacit support of the upper and middle classes. Military officials participated directly in key sectors of the economy, such as the nuclear industry and arms production.

Brazil's democratic transition began in the 1970s and was in large part led by the military, which after two decades of military rule was eager to leave economic problems to the civilians. Because military leaders controlled the transition to democracy, there were no attempts to bring Brazilian military officials to justice for destroying democracy or for engaging in widespread human rights abuses. The military was able to pressure the transitional government to pass a widespread amnesty for members of the armed forces.[17]

As a result, Brazil's military continues to be a powerful arm of the state with far more autonomy than in most other advanced democracies.[18] Article 142 of the constitution calls on the military to guarantee law and order. At the same time, democratic governments, beginning with that of President Collor de Mello, have cut military budgets (which are now among the lowest in Latin America), purged military leaders most closely connected to the authoritarian regime, redeployed troops away from population centers, and removed the military from cabinet and top bureaucratic posts. The military's national security doctrine was replaced by a new policy that focuses almost entirely on foreign threats, especially to Brazil's vast and porous Amazon borders. Some Brazilians who were victims of the military's human rights abuses have received compensation, which has further damaged the image of the military.

The two Cardoso administrations continued to assert state control over the armed forces by creating a single civilian ministry of defense to replace ministries that had existed for each branch. Upon his election, Lula tested the loyalty of the armed forces by canceling the costly purchase of fighter jets, which had been a pet project of the military.

Brazil's military today plays a much smaller role in politics, and fear of a military coup against democracy has virtually disappeared. When the military exercises its muscle domestically, it is likely to be at the behest of the civilian government.

Instead, Brazil's police forces have been the subject of a chorus of concern from human rights experts who have noted the high levels of "state violence" perpetrated against Brazil's poorest citizens. State governments control their own civil police forces (which mainly investigate crimes) and military police forces (which are uniformed and armed). The military police, like the

---

THE MILITARY AND HUMAN RIGHTS

Unlike other Latin American countries, where the human rights abuses of military regimes have been punished or at least publicly documented, Brazil's military has never owned up to its behavior during the 1964–85 military regime. Military records of the dictatorship were ordered sealed for fifty years during the Cardoso administration. In 2004, when President Lula da Silva's administration proposed opening those files, a number of top military officials made public statements justifying the repression during the dictatorship, and the minister of defense resigned in protest. The head of the PT, the president's party, responded by affirming, "We are not afraid of the military."

military itself, are governed by their own judicial system, which has in practice allowed the police to act outside the law. Off-duty officers are often hired by business owners to kill homeless street dwellers, and many of the dead have been children. The large number of such killings has exceeded the number of deaths caused by the military during the two decades of authoritarian rule, leading one observer to call Brazil an "ugly democracy."[19]

At the same time, there are serious concerns about the ability of Brazil's police to maintain a monopoly on violence. Brazil's murder rate is twice that of the United States, and private security guards outnumber the almost 500,000 military police.[20] A wave of gang violence further eroded public confidence in the police.

POLITICAL CONFLICT AND COMPETITION

The Party System and Elections

Brazil's party system has perhaps been the most vilified aspect of its democratic regime. The country has a fragmented multiparty system with weak and fickle political parties, due in large part to the electoral laws.[21] Nineteen parties currently hold seats in the legislature, and seven gained over 5 percent of the vote in the 2003 election. Opinion research consistently shows extremely low levels of party identification and low public confidence in parties.[22] As noted earlier, the weakness of political parties complicates a president's attempt to find a majority to support his legislative proposals. The president's need to bargain regularly with a number of small parties has only increased the pork barrel aspects of the Brazilian political system and has often made it hard to implement tough decisions, such as reductions in state spending.

Historically, Brazil's parties have been highly personalistic, that is, based on the leadership of a powerful or charismatic individual instead of an ideology. This feature has its roots in Brazil's patron-client politics. The military regime attempted to create a "modern" two-party system by fiat, but the two official parties did not survive the transition to democracy. Instead, the transition gave rise to an even greater proliferation of political parties. Today, the weakness of their ideological component is evident in the large number of party members who, after being elected, change affiliation or leave to create new parties.[23] This has most often occurred after the election of a president from another party, prompting legislatures to switch to the governing party in order to assure their access to patronage. Between 1991 and 1994, over half the members of the lower house changed party affiliation. Since Brazilian electoral laws allow candidates to run as members of a party without approval of the party leadership (in Brazil, any elected member of the legislature is guaranteed a place on the ballot in the

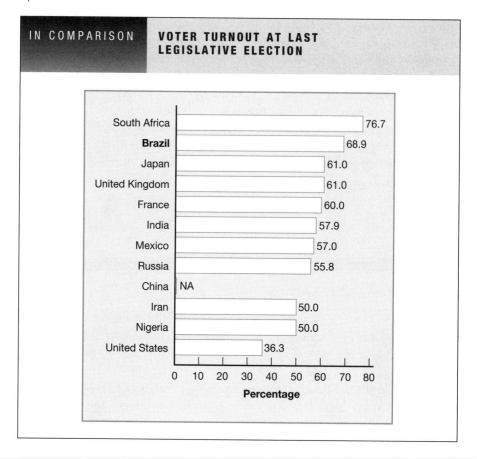

IN COMPARISON   **VOTER TURNOUT AT LAST LEGISLATIVE ELECTION**

	Percentage
South Africa	76.7
Brazil	68.9
Japan	61.0
United Kingdom	61.0
France	60.0
India	57.9
Mexico	57.0
Russia	55.8
China	NA
Iran	50.0
Nigeria	50.0
United States	36.3

following election), there is little incentive for party loyalty. Moreover, Brazil's powerful federalism further weakens party cohesion: it is common for legislators to vote across party lines with members of their state delegations to support legislation of local interest. Two presidents in the 1990s (Franco and Collor de Mello) were elected without any real party base.

The most important conservative party, the Liberal Front Party (PFL), grew out of the two "official" parties tolerated during the military regime. It is a free-market, pro-business party, differing from parties of the center mainly in its opposition to land reform and its conservative stand on social issues. Today, the PFL is the second largest party in Congress and controls four governorships. In addition, the Brazilian Labor Party (PTB) is the heir to Getúlio Vargas's political legacy but has become fairly conservative.

Two main centrist parties are the Brazilian Democratic Movement Party (PMDB) and the Brazilian Social Democracy Party (PSDB), to which former two-term president Cardoso belongs. Both parties include a mix of free-market conservatives and social democrats, and neither has a clear ideological orientation. The PMDB was the most important pro-democracy opposition party in the years of the transition and played a critical role in the move toward direct elections and a new constitution. It is currently the third largest party in Congress and controls five state governments. Cardoso and other prominent PMDB members bolted to form the PSDB in protest over the PMDB's patron-client politics. The PSDB initially distinguished itself as a social democratic alternative to the PMDB, but since Cardoso's two terms in office it has been more closely associated with free-market reforms. During Cardoso's terms in office, the PSDB grew to become the second largest party in the legislature, and it controlled the largest share of state governorships.

The Workers' Party (PT) is now the single largest political party in Congress (although it holds only three of Brazil's governorships), and it is the dominant party of the left.[24] The PT is led by the current president, Luiz Inácio Lula da Silva, whose decisive victory in the 2002 presidential election has boosted the party's fortunes. It was founded in 1980 mainly among unionized industrial workers but has grown to incorporate landless workers, rural unions, and other disaffected Brazilians. It has also attracted significant support from educated middle-class Brazilians. It claims to represent Brazil's poor, and it advocates democratic-socialist ideas. The PT's success has been growing steadily in the federal and state legislatures and in gubernatorial elections. Unlike most of Brazil's parties, the PT has practiced a high degree of internal democracy and has had fewer defections and splits. The PT was elected partly on its reputation for honesty and clean government. Its reputation was badly tarnished, however, by a series of corruption scandals in 2005 and 2006.

The dominant cleavage in the Brazilian electorate has been regional, rather than by social class, with the rural conservative northeast often pitted against

---

FROM LOCAL TO NATIONAL POLITICS

When the Workers' Party gained control of some of Brazil's most important municipalities in the 1980s, it gained experience and legitimacy. PT administrations were widely praised for the elimination of corruption and efficient administration. In one notable case, the PT administration of Pôrto Alegre implemented a participatory budget program, in which neighborhood organizations debated and voted on budgetary spending priorities. The program was expanded to other PT-controlled municipalities and has increased popular participation in politics. PT budgets differ from those of their predecessors by directing a far greater amount of resources to programs that benefit the poor.

Seats in the National Congress and Number of Governors by Party, 2003

Party	Seats (594 total)	Percentage of seats	Governors
Workers' Party (PT)	105	18	3
Liberal Front Party (PFL)	103	17	4
Brazilian Democratic Movement Party (PMDB)	93	16	5
Brazilian Social Democracy Party (PSDB)	82	13	7
Others (15 parties in Congress and 7 others at the state level)	211	36	8

Source: Adapted from Jairo Marconi Nicolau, "Dados Eleitorais do Brasil, 1982–2002," Programa de Pós-Graduação em Sociologia e Ciência Política, Instituto Universitário de Pesquisas do Rio de Janeiro, http://www.iuperj.br (accessed 7 January 2005).

the more progressive and urban south and southeast. The 2002 presidential election generally followed this pattern with Lula most strongly supported in Brazil's southeastern urban areas while his opponent, José Serra, drew his vote disproportionately from the rural northeast. Interestingly, Brazil's severe class inequality does not appear to have affected the outcome of that race. Lula did equally well among poor and wealthy Brazilians.

Despite some recent signs that the major parties are beginning to consolidate and that parties (especially on the left and in the center) are becoming more disciplined, the party system is badly fragmented. Despite Lula's resounding victory in the 2002 presidential election and despite the fact that his PT is the second largest party in Congress, Lula's supporters still control only 18 percent of the legislative seats. Even with support from parties on the left and in the center, Lula has faced difficulties passing any legislation without a lot of compromise. Party fragmentation by itself rules out any radical policy shifts under the current president.

Civil Society

Democratization has led to a mushrooming of civil society that had been stifled during the military regime. Membership in urban and rural trade unions has grown quickly. The growth of decentralized Protestant religious groups, many with a conservative political agenda, has helped to reinvigorate civil society. A host of environmental, human rights, and women's groups has emerged as well.

The return of democracy has given rise to women's rights groups, but women remain fairly marginal in Brazilian politics. However, Brazil's rapid industrialization has greatly increased the percentage of women in the workforce (now estimated at about 40 percent), although women are still paid far less than their male counterparts. Laws have been passed to try to increase women's representation. In 1998, Congress stipulated that 20 percent of the seats in the federal legislature must be held by women. The presidency of Lula, whose PT has integrated numerous women's groups, has given rise to new hopes for more equal representation.

Brazil's largest social movement is the **Landless Workers Movement (MST),** a peasant organization that has fought for land reform. It has advocated legal change but has often supported and even organized peasant seizure of uncultivated, privately owned land. This activism has been opposed, often violently, by Brazil's powerful landlords, often with the support of the police forces and with the tacit tolerance of the rural courts. Hundreds of MST workers have been killed for trying to address Brazil's extremely unequal landholding patterns. During the Cardoso administration, MST pressure resulted in a major redistribution of land to peasants.

Despite centuries of church support for the most conservative elements of Brazilian society, the Roman Catholic Church in Brazil played an essential role in mobilizing civil society to protest the military regime. Spurred by changes in Rome, especially the Second Vatican Council (1962–65), much of the Brazilian church, including some of the hierarchy, embraced a new interpretation of the role of religion. **Liberation theology,** which developed in the 1960s among a group of Catholic intellectuals that included numerous Brazilians, held that the church should use its power and prestige to teach the poor how to improve their lives immediately, in both physical and spiritual terms. Liberation theology advocated organizing small neighborhoods called **Christian Base Communities,** often in rural areas or urban *favelas,* not only for prayer, but also to learn and advocate political and social justice. These base communities were often led by "lay priests" who directly challenged the traditional church hierarchy. The National Conference of Brazilian Bishops was for a time a leading advocate of liberation theology and was a major advocate of democratization, land reform, and human rights.

SOCIETY

Ethnic and National Identity

Brazil has an extremely diverse population that has emerged from a blending of Native Americans, African slaves, and Europeans. Unlike much of Spanish

ETHNIC GROUPS

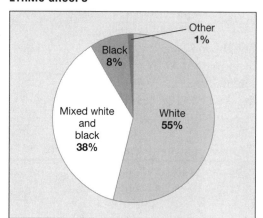

RELIGION

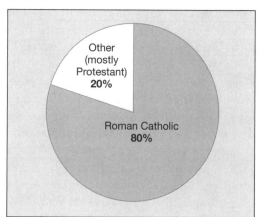

America and the United States, there was far more intermarriage among racial groups in Brazil. Today, around 40 percent of Brazilians consider themselves to be of mixed race. Brazilians have a complex vocabulary to describe the rainbow of skin colors, ranging from *preto* (black) to *mulato claro* (light brown). Despite the Brazilian myth of "racial democracy," there is a strong association between race and wealth. Wealthy Brazilians tend to be lighter skinned, and blacks are disproportionately present among Brazil's poor.[25] Relatively few blacks are found at the highest level of business or government.

Brazil has also become a religiously diverse country after centuries of domination by the Roman Catholic Church. While the vast majority of Brazilians claim to be Catholic, Brazil has seen an extraordinary explosion of Protestants, especially Pentacostal movements, over the last two decades. In addition, many Brazilians (even white Brazilians) practice one of several Afro-Brazilian religions, such as Macumba, Candomblé, or Umbanda, often in addition to Catholicism.

Ideology and Political Culture

Despite very high levels of participation in elections, due in large part to mandatory voting, and despite the growth of civil society since democracy, a look at Brazil's political culture reveals serious concerns.

Perhaps most alarming is the low level of support for democracy as a system of government. According to public opinion data, only about 37 percent of Brazilians viewed democracy as the best form of government when asked in 2005,[26] well below the Latin American average of 53 percent. Brazilians report very low levels of satisfaction with how democracy is working (only

Confidence in Democratic Political Institutions, 1996–2001	
Institution	**% Expressing Confidence**
Congress	22
Political parties	18
Judiciary	40
Public administration	29
Presidency	31
All democratic institutions (average)	28
Source: *Latinobarometro* data, reported in J. Mark Payne et. al., *Democracies in Development*, p. 31.	

22 percent of Brazilians were very or fairly satisfied with democracy in 2005), also well below the Latin American average. Research also shows that confidence in specific institutions, especially political parties and Congress, is extremely low.

POLITICAL ECONOMY

Beginning with Estado Nôvo and continuing through the military regime, Brazil's political economy could be described as capitalist but also heavily statist. Over the years, Brazil's state, through the implementation of import-substitution industrialization (ISI) policies, has played a major role in the economy by limiting imports, regulating credit, controlling the currency, regulating wages, and even owning and operating sectors of the economy. Statist policies have often resulted in spectacular economic growth, as was the case during the so-called economic miracle (1967–73), when annual growth rates averaged 11 percent. But statist policies have also been blamed for a number of serious problems that have long plagued the Brazilian economy.

Perhaps the most serious problem is inflation. An inflation rate of 90 percent was a major reason for the breakdown of democracy in 1964. The military regime was initially successful at reducing the inflation rate, but during the military period inflation still averaged 20 percent and began to skyrocket in the 1970s due to a rise in oil prices, high interest rates, and heavy state spending. Inflation eroded wages and hurt Brazil's poorest disproportionately.

Another serious problem is Brazil's debt. Brazil's military regime borrowed heavily from international lenders, and despite rapid growth rates its foreign indebtedness grew. Its long-term foreign debt has almost doubled since 1990

LABOR FORCE BY OCCUPATION

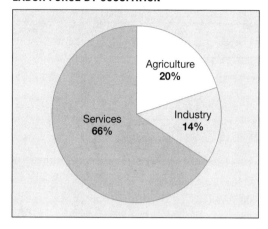

Agriculture
20%

Services
66%

Industry
14%

and in 2000 was valued at 31.5 percent of the GDP.[27] An additional problem has been Brazil's public-sector debt, which escalated rapidly with the return of democracy and increased social spending (see "Public-Sector Net Debt, 1994–2002" below).

A final problem is unemployment. Despite rapid economic growth, a large sector of Brazil's population remained jobless, and that joblessness is a chief cause of the endemic poverty and inequality. As a result, a large portion of Brazil's population (perhaps as much as two-thirds of the active workforce) makes its living in the informal sector.[28] As recently as 1995, one survey reported that over half of Brazil's workers did not contribute to the national social security system because they were not employed in a legally regulated job. The persistence of such a large informal sector deprives the state of needed tax revenue but, more important, deprives informal-sector workers of many welfare benefits.[29]

Democratization has addressed some but certainly not all of Brazil's economic problems. Democratic governments began a gradual reduction of the role of the state in Brazil's economy, but liberalization in Brazil has not been as extensive as in much of the rest of Latin America. Compared to its Latin American neighbors, the Brazilian state still has a relatively large presence in

PUBLIC-SECTOR NET DEBT, 1994–2003

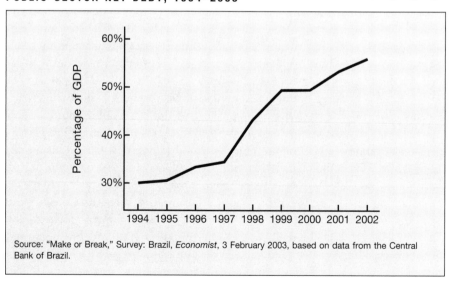

Source: "Make or Break," Survey: Brazil, *Economist*, 3 February 2003, based on data from the Central Bank of Brazil.

THE INFORMAL SECTOR: *FAVELAS* AND CABLE TV

Jardim Ângela is a typical *favela* on the outskirts of Brazil's largest city, São Paolo. A surprisingly large number of its residents enjoy cable television despite the fact that none of Brazil's cable companies have wired the area. The cable companies don't want to extend cable into the *favela* because most residents cannot afford the monthly fees. So entrepreneurs of the informal sector have installed pirated cable lines and charge a much lower monthly fee than the legal companies would. It is estimated that half a million poor Brazilians pay for pirated cable television. Rather than crack down on the illegal operations, Brazil's cable television industry has lobbied the government to pass laws that would effectively legalize such informal-sector services, hoping that they can at least gain some revenue from *favela* dwellers in a new partnership with the cable pirates.[30] It is recognition of both the important role of the informal sector and the inability of the Brazilian state to stop or regulate it.

the economy. However, starting with the presidency of Fernando Collor de Mello (1989–92), the role of the state in the economy has been curtailed and protective tariffs have been reduced. During Fernando Henrique Cardoso's two terms (1995–2002), a major policy of privatization of state assets was undertaken, ending the state monopoly in a number of key economic sectors, including energy and telecommunications. Under Cardoso, rules governing foreign investment in the Brazilian economy were liberalized.

INFLATION, 1994–2005

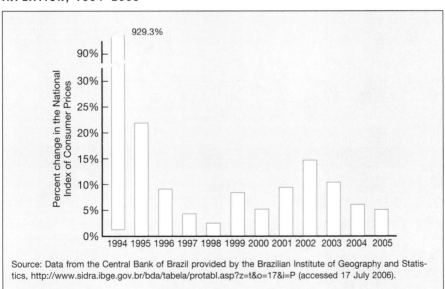

Source: Data from the Central Bank of Brazil provided by the Brazilian Institute of Geography and Statistics, http://www.sidra.ibge.gov.br/bda/tabela/protabl.asp?z=t&o=17&i=P (accessed 17 July 2006).

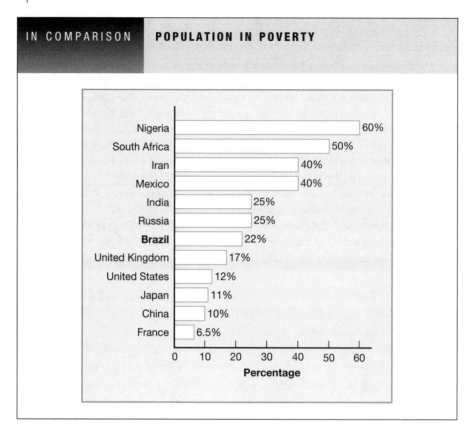

IN COMPARISON   **POPULATION IN POVERTY**

Nigeria — 60%
South Africa — 50%
Iran — 40%
Mexico — 40%
India — 25%
Russia — 25%
Brazil — 22%
United Kingdom — 17%
United States — 12%
Japan — 11%
China — 10%
France — 6.5%

Percentage (0, 10, 20, 30, 40, 50, 60)

Overall, aggregate economic growth since democratization has not attained the spectacular rates achieved during the miracle. Between 1980 and 1990, average GDP per capita fell .41 percent, and between 1990 and 2000 it grew by an average rate of 1.13 percent. However, recent democratic governments have made excellent progress in taming inflation. During the two Cardoso administrations, inflation was finally reduced to single digits (8.5 percent on average between 1995 and 2002).

Despite impressive records of aggregate growth, the most troublesome feature of Brazil's economy is its endemic poverty and persistently high levels of inequality. In 1998, the richest 20 percent of the population received 64 percent of the nation's income, while the poorest 20 percent earned only 2 percent, making Brazil the most unequal country in the world. Brazil's ranking in the 2004 United Nation's Human Development index has been falling recently: it now stands at 72, well below Mexico (52) and Russia (57).[31]

AIDS: A CASE OF SUCCESSFUL STATE POLICY

In the mid-1980s, Brazil's growth rate of HIV/AIDS infections was among the world's highest. Brazilian governments acted early to stem the epidemic but were unable to afford the costly medicines used to treat the disease. With government support, Brazilian pharmaceutical companies began manufacturing inexpensive generic drugs, although foreign producers and the U.S. government tried to stop them.

In 1999, Brazil's president Fernando Henrique Cardoso issued a presidential decree declaring the HIV/AIDS epidemic a national emergency. The decree allowed Brazilian firms to manufacture and market foreign patented medicines inexpensively under a special government license issued only in cases of national emergency. Cardoso argued that the decree was necessary because Brazil could not afford to pay for costly imported medicines to combat HIV/AIDS.

Brazil now produces eight of the twelve medicines used to treat HIV/AIDS, and it was able to reduce the cost of treatment by two thirds. As a result, almost 100,000 Brazilians have received free treatment. With its free medical treatment and an aggressive public-health campaign aimed at prevention, Brazil was able to reduce deaths related to HIV/AIDS by two thirds.

Nowhere is Brazil's poverty and inequality more evident than in education. In the first decade of Brazilian democracy, the average number of school years completed was only 3.8, and the vast majority of Brazilians never completed primary school. Only 1 percent of Brazilians attended university. The Cardoso administrations increased spending on Brazil's education system and produced a marked improvement, but a disproportionate amount of state spending continues to be directed toward a higher education system that benefits the economically advantaged.

Brazil's health-care system also reflects its massive poverty and inequality. Since 1987, all Brazilians have been formally entitled to public health care, but access and quality are very uneven. Brazil still has one of the highest infant mortality rates in the world; it has higher rates than China, Mexico, and Russia despite having a higher per capita GDP than those countries. Its life expectancy is lower than China's and Mexico's. About one third of the population lacks access to clean water.

Inadequate housing is yet another symptom and cause of poverty and inequality. The military regime did little to address housing needs, and despite increased spending on housing under the democratic governments, it is estimated that there are over 3,500 *favelas* (urban shantytowns) in Brazil, with populations ranging from several thousand to half a million.[32] Cardoso's administrations attempted to alleviate the housing crisis by distributing land to over half a million landless Brazilians, but the crisis remains acute.

The severe economic crisis of 1999, immediately following Cardoso's election to a second term, almost pulled Brazil into an economic depression. The Brazilian currency, the real, suffered a 42 percent devaluation, Brazil lost US$8 billion of its foreign reserves in one month, and inflation began to reemerge. The economy was rescued by two events: the International Monetary Fund provided a massive aid package, and Cardoso was finally able to pass a social security and pension reform package.

Despite a legacy of significant economic reform, Cardoso was less successful in other areas. His attempt to slim down Brazil's badly bloated state bureaucracy ran into serious opposition in the legislature. Public servants who run the state bureaucracy have been a relatively privileged labor elite, with a costly pension system that strains the Brazilian budget. Brazilians bear a relatively heavy tax burden that is nearly at European levels (about 40 percent of GDP) but has not been used to create a European-style welfare state.[33] Brazil does have a national social security system, but it doesn't cover the massive number of informal-sector workers. Social spending has tended to benefit the middle and upper classes instead of Brazil's poorest. As a result, Brazil's inequality has steadily worsened over the past four decades.

The election of Luiz Inácio Lula da Silva in the 2002 presidential election raised hopes for a fundamental resetting of economic priorities. Lula campaigned on a pledge to end hunger in Brazil. In office, he has steered a more cautious course. He has rejected further tax increases, and his ability to increase social spending has been constrained by Brazil's huge debt burden, commitments to state and local governments, and his inability and reluctance to reduce the state bureaucracy.

On the bright side, Brazil has become a dominant world exporter and currently has a large trade surplus (over US$20 billion in 2003). In 2002, its biggest exports were transport equipment and parts and metallurgical products, followed by soybeans, bran, and oil. Its export markets are fairly diversified, with the United States, China, and Argentina as the top three export destinations.[34]

FOREIGN RELATIONS AND THE WORLD

Until fairly recently, Brazil has not played the type of role in world politics that one might expect given the size of its territory and economy. Perhaps even more counterintuitive is that Brazil historically remained somewhat detached from its Spanish-speaking neighbors. With democratization, and especially since the presidency of Fernando Henrique Cardoso, its foreign policy has assumed a higher profile, and Brazil has become an informal leader of the developing world.

The biggest issue in Brazil's foreign relations is trade relations. Brazil is a major exporter and has sought to create free-trade agreements with its neighbors and with Europe and the United States. To date, the most important trade agreement is **MERCOSUR** (Common Market of the South; MERCOSUL in Portuguese), founded in 1991 by Brazil, Argentina, Uruguay, and Paraguay. Brazil has supported the enlargement of MERCOSUR, and Chile and Bolivia are now associate members. These countries have virtually eliminated tariffs, and within the first decade of MERCOSUR's existence there was a spectacular increase in trade among its members. Given the power of its industrial sector, Brazil has reaped a windfall with this increased trade, and its trade with MERCOSUR members now accounts for about 11 percent of its total exports. The economic crisis in Argentina and Argentine-Brazilian disputes over currency valuation slowed the momentum of MERCOSUR in the late 1990s, but since then a slow recovery of MERCOSUR trade has taken place. Many believe that MERCOSUR will eventually be incorporated into a free trade area of the Americas, which has been supported by some in the United States and Latin America.

Brazil has emerged as a world leader of attempts to create international agreements on nuclear proliferation, women's rights, environmental protection, and human rights. The Cardoso administration's successful effort to confront major multinational drug companies and to produce cheap generic medicines to treat AIDS has been a model for countries in Africa and elsewhere (see "AIDS: A Case of Successful State Policy," on p. 423).

The election of Luiz Inácio Lula da Silva to the presidency in 2002 created new strains in the normally strong U.S.-Brazilian relations. The George W. Bush administration was wary of Lula's socialist ideology and irritated by his warm relations with the Venezuelan populist Hugo Chávez. However, U.S. fears proved unfounded, and Lula's administration has acted moderately on all fronts and has continued the fiscally conservative policies of his predecessor. Lula has honored all of Brazil's debt commitments and U.S.-Brazilian relations have improved considerably. In December 2002, Lula made an official state visit to the United States. The two countries worked together to address the political crisis in Venezuela and have even collaborated on Colombia despite Lula's strong opposition to U.S. policy there.

In November 2004, Brazil sent 1,200 troops to Haiti as part of a Brazilian-commanded United Nations peace-keeping mission, the biggest Brazilian military deployment since World War II. Lula's government also founded the so-called G-20, a group of developing countries that is urging the developed world to open up markets for agricultural trade. Brazil has also campaigned for a permanent seat on the United Nations Security Council.[35]

CURRENT ISSUES

Any assessment of Brazil's democratic regime must be mixed. Brazil has managed a difficult transition to democracy and has held regular, fair elections. The recent election of Luiz Inácio Lula da Silva, the first working-class Brazilian to hold the presidency, was clearly a watershed in Brazilian politics. Brazil's economy has undergone major reform and has weathered the severe economic crises of the 1970s and 1990s. Today, Brazil is a major industrial power and a major exporter. It has gained considerable prestige and influence in the world arena.

ECONOMIC INEQUALITY AND CRIME

Nevertheless, Brazilian democracy faces a litany of challenges. First among them is the inequality and poverty that persist even as Brazil has taken enormous economic strides. It remains to be seen whether Brazil's state, even under the leadership of a president like Lula, can redirect its energy in order to improve the lot of its poor majority.

A related challenge is the epidemic of crime, which Brazilians regularly name as the country's most serious problem. Brazil's murder rate has doubled since democratization, and Brazil now has one of the highest rates of homicide by guns in the world (about 40,000 Brazilians die from gun violence each year). To a considerable extent, crime is a symptom of Brazil's endemic poverty, persistent inequality, and stubborn unemployment. Much crime in Brazil can be linked to the drug trade that has infested Brazil's *favelas*. Brazil's police have generally retreated from the *favelas*, where they are outnumbered and often outgunned.

MURDER RATES, 1980 AND 1999

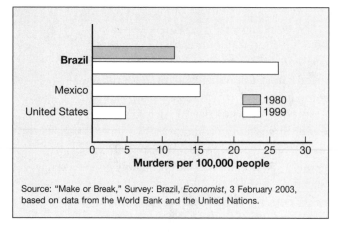

Source: "Make or Break," Survey: Brazil, *Economist*, 3 February 2003, based on data from the World Bank and the United Nations.

In July 2004, President Lula da Silva enacted a tough new gun-control law, passed by Brazil's legislature after fierce opposition from the country's powerful arms manufacturers. The law tightened rules on gun permits and created a national firearms register, with strict penalties (including a four-year prison term) for possessing an unregistered gun. The Brazilian government has begun purchasing handguns turned in by civilians in an effort to reduce gun violence, and it called a referendum in October 2005 on a proposed ban on handgun sales. The measure was rejected, however, by 63 percent of voters.

Finally, Brazilians will likely need to consider a set of institutional weaknesses that have made it difficult to address its major socioeconomic challenges. As we have seen, Brazil's electoral laws have exacerbated its weak and ineffective political parties. Weak parties have served to increase pork barrel politics and legislative gridlock. As a result, Brazilians are increasingly frustrated with how democracy works. Paradoxically, the presence of weak parties and a fragmented legislature makes it harder to reform the system.

The prospects and challenges facing Brazil can be summed up by the comments of two political scientists:

> Brazil is a country with relatively few of the regional, nationalist, ethnic, linguistic, religious divisions and conflicts that pose a threat to democracies, old and new, through most of the world. In this respect it is uniquely fortunate. But with the ninth or tenth largest economy in the world, Brazil is sixtieth or worse in international league tables of human development and is a strong contender for the title of world champion in social inequality. Can democracy be healthy, can it properly function, can it even survive in the long run, when, as in Brazil, a third of the population (some would put it much higher) live in conditions of extreme poverty, ignorance and ill health and are treated at best as second class citizens?[36]

NOTES

1. Marshall Eakin, *Brazil: The Once and Future Country* (New York: St. Martin's Press, 1998), p. 1.
2. Binka Le Breton, *Voices from the Amazon* (Hartford: Kumarian Press, 1993).
3. Eakin, *Brazil*, p. 44.
4. An excellent overview is Alfred Stepan, ed., *Authoritarian Brazil* (New Haven, CT: Yale University Press, 1973).
5. The first attempt to document the abuses under military rule was conducted secretly by the Catholic Church and first published as a book titled *Brazil, Never Again*, or *Brasil: Nunca Mais* (São Paolo: Archdiosis of São Paolo, 1985). It became an instant best seller.
6. A number of prominent political scientists have argued that presidentialism has not served Brazil's relatively young democracy well because it is less flexible and responds less well to crises. See, for example, Juan Linz, "Presidential or Parliamentary Democracy: Does It Make a Difference?" in Juan Linz and Arturo Valenzuela, eds., *The Failure of Presidential Democracy* (Baltimore: Johns Hopkins University Press), pp. 3–87.

7. In 1997, President Fernando Henrique Cardoso was able to push a constitutional amendment through the legislature that allows presidents and state governors to run for a second term. Cardoso became the first president to avail himself of that opportunity and was reelected in 1998.

8. Scott Mainwaring, "Multipartism, Robust Federalism, and Presidentialism in Brazil," in Scott Mainwaring and Matthew Soberg Shugart, eds., *Presidentialism and Democracy in Latin America* (New York: Cambridge University Press, 1997), pp. 55–109.

9. Bolivar Lamounier, "Brazil: An Assessment of the Cardoso Administration," in Jorge Dominguez and Michael Shifter, eds., *Constructing Democratic Governance in Latin America* (Baltimore: Johns Hopkins University Press, 2003), p. 281.

10. Angelina Cheibub Figueiredo and Fernando Limongi, "Congress and Decision-Making in Democratic Brazil," in Maria D'Alva Kinzo and James Dunkerley, eds., *Democratic Brazil: Economy, Polity, and Society* (London: Institute of Latin American Studies, 2003), pp. 62–83.

11. Juan Linz and Alfred Stepan, "Crises of Efficacy, Legitimacy, and Democratic State Presence: Brazil," in Juan Linz and Alfred Stepan, eds., *Problems of Democratic Transition and Consolidation* (Baltimore: Johns Hopkins University Press, 1996), pp. 166–89.

12. Fiona Macaulay, "Democratization and the Judiciary: Competing Reform Agendas," in Maria D'Alva Kinzo and James Dunkerley, eds., *Brazil since 1985: Economy, Polity, and Society* (London: Institute of Latin American Studies, 2003), pp. 93–96.

13. Predictably, Brazil's many small parties have resisted attempts at electoral reform, fearing that any such reform would likely impose a threshold and threaten their existence.

14. In 1989, the vote of one citizen of Roraima, a poor northern state, was the equivalent of 33 votes in São Paolo, Brazil's largest state. Timothy Power, "Political Institutions in Democratic Brazil," in Peter Kingstone and Timothy Power, eds., *Democratic Brazil: Actors, Institutions, and Processes* (Pittsburgh: University of Pittsburgh Press, 2000), p. 27.

15. Mainwaring, "Multipartism, Robust Federalism, and Presidentialism in Brazil."

16. David Samuels, *Ambition, Federalism, and Legislative Politics in Brazil* (Cambridge: Cambridge University Press, 2003). See p. 161, on spending levels of federal and state governments

17. Wendy Hunter, *Eroding Military Influence in Brazil: Politicians against Soldiers* (Chapel Hill, NC: University of North Carolina Press, 1997), pp. 42–71.

18. Wendy Hunter, "Assessing Civil-Military Relations in Postauthoritarian Brazil," in Kingstone and Power, *Democratic Brazil*, pp. 101–25.

19. Anthony Pereira, "An Ugly Democracy?: State Violence and the Rule of Law in Postauthoritarian Brazil," in Kingstone and Power, *Democratic Brazil*, pp. 217–35.

20. Anthony Pereira, "An Ugly Democracy?" p. 230.

21. Scott Mainwaring and Timothy Scully, "Introduction: Party Systems in Latin America," in Scott Mainwaring and Timothy Scully, eds., *Building Democratic Institutions: Parties and Party Systems in Latin America* (Stanford, CA: Stanford University Press, 1995), pp. 1–35.

22. A comparative survey in 1997 found that Brazil had the lowest level of party identification in Latin America. See J. Mark Payne, Daniel Zovatto, Fernando Cavillo-Flórez, and Andrés Allamand Zavala, *Democracies in Development: Politics and*

Reform in Latin America (Washington, DC: Inter-American Development Bank, 2002), p. 136.

23. Scott Mainwaring, *Rethinking Party Systems in the Third Wave of Democratization: The Case of Brazil* (Stanford, CA: Stanford University Press, 1999) pp. 140–45.

24. William Nylen, "The Making of a Loyal Opposition: The Worker's Party (PT) and the Consolidation of Democracy in Brazil," in Kingstone and Power, *Democratic Brazil*, pp. 126–43.

25. Timothy Power and J. Timmons Roberts, "A New Brazil?" in Kingstone and Power, *Democratic Brazil*, p. 249.

26. Data from http://www.latinobarometro.org (accessed 4 June 2006).

27. Edmund Amann, "Economic Policy and Performance in Brazil since 1985," in Kinzo and Dunkerley, *Brazil since 1985*, p. 135.

28. Timothy Power and J. Timmons Roberts, "The Changing Demographic in Context," in Kingstone and Power, *Democratic Brazil*, p. 246.

29. It also weakens trade unions and their ability to improve wages for Brazil's poorest workers.

30. Todd Benson, "Cable Pirates Thrive in Brazil," *New York Times*, 10 November 2004, p. W1.

31. United Nations, *Human Development Report 2004: Cultural Liberty in Today's Diverse World* (New York: United Nations Development Programme, 2004), http://hdr.undp.org/reports/global/2004/ (accessed 7 January 2005).

32. Power and Roberts, "The Changing Demographic Context," p. 243.

33. "Bloated, Wasteful, Rigid and Unfair," *Economist*, 4 September 2004, p. 37.

34. *Economist Factsheet, 2004*. http://www.economist.com/countries/Brazil/profile.cfm?folder=Profile-FactSheet (accessed 18 July 2005).

35. "A Giant Stirs," *Economist*, 10 June 2004.

36. Kinzo and Dunkerley, *Brazil since 1985*, p. 33.

KEY TERMS ━━━━━━━━━━━━━━━━━━━━━━━━━━━

WEB LINKS

InfoBrazil   **www.infobrazil.com** Articles on Brazilian politics and current events

IUPERJ: Programa de Pós-Graduação em Sociologia e Ciência Politica, Instituto Univeristário de Pesquisas do Rio de Janeiro
  www.iuperj.br/english/pesquisas_bancodedados.php An excellent source of online data

Latin American Network Information Center: Brazil
  lanic.utexas.edu/la/brazil An encyclopedic collection of links maintained by the University of Texas, Austin

The Workers' Party   **ww.pt.org.br**

Landless Workers Movement   **www.mst.org.br**

Links to major Brazilian periodicals   **newslink.org/sabra.html**

12 SOUTH AFRICA

Head of state and government:
President Thabo Mbeki (since June 14, 1999)

Capital: Pretoria is the seat of government;
Cape Town is the legislative capital;
Bloemfontein is the judicial capital.

Total land size: 1,219,912 sq km

Population: 44 million

GDP at PPP: .491 trillion US$

GDP per capita: $11,100

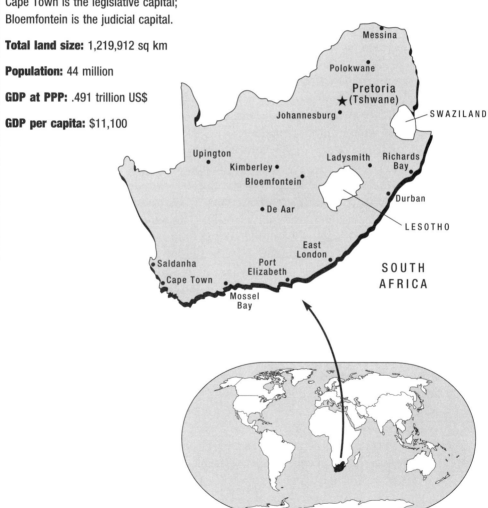

INTRODUCTION

Why Study This Case?

True to its remarkable modern history of tragedy and triumph, South Africa is a nation of paradox. The contradictions that constitute South African history and the remarkable capacity of South Africans to face and resolve them make this a fascinating case to study.

South Africa makes for a fascinating study for several other reasons as well. Like Russia, it in fact presents to students of comparative politics two cases in one. Prior to the early 1990s, South Africa's politics, society, and economy were dominated by the authoritarian racist system known as **apartheid,** or "separateness." In Afrikaans, the language spoken by the descendants of the first white settlers, the term refers to policies imposed by the ruling minority regime from 1948 to 1994 that systematically segregated races and privileged white South Africans. But with the collapse of the apartheid regime, the "new" South Africa of the past decade has been a fascinating Petri dish of unfolding multicultural democracy.

South Africa's remarkable and relatively peaceful transition from oppressive minority rule to a broad-based democracy is an even more compelling reason to study this case. Refuting the mid-1990s doomsday predictions of incendiary race wars, the overwhelming majority of South African citizens chose reconciliation over revolution, opting for ballots over bullets as a means of resolving seemingly intractable political differences. This political miracle not only stands in contrast to Africa's dismal record of failed democracies and even failed states but also offers a powerful example to other nations of the world plagued by racial, ethnic, and religious strife.

This case describes the remarkable strides South Africa has taken in the past decade. Politically, its democratically elected legislature has written and revised a constitution with broad political rights and civil liberties, and its government has convened regular nationwide elections. Socially, South Africans vanquished the world's most elaborate and overtly authoritarian racist regime and forged a common nation from its ashes. Economically, the government confounded its critics by avoiding the "easy" path of populist redistribution, instead cutting government expenditures and debt while delivering impressive gains in jobs, income, homes, and access to basic necessities for even the country's poorest citizens.

Make no mistake, however; this tale of two South Africas cannot yet boast a fairy-tale ending. The decades of political violence, social partition, and economic deprivation that victimized over 80 percent of the population have left horrible and lasting scars. Compounding the legacies of racism and authoritarianism are a host of pernicious social problems, such as rampant violent crime, brooding racial tension, and the pandemic of HIV/AIDS. As if these challenges were not enough, the remarkable success of the new government has heightened expectations for rapid economic change and social equality, and there are concerns that democracy has been successful only because the postapartheid government faces no real opposition

South Africa's leaders must now attempt to satisfy rising expectations in an atmosphere of economic stagnation. The government must balance decades of pent-up social and economic demands with the requirements of lenders and investors to maintain fiscal discipline and free markets. Without economic growth, the government will lack the very means to address South Africa's social and economic problems. The political temptation to promote affirmative action in the workplace must be weighed against the demands of the marketplace. Safeguarding the political rights of all groups in South Africa can at times necessitate overruling the will of the dominant black majority and resisting the temptation to dispense with democratic niceties.

How can the current government (or any government, for that matter) fare under such challenging circumstances? As one editorial asked, "How can a black revolutionary movement, forged by 40 years of struggle against white supremacy, transform itself into a multiracial ruling party, to run a sophisticated industrial economy? How can a new generation of leaders, without the aura of struggle, restrain the pressures towards populism and maintain a tolerant democracy when so many African governments have so noticeably failed?"[1] This case seeks to address these questions as well as the historical puzzle of why apartheid, enforced by such a small minority, managed to persist so successfully for so long and how its collapse and replacement came about under relatively peaceful circumstances.

Despite its unique history and political experience, South Africa faces many of the same issues and dilemmas as other developing countries. These include coping with the legacies of colonialism and racism, dealing with the policy trade-offs between freedom and equality, and managing the social and economic consequences of crime, poverty, and disease. The case of South Africa offers insights into these fundamental issues.

Major Geographic and Demographic Features

Historically, South Africa has been a harsh and isolated region. Ocean currents and the dearth of natural harbors impeded early European settlement of its coastline. Much of western South Africa (with the notable exception of the area around Cape Town) remains drought stricken and unsuitable for agriculture. South Africa's eastern coast and interior are subtropical and more suitable to agriculture, though the quality of the soil is generally poor. South Africa has no navigable waterways, a fact that until modern times made transportation and communication over the vast region very difficult. These factors limited the growth of a large population in pre-colonial South Africa.

Today, South Africa has about 44 million inhabitants. Unlike much of the rest of Africa, South Africa has seen its birth rates decline dramatically over the past twenty-five years, though considerable population growth is still created by emigration from South Africa's impoverished neighbors. Due to the experience of apartheid, it is common to think of South Africa's population as being neatly divided between blacks and whites. This gross simplification obscures a much more heterogeneous ethnic makeup. Three quarters of South Africans are black, but the ethnic composition of the black population is extremely diverse. About one quarter of black South Africans are Zulus, another one fifth are Xhosa (the ethnic group of former president **Nelson Mandela**), and about 18 percent are Sotho. The Tswana and Tsonga (and to a lesser extent the Venda and Ndebele) groups also have a significant presence in South Africans. Each of these ethnic groups has a different language and is concentrated in a different area. For example, Xhosas predominate in the western part of the country and in Cape Town and Port Elizabeth. Zulus are the dominant group in Durban.

Whites constitute about 10 percent of the population, and that population is also divided ethnically. Over half are **Afrikaners,** descendants of the Dutch, French, and German colonists who arrived in the seventeenth century and developed their own language (Afrikaans) and cultural traditions. Another 40 percent of South Africa's white population are descendants of English settlers who arrived in the eighteenth century. Even today these "English whites" favor English over Afrikaans and view themselves as somewhat distinct. The remaining South African whites are descendants of Portuguese migrants.

South Africans of mixed race account for 9 percent of the population. This group, largely concentrated in the Western Cape Province and KwaZulu-Natal, is widely referred to as **coloured.** The majority of coloured South Africans speak Afrikaans as their first language.

This diversity of the people is also shaped by urbanization. About half of South Africans (including most whites, Asians, and coloured people) live in an urban setting. South Africa has five cities with over 1 million inhabitants: Cape Town (2.8 million), Johannesburg (2.2 million), Durban (1.3 million), Pretoria (1.3 million), and Port Elizabeth (1.1 million). Soweto, a large black township outside Johannesburg, has between 600,000 and 2 million inhabitants.

South Africa is truly a complex, polyglot nation. The 1994 constitution recognizes eleven languages, nine of which (Ndebele, Northern Sotho, Sotho, Tsonga, Tswana, Venda, Swazi, Xhosa, and Zulu) are spoken exclusively by blacks, and some of which are very closely related to one another. One characteristic of quite a few of the languages is the distinct clicking sound that eludes non-native speakers. Quite a few blacks speak more than one African language. If there is a common language among South Africans, it is English. Virtually all whites, Asians, educated blacks, and coloureds can speak at least some English. Almost all Afrikaners are bilingual in Afrikaans and English, and many South Africans of English descent also speak some Afrikaans.

But language has often bitterly divided the South African people. Blacks long resisted the imposition of Afrikaans by Afrikaners, and the 1976 Soweto Uprising was ignited by the Afrikaner authorities' attempt to make Afrikaans the official language of instruction in all schools. Coloured South Africans, on the other hand, have recently fought to preserve the role of Afrikaans in the schools.

South Africa's neighbors have been an important focal point for many South Africans. As illustrated in the map of the region, South Africa is bordered to the north by Zimbabwe (formerly Rhodesia). Zimbabwe's transition to majority black rule, in 1980, was an inspiration to black South Africans. Botswana, also to the north, has been one of the most economically successful African nations. On its eastern border, Mozambique and Swaziland are extremely poor. Throughout much of the twentieth century, apartheid leaders frequently pointed to these neighbors (as well as much of the rest of Africa) as proof that blacks were incapable of governing themselves. Sparsely populated Namibia, a former German colony and later a United Nations protectorate, was long dominated by apartheid South Africa.

Historical Development of the State

The telling of history often reflects the perspective of those in power, so it is not surprising that South Africa's history has usually been told from the perspective of whites. Afrikaners often contend that southern Africa was largely uninhabited when their Dutch ancestors arrived at the Cape of Good Hope in 1652. The truth is far more complex. Hunters and herders populated South Africa when the Dutch arrived in the mid-seventeenth century. The Dutch East India Company officials who first established a fort in what is today Cape Town encountered tribes of Khoisans, whom they soon enslaved. When these native Africans died from disease and slavery, the Dutch settlers imported slaves, mostly from Southeast Asia.[2]

In the interior of South Africa, a variety of Bantu-speaking tribes were ending their centuries-long migration southward from central Africa,

TIME LINE OF POLITICAL DEVELOPMENT	
Year	**Event**
1652	Arrival of the Dutch at the Cape of Good Hope
1795	Cape Town captured from the Dutch by the British
1880–81; 1899–1902	Boer Wars fought between the Afrikaners and the British
1910	Formation of the Union of South Africa, dominated by English-speaking South Africans
1948	Election of Afrikaner National Party and beginning of apartheid
1960	Banning of African National Congress (ANC)
1964	Nelson Mandela imprisoned
1990	Mandela released from prison
1990–93	Transition to democracy as the result of negotiations between Mandela and President F. W. de Klerk
1994	After historic multiracial elections, ANC majority government established under Nelson Mandela
1996	Democratic constitution approved
1999	Legislative elections won by ANC; Thabo Mbeki named president

integrating with hunters and herders who had long inhabited the region. Among the largest of these tribes were the Zulu, the Sotho, and the Swazi kingdoms.

DUTCH RULE

While most of the colonial "scramble for Africa" took place in the nineteenth century, European domination of South Africa began almost two centuries earlier. Cape Town was initially settled by the Dutch East India Company to resupply ships heading to and from Dutch colonies in Indonesia. The early Dutch settlers, known as **Boers** (Afrikaans for "farmer"), quickly seized the fertile land of the Cape of Good Hope. The European residents of the Cape developed their own culture, based in their conservative Protestant **Dutch Reformed Church** and their unique language. The small and isolated Cape Colony was fairly prosperous until it was seized by the British Empire in 1795. The Dutch ceded formal control of the region to the British in 1814.

BOER MIGRATION

As Britain quickly began to integrate this new colony into its burgeoning empire, the arrival of waves of British settlers was seen as a threat to Boer society. Bristling under British rule, many Cape Colony Boers (and their slaves) undertook a migration into the interior of southern Africa that would later gain the status of heroic myth. During the **Great Trek** of 1835, the *voortrekkers* (Afrikaans for "pioneers") drove their wagons northeast to regain their autonomy and preserve their way of life. They met strong initial resistance from the Xhosa and other Bantu kingdoms, though whites had important technological advantages in these conflicts and were able to exploit the numerous divisions among the indigenous tribes.

A number of bloody battles ensued, most famously the 1838 Battle of Blood River between Zulu tribesmen and Afrikaners. During that conflict, a group of heavily outnumbered Afrikaners defeated the Zulus, with legend claiming that no whites were killed. Afrikaners still consider the Blood River anniversary an important religious holiday and celebrate it each year on December 16. By the early 1840s, Afrikaners were concentrated in the current provinces of Free State (formerly Orange Free State), North West, Gauteng (formerly Pretoria-Witwatersrand-Vereeniging), and Limpopo (formerly the Northern Transvaal).

The exhausting exodus to escape British domination, along with the bitter fighting between Boers and blacks, was in the short term a Boer success. The Boers created two states, known as the Boer republics, in which slavery, strict segregation of races, the Afrikaans language, and the Dutch Reformed Church were protected by law.

Initially the British grudgingly tolerated the interior Boer republics. However, the discovery of massive deposits of diamonds (in 1870) and gold (in 1886) changed their opinion. English-speakers flooded into the interior, and the city of Johannesburg quickly became an English-speaking enclave in the Boer-controlled Transvaal. Transvaal president Paul Kruger attempted to limit the influence of the English by denying them the vote. In 1895, diamond magnate Cecil Rhodes used the pretense of Boer discrimination against English settlers and the presence of slavery in the Boer republics to incite a rebellion among the English. President Kruger declared war on England in 1899.

THE SECOND BOER WAR

Though outnumbered five to one, the Boers fought tenaciously to defend their independence during the Second **Boer War.** To defeat the well-armed and disciplined Afrikaners, the British pioneered the use of concentration camps, in which as many as 20,000 Afrikaners and 15,000 blacks perished. By 1902, the Boers had been defeated, and the Boer republics had become self-governing British colonies. In exchange for signing a peace treaty, the Boers were promised full political rights, protections for their language and culture, and the ability to deny blacks the vote in the former Boer republics. In 1910 these regulations were formalized as the **Union of South Africa.**[3]

THE RENAISSANCE OF AFRIKANER POWER

English and Afrikaners worked together to create a single British colony, and the first prime minister of the Union of South Africa was a former Afrikaner military leader. The Native Land Act of 1913 prevented blacks from owning land except in designated "reserves" (less than 10 percent of the total land of South Africa). Discrimination against blacks continued in the former Boer republics. Only in the largely English Cape Colony were coloureds and a small number of blacks allowed to vote. Nowhere in South Africa were minority rights protected, and racial discrimination was the rule even in English-governed areas.

The first elections in the united country brought to power the South African Party (SAP), which included both English speakers and Afrikaners. But many Afrikaners, especially those in the former Boer republics, continued to deeply resent the English. The Afrikaners enjoyed full political rights, but the English controlled most of the country's wealth, especially its mineral profits and budding industry.

As has so often been the case throughout their history, the Afrikaners resisted this marginalization, but this time they did so within the political system. The formation of the **National Party (NP)** in 1914 was the most important step in their attempt to organize and mobilize the Afrikaner population. The NP demanded that Afrikaans be recognized alongside English and wanted South Africa to secede from the British Empire. In the mid-1930s, party leader Daniel Malan articulated the policies of white supremacy that later became the hallmark of apartheid. At the same time, Malan called for Afrikaner control of the state so that wealth held by the English could be redistributed to Afrikaners. Malan's goals appealed to the mass of poor white Afrikaner workers, who felt threatened by the better-off English as well as by the growing number of even poorer black workers (who vied for their jobs). The NP realized that if Afrikaners could be unified, they could not be denied power. In 1948, the NP was elected to office.

THE APARTHEID ERA

What distinguishes the apartheid era are the NP's two goals: consolidating Afrikaner power and eliminating all vestiges of black participation in South African politics. To a considerable degree, apartheid simply codified and intensified the racial segregation that existed in the mid-twentieth century. During an era when racial discrimination was being challenged in virtually every other country, Afrikaner leaders sought to construct elaborate legal justifications for it.

HENDRIK VERWOERD AND THE "LOGIC" OF WHITE RULE

The leading ideologue and architect of apartheid was Hendrik Verwoerd, a professor at South Africa's leading Afrikaner university and prime minister from 1958 to 1966. Verwoerd argued that the population of South Africa contained four distinct "racial groups" (white, African, coloured, and Indian) and that whites, as the most "civilized" racial group, should have absolute control over the state. Verwoerd and the advocates of apartheid further argued that Africans belonged to ten distinct nations, whereas the other racial groups belonged to only one nation each. By this logic, whites were the largest nation in South Africa and were therefore justified in dominating the state.

The Population Registration Act of 1950 divided South Africa into Verwoerd's four racial categories and placed every South African into one of those categories. Once Africans were divided into races, the apartheid architects argued that blacks (about three quarters of the population) were not citizens of South Africa. According to the **Group Areas Act** of 1950, blacks were deemed to be citizens of ten remote "tribal homelands" (dubbed **Bantustans**), whose boundaries and leaders were decreed by the government. The Bantustans, somewhat akin to American Indian reservations, constituted only around 13 percent of South Africa's territory and were usually made up of noncontiguous parcels of infertile land separated by white-owned farms. The NP chose black leaders (often tribal chiefs) loyal to the party goals to head the Bantustan governments. All blacks in South Africa were in effect "guests" and did not enjoy any of the rights of citizenship. The 1971 Bantu Homelands Citizenship Act allowed the government to grant "independence" to any Bantustan, and though government propagandists defended the measure as an act of "decolonization," in reality it had little impact. Over the next decade, many Bantustans became "independent," though no foreign government would recognize them as sovereign countries.

Racial segregation in the rest of South Africa went even further. Members of each of the four racial groups were required to reside in areas determined by the government. The vast majority of blacks who lived and worked in white areas were required to carry internal visas at all times. Each year, failure to carry such a pass resulted in hundreds of thousands of deportations to a "homeland" that, more often than not, the deportee had never before set foot in. The apartheid authorities created new racial categories and designed separate residential areas for South Africans of Asian descent, or of mixed race, often forcibly relocating them. In the largest cities, entire neighborhoods of nonwhites were uprooted and moved to new racially segregated townships, such as Soweto (outside Johannesburg). Other infamous laws reinforced racial segregation. The Prohibition of Mixed Marriages Act (1950) banned relations across racial lines, and the Reservation of Separate Amenities Act (1953) provided the legal basis for segregating places as diverse as beaches and restrooms.[4]

The apartheid system retained many of the trappings of a parliamentary democracy. Apartheid South Africa had regular elections, a fairly vigorous press, and a seemingly independent judiciary. However, the vast majority of South Africans were disenfranchised and utterly powerless. The regime tolerated mild opposition on some issues but ruthlessly quashed individuals and groups that actively opposed apartheid itself.

Indeed, the apartheid regime met resistance from its very inception. The most important organization resisting racial discrimination was the **African National Congress (ANC).** Founded in 1912 as the South African Native National Congress and renamed in 1923, it was a largely black organization that sought the extension of suffrage to blacks. The ANC was initially nonviolent and politically moderate in its calls for multiracial democracy. Under the leadership of Nelson Mandela, it led a series of nonviolent civil disobedience campaigns against apartheid laws.[5]

Fierce repression of this protest by the apartheid regime had several consequences. First, some blacks tiring of the nonviolent, gradualist approach of the ANC, created more radical organizations, such as the Pan African Congress (PAC), founded in 1959. Second, the apartheid leaders, alarmed by the growing resistance, banned the ANC and the PAC. Third, the repression (especially the government slaughter of protesters during the Sharpeville Massacre of 1960) persuaded ANC leaders to initiate military action against the apartheid regime. The government countered by arresting Mandela and other top ANC leaders in 1963 and sentencing them to life in prison. The ongoing repression led to the incarceration and murder of thousands of South Africans who actively resisted apartheid.

Although not all whites supported the apartheid system, the NP skillfully retained the majority's allegiance. For Afrikaners, the NP dramatically improved their political and economic status, making them dependent on the perpetuation of the status quo. The NP played on English-speaking whites' fears of black rule. Moderate white critics of apartheid were mostly tolerated, as they generally held little sway among the white population.

Though the NP subdued most domestic resistance to apartheid, the system faced growing hostility from abroad. The end of colonialism created independent African states that supported the ANC, and the United Nations condemned apartheid as early as 1952 and imposed an arms embargo on South Africa in 1977. Nevertheless, in the context of the cold war, South Africa was able to gain support (from the United States in particular) by portraying its fight against the ANC as a struggle against communism. Moreover, the world's major capitalist powers had lucrative investments in South Africa and were ambivalent about promoting black rule.

THE TRANSITION TO DEMOCRACY

There was nothing inevitable about South Africa's transition from apartheid to majority rule. Five categories of factors need to be considered to explain the momentous political shift that culminated in South Africa's first free elections in 1994.

1. *Demographic pressure and growing unrest:* The growth of opposition to apartheid had at its core a demographic component. The proportion of whites in the population had dropped from a high of 21 percent in 1936 to only 10 percent in 1999. Not only was the black population growing more quickly, but it was increasingly concentrated in urban areas, which were more subject to political mobilization. Most of these newly urban blacks lived in squalid conditions in South Africa's townships, the population of which doubled between 1950 and 1980. These demographic trends meant that despite largely successful efforts to deny blacks political power, their economic power and significance were rapidly expanding.

As a result of these changes, opposition to apartheid during the 1980s assumed dimensions previously unknown in South Africa. The creation of the **United Democratic Front (UDF)** in 1983 effectively united trade unions and the major black and white apartheid opposition groups. The number of protests, strikes, boycotts, and slowdowns grew, requiring ever-greater levels of repression by the apartheid regime. In July 1985, the government imposed a virtually permanent state of emergency, leading to massive arrests of suspected opposition members. In 1988, the government banned the UDF and the largest trade union confederation.

2. *Economic decline:* By the 1980s, the deficiencies in the apartheid economic model had become increasingly apparent. During this decade, South Africa's economy was among the most stagnant in the developing world, growing at an average rate of only about 1 percent. The apartheid economic system had clearly raised the standard of living for South Africa's whites, especially Afrikaners, but it had also led to serious distortions that were by now beginning to take a toll.

The apartheid state, with its convoluted and overlapping race-based institutions and its subsidies to the entirely dependent black "homelands," was costly and inefficient. The mercantilist apartheid policies of self-sufficiency and protectionism led to the creation of industries and services that were not competitive with those of other developing countries. The system of racial preferences and job protection that was a cornerstone of apartheid clearly hindered economic development and economic efficiency.

3. *Internal reforms:* By the mid-1970s, even leading Afrikaner politicians were convinced that apartheid was an anachronistic system that needed reform if it was to survive. The reforms that followed paved the way for a future transition to democracy. Prime Minister P. W. Botha, who took power in 1978, promised to dismantle apartheid and enacted some minor reforms. However, Botha was unwilling to push the reforms very far. The next leader, President **F. W. de Klerk** (1989–94), repealed the Reservation of Separate Amenities Act, the Group Areas Act, and the Population Registration Act. De Klerk legalized black political parties, including the ANC and the PAC, and freed their leaders. The crisis of apartheid served to split the traditionally unified Afrikaner leadership, opening the window to reform.

4. *The changing international context:* During the 1980s, many countries imposed embargoes on South Africa, limiting trade and foreign investment, though powerful nations like the United States and the United Kingdom continued to trade with the regime into the 1990s. Of greater importance was the winding down of the cold war in the 1980s. On the one hand, it deprived the South African regime of a key source of international legitimacy: the decline of communism weakened its claim that it was facing a communist insurgency. On the other hand, the collapse of the Soviet Union and the Soviet bloc weakened the ANC sectors that promoted Communist revolution in South Africa.

5. *Skilled leadership:* Finally, South Africa's transition would likely not have occurred (or at the very least would not have been as peaceful or successful) had skilled leaders not managed the transition. F. W. de Klerk's role in forcing Prime Minister Botha's resignation and his courageous decisions to free Mandela and legalize the ANC were essential to the transition. De Klerk used his unblemished credentials as a National Party stalwart to convince NP die-hards to accept the transition. He was able to convince most Afrikaners that their interests would be safeguarded during and after the transition.[6]

Likewise, Nelson Mandela risked a great deal by negotiating the terms of the transition with the NP government. Mandela and the ANC leadership agreed to power sharing and numerous guarantees in order to assuage white fears and were able to restrain radicalized blacks who wanted quick redress for decades of abuse. Mandela's knowledge of Afrikaner language and culture (gained through decades of study in prison) undoubtedly helped him negotiate with his Afrikaner opposition. His ability to eschew bitterness and revenge after his twenty-seven-year prison term impressed even his strongest opponents. Still, the negotiations between the black leadership and the NP were protracted and difficult. De Klerk and Mandela faced serious opposition from radical sectors of their own camps. Nevertheless, an interim constitution was approved in 1993, paving the way for democratic elections and majority rule in 1994. In recognition of their important role in the South African transition, de Klerk and Mandela were awarded the 1993 Nobel Peace Prize.

NELSON MANDELA: DEMOCRATIC SOUTH AFRICA'S FOUNDING FATHER

The remarkable story of Nelson Mandela parallels the turbulent history of modern South Africa. Mandela's father was a Xhosa-speaking tribal chief in the Eastern Cape Province. Mandela was expelled from the University College of Fort Hare for demonstrating against racism but went on to earn a law degree and was one of the first blacks to practice law in South Africa. He became deeply involved in the ANC and was appointed one of its four deputy presidents in 1952.

Mandela helped move the ANC in a more radical direction after NP governments began construction of the apartheid regime in 1948. The ANC was banned in 1960 after it led nationwide protests against apartheid. In response to the Sharpeville Massacre of that same year (in which police massacred sixty-nine unarmed protesters), the ANC abandoned its strategy of nonviolent protest, and Mandela was named its first military commander. Mandela was sentenced to life in prison in 1964 and was held with other ANC leaders on Robben Island. From his cell, he was able to direct the anti-apartheid struggle, learn Afrikaans, and write his autobiography.

When Mandela was released in February 1990, he immediately assumed the role of representative of the black majority in the negotiations for a democratic transition. After Mandela received the Nobel Peace Prize in 1993, his ANC won a landslide victory in the country's first multiracial elections, and Mandela became South Africa's first black president. While in office, Mandela did much to heal the racial divide, taking special pains to respect the culture of the Afrikaners. His decision to step down in 1997 and make way for a younger generation of ANC leaders was another sign of Mandela's commitment to democracy.

POLITICAL REGIME

Political Institutions

During the apartheid regime, South Africa enjoyed a set of democratic institutions, but these applied only to the white population. Nonwhites had much more limited political rights or none whatsoever. As a result, few considered the country to be a true democracy. After the political transition in 1994, however, political rights were extended to the population as a whole, regardless of race. South Africa is now a democracy with broad political rights and civil liberties commensurate with those found in advanced democracies. Ironically, South Africa's long tradition of democratic institutions, albeit highly restrictive ones, helped smooth the transition to multiracial democracy. The architects of the 1994 transition did not need to create an entirely new democratic system from scratch but merely reformed existing democratic institutions and extended them to the entire population.

ESSENTIAL POLITICAL FEATURES

- Legislative-executive system: prime ministerial
- Legislature: Parliament
- Lower house: National Assembly
- Upper house: National Council of Provinces
- Unitary or federal division of power: unitary
- Main geographic subunits: provinces
- Electoral system for lower house: proportional representation
- Chief judicial body: Constitutional Court

THE CONSTITUTION

The new democratic regime is fundamentally enshrined in the South African constitution, approved in 1996. This document reflects the delicate nature of the country's transition to democracy, in which new democratic rights had to be provided to the disenfranchised black majority while those of the white minority had to be protected.

The constitution attempts to balance majority and minority concerns carefully, affirming the basic values of human rights regardless of "race, gender, sex, pregnancy, religion, conscience, belief, culture, language and birth," a list far more detailed than that of most democratic constitutions. Eleven official languages are recognized. The constitution also upholds citizens' rights to housing, health care, food, water, social security, and even a healthy environment. Reacting to decades of apartheid authoritarianism, the constitution includes unusually detailed provisions limiting the powers of the state to arrest, detain, and prosecute individuals. Finally, it enshrines the principle of affirmative action, stating that in order to achieve greater equality, laws and other measures can be used to promote or advance individuals who have been discriminated against.

The constitution also firmly protects the rights of property, however, an element that ensured the white population that their property would not be seized by a black-dominated government. Perhaps most important, the constitution defines itself as the supreme law of the land: parliament must act within its confines, and the new Constitutional Court can strike down unconstitutional behavior. This is a departure from the past, when the parliament and the government reigned supreme and could change and reinterpret laws as they saw fit, with no higher legal power to restrain them.

The Branches of Government

The South African government is based on British institutions, with some variations. For most of the apartheid period, South Africa had a bicameral parliament and a prime minister, with a ceremonial president as head of state. Since 1994, the South African system has been transformed into one similar to that seen in many other democracies, with a bicameral parliament and a Constitutional Court. Interestingly, as a result of historic compromises between Afrikaner and English-speaking whites, South Africa has three capitals. The seat of government is located in Pretoria, the traditional heart of Afrikaner power and the center of the former Boer republics. Cape Town, where English influence was strongest, is the legislative capital. South Africa's judicial capital is located in Bloemfontein.

THE PRESIDENCY AND THE CABINET

The chief executive of South Africa is the president. This title is rather confusing, however, given that, like a typical prime minister, the president is chosen from the National Assembly, the lower house of the legislature, by its members and can be removed by a vote of no confidence. Yet, there is no division between the head of state and the head of government, as is found in most parliamentary systems, so the South African president serves in both capacities. Like most prime ministers, the president chooses a cabinet of ministers, signs or vetoes legislation presented by the National Assembly, and can refer legislation to the Constitutional Court as necessary. The president may also call national referenda, dissolve the National Assembly, and (in some situations) call new elections. If the president wishes to dissolve the National Assembly, a majority of the lower house must support the dissolution and three years must have passed since it was first elected. The president is unable to call the kinds of snap elections seen in other parliamentary systems.

Where the presidency does diverge from typical prime-ministerial offices it serves to strengthen the institution. As head of state and head of government, the president can not only exert authority over the cabinet and government policy (like a typical head of government), but can also speak on behalf of the nation and represent the country on the world stage (as a head of state does). Moreover, South African presidents can be removed by the legislature, but only with great difficulty. A vote of no confidence requires the support of two thirds of the members of the National Assembly and can be taken only on the grounds of a substantial violation of the law or constitution, serious misconduct, or an inability to perform the functions of the office—circumstances akin to an impeachment. Theoretically, the National Assembly cannot simply dismiss the president because it opposes a given policy. This provision remains untested, however, as there have been only two presidents since the 1994 transition, and a vote of no confidence has not yet been attempted. To date, the overwhelming power of the ANC in the National Assembly, combined with the prestige of Nelson Mandela as the first president, has given the office a great deal of authority.

THE LEGISLATURE

South Africa has a bicameral parliament. The lower and more powerful of its two houses, the National Assembly, currently has 400 members. Members

FILLING BIG SHOES: THABO MBEKI

South Africa's current president, **Thabo Mbeki,** was born in 1942 in southeastern South Africa. He is the son of legendary African National Congress (ANC) leader Govan Mbeki, a close colleague of Nelson Mandela. The younger Mbeki became an ANC activist in high school and earned a degree in economics through a correspondence program with the University of London. After he worked for two years in the ANC underground (1960–62), the party sent Mbeki to the United Kingdom, where he earned a graduate degree in economics at the University of Sussex. After several years of Soviet military training, Mbeki moved to Zambia and became the youngest member of the ANC National Executive Committee.

After the ANC was legalized in 1990, Mbeki returned home to participate in the negotiations for the transition to democracy, and became first deputy president after the 1994 elections. Nelson Mandela's chosen successor, Mbeki became ANC president in late 1997 and president of South Africa after the ANC's electoral victory in 1999. He has had difficulty filling the shoes of the legendary Mandela and is widely perceived as more intellectual and aloof. His controversial stance on HIV/AIDS, his support for the growing authoritarianism of neighboring Zimbabwe, and his seeming intolerance of criticism have made him a more controversial leader than Mandela was.

serve for five-year terms, and are charged with electing and removing the president, preparing and passing legislation, and approving the national budget. As in Britain, the lower house has a weekly "question time," when members can question the cabinet and the president. Question time can become a heated affair, with members of the opposition parties grilling the cabinet and casting aspersions on one another. Given the racial divisions in the country, however, such debate is also limited (for example, when one white member of parliament commented that a black member of the cabinet lacked intelligence, he was rebuked for using racial stereotypes).

The upper house is the National Council of Provinces. Its ninety members are indirectly elected by the nine provincial legislatures and include the premier of each province. Each province, regardless of its size or population, sends ten delegates. The power of the National Council depends on the type of legislation under consideration. When the National Assembly is dealing with national policy (such as foreign affairs or defense), the National Council has relatively little influence. When proposed legislation affects the provinces, however, the National Council can amend or reject measures, forcing the two houses to form a mediation committee to hammer out a compromise. Ultimately, the National Assembly can override the upper house with a two-thirds vote. In short, the National Council exists to ensure that local interests are heard at the national level, which is especially important when the provinces are distinguished by ethnicity, language, and culture.

THE JUDICIAL SYSTEM

Another important component of the transition to democratic multiracial rule in South Africa is the Constitutional Court. This body hears cases regarding the constitutionality of legislation on the separation of powers among the branches of government. Its eleven members serve twelve-year terms and are appointed by the president on the basis of the recommendations of a judicial commission. The commission is made up of government and nongovernment appointees who evaluate candidates' qualifications and take racial and gender diversity into account. To date, the court has shown a tendency for activism; in 1997, for example, it struck down the country's death penalty despite public sentiment in favor of capital punishment, and in 2002 it ruled that the government was obligated to provide treatment for persons with AIDS.[7]

The Electoral System

The current electoral rules in South Africa mark a significant departure from the past. Under apartheid, the country used the British single-member district, or plurality, system. As part of the transition to democracy, South Africa had to decide what election method would best represent the needs of a diverse public and help consolidate democratic legitimacy by creating an inclusive system. The result was the creation of an electoral system based on proportional representation (PR). Voters now cast their votes not for individual candidates but for a party, which is designated on the ballot by name, electoral symbol, and the picture of the head of the party (to ensure that illiterate voters are not excluded). The number of seats a party wins is divided proportionally to reflect the percentage of the total vote they received. At elections, voters are given two ballots: one for the national legislature and one for their provincial legislature.

Overall, the electoral system in South Africa has successfully created an inclusive political atmosphere and has averted conflict and violence.[8] However, some critics have argued that the use of PR has created a disconnect between the National Assembly and the citizens. Because members of parliament are tied to their party instead of their constituency, they are not accountable to local communities. Political parties can stifle internal dissent and limit the independence of legislators by threatening to remove them from the party electoral list if they stray too far from the party's wishes. Critics inside South Africa have suggested that the country consider adopting a mixed electoral system, in which some percentage of the seats are filled by plurality while the remaining are filled by PR. This would give voters a local representative with whom they could identify, as well as the ability to cast their vote for a particular party. After some discussion on electoral reform earlier in the decade, however, such suggestions have faded and the current system has become institutionalized.

Local Government

Below the national level, South Africa is divided into nine provinces, each with its own elected assembly. Members are elected for a term of five years (with elections for the national and provincial legislatures occurring simultaneously) and in turn elect a premier to serve as the province's chief executive. The provincial assemblies have their own constitutions, pass legislation, and send delegates to the National Council of Provinces.

It is difficult to call South Africa a federal state, however, and the concept itself is a politically charged issue. During the transition to democracy, the ANC in particular looked upon federalism with a great deal of suspicion. At that time, the National Party (NP) architects of apartheid, favored federalism as a way to limit the ANC's power, while some Afrikaners in fact hoped that a federal right to self-determination could pave the way for outright secession. The Zulu-based Inkatha Freedom Party also called for self-determination— and an independent Zulu state. The 1996 constitution reflects these concerns by supporting regional and ethnic diversity. Still, the constitution gives the central government the ability to overturn local legislation relatively easily, and any powers not delimited by the constitution reside with the central, not the local, government. Provinces also have limited power to levy taxes, giving them little financial autonomy.

POLITICAL CONFLICT AND COMPETITION

The Party System and Elections

During apartheid, few political parties existed and the National Party (NP) dominated politics from 1948 until 1994. The main opposition was the weak Progressive Federal Party, which opposed apartheid laws and favored multiracial democracy within a federal framework. The enfranchisement of the nonwhite population has dramatically changed the political spectrum, though as in the past it remains dominated by one major party. National elections are held at least every five years, and those differences that do exist

Average Voter Turnout, 1945–2000

Country (number of elections)	Eligible Voters Voting (%)
South Africa (1)	**85.5**
United Kingdom (15)	74.9
Japan (21)	69.0
Iran (2)	67.6
France (15)	67.3
India (12)	60.7
Russia (2)	55.0
United States (26)	48.3
Mexico (18)	48.1
Brazil (13)	47.9
Nigeria (3)	47.6
China	NA

Source: "Turnout in the World: Country by Country Performance," International Institute for Democracy and Electoral Assistance

http://www.idea.int/vt/survey/voter_turnout_pop2.cfm (accessed 27 January 2006).

between the parties are driven as much by race and ethnicity as they are by ideology.

Currently the dominant party, the African National Congress (ANC) led the struggle against white rule starting in 1912. During the ANC's long period underground and in exile, it developed an ideology strongly influenced by Marxism, favoring the nationalization of land and industry. Economic equality was seen as a necessary mechanism in overcoming racial discrimination. The ANC cultivated relations with Communist countries like the Soviet Union and China and at home formed an alliance with the much smaller South African Communist Party (which still operates within the framework of the ANC). Many white South Africans, including some opponents of apartheid, were troubled by the ANC's demands for radical political and economic change. Since winning power in 1994, however, the ANC has stood for racial and gender equality and a strong state role in the expansion of economic opportunities for nonwhites, but it has also embraced property rights and rejected any calls to seize land or businesses. The ANC thus walks a fine line, preserving the status and power of the white minority while attempting to provide jobs, education and social services to the much poorer black majority. As such, its ideology is unclear, encompassing a mixture of social democratic and liberal views, a lingering sense of militancy, and an emphasis on unity. The ANC has consistently increased its share of the vote in each election since 1994.

The overwhelming preponderance of ANC power raises concerns. Some observers fear that the party has so easily embraced democracy after its long struggle in part because the party has done so well. Were the ANC to face losing power, it might not look upon the democratic process so favorably. These concerns have been heightened in particular by Thabo Mbeki's tenure in office, as his rhetoric and that of the ANC have grown increasingly intolerant of those who challenge it.

The overwhelming presence of the ANC in parliament dwarfs the opposition parties. Among them is the **Democratic Alliance (DA),** successor to the old Progressive Federal Party. The DA is primarily liberal, favoring a small state, individual freedoms, privatization of state-run firms, and greater devolution of power to local governments. Public support for the DA has grown since the 1994 elections, but its primary base of support remains the white and mixed-race population. In order to become a viable challenger to the ANC, it will have to broaden this base.

The third political group in South Africa is the **Inkatha Freedom Party (IFP),** which has played an ambiguous role in apartheid and post-apartheid politics. The IFP, founded in 1975 by Zulu chief Mangosuthu Buthelezi, challenged apartheid institutions but also participated in local government in the KwaZulu "homeland," one of the remote areas created to remove blacks from desirable areas and deprive them of basic citizenship. During the 1980s, animosity grew between the IFP and the ANC: the ANC saw the IFP as having been co-opted by the government, while the IFP viewed the ANC as dominated by ethnic Xhosas who did not represent Zulu interests. The animosity soon erupted into violence, which was abetted by the apartheid regime as a way to weaken both sides. After the first democratic elections, however, the ANC was careful to bring members of the IFP into the government cabinet, helping to diffuse much of the tension between the two parties. The IFP was embarrassed in 2004, however, having failed to do well even in the elections for KwaZulu's provincial legislature, and the party is no longer a part of the government. Fears that the IFP could represent a threat to the stability of the country have disappeared.

Aside from those three main parties, few actors show much influence in South African politics. The National Party, which created apartheid and ran the country for over four decades, tried unsuccessfully to recast itself as a multiracial party and renamed itself the New National Party (NNP). Even more bizarre, the NNP threw its support behind the ANC, claiming that this action would allow it to play a constructive role in policy making rather than simply sitting on the sidelines as an opposition party. Less charitable observers

South African National Assembly Elections, 1999 and 2004

Party	1999		2004	
	% of Vote	Seats Won	% of Vote	Seats Won
African National Congress	66	266	70	279
Democratic Alliance	10	38	12	50
Inkatha Freedom Party	9	34	7	28
New National Party	7	28	2	7
Others	8	34	9	36
Total	100	400	100	400

have viewed it as a purely tactical move to try to shore up its power in the face of declining public support. The gamble did not pay off in the 2004 elections, however. In April 2005, the NNP disbanded. The DA hopes to capture many of its former supporters in the next election.

Civil Society

As we have discussed, the exclusionary nature of the apartheid regime was built upon the policy of destroying black opposition, which it carried out by weakening any form of organized resistance. Black civil society was crushed to an extent not seen elsewhere in colonial Africa, with traditional institutions undermined, co-opted and repressed wherever possible. Yet even with such pressure, anti-apartheid nongovernmental organizations (NGOs) continued to form and were vital in organizing the resistance that would help bring about democracy.

In the aftermath of apartheid, however, civil society in South Africa has remained weak, for a number of reasons. One major problem is simply the legacy of the past: having had civil society effectively stifled for decades, South Africans have found it hard to create civic values. This is not unusual; with the fall of highly repressive regimes (like the Soviet Union), new democracies often experience a civil vacuum, in which the public is unfamiliar with and mistrustful of civic participation. A second problem lies with the ANC itself. During the transition period, the ANC relied heavily on a variety of NGOs to build public support. After 1994, the ANC co-opted many of these formerly autonomous groups, bringing them under its direction. This, too, has stunted the emergence of an independent civil society.

With the exception of political protest, public activism remains low in South Africa. A 2000 survey of seven southern African countries showed that the South Africans' civic and political participation was among the lowest in the region.[9] This may be an inevitable reflection of a new democracy, but it may also point to a long-term detachment of South Africans from public life, a detachment that could hinder further growth of democracy.

Given these problems, what elements of civil society (if any) play a prominent role in South Africa? One is organized labor, in particular the **Congress of South African Trade Unions (COSATU),** formed in 1985 to promote workers' rights and oppose apartheid. In postapartheid South Africa, COSATU remains powerful in defending labor interests. Like many other organizations that were involved in the battle against apartheid, COSATU is strongly tied to the ANC, through what is known as the Tripartite Alliance, which links COSATU, the ANC, and the South African Communist Party. In spite of this alliance, COSATU is openly hostile to the government's liberal economic policies, and this hostility has generated friction. COSATU has also been vocal in opposing the anti-democratic actions of the current government in neighboring Zimbabwe, which the ANC supports. COSATU has considered severing its ties to the ANC, but like other civic actors, it fears that doing so will result in its political marginalization.

A second important element of civil society is the media. Since 1994, electronic and print media have expanded substantially, making for a relatively well informed public. South Africans place a high degree of trust in the media, more so than they place in any of the state institutions, perhaps due in part to the ethnic integration of television and other outlets. Finally, the AIDS epidemic has recently led to the formation of numerous groups that have challenged the government's weak response to the crisis. Ironically, this horrible epidemic may help foster a new and positive wave of civil activism.

SOCIETY

Given the historical ethnic diversity of South Africa's inhabitants, as well as the colonial and national policies of systematic racial discrimination, it is no surprise that South African society has been (and in many ways remains) significantly divided along racial and ethnic lines. In fact, one of the most tragic effects of apartheid was that the social policy of racial segregation was compounded—indeed, was reinforced—by political persecution and economic discrimination.

What is surprising is the extent to which both groups and individuals in contemporary South Africa identify with the South African nation and express patriotism toward the state. Unfortunately, this shared national identity has

ETHNIC GROUPS

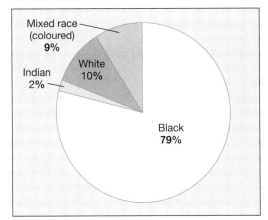

Mixed race (coloured) 9%

Indian 2%

White 10%

Black 79%

RELIGION

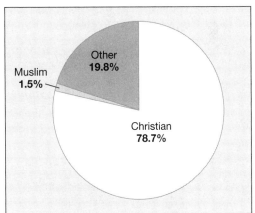

Other 19.8%

Muslim 1.5%

Christian 78.7%

not easily been translated into domestic peace or tolerance among the country's various groups. Despite South Africa's ability to avoid much of the ethnic violence and civil war that plagues other portions of the continent, there is much truth to President Thabo Mbeki's indictment that South Africa remains in many ways two nations: one, wealthy and largely white; the other, poor and largely black.

The challenge for South Africa as it moves from a political culture of racism to one of reconciliation is to forge the varying notions of South African identity into a common, multicultural concept of what it means to be South African, one that reconciles national unity with democratic pluralism.

Ethnic and National Identity

As should be clear, South Africa is truly a multiracial and multiethnic society. Under apartheid, government not only enforced policies of separate racial development but also utilized its "homelands" policy to divide and conquer the country's many ethnic and tribal groups. Although Bantustans (homelands) were legally dissolved in 1994, many citizens (particularly urban blacks) had never identified with or even visited their alleged homeland. Nonetheless, black Africans, particularly rural blacks, remain in many ways tribal in their social relations and political behavior, with tribe or ethnic group remaining their primary identification.

Like black South Africans, the white population has a long history of ethnic division, stemming from the colonial-era conflict between the Afrikaners and the British. A century of sporadic violence between the Afrikaners and the English culminated in the 1910 establishment of the Union of South Africa.

The English minority dominated the Union politically, economically, and culturally. In fact, it was the fear of English dominance that inspired the formation and growth of the Afrikaner National Party (NP) and its policies of cultural and racial purity during the first half of the twentieth century. Apartheid allowed Afrikaners to separate the minority whites from the majority blacks and to culturally dominate the white English subculture.

But whereas racial and tribal groups were fastidiously segregated under apartheid, language has rendered the multiethnic fabric of South Africa far more complex. Indeed, linguistic differences have brought groups together and pushed them apart. Nine languages spoken exclusively by blacks are now enshrined in the constitution. Though violently resisted by blacks during apartheid, Afrikaans remains the preferred tongue of not just Afrikaners but also most coloured South Africans. As is true in many polyglot former colonies, the English language serves to some extent to unify the country's citizens.

Similarly, religion has both unified and divided South African society. More than two thirds of all South Africans, including most whites and coloureds and nearly two thirds of blacks, identify themselves as Christian, and over three quarters describe themselves as religious.[10] The Dutch Reformed Church—dubbed the National Party in prayer—played a particularly important role in unifying Afrikaners (first against the British, then against black Africans) and providing divine justification (at least in the eyes of its members) for their separate and superior status.

As with racial discrimination in America, the dismantling of legal racism in South Africa and the national strides taken toward reconciliation have not fully eliminated racial prejudice or distrust. Levels of black-on-white violence and even black-on-black violence climbed during the 1990s, particularly in the townships, with murder rates in South Africa now nearly ten times higher than those in the United States.

Despite persistent racial tensions, South Africans enjoy a remarkably high level of nationalism and patriotism, as was noted above. And while the apartheid state essentially excluded all non-whites from political life, citizenship is now universally shared. However, legacies of division and exclusion combined with a perceived inability of the African National Congress (ANC) government to deliver socioeconomic benefits, have dampened citizen participation and increased levels of political apathy since the dissolution of apartheid. Recent polls show that support for democracy, trust in government, and satisfaction with government policy have all declined in recent years.[11]

Ideology and Political Culture

Although it may be troubling for the future of South African democracy, a relative decline in levels of political interest since the tumultuous early 1990s should not be surprising. Since the fall of apartheid, political ideologies have also become less pronounced and more pragmatic. In the old South Africa, Afrikaner politicians and intellectuals combined and refined political and theological ideas to form an ideology of racist authoritarianism. And like many other movements of resistance in colonial and postcolonial settings, the ANC and other revolutionary opponents of apartheid (including the South African Communist Party) adopted radical socialist principles of economic egalitarianism and revolutionary political violence. Now the ANC government has reached out to both white capitalists and black voters, embracing liberal capitalism, and promoting electoral democracy and handily winning two national elections.

Likewise, differences among the very disparate political cultures of apartheid South Africa—not just between ruling whites and oppressed blacks but also between the subcultures of Afrikaners and English and even between the Zulu and the Xhosa—have narrowed. Many South Africans have genuinely embraced the new culture of social inclusion and political participation and have supported efforts to integrate former adversaries and divided communities.

Certainly the highest-profile effort of bridge building was the **Truth and Reconciliation Commission.** Convened in 1995 and led by Archbishop **Desmond Tutu,** the commission was charged with two goals: (1) establishing the "truth" of crimes committed (on all sides) from the time of the 1960 Sharpeville Massacre through the outlawing of apartheid in 1994 and (2) using that truth as the essential foundation for healing the deep wounds of the era. The commission was given the authority to hear confessions, grant amnesty to those who were deemed to have told the complete truth, and provide recommendations for promoting long-term reconciliation (including reparation payments). While the commission uncovered a great deal of horrific "truth," much controversy surrounded the final report. Though not surprising given the enormity of the crimes, genuine reconciliation has remained elusive.

Nonetheless, many observers remain optimistic that ANC-governed South Africa can overcome the tragedies of the country's history as well as its current social and economic woes, including endemic crime and violence. They argue that both the South African people and political culture have shown a remarkable capacity to avoid conflict even in the face of serious economic and social problems. Scholars note "countervailing sources of stability" in South Africa's political culture, including a pervasive tradition of collective decision making (known as ubuntu), the ANC's proven pragmatism and political discipline, and the "prudential caution" of whites and blacks forged during the period of transition. Perhaps most important, with the rise of a new black capitalist class, the country has seen the gradual emergence of a multiracial elite.[12]

POLITICAL ECONOMY

One cannot separate the social challenges confronting South Africa today from the economic challenges. Not surprisingly, these challenges are also inherently political. Having vanquished the demon of apartheid, South Africa faces rising crime rates, the rapid spread of HIV/AIDS, and a growing brain drain of skilled young white professionals. These social problems in turn are rooted in unemployment, growing income inequality, and persistent poverty among South Africa 's poorest.

The African National Congress (ANC) government must adopt policies that can both ameliorate these problems without alienating its broad and disparate constituencies and preserve South Africa's nascent democracy and fragile civil liberties. Moreover, successful democratic transition has not guaranteed the economic transformation of South Africa. In fact, it has in some ways made it more problematic, as issues of equality—delayed in the name of promoting political freedom—have taken on more significance.

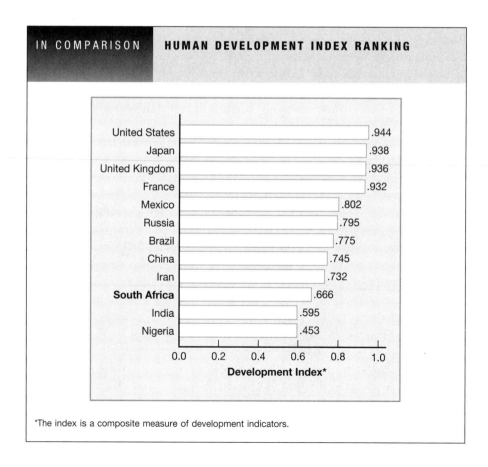

IN COMPARISON   HUMAN DEVELOPMENT INDEX RANKING

	Development Index*
United States	.944
Japan	.938
United Kingdom	.936
France	.932
Mexico	.802
Russia	.795
Brazil	.775
China	.745
Iran	.732
South Africa	.666
India	.595
Nigeria	.453

*The index is a composite measure of development indicators.

To its credit, the government has made strides in improving the economy by curtailing debt, reversing inflation, and expanding exports. It has also improved employment opportunities and income for the growing black middle class, and for South Africa's poor it has greatly expanded access to basic necessities, such as water, electricity, and housing. By African standards, the South African economy is highly developed. Its companies have also become major investors elsewhere in the region.[13] South Africa's economy is also highly diversified, although still fairly dependent on the country's large mineral resources, particularly gold and diamonds.

LABOR FORCE BY OCCUPATION

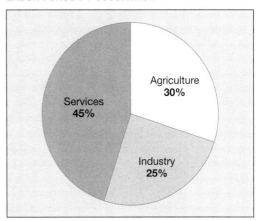

Historically, both British- and Afrikaner-controlled governments sponsored political economic systems that favored their own. In the early twentieth century, government policy facilitated English ownership and control of mines and other industries, even in Afrikaner-dominated regions of the country. Squeezed by wealthier and more highly skilled English from above and by cheaper black labor from below, Afrikaners sought political power in large part to redress what they saw as economic oppression.

With this power, the National Party (NP) promoted essentially mercantilist policies of import substitution to promote local, and more specifically, Afrikaner industry. Though those policies were initially adopted to nurture an Afrikaner capitalist class, by the 1970s the international economic sanctions imposed on South Africa gave the state little option but to substitute local production and markets for those lost abroad. During its tenure, the NP government intervened extensively in the marketplace, imposing high tariffs and other trade barriers on imports, bestowing lucrative government contracts on favored firms, establishing **state-owned enterprises (SOEs)** in such key industries as weapons, steel, and energy production, and using oligopolist profits from gold and diamond exports to fuel industrialization.

Throughout the 1970s, the South African economy thrived and Afrikaners prospered. At the same time, the absence of economic opportunity for black Africans and the prohibition against the formation of black trade unions kept black labor costs artificially low, encouraging foreign investors eager to take advantage of the cheap labor and relative stability that authoritarian South Africa promised. During the 1980s, however, foreign firms and countries faced growing moral and legal pressures to divest their South African interests. At that time, too, multiracial trade unions (including the COSATU) were legalized and began demanding higher wages. Finally, the government began to face a shortage of skilled labor. Limiting access to education for blacks meant that the economy could not depend on a large pool of educated workers. These pressures dealt severe—and some would say ultimately fatal—economic blows to the apartheid state.

Given the history of policies benefiting the English and the Afrikaners, many expected that the victorious ANC would adopt interventionist policies to redress the discrimination and exclusion that blacks had experienced for generations. Not only did such policies promise to be popular with the ANC's majority black constituency, but this kind of progressive state intervention, designed to redistribute wealth and promote greater equality, was also in harmony with the long-standing socialist ideological heritage of the ANC. White property owners feared that a great share of their economic assets would simply be seized by the state. This, then, would be state manipulation of the market by the left rather than the right—but state intervention all the same.

The ANC's approach to the economy was much less radical than expected, and in many ways it pursued a liberal political economic model. In 1994, Nelson Mandela announced the **Reconstruction and Development Plan (RDP),** which focused on meeting the basic needs of South Africans living in poverty. The ANC argued that safe drinking water, housing, electricity, jobs, affordable health care, and a safe environment had to take precedence over economic growth.

Within two years, however, the ANC government had recognized that the huge costs of the RDP were unsustainable in the absence of substantially more foreign investment and more rapid economic growth. In addition, the recent failure of communism in Eastern Europe and the Soviet Union and the increasing popularity of neoliberal market solutions within international development circles helped turn the ANC leadership away from its socialist roots. In 1996, the government adopted a plan of liberal macroeconomic structural adjustment known as **Growth, Employment, and Redistribution Program (GEAR).** GEAR called for opening trade, privatizing SOEs, and otherwise limiting the role of the state in the marketplace in an effort to stimulate growth and attract foreign investment.

Not surprisingly, this dramatic shift in redistributive priorities and interventionist policies has angered the ANC's longtime allies on the left, COSATU and the South African Communist Party. In labor protests against GEAR, COSATU leaders have called the GEAR privatization of the SOEs "born-again apartheid" and have predicted devastating consequences for South Africa's working poor. The government finds itself in the position of being praised by the International Monetary Fund for promoting GEAR privatization but under attack from its erstwhile anti-apartheid allies.

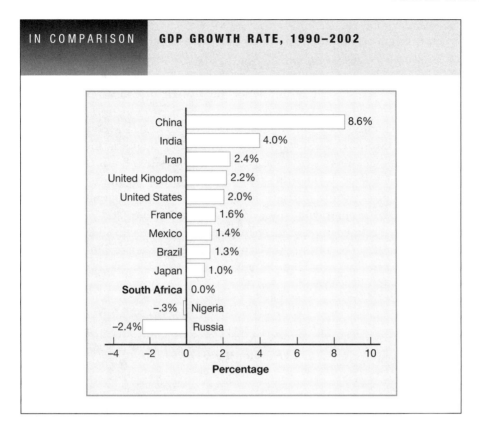

IN COMPARISON   **GDP GROWTH RATE, 1990–2002**

China   8.6%
India   4.0%
Iran   2.4%
United Kingdom   2.2%
United States   2.0%
France   1.6%
Mexico   1.4%
Brazil   1.3%
Japan   1.0%
South Africa   0.0%
−.3%   Nigeria
−2.4%   Russia

-4   -2   0   2   4   6   8   10

Percentage

Facing this catch-22, the government is trying to please all sides. On the one hand, the ANC government remains committed to land reform and basic health care and funds programs to provide water, electricity, phones, and housing to the poor. On the other hand, the government continues to woo foreign investment by cutting inflation, lowering taxes, and keeping a lid on its spending. It has also targeted key industries and manufacturing sectors, offering low-interest loans and other incentives for investment. As in other developing economies, the government has promoted microcredit, or small-loan initiatives designed to assist the very poorest in starting businesses. So far, GEAR and related policies have borne some fruit, in the form of increased growth rates that, it is hoped will help reduce unemployment over the coming decade. But there are still serious obstacles to be overcome.

Chief among these is persistent income inequality. Despite the ANC government's affirmative action efforts and the emergence of a small but growing black middle and upper class, the white minority still dominates the economy. South Africa has one of the greatest levels of income inequality in the world. Moreover, while the rising income of some blacks and the government's redistribution efforts have led to a decline in inequality between races, overall inequality among all South Africans continues to increase. The danger is that a white economic elite will simply be replaced by a black one, with income redistribution no better (and perhaps worse) than before apartheid.

This pernicious inequality has certainly fed into a second problem: crime. The rate of violent crime in South Africa, including murder, rape, and vehicle hijackings, is extremely high. Nearly 20,000 South Africans are murdered each year, a rate nine times greater than the U.S. average. Carjackings, often resulting in death or serious injury, are commonplace and have increased dramatically since 1994. Unemployment and poverty, particularly in the townships, and corruption in the police force exacerbate this problem. Crime not only undermines the social fabric but also deters domestic and international investment and diverts to security resources that could be spent elsewhere.[14]

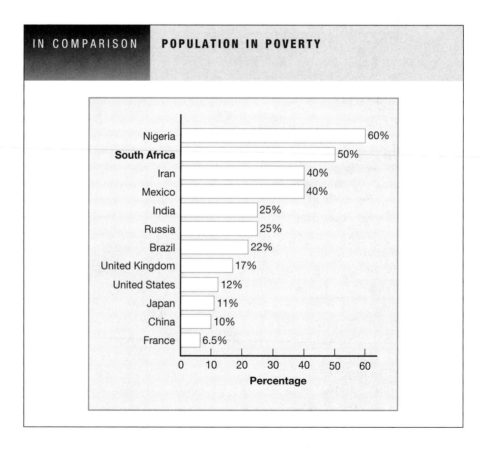

IN COMPARISON   POPULATION IN POVERTY

A third challenge is the growing HIV/AIDS epidemic. It is estimated that nearly 10 percent of South Africans over the age of two are HIV positive, one of the highest rates in the world, and some 600 South Africans die of the disease every day. Despite increasing access to affordable drugs, most of those infected will die of the disease. This is not just a human and social tragedy; it will and already has had huge consequences for the economy. It is estimated that the AIDS pandemic will cut .5 percent from South African GDP growth each year over the next ten years. The health-care system is under-funded and grossly inadequate, and corporations are increasingly wary of investing in personnel, given the mortality odds facings their employees. Compounding this problem is a high degree of stigma attached to those with AIDS, as well as the questionable handling of the issue by Thabo Mbeki and other ANC politicians, who questioned the causal link between HIV and AIDS and resisted conventional drugs and drug protocols prescribed in the West, citing scientifically dubious theories and charging the West with racist views of African sexuality. Pressure from international and domestic activist groups and from Nelson Mandela (whose son died of AIDS) is slowly raising awareness and the level of treatment, but treatment remains limited in the face of this devastating epidemic.[15]

A final challenge worth noting is the loss of human resources through the emigration of skilled workers. The brain drain is sometimes dubbed "white flight" because a high proportion of those leaving are young white professionals who are increasingly skeptical of their prospects in their native South Africa. The brain drain is particularly noticeable in the English-speaking population, whose ties to the country are not as old as those of the Afrikaners. It is estimated that nearly 50,000 whites have emigrated from South Africa since 1994.[16] In order to develop and diversify its economy, South Africa needs not only to create, but also retain, its most skilled workers, both black and white.

FOREIGN RELATIONS AND THE WORLD

As South Africa's domestic institutions and politics are still in transition, so, too, are its relations with the outside world. Under apartheid, South Africa was largely isolated from the outside world, limited in its economic and diplomatic ties. This isolation helped reinforce a siege mentality among the white population and directed much of the politics of the country inward. Relations with the rest of Africa were particularly hostile, often limited to military skirmishes with neighboring countries that harbored or supported the African National Congress (ANC). With the move to multiparty rule, South Africa was able to break out of its isolation, rebuilding ties in the region and in the international community as a whole.

As can be expected, however, the realities of this transition have been somewhat more complicated. For most observers, this has been most obvious in the often prickly relationship between the ANC and members of the international community, whether they are other governments, intergovernmental organizations, or nongovernmental organizations (NGOs). As we have noted, President Thabo Mbeki has bristled at suggestions that the government has been derelict in its response to the AIDS crisis and in addressing some of the main issues involved, such as sexual assault. ANC leaders (including Nelson Mandela) have accused the international community of double standards and racism, treating South Africa as if it were still a colony of the imperial powers. Ironically, in some ways this defensiveness is reminiscent of the rhetoric of the apartheid-era National Party (NP), which also angrily rejected criticism from the international community. Perhaps this should not be surprising. In spite of the wide ethnic, economic, and other divisions among South Africans, surveys have found a deep vein of patriotism that has persisted over the past decade, with over 90 percent of those surveyed saying that they are proud to be South African.[17] Such strong patriotism is less likely to tolerate external criticism, especially if it originates in the developed world.

Yet when we shift our focus from the international community to Africa alone, our perspective of South Africa changes. In the international community, South Africa is still a struggling country that confronts a series of major obstacles. But in Africa, South Africa is a regional powerhouse. On the economic front, its economy alone makes up nearly 45 percent of *all* of sub-Saharan Africa's GDP. By virtue of this large GDP and its vibrant private sector, South Africa has become central to trade and investment on the continent. South African exports to other African countries have risen substantially over the past decade, fostered in part by the lowering of trade barriers across the region. South Africa has also become a major investor in many neighboring countries. South African multinationals now play an important role in retail, banking, telecommunications, and other sectors in the region. As a result of this dominant economic presence, there has been a growing resentment of what is seen as a kind of South African imperialism, the effects of which are thought to be undermining local African businesses and increasingly controlling the regional economy.[18] Inside South Africa, these actions have also been criticized as running counter to the goals of economic development within South Africa itself. Furthermore, at the other end of this relationship, the far better economic conditions in South Africa have attracted millions of illegal immigrants over the past decade, fueling xenophobia among the South African population and mistreatment of immigrants by the police, immigration officials, and the public as a whole.

South Africa's regional power has expanded in the diplomatic sphere as well. An important element of this growing influence is the country's role in the formation of the **African Union (AU),** which replaced the Organisation of African Unity (OAU) in 2002. In many ways inspired by the European Union, the AU seeks to depart from the OAU in pursuing greater political and economic integration across the continent. As the first head of the AU, Thabo Mbeki sought to position the organization as a mediator between African states and the advanced democracies. Mbeki also helped create the **Southern African Development Community (SADC),** a thirteen-member body that is also concerned with regional economic integration and cooperation in southern Africa.

A cornerstone of regional integration and cooperation has been the **New Partnership for Africa's Development (NEPAD).** NEPAD proposes that the developed world's support for African countries would, unlike past aid or loan programs, be tied to commitments to the rule of law and democracy. Progress toward this goal is to be monitored by the AU. If the AU is able to show progress in tying aid to economic and political progress in the region, it will no doubt boost the organization's power and with it the regional and international authority of South Africa.

Finally, South Africa has been directly involved in peacekeeping and peace-making in the region. In recent years the South African government has worked at brokering an end to civil conflicts in the Congo, Angola, Liberia, and Burundi, and has troops on the ground as peacekeepers or observers in several African countries.

Thus South Africa's role in the region has been transformed from pariah to continental leader and mediator with the advanced democracies. But this power comes with its own costs. In many ways, South Africa has become a regional hegemon—that is, a dominant power that is able to set the rules for the region, adjudicate disputes between countries, and punish those who fail to go along. That South Africa has not only the most powerful army on the continent but also a sophisticated arms industry (as a legacy of apartheid) only reinforces this authority.

That power comes with a certain degree of contradiction is true for any important actor in the international system, and in that respect, South Africa is no different from any other country with more power than its neighbors. What complicates matters for South Africa, however, is the way in which its new regime has been built on moral authority—the need for democracy, multiethnicity, and tolerance. As a result, South Africa has been at the forefront of promoting democracy in the region through its own diplomatic efforts and through participation in the AU and the SADC. Yet its efforts have often been viewed in the region as patronizing, not unlike the behavior of the advanced democracies toward South Africa that Mbeki often condemns. This view is reinforced by the perception of double standards. We have already noted that in the economic realm some observers see South Africa's economic relations with the continent as one of domination. NEPAD, too, has been criticized by some Africans as an attempt to bring a neo-liberal version of GEAR to the rest of Africa, thereby primarily benefiting South African economic interests.[19]

In the diplomatic sphere as well, South Africa's calls for greater democracy in the region have rung hollow in the face of its support for Zimbabwe, whose deepening authoritarianism is made possible in part by South African diplomatic and economic support (see "Current Issues"). As with many other countries around the world, South Africa has found that its increased international power has led to a clash of morality, stability, and self-interest.

CURRENT ISSUES

ZIMBABWE

Since the fall of apartheid, South Africa has sought to develop a role as an important regional actor, leading both by economic example and by moral example. But in the past few years, this position has been caught up in the politics of its neighbor Zimbabwe.

Like South Africa, Zimbabwe (formerly known as Rhodesia) is a former British colony in which a small white elite once dominated the black majority. Just as the African National Congress (ANC) fought a guerrilla campaign against the South African government, in Zimbabwe a movement known as Zimbabwe African National Union (ZANU), led by Robert Mugabe, struggled to end white rule. After years of violent conflict, the government agreed to open elections in 1980, which ZANU won. As in South Africa, the transition from white rule was predicated on allowing the white minority to maintain its economic domination over the country. Unlike South Africa, however, the transition led to conflict among different indigenous African ethnic groups and thousands of deaths.

The ZANU victory served as an inspiration for South Africans opposed to apartheid. Over time, however, it also became a more negative example. During the 1980s, ZANU (merged with its main rival, the Patriotic Front, to become ZANU-PF) consolidated power in the hands of the party and President Mugabe. Economic mismanagement and corruption followed, undermining political authority. In the late 1990s, as public opposition grew, a new party rose to challenge ZANU-PF, known as the Movement for Democratic Change (MDC). Fearing the MDC and seeking to shore up his own authority, Mugabe turned on both the MDC and white landowners, who controlled most of the farmland in Zimbabwe. Mugabe encouraged his supporters to seize white-owned land and to harass and kill members of the MDC. The international community condemned these tactics, but Mugabe dismissed the criticism as the machinations of imperialist oppressors.

The South African government took a different position, however. President Thabo Mbeki and the ANC expressed its support for Mugabe even in the face of increasing repression, and the South African government extended financial support when the rest of the international community had withdrawn its aid. In 2005, Zimbabwe held parliamentary elections that were widely regarded as rigged. Yet the South African government declared the elections free and fair, as it had done in response to similar elections in 2002.

Why would democratic South Africa support a neighboring dictatorship? Different factors may be at work. Some observers argue that the ANC and the ZANU-PF share a bond in the struggle against white rule. Both have since chafed at what they see as the lecturing of the international community, a reaction that has also characterized Mbeki's intransigence on AIDS. Others emphasize that the South African government, concerned about the complete breakdown of authority in Zimbabwe, would rather back Mugabe than face chaos on its border.

But the South African government's position is not shared by everyone in the country. The COSATU has strongly supported the MDC and condemned Mbeki's support, whereas such national figures as Nelson Mandela and Archbishop Desmond Tutu have called for Mugabe to step down and have indirectly or directly challenged ANC policies on the matter.

There is a final worrying element in the situation. Mbeki and the ANC may be motivated by the same kind of power politics that has motivated many regional powers around the world, whereby ideals give way to issues of security and stability. But it may also be that many members of the ANC sympathize with both ZANU-PF's desire to monopolize their hard-won power and their unwillingness to give it up through the democratic process. It is unlikely, but worth considering, that Zimbabwe could be South Africa's future.

DEMOCRACY AND THE POWER OF THE AFRICAN NATIONAL CONGRESS

The ANC played a crucial role in ending apartheid and consolidating democracy after 1994. It was rewarded with three massive electoral victories, and it has enjoyed an absolute majority since the democratic transition. The popularity of the ANC and its leaders has made it very difficult for opposition parties to gain a foothold. The Democratic Alliance has never mustered more than 12 percent of the vote and the Zulu-based Inkatha Freedom Party has recently worked closely with the ANC. The New National Party disbanded and its legislators joined the ANC.

The dominance of the ANC and the weakness of the opposition have raised concerns about possible abuses of power. The ANC has generally acted with caution in order to not antagonize opposition parties and South Africa's various ethnic and religious minority groups. Corruption, however, may be a more serious challenge for the ANC. A series of influence-peddling scandals have rocked the ANC in recent years.

In June 2005, president Mbeki fired deputy president Jacob Zuma, who was facing charges of influence-peddling in his dealings with wealthy entrepreneurs. Zuma, a close friend of Mbeki, was extremely popular among the rank and file and the pro-ANC trade unions, and he was expected to be Mbeki's successor. His firing was viewed as a sign that Mbeki and the ANC would not tolerate corruption.

South Africa has yet to experience political alternation. Other democracies, like Japan, have been dominated by a single political party. Nevertheless, the dominance of a single party may threaten democracy in the long run.

NOTES

1. Anthony Sampson, "Men of the Renaissance," *Guardian* (London), 3 January 1998, p. 19.
2. For a discussion of South African history, see Leonard Thompson, *The History of South Africa* (New Haven, CT: Yale University Press, 2001).
3. For more on this conflict, see Thomas Packenham, *The Boer War* (New York: Random House, 1979).
4. African History: Apartheid legislation in South Africa, http://africanhistory.about.com/library/bl/blsalaws.htm, contains a detailed list of the apartheid legislative acts.
5. For more on the emergence of the struggle against apartheid and Mandela's role in it, see Nelson Mandela, *Long Walk to Freedom: The Autobiography of Nelson Mandela* (Boston: Little, Brown, 1996).
6. For de Klerk's own perspective on the transition from apartheid, see F. W. de Klerk, *The Last Trek: A New Beginning* (New York: St. Martin's Press, 1999).
7. J. L. Gibson and J. A. Caldeira, "Defenders of Democracy? Legitimacy, Popular Acceptance, and the South African Constitutional Court," *Journal of Politics* 65, no. 1 (February 2003), pp. 1–30.
8. Andrew Reynolds, "Constitutional Engineering in South Africa," *Journal of Democracy* 6 (1995), pp. 86–99.
9. Robert Mattes, Yul Derek Davids, and Cherrel Africa, "Views of Democracy in South Africa and the Region: Trends and Comparisons," *Afrobarometer Paper #8* (October 2000), http://www.afrobarometer.org/papers/AfropaperNo8.pdf (accessed 3 August 2005).
10. Ronald Inglehart et. al., eds., *Human Beliefs and Values: A Cross-Cultural Sourcebook Based on the 1999–2002 Value Surveys* (Mexico City: Siglo XXI, 2004).

11. Those data are cited in Robert Mattes, "South Africa: Democracy without the People?" *Journal of Democracy* 13 (2002), pp. 22–36.

12. Daniel O'Flaherty and Constance J. Freeman, "Stability in South Africa: Will It Hold?" *Washington Quarterly* 22 (Autumn 1999), and "Africa's Engine," *Economist*, 15 January 2004.

13. "Africa's Engine," *Economist*, 15 January 2004.

14. For more on murder, see Rob McCafferty, Murder in South Africa: A Comparison of Past and Present (Claremont, South Africa: United Christian Action, 2003). http://www.christianaction.org.za/newsletter_uca/murder_southafrica.doc.

15. Adele Baleta, "South African President Criticized for Lack of Focus on AIDS," *Lancet* 14 February 2004, p. 541.

16. "If Only the Adults Would Behave Like the Children,"*Economist*, 21 April 2005.

17. David Mattes, "Understanding Identity in South Africa: A First Cut," *Afrobarometer Paper* 38 (June 2004), http://www.afrobarometer.org/papers/AfropaperNo38.pdf (accessed 3 August 2005).

18. See Chris Landsberg, "Promoting Democracy: The Mandela-Mbeki Doctrine," *Journal of Democracy* 11 (2000), pp. 107–121.

19. Henning Melber, "South Africa and NEPAD—Quo Vadis?" *Policy Brief* 31 (June 2004), Centre for Policy Studies, http://www.cps.org.za/cps%20pdf/polbrief31.pdf (accessed 3 August 2005).

KEY TERMS

WEB LINKS

African Studies Internet Resources: South Africa, Columbia University
    Libraries **www.columbia.edu/cu/lweb/indiv/africa/cuvl/SAfr.html**
South African Government **www.gov.za**
Truth and Reconciliation Report **www.gov.za/reports/2003/trc/index.html**
African National Congress **www.anc.org.za**
The Democratic Alliance **www.da.org.za**
Inkatha Freedom Party **www.ifp.org.za**
Institute for Democracy in South Africa **www.idasa.org.za**
Overview of Soweto township **www.soweto.co.za**

13 NIGERIA

Head of state and government:
President Olusegun Obasanjo
(since May 29, 1999)

Capital: Abuja

Total land size: 923,768 sq km

Population: 129 million

GDP at PPP: .125 trillion US$

GDP per capita: $1,000

NIGERIA

INTRODUCTION

Why Study This Case?

N igeria stands out in ways that are both impressive and disheartening. First, Nigeria is noteworthy for its sheer size: it is the most populous country in Africa. Second, unlike many other African countries, Nigeria is blessed with a great deal of natural wealth, from oil to agriculture. Following independence from British rule in 1960, those assets would have been expected to make Nigeria a major regional, if not global, actor.

Yet exactly the opposite happened, and Nigeria has become renowned for all that can go wrong. For most of the time since independence, the country has been under military rule. Those long periods of military dictatorship coincided with widespread corruption, with oil revenues and other resources siphoned off to line the pockets of those in power. In spite of earning billions of dollars in oil exports, Nigeria has become one of the poorest and least developed countries in the world. It would seem to be an excellent example of a country in which natural resources have been used by those in power to buy supporters and repress the public.

Yet the long era of military rule may now be at an end. In 1999, Nigeria returned to civilian rule, and since then a fragile democratic system has taken hold. Still, much remains to be done. Nigeria lacks the rule of law and continues to be recognized as one of the most corrupt countries in the world. The state also has questionable control over the monopoly of violence, both in terms of civilian control over the military and the country's widespread criminal and political violence. The standard of living for the average Nigerian remains very low, far below what the country's wealth should ensure. If it is to succeed, the country must confront these challenges while facing a large foreign debt, incurred while billions of dollars in oil revenue were stolen by those in power.

If the legacy of its military rule were not enough of a challenge for Nigeria, a second concern derives from its sheer size. Nigeria is a diverse country encompassing numerous ethnic groups, whose local interests have been reinforced by corruption and federalism. For the past thirty years, military rule has largely kept fractiousness in check, but tensions and violence have surfaced with democratic rule. Most disturbing is a growing ethnic rift between the Muslim north and the Christian and animist south. At a time when many global conflicts center on religion and religious fundamentalism, the prospect of increasing tension among faiths in Nigeria leads some observers to worry that in the long run the country will be ungovernable and will return to authoritarianism, civil war, or both. Is Nigeria doomed to be a failed state?

Nigeria thus provides a fascinating, if daunting example of the possibilities and potential limits of state power and democracy. Can the change from military rule to democracy help bring stability and prosperity to Nigeria? Or are the problems of state capacity and autonomy such that democracy cannot help improve them—and might even make them worse? We will consider these tensions as we investigate Nigeria's political heritage, current institutions, and political prospects.

Major Geographic and Demographic Features

We have noted that one of Nigeria's most impressive features is its sheer size. Nigeria is the largest country in Africa in terms of population and among the top ten in the world. Lying along the western coast of the continent, Nigeria has a diverse climate and geography. The Niger-Benue river system divides the country into distinct regions. The north is relatively arid and known for its grasslands, while the south is characterized by tropical forests and coastal swamps. Nigeria's geography and climate (particularly in the south) are favorable to agriculture, such that nearly one third of the land is arable—compared with only 15 percent of the land in China and 20 percent of the land in the United States. Until oil became a major export commodity, cocoa and nuts were a major source of foreign trade.

Nigeria's best-known region is the **Niger River Delta.** The Niger River enters the sea at that point, creating a vast swampy area of over 5,000 square miles. It is the third-largest wetland in the world, after the Netherlands and the Mississippi Delta, and home to an enormous range of plants and animals. The Niger Delta is also home to approximately 10 million people, who traditionally have been engaged in farming and fishing. The complicated topography of the area has limited interaction, integration, and assimilation, thus fostering a large variety of ethnicities—by some estimates, over a dozen groups speaking about twenty-five languages inhabit the delta. It is also one of the poorest regions of the country, with limited infrastructure and development.

But the Niger Delta is also the source of Nigeria's oil and the vast majority of the country's exports. Oil production in the delta has contributed to the national corruption spoken of earlier, and at the local level, too, its effects have been profound. The first and most commonly cited local effect is environmental degradation. In the nearly half century since oil production began, there have been more than 4,000 spills, whose effects on the wetlands and population are a source of intense domestic and international controversy.[1] Oil production has also abetted ethnic conflicts in the region, with groups on occasion attacking oil facilities in order to draw attention to their demands or seek ransoms. Finally, oil production has exacerbated intergroup hostility in the delta as some groups have perceived that others have benefited disproportionately from the industry.[2] Given the importance of oil to Nigeria, the problems of this region significantly affect the security of the country as a whole.

The diversity that marks the delta is mirrored across the country as a whole. Nigeria is home to some 250 ethnic groups. Dominant among them are the **Hausa** and the **Fulani,** who are overwhelmingly Muslim and concentrated in the north; the **Igbo** (also spelled Ibo), who are predominantly Christian and concentrated in the southeast; and the **Yoruba,** who inhabit the southwest and whose members are divided among the Christian, Muslim, and local animist faiths.

Nigeria's large population is a function of its growth rate. In the past twenty years, the country's population has doubled, with the result that nearly half the population is now under the age of fourteen. According to some projections, the country will increase by another 40 million people in the next decade, with Lagos becoming one of the ten largest cities in the world.[3] The presence of a large, rapidly growing, ethnically and religiously diverse population will complicate development, stability, and governance.

Historical Development of the State

Like most other less-developed countries, Nigeria has a history marked by local political organization, imperial control, and recent independence and instability. Contrary to common assumptions, however, pre-colonial Nigeria was neither undeveloped nor unorganized. Rather, the region was marked by varying degrees and kinds of political and social organization, some of which were highly complex and wide ranging. Although we cannot explore each of them in depth, we can point to some of the earliest and most powerful examples.

Nigeria was the setting for several early kingdoms. Over two thousand years ago, the members of the Nok society, located in what is now central Nigeria, fashioned objects out of iron and terra-cotta with a degree of sophistication unmatched in West Africa, though little else is known about their civilization. As the roots of today's dominant ethnic groups began to take shape, new forms of political organization also emerged. Around 1200 C.E., the Hausa to the north established a series of powerful city-states, which served as conduits of north-south trade. In the southwest, the Yoruba kingdom of Oyo extended its power beyond the borders of modern-day Nigeria into present-day Togo. This kingdom grew wealthy through trade and the exploitation of natural resources, facilitated by its location along the coast. In the southeast, the Igbo maintained less centralized political power, though they, too, had a precedent of earlier kingdoms and would come to play a central role in modern Nigerian politics.

TIME LINE OF POLITICAL DEVELOPMENT

Year	Event
300s B.C.E.	Jos plateau settled by the Nok people
1100s C.E.	Hausa kingdom formed in the north; Oyo kingdom formed in the southwest
1472	Portuguese navigators reach the Nigerian coast
1500s–1800s	Slave trade develops
1807	United Kingdom bans the slave trade
1809	Sokoto caliphate founded
1861–1914	Britain acquires Lagos and establishes a series of Nigerian protectorates
1960	Nigeria achieves independence and creates the First Republic
1966	After a military coup, the Federal Military Government is established
1967–70	In Nigerian Civil War, Biafra fails to win independence
1975	General Olusegun Obasanjo comes to power and initiates a transition to civilian rule
1979	Elections bring Shehu Shagari to power, establishing the Second Republic
1983	Muhammadu Buhari seizes power
1985	Ibrahim Babangida seizes power
1993	Transition to civilian rule (the Third Republic) fails; Sani Abacha seizes power
1995	Activist Ken Saro-Wiwa executed
1998	Abacha dies; Abdulsalam Abubakar succeeds him as the military head of government
1999	Military rule ends and the Fourth Republic is established; Olusegun Obasanjo elected president
2000	Sharia law adopted by twelve northern states
2000–02	Ethnic and religious clashes leave several thousand dead
2003	Obasanjo re-elected to a second term as president

ISLAM AND THE NIGERIAN NORTH

The fortunes of those and other peoples in what is now Nigeria changed dramatically as contact with peoples, politics, and ideas from outside West Africa increased. The first important impact came not from Europe, however, but from the Middle East, with the spread of Islam. By the eleventh century, Islam had found its way into the Hausa region of northern Nigeria, carried along trade routes linking the region to North Africa and beyond. By the fifteenth century, Islam had brought literacy and scholarship to the region through the Arabic language, though the religion remained largely confined to the Hausa elite. By the late eighteenth century, however, an increase in contact with Islamic regions led to an increase in conversions to the faith. The religion's growing influence was solidified by the leadership of Usman dan Fodio (1754–1817). A religious scholar, Usman played an important role in spreading Islam among the Hausa and Fulani. Usman found widespread support among the peasantry, who felt oppressed under the city-states' warring monarchies and saw in Islam's message a promise of greater social equality. Their embrace of Islam in turn alarmed those in power, eventually precipitating a conflict between the city-states and Usman. Following an initial conflict, Usman declared jihad against the Hausa city-states in 1804 and by 1808 had overthrown the ruling monarchs, establishing what became known as the Sokoto caliphate. The Sokoto caliphate became the largest empire in Africa at the time and provided a uniform government to a region previously racked by war. Islam would now play a central role in western Africa and in the eventual establishment of an independent Nigerian state.

EUROPEAN IMPERIALISM

As Islam and centralized political organization spread across the north, the south experienced similarly dramatic effects with the arrival of the European powers. As far back as the late fifteenth century, Europeans had begun arriving along Nigeria's coast, purchasing from indigenous traders agricultural products as well as slaves (often captives from local wars). From the seventeenth to the nineteenth century, Europeans established several coastal ports to support the burgeoning trade in slaves, with the United Kingdom becoming the major trading power. During that time, over 3 million slaves were shipped from Nigeria to the Americas. In 1807, the United Kingdom declared the slave trade illegal and established a naval presence off Nigeria's waters for enforcement, though an illegal trade continued for another half century. The precipitous decline in the region's major export contributed to the collapse of the Oyo Empire and to warfare among the Yoruba, which in turn paved the way for an expanded British presence in the interior. The colonial presence further expanded as British industrialization generated ever-greater demand for resources such as palm oil, cocoa, and timber. That demand radically changed the nature of agricultural production and encouraged the greater use of local slavery to produce these goods. At the same time, British missionaries began to proselytize in the coastal and southern regions, converting large numbers of Igbo and Yoruba to Christianity.

By 1861, the British had established a colony at Lagos, and by the 1884–85 Berlin Conference other European powers had recognized the United Kingdom's "sphere of influence" along the coast. Fearing French and German encroachment in the interior, the United Kingdom quickly joined the European powers' "scramble for Africa" by asserting its authority far inland. Through a combination of diplomacy, co-optation, and force, the United Kingdom established control over both the north and the south. In many areas, the British relied upon a policy of indirect rule. For example, as the Sokoto caliphate was brought under British control, local leaders were allowed to keep their positions, co-opted as part of the new state bureaucracy. Furthermore, **sharia,** or Islamic law, was respected in noncriminal matters, and in that region Christian proselytizing was prohibited. Such policies helped limit local resistance but increased the power of some ethnic groups over others, giving them greater authority within the imperial administration. In areas where indirect rule was less successful, as among the Igbo, resistance was much more significant. In 1914, the various protectorates in the area under British control were unified under the name Nigeria, though the country remained highly decentralized administratively, reflecting its distinct regional differences.

Following unification, Nigeria experienced dramatic change under imperial rule. A modern infrastructure was developed, with the construction of ports, roads, and railways to help facilitate economic relations. Agricultural production continued to play an important role in exports. Within Nigerian society, development meant the establishment of Western educational policies and institutions, especially in regions where Christian missionaries were active. In general, indirect rule meant the development of a new elite who were more Westernized and more conscious of the complexities of imperialism. The creation of a colonial legislative council and local elections for some of the seats introduced the idea of democratic representative institutions, no matter how limited.

It might be thought that the development of a Westernized elite would serve to perpetuate imperial control. Instead, exposure to Western ideas often served as the foundation for resistance as Nigerians embraced the heretofore alien concepts of nationalism and sovereignty. Such ideas were not easily planted in Nigeria's complex political terrain. For some activists, anti-colonialism meant a greater role for Nigeria and other African states in the Commonwealth of Nations (the loose affiliation of former British colonies opposed to complete independence). For others, it meant a reassertion of pre-colonial political structures that had been destroyed or weakened by British rule. As economic development, urbanization, and state centralization increased the integration of Nigeria as whole, however, there began to emerge the tentative notion of a Nigerian nation and state that could be independent from colonial rule.

Following World War II, Nigeria saw the rapid expansion of various civil society organizations, ranging from political parties and ethnic movements to labor unions and business movements. Among the numerous political leaders who emerged during this time was Benjamin Nnamdi Azikiwe (1904–96). Born in northern Nigeria, Azikiwe studied and taught in the United States before returning to Nigeria in 1938. He established a daily newspaper and in 1944 helped found the National Council of Nigerian Citizens (NCNC), which advocated national unity and self-government. While the NCNC sought to appeal to all Nigerians, it drew heavily from the Igbo, while other political parties, such as the Northern People's Congress (NPC) and the Action Group Party (AGP), were backed by Hausa Muslims and the Yoruba, respectively.

The British government attempted to deal with the rising tide of Nigerian activism, strikes, and competing demands by reforming the local constitution, creating regional assemblies, and formalizing the decentralized nature of imperial rule through a system of federalism. Executive power remained in the hands of a British governor, but increasingly authority devolved on the local level. Thus, while Nigerian nationalism became a potent force among some political elites, the decentralization of power reinforced regional tendencies. By the late 1950s, an array of constitutional reforms had effectively created autonomous regions in the north, west, and east, with the goal of eventual national independence while remaining within the Commonwealth. The new federal political structure consisted of three regions (Northern, Western, and Eastern), a directly elected House of Representatives, a Senate whose members would be indirectly elected by the regional assemblies, a prime minister, and a governor general, who would serve as the representative of the British monarchy. Azikiwe was appointed governor general. On October 1, 1960, Nigeria formally gained its independence (creating what is known as the **First Republic**), absent much of the violence and destruction that plagued decolonization elsewhere. It also enjoyed ongoing industrialization, strong exports, and the promise of oil revenues, whose potential was just beginning to be explored.

INDEPENDENCE, CONFLICT, AND CIVIL WAR

The relative peace and the promises of an independent Nigeria quickly experienced tension, however. Elections in 1959 had given the NPC nearly half the seats in the House of Representatives, leading it to form a coalition with the NCNC. That coalition battled over some of the most essential questions regarding Nigerian statehood, including the scope of central versus local powers and national versus regional identity. Meanwhile, the AGP fragmented as a result of internal disputes and electoral setbacks. The infighting eventually spread across the Western Region, which the AGP controlled, leading to riots, the collapse of the regional legislature, emergency rule, and a conspiracy by some AGP leaders to overthrow the central government.

The dynamics of the Action Group crisis were not unique to the Western Region. Various groups across Nigeria demanded that the federal system be further decentralized to make way for additional states, while other groups and leaders opposed such tactics, fearing they would undermine their own territorial authority or even lead to the breakup of the country. Fragmentation was of particular concern to the NPC. As the Northern Region was allocated over half the seats in the House of Representatives, the NPC feared that any restructuring of federalism would undermine its power. Such concerns even extended to the national census, which each side hoped would bolster its allocation of seats. Sharply contested elections and electoral alliances were marked by ethnic tensions and electoral discrepancies. The ethnic conflict was sharpened by economic differences, with each group viewing the state as a means to siphon off wealth for its own people.

In the violent aftermath of the contentious 1965 regional assembly elections in the Western Region, 2,000 people died. In the midst of the increasing disorder, a group of army officers, primarily Igbos, staged a coup d'état, assassinating the prime minister, the leaders of several political parties, and a number of military officials from the north. The constitution was suspended and political parties banned, and the new military government called for a unitary government and the end to northern domination. The coup failed to impose order, setting off civil war instead. Conflict erupted between northern and Igbo troops, and the coup leaders were in turn overthrown, and many of them were killed. Many Igbo living in the north were also massacred, and Igbo leaders who had supported the coup and an end to federalism as a way to weaken northern power now believed that their people and region had no future in a multiethnic Nigeria.

In May 1967, the Igbo-dominated Eastern Region seceded from Nigeria, declaring itself the **Republic of Biafra.** Although the Biafrans were outnumbered and outgunned, they held off the Nigerian military for three years, helped in part by international supporters, who believed that the Nigerian government was conducting a genocidal war against the Igbo. Azikiwe, who had been dismissed from his post by the military government, became a prominent supporter of Biafran independence. In 1970, Biafra was defeated.

Although the defeat did not lead to the Igbo extermination that many had feared, the war itself exacted huge costs in terms of military and civilian life— estimates range from 500,000 to 3 million fatalities.[4]

THE MILITARY ERA

The armed forces brought an end to the Nigerian Civil War, but their role in the politics of Nigeria was just beginning. The 1966 countercoup in response to the takeover by Igbo army officers established the Federal Military Government (FMG), which initially claimed that it would soon return power to civilian control. **General Yakubu Gowon,** who came to head the FMG in 1966, argued that in advance of any such transition, Nigeria needed to undergo dramatic state and economic reform. Dominated by none of the three main ethnic groups, the FMG broke Nigeria into a number of federal states, hoping to weaken regional and ethnic power. The government also sought to move the country away from its reliance upon agriculture by stimulating industrialization through a policy of import substitution. This shift was made possible in part because agricultural exports were declining in favor of oil, which was emerging as a major source of revenue. By the 1970s, Nigeria had become one of the top ten oil-producing countries in the world. The result was rapid if uneven development of the country in numerous areas.

The FMG had come to power with a certain degree of public support, given its call for an end to divisive ethnic-based politics and the creation of an effective state. Yet in reality, military rule simply replaced one form of patronage with another, tapping oil revenues as a way to enrich those in power and their supporters. By the mid-1970s, Gowon's political authority had deteriorated in the face of public animosity in reaction to widespread corruption, crime, and stagnating economic development. In 1975, Gowon was overthrown in a bloodless coup that brought General Murtala Muhammed to power. Muhammed began to crack down on corruption and took the long-delayed steps necessary for the return of civilian rule, thereby becoming widely popular with the public. But within a year, Muhammed himself was assassinated in a failed coup attempt, which brought to power **General Olusegun Obasanjo,** who continued Muhammed's plans for the restoration of civilian rule. A new constitution enacted in 1979 ushered in the **Second Republic,** under which the old parliamentary system was replaced by a presidential system, in the hope of strengthening central authority and preventing a breakdown like the one that had occurred a decade earlier. Democratic elections were held in 1979, and Obasanjo willingly retired from political and military life; subsequently, he became active with various intergovernmental and nongovernmental organizations (NGOs), such as the World Health Organization and Transparency International. Obasanjo's apparent respect for the rule of law while in power and his prominent international role thereafter have made him one of the most prominent Nigerians of the last twenty years and favored his return to politics.

The 1979 presidential elections resulted in a victory for the northerner Shehu Shagari (narrowly defeating the perennial candidate, Azikiwe) and the reemergence of several traditional parties that had dominated Nigeria before military rule. Shagari's civilian government faced numerous obstacles. In addition to the ethnic factionalism that continued to plague politics, state revenues declined dramatically in 1981 after a drop in oil prices. The resultant economic recession fostered unrest, and the government was burdened by the use of public spending and corruption to award supporters and buy off the public. Inflation and foreign debt increased, and capital fled. When the Shagari government sought to stay in power in 1983 by rigging elections, the military re-entered the picture.

After 1983, Nigeria experienced another decade and a half of military rule, a period dominated by two men: **General Ibrahim Babangida** and **General Sani Abacha.** Babangida, an ethnic Gwari and a Muslim, had the unenviable task of dealing with Nigeria's mounting economic crisis. He implemented a structural-adjustment program backed by the International Monetary Fund and the World Bank that dramatically worsened the lives of average Nigerians by cutting back on public spending. In politics, too, while Babangida asserted that he would restore civilian rule, he increased tension by packing the military government with northerners, only deepening regional and ethnic resentments. In the late 1980s, Babangida sought to initiate a civilian transition under his control, even to the point of creating new political parties and platforms. Under growing public pressure, presidential elections for this **Third Republic** were held in 1993, but Babangida quickly annulled the results, an action that set off a wave of public protests, strikes, and the fear of a new civil war. Babangida stepped down in the face of the unrest, installing a caretaker civilian government. Within three months, Babangida's second in command, Sani Abacha, a northerner, had taken the reins of power for himself in yet another military coup.

Abacha's government lacked many of the skills that had allowed Babangida to remain in power for such a long time. While Babangida sought to co-opt his opponents as much as possible, using force only as a last resort, Abacha regularly employed violence as a means of public control. Political leaders and activists involved in the 1993 elections and ensuing crisis were arrested, and Abacha used his North Korea–trained Special Bodyguard Unit to repress and murder critics of the regime. In 1995, a number of civilian and military officials were imprisoned for allegedly plotting against Abacha, among them former President Obasanjo. The writer and environmentalist Ken Saro-Wiwa, a critic of the regime and of the Shell company's role in Nigeria, was also arrested and executed for his opposition to the regime (see the box on p. 486).

Saro-Wiwa's execution led to Nigeria's expulsion from the Commonwealth of Nations and to sanctions by the United States and the European Union. Not only did Abacha repress the Nigerian people, but it is estimated that during his rule he also stole as much as US$6 billion from the state. This dark period ended suddenly in 1998, when Abacha died of a heart attack (some observers suspect that he was poisoned). Perhaps realizing the dangers of military rule, the general who succeeded Abacha rapidly carried out a democratic transition and released all political prisoners. In 1999, free presidential elections were held, bringing Obasanjo to power again as head of the **Fourth Republic.**

POLITICAL REGIME

Nigeria's uneven record of governance presents a compelling study of political regimes and a sober lesson in the challenges facing postcolonial countries struggling to institutionalize stable government. Nigeria has experimented with an assortment of political regimes and experienced more than its share of political turmoil in less than fifty years of independence. The country has vacillated between authoritarian military regimes and democratic civilian republics—both parliamentary and presidential—and has had a variety of federal, state, and local political arrangements.

The most prominent form of governance in independent Nigeria has been **patrimonialism,** in which the personal rule of an authoritarian leader has been shored up by the economic privileges he bestows upon a coterie of loyal followers. Not surprisingly, the divisiveness, corruption, and illegitimacy of patrimonialism has meant that the bullets of military coups, rather than the ballots of electoral democracy, have more frequently determined Nigerian regime shifts and changes in government.

Each of those shifts has shared at least two features: each new regime has come to power promising improved governance, and each has largely failed to deliver on its promise. Whether military or civilian, authoritarian or democratic, no regime has worked particularly well in Nigeria. On a brighter note, the current Fourth Republic, ushered in with the transition to civilian democracy in

---

ESSENTIAL POLITICAL FEATURES

- Legislative-executive system: presidential
- Legislature: National Assembly
- Lower house: House of Representatives
- Upper house: Senate
- Unitary or federal division of power: federal
- Main geographic subunits: states
- Electoral system for lower house: single-member district plurality
- Chief judicial body: Supreme Court

1999, has successfully sponsored two elections (and is preparing for a third in 2007), kept the military in its barracks, and survived longer than any of its democratic predecessors. Perhaps most important, Nigerians seem willing to keep trying. As one observer noted, "Although they have badly botched it up when they achieve democratic rule, Nigerians refuse to settle for anything less."[5]

Because of that tenacity, even though military regimes have ruled Nigeria nearly twice as long as civilian republics, over the years Nigerians have developed a number of important components of successful democracy. These include a diverse and vigorous media, an educated and often critical elite, outspoken human rights organizations, a growing middle class, and a respected legal profession and judiciary. In short, Nigerians have sought to establish the rules and procedures of an effective political regime, but political instability, ethnic disunity, and bureaucratic corruption persist. Long periods of authoritarian oppression have alternated with shorter periods of what appears to be democratic chaos.

The primary focus of the following discussion is the nature of the current civilian democratic regime, but it also touches on the more prevalent authoritarian regimes that preceded it. For, like its two predecessors, if this democratic regime is unable to deliver on its promises and devolves into corruption and chaos, history has shown that authoritarian rule will likely replace it. Nigerians may dislike military rule, but they have also shown little patience for bad democracy.

Political Institutions

THE CONSTITUTION

Since independence, Nigeria has been governed by six constitutions (after having been governed by four during the colonial era). The problem for Nigerian political leaders has not been coming up with rules of good governance but, rather, abiding by them.[6] Well-meaning leaders have oftentimes sought in good faith to revise legal norms to better accommodate both the developmental and the democratic aspirations of the Nigerian people, as well as the realities of their ethnic and religious differences. Too often, however, neither military rulers nor civilian elites (nor foreign multinational corporations, for that matter) have felt bound by those rules.

The British established colonial Nigeria's first constitution in 1922 and then rewrote it three times to reflect the decentralized federal arrangements they imposed to accommodate the colony's regional economic and ethnic divisions. Nigeria's first national constitution, promulgated in 1960, reflected the colonial imprint in at least two important ways. First, like all former British colonies, independent Nigeria established itself as a constitutional monarchy with a Westminster-style parliamentary democracy: the British monarch remained the head of state, legislative authority was placed in the hands of a bicameral parliament, and executive power was vested in a prime minister and cabinet. Second, the federal nature of the Nigerian state was further institutionalized with the codification of the regional division of Nigeria into the Hausa- and Fulani-dominated North, the Igbo-dominated East, and the Yoruba-dominated West.

In 1963, after only three years of independence, Nigeria reconstituted itself as a republic, replacing the queen of England as head of state with its own elected but largely ceremonial president. The revised parliamentary system ostensibly remained in place over the next decade and a half, though military rule for most of that period precluded its functioning. When the military finally acceded to civilian rule in 1979, the constitution of the Second Republic established an American-style presidential system with a directly elected president (as both head of state and head of government), a bicameral legislature, and a separate constitutional court. Subsequent constitutions (of 1989, 1995, and 1999) have retained the presidential system. Nigeria's current Fourth Republic, established in 1999, is thus a federal democratic republic with a presidential executive and a bicameral legislature.

The Branches of Government

THE EXECUTIVE SYSTEM

Nigeria's frequent leadership changes are in large part a consequence of the substantial social, economic, and political challenges facing this postcolonial country. Those changes and challenges have in turn fostered the personal rule of authoritarian leaders and hampered efforts to institutionalize more legitimate executive rule. As the following table indicates, in its nearly five decades of independence, Nigeria has been ruled for most of three decades by patrimonial strongmen. Elected civilian rule has been infrequent, consistently giving way to military rulers. Generally speaking, military and civilian rulers alike have possessed substantial, if frequently short-lived, political power.

Nigeria's current president, Olusegun Obasanjo, is only the third democratically elected executive to govern Nigeria and the only president to have been reelected to that office (in 2003) for a second term. An ethnic Yoruba from southwestern Nigeria, even he ruled Nigeria as a military head of government (from 1976 to 1979), and even now he is often criticized for bypassing the legislature and ruling by decree on important matters.[7] Nonetheless, Obasanjo is rightly seen as a champion of democracy in Nigeria. He presided over the voluntary transition to civilian rule in 1979, at the end of his first (unelected) stint in office—a promise often made by Nigeria's coup leaders but heretofore never kept. He was imprisoned by General Sani Abacha dur-

STRUCTURE OF THE GOVERNMENT

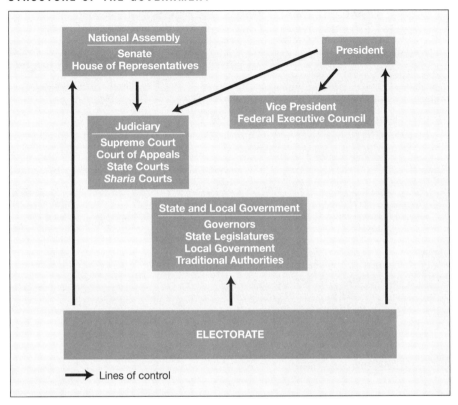

National Assembly
Senate
House of Representatives

President

Vice President
Federal Executive Council

Judiciary
Supreme Court
Court of Appeals
State Courts
Sharia Courts

State and Local Government
Governors
State Legislatures
Local Government
Traditional Authorities

ELECTORATE

→ Lines of control

ing the 1990s and released only after Abacha's sudden death in 1998. He and other opponents of Abacha formed the **People's Democratic Party (PDP),** successfully won the presidency in the following year's election, and won reelection in 2003. The constitution permits the president to hold office for no more than two terms of four years each, and efforts by some of Obasanjo's closest allies (not surprisingly, those who are reaping the most political and monetary benefit from his rule) to push through a constitutional amendment allowing Obasanjo to remain in power longer failed in 2006. Obasanjo has maintained he would prefer to return to his "beloved chicken farm."[8]

As in the U.S. presidential system, the president of Nigeria is directly elected by the people and nominates his or her own running mate, who automatically becomes vice president if the president is elected. The president also appoints ministers to the Federal Executive Council, or cabinet, which is charged with initiating and implementing the policies and programs of the federal government. In a nod to Nigeria's ethnic challenges and in an effort to avoid favoritism (if not clientelism), the constitution requires the president to appoint ministers from each of the states of the Nigerian republic. This

Nigerian Heads of Government

Name (Tenure)	Ethnicity (Religion)	Office	Path to Power	Regime Type
Abubakor Tafawa Balewa (1960–66)	Hausa-Fulani (Muslim)	Prime minister	Elected (indirectly)	Parliamentary democracy (First Republic)
Johnson T. U. Aguiyi-Ironsi (1966)	Igbo (Christian)	Military head of government	Coup	Authoritarian military rule
Yakubu Gowon (1966–75)	Tiv (Christian)	Military head of government	Coup	Authoritarian military rule
Murtala Muhammed (1975–76)	Hausa-Fulani (Muslim)	Military head of government	Coup	Authoritarian military rule
Olusegun Obasanjo (1976–79)	Yoruba (Christian)	Military head of government	Coup	Authoritarian military rule
Shehu Shagari (1979–83)	Hausa-Fulani (Muslim)	President	Elected (directly)	Presidential democracy (Second Republic)
Muhammadu Buhari (1983–85)	Hausa-Fulani (Muslim)	Military head of government	Coup	Authoritarian military rule
Ibrahim Babangida (1985–93)	Gwari (Muslim)	Military head of government	Coup	Authoritarian military rule
Ernest Shonekan (1993)	Yoruba (Christian)	Interim head of government	Appointed	Civilian puppet rule (proposed Third Republic)
Sani Abacha (1993–98)	Kanuri (Muslim)	Military head of government	Coup	Authoritarian military rule
Abdulsalam Abubakar (1998–99)	Gwari (Muslim)	Military head of government	Assumed power	Authoritarian military rule
Olusegun Obasanjo (1999–present; relected 2003)	Yoruba (Christian)	President	Elected (directly)	Presidential democracy (Fourth Republic)

quota system, what Nigerians refer to as the **federal character principle,** is also used with federal appointments and civil service positions in the government bureaucracy.[9] Each ethnic group is allotted a certain portion of federal positions based on its regional population. The federal-character principle may have spread the spoils of office among the various groups but has done little to prevent corruption. Bribery, waste, and rent seeking remain the norm in Nigeria's largely dysfunctional civil service, which "absorbs most of the budget but delivers little in the way of service."[10]

THE LEGISLATURE

Although in practice the president and his cabinet initiate budgetary legislation and most other important bills, the constitution designates the National Assembly, Nigeria's federal legislature, as the highest law-making body. This bicameral legislature consists of a lower House of Representatives and an upper Senate, with both representatives and senators serving four-year renewable terms. Elections for both houses are held the week preceding the presidential election.

The House of Representatives contains 346 seats, with each member representing an individual district. The 109 seats in the Senate are divided among Nigeria's thirty-six states and the federal district of Abuja. Despite their appointed constitutional roles, both chambers of the National Assembly have served as little more than rubber stamps for the executive branch, even during periods of democratic rule. This circumstance is in part a result of the same party controlling both branches of government, but it is also a result of the legislature's lack of experience, expertise, and staff support. In recent years, however, the National Assembly has demonstrated less compliance in passing budgetary bills and has become more vocal in expressing the demands of regional and even local interests.

These regional disagreements speak to the huge political challenge an increasingly democratic Nigeria faces in overcoming its seemingly intractable ethnic divisions, as we discuss later in this case. Some critics have argued that a prime ministerial or parliamentary system might better address Nigeria's challenges of cultural pluralism, by reducing conflict between the executive and legislative branches. Others have called for a unicameral legislature or even the rotation of the presidency and other key executive posts among the dominant ethnic groups, as is done with civil service appointments.

THE JUDICIAL SYSTEM

Nigeria inherited a colonial legal system that combined British common law with an assortment of traditional or customary laws that the colonial government had permitted to handle local matters (including sharia, which predominated in the Northern Region). This legacy fostered a court system

---

KEN SARO-WIWA: PLAYWRIGHT AND ENVIRONMENTAL ACTIVIST

Kenule Benson Saro-Wiwa was born in 1941 to an Ogoni family, members of an ethnic minority of southern Nigeria, on whose land in the Niger Delta rich oil reserves were discovered. By the 1980s, Saro-Wiwa had become known internationally for his novels and plays, many written in Nigerian pidgin, or "rotten" English. At the same time, Saro-Wiwa became increasingly involved in political efforts to force the Shell oil company and the Nigerian government to take greater responsibility for the environment and share a greater portion of the oil wealth with the Ogoni, whose lands the oil rigs were despoiling. With others, Saro-Wiwa founded the **Movement for the Survival of the Ogoni People (MOSOP)** in 1990. MOSOP challenged the government's revenue-sharing formulas, which kept the bulk of the oil wealth flowing to national government coffers. With allied groups, MOSOP also disrupted production, compelling Shell first to curtail oil extraction in the Ogoni region and ultimately to abandon its operations there altogether. By interfering in this "stream of petroleum revenues that fed the dictatorship,"[11] MOSOP raised the ire of General Sani Abacha's military government, which in 1994 ordered a brutal crackdown on Ogoni activists and sympathetic Ogoni villages. Saro-Wiwa and other activists were arrested that year on trumped-up charges and as civilians brought before a special military tribunal. The following year, the show trial had returned a verdict of guilty, and in November of 1995 the government hanged all nine of the defendants despite an international outcry and efforts to intervene by international human rights groups and the leaders of dozens of countries.

---

and rule of law that historically, even during periods of military rule, retained a degree of independence and legitimacy. However, the Abacha military dictatorship (1993–98) flouted this independence, routinely ignoring legal checks and using an intimidated judiciary to silence and even eliminate political opponents. Although Abacha used the courts to persecute many of his enemies (including those alleged to have plotted coups against him in 1995 and 1997), the most infamous case of "judicial terrorism" was the 1994 Abacha military tribunal that resulted in the execution of the noted playwright and activist **Ken Saro-Wiwa**.[12]

With the return to democratic rule, an effort has been made to reestablish the legitimacy and independence of the judiciary. The 1999 constitution establishes a Supreme Court, a Federal Court of Appeals, and a single unified court system at the national and state levels. Individual states may also authorize traditional subsidiary courts, however, giving the customary legal systems significant judicial clout. The most controversial of the traditional systems have been the Islamic sharia courts, which now function in twelve of the predominantly Muslim northern states. As discussed later in this case, Nigerians

have contended heatedly and, in some cases, violently over the role and jurisdiction of the sharia courts.

The Electoral System

As in the United States, Nigerians directly elect their president and separately
elect members of both chambers of their legislature, the National Assembly.
But unlike the system in the United States, in Nigeria presidents, senators,
and representatives all serve four-year terms, with elections for all three offices
held in the same year. In an effort to assure that the president serves with a
national mandate, Nigeria's constitution requires that the winning presidential candidate obtain both a plurality of votes and at least 25 percent of the
ballots cast in at least two thirds of the states. This requirement became an
issue of contention in the 1979 election, when the Supreme Court was called
upon to determine what constituted two thirds of Nigeria's then nineteen states
(there are now thirty-six). Ultimately, the court ruled that Shehu Shagari's victory in twelve states—not the thirteen demanded by the opposition—sufficed,
and Shagari was named president. As in France, the constitution holds that
if no candidate succeeds in reaching the two-thirds threshold in the first round,
a second round of voting takes place a week later, pitting the top two candidates against each other in a runoff.

All 360 seats in the House of Representatives are contested in single-
member districts apportioned roughly equally by population. The 109 members of the Senate are also elected from single-member districts, with each of
the thirty-six states divided into three districts. The federal district, or "capital territory," of Abuja elects one senator in a single-seat constituency for the
109th seat. These winner-take-all plurality systems have allowed just three
parties to dominate both chambers of the National Assembly. Four additional
smaller parties have managed to win either one or two seats in the House.
The success of the smaller parties reflects the geographic concentration of
ethnic groups willing to vote in blocs large enough to win a plurality of votes
in the less-populous lower-house electoral districts, such as the districts dominated by the Kanuri minority of northeastern Nigeria.

Local Government

Constitutionally, Nigeria is a federal republic with national, state, and local
levels of governance. Although Nigeria's military governments sought to establish a unitary system, the gaping ethnic divisions within the country have
prevented governments of all stripes from truly unifying the nation and centralizing political authority. These divisions reflect the ethnic diversity of Nigeria and the legacy of colonial rule.

In 1970, the Federal Military Government divided the republic into twelve states following the Nigerian Civil War, which nearly split the country permanently. The number of states grew to nineteen in 1976, thirty by 1991, and thirty-six by 1996, plus the Federal Capital Territory. The number of local government units has varied even more substantially, reflecting the uncertainty of how federalism should be constituted in Nigeria. The democratic government elected in 1979 doubled the number of local authorities to more than 700. In 1983, the military government downsized the number to 300, but it has since increased to nearly 800.

With a history of interregional instability and suspicion and relatively weak state capacity, the countervailing demands of centralization and devolution will certainly persist in Nigeria. On the one hand, the national government's control of the lion's share of oil revenues has provided the patrimonial glue that keeps the local regions dependent upon the center. But as increasingly diverse and articulate voices have entered an increasingly democratic political arena, the calls for enhanced state and local autonomy have grown louder. Those demands range from expanded state control over the budget (and for the oil-rich Niger Delta, local control over its oil revenues) and a separate military for each region to full-fledged dismemberment of Nigeria.

To date, local and even state governments have enjoyed little autonomy from the national government and have no means of generating revenue. Put simply, the central government controls the purse strings, and the Nigerian purse depends almost completely upon oil revenues. Not surprisingly, as oil revenues have expanded, so has the public sector at all levels and the levels of corruption associated with that patronage. At the same time, the expansion of oil revenues has led to increased disputes over the percentage—known as the **derivation formula**—that should accrue to the oil-producing localities.[13]

Other Institutions: The Military

Although the Fourth Republic has managed to sponsor two successive and relatively peaceful democratic elections, independent Nigeria's tumultuous history cautions us not to become too confident that the military will remain in its barracks. Nigeria's experience with military-in-government (military officers as political leaders) has left a deep impression on Nigerian politics. It is not a coincidence that most of Nigeria's most powerful leaders (including former coup leader and current president Obasanjo) boast a military background. As is the case elsewhere in postcolonial Africa and in much of the developing world, the military has served as one of the few stable avenues of meritocratic social mobility; it has long been able to attract many of Nigeria's best, brightest, and most ambitious.

This avenue has been particularly important for the ethnic Muslims of northern Nigeria, who have been educationally and economically disadvantaged in comparison with southern Nigerians. Although the south is the source of Nigeria's oil, for many years the north controlled the army and used that control, in the form of military dictatorships, to redistribute oil wealth. Time will tell whether Nigeria's military is prepared to make its most recent withdrawal from public life permanent.

POLITICAL CONFLICT AND COMPETITION

The Party System

Politics in oil-rich, patrimonial Nigeria has been described as a "contest of self-enrichment."[14] Whether these political contests have been fought with ballots or bullets, the stakes are indeed high, the competition fierce, and the corruption and violence all too common.[15] Not surprisingly, political parties and the party system have fared best under democratic regimes and have withered during periods of military rule. Political parties first began forming during the colonial period and did so quite naturally along ethnic lines even as early advocates of democracy sought to establish multicultural and issue-based platforms. Although the names of the dominant parties have changed over time, the parties that emerged during each era continued to reflect the ethnic divisions, despite efforts of democratic and even some military regimes to establish cross-ethnic national parties.

It makes more sense to discuss Nigeria's parties in terms of their ethnic identity and, therefore, their geographic location than to try to place them on a left-right political continuum. This regional party identity has exacerbated ethnic tensions and complicated efforts to establish democratic institutions and legitimize national party politics. Moreover, most state and local contests are also dominated by the region's dominant party, a circumstance that allows the party to control the state assembly and effectively capture the seats in the national Senate and House of Representatives as well. This reminds us that in Nigeria all politics is in the first instance local, and in communities, ethnicity and clientelist networks have traditionally meant everything.

Although the two most recent elections (1999 and 2003) under Nigeria's increasingly democratic Fourth Republic offer hope for the establishment of cross-ethnic parties with national appeal, the strengthened democracy has also given stronger voice to persistent sectarian and even separatist demands. The centrifugal push of growing communal violence between the Muslim north and the Christian south weakens the centripetal pull of increasingly legitimate national electoral contests.

Elections

Colonial-era parties survived through the First Republic (1960–66) but were banned from the onset of military rule until Olusegun Obasanjo, as leader of a military coup, seized power in 1976. Obasanjo legalized the establishment of political parties in 1978, and some 150 parties were formed in that year alone. In 1979, Obasanjo's elected successor, Shehu Shagari, sought to impose order on this political cacophony by compelling the formation of nationwide parties. The constitution of the Second Republic specified that any successful presidential candidate must win at least one fourth of the vote in at least two thirds of the states. The election commission required that all parties open membership to all Nigerians and that the parties' leadership come from at least two thirds of the states. In all, five parties were deemed viable contenders in the 1979 and 1983 elections. Military coups in 1983 and 1985 (in part the result of the widespread corruption and failure of the Second Republic) once again banned political parties.

Ibrahim Babangida, the military ruler from 1985 to 1993, charged his National Election Commission with reforming the party system to produce a two-party system. But fears that such a system would lead to a dangerous political division between the Muslim north and the Christian south led the commission once again to approve five parties. Dissatisfied, Babangida dissolved the commission and established two national parties, one neatly placed "a little to the left of center and one a little to the right."[16] The government built headquarters for each party, gave each one start-up funds, and even named them (the Social Democratic Party and the National Republican Convention). Babangida called for local elections in 1990 and announced plans to hand over power to civilians with a presidential election in 1992.

Although the election was postponed until 1993, it took place fairly. But because the winner was a southern (Yoruban) civilian distrusted by the northern military generals, the military nullified the results and charged the apparent victor with treason. The military installed an interim puppet president, who was quickly pushed aside by General Sani Abacha. Abacha called for elections in 1996, and his military government certified five parties—all loyal to him. Not surprisingly, all five nominated Abacha as their candidate for president.

Abdusalam Abubakar, Abacha's military successor, dissolved the five parties and called for presidential elections in 1999. In another effort to foster political parties with a "federal character," the election commission approved only parties that maintained well-established national organizations. Nine parties qualified for local elections, and the three parties with the highest votes in those elections were permitted to participate in the national legislative and presidential elections. Not surprisingly, each of those parties once again reflected its regional base in one of the country's main ethnic groups: the People's Democratic Party (PDP), representing the northern Hausa; the **All People's Party (APP)** of the eastern Igbo; and the **Alliance for Democracy (AD)** of the western Yoruba.

Significantly, however, the 1999 election appears to have marked a watershed for Nigerian national politics. PDP supporters—with strength in the

Muslim north, home of many of Nigeria's military leaders—chose to support Obasanjo, a retired general but a southern Christian Yoruban. The AD chose to throw its support behind the APP contender rather than field its own candidate. Obasanjo won with 62.8 percent of the vote, and a "relieved public" overlooked the many flaws in the election and largely accepted the results that ushered in the Fourth Republic.[17]

Nigeria's most recent election, in 2003—the first sponsored by a civilian government in twenty years—has continued this trend. There were in fact four elections, all held in April; contests for the two chambers of the legislature were followed a week later by the presidential election, and state assembly races were held the following week. Turnout for the legislative election was just under 50 percent; turnout for the presidential race was nearly 70 percent. With newly relaxed criteria for party registration, some thirty parties fielded twenty presidential candidates in a wide-open field.

Although there were once again numerous charges of corruption and fraud, Obasanjo and the PDP swept the presidential, Senate, House, and state elections. In 1999, in spite of his Yoruban credentials, Obasanjo did not win support from the Yoruban Alliance for Democracy, which feared he was little more than a military stooge for the north. But in 2003, having demonstrated his good intentions, Obasanjo earned the full support of not just the

Results of Nigeria's National Elections, 1999 and 2003

Region/Ethnicity Party Election Year	North/ Hausa PDP	East/ Igbo APP/ANPP*	West/ Yoruba AD	Other parties	Total
Presidential Vote (%)					
1999	62.8	37.2	no candidate	—	100
2003	61.9	32.2	no candidate	5.9	100
Senate Seats					
1999	65	24	20	0	109
2003	73	28	6	0	107**
House Seats					
1999	212	79	69	0	360
2003	213	95	31	7	346**

Source: Adapted from Peter M. Lewis, "Nigeria: Elections in a Fragile Regime," *Journal of Democracy* 14(2003), p. 143.

*The APP renamed itself the All Nigeria People's Party after a merger with a smaller independent party in 2003.

**Contested returns from some districts reduced the total number of candidates seated in both the Senate and the House in the 2003 election.

Nigerian Attitudes toward Nondemocratic Alternatives, 2000–2003			
	2000	**2001**	**2003**
Percent who disapprove or strongly disapprove of . . . *			
Presidential "strongman"	83%	71%	72%
Military rule	90%	81%	69%

Peter Lewis and Etannibi Alemika, "Seeking the Democratic Dividend: Public Attitudes and Attempted Reform in Nigeria," *Afrobarometer Paper* 52 (October 2005), p. 10.

*The question posed was, "There are many ways to govern a country. Would you disapprove or approve of the following alternatives?

PDP but of the AD as well. The weaker showing for the AD in the legislative races also reflects the logic of the winner-take-all plurality system's favoring two parties. The PDP's main challenger was the Igbo-based APP—newly named the All Nigeria People's Party (ANPP); it finished a distant but respectable second in all three national races. Obasanjo's reelection was widely seen as a vote of confidence for his performance since 1999 by a broad majority of Nigerians across ethnic and regional lines. Promising to abide by the constitutional limit of two terms, Obasanjo has the opportunity in 2007 to be Nigeria's first civilian leader to hand power to another.

Despite these consecutive affirmations of the democratic process in Nigeria and the high expectations of the Nigerian people, endemic government corruption, rising communal violence, and persistent economic misery have tested Nigerians' patience for democratic rule. When asked in 2003 if the present system of elected government "should be given more time to deal with inherited problems," only 58 percent of Nigerians said yes, compared with nearly 80 percent in 2000. More troubling is that authoritarian alternatives to Nigeria's struggling democracy are becoming more palatable to many Nigerians, as shown in the table above. Despite or perhaps because of Nigeria's many problems, governments of the Fourth Republic must start delivering on promises of better times if they hope to avoid the fate of the earlier republics.

Civil Society

Neither the British colonial government nor the series of military authoritarian regimes has been able to squelch Nigeria's rich tradition of activism and dissent. Even Abacha's oppressive dictatorship in the 1990s could not fully muzzle what one foreign observer referred to as Nigerian citizens' "defiant spunk."[18] In Nigeria's relatively short postcolonial history, a wide variety of formal interest groups and informal voluntary associations has emerged and persisted. Under the relaxed environment of the Fourth Republic, these groups and organizations have proliferated and strengthened. Some of them, particularly professional associations and other nongovernmental organizations (NGOs), have drawn their support from across Nigeria's cultural spectrum and have functioned in ways that promote national integration. Others, particularly those based on ethnic and religious identities, are among the most resilient of groups and in some cases serve to fragment Nigerian society.

Formal and informal ethnic and religious associations were the first groups in Nigerian society and remain the most cohesive. Some of these groups have long served as important vehicles of mutual trust for promoting the economic interests of their members, for example, by mobilizing savings or investing in a business. Others have formed to protect or promote the ethnic or local interests of a particular minority group. In the early years of independence, some groups provided the foundation for the subsequent formation of political parties. One of the most important of the issue-based minority associations is the Movement for the Survival of the Ogoni People, or MOSOP. As noted in the Political Regime section, this group, established by Ken Saro-Wiwa in the 1990s to defend the interests of the Ogoni, has employed a variety of legal and extra-legal political tactics to secure more financial benefits with fewer environmental costs from foreign-operated oil interests in the Niger Delta.

The volatile potential of conflict between Christian and Muslim religious institutions and groups has been mitigated by the numerous divisions and differences within each religious tradition. Although Muslims of the north share a common faith and have banded together in defense of certain interests (such as the maintenance and expansion of the scope of sharia law), there are numerous schisms within the faith as well. For example, the Tijaniyah variety of Sufi Islam, practiced among lower-class Hausa Muslims, is quite distinct and in many ways at odds with the orthodox Sunni Islam practiced by the Hausa and Fulani Muslim elite. In fact, some liberal Muslim groups favor secular government and oppose the implementation of sharia. Christian-based politics in the south is similarly far from monolithic.

Modern civic associations such as trade unions and professional organizations played a prominent role in the anti-colonial struggle and have been relatively active in promoting their particular and at times more collective interests since the time of independence. Unions representing workers in the all-important petroleum industry—for example, the National Union of Petroleum and Gas Workers (NUPENG)—have been particularly influential. Formal associations such as those representing legal, medical, and journalism professionals have begun to articulate the political interests of Nigeria's growing professional class. Particularly since the end of military rule and the establishment of the Fourth Republic, NGOs promoting issues such as development, democracy, and civil rights have exerted more influence in Nigerian politics.

SOCIETY

Ethnic and National Identity

It should be quite clear by now that one of the central factors defining Nigerian politics is group identity. Ethnicity is a powerful force, given the historical rivalry among Yoruba, Igbo, and Hausa and Fulani peoples. In addition, nearly one third of the population belongs to none of those groups, further complicating the ethnic map. This diversity has created significant problems for the consolidation of democracy, as there are temptations for each group to see politics in zero-sum terms. That is, an electoral victory by a Hausa candidate, for example, is viewed as a blow to the interests of the Yoruba, and vice versa. Such centrifugal tendencies were largely responsible for the collapse of civilian government in 1966 and of course for the Nigerian Civil War. Subsequent military leaders often sought to play on the fears of ethnic conflict as a justification for authoritarianism, arguing that democracy only exacerbated the fault lines between regions and peoples. Changes in federalism (creating more territorial divisions) and the executive (replacing a parliamentary system with a presidential one) similarly reflected the desire to weaken local authority and move more power to the center. Even the capital was moved, in 1991, from Lagos to Abuja, a city built from scratch in the center of the country.

How has the transition to democracy affected ethnic relations? Since the end of military rule, communal violence has risen, as the state is no longer

ETHNIC GROUPS

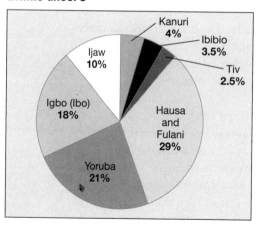

RELIGION

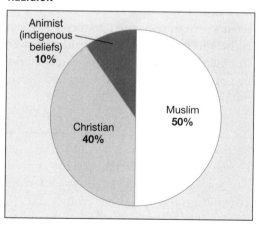

able to suppress the public as it pleases and as the struggle for control over the state has returned to the populace. Since the return to civilian rule in 1999, it is estimated that such conflicts have taken over 12,000 lives and displaced 750,000 Nigerians.[19] This violence often has economic motives, with its origins in conflicts over access to state funds, oil revenues, jobs, or other resources. Moreover, it is frequently asserted that political elites capitalize on these conflicts as a way to build their base of support, even to the point of inciting conflict through words and actions (such as paying supporters to attack rival groups).

The conflicts also have a religious component. In recent years, there has been a deepening fissure between Muslims, who are concentrated in the north, and Christians and animists, who are concentrated in the south. The catalyst has been the role of sharia, or Islamic law. As noted in the Introduction, under British rule Islamic law was preserved in the north and continued to serve an important, if limited, role. The practice was continued under independent Nigeria, and by the 1980s Islamic groups had begun to press the regime of Ibrahim Babangida to allow for the expansion of sharia in the north as well as in higher courts, where it then had no authority.

While the repression of Sani Abacha's regime froze much of that activism, it quickly revived with the onset of civilian rule. Muslim leaders and the Muslim public saw the expansion of sharia as a way to overcome the corruption of the military era and reassert their rights in a democratic system. Some political leaders also clearly saw the issue in a more cynical light, as a way to garner public support. Shortly after the 1999 elections, a number of northern states made sharia the primary law, extending it to criminal and other matters. This legal system includes an extreme punishment for adultery and apostasy (leaving the faith): death by stoning. The imposition of sharia has touched off some of the worst violence under civilian rule; in one incident in 2000, clashes between Christians and Muslims in the town of Kaduna left 2,000 dead. The tension over sharia also grabbed international attention when two women were sentenced to be stoned to death for committing adultery. Although the verdicts were eventually overturned by higher courts, the seeming incompatibility between secular national law and an expansive regional use of sharia remains a serious and potentially destabilizing issue.[20]

Ideology and Political Culture

Could the conflicts between north and south, between Christian, Muslim, and animist, lead to civil war, another military coup, or the dissolution of the country itself? Perhaps. As we have seen, political parties in Nigeria tend to be built around individual leaders and ethnic groups, meaning that ideology plays a limited role compared with more narrow communal concerns, in contrast to a country like South Africa, where ideology plays a much stronger role in the party system. Similarly, it is commonly asserted that Nigerians have a low sense of patriotism or pride in their state, presumably a result of their stronger local identity and the legacy of military rule. The Nigerian novelist and political activist Chinua Achebe once described Nigerians as "among the world's most unpatriotic people," which, he argued, was a serious impediment to prosperity and democracy.[21]

In spite of these concerns, however, there are aspects of Nigerian political culture that continue to lend support to the state and the democratic regime. A 2003 survey of Nigerians showed that despite the tensions and disappointments that have followed the return of civilian rule, nearly 70 percent continued to support democracy and reject military rule. Nigerians also express strong opposition to a political system dominated by a single party or leader, an attitude quite different from that in many other African democracies, where such domination is common. Over time, Nigerians have come to base their support for democracy less on economic performance and more on trustworthy leaders and similar factors—quite the opposite of what is expected in less-developed countries with weakly institutionalized democracy.[22] Moreover, in contrast to Achebe's assertion, surveys show that Nigerians exhibit a high degree of pride in their broader national identity. Those views, if sustained, may help limit communal tension and build ties across ethnic and religious divisions.

POLITICAL ECONOMY

The misfortune of the Nigerian economy has been a constant theme throughout our discussion. The economic difficulties that Nigeria has faced since independence are not unusual among less-developed countries, but they are particularly egregious given that Nigeria is one of the world's largest oil producers and has earned hundreds of billions of dollars from its steady export of the product, making up 90 percent of the its foreign-currency earnings. In fact, Nigeria's economic difficulties exist not in spite of its oil resources but in large part because of them. Nigeria's predicament is an excellent example of what scholars sometimes refer to as the **resource curse.** Natural resources that are abundant and state controlled often serve to support authoritarian rule by giving the ruling regime the means to buy off the public and pay for repression. It is also argued that natural resources tend to distort an economy by diverting it from other forms of development. This situation can be seen in other oil-producing economies, such as Iran.

Each of these factors is evident in the development of Nigeria's political economic system. Like other less-developed countries, in the years following independence Nigeria opted for a system of import substitution, creating tariff barriers and parastatal industries with the objective of rapidly industrial-izing the country. This ambitious program was made possible by oil sales, which during the 1970s benefited from high prices. However, these programs suffered from policies directing resources toward certain industries for polit-ical reasons, without a clear understanding of whether the investments would be profitable. For example, US$8 billion was spent in the attempt to create a domestic steel industry that in the end produced barely any steel.[24] The decline in oil prices in the 1980s and the subsequent economic crisis and substantial foreign debt led Nigeria to initiate a policy of structural adjustment that moved the country away from import substitution, although the economy remained highly regulated and closed to trade.

The limited reforms also did not address the fact that the country remained dependent upon oil exports and that the revenues from those exports were in the hands of the military. As the public suffered from the effects of structural adjustment, such as unemployment and inflation, the regime of Ibrahim Babandiga used its financial resources to co-opt some opponents while repressing others. Economic reforms also facilitated this patrimonialism, as newly liberalized markets or privatized state assets could be doled out in return for political support—not unlike the "insider privatization" that plagued Rus-sia in the 1990s.

By the time of Sani Abacha's regime, corruption had reached such heights as to be described by one scholar as outright "predation" under an "avaricious dictatorship."[25] The Nigerian economy not only suffered from the outright theft of state funds, but also became a center for illicit activity, including narcotics trafficking, human trafficking, money laundering, and perhaps best known, the so-called 419, or advance-fee, scams (see Current Issues). One might argue that corruption should not be a central focus if it has helped provide funds for eco-nomic development, but the reality is that little of this wealth was re-invested in the country. Over the past thirty years, Nigeria has had a negative GDP growth rate and has suffered from a high degree of income inequality. It boasts the dubious distinction of being one of the world's most corrupt countries (surpassed only by Bangladesh and Haiti) as well as a nation with one of the world's lowest life expectan-cies. Per capita income is lower now than it was in 1975.[26] Corruption, inequality, and poverty are clearly connected.

The Fourth Republic thus faces an enor-mous challenge in righting the Nigerian economy and breaking with the practices

LABOR FORCE BY OCCUPATION

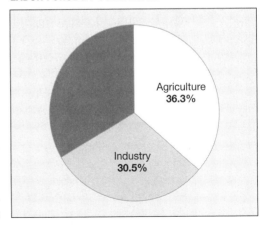

Agriculture
36.3%

Industry
30.5%

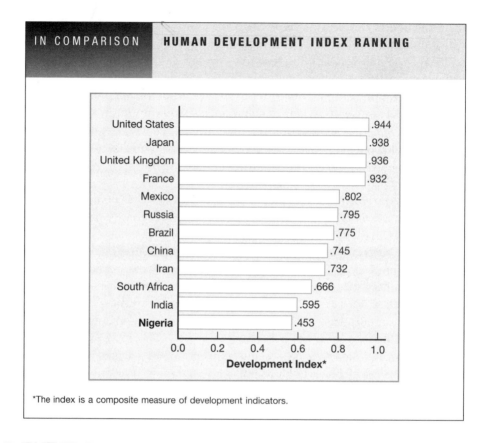

IN COMPARISON　HUMAN DEVELOPMENT INDEX RANKING

	Development Index*
United States	.944
Japan	.938
United Kingdom	.936
France	.932
Mexico	.802
Russia	.795
Brazil	.775
China	.745
Iran	.732
South Africa	.666
India	.595
Nigeria	.453

*The index is a composite measure of development indicators.

of previous regimes. Olusegun Obasanjo's government has taken several important steps, developing a wide-ranging reform program known as the **National Economic Empowerment and Development Strategy (NEEDS).** NEEDS has tackled several important areas. First, it has increased the transparency of government finances, for example, by auditing the accounts of various levels of government to oversee how money is being spent and by making the findings available to the public. Second, it has prompted the government to address the corruption problem and improve the rule of law, for example, by creating an Economic and Financial Crimes Commission to pursue theft and money laundering (and seizing over US$500 million in the process).[27] NEEDS also focuses on the country's inadequate infrastructure, seeking to boost electricity production, improve transportation, increase telecommunications, and expand access to sanitation and clean drinking water. The goal, then, is to reform the state while expanding basic social expenditures across Nigeria. If successful, NEEDS could dramatically improve the lives of average Nigerians and increase domestic business and foreign investment.

The long-term success of NEEDS will of course hinge on one critical factor: oil. As oil prices have risen of late, the Nigerian government has found itself in a better financial position, but as we know from the past, such windfalls reap no long-term benefits if they are stolen or spent unproductively. Realizing this, the Obasanjo government has earmarked some of the oil revenues for a stabilization fund that can be drawn from if and when oil prices fall. The government has also taken on corruption within the oil industry. But huge problems remain, reflecting the enormous impact that the oil industry has on Nigeria.

In the oil-producing Niger Delta, conflicts over the resource continue to take place between local groups and the central government. International oil producers who operate in Nigeria, such as Shell and Chevron, have worsened matters by regularly providing payments to local leaders as tribute for operating in their community. This practice has increased conflict between ethnic groups in the delta and between community leaders and unemployed youth, with each group vying for a share of the funds. A result has been the spread of armed militias, often linked to political parties, battling—often violently—over oil. Among their activities are "bunkering" (illegally siphoning oil from pipelines—perhaps as much as 40 percent of all that is produced), seizing or destroying facilities and kidnapping foreign oil-industry workers for ransom, and staging attacks on rival groups. Solving this conflict will not be easy; it will require more effective policing, local governance, and central control over the actions of foreign oil producers.

FOREIGN RELATIONS AND THE WORLD

Nigeria's foreign policy has undergone several shifts in emphasis since independence, reflecting international and domestic influences. The country's gradual transition from colonialism has meant that it did not undergo revolution or a protracted war of independence, either of which might have dramatically reshaped its relationship with the outside world. As a result, during the cold war Nigeria remained clearly within the pro-Western camp and retained its ties to the United Kingdom through membership in the Commonwealth of Nations. However, Western sympathy for the Biafrans during the 1967–70 Nigerian Civil War and the West's refusal to provide arms to defeat Biafra steered Nigeria toward nonalignment. Nigeria has also sought to play an important regional role by helping to lead several international governmental organizations focused on Africa. One such body is the Economic Community of West African States (ECOWAS), with a membership of fifteen West African countries. ECOWAS was created as an instrument of regional integration, not unlike the European Union in its early stages. The process of economic integration has been slow, however, although ECOWAS has actively met its obligation to intervene in armed conflicts in member states. Thus it has dispatched peacekeeping troops to help resolve civil conflicts in Liberia and Sierra Leone. As the largest ECOWAS member state by far, Nigeria has borne the brunt of the peacekeeping efforts. Nigeria has similarly been active in deploying peacekeepers for far-flung UN missions, as in Lebanon and along the Indian-Pakistan border. In spite of these important responsibilities, Nigeria's international relations declined steadily under the Sani Abacha regime, and by 1995 the country has been suspended from the Commonwealth and subject to sanctions by the European Union and the United States following the execution of Ken Saro-Wiwa. With democratic elections, however, Nigeria is gaining status as a regional and, perhaps, a global actor.

In the coming decades, it is likely that Nigeria will become more important on the international scene. Whether this change will contribute to global security and prosperity is an open question, however. One main reason why Nigeria may grow in importance takes us back to a recurrent theme of this case, and that is oil. It is estimated that Nigeria has some 34 billion barrels of oil reserves. Whereas that is only a fraction of the reserves of major oil-producing states such as Saudi Arabia, it nevertheless makes Nigeria one of the world's major producers. The vast majority of Nigerian oil is exported to Europe, Asia, and North America, making it an important trading partner. Instability in the Middle East and economic development in Asia may further push Nigeria into the forefront of energy production. China and India, for example, have shown interest in investing in Nigeria's oil industry, raising the possibility that the country will find itself caught in a political struggle as the United States, Europe, and Asia vie for access to its oil. Recognizing its increased status on the world stage, Nigeria has been pushing for representation as a permanent member of the United Nations Security Council, which currently has no permanent African member (the permanent members are the United States, the United Kingdom, Russia, China, and France).

A second factor is regional. As the most populous country in Africa, Nigeria stands to play a key role on the continent in helping to bolster democracy and stability. In addition to its role in ECOWAS, Nigeria has long been an important player in the Organisation of African Unity (OAU), which was created in 1963. Within the OAU, Nigeria was a strong opponent of white rule in Rhodesia (now Zimbabwe) and South Africa and with its own transition to democracy has stressed its commitment to democratic rule in Africa. This attitude can be seen in the recent transformation of the OAU. In 1999, its members agreed that the body should broaden its responsibilities in order to actively pursue a process of greater regional integration (not unlike the original intentions of ECOWAS in West Africa). In 2002, the OAU officially renamed itself the African Union (AU) and declared a new mandate for its member states, known as the New Partnership for Africa's Development, or

NEPAD. NEPAD's primary goals are to eradicate poverty, sustain growth, integrate Africa into the process of globalization, and empower African women.

To that end, the AU and NEPAD have broken with past practices by serving as an intermediary between international donors and African states and holding the latter accountable for enforcing the rule of law and making certain that foreign aid is properly spent. Nigeria and South Africa have become the leading members of the African Union, with Nigeria taking a strong line on supporting democracy on the continent. For example, as Zimbabwe's government under Robert Mugabe slid deep into authoritarian rule over the past decade, Nigeria supported the country's suspension from the Commonwealth of Nations, and President Olusegun Obasanjo has since repeatedly clashed with Mugabe over his dictatorial rule. Both Nigeria and South Africa can be expected to grow in influence across the continent, with the former benefiting from its size while the latter benefits from its more developed economy. Some observers of Africa have called Nigeria and South Africa the China and Japan of Africa.

Finally, Nigeria's presence in the international system will depend to a great extent on how its democracy fares. A slide toward authoritarian rule will undoubtedly weaken the country's regional and international authority and in the process damage institutions like the AU and NEPAD. Another worry is that the history of conflict between northern and southern Nigeria could embroil the country in the current international struggle against violent Islamic extremism. Recent clashes among Nigerian Muslims, Christians, and animists have their impetus in disputes that date back many generations. As in many other parts of the world, however, local ethnic or religious conflicts might become radicalized and internationalized and drawn into the loose ideology of Al Qaeda and its supporters. What role, if any, such groups may have in Nigeria is unclear, although their presence in Africa is long-standing. Al Qaeda staged devastating attacks on U.S. embassies in Kenya and Tanzania in 1998, and its operatives may have been active in nearby Liberia before and after 2001. Nigeria's widespread criminal activities may also be attractive to terrorists, as a means of raising funds and laundering money. Some observers express concern that the long-standing ethnic and religious tensions in Nigeria will provide a platform for terrorist activity, especially attacks on the country's oil facilities. As a result, the United States has significantly increased its military support for West African countries, including Nigeria. Closer ties with the United States increase the risk of exacerbating tensions in Nigeria's Muslim community, however, and so could play directly into the hands of terrorists.[28] Nigeria will undoubtedly become more connected to the globalizing world in the coming decade, but such a connection will require balancing domestic tensions with regional and international pressures. It will not be easy.

CURRENT ISSUES

419 SCAMS

Many readers of this case have received an e-mail message stating that if they provide financial support up front, they will receive a share of a large sum of money from overseas. Those offers are known as 419, or advance-fee, scams. Such confidence games, long known as spanish-prisoner cons, date back to sixteenth-century Europe. What is notable about the recent permutation, however, is the frequency with which the scam has originated in Nigeria—indeed, the term "419" stems from the Nigerian legal code banning such activities. The Nigerian scams appear to have begun in the 1980s, around the time of the decline in oil prices, and were tolerated, if not abetted, by the government. The most common version is an unsolicited letter from a Nigerian claiming to be a senior civil servant. The letter writer is seeking a partner in whose account he can deposit several million dollars, money that supposedly was overpaid on a government contract. The partner is offered a share of the funds for his or her assistance but first must help defray the cost of a number of bribes or licenses. Gullible (and greedy) recipients of such letters have sent substantial amounts of money to Nigeria, billions of dollars, according to some estimates. In some cases, individuals have been lured to Nigeria to complete the supposed transaction, only to be kidnapped or killed. In addition to defrauding unwitting marks, the cons have deterred prospective legitimate investors, who are unwilling to risk having to distinguish between a business opportunity and a scam.

In recent years, the Nigerian government has cracked down on the 419 scams, with the Economic and Financial Crimes Commission seizing over $700 million between 2003 and 2004 and arresting over 500 people. With the proliferation of e-mail, however, it has become much easier for scam artists to distribute their bogus stories of covert wealth, and they have moved on to new territory, focusing new variants on eBay customers, for example. Nigerian expatriates have apparently moved the scams abroad, to Europe and South Africa. The 419 scams demonstrate the lack of the rule of law in Nigeria, as well as how that condition, facilitated by globalization, can spill over into the international system.

NOTES

1. Ike Okonta and Oronto Douglas, *Where Vultures Feast: Shell, Human Rights, and Oil* (San Francisco: Sierra Club Books, 2001).
2. *The Niger Delta: No Democratic Dividend* (New York: Human Rights Watch, 2002).
3. *World Urbanization Prospects: The 2003 Revision Population Database* (New York: United Nations, 2004).
4. Charles R. Nixon, "Self Determination: The Nigeria/Biafra Case," *World Politics* 24:4 (July 1972), pp. 473–497.

5. Blaine Harden, *Africa: Dispatches from a Fragile Continent* (Boston: Houghton Mifflin, 1990), p. 247.

6. Julius O. Ihonvbere, "How to Make an Undemocratic Constitution: The Nigerian Example," *Third World Quarterly* 21 (2000), pp. 343–66.

7. "A Reporter's Tale," *Economist*, 28 February 2004, p. 46.

8. "A Troubled but Lingering President," *Economist*, 4 August 2005.

9. The 1999 constitution states that the "composition of the Government of the Federation or any of its agencies and the conduct of its affairs shall be carried out in such a manner as to reflect the federal character of Nigeria and the need to promote national unity, and also to command national loyalty thereby ensuring that there shall be no pre-dominance of persons from a few states or from a few ethnic or other sectional groups in that government or in any of its agencies." See E. Ike Idogu, "Federalism and Ethnic Conflict in Nigeria," *Journal of Third World Studies* (Spring 2004).

10. "A Reporter's Tale."

11. Howard French, *A Continent for the Taking* (New York: Alfred A. Knopf, 2004), p. 38.

12. For the term *judicial terrorism*, see Shu'aibu Musa, "Shades of Injustice: Travails of Muslim Activists in Nigeria in the Hands of Successive Regimes," paper presented at the International Conference of Prisoners of Faith, London, 17 February 2002 (London: Islamic Human Rights Commission, 2002), http://www.ihrc.org.uk/file/02feb17drmusaSHADES%20OF%20INJUSTICE.pdf (accessed 3 November 2005).

13. Idogu, "Federalism and Ethnic Conflict in Nigeria."

14. French, *A Continent for the Taking*, 2004, p. 27.

15. Ike Okonta, "Nigeria: Chronicle of a Dying State," *Current History* (May 2005), pp. 203–08.

16. Harden, *Africa: Dispatches from a Fragile Continent*, p. 306.

17. Peter M. Lewis, "Nigeria: Elections in a Fragile Regime," *Journal of Democracy* 14 (2003), p. 133.

18. French, *A Continent for the Taking*, p. 42.

19. Freedom House, *Freedom in the World 2004: The Annual Survey of Political Rights and Civil Liberties*, http://www.freedomhouse.org (accessed 27 February 2006); Michael Bratton and Peter Lewis, "The Durability of Political Goods? Evidence from Nigeria's New Democracy," *Afrobarometer Paper* 48 (April 2005).

20. Vincent O. Nmehelle, "Sharia Law in the Northern States of Nigeria: To Implement, or Not to Implement, the Constitutionality Is the Question," *Human Rights Quarterly* 26:3 (2004), pp. 730–59.

21. Chinua Achebe, *The Trouble with Nigeria* (London: Heinemann, 1983).

22. Bratton and Lewis, "The Durability of Political Goods?"

24. "A Tale of Two Giants," *Economist*, 13 January 2000.

25. Peter Lewis, "From Prebendalism to Predation: The Political Economy of Decline in Nigeria," *Journal of Modern African Studies* 34:1 (March 1996), pp. 79–103.

26. International Monetary Fund, "Nigeria: Selected Issues and Statistical Appendix," *IMF Country Report* 05/303 (August 2005) http://www.imf.org/external/pubs/ft/scr/2005/cr05303.pdf (accessed 27 February 2006).

27. International Monetary Fund, "Nigeria: 2005 Article IV Consultation Concluding Statement," International Monetary Fund, March 25, 2005. www.imf.org/external/np/ms/2005/032505.htm (accessed 27 February 2006).

28. Princeton N. Lyman and J. Stephen Morrison, "The Terrorist Threat in Africa," *Foreign Affairs* (January/February 2004), pp. 75–86.

KEY TERMS

General Sani Abacha   p. 479
All People's Party (APP)   p. 490
Alliance for Democracy (AD)
   p. 490
derivation formula   p. 488
General Ibrahim Babangida   p. 479
federal character principle   p. 485
First Republic   p. 476
Fourth Republic   p. 480
Fulani   p. 472
General Yakubu Gowon   p. 478
Hausa   p. 472
Igbo   p. 472
Movement for the Survival of the
   Ogoni People (MOSOP)   p. 486

National Economic Empowerment
   and Development Strategy
   (NEEDS)   p. 498
Niger River Delta   p. 471
General Olusegun Obasanjo   p. 478
patrimonialism   p. 480
People's Democratic Party (PDP)
   p. 483
Republic of Biafra   p. 477
resource curse   p. 496
Ken Saro-Wiwa   p. 486
Second Republic   p. 478
sharia   p. 475
Third Republic   p. 479
Yoruba   p. 472

WEB LINKS

Nigeria Direct: Official Government Gateway   **www.nigeria.gov.ng/**
Niger Delta Development Commission
   www.nddconline.org/The_Niger_Delta
African Studies Internet Resources: Nigeria, Columbia University Libraries
   www.columbia.edu/cu/lweb/indiv/africa/cuvl/Nigeria.html
The Guardian (Nigeria)   **www.ngrguardiannews.com**
IRIN News.org   UN Office for the Coordination of Humanitarian Affairs
   www.irinnews.org/frontpage.asp?SelectRegion=
   West_Africa&SelectCountry=Nigeria
Economic and Financial Crimes Commission   **www.efccnigeria.org**